# ROUTLEDGE LIBRARY EDITIONS: HISTORICAL SECURITY

Volume 5

# STUDIES IN SECRET DIPLOMACY

# STUDIES IN SECRET DIPLOMACY
During the First World War

W. W. GOTTLIEB

LONDON AND NEW YORK

First published in 1957 by George Allen & Unwin Ltd

This edition first published in 2021
by Routledge
2 Park Square, Milton Park, Abingdon, Oxon OX14 4RN

and by Routledge
52 Vanderbilt Avenue, New York, NY 10017

*Routledge is an imprint of the Taylor & Francis Group, an informa business*

© 1957 W. W. Gottlieb

All rights reserved. No part of this book may be reprinted or reproduced or utilised in any form or by any electronic, mechanical, or other means, now known or hereafter invented, including photocopying and recording, or in any information storage or retrieval system, without permission in writing from the publishers.

*Trademark notice*: Product or corporate names may be trademarks or registered trademarks, and are used only for identification and explanation without intent to infringe.

*British Library Cataloguing in Publication Data*
A catalogue record for this book is available from the British Library

ISBN: 978-0-367-61963-3 (Set)
ISBN: 978-1-00-314390-1 (Set) (ebk)
ISBN: 978-0-367-64420-8 (Volume 5) (hbk)
ISBN: 978-1-00-312446-7 (Volume 5) (ebk)

ISBN: 978-0-367-64431-4 (pbk)

**Publisher's Note**
The publisher has gone to great lengths to ensure the quality of this reprint but points out that some imperfections in the original copies may be apparent.

**Disclaimer**
The publisher has made every effort to trace copyright holders and would welcome correspondence from those they have been unable to trace.

# Studies in Secret Diplomacy

### during the First World War

―►―◄―

### W. W. GOTTLIEB

*LONDON*

**GEORGE ALLEN & UNWIN LTD**
RUSKIN HOUSE MUSEUM STREET

*First published in 1957*

*This book is copyright under the Berne Convention. Apart from any fair dealing for the purposes of private study, research, criticism or review, as permitted under the Copyright Act, 1911, no portion may be reproduced by any process without written permission. Enquiry should be made to the publisher*

*Printed in Great Britain
in 10pt. Times Roman type
by C. Tinling & Co., Ltd.
Liverpool, London and Prescot*

*To My Wife*

*whose part in this work
has been greater
than I can convey*

☥

# INTRODUCTION

THE First World War has been described in very similar terms by statesmen as different as Churchill and Lenin. For the one it was 'The World Crisis', for the other 'the greatest historical crisis, the beginning of a new epoch'. The explosion of 1914 certainly was a —probably the—decisive turning point in Modern History. In the ensuing four years, processes were at work to bring about the overthrow of the Tsarist, German, Austro-Hungarian and Turkish Empires. They gave rise to the emergence of national States in Central, Eastern and South-Eastern Europe, the expansion of Italy and Japan, the birthpangs of new China, the shape of things to come in the Levant. They led to the relative weakening—despite enlargement—of Britain and France, the accession of the U.S.A. to predominance, and the establishment of the Soviet Socialist Republic. The unprecedented scale of military and naval operations was matched by popular movements of unparalleled sweep and by secret Diplomacy of uncommon intensity and scope.

A time so big with events and consequences warrants the closest examination. But whereas much has been written on its political and social aspects, there are few diplomatic histories of the War. Although literature on the Diplomacy of the pre-1914 and post-1918 periods is plentiful, there is too little on the tormented years between. I have, therefore, tried to contribute towards filling the gap.

The two Studies which make up this book deal with the complex problems associated with the intervention of Turkey and Italy. They show that the international frictions which engendered the War were exacerbated by it. That this is so is seen in the efforts of the belligerent Governments to enlist allies or—if the paradox may be allowed—to make enemies, to safeguard their internal régimes, to defend and enhance their external status in the face of friend and foe, and to worry out the Secret Treaties, which bedevilled (and go far to explain) the peace settlements and the era they ushered in. The Studies are focused upon Turkey and Italy because those Powers were the first to enter the European War and the involvement of the former went far to determine that of the latter. A volume on the Balkans and the Near East, on which I am now engaged, will carry the story further. The present work, however, is complete in itself, and the reader will find, I think, that the pattern of international relations which emerges is one which has a more general application.

The material I have used confirms that diplomatic activity is not a professional exercise *per se*. It is not, despite the unquestionable influence of the personal element, the product of either the goodwill or evil intentions, the blunders or master-strokes of individuals or nations. It is, at root, the result of objective causes, the international play of forces compounded, within each country, of such factors as national history and tradition, domestic politics, strategy, the fluctuations of public opinion, and the whole social and economic structure. A better appreciation of the way in which the foreign policy of every Power affects every other comes when the separate strands in each have been unravelled. It has been said that behind the public record of diplomatic activity there is an unwritten chronicle of secret moves. The relevance of this silent history is obvious. It seemed worth while, therefore, to attempt a systematic inquiry into it, and to make an assessment of underlying motives and of techniques employed. This investigation has taken me into the workshop of secret diplomacy.

In order to render as authentic an account as I could, I have, for the most part, presented the story of each move and countermove in the participants' own words, with numerous quotations from their memoranda and dispatches. Where it seemed likely to shed more light on an issue, I have put into the chronological sequence historical flashbacks or sketched in the social, economic and political background. In handling the Russian papers, I have used the dates of the Western calendar, and given Slav names a uniform phonetic spelling.

The basic sources of my evidence are almost entirely new. The full range of Adamov's and Pokrovski's compilations of confidential war-time diplomatic correspondence, which include non-Russian telegrams intercepted and deciphered in Petrograd, is not known to the English reading public. This is true, above all, of the huge collection entitled *Die Internationalen Beziehungen im Zeitalter des Imperialismus* which, together with *Das Zaristische Russland im Weltkriege*, I have used in their German translations because these alone were permanently available to me. I have, however, checked them with the Russian originals. The *Documenti Diplomatici Italiani* are equally unfamiliar and important. Since only the first volume of the war series has so far appeared, I have been unable to draw on it beyond October 1914. But if subsequent parts follow the same lines, I have reason to suppose that they will still further support my arguments. The German Foreign Ministry Archives captured by the Allies in the recent War and, for want of a better name, cited here as *Die Geheimakten des Deutschen Aussenamtes* are also substantially untrodden ground. As they consist of a very large number of cartons containing photostats and microfilms of thousands of documents filed but not organized for publication, I have not been able to provide the convenience of reference to them in my footnotes. The time-consuming work

# INTRODUCTION

involved would have entailed serious delay which the nature of the material did not seem to warrant. I would say, however, that, although I found in them no new gems, the files on 'The Treaty of Alliance between Germany, Austria-Hungary and Italy' (G.F.M. 11/22-27) lend weight to the thesis I had already formed from information gleaned elsewhere—particularly where it concerns Berlin's ceaseless pressure in Vienna for Italy's benefit, and the whole of the intricate relationships between those three Powers discussed in chapters XVII, 3-5; XIX; XX; XXI, 2-3 and XXIII, 3, 5, 6, 9 below. The muster of original evidence is completed by the highly illuminating *Carteggio Avarna-Bollati*, and *The Lansing Papers* of the U.S. State Department.

Then there are such earlier but still mainly untapped sources as the Reports of the Dardanelles Commission, the data, documents and letters published by Churchill, Grey, Trevelyan, Storrs, Conrad, Tisza, Macchio, Poincaré and Salandra, and the dispatches in the Italian Green and the Austrian Red Books. All this material I have supplemented with extracts from the older sets of records issued by Gooch and Temperley, Kautsky, Pribram and the Austrian Foreign Office, and with direct or circumstantial evidence from the revelations and recollections of statesmen, politicians, soldiers and diplomats. I need only mention the gold to be mined from the disclosures of, for example, Sabini, Marescotti, or Flotow. For vital background matter I have relied on standard and reference works, Foreign Office Handbooks, histories, economic and financial monographs, and biographies. I have also consulted the English, Russian, German, Austrian, Italian, French and American press of the times.

After a survey of the material comes the question of its treatment. Collections of diplomatic documents are open to the charge of incompleteness and selection. But, of my basic sources, those most likely to be proof against this are the Russian papers. For however distasteful some testimonials might have been to the Tsarist and the Allied Cabinets, the Soviet Government, under whose auspices they were published, could have had no reason to suppress them. In every case, moreover, where collation was possible, I found these dispatches repeated or referred to by Churchill, Grey, Trevelyan, Poincaré, Paléologue, or the *Documenti Diplomatici*. The Wilhelmstrasse, presumably, had no time to tamper with its archives before their capture. Any gaps there may be in the other records can be narrowed or bridged by making use of all the material now available and fitting together scattered facts. Memoirs, Diaries and Letters invite the objection that some at least were written as personal or national apologias, that they may have been doctored on publication, and may show bias. The careful historian will take this into account.

A*

But he will detect in them few outright falsehoods. He will recognize in the display of subjective motives (such as those of Salandra and Djemal Pasha) the hard core of historical fact. He will see that what some authors (Burián) thought well to omit, is broadcast by others (Tisza). He will meet chroniclers so eager to vindicate themselves (Sabini, Macchio, Bülow, Giolitti) that they uncover secrets of capital importance. He will find the assertions of Conrad echoed on the other side by Hindenburg and Ludendorff and borne out years after by Redlich, and those of Salandra confirmed by the *Documenti Diplomatici*. He will learn much from the entries of Lloyd George, Rodd, Dumaine, Karolyi, Sanders and Szilassy. He will gain valuable insight from the neutral eye-witness reports of Morgenthau, Einstein, Page. And he will appreciate, in these personal 'dossiers', the value of the psychological undertone, the revealing comment (Asquith, Poincaré, Bertie), the studied or unintentional indiscretion (Melas, Tirpitz, Moukhtar), which provide missing links and light up hitherto bewildering obscurities.

My method of handling the material then—as the cross-references in my footnotes indicate—has been to test and compare, to verify, corroborate and integrate. So treated, the whole body of this evidence would seem to allow some general conclusions on the laws and logic of the diplomacy of imperialism and power politics. The most striking phenomenon, perhaps, to emerge from these Studies is the ceaseless diplomatic war among the Allies in each coalition behind their clash of arms with the enemy. Another is the perpetual striving of the enemy to divide his opponents by exploiting these divergencies. A third is the intimate connection between the domestic struggle for or against intervention and the external diplomatic contest. A fourth is the unconcern with which some, at any rate, of the warring Governments disposed of the freedom of weaker and smaller nations for which they claimed to be fighting—*vide* the genesis of the Secret Treaties affecting Turkey and Italy. These latter bring also into relief the inseparability of international problems apparently unrelated. It will be seen, for example, how the Constantinople Agreement begot the secret London Treaty, why Vienna defied Berlin over Italy, or what the Dardanelles campaign had to do with the ambitions of Petrograd. In the light of material hitherto unused and by co-ordinating all the data now at hand, I have tried to present evidence which is fresh, to reinterpret where it seemed necessary facts already known, and s to lay open to scholar, student and general reader a new aspect of the history of 1914-18.

W.W.G.

*Glasgow, September 1956*

## ACKNOWLEDGEMENTS

GRATEFUL acknowledgement is made to the Carnegie Trust for the Universities of Scotland and the University Court of the University of Glasgow who have made publication possible.

My appreciation is due to Mr. G. P. Gooch, D.Litt., C.H., F.B.A., for invaluable advice and support. For unstinted help by discussion, consultation and advice I am greatly indebted to Mr. N. C. Anderson, M.A., L. ès L., Lecturer in French, Mr. J. F. R. Corlett, B.A., Lecturer in Modern History, Mr. J. D. Dawson, B.A., Ph.L., S.T.B., Lecturer in Philosophy, University of Glasgow, Mr. M. H. Dobb, M.A., Lecturer in Economics and Fellow of Trinity College, University of Cambridge, Mr. E. J. Hobsbawm, Ph.D., Lecturer in History, Birkbeck College, University of London, Mr. Ph. R. Horne, M.A., B.Litt., Lecturer in Italian, University of Glasgow, Mr. V. Kiernan, M.A., Lecturer in History, University of Edinburgh, and Mr. J. H. Warrender, M.A., Head of the Political Science Department, University of Glasgow. Mr. Corlett, Mr. Dobb, Mr. Kiernan and Mr. Warrender have also read the whole or parts of my MS. and improved it by comments and suggestions, but they must not be identified with my opinions and conclusions for which I alone am responsible. I am glad to record my gratitude to Mrs. Marjorie Barnett, B.A. (Oxon.) for untiring and sympathetic editorial help and to all those friends who have assisted me in other substantial ways.

For research facilities I am indebted, above all, to the Library of the University of Glasgow, the London Library, the Public Record Office, the Library of the British Museum, the National Central Library, the Institute of Historical Research, the School of Slavonic Studies in the University of London, the Mitchell Library and the Knightswood Library in Glasgow.

I am obliged to the following for permission to quote from the works mentioned in brackets below: The Controller of H.M. Stationary Office (Dardanelles Commission, *First Report, Supplement to the First Report, The Final Report. British Documents on the Origins of the War, 1898-1914.*); Messrs. Edward Arnold (Publishers) Ltd. (Salandra, *Italy and the Great War.*); Sir Winston S. Churchill and Odhams Press Ltd. (Sir Winston S. Churchill, *The World Crisis 1911-1914, The World Crisis 1915.*); the Executor of the late Viscount Grey of Fallodon and Messrs. Hodder & Stoughton, Ltd. (Viscount Grey of Fallodon, *Twenty-Five Years.*); Messrs. Hutchinson & Co. (Publishers) Ltd. (Djemal Pasha, *Memories of a Turkish Statesman 1913-1919.* Ambassador H. Morgenthau, *Secrets of the Bosphorus.*

M. Paléologue, *An Ambassador's Memoirs*.); Messrs. Longmans, Green & Co. Ltd. (Trevelyan, G.M., *Grey of Fallodon*.); and Oxford University Press, Inc., New York (Diplomatic Documents Relating to the Outbreak of the European War. Part I: *The Austro-Hungarian Red Book No. 2*. Part II: *The Italian Green Book*.). Fuller details, and particulars of other publications from which quotations have been made are given in the Bibliography.

CONTENTS

INTRODUCTION *page* 7

PART ONE: *The Great Powers Over Turkey*

I PRELUDE TO WAR
1. British, French and German interests in Turkey 19
2. Turkey: the domestic scene 24
3. The Turkish brand of imperialism 27
4. Germany and the Ottoman Empire 30

II THE DISPOSITION OF TURKEY
1. Overtures to the Triple Entente and Alliance with Germany 34
2. Russia's policy towards Turkey 39
3. Turkey: grounds for war with the West 42
4. Britain, France, and the importance of keeping Russia in the War 45
5. Great Britain and the Arabs 48
6. The Entente fails to satisfy the Porte 53
7. Germany's all-out effort in Constantinople 57
8. The Young Turks decide on war 60

III RUSSIA, CONSTANTINOPLE AND THE STRAITS
1. Russian economy, strategy and imperialism 63
2. The partition of the Ottoman Empire, I: London and Petrograd 66
3. The partition of the Ottoman Empire, II: Paris and Petrograd 72
4. The British in Egypt, the French in Morocco, the Russians in a quandary 73

IV CHURCHILL AND THE DARDANELLES
1. Churchill's naval and political strategy 77
2. British and French divergencies over Turkey 80
3. The political background of the naval operation 82
4. Extending the British Empire in the Levant 84

V THE DIPLOMATIC WAR AMONG THE ALLIES
1. Russian reactions to Churchill's plan 88
2. Petrograd demands Constantinople and the Straits 90
3. British expedients: internationalization, Greek involvement, compromise 93
4. Paris and the *fâcheux incident*. The Franco-Russian bargain 98
5. French imperialism in the Middle East; conflict with Britain 101
6. Outbidding Germany in Russia 104

## VI THE SECRET AGREEMENTS BETWEEN BRITAIN, FRANCE AND RUSSIA

1. The political context of Gallipoli — page 106
2. In Constantinople. Turks and Greeks. The Armenian massacres — 109
3. Peace feelers and their failure — 110
4. The Bulgarian imbroglio — 112
5. The Russian play for Constantinople — 115

## VII WITHDRAWAL

1. The drama of Gallipoli — 119
2. The diplomatic wrangle over hypothetical details — 122
3. Churchill's resignation and the abandonment of the Dardanelles — 127
4. The rift between Russia and her Allies — 129

## PART TWO: *Italy Among the Great Powers*

## VIII BEFORE 1914

1. The zig-zag course of Italian diplomacy — 135
2. German investments and influences in Italy — 138

## IX ITALY'S SOCIAL AND ECONOMIC STRUCTURE — 141

## X THE PURSUIT OF EMPIRE — 146

## XI PEACE OR WAR

1. The Italian friends of Vienna and Berlin — 150
2. The Italian champions of the Entente — 153
3. Italy's conflicts with her Austrian Ally — 155
4. The Albanian and the Serbian cockpits — 157

## XII THE CRISIS IN THE TRIPLE ALLIANCE

1. A *fait accompli* and an intrigue — 162
2. 'Do you think it useful to know the truth?' — 166
3. The dispute over Article VII — 169

## XIII NEUTRALITY

1. The ephemeral neutrality — 174
2. The reasons for marking time — 178
3. The Italian Socialist Party and war — 179
4. The genesis of Mussolini — 183
5. Propaganda and the role of the press — 187

## XIV THE DIPLOMATIC DUEL BETWEEN ITALY AND AUSTRIA-HUNGARY — 190

CONTENTS

### XV ITALY AND THE TRIPLE ENTENTE

1. Soundings in Petrograd and London *page* 198
2. London, Vienna and the balance of power 201
3. Britain's response to Italy 203
4. Paris-Vienna 209
5. Italy explores possibilities in Paris: Nice, Corsica, Savoy and Tunis 211

### XVI EXTRA-DIPLOMATIC FACTORS

1. British, French and Belgian investments in Italy 224
2. Informal contacts; creating a war atmosphere; the uses of money 227

### XVII 'SACRED EGOISM'

1. The Government of *sacro egoismo* 231
2. The 'protection' of Albania 234
3. Italy's diplomatic offensive in Vienna 238
4. German pressure in Vienna 240
5. The fall of the Austro-Hungarian Foreign Minister 243

### XVIII AUSTRIA-HUNGARY

1. The social scene 247
2. The Dual Monarchy and the Yugoslavs 250
3. Sarayevo and war with Serbia 254
4. Habsburg imperialism in the Balkans 256

### XIX TENSION BETWEEN AUSTRIA-HUNGARY AND GERMANY

1. *Mitteleuropa*, the Adriatic and the Road to Baghdad 260
2. Financial, economic and political dependence on Germany 261
3. Differences over strategy 264
4. Political divergencies 269
5. Rival designs in Poland and Russia. Seeking a decision: East or West? 272
6. Cancelling out the Ally's prospective gains 277

### XX THREE CRAFTSMEN OF DIPLOMACY

1. Implications of the appointment of a new Foreign Minister 281
2. Prince Bülow's mission and the Banca Commerciale Italiana 283
3. The tussle over Trieste 286
4. 'The Minister of the Underworld' and his programme 288

### XXI A DIPLOMATIC TRIANGLE: ROME-BERLIN-VIENNA

1. A separate peace between Austria and Russia? 296
2. Berlin and Vienna 300
3. Vienna and Rome 304

## XXII THE SECRET TREATY OF LONDON

1. Italy and Turkey — page 312
2. Italy tries to divide France and Russia — 314
3. The origins of the Italo-British partnership — 317
4. London and Petrograd — 319
5. Franco-Italian rivalry in the Balkans. Anglo-French interests in the Mediterranean and Africa — 323
6. Italian imperialism in the Balkans and the Yugoslavs — 326
7. The struggle between Italy and Russia over the Balkans — 331
8. Britain and France versus Russia — 334
9. Strife — 338
10. Difficulties between Britain and Italy — 344
11. France tables a formula — 346
12. Russia and the Yugoslavs — 348
13. Dealing in lands and people — 349
14. Agreement over Constantinople and compromise over Italy — 354

## XXIII THE FINAL STRUGGLE

1. Inside Italy — 359
2. Engineering a break — 361
3. The Central Powers work for a change of Cabinet in Rome — 367
4. Vatican diplomacy — 370
5. Erzberger as a go-between — 375
6. Plot and counterplot — 381
7. D'Annunzio, poet-mercenary — 386
8. Piazza politics. King and Constitution — 388
9. Austria-Hungary, like Italy, is bent on war — 391
10. The last obstacle. The balance sheet — 399

BIBLIOGRAPHY — 403

INDEX — 413

PART ONE

*The Great Powers
over Turkey*

CHAPTER I

## *Prelude to War*

### 1

#### BRITISH, FRENCH AND GERMAN INTERESTS IN TURKEY

ON the outbreak of war in 1914, both belligerent coalitions burst into complex and conflicting diplomatic activity. The Foreign Offices were intensely preoccupied with the disposition of the neutral States.

In the Ottoman Empire the initial advantage appeared to lie with the Entente. Britain and France had vast economic and financial interests in the country. Sir Ernest Cassel had founded, and controlled, the so-called National Bank of Turkey, of which the oil magnate Gulbenkian (a British subject since 1902) was a director. Armstrong and Vickers owned the Golden Horn and Stenia docks, held contracts for modernizing arsenals, and building a floating dock and ship-yards at Ismid, and had orders for a dreadnought, two cruisers, six destroyers and two submarines. The Anglo-Persian Oil Company and Shell possessed 75 per cent of the shares of the Turkish Petroleum Company which had a monopoly in the Sultan's realm, and of which the moving spirit was Gulbenkian. British concerns operated the Smyrna-Aidin Railway and its branch lines, the lucrative emery deposits in the vilayet of Aidin (E. Abbott), and a cotton mill, much of the shipping and insurance business, the most prominent foreign mercantile firms (Whittal & Co.) and the Telephone Company in Constantinople. They had the largest cotton-seed oil plant at Mersina, engineering and machinery stores at Beirut, Aleppo (White & Son) and Baghdad, two factories for yarn-dyeing, a cloth mill, limited liability companies dealing in carpets, cloth, figs and oil, and a commanding position among the European commercial houses (MacAndrews & Forbes, Whittal & Co.) in Smyrna. They were paramount in Turkey's imports of textiles and coal, and had concessions for shipping on Lakes Beyshehir and Egerdir, road transport between Baghdad and Bakuba, lead mining near the Dardanelles, railway extensions, and port development in Trebizond and Samsun. The Euphrates and Tigris Steam Navigation Company, in which H. B. Lynch of London predominated, was the principal carrier of merchandise between Baghdad and Basra. By 1910, some 96 per cent of the boats coming into the latter port represented British trade. The commerce of these two cities, valued at £2,500,000 in 1903, was mainly in the hands of English and Indian business men.

Lord Inchcape, the Chairman of the British India Steam Navigation Company, had exclusive shipping rights on important stretches of the Tigris and the Euphrates, on the Shatt el-Arab and their tributaries and canals. The Zionist financial institutions, such as the Jewish Colonial Trust, the Anglo-Palestine Company which promoted Jewish undertakings, and the Jewish National Trust, functioned as British corporations.[1]

As for the French, Creusot had a commission from the Porte for two submarines, and the Chantiers de la Méditerranée for six destroyers. Other groups owned wholly, or in great part, the wharves, docks and warehouses, the waterworks, the electricity board and the telephones in Constantinople, the Lighthouses Administration, the Heraclea coal-fields, the Balia-Karaïdin lignite and lead mines, the Arghana and Ak Dagh Syndicates, the Karval mines, the Pilot, Tugboat and Salvage Company, the Orosdi Back concern, the Société Immobilière Ottomane, the Société Nationale de Commerce, d'Industrie et d'Agriculture, the Société Générale d'Entreprise des Routes, and had concessions for port construction in Haifa, Jaffa, Tripoli, Beirut, Zunguldak, Panderma, Ineboli and for railways in Armenia, Anatolia, Syria. The railway network of Panderma-Soma-Magnesia, Smyrna-Kassaba-Aifium Karahissar, Mudania-Brusa, Beirut-Rayak-Damascus, Rayak-Homs-Hama-Aleppo, Tripoli-Homs and Jaffa-Jerusalem, the big business houses of Beirut, the Smyrna Quay Co., and the Land Bank, were further strongholds of French enterprise. With the aid of the Banque Périer, £2,000,000 had been raised for the Navy. Parisian financiers had a 30 per cent share in the Baghdad Line, and the Crédit Lyonnais was firmly entrenched in Turkey. Of the Ottoman Public Debt, which totalled 143,200,000 T. liras (one T. lira equalled about eighteen shillings), 62·9 per cent were due to France, and 22·3 per cent to Britain. The Imperial Ottoman Bank, which enjoyed the prerogatives of a State Bank, was owned by Franco-British capital. It controlled the Tobacco Monopoly

---

[1] Baster, *The International Banks*, 107–8, 112. Bentwich, *England in Palestine*, 16. Connell, *Manifest Destiny*, 73, 80. Djemal Pasha, *Memories of a Turkish Statesman*, 91–5, 99–100. Perris, *The War Traders*, 68, 70. 'Les intérêts pétroliers français dans le Proche-Orient'. *Politique Étrangère*, 4 Oct. 1952. pp. 276–7. *The Times*, 21 July 1955, p. 12. The Euphrates and Tigris Steam Navigation Co. and Britain's 'exceptional' commercial position in the Mesopotamian delta are discussed in the Memoranda, British Foreign Office to Cambon and Benckendorff, 4 June 1907, and Sir E. Grey to Sir G. Lowther, 20 April 1910. *British Documents on the Origins of the War (1898–1914)*. Edit. by Gooch and Temperley. Vol. VI. NN 250 and 352, pp. 356 and 470. Also *The Times*, 23 Sept. 1912, p. 3, and Post Office London Directory, 1914, p. 905. *Turkey in Europe*. Foreign Office Handbooks, No. 16, pp. 72–3, 78, 102, 106, 110. *Anatolia*. F. O. Handbooks, No. 59, pp. 44, 49, 89–91, 97–9, 103, 113. *Syria and Palestine*. F. O. Handbooks, No. 60, p. 126. *Mesopotamia*. F. O. Handbooks, No. 63, pp. 50–1, 96–7, 114.

(40,000,000 francs), various utilities, railway and industrial issues, and a wide branch system with multifarious business ramifications. At the same time it embodied, through a majority of French shareholding, the concentrated power of Schneider-Creusot and the Bourse. Although the head office was located in Constantinople and there were alternate Anglo-French Director-Generalships, its loan and other financial operations were determined from Paris. Among the directors of the Ottoman Bank were commonly politicians of the Third Republic or regents of the Banque de France. In Near-Eastern diplomacy it was both a prompter and an agent of the Quai d'Orsay.[1]

This was reflected in Turkey's government services. A certain Monsieur Joly was Inspector-General of Finance. A compatriot of his directed the police, another the Tobacco Monopoly. Sir Richard Crawford had effective charge of Customs. Mr. H. Woods was economic adviser. Other Britons acted as advisers to the Ministries of the Interior, Justice, and Public Works, and to the Civil Service. Sir Vincent Caillard, a member of the board of Vickers, was chairman of the Ottoman Public Debt Council. The British Naval Mission under Admiral Limpus occupied a key position in the Fleet. By means of posts and investments of such magnitude—three thousand millions of French capital alone—Britain and France had reduced the sprawling Turkish Empire economically and financially to a semi-colony.[2]

But since the Kaiser's call on Abdul Hamid II in 1889, Germany had been gaining ground on the earlier arrivals. Between 1887 and 1910, her proportion of Turkey's imports rose from 6 per cent to 21 per cent, and Austria-Hungary's from 13 per cent to 21 per cent. In the same period, the intake of British goods fell from 60 per cent to 35 per cent, and of French goods from 18 per cent to 11 per cent. While France accounted for 25·9 per cent and Britain for 16·9 per cent of the foreign money invested in Turkish enterprise (apart from the Ottoman Public Debt), Germany alone attained 45·4 per cent. Her commerce was boosted by the Deutsche Palästinabank, the

---

[1] Adamov, *Konstantinopol i Prolivy*, II. p. 157, footnote 1; p. 334, footnote 2; pp. 335, 352-3. Baster, 27, 35, 101-3, 107-12. Cumming, *Franco-British Rivalry in the Post-War Near East*, 11, 12. Djemal, 86, 95, 102. Miller, *Ocherki noveishei istorii Turtsii*, 11, 16-17. Perris, 70. *Turkey in Europe*. Foreign Office Handbooks, No. 16, pp. 72-3, 76, 134, 137. *Anatolia*. F. O. Handbooks, No. 59, pp. 42, 44, 51, 61, 64, 86-8. *Syria and Palestine*. F. O. Handbooks, No. 60, pp. 69, 74, 79, 84, 89, 126, 139-40, 144. For the connections between the Ottoman Bank and Schneider-Creusot see Hallgarten, *Imperialismus vor 1914*, I. 521. II. 141.

[2] Toynbee, *Turkey—A Past and a Future*, 79. Einstein, *Inside Constantinople*, 260. Sanders, *Five Years in Turkey*, 13. Ryan, *The Last of the Dragomans*, 92. Adamov, II. pp. 329, 345. Djemal, 84, 99-101. Miller, 11, 26. Perris. 30. *The Times*, 4 Nov. 1952, p. 8.

Levante-Kontor, and notably the Deutsche Orientbank which had been established by the massive combination of the Dresdner Bank, the Discontogesellschaft, the Schaaffhausenscher Bankverein and the Nationalbank für Deutschland. Her war plants, especially Krupp's and the Mauser works, were suppliers to the Sultan's Army. Her holdings in the Ottoman Debt increased from 4·7 per cent in 1881, when she had the sixth place among Turkey's creditors, to 20 per cent in 1912 when they were second only to those of France. By 1914, German concerns controlled the Tramway Company, the Metropolitan Railway, the electricity supply, and numerous firms in Constantinople, the passenger steamship service of the Golden Horn, the Ost-Europäische Telegraphengesellschaft, the port and waterworks of Haidar Pasha, the Mersina-Tarsus and Adana Railway, and a sector of the Heraclea mines (the Ruhr magnate Stinnes and the Deutsche Bank). They had harbour concessions at Alexandretta and Mersina, navigation rights on Lake Beyshehir, irrigation systems in the Konia oasis and the Adana plain, a carpet factory at Urfa, a cotton mill at Adana, mining concessions along some of their principal railway tracks, and vast trading interests in Syria and Palestine. Berlin Finance—together with the Wiener Bankverein—was responsible for the Oriental Railway connecting Constantinople with Central Europe. Above all, the Deutsche Bank owned the Anatolian Railway comprising the lines Haidar Pasha-Ismid-Angora, Hamidie-Bolu, and Eskishehir-Konia, the Company for the Operation of the Oriental Railways, the Bank for Oriental Railways, and the Imperial Ottoman Railway Company which had been set up (in co-operation with Turkish, Austrian, Swiss, French and Italian houses) for the purpose of extending the route from Konia to Baghdad and Basra. By 1914, the new artery stretched as far as Aleppo, Alexandretta and beyond the Euphrates.[1]

The Berlin-Baghdad Line, the embodiment of the *Drang* to the Middle East, was reaching out for the copper of the Taurus, the oil of Kerkuk, the tobacco, wool, cotton, grain and fruits of Mesopotamia and Kurdistan, and one of the richest markets in the world for German manufactures. By pushing towards the Persian Gulf, its

---

[1] Riesser, *The German Great Banks and their Concentration*, 434, 436–7, 445–6, 453–4, 474, 494, 512. Yerusalimski, *Vneshnyaya politika i diplomatiya germanskovo imperializma*, 191, footnote 46; 193. Bowman, *The New World*, 412. Menne, *Krupp Deutschlands Kanonenkönige*, 154–5. (This author shows that over 1,000 artillery pieces were ordered at Krupp's in 1885–86 alone). Schreiner, *Zur Geschichte der deutschen Aussenpolitik*, I. 252. Adamov, II. p. 157, footnote 2; pp. 352–3. Toynbee, *Turkey P. F.*, 46, 55. Miller, 11. *Politique Étrangère*, 4 Oct. 1952, pp. 276–7. *Turkey in Europe*. Foreign Office Handbooks, No. 16, pp. 63–9, 72, 80, 103, 110–11, 137. *Anatolia*. F. O. Handbooks, No. 59, pp. 44–6, 49, 54, 69, 86, 99. *Syria and Palestine*. F. O. Handbooks, No. 60, pp. 68–9, 80, 83–4, 127, 144. See also Feis, *Europe the World's Banker*, map opposite p. 348.

aim was to divert the Levantine, Indian and Far Eastern trade from the sea lanes to London overland to the Reich. Moreover, a safe position in the interior of Asia Minor gave it unique strategic value for the imminent struggle with Britain. Dr. P. Rohrbach, one of the most vehement advocates of German imperialism, besides enumerating, in *Die Bagdadbahn*, the economic advantages it would entail, wrote that:

'England can be attacked . . . on land in one place only . . . in Egypt. With the loss of Egypt, England would lose not only the mastery over the Suez Canal and the link with India and Asia, but presumably also her possessions in Central and East Africa. The conquest of Egypt by an Islamic Power like Turkey, moreover, could have dangerous repercussions on England's sixty million Moslem subjects in India, and also on Afghanistan and Persia. But Turkey can only think of India if she has a developed railway system in Asia Minor and Syria. . . .'

The latter's railways,

'if the need arose . . . would be the direct instrument . . . for pressure upon England in the direction of Egypt.'[1]

The Baghdad Line was closely connected with the German electrical, building (Siemens Bau A/G), heavy and export industries. Its sponsor, the giant Deutsche Bank (acting in conjunction with the Dresdner Bank, the Discontogesellschaft and others) became a prime mover and promoter of Hohenzollern policy in Turkey. Such was its influence that its correspondence found its way into State dispatches, and the Embassy in Constantinople was hardly more than its agency. Assuming a prominent role in the Porte's finances, it captured for Germany several Turkish loans. Challenging the Imperial Ottoman Bank at every step, it was guided in all its transactions by the motto that 'the skirmishes of the political advance posts are fought out on the financial ground'.[2] The Ottoman Bank, it is true, still towered above the younger rival, and the Franco-British financial entrenchment was, on the whole, the more formidable. But the supply to Turkey of four torpedo-boats by the Schichau yards in Danzig in 1910 made significant inroads into the preserves of Armstrong and Vickers. In 1911, the Deutsche Bank acquired 25 per cent of the shares of Gulbenkian's Turkish Petroleum Company. By 1913, the Hamburg-Amerika Line, which seven years

---

[1] *Die Bagdadbahn*, 1st edit. 1902, 2nd edit. 1911. See Schreiner, I. 250; also 251–2, 256–7, and Toynbee, *Turkey P. F.*, 48; also 52. Miller, 14, 23, 24. Yerusalimski, 540. Bowman, 409, 411. Hallgarten, II. 132.

[2] Riesser, 474; also 434, 445, 494. Miller, 15. For the role of the German Embassy in Constantinople as an agency of the Deutsche Bank see Hallgarten, II. 296, and *ibid*. footnote 5; 297; also 142. Schreiner, I. 252–4.

earlier had began to attack Britain's virtual monopoly of the seaborne trade of Mesopotamia, had captured so much of the transport business to and from Basra that the British shippers were forced to compromise with their competitor on something like dictated terms. Above all, the arrival of General von Sanders's Military Mission in December 1913, and his *de facto* command of the Sultan's Army, which—as the German Ambassador wrote—was designed 'to check British influence',[1] illustrated the marked increase in German power, and the extent to which it was accepted at the Golden Horn.

2

TURKEY: THE DOMESTIC SCENE

The Porte's submission to Germany was largely due to internal causes. The overthrow of Abdul Hamid's feudal autocracy by the Young Turk 'Committee of Union and Progress' in 1908 was a bourgeois revolution.[2] It was inaugurated by promises and expectations of liberal reforms. But since the mass of the people did not take part independently, actively, with an economic and political programme of their own, the movement produced but a veneer of change. As early as October 1911, the Congress of the Committee passed a resolution that 'the formation of new parties ... must be suppressed and the emergence of new "liberal" ideas prevented';[3] and soon after the coup of January 1913 against an interregnum of the old régime, government withered into dictatorship. The Committee of some 40 members, with branches in all larger cities, ruled in secret, manipulating elections, filling offices, distributing patronage and staffing the administration with its henchmen. Abdul's successor, the 72-year old Mehmed V ('an imbecile' in English eyes, a 'gentleman' of 'much knowledge and wisdom' to the Germans[4]) was impotent. Parliament was a puppet show. The Grand Vizier and Foreign Minister Said Halim, a rich Egyptian princeling whose heavy contributions to the party funds matched his aspirations for the Khedivate, served as a pliant and decorative figure-head. Power was in the hands of a triumvirate which, rising by assassination, continued a system of terror so that 'instead of having one Abdul Hamid, Turkey now discovered that she had several'.[5]

[1] Sanders, 2; also 3. Hallgarten, II. 138. Yerusalimski, 194, 264. Miller, 26. *Mesopotamia*. Foreign Office Handbooks, No. 63, pp. 98–101, 114. The pioneer work in reorganizing the Turkish Army had, of course, been done by General von der Goltz in 1885 to 1895 and again in 1910.
[2] Lenin, *The State and Revolution. Collected Works*, XXI. 2, p. 180.
[3] Toynbee, *Turkey P.F.*, 25.
[4] Ryan, 90. Sanders, 4.
[5] Morgenthau, *Secrets of the Bosphorus*, 9.

Of these, Djemal, the Minister of Marine, Governor of Istanbul and Head of the Police, was as notorious for gambling as for judicial murders. Talaat, in whom ability and force were blent with utter ruthlessness, had risen from humble beginnings as a telegraphist to the position of manager of the Committee and Home Minister in the Cabinet. The most prominent of the trio, Enver, as War Minister appointed himself Chief of Staff and purged or imprisoned hundreds of fellow officers in order to crush political opponents. Capable, remorseless, bold, he was nicknamed 'Napoleonlik' (Little Napoleon), though less for his military campaigns in Libya and the Balkans, which were pedestrian, than for Bonapartist ambitions which led him to play the 'man of destiny', take a wife from the Imperial House, cover up his pauper's origin by fabulous luxury, and invest in real estate. 'Someone has got to govern Turkey', Talaat once told the American Ambassador, 'why not we?'[1]

This insouciance contrasted grimly with the state of the country. Capitulations (Treaty rights), concessions and credit gave alien citizens and concerns a status of unequalled privilege. The permanent 'Council of the Ottoman Debt', representing the international lenders, disposed of the main revenues: the tobacco and salt monopolies, the stamp and customs duties, the spirits, fisheries and much of the land taxes. Britons, Frenchmen, Italians, Americans and Germans maintained their own consular courts, prisons, schools and post offices. Interest payments and loan amortization drew some £ T7,426,000 (about £6,800,000 sterling) annually out of the country.[2] The Government's right of taxation over Western nationals was practically nil. Municipal enterprise, power plants, harbours and sea transport even in coastal waters were run by, and for, European capital. Railways were built not for the benefit of the Turkish economy, but to carry raw materials to the ports and foreign goods to the interior. Investments from abroad concentrated on the exploitation of natural resources rather than finishing processes. The tariff system, which was immutable without the consent of the Powers, favoured the unimpeded influx of their manufactures. The 1913 law for 'the encouragement of industry' in Turkey, therefore, was stillborn. Customs dues were uniform and so low (11 per cent *ad valorem*) that native industry was defenceless against incoming commodities. External trade was monopolized by foreigners or Greek, Armenian and Jewish compradors who could sell cheaply enough to kill local business. Of more than a thousand merchants

---

[1] Morgenthau, 14; also 8–15, 19–21, 74–5, 91, 112–13, 187. Toynbee, *Turkey P.F.*, 23, 25, 39. Ryan, 83–6. Sanders, 7–8, 19 Miller, 22–3. Savinski, *Recollections of a Russian Diplomat*, 228. Erzberger, *Souvenirs de Guerre*, 84.
[2] Ahmed Emin, *Turkey in the World War*, 92. In the 1911–12 budget—30·7 per cent went for payments on the Public Debt. *ibid*. 94.

registered in Constantinople in 1911, not more than seventy were Turks. In the whole of Asia Minor, only a few purely Turkish firms engaged in foreign commerce. The result was a huge preponderance of cheap articles from overseas. The commercial balance was adverse. In 1913, for example, imports worth 40,800,000 T. liras dwarfed the export total of only 21,400,000 T. liras. There was a chronic budget gap.[1]

The widespread poverty, for which these conditions were responsible, crippled the purchasing power of the people to such an extent that imports, in 1912, averaged about £1 17s. per head, compared to some £8 4s. for France and £26 2s. for Belgium. Corruption and embezzlement, fostered by the system of Capitulations, and official neglect depressed to rock bottom the living standards of the masses. Among those hardest hit was the peasantry. The early Young Turk promises of land distribution went with the wind. The cadastre and mortgage laws benefited the well-to-do. A minority of landlords (beys) and wealthy farmers—five per cent of the rural population—owned two-thirds of the arable soil. The bulk of the peasants, accounting for 87 per cent of all the farms, had only 35 per cent of the land, and eight per cent of the peasants had none. While individual estates included as much as 15-20,000 hectares, and those of the Church very much more, the average family languished on half a hectare per head. Under the prevailing land tenure, generally up to half of the produce was paid in kind for the lease of a plot. The main agricultural tax, officially 12·5 per cent in kind, in fact consumed through tax farming 30 to 40 per cent of the harvest. As the incentive to tillage was therefore paralysed, only 17 to 18 per cent of the cultivable ground was actually used. Chemical fertilizers and regular irrigation were unknown. The two or three-field system and the wooden plough symbolized the agrarian stagnation. And the countryman was as much at the mercy of famines, freaks of nature and pests as of the tax-gatherer and conscription sergeant, infant mortality and syphilis from the garrison towns.[2]

The urban worker fared no better. The old highly developed handicrafts were ruined by mass imports of cheap manufactures. The incomplete census of 1913 in six of the principal industrial centres, omitting coal mines, showed some 269 enterprises (in which only

[1] Emin, 91, 93, 113. Toynbee, *Turkey P.F.*, 44. Morgenthau, 73-4. Miller, 12-17. Miller, 'Turtsiya pod gnetom germanskovo imperializma v gody pervoi mirovoi voiny.' *Istoricheski Zhurnal*, 1942. No. XII. pp. 12-14. Bowman, 435-7. Adamov, II. 327, footnotes 1, 2. The budget deficit for 1911-12 came to over £ T 22,638,000. 'The deficits were covered by foreign loans . . . which in all amounted to about £ T 20,000,000 . . . every successive loan only increased the general burden. . . .' See Emin, 94. Also *The Lansing Papers*, I. 771-2.

[2] Emin, 80-3. Miller, 18-20. *Istoricheski Zhurnal*, 1942. No. XII. pp. 13-14. Bowman, 435, 437, 442-3. Toynbee, *Turkey P.F.*, 38. Erzberger 82.

15 per cent of the invested capital was Turkish) with approximately 16,000 operatives. Strikes were forbidden. The Trade Unions, formed soon after 1908, and the Socialist Party with its few Members of Parliament, were tolerated because they were too weak to threaten the régime. But when leaders like Mustapha Suphi began to organize the working class, the full force of repression fell upon the Left in 1913-14.[1] The American Ambassador Morgenthau, arriving in the Ottoman Empire in the last year of peace, found 'the nation more degraded, more impoverished, and more dismembered than ever before'.[2] The few new bills of the Government were as barren as their protests to the Powers against interference and restrictions.[3] The Young Turk Revolution accomplished neither democratization nor liberation from dependence on foreign imperialism. And when the War came, the people were sold like oriental slaves in the market of foreign policy.[4]

3
### THE TURKISH BRAND OF IMPERIALISM

The international position of the Young Turks, like their internal régime, had quickly deteriorated after a hopeful start. In July 1908, at Salonika, Enver had declared: 'We are ... brothers ... Under the same blue sky we are all proud to be Ottomans'.[5] The 'Committee of Union and Progress' forecast the complete transformation of the Turkish Empire, in which the oppressed races would turn from 'Giaours' (swine) into equals, and religious and national differences sink in a common citizenship. The inclusion of a Moslemized Jew, a Circassian, a Christian Arab and an Armenian in the Cabinet denoted the tendency to share parliamentary government, public office and cultural freedom. The non-Turkish elements, however, withstood all blandishments. The Balkan Wars, when the Porte's Hellenic, Bulgarian, Serbian, Albanian and Macedonian subjects gave their allegiance to its enemies, blighted the doctrine of Ottomanism. A substitute was discovered in Turkism as a conception of Turkish racial superiority. Springing from a group of Macedonian Turks in Salonika about 1909 and a band of Turkik refugees from Tsardom in Constantinople,[6] this movement which

[1] Emin, 91-3. Miller, 17-18, 20. The Socialist Mustapha Suphi sought refuge in Russia in 1914. See Carr, *The Bolshevik Revolution*, III. 74, 304.
[2] Morgenthau, 7. [3] Morgenthau, 73-4.
[4] See Amb. Bompard, 'L' Entrée en guerre de Turquie'. *Revue de Paris*, 15 July 1921. p. 287. Also Morgenthau, 8.
[5] Morgenthau, 7.
[6] A pamphlet published in Egypt early this century by Jusuf Akçura, a Tatar exile from Russia, had great influence in spreading Turkism in the Ottoman Empire. See B. Lewis, 'Islamic Revival in Turkey.' *International Affairs*, XXVIII. 1 Jan. 1952. p. 38.

produced literary, sports, scouts' and students' societies, intellectuals' clubs, and periodicals, was soon infected by an aggressive nationalism. From advocacy of the national language, art, history and consciousness, it was but a step to persecution of Greek communities, to general Turkifying trends, and a sweeping programme of expansion to efface the loss and shame suffered in Libya and the Balkans.[1] As early as October 1911, the Congress of the 'Committee of Union and Progress' resolved that 'the nationalities are a *quantité négligeable*'.[2] In 1912, the *Turk Jourdou* ('Turkish Hearth') association proclaimed that the Turks 'constitute the most important element in Islam'.[3] As the publicist Tekin Alp wrote:

'The Turks realized that, in order to live, they must become essentially Turkish. . . . The Turkish nation turned aside its gaze from the lost territory and looked instead upon Turania, the ideal country of the future'.[4]

Zia Goek Alp, leader of the Turkish national movement, announced:

'The country of the Turk is not Turkey . . . it is a great and eternal land, "Turan".'[5]

The quick transition to chauvinism, arising in part from anger with the aliens' economic stranglehold and manifesting, at the same time, its own predatory tendencies, launched the régime into 'Pan-Turanianism', that is the submission of all 'Turanians' to the domination of Istanbul.[6]

That Finland and Hungary were to be included in the scheme might, like the hero-worship of Attila and Jenghis Khan,[7] be discounted as a joke. More serious was the tension with Greece over the Aegean islands lost in 1913, which made the bankrupt Porte spend £2,500,000 on a dreadnought (hapless officials being compelled to sacrifice a month's salary for the new Navy Fund),[8] and brought her to the brink of war. Worse still were the hallucinations about a 'Greater Turkey':

'There are now sixty to seventy million Turkish subjects of various states in the world. . . . Now that the Ottoman Turks have awakened from their sleep of centuries they do not only think of themselves but hasten to save the other parts of their race who are living in slavery and ignorance. . . . Irredentism . . . is a political and social necessity for the Turks. . . . If

[1] Djemal, 97. Emin, 64. Ryan, 88.
[2] Toynbee, *Turkey P.F.*, 26.     [3] Emin, 193.
[4] *The Turkish and Pan-Turkish Ideal*, published by G. Kiepenheuer, Weimar, 1915. See Toynbee, *Turkey P.F.*, 17.
[5] Emin, 194.
[6] Morgenthau, 31-2, 78-9, 114, 185-6. Emin, 64, 188, 190-2. Toynbee, *Turkey P.F.*, 15, 17-18, 26, 37. Miller, 20-1.
[7] Bowman, 433. Toynbee, *Turkey P.F.*, 19.     [8] Ryan, 86, 88.

all the Turks in the world were welded into one huge community, a strong nation would be formed....'[1]

Among 'the objects of Turkish Irredentism' there figured 'Siberia, the Caucasus, the Crimea, Afghanistan ... the alluvial plains of the Volga and the Kama in European Russia ... inhabited by four or five million Turks....' Hence:

'The Pan-Turkish aspirations cannot come to their full ... realization until the Muscovite monster is crushed.... If the Russian despotism is ... to be destroyed by the brave German, Austrian, and Turkish armies, thirty to forty million Turks will receive their independence. With the ten million Ottoman Turks this will form a nation ... advancing towards a great civilisation which may perhaps be compared to that of Germany.... In some ways it will be even superior to the degenerate French and English civilisations'.[2]

The war-time dreams about hegemony in Persia, Afghanistan and Moslem India, too, began of course before 1914. The President of the Chamber, Halil, that summer, invoked memories of Salonika and 'green' Monastir,[3] while the Committee and the Cabinet adopted what Djemal calls 'an active foreign ... policy' to gain for Turkey 'her true place among the nations.'[4]

A converging line was pursued by re-hashing Abdul-Hamidian Pan-Islamism. The Young Turks, as Tekin Alp admitted, 'realized only too clearly that the still abstract ideals of Nationalism could not be expected to attract the masses, the lower classes, composed of uneducated and illiterate people. It was found more expedient to reach these classes under the flag of religion'.[5] The old appeal for the unification of all Moslems under the Caliphate was 'to combine the movement of liberation against European and American imperialism with the consolidation of the position of the khans, landlords, mullahs, and so forth'.[6] It was also to cement the Turkish hold on the Arabs, pave the way to the reconquest of Egypt, and open the gates of North Africa. Tekin Alp wrote:

'The united Turks should form the centre of gravity of the world of Islam. The Arabs of Egypt, Morocco and Tunisia, the Persians, Afghans, etc. .... must present a perfectly united front'.[7]

---

[1] Tekin Alp, *Thoughts on the Nature and Plan of a Greater Turkey*. See Toynbee, *Turkey P.F.*, 30-1.
[2] Tekin Alp, *The Turkish and Pan-Turkish Ideal*. See Toynbee, *Turkey P.F.*, 35-6.
[3] Ryan, 89. Many Young Turk leaders and officials, who used to own landed property in Macedonia which had been lost in the Balkan Wars, had a personal interest in Irredentism. See Emin, 64.
[4] Djemal, 97.   [5] See Toynbee, *Turkey P.F.* 21.
[6] Lenin, *Sochineniya* (*Works*). 3rd edit. XXV. 289.
[7] *The Turkish and Pan-Turkish Ideal*. See Toynbee, *Turkey P.F.*, 35; also 34.

The peculiar blend of the two ideologies—political Pan-Turanianism and religious Pan-Islamism—produced a form of Turkish imperialism which was profoundly disturbing to Britain, France and Russia.[1]

## 4
### GERMANY AND THE OTTOMAN EMPIRE

This circumstance, among others, endeared the Ottoman Government to Berlin. Germany, on the threshold of a decisive struggle, could not but welcome a factor so likely to divert, disrupt, perhaps dismember, her principal antagonists. Nor was the Turkish Empire merely a strategic base for political and military attack. It was, above all, one of the great markets of the world, and the enormous entrenchment there of German capital, clashing with Franco-British investments, induced William II to seek exclusive control. Already in Abdul Hamid's reign, the Kaiser's influence was great. It was not only that he refrained from joining the other Powers in pressing reforms on the Sultan; he provided training for the latter's officers, and gave the Porte subsidies and diplomatic support.[2] The year 1908, far from curtailing it, increased the ascendancy of the Reich. The Western financial and commercial pioneers had selected their chief native right-hand men (compradors) mainly from the local Greek and Armenian middle class. The German late-comers relied on, and encouraged, the compradors from the rising Turkish bourgeoisie. Hence, when the bourgeois revolution put the Young Turks in the saddle and they began, in turn, to promote the national compradors, they found themselves, through these, tied to Berlin,[3] and neither could nor wished to reverse the process.

Without experience, short of money and adequate arms, and facing enemies at home and abroad, Enver and his friends were conscious of being cajoled and flattered by the Herrenvolk, but scorned by the other side. After the Libyan and notably the Balkan Wars, Turkey—at a discount as a military factor—was the object of ill will at the London Conference and the butt of Western statesmen and journalists. London, Paris and Petersburg, refusing to consider her régime as permanent, backed the internal opposition.[4] As Moukhtar Pasha, the Turkish Ambassador in Berlin, reported,

[1] Emin, 76. Morgenthau, 80. *Diplomaticheski Slovar*, II. 789, 966. *Istoriya Diplomatii*, edit. by Potemkin, II. 268.
[2] Hallgarten, II. 136. *The Balkans*, 70.
[3] Miller, 16. The reluctance of the Young Turks to accept loans from France on conditions amounting to financial tutelage facilitated the penetration of Turkey by German capital. Baster, 111.
[4] Moukhtar Pacha, *La Turquie, l'Allemagne et l'Europe*, 249, 268.

the British and French, since 1913, were negotiating the partition of the Ottoman Empire into zones of influence. On August 21st 1913, he sent warning 'of the intention of the Western Powers to dismember Turkey sooner or later'.[1] The Porte watched France tightening her hold on Syria, the Lebanon, the Holy Land, and enmeshing other portions of the country. It watched Britain upholding the new frontiers in the Balkans and Aegean, extending control in Egypt, the Persian Gulf and half of Persia and, as Djemal wrote later, striving 'to possess Mesopotamia, possibly Palestine also', seeking 'exclusive influence over the whole of the Arabian Peninsula', and desirous that 'the title "Caliph of Islam" held by the Ottoman Sovereign should be transferred to some insignificant individual in one of the countries under her influence'.[2] It watched Russia who had fought the Ottoman Empire more than once, freed Bulgaria and Rumania, backed the Armenians, pushed into North Persia, and was stretching out for Constantinople and the Straits. The fear of, and hostility to, Tsardom was foremost in deciding Turkey's orientation, and the Alliance of her former 'protectors'— Britain and France—with Nicholas II was viewed as an ill omen.[3] Such a combination could only mean that the 'sick man on the Bosphorus' was condemned to death.

The Reich, on the other hand, could plead that it alone among the European Powers had not taken any Ottoman territory. As one of the younger imperialist States, it had no basic share in the Capitulations so hateful to the Young Turks.[4] Moreover, since the Triple Entente had embarked on a policy of which the only logical conclusion was partition, Germany must of necessity endeavour to preserve the estate intact. Rohrbach, in *Die Bagdadbahn*, asserted that the only means of meeting British aggression was to see to the 'strengthening of Turkey'.[5] The University Professor Wiedenfeld, in his book on German-Turkish economic relations, emphasized that

'our common political aims, and Germany's interest in keeping open the land-route to the Indian Ocean, will make it more than ever imperative for us to strengthen Turkey economically . . . and to put her in a position to build up . . . a body politic strong enough to withstand all external assaults.'[6]

As Djemal was to write later,

'Germany regarded Turkey as a link in the commercial and trading chain, and thus became her stoutest champion against the Entente Govern-

---

[1] Moukhtar, 248–9.  [2] Djemal, 113; also 112. Cf. pp. 49–50 below.
[3] Morgenthau, 15–17, 81. Djemal, 111.  [4] Erzberger, 77. Morgenthau, 18.
[5] *Die Bagdadbahn*, 1911 edit. p. 19. Schreiner, I. 250; also 255.
[6] Dr. K. Wiedenfeld, *Die deutsch-türkischen Wirtschaftsbeziehungen*. Duncker und Humblot, 1915. See Toynbee, *Turkey P.F.*, 47.

ments which wanted to dismember her, particularly as the elimination of Turkey would mean the final "encirclement" of Germany. ... The only way in which she could escape the pressure of the iron ring was to prevent the dismemberment of Turkey'.[1]

While Britain, France and Russia were each tugging at the best portions of the Empire from outside, the Reich was endeavouring to hold it together by capturing the whole from within. Krupp was bribing members of the Government, and the Deutsche Bank the Young Turk Parliamentary deputies. Germany's armaments cartels (Krupp and Blohm und Voss), abetted by General Mahmud Shevket Pasha who had spent ten years with the Mauser Company in Swabia, were pumping weapons into the country. Her agents were encouraging the Porte in its nefarious domestic practices. Her diplomats were profuse in assurances not only of 'territorial disinterestedness', but of what Helfferich calls her 'positive concern for the maintenance of Turkey's integrity, independence and economic, military and political consolidation'.[2] And as that consolidation was aimed at the Entente, German imperialism sought to enlarge the offensive by stimulating and inciting the Pan-Turanian and Pan-Islam tendencies.[3]

The impact of Potsdam did the rest. Enver, having served as Military Attaché in Berlin (1909-1911), was dazzled by the jackboot and scabbard, and had implicit faith in the Prussian Army. The curl of his moustache à la William II showed the extent to which he aped all things German. His former hosts were quick to perceive in him their instrument. His 1913 putsch, which was spurred on by German High Finance, overthrew the Anglophil Cabinet in Constantinople,[4] and was a victory for the Kaiser. So was Enver's elevation to the Ministry of War and personal control of the Army. As the Army was the ultimate arbiter of the régime, his power grew so absolute that even Talaat, the party boss, became dependent on him. Talaat, moreover, realized that his annexationist schemes required military backing which only the Reich could supply. Warned that Turkey, by her new alignment, would suffer the fate of Egypt, he replied: 'We shall use Germany to help us reconstruct and defend the country until we are able to govern ... with our own strength. When that day comes, we can say good-bye to the Germans within

[1] Djemal, 113. See also *The Lansing Papers*, I. 767.
[2] Helfferich, *Der Weltkrieg*, II. 52. Also Erzberger, 77. Hallgarten, II. 136, footnote 5; 139 and *ibid.* footnote 7; 140, 271, 273, 296. Emin, 66, 69, 181. Toynbee, *Turkey P.F.*, 49. Yerusalimski, 198, 207, 248. Skoda, whose agent was Enver's brother-in-law, also armed Turkey during the Balkan Wars. Hallgarten, II. 273, footnotes 2 and 3.
[3] Miller, 35. *Diplomaticheski Slovar*, II. 966.
[4] Hallgarten, II. 295, 297. *Diplomaticheski Slovar*, II. 965.

twenty-four hours'.[1] Meanwhile, the Ambassador von Wangenheim, playing on the ambitions and foibles of the two rulers, in effect ruled them both. The Military Attaché von Strempel, the trusted agent of German Heavy Industry, was thoroughly at home at the Ottoman Ministry of War. Liman von Sanders's transformation into 'Liman Pasha', Marshal of Turkey and Inspector-General of the Army was accompanied by the appointment of German officers to senior commands, the training of Turkish soldiers in the Reich, and constant drilling around Constantinople. In July 1914, the Sultan attended a gala review, from which the Representatives of the Entente were conspicuously absent. 'What in January had been an undisciplined, ragged rabble,' the American Ambassador wrote later, 'was now parading with the goose-step . . . clad in . . . field-grey'.[2]

Thus, while Britain and, to an even greater degree, France were still economically and financially paramount in the Ottoman Empire, the Reich already enjoyed military and political supremacy. On the eve of Sarayevo, the Porte was, in practice, an agency for German imperialism.

---

[1] Morgenthau, 21.
[2] Morgenthau, 30; also 17–21, 26–7. Djemal, 83, 102. Hallgarten, II. 295–6. Sanders, 5–7. Miller, 22. Pears, *Forty Years in Constantinople*, 340.

## CHAPTER II

# The Disposition of Turkey

1

### OVERTURES TO THE TRIPLE ENTENTE AND ALLIANCE WITH GERMANY

NO sooner had the Bosnian pistol shots brought down the avalanche, than Wangenheim in Constantinople pressed for Alliance.¹ He found the Cabinet divided between his clients and those who understood the risks the Enver group was running. Djemal, believed to favour a Western orientation, went to Paris early in July 1914. Whether he was sincere or merely bent on an alibi for the triumvirate, he had a few talks with the Foreign Minister Viviani. The latter, busy with his own and President Poincaré's imminent visit to Nicholas II, referred him to the Director of Political Affairs at the Quai d'Orsay.²

The Pasha's first topic was the Aegean archipelago lost, by decree of the Powers, to Greece after the Balkan Wars. Turkey was ready to forgo some of the islands. But Imbros and Tenedos commanded the entry to the Dardanelles. Khios and Mitylini (Lesbos) controlled the approach to Smyrna, her greatest Mediterranean port and terminus of all the railways to inner Anatolia. From these four points, the Greeks, who had revealed their intentions by the recent redemption of Crete and had, in the Hellenic colonies, a Trojan horse on the Turkish shore, threatened the vitals of the Ottoman Empire. The Porte, therefore, felt it had a serious grudge and a case for the return of the islands. 'You consider it a wise policy always to back the Greeks', Djemal said to the French, 'but ... one day we shall be in a position to be more useful to you than the Greeks. The Ottoman Government says to itself: "The object of ... France and England is to forge an iron ring around the Central Powers". That ring is closed except in the South-East. ... If you want to close your iron ring ... you must try to find some solution of this question of the islands. ... You must take us into your Entente and at the same time protect us against Russia'.³

---

¹ *Diplomaticheski Slovar*, I. 479.
² Djemal, 104–5. On the divisions in the Turkish Cabinet see *Diplomaticheski Slovar*, I. 554. *Das Zaristische Russland im Weltkriege*, p. 22. Stieve, *Isvolski im Weltkriege*, p. 76.
³ Djemal, 105–6. In the original: 'South-West', which is obviously an error. For the question of the islands see Morgenthau, 30–1. *The Balkans*, 231. Adamov, I. 178, footnote 2; 230, footnote 2.

34

## THE DISPOSITION OF TURKEY

But these, from the standpoint of France and Britain, were impossible demands. Their support of Greece[1] was part of a deliberate policy of gaining Balkan accessories to the 1914 coalition. A crucial feature of that coalition was the Alliance with Russia at the expense, to some extent at least, of the Turks—and not a Turkish alliance with guarantees against Russia. Viviani, in consequence, refrained from negotiations. His officials, waiting for a 'joint decision' at Petersburg, avoided commitment, and Djemal was fobbed off with receptions and an Order of the *Legion d'Honneur*. His instructions had been to 'emphasize... how much importance we attach to the friendship of France'. But her answer, as he recollects, 'was only a veiled refusal... under no circumstances would she vouchsafe us her help'.[2]

Meanwhile, Herr Wangenheim was waiting, watching, wooing. Turkey, as General Sanders testifies, was expected by the Reich 'not only to defend the Straits and protect her frontiers... but conquer Egypt, free Persia, prepare the creation of independent states in Trans-Caucasia, threaten India from Afghanistan... and... furnish active assistance in European theatres....'[3] The Sultan was to light for William II the fuses of a 'Holy War', rousing the Moslems against their British, French and Russian overlords.[4] Ottoman adherence would enable German diplomacy militarily and politically to impress and intimidate the Balkans. It promised to feed Germany's Army with metals, cotton, wool, fats and other raw materials, while severing the artery between East and West. To close the Dardanelles was to dry up the occidental flow of Russia's grain and ruin her economy, to choke off her imports of arms from Vickers and Creusot and paralyse her fighting strength. It was not too much to hope that such a blockade might detach Nicholas II from his friends. To shut the Straits meant also to deprive Britain, France and Italy of a source of food and stop the Tsarist troops from being shipped to France. The Entente, in short, would be neutralized, Germany's encirclement broken and the War won by the Central Powers, if they enrolled the Crescent as an Ally.[5]

The Turko-German parleys, supported by the Austro-Hungarian

---

[1] According to Moukhtar, 274–5, the British Foreign Office, since General Sanders's arrival in Constantinople, was increasingly orientated on Athens.

[2] Djemal, 103, 106; also 107. Emin, too, argues that the Entente was 'inactive' in regard to winning Turkey. See p. 70. Also Moukhtar, 262, Miller, 25, 37.

[3] Sanders, 326.

[4] As early as 1889, Friedrich Naumann anticipated that 'the Caliph of Constantinople will once more uplift the standard of the Holy War. The Sick Man will raise himself for the last time to cry aloud to Egypt, to the Sudan, to East Africa, Persia, Afghanistan, and India: "War against England".' See Emin, 180–1.

[5] Bethmann-Hollweg, *Betrachtungen zum Weltkriege*, II. 12. Helfferich, II. 54, 64, 199–200. Erzberger, 77. Morgenthau, 3, 4, 71, 105. *Diplomaticheski Slovar*, I. 479.

Ambassador, continued throughout the crisis of July 1914. Early that month, Enver met the Chief of Staff Moltke in Berlin. When Djemal, returning home with empty hands, saw the draft of the Turco-German Treaty, he found it 'an excellent compact between two independent Governments', and accepted it 'without hesitation'.[1] Under its terms, the Reich pledged its support to the Porte in 'abolishing the capitulations', obtaining from Bulgaria an 'agreement corresponding to Ottoman interests in the division of the territories to be conquered in the Balkans', regaining the Aegean archipelago (including Crete),[2] if Greece should go against them, extending Turkish territory at the cost of Russia, 'so as to secure direct contact . . . with the Moslem populations' there (that is the conquest of Russian Armenia), and receiving 'appropriate compensation' for the losses to be incurred in the War. In return, the Turks undertook to side with the Austrians and Germans against the Tsar. On August 2nd and 6th, documents to that effect were signed in secret.[3]

Paradoxically, the clinching of the Alliance, instead of quashing diplomatic activity, gave it a fresh impetus. 'If the English, French and Russians', Djemal claims to have warned his colleagues, 'made a sudden attack on the Dardanelles and the Bosphorus . . . advanced on Erzerum, and after occupying Constantinople and Erzerum approached the interior of Anatolia . . . our Army would be unable to complete its mobilization . . . and the downfall of the Ottoman Empire would be decreed at the very outset'.[4] Turkey was militarily so weak that her immediate belligerency could only be a liability to the Central Empires. Time was required to get ready, and to acclimatize opinion, including that of a section of the Cabinet. The Kaiser, therefore, was content for a while with alarming Russia, pinning down British forces in Egypt and deterring Greece and Rumania from aiding the Serbs. He reckoned, too, that a quick defeat of France would reduce the price to be paid the Turks. It was with his consent that the Porte, though ordering general mobilization and a state of siege, proclaimed itself 'strictly neutral'.[5]

The respite was useful in more than one respect. The very fact that the critical step had been taken provided the triumvirate with food for thought. Their premature commitment had paralysed

[1] Djemal, 109, 114. The quotations are from his book.   [2] Pears, 352.
[3] Klyuchnikov i [and] Sabanin, *Mezhdunarodnaya politika noveishevo vremeni*, II. pp. 8–9, 17, reproduce the complete text of the Secret Agreements. Moukhtar, 253–4, gives the text of what is, essentially, the Military Convention. Reports had it that Germany also promised the Young Turks Tiflis, Tabriz and Cairo. See Einstein, p. XIV. On 6 Aug. '14, an understanding was also arrived at between Turkey and Bulgaria.
[4] Djemal, 116.
[5] Helfferich, II. 55–6. Morgenthau, 62–3. Adamov, I. 90–1. Miller, 29.

## THE DISPOSITION OF TURKEY 37

initiative. 'If we had waited,' Djemal asked himself, 'would not [the Entente] have made us . . . more profitable proposals?'[1] Neutrality, the *sine qua non* for war preparation, was also the means of recovering freedom of choice. It would, some leaders urged, enable a strengthened and well-armed Turkey to decide whether to stay with Germany on better terms, or to keep out of the War in return for a handsome reward from the Entente. As for the compact with Berlin, the Young Turks, if it came to that, had no more need to be squeamish over a scrap of paper than their European tutors. Was not Italy's indifference to the Triple Alliance creating a precedent?[2] Had not the Reich violated Belgium? Britain's belligerency, moreover, wholly upset the international scene. The German Treaty offered no protection against such a contingency.[3] The Porte's original obligation to fight Russia led all of a sudden straight into a great war. It would have been easy to argue that the Treaty just concluded was no longer valid. Since Germany, at this juncture, had no effective powers of coercion, the Porte could take an independent line.[4]

Accordingly, a series of soundings was taken in various capitals. Talaat, seeking to re-insure Ottoman prospects in the Central coalition, journeyed to Sofia and Bucharest. In the latter, he met Hellenic delegates, ostensibly to settle the islands problem, but actually ready to make a break. In fact, no agreement was reached, and as the Turks had apparently decided to wait for a suitable moment to resort to force,[5] the issue was adjourned to the Greek calends. Simultaneously and principally Talaat strove to win Bulgaria and Rumania for an anti-Russian alignment, only to find that both preferred to wait on events.[6] The Finance Minister Djavid Bey asked Bompard, the French Ambassador in Constantinople, for a positive offer, such as a written fifteen to twenty years' guarantee of territorial integrity and the suppression of the Capitulations, so as to counter the German bribes.[7] Djemal handed the British Envoy a list of conditions on which, as he avowed subsequently, 'we might possibly join the Entente'.[8] The Grand Vizier, in order to dis-

---

[1] Djemal, 110–11.     [2] See part II. pp. 169–73.
[3] Nor against war with a Balkan State.
[4] *Diplomaticheski Slovar*, I. 480. Miller, 30. Emin, 68.
[5] Izvolski to Sazonov, 27 Aug. 1914. Stieve, p. 82. Giers to Sazonov, 4 Sept. '14. *Das Zaristische Russland*, p. 39. Also Ryan, 98.
[6] Poklevski to Sazonov, 25 Aug. '14. *Die Internationalen Beziehungen im Zeitalter des Imperialismus*, II. 6. I. No. 159, pp. 119–20. Izvolski to Sazonov, 27 Aug. '14. Stieve, p. 82. Poincaré, *Au service de la France*, V. 125, 153. Ryan, 98. Jonescu, *Some Personal Impressions*, 88–9, 177–82.
[7] Poincaré, V. 141. Bréal, *Philippe Berthelot*, 137. Djemal, 123. This request was also made to the British and Russian Ambassadors. See Giers to Sazonov, 19 and 20 Aug. '14. *Das Zaristische Russland*, pp. 30–1.
[8] Djemal, 123.

organize the latter, whispered into Sir Louis Mallet's ear how worried he was about Russia's intentions, and how anxious to have Western protection.[1] Meanwhile, Enver—in confidential talks with the Russian Military Attaché—proposed unblushingly a five to ten years' alliance with the Tsar. Alleging that, contrary to current opinion, Turkey was not yet tied by any agreements to the Central Powers, and vowing the utmost goodwill towards the Northern neighbour, he offered to withdraw his troops from the Caucasian frontiers, to remove the German instructors, and to lend Russia an army in the Balkans to act against any one state hostile to her, or to operate jointly with Bulgaria against Austria. In exchange, he demanded the Aegean islands from Greece and the Moslem-inhabited parts of Western Thrace held by Bulgaria. For these amputations, Athens would be compensated in Epirus, Sofia in Macedonia, and Belgrade in Bosnia-Herzegovina. The outcome would be a South- and Mid-Eastern bloc against, and at the expense of, the Austro-Hungarian Empire[2] with which the Porte had just entered into solemn diplomatic union.

The Russian Foreign Minister Sazonov instructed his spokesman to continue the discussions 'in a friendly spirit, if only to gain some time, avoiding commitments of any kind'.[3] This caution was due to his knowledge of 'Napoleonlik's' notorious addiction to Pan-Turanianism and subservience to the Reich. Sazonov had received strong hints, if not more, of the conclusion of the Turco-German Alliance.[4] His scepticism was further increased by reports that the Turks, at this very time, were sounding Sofia on the subject of a military convention, and that his Ambassador in Constantinople, Giers, had had 'exactly the same proposals' from the Bulgarian Minister there, which 'proves beyond doubt that, with the support of Austria and Germany, Turkey and Bulgaria had been seeking to reach agreement on the line both would take in the present crisis'.[5] The Ottoman overture was probably meant to embroil Petrograd with the Bulgarians, Rumanians and Greeks who just then needed more than careful treatment. But whether or not Enver was in earnest

[1] Sazonov to Benckendorff, 16 Aug. '14, quoting Buchanan. *Das Zaristische Russland*, p. 25.
[2] Giers to Sazonov, 5 and 9 Aug. '14. *Das Zaristische Russland*, pp. 7–8, 13–14. Sazonov to Benckendorff and Izvolski, 16 Aug. '14. *ibid.* 26. Enver's proposal was endorsed by the Grand Vizier. See Giers to Sazonov, 10, 14 and 18 Aug. '14. *Das Zaristische Russland*, pp. 16, 21. Adamov, II. 237, footnote 1. On 11 Aug. '14, Sazonov informed his Minister in Bucharest that Djemal had arrived in Petrograd. *Das Zaristische Russland*, p. 22, footnote 8.
[3] Sazonov to Giers, 6 Aug. '14. *Das Zaristische Russland*, p. 11.
[4] Giers to Sazonov, 5 Aug. '14, *ibid.* p. 10. Savinski to Sazonov, 7 Aug. '14. Giers to Sazonov, 8 Aug. '14. *Internationale Beziehungen*, II. 6. I. p. 14, footnote 1.
[5] Giers to Sazonov, 5 Aug. '14. *Das Zaristische Russland*, p. 9.

(it has still to be proved that the acceptance of his demands would not have severed the Porte from the Central Powers), Sazonov, while sympathizing with parts of this scheme, sought not a Turkish alliance at the expense of the Balkans, but a Balkan bloc at the ultimate expense of the Ottoman Empire. It was in accordance with this policy that he offered Bulgaria a slice of Serbian Macedonia, to which he was soon to add Turkish Thrace down to the Enos-Midia Line. The talks with Enver, therefore, were to be pursued in a desultory fashion 'until I have had a reply from Sofia'.[1] Nor was he prepared to concede to the Sultan any territorial acquisitions other than one island in the Aegean. Hence the Turkish Chargé d'Affaires in Petrograd was offered, instead of 'questionable conquests', a guarantee of his country's integrity and, as a reward for an understanding, the recovery of Germany's economic, railway and other concessions in Asia Minor.[2] Considering how greatly the Turks desired to shake off the Capitulations and that, as Giers wired, 'what matters to the Porte is exactly territorial gain',[3] Sazonov's answer clearly was not intended to give satisfaction. But even if the arrangement with Enver had been wanted in Russia, it would have been precluded by her industrial, financial and political dependence on Britain and France.

2

RUSSIA'S POLICY TOWARDS TURKEY

The striving of Russia's rulers for Constantinople and the Straits (as well as the Franco-British resistance to it) was traditional. Although the Russians had almost no share in the economy and finance of the Ottoman Empire,[4] the Tsarist military-feudal imperialism menaced her with its predatory tendencies. These were strongly reinforced by the rapid German-sponsored rearmament of Turkey and her simultaneous conquest from within by the Reich. It was not only that these factors threatened to bar the Russian road to 'Tsargrad' and to encourage a Turkish attack on Batum. To surrender the Straits to Germany, as Sazonov informed his Sovereign in December 1913, 'would be tantamount to subjecting the whole economic development of Southern Russia to that State'.[5] The

---

[1] Sazonov to Giers, 10 Aug. '14. *Das Zaristische Russland*, p. 15. Sazonov to Savinski, 30 Aug. '14. *ibid*. p. 80.
[2] Sazonov to Giers, 14 Aug. '14. Sazonov to Benckendorff, 15 Aug. '14. *ibid.* pp. 21, 23.
[3] Giers to Sazonov, 13 and 19 Aug. '14. *ibid*. pp. 20, 29.
[4] No Turkish securities were held by Russians. The solitary Russian Bank for Foreign Trade in Constantinople could not be compared to the financial giants of the other Powers. See *Das Zaristische Russland*, p. 57. Also Adamov, II. p. 353.
[5] Hallgarten, II. 340; also 140. Adamov, II. p. 347. Miller, 11, 28.

seizure of Constantinople, therefore, became a matter of prime importance in which the usual imperialist considerations were blended with strategic requirements and the need to defend the Russian economy. 'We knew', Sazonov wrote later, 'that this fundamental and age-long problem... could only be settled in connection with a European war....'[1] Nor could Russian diplomacy have been unaware of Franco-British designs in, and their implications for, the Middle East.[2] On February 21st 1914, the Foreign, War and Naval Ministries, with the approval of Nicholas II, decided jointly, 'in the event of a large European war, to solve the "Eastern" question in Russia's favour, that is by establishing her domination in Constantinople, the Bosphorus and the Dardanelles.'[3]

But in the summer of 1914—owing to the undiminished opposition of France and Britain to such a programme—Sazonov's immediate aim was not annexation ('Russia in 1914 was making no such pretensions, at least openly...' the American Envoy has recorded),[4] but to obtain free passage for her Navy through the Straits. When the world crisis broke, the Tsarist General Staff ruled out parallel operations against the Central Powers and the Ottomans.[5] Moreover, the British Ambassador Buchanan was instructed by his Chief to impress upon the Russian Foreign Minister the supreme need for helping France in the struggle with Germany. 'The British and French Ambassadors have expressed the hope that... we shall keep back no troops for the defence of the Caucasian frontiers.'[6] That is why, until decisions had been reached on the principal fronts, it was desirable to keep the Porte quiet.[7] Military necessity was reinforced by the political argument that Turkey's belligerency against the Entente would inflame the smouldering Greek and Bulgarian aspirations regarding Constantinople. If they took up arms for such a cause, victorious Russia would be confronted with awkward rivalries.[8] Hence Sazonov's protracted negotiations with Enver, and his efforts to recommend them to his Allies. He instructed the Russian Ambassador Benckendorff to state in London that, 'as we

[1] Sazonov, *Fateful Years*, 242.   [2] See pp. 49–51, 80–1 below.
[3] Memorandum by Nemitz, the Chief of Black Sea Operations, Naval Staff, 14 Dec. '14. Adamov, I. No. 3, p. 185.
[4] Morgenthau, 16. For the Russian policy at the time see Miller, 28.
[5] *Diplomaticheski Slovar*, I. 479. Adamov, I. p. 90.
[6] Sazonov to Izvolski and Benckendorff, 15 Aug. '14. *Das Zaristische Russland*, p. 23.
[7] Sazonov to Kudashev, Director of the Diplomatic Chancellery attached to the General Staff, and to Giers, 29 Aug. '14. *Das Zaristische Russland*, p. 35. The French Ambassador in Petrograd, Paléologue, wired on 12 Aug. '14 that the Russian Government contemplated no action prejudicial to the integrity of the Ottoman Empire. See Poincaré, V. 82. 'Russia had been genuinely anxious to avoid war with Turkey...' Grey, *Twenty-Five Years*, II. 168.
[8] *Diplomaticheski Slovar*, I. 479.

are at war with Germany and Austria, we must endeavour to avoid a collision with Turkey....'[1] He proposed that the Porte should be offered a three-Power guarantee of territorial inviolability, discussions on a new diplomatic combination, a modification of the Capitulations as a first step towards their abolition, the acquisition of all the German economic concessions, especially those for the Baghdad Railway, and—as a positive gain—the island of Lemnos which had been seized by the Greeks in 1913. In return for these benefits, Turkey was to bind herself to demobilize and observe neutrality.[2]

To secure Turkish neutrality was also the professed purpose of Britain and France. President Poincaré claims that French diplomacy exerted itself to prevent Ottoman belligerency.[3] Sir Edward Grey asserts that, apart from the seizure of the Turkish ships, everything conceivable was done to make it easy and even profitable for Turkey to remain neutral'.[4] 'Our policy is to keep Turkey out of the War by backing up the moderates . . .', the chief British Dragoman wrote in a private letter.[5] Nevertheless, Sazonov's suggestions—except for the territorial guarantee—were turned down. His idea of compensating Greece for the abandonment of Lemnos by giving her territory in Epirus was certain to antagonize Italy. Whilst Russia could lose little if inroads were made into the Capitulations, the Entente would forfeit much. Whereas the Russians could only gain from Germany's economic and financial eviction from the Near East, the French investors, in particular, were afraid of creating a precedent likely to affect their interests. An understanding with the Porte, moreover, would have been in conflict with the intentions of the Entente. Benckendorff, the Ambassador in London, therefore, cabled to Petrograd: 'Grey is positively against the idea of offering any territorial extension, such as the offer of Lemnos. This would, in his view, give rise to wavering in Greece. . . . Grey is anxious to

---

[1] Sazonov to Benckendorff, 6 Sept. '14. *Internationale Beziehungen*, II. 6. I. No. 226, p. 171.

[2] Sazonov to Benckendorff and Izvolski, 15 Aug. '14. *Internationale Beziehungen*, II. 6. I. No. 100, pp. 73–4. Stieve, p. 53. Sazonov to Benckendorff and Izvolski, 16 Aug. '14. *Das Zaristische Russland*, p. 25. Also Poincaré, V. 112, 117, 142.

According to an undated telegram from Paléologue, Sazonov had originally intended to 'attract the Porte to our side.' (See Adamov, I. p. 226, footnote 1). On 11 Aug. '14, Poincaré noted that Russia was trying to draw Turkey 'into the wake' of the Triple Entente. (Poincaré, V.7. Also Moukhtar, 257–8). Whether this information was correct or not, active co-operation between Russia and Turkey was precluded by the nature of Enver's demands (see above), and by the probable tendency in Petrograd to conclude 'an alliance . . . under conditions which would have amounted to a protectorate'. (Emin, 66). But, above all, Sazonov must have modified his policy in order to meet that of Britain and France.

[3] Poincaré, V. 62, 112.   [4] Grey, II. 166.

[5] 21 Aug. '14. Ryan, 97–8; also 96. Morgenthau, 62–3.

believe in Greece as a prompt and sure Ally in the event of a break with the Turks'.[1] And from Paris, the Ambassador Izvolski reported to Sazonov that in the Foreign Minister 'Doumergue's opinion, which is shared by the London Cabinet, it would be dangerous . . . to come forward with formal statements' on the economic concessions in Asia Minor, as 'this could provide the German party in Constantinople with weapons against us'.[2]

### 3
### TURKEY: GROUNDS FOR WAR WITH THE WEST

In fact, however, that party already had a most powerful weapon against the West. Two battleships, the *Sultan Osman* and the *Reshadieh* were built for Turkey by Armstrong, Whitworth and Co. before the War. Part of the £7,000,000 sterling, disbursed for them in advance, had been collected in a wave of public patriotism. Money was raised by subscriptions at every door, at popular fairs, or by women selling their hair. Official propaganda proclaimed that to develop the Navy was the royal road to the recovery of the Aegean islands and the reckoning with Greece. In Djemal's words, 'our one object in life was to make our Fleet superior to the Greek Fleet. . . .'[3] Late in July 1914, a Turkish crew of 500 was waiting on the Tyne to take over the first dreadnought—when Churchill, the First Lord of the Admiralty, suddenly on the 31st requisitioned both.[4]

The British Government, in getting into gear for war, obviously had to take into account that the Porte might line up with Germany. Churchill says that 'we could not afford to do without these two fine ships. Still less could we afford to see them . . . used against us'. Had they been handed over to the Turks, a corresponding force would have had to be employed to watch them. 'Thus the British numbers would have been reduced by two instead of being increased by two'.[5] Moreover, the Russian Admiralty did not desire the delivery of the two vessels.[6] As the contract for these allowed for pre-emption, and Turkey was offered financial compensation,

---

[1] Benckendorff to Sazonov, 17 Aug. '14. *Internationale Beziehungen*, II. 6. I. No. 118, p. 89. For the French objections to the transfer of Lemnos see Poincaré, V. 117.
[2] Izvolski to Sazonov, 21 Aug. '14. Stieve, p. 67. The French Ambassador in Constantinople opposed Sazonov's suggestion. Adamov, I. p. 226, footnote 1.
[3] Djemal, 95 (cf. Pears, 350); also 91. Emin, 65. Moukhtar, 270 and *ibid.* footnote 1.
[4] Churchill, *The World Crisis, 1911-1914*, p. 209.
[5] Churchill, *1914*, p. 209.
[6] Giers to Sazonov, 2. Aug. '14. *Das Zaristische Russland*, p. 6. Also Gooch, *Recent Revelations of European Diplomacy*, 104.

Britain, it was claimed,[1] acted within her legal rights. But if she had wanted deliberately to incense the Turks and drive them into the Kaiser's arms, she could not have chosen a more effective means. The explosion of anger in Constantinople ranged from a furious protest by the Government (on August 7th) against a breach of international law to wild press attacks and invocations of 'A Thousand Curses' on the faithless friend. Enver and the Germans found it easy to fan the flames. Here was a justification for the call to arms. '... in the struggles ... between the Turkish war party and those who favoured neutrality', Churchill writes, 'this episode seemed to have weight.'[2] The American Ambassador was more explicit: 'The transaction gave Wangenheim the greatest opportunity of his life.'[3]

Nor was this the only cause the German Envoy was given for rejoicing. The Reich had two formidable cruisers, the *Goeben* and the *Breslau*, as part of a Central Powers squadron in the Mediterranean. The Russian Naval Staff and Foreign Ministry had foreseen the danger that both vessels might pass into the Sultan's possession.[4] On August 7th 1914, Sazonov instructed Izvolski that 'the Admiralty considers it possible that Austria will attempt ... to send her Fleet to the Black Sea, where it would undoubtedly have preponderance over ours, after being reinforced by German and perhaps Turkish ships ... it is extremely desirable to ascertain as soon as possible, what we can count upon in the way of French and British countermeasures to such an operation'.[5] On the 11th, he requested his Ambassadors in London and Paris to inform the respective Governments, in reference to the *Breslau* and the *Goeben*, that 'we consider it of the utmost importance ... that the passage of the two ships should be prevented ... by force'.[6]

Meanwhile, the Allies had followed closely the movements of both men-of-war. By August 1st, when the two cruisers were at Brindisi, practically the whole British Fleet was at Malta. Admiral Milne, the Commander-in-Chief, had orders that his 'primary task' was to assist the French in guarding their African army trans-

---

[1] Grey, II. 166: 'This was quite legal'. See also Toynbee and Kirkwood, *Turkey*, 55. On the other hand, Djemal wrote later (p. 112) that, since Britain was not at war at the time, she was not entitled to take such action. Giers reported to Sazonov on 7 Aug. '14 that the Porte had been assured by British legal opinion that 'English law does not admit of such a confiscation by the English Government'. *Internationale Beziehungen*, II. 6. I. p. 10, footnote 5.
[2] Churchill, *1914*, p. 482. Ryan, 95. Moukhtar, 269-70, 272-4. Pears, 350. Giers to Sazonov, 5 Oct. '14. *Das Zaristische Russland*, p. 51.
[3] Morgenthau, 49. Also *The Lansing Papers*, I. 766.
[4] A telegram from the Russian Chargé d'Affaires in Constantinople, 21 Jan. '14. Adamov, I. p. 225, footnote 1.
[5] Sazonov to Izvolski, 7 Aug. '14. Stieve, p. 27.
[6] Sazonov to Izvolski, 11 Aug. '14. Stieve, p. 45. A telegram to the same effect was also sent the day before. *ibid*. p. 39. Also Corbett, *Naval Operations*, I. 90.

ports. He was also to detach Rear-Admiral Troubridge's squadron 'to shadow the *Goeben*',[1] and prevent her escape into the Adriatic. On August 3rd, Admiral de Lapeyrère sailed from Bizerta with identical instructions to protect the troop convoys and 'to watch' the *Goeben*.[2] On August 4th, Berlin—not free from doubt about the new Ottoman Ally—directed the *Goeben* and the *Breslau* to the Dardanelles. William II informed the King of Greece that the two ships would join the Turkish Navy for combined action, and the communication was transmitted to the Chief of the British Naval Mission in Greece, who must obviously have sent it on to London.[3] On the same day, the *Goeben* and the *Breslau* revealed their whereabouts by shelling Bona and Philippeville. Still the British ban on attack remained in force, and H.M.S. *Dublin* had idly to watch them go by. On the 5th, the Ambassador Sir Rennell Rodd in Rome learned that they had anchored in Messina, and Poincaré noted that French units were sent after them.[4] 'They formed no match for the large British and French naval forces which were roaming through the Mediterranean. . . .'[5] But none of these came on to the scene. Only the little *Gloucester*, sighting the *Breslau* and the *Goeben* on the 6th, remained 24 hours on their heels, but avoided action, and despite much movement and bustle by Troubridge's ships she was left to make the chase alone. Seeing the enemy pass Cape Matapan ('route à l'Est', as Poincaré recorded),[6] that is leaving behind the Adriatic, she was recalled by Milne without being replaced by any other cruiser. It was not until midnight on August the 7th/8th that the Admiral left Malta, steaming leisurely along the coast of Greece, and not until the 10th that he entered the Aegean, some 60 hours after the *Goeben* had passed the Cervi Channel. And when the *Goeben* and the *Breslau* reached the safety of the Dardanelles on the 10th, the pursuers did not arrive outside until two days later, and simply contented themselves with blockading the Straits.[7] While this was going on, the French Ambassador was urging upon Sazonov that no Russian warships should approach the Bosphorus.[8] Admiral Condouriotis (as Melas, the Secretary of the King of Greece, recollects), 'thinking that the British were going to force the Straits',

[1] Corbett, I. 35.
[2] Bertie to the Foreign Office, 3 Aug. '14. Corbett, I. 35–6.
[3] Abbott, *Greece and the Allies*, 10 and *ibid.* footnote 1. Melas, *Ex-King Constantine and the War*, 211.
[4] Rodd, *Social and Diplomatic Memories*, III. 211. Poincaré, V. 10.
[5] Morgenthau, 47; also 46, 48.    [6] Poincaré, V. 40.
[7] Churchill, *1914*, pp. 255–6, 482. Asquith, *Memories and Reflections*, II. 26. Corbett, I. 33–6, 54–71. Melas, 214. On 9 Aug. it was known in Paris that the two German cruisers were in the Aegean, and Poincaré noted 'the strong probability' that they would aid the Turks in attacking Russia. See Poincaré, V.5.
[8] An undated telegram from Paléologue. See Adamov, I. p. 226, footnote 1.

THE DISPOSITION OF TURKEY  45

asked, 'to be allowed the honour of placing himself . . . with the Greek flotilla at the head of the attacking squadron. . . . The reply . . . was that: "The British squadron, having no orders, could do nothing" . . . And to think that the Dardanelles in those days were only defended with some old catapults.'[1]

4

THE IMPORTANCE OF KEEPING RUSSIA IN THE WAR

The bloodless victory of the *Goeben* and the *Breslau* provided Germany with the means to exert pressure on the Porte, and Enver with an unanswerable argument. In Constantinople the scales sank heavily on the side of war.[2] Sazonov stormed in a telegram to Benckendorff in London that the arrival of the *Goeben* has put the Tsarist Black Sea Fleet 'in a most difficult position, which is all the more regrettable since the English had the means of preventing her passage through the Dardanelles'.[3] But the British Admiralty, accepting Milne's explanations of his failure, exonerated him from blame. For, although the Toulon Fleet had proved sufficient to secure the Western Mediterranean, his original orders to pay primary attention to the French army transports had not been cancelled. The Court Martial which tried Troubridge on the same count 'found that he had acted in accordance with his instructions' as he had, in fact, closed the Adriatic to the two German ships, and he was 'fully and honourably acquitted'.[4] The Captain of the *Gloucester*, on being awarded the Companionship of the Bath, was officially commended for his 'combination of audacity with *restraint* . . . and strict conformity to orders'.[5] The Chief of the French Naval Staff, referring to the alleged sale of the two cruisers by Germany to the Sultan, said to the Russian Naval Attaché in Paris that no one can forbid a belligerent to weaken himself if he so chooses.[6] The British Foreign Secretary remarked to Benckendorff that he preferred 'to see the two ships in Turkish hands rather than in German hands in the Mediterranean'.[7] And Asquith, the Prime Minister, admitted to

---

[1] Melas, 215; also 210–11, 147. Adamov, I. p. 225, footnote 1.
[2] Giers to Sazonov, 12 Aug. and 5 Oct. '14. *Das Zaristische Russland*, pp. 18 and 51. Also Grey, II. 164.
[3] Sazonov to Benckendorff, 13 Aug. '14. *Das Zaristische Russlard*, pp. 20–1.
[4] Corbett, I. 67–8.
[5] Corbett, I. 66–7. *The Times*, 15 Sept. 1952. The italics are by the present author.
[6] Izvolski to Sazonov, 13 Aug. '14. *Internationale Beziehungen*, II. 6. I. No. 89, p. 61.
[7] Benckendorff to Sazonov, 12 Aug. '14. *Internationale Beziehungen*, II. 6. I. No. 76, p. 52. But on 17 Aug. Churchill wrote to Grey that 'we have to keep two British [battle] cruisers, which are urgently needed elsewhere, waiting with other vessels outside the Dardanelles' to watch the *Goeben* and the *Breslau*. See Churchill, *1914*, p. 483; also Corbett, I. 88.

his Diary: 'As we shall insist that the *Goeben* shall be manned by a Turkish instead of a German crew, it does not much matter, as the Turkish sailors cannot navigate her except on to rocks or mines'.[1]

Such unconcern, verging on satisfaction, was attributed to the relief of having removed from Egypt and French North-Africa the threat of bombardment. The startling inactivity of the Entente Admirals Milne and de Lapeyrère was explained on the grounds that their squadrons had been 'otherwise engaged'.[2] Sir Edward Grey, in his Reminiscences, affirms that 'we did not know at the time that Turkey already had a Secret Treaty binding her to join Germany'.[3] The failure to follow and destroy the two cruisers in the Dardanelles was justified by respect for international law. The Conventions of 1856 and 1871 closed the Narrows to foreign warships so long as Turkey was at peace. Although the Germans had broken this regulation, Great Britain, it was said, would not violate the sanctity of treaties. But less charitable commentators have contrasted this moral rectitude with the fact that 'only a week previously the First Lord of the Admiralty, in defiance of international law, had ordered the retention of two Turkish men-of-war'.[4] Contrary to Grey's plea of ignorance, the Head of the British Naval Mission, Vice-Admiral Mark Kerr, on August 4th, had learned from the King of Greece that, according to a communication from William II, the latter had signed an Alliance with Turkey.[5] In the opinion of the King's Secretary, 'if the British had wanted, they could have prevented these two ships from entering the Dardanelles'.[6] And the Ottoman Ambassador in Berlin, Moukhtar Pasha, telegraphed to the Grand Vizier that 'considering the displeasure and complications, which a Russian attack on Constantinople would produce in England', 'the British Navy, having enabled the German ships . . . to take cover in the Sea of Marmora, has, with the Machiavellianism characteristic of the Foreign Office', foiled any possibility of action by the Russian Black Sea Fleet.[7]

The U.S. Ambassador in Constantinople relates that he had 'often speculated on what would have happened if the English battle-cruisers, which pursued the *Breslau* and *Goeben* . . . had not been too gentlemanly to have violated international law. Suppose

[1] 12 Aug. '14. Asquith, II. 26.
[2] *The Times*, 15 Sept. 1952. Cf. Cambon, *Correspondance*, III. 94.
[3] Grey, II. 164. The same plea is made by Ryan, 96.
[4] Alastos, *Venizelos*, 143, footnote.
[5] Abbott, 10. Also Melas, 212.    [6] Melas, 210.
[7] Moukhtar to Said Halim, 17 Oct. '14. Deciphered in the Russian Foreign Ministry. Adamov, I. No. 16, pp. 225–6. 'What an outrage on the part of the Turks letting the . . . *Goeben* and *Breslau* enter the Dardanelles', the British Ambassador in Paris commented on 14 Aug. '14. Bertie, *The Diary*, I. 16.

that they had entered the Straits, attacked the German cruisers . . . and sunk them. . . . Not improbably the destruction would have kept Turkey out of the War'.[1] Grey has confirmed that 'if the two German cruisers . . . had not got to Constantinople . . . the Turks might have been a long time before they acted on that Treaty [of August 2nd 1914], or might never have acted on it at all'.[2] But, as Sir George Buchanan wired from Petrograd: 'There is much ground for assuming that war with Turkey is bound to be sympathetically received by wide circles of Russian society, who are convinced that Russia will draw no great benefits from the War with Germany and Austria'.[3]

It was no secret that, while Tsarist society was divided on the virtues of fighting the Central Empires, it was unanimous in longing to add the Sultan's metropolis and the Black Sea outlets to the possessions of Nicholas II. It was equally well established that the West, in its struggle with Germany, depended on the millions of his soldiers and on the stability of the Eastern front. As early as August 9th 1914, President Poincaré found that 'it is time for Russia to start her offensive in order to relieve the pressure which is being brought to bear on Belgium and ourselves'. On September 9th, he recorded that Russia was giving France 'valuable aid'. On October 19th, he clamoured for the Russian 'steamroller'.[4] From London, on August 13th, Grey wired to Buchanan that, since the Russians 'are holding back' part of their troops against the event of war with Turkey, the Ambassador should insist in Petrograd that the chief aim of the Allies was the speediest defeat of Germany as 'otherwise France and England would find themselves in a critical position'. Towards the end of August, Buchanan passed on to Sazonov a proposal from the British Government that three to four Russian corps should be sent via Archangel to the French front.[5] In the circumstances, the Porte's belligerency and the prospect of its defeat would be the strongest incentive to the Tsar to remain in battle till the end. But just the expected Turkish downfall prompted London and Paris to seek a means of preventing Petrograd from achieving her aims. As the brotherhood-in-arms removed none of the basic differences among the partners, it did not weaken the fundamental opposition of the

[1] Morgenthau, 51.
[2] Grey, II. 164. This is also the view of Prince Christopher of Greece. See *Memoirs*, 124.
[3] Buchanan to Grey, 29 Oct. '14. Adamov, I. No. 17, p. 227. Deciphered in the Russian Foreign Ministry. The quotation is a retranslation from the Russian translation of the original.
[4] Poincaré, V. 53, 272, 386; also 69, 70, 223, 301.
[5] Grey to Buchanan, 13 Aug. '14. Deciphered in the Russian Foreign Ministry. *Internationale Beziehungen*, II. 6. I. p. 48, footnote 1. The quotation is a retranslation from a translation of the original. Sazonov to the Director of the Diplomatic Chancellery of the Russian General Staff, 30 Aug. '14. *Internationale Beziehungen*, II. 6. I. No. 189, p. 143.

Western Powers to Tsarism's age-old dream. All this may explain why the *Goeben* and the *Breslau* were allowed to reach the Golden Horn. Their presence, Morgenthau writes, 'made it inevitable that Turkey should join her forces with Germany's'. At the same time, 'with them the Turkish Navy became stronger than the Russian Black Sea Fleet,[1] and thus made it certain that Russia could make no attack on Constantinople'.[2] It looked very much like a case of dangling the carrot before the donkey.

5

GREAT BRITAIN AND THE ARABS

The other reason why Britain and France were not disconcerted by the probability of the Porte's active hostility was that they had revolutionized their Near-Eastern policy. They had propped up and protected the Empire of the Crescent so long as it was a matter of keeping out the Tsar, and retaining in their own hands the internal controls. The Tsarist threat, however, paled before the overwhelming menace of the Reich. Under German hegemony, the Ottoman régime was rapidly becoming a military danger to the possessions and communications of the Entente. In diplomacy, London's relations with Constantinople, as Ryan had cause to know, were 'impaired by the chauvinistic attitude of the Young Turks, and more particularly by differences in regard to the Baghdad Railway, the Persian Gulf and the Arabian Peninsula'. British trade and shipping in Mesopotamia, according to a Foreign Office historian, suffered from 'persistent efforts on the part of the Turkish Government to whittle down such rights as were possessed . . . by Great Britain and her subjects'.[3] The penetration of Turkey by Germany, rapidly approaching the stage of conquest from within, and aggravated by the spread of Pan-Turanian agitation, destroyed the value of Ottoman integrity in Western eyes. As early as August 21st 1913, Moukhtar Pasha, the Ambassador in Berlin, warned the Porte that, judging by the European press, 'the conclusions to be drawn from the political situation brought about by the Balkan Wars are such

---

[1] Poincaré was well aware that the *Goeben* and the *Breslau* would provide Turkey with a '*force navale*'. 10 Aug. '14. Poincaré, V. 56.
[2] Morgenthau, 51. H. D. Napier, *The Experiences of a Military Attache in the Balkans*, p. 11, says: '. . . had this incident been handled diplomatically with firmness the Turks would have surrendered these two German vessels and have remained neutral'. According to the *Diplomaticheski Slovar*, II. 467, the entry of the *Goeben* and the *Breslau* into the Straits was also expected to intensify the Russo-German antagonism in the Near East, and so to increase Russia's dependence on Britain and France.
[3] Ryan, 82–3. *Mesopotamia*. Foreign Office Handbooks, No. 63, p. 96. Also Toynbee, *Turkey P.F.*, 49.

as to convince us of the intention of the Western Powers, sooner or later, to dismember Turkey.'[1]

Meanwhile, as far back as November 1912, Arabs from the Lebanon and Damascus had requested British assistance in their struggle against the Turks. A delegation of Syrian notables asked Lord Kitchener, the High-Commissioner in Cairo, for their country to be annexed to Egypt.[2] Kitchener, according to authoritative evidence, foresaw 'that if Turkey were ranged against Britain, as she must be as the Ally of Germany . . . Arab co-operation would be clearly useful as a means of discouraging Jihad [the Holy War] . . . and of thwarting German ambitions in the Middle East'.[3] Moreover, 'Lord Kitchener, no less than His Majesty's Government, was aware of the importance of extending British influence in Western Arabia as well as on the coast of the Persian Gulf and with Ibn Saud'.[4] A Caliphate independent of Ottoman control, and a Trans-Arabian railway were under consideration in London. Iraq was desired not only for her resources, but also for the defence of India and as a repository for the latter's emigrants. The head of the Persian Gulf was regarded as essential for the protection of the Anglo-Iranian oil fields. The Holy Places of Islam, master-key to the loyalty of millions of believers, 'had a special significance . . . and hence Kitchener and their keeper, the Sharif Husain, were in touch before Turkey had openly joined . . . Germany.'[5]

The Sharif, as host to the continuous stream of pilgrims, had inherited and amassed great wealth from their obligatory offerings. In control of the tribes around, and the inhabitants of, Mecca and Medina, he struggled for power with his overlord in Constantinople. He resented the determination of the Turks to build a railway to Mecca, which threatened to curtail the autonomy he had won, and to lead to the ruin of the camel owners. He was, therefore, in communication with Arab dignitaries at Beirut and Damascus who, like him, sought a measure of independence from the Sultan.[6]

The British, with their 'intelligence system that extended over most of Africa and Arabia',[7] were well aware of this trend for

---

[1] Moukhtar, 248-9; also 268. Djemal, 101, 111-12. Toynbee and Kirkwood, *Turkey*, 55.
[2] Gooch and Temperley, X. 2, pp. 824-5.
[3] Bertram Thomas, *The Arabs*, 298.
[4] Gooch and Temperley, X. 2, p. 825. Also Hourani, *Great Britain and the Arab World*, 16-17. Cf. *Mesopotamia*. Foreign Office Handbooks, No. 63, p. 43: 'No Power in the world has any claim comparable with that of Great Britain to control the destinies of Mesopotamia.'
[5] B. Thomas, 298-9. Also Gooch and Temperley, X. 2, pp. 825, 829, 835. Hourani, 16-17.
[6] Storrs, *Orientations*, 143, footnotes 1 and 2. Wingate, *Wingate of the Sudan*, 178-9.
[7] Wingate, 177, 180.

separation. British officials mixed with the Arab national movement and Arab rulers. In 1912, Husain's son Abdullah saw Kitchener in Cairo. On February 5th 1914, he was again received by the High Commissioner. As he recalled subsequently, 'things had come to such a pass between the Porte and the Sharif, and indeed between the Turks and Arabs in general, that a conflict seemed inevitable. I decided to speak openly to Kitchener. . . . When I asked him . . . whether, in the event of a rupture, the Sharif could count upon any support from Great Britain, Kitchener replied negatively'. When Abdullah reminded him that Britain had intervened in the dispute between Constantinople and the Sheikh of Kuwait to set up an effective protectorate over the latter's domain, Kitchener laughed . . . he said that he would make a point of reporting our conversation to his Government'.[1] Indeed, in a report dispatched on April 4th, he emphasized *inter alia* that 'we cannot afford to lose sight of the interests which Great Britain must always take in the Holy Places. . . .'[2] Towards the end of April, Abdullah met Ronald Storrs, the High Commissioner's Oriental Secretary, who under Kitchener's 'instructions told him [Abdullah] that the Arabs of the Hedjaz could expect no encouragement from us. . . .'[3]

But the Sharif's son did not appear to be discouraged. His talk with Storrs, he recollected, was 'a long and cordial' one.[3] Significantly, the British Ambassador in Constantinople, already on March 18th 1914, could write to Grey that 'Arab Officers in the Turkish Army . . . have visited His Majesty's Embassy and have inquired what would be the attitude of His Majesty's Government in certain eventualities'.[4] In the early part of 1914, too, the British Consul at El-Bahiern negotiated with Emir Ibn Saud of the Nejd, and reached complete commercial and political agreement on the Persian Gulf. Ibn undertook to protect British interests in the Nejd and renounced all his rights to Muscat. In return, he was promised arms and munitions for action in Syria and Mesopotamia against the Turks.[5] On September 24th 1914, that is well before Turkey took up arms, Kitchener, now Secretary of State for War, instructed Storrs

---

[1] Gooch and Temperley, X. 2, p. 832; also Kitchener to Grey, 6 Feb. '14. *ibid.* p. 827. Wingate, 179.

[2] Kitchener to Grey, 4 April '14. Gooch and Temperley, X. 2, p. 830. According to Liddel Hart, *T. E. Lawrence*, 1934, p. 61, and other authorities, some acquiescence in a possible Arab revolt was winked at by Lord Kitchener, and the Arab press made positive assertions to that effect. See Gooch and Temperley, X. 2, p. 826.

[3] Kitchener to Tyrrell, 26 April '14. Gooch and Temperley, X. 2, p. 831; also 832. Storrs confirms that Abdullah 'had unlocked his heart during his visit to Cairo that . . . spring'. Storrs, 172; also 142–3.

[4] Gooch and Temperley, X. 2, p. 828.

[5] Cumming, 14, quoting E. Jung, *La Révolte arabe*, I. 104.

'to send secret and carefully chosen messenger from me to . . . Abdallah [Abdullah] to ascertain whether "should present armed German influence in Constantinople coerce Sultan . . . and Sublime Porte to acts of aggression . . . against Britain, he and his father and Arabs of the Hedjaz would be with us. . . ."[1]

A special agent with a letter from Storrs to Abdullah and a 'suitable gift' reached Mecca about October 9th (in the same month, a Captain of the Royal Navy was directed to get in touch with Ibn Saud) and, a few days later, transmitted the British message to the Grand Sharif Husain who replied: 'The Ottoman Empire . . . has made war upon our rights . . . my heart is open to S[torrs] . . . Stretch forth to us a helping hand and . . . we shall help those who do good'.[2] The benefactors of the Arab world were not confined to London. Before long, M. Jung, a former French Vice-Resident in Tonkin, urged upon Poincaré the need to 'proclaim . . . Arab independence in Syria, Palestine, Mesopotamia, Hedjaz, Assir, Yemen (and also that of Armenia) . . .' and 'to have an Arab Caliph named in Mecca. . . .'[3] As early as March 1914, the British Ambassador in Constantinople could write to Grey that

'the Turkish Government are probably aware of the inclination of the Arabs to look to His Majesty's Government for sympathy in their movement and even for eventual protection if they are successful in achieving their independence. . . . If these projects should mature and if the Arabs are eventually successful in defeating the Ottoman armies . . . Turkish rule, as it exists to-day, would presumably disappear. Europe might then be faced with the question of a partition of the Turkish Empire. . . .'[4]

The revolution in the Near-Eastern policy of Britain and France would seem to have been the reason why, already in 1911, when Constantinople sought British protection against the Italian attack on Libya, her offer of a permanent alliance was refused,[5] and why, by 1913-1914, the old Anglo-Turkish friendship had been so impaired that attempts at improvement, as Ryan says, were rendered 'to a great extent nugatory'.[6] It would explain why Djemal's overtures in Paris in July 1914 were rebuffed, the Turkish ships were

---

[1] Storrs, 173.
[2] Storrs, 174–5. The British Agent returned to Cairo with a letter for Storrs. ibid. 176. Also Cumming, 33. When the War with Turkey broke out, Britain at once got into touch with Husain 'to persuade him, by offers of assistance and guarantees of his future . . . independence, to throw off the Turkish supremacy'. In December 1914, a letter was sent to him, via Cairo, which inaugurated the long and tortuous negotiations that led to the Arab revolt in June 1916. Wingate, 181.
[3] 7 Nov. '14. Cumming, 14 15.
[4] Mallet to Grey, 18 March '14. Gooch and Temperley, X. 2, p. 828.
[5] Churchill, *1914*, pp. 480–1.
[6] Ryan, 83. Also Emin, 66. Moukhtar, 264.

withheld by Britain, the *Goeben* and the *Breslau* given a free pass, and the Porte's demands dismissed by Grey as 'excessive'.¹ It would also show why the Entente's Representaives (as the Finance Minister Djavid complained to the Russian Envoy who repeated it to Sazonov) 'were making it more difficult for the moderate members of the Cabinet to restrain Turkey from war'.² Djavid reproached the French Ambassador in Constantinople with the fact that, while Wangenheim was lavish with promises, the West made no concrete offer. When he mentioned the suppression of the Capitulations, Bompard replied that France, of course, was prepared 'to go very far in that direction',³ but that was as far as it went. Ponceau, a senior official at the Quai d'Orsay, 'implied that [as Izvolski wired to Petrograd] it might perhaps be more advantageous to push Turkey over into the enemy camp in order to finish her off....'⁴ M. Delcassé —the Russian Ambassador reported—'does not believe that negotiations with Turkey could lead to anything, and considers it more expedient ... to ensure the restoration of the Balkan bloc against Turkey'.⁵ As soon as Delcassé was appointed Foreign Minister, he suggested that Bulgaria should be induced to join the Serbs and Greeks and that she 'should be granted at once a compensation at Turkish expense'.⁶ According to a cable from the Sultan's Envoy in Paris, Rifaat, Delcassé went so far as to tell him that 'the inviolability of the Ottoman Empire is no longer a dogma for France'.⁷ As for Britain, Churchill has confessed that 'from the very beginning of the War I hoped for nothing from Turkey....'⁸ Relations in July-August 1914, as Asquith, the Prime Minister, has declared, were 'in a state of extreme tension'.⁹

'We all', a stalwart of the British colony in Constantinople wrote later, 'saw ... that Turkey was drifting into war. We all ... asked ourselves whether it might not have been avoided by England'.¹⁰ But it would have been pointless to destroy German imperialism

¹ Grey to Mallet, 22 Aug. '14. Grey, II. 167.
² Giers to Sazonov, 6 Sept. '14. *Das Zaristische Russland*, p. 40. Also Giers to Sazonov, 19 Aug. '14. *ibid.* p. 30. The Ambassador Moukhtar wrote later that the Western Powers 'were no longer inclined to arrest the fall of Turkey. Otherwise, it would have been easy for them to checkmate the agitations of the Germanophils' in Constantinople. Moukhtar, 258.
³ 21 Aug. '14. Poincaré, V. 142; also 141.
⁴ Izvolski to Sazonov, 10 Aug. '14. Stieve, p. 38.
⁵ Izvolski to Sazonov, 17 Aug. '14. *Internationale Beziehungen*, II. 6. I. No. 120, pp. 89–90. The British Minister to Sofia was said to have supported this scheme by dwelling on the need for a Balkan bloc of 'Christian' States. Giers to Sazonov, 6 Sept. '14. Stieve, p. 108.
⁶ Izvolski to Sazonov, 27 Aug. '14. *Internationale Beziehungen*, II. 6. I. No. 166, pp. 124–5.
⁷ Giers to Sazonov, 6 Sept. '14. *Das Zaristische Russland*, p. 40.
⁸ Churchill, *1914*, p. 482.
⁹ Asquith, *The Genesis of the War*, 223.   ¹⁰ Pears, 347.

and still leave intact its active cells in Turkey. There would have been no sense in a War which, intended for the redistribution of imperial possessions and power, omitted the greatest prize of all.

6

THE ENTENTE FAILS TO SATISFY THE PORTE

'Winston, in his most bellicose mood, is all for sending a torpedo flotilla through the Dardanelles . . .' the British Premier noted on August 17th.[1] But it was not yet zero hour. The first Turkish target, in the event of hostilities, would certainly be the Suez Canal. The forces for its defence could not be spared from the Western front. A delay of weeks was required for the arrival in France and on the Nile of troops from India and the Dominions. Moreover, as Grey states, 'an Indian personage of very high . . . influence in the Moslem world . . . urged earnestly that Turkey should be kept out of the War . . . it might cause great trouble for Moslem British subjects. . . .'[2] Lord Kitchener and other Ministers, therefore, as Asquith noted at the time, 'in the interests of the Mussulmans in India and Egypt . . . are against our doing anything at all which could be interpreted as . . . taking the initiative against Turkey'.[3] It was vital to Britain (and for the same reasons to Russia)[4] that, in the event of a clash, as Asquith puts it, 'it should be clear that it was the deliberate and unprovoked act of the Ottoman Government'.[5] The Foreign Secretary told the Russian Ambassador that, as the latter wired, 'the present German efforts would, in the near future, cause Turkey to act, which would make her and Germany patently responsible for the War'. One ought 'to allow the situation to develop . . . without running ahead'.[6]

The British, therefore, rejected Sazonov's proposal for joint representations to Constantinople regarding the alleged purchase of the *Goeben* and the *Breslau*, and, like the French, contented themselves with ineffective general protests. Threats or coercive measures were ruled out.[7] Churchill, recalling the episode of the two ships, states that 'the British Government had a right to assume that they

[1] Asquith, *Memories and Reflections*, II. 26; also Churchill, *1914*, p. 483.
[2] Grey, II. 165.
[3] Asquith, *Memories and Reflections*, II. 26. Also Churchill, *1914*, p. 483.
[4] Sazonov to Kudashev, 30 Aug. '14. *Das Zaristische Russland*, p. 36.
[5] Asquith, *The Genesis of the War*, 224.
[6] Benckendorff to Sazonov, 28 Aug. '14. *Internationale Beziehungen*, II. 6. I. No. 176, p. 133. Also Grey, II. 167.
[7] Benckendorff to Sazonov, 10, 12 and 14 Aug. '14. Giers to Sazonov, 11 Aug. Sazonov to Giers, 11 Aug. Sazonov to Benckendorff, 12 Aug. Izvolski to Sazonov, 15 Aug. '14. *Internationale Beziehungen*, II. 6. I. No. 55, p. 37, and *ibid.* footnote 2; p. 52, footnote 2. No. 97, p. 71. No. 103, pp. 76–7. Giers to Sazonov, 13 Aug. '14. *Das Zaristische Russland*, p. 19. Djemal, 119, 122.

would be interned and disarmed'.[1] This was, no doubt, what international law would demand. But was it likely that the Germans, after their transgression in Belgium, would now allow Turkey to apply the law to them? Djemal claims that the Porte intented to make a show of legal compliance. However, as the Turks were caught between Wangenheim's veto and their own desire to play for time, they concocted with Berlin the myth that the two men-of-war, previously bought for so many million marks, had been delivered under contract. The Ottoman press, says Djemal, was told 'to speak enthusiastically of the . . . compensation for the *Sultan Osman* and the *Reshadieh*, of which the English had robbed us'.[2] Churchill, meanwhile, communicated to Grey the Admiralty's consent to the 'transfer' of the *Goeben* and the *Breslau*. But he added: 'The essential condition to insist on is that all the German . . . crews of both ships must, without exception, be at once repatriated. . . . In these circumstances, the Admiralty would allow the [British] Naval Mission to remain'.[3] This was, in fact, insisted upon. Admiral Limpus called on the Minister of Marine and, so the latter recollects, 'assured me that, as the two ships came under his direct command, he would have the selected officers and men ready. . . .'[4] Djemal's reply (even while the Grand Vizier was vowing that the Kaiser's crews would be sent home)[5] was to dismiss all British sailors from his Fleet and, by German request, to appoint as its Commander-in-Chief Admiral Souchon who had brought in the *Goeben* and the *Breslau*. The offending vessels, adorned with Turkish names, retained their original personnei –clad in new uniforms and the fez.[6] Britain turned a blind eye to the masquerade. It is a moot point whether she could have seriously expected that the Turks either would or could abide by the rules of neutrality. According to Asquith, she did not.[7] The purpose of her protests was simply to record the fact of the breach. 'The presence of the *Goeben* and the *Breslau* [in Morgenthau's words] was a standing *casus belli*'.[8]

---

[1] Churchill, *1914*, p. 482.   [2] Djemal, 120. Moukhtar, 278.
[3] Churchill to Grey, 12 Aug. '14. Churchill, *1914*, pp. 482–3. Benckendorff to Sazonov, 14 and 15 Aug. '14. *Internationale Beziehungen*, II. 6. I. No. 97, p. 71; No. 101, p. 75.
[4] Djemal, 120–1.
[5] Giers to Sazonov, 11, 13 and 15 Aug. '14. *Internationale Beziehungen*, II. 6. I. p. 37, footnote 2; p. 61, footnote 3; p. 77, footnote 1. Benckendorff to Sazonov, 14 Aug. '14. *ibid.* II. 6. I. No. 97, p. 71.
[6] Djemal, 118–22. Although Giers reported to Sazonov, on 19 Aug., that some German sailors had left the ships and been replaced by Turks (*Internationale Beziehungen*, II. 6. I. p. 77, footnote 1), Morgenthau states in his book that 'still Germany manned and officered the cruisers'. See p. 64, also 49, 50. Churchill *1914*, p. 483. Ryan, 102.
[7] Asquith, *The Genesis of the War*, 223.
[8] Morgenthau, 64. Also Djemal, 199. Grey, II. 168. Ryan, 102.

## THE DISPOSITION OF TURKEY

The case of the Entente against the Porte was further built up by the draft Declaration presented by Britain, France and Russia in Constantinople, on August 30th, that

'they are prepared to guarantee the integrity of Ottoman territory against any hostile designs during the present War, and to examine in a friendly spirit the demands which the Sublime Porte would wish to address to them in the economic and juridical sphere'.

The three Ambassadors, as Giers reported, added that they would make this statement official,

'as soon as the Porte, for its part, has expressed readiness to give a written assurance that it will preserve strict neutrality throughout the War'.[1]

This, to be sure, was a direct offer, but—compared to the lavish German baksheesh—the three Powers, as Morgenthau writes, 'had only one consideration to offer Turkey',[2] and she was bound to find it meagre. Her inviolability was to be guaranteed merely for the duration of the current conflict.[3] Grey—but not Poincaré—mentions in his Memoirs 'a promise . . . that in any terms of peace . . . her independence and integrity should be preserved'.[4] But even if this were so, the Turks could not help suspecting the sincerity of the pledge. They had a feeling that one reason, at least, for the retention of their ships by Britain was that she wanted to prevent them 'from securing superiority over the Greek Fleet in the Aegean'.[5] They knew that, as Djavid and the Grand Vizier complained to the French and Russian Ambassadors, the three Foreign Ministers, at this very

[1] Giers to Sazonov, 30 Aug. '14. *Das Zaristische Russland*, p. 37. Poincaré, V.210. Churchill, *1914*, p. 486. Miller, 38. Sazonov's demand for the demobilization of Turkey was dropped because of Franco-British opposition. See Izvolski to Sazonov, 17 Aug. '14. Stieve, p. 59.
[2] Morgenthau, 63.
[3] This limitation which, strangely enough, is not mentioned in the text given by Poincaré (V. 210) was not contained in either Grey's instructions to Mallet, 22 Aug. '14 (Grey, II. 167), or Sazonov's draft of 28 Aug. '14 (*Internationale Beziehungen*, II. 6. I. No. 173, p. 129). This latter expressed the Triple Entente's unreserved willingness 'to guarantee the integrity of Ottoman territory'. On 29 Aug. '14, Benckendorff cabled to Petrograd a new version by Grey whereby Turkey's 'integrity would be guaranteed against any attempt to take advantage of the present War to attack her.' (*Das Zaristische Russland*, p. 38, footnote 16. Cf. also Grey to Bucharan, 17 Aug. '14. Deciphered in the Russian Foreign Ministry. *Internationale Beziehungen*, II. 6. I. No. 119, p. 89). According to Miller (p. 38), this clause was inserted as a bait to Russia. Sazonov, at that time still anxious for Turkish neutrality, notified Giers, 2 Sept. '14, that he had consented to the British amendment 'only in order to avoid delay'. (*Internationale Beziehungen*, II. 6. I. p. 129, footnote 4; see p. 130). But already on 1 Sept. '14, the Turkish Finance Minister Djavid had criticised the amendment limiting the Entente's guarantee to the duration of the War. Giers to Sazonov, 1 Sept. '14. *Das Zaristische Russland*, p. 38.
[4] Grey, II. 166. Also Trevelyan, *Grey of Fallodon*, 301.
[5] Talaat's statement at the Congress of the 'Committee of Union and Progress', after the Armistice. Moukhtar, 272.

time, proposed to buy Bulgaria with Turkish territory up to the Enos-Midia Line.¹ They reflected that, in the clause on the economic concession, there was no mention of Asia Minor—or in particular of the Baghdad Railway²—and that at any rate the economic advantages to be won were still in the hands of Germany as yet far from defeated. They were only too well aware of the three Powers' economic involvement in, and political designs on, the Near East. The Entente, Talaat said to Morgenthau, 'promised that we should not be dismembered after the Balkan Wars, and see what happened to European Turkey then'.³

The Porte wanted not doubtful benefits, but tangible advantages. Djemal demanded from Sir Louis Mallet the abolition of the Capitulations, the restoration to Turkey of the Aegean islands and Western Thrace, a solution of the Egyptian question, the return of the confiscated ships, security against Tsarist interference and attack—and all this as part of an alliance which would underwrite these claims.⁴ The Turkish Ambassador in London maintained that their negotiations would surely succeed if the Triple Entente invited the Porte to join them rather than to remain neutral. Lord Kitchener, however, to whom the Aga Khan communicated these remarks, answered that, in the latter's words, 'the Allies had no desire to bring Turkey into the War on their side'.⁵ Whitehall conceded in principle an easing of the economic fetters. But—in view of the resolution passed by the Young Turk Congress of 1911 that 'the reorganisation of the administration of justice was less important than the abolition of the Capitulations'⁶—Sir Edward Grey excluded modifications in the juridical *status quo*, until 'a scheme ... is set up which will satisfy modern conditions'.⁷ Discussions on Egypt and the islands,

¹ Giers to Sazonov, 30 Aug. and 6 Sept. '14. *Das Zaristische Russland*, pp. 36-7, 40.
² Whereas Britain apparently was prepared to offer Turkey the German economic concessions in Asia Minor (Grey to Buchanan, 18 Aug. '14. Deciphered in the Russian Foreign Ministry. *Internationale Beziehungen*, II. 6. I. No. 124, p. 92), the reference to Asia Minor in Sazonov's draft was omitted on French insistence. See Giers to Sazonov, 18 Aug. '14. *Internationale Beziehungen*, II. 6. I. p. 74, footnote 7. Sazonov to Izvolski, 20 Aug. '14. *Das Zaristische Russland*, p. 32; also 28 Aug. '14. *Internationale Beziehungen*, II. 6. I. No. 172, p. 129.
³ Morgenthau, 64. Also Burián, *Austria in Dissolution*, 131. In the opinion of the Aga Khan, 'the Turks were justifiably suspicious of "guarantees" ... offered by the Western Powers'. *The Memoirs of Aga Khan*, 133. Poincaré, in his Diary, admitted that, coming after the French defeats, the Entente's guarantee 'would have little chance of being accepted'. 29 Aug. '14. Poincaré. V. 210.
⁴ 20 Aug. '14. Djemal, 123. Emin, 71.
⁵ Aga Khan, 133. Also Emin, 70. Moukhtar, 258.   ⁶ Toynbee, *Turkey P.F.*, 39.
⁷ Grey to Mallet, 22 Aug. '14. Grey, II. 167. This tallies with the Aide-Memoire, British Embassy, Petrograd, to Sazonov, 23 Aug. '14. *Internationale Beziehungen*, II. 6. I. No. 148, p. 110. The French Government, too, opposed an unconditional cancellation of the Capitulations. See Giers to Sazonov, 20 Aug. '14. *ibid*. II. 6. I. p. 102, footnote 1.

he suggested, should be postponed. The fear of Russia was to be allayed by the guarantee of Ottoman integrity.[1] This negative approach, moreover, was coupled with positive demands on Turkey. 'Nothing was asked from her in return', the Foreign Secretary has affirmed, 'no help, no facilities for the Allies . . . nothing except that she should remain neutral'.[2] But that innocuous formula implied that, as Grey instructed Mallet, she should 'repatriate at once the German officers and crews of . . . the *Goeben* and *Breslau*, and give a written assurance that she will afford all facilities for . . . uninterrupted passage of merchant vessels' through the Straits.[3]

'But in that case', so Djemal argues, 'Russia would have emerged from the World War so strong that she would certainly not have waited to seize Constantinople and the Eastern provinces of Asia Minor'. As for Britain and France, 'their object was patently as follows: "For the moment let us prevent Turkey from doing anything to our disadvantage. During the War we will preserve our association with Russia and thereby bring it to a victorious conclusion. Then we can . . . on the pretext of reforms grant the Arabian provinces autonomy so that they will easily fall under our protection and control".'[4] Turkey saw clearly that she would preserve neutrality at her peril.

Her reaction was to close the Dardanelles. The immediate reason was that one of her destroyers was stopped from putting out to sea by an Allied squadron. And on September 27th: 'Down went the mines and the nets . . . the lighthouses were extinguished; signals were put up . . . that there was "no thoroughfare" . . .' The hundreds of ships which crowded the roadsteads left. 'In a few weeks the Bosphorus and adjoining waters had become a desolate waste'.[5]

7

GERMANY'S ALL-OUT EFFORT

This act, at the same time, showed that Berlin was tightening the screw. As long as the Germans had hopes of beating France at one stroke, they were not averse to Turkish non-belligerency. But the beer-cellar dreams of another Sedan dissolved in blood and

[1] Djemal, 123–4. Moukhtar, 264.
[2] Grey, II. 166.
[3] Grey to Mallet, 22 Aug. '14. Grey, II. 168. This demand was endorsed by France and Russia. The latter also desired a cessation of all Turkish activity in Persian Azerbaidjan. Aide-Memoire, Russian Foreign Ministry to British Embassy, Petrograd, 23 Aug. '14, and Sazonov to Giers, 23 Aug. '14. *Internationale Beziehungen*, II. 6. I. p. 111, footnote 1. Izvolski to Sazonov, 24 Aug. '14. Stieve, p. 72. Sazonov to Giers, 16. Aug. '14. *Das Zaristische Russland*, p. 25.
[4] Djemal, 124.
[5] Morgenthau, 69, 72; also 68. Mallet to Grey, 27 Sept. '14. Giers to Sazonov, 27 Sept. '14. Adamov, I. p. 92 and p. 158, footnote 2.

mire on the Marne. Russia was sweeping across Galicia. The spectre of a protracted war on two fronts could only be laid, if the British forces were drained away in Egypt and those of the Tsar in the Caucasus, if communications between East and West were cut, and Turkish lives thrown into the Kaiser's war machine.[1] Mesopotamia, Armenia and the Straits were still as vulnerable as before. A success against Suez, owing to Britain's preparations, grew more improbable. Turkey's one land-link with Europe—the Orient Line—and the Anatolian and Baghdad Railways connecting Constantinople with the interior of the Empire and its peripheries, had single tracks and diverse gauges and were short of engines, rolling stock and fuel. The branch arteries were underdeveloped. Because the Taurus tunnel was incomplete, the trains to Syria, Palestine and Iraq had to be unloaded north of the mountain, and cargoes carried by camels or waggons over the peaks. The Amanus range presented the same difficulty. The Baghdad Line itself stopped some 700 miles from its goal. Such main roads as existed were bad. The Turkish Fleet was inferior both to the British and the French. The Army, dispirited and weary from previous wars, lacked ammunition, lorries (supplies depended on ox carts and pack animals), equipment, uniforms and boots. When General Sanders took over, he found the troops unpaid, undernourished, ragged and ill cared for by their officers. The vermin infested barracks were as primitive as the cooking and the sanitation. In the military hospitals, the sick 'lay confusedly mixed, often in the same bed, when there was one', or 'in dense rows in the hallways, some on mattresses, some on blankets . . . a large number of these wasted soldiers died daily. . . .'[2] Nor does he mention improvements in the autumn of 1914. Yet Wangenheim, brandishing the Treaty of Alliance, 'became more and more imperious'.[3]

The Alliance, at this stage, was already backed by force. The *Goeben* and the *Breslau* upset the balance of power at the Golden Horn. Their guns, easily trained on the capital, changed the nature of Turkish-German relations. The Enver faction was strengthened, that of the neutralists terrorized. With the recall of the British Naval Mission on September 9th, Wangenheim, Sanders and Souchon became the masters.[4] A flow of officers, service-men, mechanics,

[1] Morgenthau, 58, 62–3, 70. Djemal, 127–8. *Diplomaticheski Slovar*, I. 480–1.
[2] Sanders, 11; also 9–12, 27–30, 73, 75. Helfferich, II. 56. Morgenthau, 21–2. Emin, 86, 88.
[3] Djemal, 128; also 117. Erzberger, 77. Conrad, *Aus meiner Dienstzeit*, IV. 418. According to Garroni to San Giuliano, 15 Aug. '14, the German-Austrian pressure in Constantinople for war was 'unheard of'. *I Documenti Diplomatici Italiani*, 5. Serie. Vol. I. No. 263, p. 151.
[4] Miller, 34, 37. Djemal, 119. Morgenthau, 51. Churchill, *1914*, p. 491. Also Garroni to San Giuliano, 15 and 23 Aug. '14. *Documenti Diplomatici*, 5. I. No. 262, p. 150; p. 236, footnote 2.

artillery and munitions came from the Reich. Its agents acquired the big daily *Ikdam* and the *Osmanischer Lloyd*, secured the suppression of the pro-French *Jeune Turc*, and fed the venal press with hymns of hate. Britain was flayed for seizing the Turkish ships and joining up with the Tsar. The Russian bogey, inflated beyond measure, was blamed for all the country's ills. The papers were exaggerating or inventing victories for the Germans and defeats for the other side. Outsize maps, in shop windows and on walls, indicated the Ottoman territories lost to the Triple Entente and its friends. William II was promoted protector of Islam, and stories were spread that the latter-day Siegfried had become a disciple of the Prophet.[1]

The Capitulations, too, were thrown into the fires of anti-Westernism. The Porte, faced with Anglo-French intransigence, and exploiting the divisions of Europe, suddenly, on September 9th, cast off the age-old shackles. The move was also designed to reconcile the public to mobilization and the other sacrifices. Great popular rejoicings greeted the restoration of national sovereignty. This threat to their 'rights' brought the belligerents to an amazing, if brief, show of solidarity. While their respective peoples were destroying each other, the Ambassadors of the Entente and the Central Empires drew up, with the Italian Envoy's help, identical notes of refusal to recognize the unilateral act. Yet no sooner were the replies delivered than Wangenheim and his Austro-Hungarian colleague informed Constantinople that their Governments accepted the *fait accompli*. As the restrictive régime could not legally be ended without the consent of all the Powers, the risk to the interests of Germany and Austria was nil. At the same time, though sharing in the general protest, they shifted its onus, in Turkish eyes, on to the French and British.[2]

Next came the simple question of cupidity. The Treaty of Alliance had said nothing about money or in particular about cash in advance. The Young Turk leaders, therefore, wished to turn the present German importunities to their own profit. The Treasury was emptier than ever. With a steep drop in customs revenue, and the last loan from France running out, it was impossible to embark on war. Djemal also implies that, with mobilization completed, this question was raised as an excuse for postponing action. 'We, therefore, asked the Germans to settle the financial problem'.[3] On October 11th, they

---

[1] Giers to Sazonov, 3, 5, and 23 Oct. '14. *Das Zaristische Russland*, pp. 49, 51, 57. Morgenthau, 65–6. Emin, 70. Pears, 343, 348–9.
[2] Giers to Sazonov, 5 Oct. '14. *Das Zaristische Russland*, pp. 52–3. Ryan, 98–9. Poincaré, V. 277. Miller, 41. Garroni to San Giuliano, 9, 10 and 15 Sept. '14. *Documenti Diplomatici*, 5. I. NN 630. 633. 635. 689, pp. 364, 367–9, 400.
[3] Djemal, 129.

received a loan of 100 million francs in gold, and Wangenheim 'looked at us as much as to say: "Now, don't start thinking of any more objections".'[1]

The rest was provocation. Despite the Ambassador's promptings, the Porte continued to hesitate. The Galician and Marne events, which made Berlin insistent, chilled the Turks. The Crown Prince Izzedin, and the majority of Ministers—including the Grand Vizier—stood for neutrality. The Germans decided to force their hands. At the same time, in view of the diplomatic struggle over the Balkans, the Hungarian Premier Tisza urged that Turkey's Fleet should challenge that of the Tsar—or else 'the predominance of Russian naval power in the Black Sea will impress Rumania and Bulgaria'.[2] All this was arranged over luncheon at Wangenheim's Embassy. And so, the *Goeben* and the *Breslau* with a Turkish cruiser and destroyers steamed out of the Bosphorus and, on October 29th and 30th 1914 (while Egypt was being invaded by an Ottoman army) bombarded Odessa, Sevastopol, Theodosia and Novorossisk—without a declaration of war.[3]

A section of the Government, taken unawares and shocked by what they felt to be the imminence of disaster, resigned. The Grand Vizier intended to follow suit, but found the lure of office stronger than the dictate of duty. Talaat and Djemal, in spite of their denials, were implicated in, or at least had knowledge of, the plot hatched in cold blood by Enver with General von Sanders and Admiral Souchon. The triumvirate, a small minority but ruthlessly resolute and drawing strength from their subservience to Germany, prevailed. Their earlier parleys with the three Entente Ambassadors revealed themselves as crude deception. Djemal has admitted that 'we had declared our neutrality solely with the object of gaining time . . . and were simply waiting for the completion of our . . . mobilization'.[4]

8

THE YOUNG TURKS DECIDE ON WAR

The Sharif Husain of Mecca wrote to the Sultan: '. . . the Southern portions of the Empire, Basra, Yemen and the Hedjaz, are exposed to attack from hostile navies. The Government cannot rely on the inhabitants of these outlying provinces to defend themselves . . .'[5]

[1] Djemal, 129. Also Miller, 43. Pears, 352.
[2] Tisza to Berchtold, 11 Oct. '14. Tisza, *Briefe (1914–1918)*, I. 93.
[3] Morgenthau, 78–81. Pears, 352–3. Potemkin, II. 271. Churchill, *1914*, p. 495. Poincaré, V. 424–5. Miller, 43–4. Szilassy, *Der Untergang der Donaumonarchie*, 279.
[4] Djemal, 122; also 130–2. Moukhtar, 286–7. Morgenthau, 81–2. Ryan, 105. Erzberger, 77. Adamov, I. p. 91. *The Lansing Papers*, I. 766.
[5] *Memoirs of King Abdullah of Transjordan*, 128–9.

The Ottoman Ambassador wired from France: 'The low level of life and primitive development of Turkey require a long and peaceful growth. The deceptive attraction of possible military successes can only lead to our annihilation. . . . The Entente is ready to condemn us to death, if we act as its enemies. Germany has no interest in saving us. . . . In case of defeat she will use us as a means of satisfying the appetite of the victors; in case of victory she will turn us into a protectorate'.[1] The Rumanian statesman T. Jonescu warned Talaat: 'A victorious Germany . . . will never commit the folly . . . of giving you the Caucasus or Egypt. She would take them for herself if she could. . . .'[2] The ruling trio could not deny that the Reich had allowed its Austro-Hungarian and Italian Allies 'to rob us' of Bosnia-Herzegovina and of Tripolitania, withheld its help in the Balkan Wars and was out 'to exploit us economically'.[3] It was not difficult to guess that Turkey herself, as the Foreign Minister Jagow had written to Wangenheim, was only safe from Germany 'until we . . . are ready for annexation'.[4] It was, above all, elementary that, since the Near-Eastern question arose generations ago, Ottoman survival depended on a division between Britain, France and Russia. To challenge the three in coalition was next door to committing suicide.

But the very fact that it was a small unpopular minority spurred on the Enver group. They needed an outward success, a striking military exploit to win support in the country and consolidate their power. A reckless and unscrupulous spirit of adventure impelled them to risk everything with a gambler's throw.[5] Another motive was the predatory programme of Turanianism which produced, on the day of decision, this proclamation from the Government:

'Our participation in the World War represents the vindication of our national ideal. The ideal of our nation . . . leads us towards the destruction of our Muscovite enemy in order to obtain thereby a natural frontier to our Empire, which should include and unite all branches of our race.'[6]

Nor could the Porte remain a passive witness of the struggle, on the outcome of which depended its existence. 'It was realized', the Austro-Hungarian Foreign Minister Burián writes, 'that the combatants would scarcely respect Turkey's neutrality . . . where extensive Turkish territory was necessary to them or in their way'.[7] As both sides were fighting over Turkey, the War—whether or not she stood apart—would settle her future. The one hope of correcting

[1] 28 Sept. '14. Emin, 74.     [2] Jonescu, 181–2.
[3] Djemal, 99.
[4] Brandenburg, *Von Bismarck zum Weltkriege*, 393.
[5] Emin, 68. Miller, 34. Abdullah, 129. Toynbee, *Turkey P. F.*, 49.
[6] Toynbee, *Turkey P.F.*, 31.
[7] Burián, 130–1. Also Helfferich, II. 53. Moukhtar, 258. Adamov, I. p. 90.

her fortunes was intervention. '... we had only two ... courses open to us', Djemal reflects, 'we could either ally ourselves with the English and French ... and in that way secure ourselves against Russia, or we could join the Central Powers and assist in the destruction of Russia. After declining our alliance, France and England had required us to remain neutral and keep the Straits open for the benefit of our worst enemy. The Central Powers, on the other hand, allowed us to come in with them'.[1] They shielded Turkey against encroachments by her Balkan neighbours and dismemberment by the Triple Entente, and, it was believed, conceded to her under the 'Alliance ... based upon equality of rights'[2] a seat at the peace conference and a direct claim to annexations. 'There was, of course, a possibility that the Central Powers might be beaten, and in that case a catastrophe for us was a certainty. But ... if we had remained neutral and left the Straits open, the inevitable victory of our enemy would have sealed our fate with equal certainty'.[1]

The reaction of Britain, France and Russia to the Black Sea outrage was to inform the Porte that, unless it dismissed all the Germans serving in its forces, it would be responsible for a state of war. This was a necessary, but from the outset patently impossible request. The three Ambassadors asked for their passports on November 1st. Sir Edward Grey's main concern was that 'by this time the Indian troops were through the Canal and the manner of Turkey's entry into the War made it clear ... that the Allies and not Turkey were the injured party. These two objectives diplomacy had attained'.[3] Poincaré's references to the crisis are equally placid.[4] And when the Ottoman Chargé d'Affaires in Petrograd, expressing his Government's 'infinite regret' at 'the hostile action provoked by the Russian Fleet', professed a desire for conciliation, Sazonov dismissed the imputation of guilt and retorted that 'it is now altogether too late for any negotiations ...'[5] The immediate effect of Turkish belligerency was to free Tsarism from restraint. Nicholas's Manifesto of November 2nd proclaimed that

'this reckless intervention by Turkey will only hasten her doom and open Russia's path towards the solution of the historic task, bequeathed to her by our ancestors, on the shores of the Black Sea'.[6]

[1] Djemal, 125. Also Emin, 73.   [2] Djemal, 114; also 113.
[3] Grey, II. 168-9. The quotation is from his book. Also Ryan, 96.
[4] See Poincaré, V. 425.
[5] Sazonov to Izvolski and Benckendorff, 1 Nov. '14. *Internationale Beziehungen*, II. 6. I. NN 445, 446, p. 355. Churchill, *1914*, p. 495. Djemal, 131. Djavid, by orders of his Government, sounded the three Ambassadors on the possibility of an arrangement but had to admit that it was impossible for Turkey to comply with the Entente's request. Poincaré, V. 426. Morgenthau, 82.
[6] Adamov, I. p. 364, footnote 4. Paléologue, *An Ambassador's Memoirs*, I. 178.

CHAPTER III

# Russia, Constantinople and the Straits

1

RUSSIAN ECONOMY, STRATEGY AND IMPERIALISM

THE nature of Russia's task in the Black Sea was delineated, in November 1914, by Bazili, a high official of the Petrograd Foreign Ministry, in an Aide-Memoire for Sazonov.[1] The traditional closure of the Straits, as he showed, not only barred the Russian Black Sea Fleet from the Mediterranean and the oceans of the world, it paralysed the movement of men-of-war from her Southern ports to the Baltic or Far East and vice versa, restricted the use of her naval ship-yards in Odessa and Novorossisk to local needs, and precluded a strengthening of her forces there in an emergency.[2] This strategic consideration was reinforced by economic necessity. Ukrainian grain Caucasian oil, and manganese and, to some extent, West-Siberian dairy produce, had their only outlet through the Bosphorus and the Dardanelles.[3] Land transport, twenty five times dearer than maritime traffic, was uneconomical for these bulk cargoes. Hence, in the decade ending in 1912, the flow of Russia's commodities through the Narrows averaged 37 per cent of her exports. In 1911, of the total of outgoing goods valued at 1,591,000,000 roubles, 568,000,000 worth, that is over one third, went by that route. Its importance was magnified by the projected industrial development of the Ukraine, with its abundance of iron and coal, and the exploitation of Trans-caucasian and Persian resources. The urgency of the problem was brought home to the Russian bourgeoisie by the extent to which business was affected through the temporary shutting of the sea gates by Turkey in her Wars with Italy (1911) and the Balkans (1912-13). In 1912, Russia's Black Sea exports dropped from the 568,000,000 roubles of the year before to 433,000,000, and her commercial balance was 100,000,000 roubles less than in each of the three preceding years.[4]

That is why, in December 1913, Sazonov had informed the

[1] Aide-Memoire *On our Aims in the Straits* by the Vice-Director of the Chancellery of the Foreign Ministry, N. A. Bazili, Nov. '14. Adamov, I. No. 2, pp. 156–181.
[2] *ibid.* 159, 161–2.
[3] From 70–90 per cent of the total Russian exports of oil, manganese and cereals went by way of the Straits. Bowman, 409–10.
[4] Bazili's Aide-Memoire, Nov. '14. Adamov, I. No. 2, p. 157.

Tsar: 'The Straits in the hands of a foreign State means the submission of the whole of Southern Russia to that State'.[1] They were, it was urged upon him twelve months later, 'the vital nerve of our whole economic life'.[2] Bazili's Aide-Memoire stated: 'The dependence of this trade road . . . on the arbitrariness of an alien land Power and the state of its international relations . . . conflicts with our paramount State interests'. These could only be served by 'the complete subjection of the whole sea route through the Straits . . . to our authority'.[3] Such whispers, reverberating beyond the intimacy of the Minister's study, were soon to swell into a public chorus. 'The opening of a free exit from the Black Sea', the economist Tugan-Baranovski announced 'will inaugurate brilliant prospects for the development of our entire South'.[4] The Liberal professor Trubetskoi proclaimed that Constantinople 'is for us the problem of our daily bread . . . of all our political might, and of our cultural mission, of the very spiritual ego of Russia'.[5] And P. Milyukov, the Chief of the 'Cadets'—the leading middle-class party—assured the Entente that the acquisition of the Bosphorus and the Dardanelles by Russia would have 'nothing in common with annexationist tendencies to which the partisans of the future organized peace of Europe want to put a stop. . . . The possession of Constantinople and the Straits is the end, and not the beginning . . . the liquidation of the problem of the Straits will make it possible solemnly to store away in the sanctuary of history the "Eastern Question" which has tormented Europe for so long'.[6]

But the idea that Tsarism would be able to perform such feats was, at best, a Liberal illusion. Control of the Black Sea outlets, Bazili wrote, is not confined to the Narrows. It was pointless to consider the Dardanelles without Imbros and Tenedos which dominate their mouth, and Lemnos and Samothrace commanding the space further out. 'The strategic task of securing our exit into the Mediterranean, therefore, cannot be solved without reference to the fate of these islands'.[7] The acquisition of Constantinople and the Straits would make Russia a Mediterranean Power. This made it necessary to secure herself in the Eastern basin of that sea. 'Russia', according to

---

[1] Memorandum, 6 Dec. '13. See Adamov, I. p. 183 and *ibid.* footnote 1.
[2] Aide-Memoire by the Chief of Black Sea Operations of the Naval Staff, Nemitz, 14 Dec. '14. Adamov, I. No. 3, p. 183.
[3] Nov. '14. Adamov, I. No. 2, p. 158.
[4] *Chevo zhdet Rossiya ot voiny* (*What Russia Expects of the War*). Petrograd, 1915, p. 23. Adamov, I. p. 90.
[5] *Natsionalny vopros* (*The National Question*). Moscow, 1915. Adamov, I. p. 97.
[6] *Voprosy Mirovoi voiny* (*Problems of the World War*). Petrograd, 1915, p. 548. Adamov, I. p. 94.
[7] Aide-Memoire, Nov. '14. Adamov, I. No. 2, p. 163.

a naval spokesman, 'was always aware of the really *vital\** significance for her Empire of her political position in the Balkan Peninsula and the Narrows which lead from "Tsargrad" east and westward. . . . It is only by obtaining a firm footing on the Bosphorus and the Dardanelles that Russia will actually be able to fulfil her historic vocation which consists in the political unification, internal pacification of, and the bestowing of "European" culture on, the peoples of all Eastern Europe and the greater part of Asia'.[1] While vague on the latter, he was explicit on the Balkans. Though Russia was disinclined to 'absorb the independent Slav nations', her policy was to become their 'common political centre, a role in which the Habsburg Monarchy and the Ottoman Empire have failed and are, therefore, being taken off the stage of history by the hand of fate'. Nicholas II, in short, was to assume the place of Francis Joseph and Mehmed V as 'the arbiter and protector of the Slav nations.'[2] The Foreign Ministry, echoing through Bazili, the theme of 'predominance in the Balkan world and Asia Minor', went further: 'the Straits are an excellent operative base for the Fleet in the Mediterranean'—'freedom of navigation for our warships through the Straits would enable us to employ our Navy as a threat in the Mediterranean' and, provided that large Russian naval forces were developed, 'could greatly increase our influence in the world'.[3]

These trends were natural in such a society as that of Old Russia. Tsarist imperialism, with its feudal survivals, was just a less efficient, less up-to-date copy of that of the other Powers. The pressure of economic need was intermixed with expansionism, the dictate of security with aggressiveness. In December 1913, Sazonov had suggested to Nicholas II that Russia required the Straits not only for 'economic but also for purely political reasons'.[4] For the associations of Russian nobles, industrialists, business men and the Cadets, the acquisition of Constantinople and the Straits was not an aim in itself but the prelude to ultimate supremacy in the Near East and the possession of naval power in the Mediterranean.[5] It was a matter of obtaining the keys not only to one's own domain but also to what others considered to be their preserves.[6]

[1] Aide-Memoire by Nemitz, 14 Dec. 14. Adamov, I. No. 3, p. 182; also 127.
[2] *ibid.*, p. 184.
[3] Aide-Memoire, Nov. '14. Adamov, I. No. 2, pp. 164–5, 160–1.
[4] Adamov, I. p. 184.
[5] Some publicists stated that Russia must acquire 'Anatolia and the Black Sea coast, plant herself firmly on the Armenian plateau and take her share of the Mesopotamian regions . . . Alexandretta and Smyrna must become the bases of our economic influence in the Mediterranean'. Pletnev in *Golos Zhizni*, (*The Voice of Life*), No. 3: Arktur, *Osnovniye voprosy vneshnei politiki Rossii* (*Fundamental Problems of the Foreign Policy of Russia*). Adamov, I. p. 97.
[6] Adamov, I. pp. 95, 97, 184. II. p. 102.
\* Italics in the original.

## 2
### THE PARTITION OF THE OTTOMAN EMPIRE
### I: LONDON AND PETROGRAD

In British and French eyes, therefore, Milyukov's programme could not be 'the end', but only a beginning.[1] It raised new problems in their stubborn endeavours to contain the Empire of the Tsars, affected their interests in the Levant, and cut across their own designs in the area from the Aegean to the Persian Gulf. Anticipating the doom of the Sultan's realm, they sought in the Balkans an alternative base for power. Hence Britain's irritation with Russia's 'absurd and obsolete claim that she is the protectress of all Slav States', reflected in the Ambassador Sir Francis Bertie's Diary on the eve of the common War.[2] Hence also Poincaré's ill-humoured comments on the Generalissimo Nikolai Nikolayevich's Appeal to the Poles, Czechs, Slovaks, Croats and Serbs, which proclaimed publicly on August 14th the Slav mission of Petrograd—'an announcement of disguised annexations on which no agreement was concluded between Russia and us. . . .'[3] As for the Straits, the Committee of Imperial Defence in London had been unanimous in 1908 that free Russian egress from the Black Sea 'would not fundamentally alter' the balance of power in the Mediterranean.[4] With Alexandria in British hands, the much-heard argument that Suez was safer with the Russian Fleet in Sevastopol than if it were in Constantinople was dispelled. But Constantinople was Turkey's largest centre of trade which handled, in 1911, nearly a third of all her imports. In 1913-14, the British tonnage of approximately 6,500,000 there dwarfed that of every other country. Constantinople, moreover, was the *entrepôt* between the Ukraine, Transcaucasia, Mesopotamia and Persia, and served as one of the transit centres of the world. Britain's share in the commerce of the whole of that region in 1913-14 can be gauged from her shipping total of some 14,000,000 tons (against Russia's 5,500,000 and France's 4,000,000) in the Red Sea, the Persian Gulf and the Black Sea.[5] The City and Whitehall, far from wishing the Black Sea to become a Russian lake, had themselves an eye on the lands to the South of it.

Mr. N. Buxton's picture of a Turkey reduced to four provinces with only one port, and her people 'allowed to organize themselves . . .

---

[1] See Adamov, I. pp. 94, 100.
[2] 27 July '14. Bertie, I. 2.
[3] 15 Aug. '14. Poincaré, V. 101.
[4] Headlam Morley, *Studies in Diplomatic History*, 241-2.
[5] Bowman, 416; also 409. Russia, Germany, Austria, Greece and Italy had a tonnage of only about 1,000,000 each in Constantinople.

in a quiet pastoral state—a happy prospect. . . .'¹ may have been far-fetched. But before it appeared in print, Lord Kitchener had cabled his 'Salaams' to Abdullah and promised that 'if Arab nation assist England in this War, England . . . will give Arabs every assistance against external foreign aggression'.² Edmund de Rothschild confided to Sir Francis Bertie that he had the support of Lloyd George, Grey, Samuel and Crewe for a British protectorate in Palestine³. Delcassé notified the British Envoy of French wishes for Syria as 'a matter of sentiment',⁴ and the Foreign Secretary, with pained surprise, inquired of the Ambassador Paul Cambon: 'But you are not going to ask me to admit that Alexandretta is part of Syria?'⁵ The thousand and one schemes fathered by Lord Kitchener and the Sharif Husain—the making of Arab kingdoms, the appointment of a new Caliph,⁶ and so forth—were taking shape and were bound to be affected if Constantinople, the key to the Orient, and the Narrows were in rival hands. In spite of repeated attempts— during the Turko-Italian and Balkan Wars, in Sazonov's visit to Balmoral and the conclusion of a naval agreement with France in 1912, and in the naval discussions with Britain as late as May 1914— Russia failed to lift the 'Tsargrad' tabu.⁷

But the 'partition of the Turkish Empire', which had been mooted in the Ambassador Mallet's letter,⁸ was bound up with the Great War and unthinkable without Russia. The Western Allies, to attain their objectives, had to secure the Russian steamroller.⁹ For all Poincaré's later denials,¹⁰ the British Ambassador in Paris wrote that, 'when the President of the Republic was at Petersburg in July [1914], hopes, and perhaps more than hopes, were held out to the Russian Government that the French Government would not make objection to Russia having Constantinople.'¹¹ From the end of August

⁴ Buxton, *The War and the Balkans*, April 1915, p. 111.
² Kitchener to Abdullah, 31 Oct. '14. Storrs, 176.
³ 25 Jan. '15. Bertie, I. 105.
⁴ Bertie's formulation. 24 Feb. '15. Bertie, I. 120. Also B. Thomas, 296. Hourani, 16. The French Ambassador in Petrograd claimed also Palestine for France. Paléologue, I. 193.
⁵ 28 March, '15. Bertie, I. 135.
⁶ On 30 Oct. '14, Bertie noted in his Diary, I. 60, that 'we shall have to go in for an Arab Caliphate'.
⁷ Headlam Morley, 241, 245-8, 250. Adamov, II. p. 16. *Diplomaticheski Slovar*, II. 572. Sazonov, 247.
⁸ See p. 51 above.
⁹ Churchill says that Russia 'was all the time vital to our hopes of general victory'. *1915*, p. 198. Grey, II. 177. See also p. 47 above.
¹⁰ See Poincaré, V. 115; VI. 88, 95.
¹¹ 28 March '15. Bertie, I. 135. Delcassé, according to his biographer, promised Russia more than once his backing for the annexation of Constantinople and the Straits in exchange for her support for the return of Alsace-Lorraine, colonial acquisition, and the economic, military and political weakening of Germany. Porter, *The Career of Théophile Delcassé*, 329.

1914, Sir Edward Grey, with much circumspection, began to hint to the Russians that Turkey's fate was sealed, her adherence to Germany unavoidable, and that she would have to bear 'the most extreme' consequences.[1]

Thereupon, Sazonov, on September 14th and 26th, informed the British and French Ambassadors that Russia demanded—in addition to the lower reaches of the Nyemen and Eastern Galicia—'the permanent freedom of the Straits'. This was to be guaranteed by their internationalization, the disarmament of the Dardanelles and the establishment of a Russian station at the mouth of the Bosphorus. And, as he recollects, he warned the two Envoys, in the event of failure to attain this object, 'of my firm decision to resign my post for which there were plenty of candidates of less definite political orientation than myself'.[2]

Sazonov was susceptible to the pressure of the bourgeois sections in the Duma which sympathized with the West, and whose main ambition centred on Constantinople. His reactionary pro-German opponents argued that no serious advantage could be expected from the defeat of the Central Powers, and that Tsarism, far from sharing the Franco-British interest in crushing the Reich, needed the latter as a check on the liberal and imperialist proclivities of England. Western opposition to Sazonov's wishes, therefore, was bound to play into the hands of his political adversaries, discourage his friends, undermine his position, and damage the Entente. Hence, he must be allowed to uphold a 'national' policy on which both factions in Petrograd were agreed. This entailed concessions on the Straits.[3] These were dictated, too, by the military situation. The Russian invasion of Prussia at the height of the Marne was, as Churchill testifies, 'decisive upon the fate of the battle'.[4] Grey says that '... the only hope of holding out in the decisive theatre of war was that Russia should press her advance on the Eastern side ... it was the energy and tremendous sacrifice with which Russia made this advance that saved the Allies in the autumn of 1914. ... The whole-hearted effort and all the strength of Russia were needed in the early stages to save the Allies. ...'[5] But the toll taken was such that, by the end of the year, she had over 1,350,000 killed, wounded and missing. The arms shortage, the British Military Representative

---

[1] Benckendorff to Sazonov, 28 Aug. '14. *Internationale Beziehungen*, II. 6. I. No. 176, pp. 132–3.

[2] Sazonov, 249; also 248, 250–1. Paléologue to Delcassé, 14 and 26 Sept. '14. Deciphered in the Russian Foreign Ministry. *Internationale Beziehungen*, II. 6. I. No. 256, pp. 193–4. Adamov, I. No. 15, pp. 223–4. Poincaré, VI. 88, 164–5. Sazonov also desired that Western Posnania and parts of Silesia and Western Galicia should be included in a 'restored' Poland.

[3] Adamov, I. p. 112. Sazonov, 242–3. Trevelyan, 282.

[4] Churchill, *1915*, p. 25.     [5] Grey, II. 177.

reported, was beginning to paralyse her operations on the Eastern front. Deadlock prevailed in the West. Churchill, recapturing the mood of those days, writes: 'If only the will-power of Russia did not fail . . . if she could be encouraged to dwell on the prizes of victory. . . .'[1] Only the prospect of 'Tsargrad'—alpha and omega of all religious and political agitation—could enable Nicholas II to keep the 'mouzhik' in the trenches.[2]

The hesitations which the British Foreign Office may still have felt were overcome by diplomatic pressure from Sazonov. On November 6th 1914, he notified Benckendorff, his Envoy in London, that Russian troops operating against Turkey would be compelled to violate Persia's neutrality. Already before 1914, Petersburg and Constantinople had earmarked Persian Azerbaidjan as a base from which to outflank one another. In view of the impotence of the Teheran Government both sides hastened now to exploit the strategic advantages of that province. Not unnaturally the Russian Generalissimo wished to forestall the enemy. But Grey frowned on such action, lest—he replied through Buchanan—an analogy should be drawn between it and the German violation of Belgium.[3] He also professed anxiety lest Russia's incursion into a neutral Moslem country should provoke anti-Entente ferment among the Mohammedans of the East.[4] He said nothing about the importance of Persia in Britain's imperial scheme in Asia (the defence of India, Anglo-Iranian oil, and the containment of Russia) or about the possibility that an offensive against the Ottoman Empire from that direction might spread to Mesopotamia. But he must have felt strongly enough on the subject to urge upon the Russians that, in Benckendorff's words,

'the basic principle of the political harmony between the three Allied Entente Powers is the protection of the inviolability and neutrality of second-rate Powers. . . . This principle is to an equal degree the most essential guarantee that the same complete harmony will be preserved when it comes to future negotiations which are going to be of the very highest importance from the viewpoint of our most direct interests.'

Russia's contemplated step in Persia, the Ambassador added,

'would give rise to apprehension concerning a [Russian] military hegemony taking the place of German hegemony, an apprehension not wholly dispelled and capable of producing the greatest difficulties in the fulfilment

---

[1] Churchill, *1915*, p. 28; also 26–7.
[2] *Das Zaristische Russland*, p. XIII. Sazonov, 245. Paléologue, I. 151.
[3] Aide-Memoire, British Embassy, Petrograd, to Sazonov, 14 Nov. '14. Adamov, I. No. 23, pp. 233–4.
[4] Benckendorff to Sazonov, 9 Nov. '14. Adamov, I. No. 18, p. 228.

of our desires regarding the Dardanelles and Constantinople, which are now no longer meeting with any serious opposition in England'.[1]

Grey even went so far as to imply that, if Russia persisted, Britain would have to send larger forces to the East,[2] the least consequence of which would obviously be a weakening of the Western front, and the worst a collision between the Allies.

The warning: 'hands off Persia', however, was softened by the rejoinder that, 'the basic aim of the War remains the rout of Germany', which would also decide the destiny of Turkey. Grey suggested, on November 9th, that if Russia respected Persia's frontiers, contented herself with attacking Turkey from the Caucasus, or even with 'more dilatory tactics' on that front and, for the rest, concentrated her main efforts on the Germans, then, as Benckendorff reported, 'if Germany is crushed, the fate of the Straits and Constantinople cannot this time be decided in any other way than in conformity with our interests'.[3] Buchanan informed Sazonov 'that the wishes and interests of Russia in the question of Imbros and Tenedos must be taken into account'.[4] And on November 13th, Benckendorff cabled that King George V had said to him: 'Constantinople . . . must be yours'.[5]

Under the double impact of threat and promise, Sazonov dropped his Persian plan. Indeed, he abandoned more. To obtain recognition for Russia's demand for the Straits, he admitted later, 'I was . . . aware that . . . I had to offer some compensation. . . .' Despite the Tsargrad 'gift' from King George, 'I was of the opinion that our laying claim to that town made it more difficult to settle the question of the Straits. . . .'[6] The Foreign Minister was guided by such arguments as those presented by the Russian Chief of Black Sea Operations, Nemitz, on December 14th 1914. The latter, in a secret Aide-Memoire, emphasized that

'it is necessary to occupy in the Straits a military position whereby the maritime route from the Mediterranean to the Black Sea would be under the due protection of the Russian Fleet and a Russian fortress'.

But

'immense interests of "world" significance have for ages accommodated themselves and intertwined most intricately and subtly in Constantinople. . . .'

[1] Benckendorff to Sazonov, 13 Nov.' 14. Adamov, I. No. 22, pp. 232-3.
[2] Benckendorff to Sazonov, 9 Nov. '14. Adamov, I. No. 18, p. 228.
[3] ibid.
[4] Aide-Memoire, British Embassy, Petrograd, to Sazonov, 12 Nov. '14. Adamov, I. No. 20, p. 231.
[5] Benckendorff to Sazonov, 13 Nov. '14. The words 'must be yours' are in English in the original. Adamov, I. No. 21, pp. 231-2. Sazonov, 252.
[6] Sazonov, 249, 245; also 250.

Owing to these international interests—religious, economic and political—

'Turkish power in Constantinople has, strictly speaking, long been fictitious, and all the above factors jostle and pursue well-nigh freely *their own courses, directed and supported from the great European and other world centres.* The State which acquires Constantinople by force will at once come into contact and collision with all these vast factors behind which stand all the great Powers of the world.'

Tsarism, therefore, would either have to avoid clashes with its rivals, in which case its authority in Tsargrad would be 'as ficticious as that of the Turkish Sultan', or take up the struggle with them and

'very soon find itself in heavy, acute and protracted conflicts with many European great Powers and, in the end . . . be compelled to retreat from a "world" status in Constantinople.'

And as Russia

'can desire . . . neither a fictitious rule in Constantinople nor conflicts with Europe',

she must dominate the Straits and the Constantinople region in

'a *manner* . . . which, while it secures Russia's interests, enables her at the same time not only to avoid weakening, but actually to consolidate, her international position. . . . From this viewpoint it appears essential but also sufficient . . . to affirm that the Straits are absolutely indispensable to us . . . but that we do not at all require Constantinople as a city. . . .'[1]

And so Sazonov submitted to Western insistence that 'Tsargrad' should be internationalized.[2]

It was on this basis that he was informed by the British Embassy on November 14th that

'however much Russia or Great Britain may confine themselves to a defensive attitude against Turkey till the issue against Germany—the issue on which all others depend—is successfully concluded, Sir E. Grey regards the conduct of the Turkish Government as having rendered inevitable a complete settlement of the Turkish question, including that of the Straits and of Constantinople, in agreement with Russia. . . .'[3]

---

[1] Aide-Memoire by Nerntiz, 14 Dec. '14. Adamov, I. No. 3, pp. 191–2; also 195. Italics in the original.
[2] Sazonov, 250–1. Poincaré, VI. 87–8.
[3] Aide-Memoire, British Embassy, Petrograd, 14 Nov. '14. Adamov, I. No. 23, pp. 233–4. The Aide-Memoire insisted, at the same time, on 'the necessity of concentrating all our efforts against the Germans'.

## 3

### THE PARTITION OF THE OTTOMAN EMPIRE
### II: PARIS AND PETROGRAD

France, in regard to Tsarist desires, differed from Britain only in this: while less preoccupied with the Straits, she was even more eager to dispel the 'Tsargrad' dream. As early as August 11th 1914, the Quai d'Orsay—on the grounds that the Porte dreaded a Tsarist victory—sought to commit Russia to a guarantee reassuring the Turks [and thereby also the French] about her intentions.[1] On August 17th, the Ambassador Paléologue admonished Sazonov: 'You will not overlook . . . that preserving the territorial integrity and political independence of Turkey remains one of the guiding principles of French diplomacy'.[2] But this being understood, Delcassé was not averse to the Russians' poaching upon British naval preserves in the Mediterranean. A telegram from Izvolski to Petrograd quotes the French Foreign Minister as earmarking for France, apart from Alsace-Lorraine, 'the destruction of the German Empire' and 'rectification of some colonial frontiers' in Africa. He made no reference to the Near East beyond endorsing the Freedom of the Straits, 'wherein Russia would meet with far-reaching support from France who could, in this matter, exert an influence on Britain that would be useful to us'.[3] The need for such backing probably induced Sazonov to give this reassuring answer to Paléologue's searching enquiries into the meaning of Nicholas's Manifesto on Russia's 'historic tasks' in the Black Sea: 'We must have tangible guarantees on the Bosphorus. As regards Constantinople, personally I don't want the Turks to be cleared out'.[4] On November 21st, the Tsar said to the French Ambassador: 'We must *dictate* the peace'. He desired 'the destruction of German militarism' and, in return for a *carte blanche* for British and French war aims, 'a rectification of the frontier' in East Prussia by extending his territory to the mouth of the Vistula. He repeated Sazonov's earlier demands regarding Poland, and claimed for Russia the Northern half of Bukovina, Turkish Armenia and 'lastly . . . a free passage through the Straits. . . .' Paléologue pressed the Monarch 'to enlighten' him further. Nicholas: ' . . . the Turks must be expelled from Europe. . . . Constantinople must . . . be neutralized . . . Western Thrace to the Enos-Midia line

[1] Izvolski to Sazonov, 11 Aug. '14. *Das Zaristische Russland*, p. 18. For Doumergue's instructions to this effect to Paléologue, 10 Aug., see Poincaré, V. 62.
[2] Paléologue's telegram, 17 Sept. '14. Poincaré, V. 115.
[3] Izvolski to Sazonov, 13 Oct. '14. *Internationale Beziehungen*, II. 6. I. No. 385, p. 304.
[4] 2 Nov. '14. Paléologue, I. 178.

should be given to Bulgaria. The rest, from that line to the shores of the Dardanelles... would be assigned to Russia....'—'... Your Majesty will forgive me for interrupting again to remind you that, in Syria and Palestine, France has a precious heritage of historical memories and moral and material interests. May I assume that Your Majesty would acquiesce in any measures the Government of the Republic might think fit to take to safeguard that inheritance?'— 'Certainly'.[1]

## 4
### THE BRITISH IN EGYPT, THE FRENCH IN MOROCCO, THE RUSSIANS IN A QUANDARY

The Tsar's deference betokened not so much political amiability as diplomatic impotence. Sazonov was not unaware that he had bought Britain's promise regarding the Straits at the price of abandoning, in Azerbaidjan, the only operations against Turkey which had a chance of success. He must have suspected that he had been caught with a bait designed to keep Russia in the War—'a bait without risk, since the realization of that agreement was more than doubtful'.[2] His uneasiness was deepened when he found the British Aide-Memoire of November 14th, as he cabled to Benckendorff, 'more restrained in expression' than Grey's oral statements. He hastened to request 'that Buchanan should be instructed to repeat the communication made to me, but in words closer to those in which Grey spoke to you'.[3] There is no record of Sir Edward's having complied. Instead, there remained in the British Aide-Memoire the crucial proviso that the 'settlement' of the question of Constantinople and the Straits 'will, of course, be reached after the defeat of Germany'.[4] This meant that Russia's war effort and war aims were subordinated to the principal purpose of her Allies. No matter how great her sacrifices, if the struggle ended in compromise, she had no claim on Britain.

The British Government, on the other hand, secured, apart from maximum Russian co-operation, immediate and tangible benefits. They 'saved' Persia—for themselves. Without waiting for victory, they notified Sazonov of England's intention to annex Egypt.[5]

[1] Paléologue, I. 191–3 (Italics in the original). Poincaré, VI. 90–1. 165. See also Paléologue to Delcassé, 22 Nov. '14. *Internationale Beziehungen*, II. 6. II. No. 546, pp. 468–9.
[2] Rosen, *Forty Years of Diplomacy*, II. 102.
[3] Sazonov to Benckendorff, 16 Nov. '14. Adamov, I. No. 24, p. 234.
[4] Aide-Memoire, British Embassy, Petrograd, 14 Nov. '14. Adamov, I. No. 23, p. 234.
[5] Sazonov to Benckendorff, 18 Nov. '14, quoting an Aide-Memoire from Buchanan. Adamov, I. No. 25, p. 234; also 113.

Cyprus, held since 1878 and several times on the verge of being returned to Greece, was swallowed up on November 7th 1914 with no more ado than Poincaré's mordant comment that its 'inhabitants, most of whom are Greeks, never know the fate in store for them'.[1]

Such trouble as did arise was not of Russia's making. On November 3rd, the Ambassador Cambon cabled Delcassé that Grey had foreshadowed the proclamation of a British protectorate in Egypt. 'In return for our acquiescence, we demand', the French President noted, 'recognition of our Moroccan protectorate. . . .'[2] Some days later he wrote: 'It appears that the principal political personages in Cairo are opposed to a British protectorate which would leave Ottoman nationality to the Egyptians. They are said to prefer annexation. . . . The English Government inform us that they intend to adopt that solution and would not object to our . . . annexing Tunisia and Morocco'.[3] But, shortly before, a French detachment had been attacked and annihilated by Moroccan 'rebels'. In the prevailing tension, a tightening of France's rule would have had the effect of blowing on a hot coal. The hostilities with Turkey made it particularly dangerous to irritate the local Moslems. Moreover, such a demonstration of imperialism in practice would have embarrassed the Entente's claims to be crusading for the rights of small countries. Delcassé, intimating to Grey the undesirability of German assertions that Britain was in a hurry to gather the fruits of war, asked him to refrain for the duration from Egyptian *faits accomplis*. He said nothing of his own distaste for a premature British entrenchment in the heart of the Levant. The danger of differences among the Allies was one of the reasons which induced Grey to drop his project.[4] Another was that 'the Egyptian Ministers had accepted the . . . responsibility of Administration and secured the support of the religious party with a view to a . . . protectorate. Had Britain annexed Egypt they must have resigned to a man, with consequences none could foresee'.[5] And so, on December 18th, simultaneously with the recognition of French desires in Morocco, Britain announced her protectorate in Cairo and the replacement of the pro-Turkish Khedive by one more amenable to her. The risk of causing ferment in the Middle East, invoked against Russian action in Persia, was now ignored. The Russian Government, meanwhile, heedless of the Anglo-French by-play, had hastened to express approval of the annexation 'with particular pleasure'.[6] Nicholas's comment 'excellent'[6] betrayed

---

[1] 7 Nov. '14. Poincaré, V. 428.  [2] 6 Nov. '14. Poincaré, V. 427.
[3] 15 Nov. '14. Poincaré, V. 435. According to Storrs, p. 159, the decision for annexation was taken on 15 Nov. '14.
[4] Poincaré, V. 434–5, 443–4, 470. Grey, II. 171.
[5] Storrs, 159.
[6] Sazonov to Benckendorff, 18 Nov. '14. Adamov, I. No. 25, pp. 234–5.

the hope that Britain's acceptance of the Egyptian *avance* made the Dardanelles deal a certainty.[1] Nevertheless, Sazonov was worried. Considering 'as firmly acquired only . . . that which we have obtained by ourselves . . .',[2] he wrote to General Yanushkevich, the Chief of Staff, on December 21st 1914 that it was imperative 'for Russia to get possession of both Straits. . . . This will not be achieved by diplomatic action alone'; and he inquired 'what military operations had been decided upon for the actual penetration and seizure of the Narrows and their environs. . . .'[3]

But Russia had made no peace-time preparations for the attack. The Black Sea Fleet, short of dreadnoughts, fast mine-layers and modern submarines, was only just equal to the Turkish Navy. The loss of one or two ships would upset the precarious balance. Each single unit was inferior to the *Goeben* in speed and armament. Flaws in construction limited the amount of fuel they could carry, and from the nearest Russian coaling base it took 24 hours to reach the Bosphorus. Owing to weakness in transport, only small contingents could be expected to land on the Asiatic coast near the Straits, and reinforcement would be slow. The prospect, then, was one of immediate repulse or hazardous marches. Nor would good furtune on that side, however improbable, be enough. The conquest of the Bosphorus could only be consummated on its European shore.[4] Even if this were feasible from the aspect of Balkan politics (which it was not), troops of sufficient numbers could not be spared. Already grave defeats had been suffered in Poland and East Prussia. Already the Tsar's Army was reduced by rifle and shell shortage to defence on the Austro-German fronts, and Lord Kitchener warned the Russian High Command on December 22nd that this might affect the Western theatre.[5] Nicholas's generals were bound, by long-standing agreement with France, to concentrate on the principal foe.[6] Enver's sweeping Caucasion offensive, moreover, wholly precluded a fresh dispersal of Russian strength.[7] Hence, Yanushkevich answered Sazonov on December 25th that 'in the present circumstances . . . the question of allocating special forces for taking possession of the Straits cannot be raised until we have achieved a decisive success over our Western

[1] Adamov, I. p. 114.   [2] Adamov, II. p. 133.
[3] Adamov, II. No. 1, p. 115.
[4] Bazili to Sazonov, 28 Dec. '14. Adamov, II. No. 4, p. 119. Also Aide-Memoire by Nemitz, 14 Dec. '14. Adamov, I. No. 3, p. 189. The Generalissimo's draft reply to Kitchener, undated. Adamov, II. No. 15, pp. 134–5.
[5] Aide-Memoire by Nemitz, 14 Dec. '14. Adamov, I. No. 3, p. 186. Bazili to Sazonov, 27 Dec. '14. Adamov, II. No. 3, p. 117 and *ibid*. p. 117, footnote 1.
[6] Adamov, II. p. 13 and *ibid*. footnote 1.
[7] Adamov, I. p. 293, footnote 2.

enemies'.[1] And as the anxious Foreign Minister, nevertheless, did raise it again,[2] there came the Generalissimo Nikolai Nikolayevich's ruling: 'On our own, we cannot seize the Straits in any way, whatever'.[3]

The Stavka (General Headquarters) did more than dash Sazonov's hopes of solving the problem by independent military action. Seeking relief from their own difficulties—especially the crisis in the Caucasus—they took a course directly opposed to his. On December 30th 1914, Nikolai Nikolayevich, while promising that Russia, 'contrary to her own interests', would continue to deal Germany the main blows and thereby denude the Caucasian front to danger point, inquired through the British Representative at his Headquarters whether England could not divert the Ottoman armies by 'bringing pressure to bear upon Turkey in her most vulnerable and sensitive spots'.[4]

---

[1] Adamov, II. No. 2, p. 116.
[2] Sazonov to Yanushkevich, 29 Dec. '14. Adamov, II. No. 5, pp. 121–2.
[3] Aide-Memoire by Kudashev, 31 Dec. '14. Adamov, II, No. 6, p. 122.
[4] Aide-Memoire, Kudashev to Sazonov, 31 Dec. '14. Adamov, II. No. 11, pp. 128–9; also 13. Buchanan's telegram, received in London 2 Jan. '15. Churchill, *1915*, p. 93. Dardanelles Commission, *First Report*, p. 15.

CHAPTER IV

# Churchill and the Dardanelles

1

## CHURCHILL'S NAVAL AND POLITICAL STRATEGY

THE Russian request disturbed the brooding indecision produced by deadlock in the West. 'The great struggles of 1914', in the words of Lloyd George, 'had shattered every military dream . . . on both sides'.[1] The Germans had failed before Paris, at Ypres and on the way to the Channel ports, and were no more likely to succeed in future. Their Fleet hid in its fortified bases, and the Royal Navy could not draw it out. The Entente Commands, facing a barrier of trenches from the North Sea to the Alps, were unable to outflank the enemy. So they resorted to the blockade, attrition and, as Churchill recollects, 'the forlorn expedient of the frontal attack',[2] although they lacked the guns and equipment to break through. And the outlook for the New Year, like the pattern of the old, was one of 'the torture, mutilation or extinction of millions of men. . . .'[3]

But there were in both countries those who understood that 'nearly all the battles which are regarded as masterpieces of the military art . . . have been battles of manoeuvre. . . .'[4] If Germany was impregnable in Flanders and France, she had her Achilles heel in South-Eastern Europe. The Austrian Empire, it was argued, was inferior to the Reich in organization, material and direction, and its Army was largely recruited from races hostile to their rulers and friendly to the Triple Entente. A blow dealt to it from the Balkans would isolate Turkey, rally Greece, Rumania and Bulgaria, bring in Italy, arouse the Habsburg Slavs, and open the road to Vienna. Germany would either have to aid Austria and thus attenuate her own lines, or else abandon her to her fate. In either case, a diversion in the East, coupled with a strategy of defence in the West, was bound to be decisive. From October 1914, several French generals, notably Gallieni, and, in the Cabinet, the Minister of Justice, Briand, urged an expedition to Salonika.[5]

In Britain, the principal advocate of manoeuvre was Churchill. A 'glance upon each of the flanks of the battle line', he writes,

---

[1] Lloyd George, *War Memoirs*, I. 359; also 363, 370.
[2] Churchill, *1915*, p. 19; also 18, 46, 174. Dardanelles C. *First Report*, 19.
[3] Churchill, *1915*, p. 20.     [4] Churchill, *1915*, p. 21.
[5] Suarez, *Briand*, III. 87–90. Poincaré, VI. 2–3. Lloyd George, I. 363–4, 367, 384–5.

77

prompted the question: 'should we strike through the Belts at the Baltic, or through the Dardanelles at Constantinople and the Black Sea?' He was tempted by the prospect of gaining 'the command of the Baltic, and the consequent letting loose of the Russian armies upon . . . the unprotected . . . seaboard of Germany'.[1] But the Northern states, defenceless against Germany and frightened of Tsarism, refused to co-operate. Russia showed little liking for such an extension of British naval power.[2] The project, 'so vast, so critical and dependent on so long a succession of events',[3] was allowed to fade. Instead, the First Lord of the Admiralty threw his energies into the Southern scheme. Its 'period of origin and inception commenced at the outbreak of the War with Germany. . . .'[4] From the end of August 1914, he proceeded on the assumption that Turkey would be among Britain's enemies.[5] On September 1st, he informed General Douglas, the Chief of the Imperial Staff, that he himself and Lord Kitchener would 'work out a plan for the seizure, by means of a Greek army . . . of the Gallipoli Peninsula, with a view to admitting a British Fleet to the Sea of Marmora'.[6] On November 25th, that is soon after Grey's assurances to Russia regarding the Narrows, the War Council discussed the attack which, Churchill urged, would 'enable us to dictate terms at Constantinople'.[7] On December 28th, Hankey, the Secretary of the War Council, suggested that Germany might 'be struck most effectively, and with the most lasting results on the peace of the world, through . . . Turkey'.[8] Throughout these months, however, Entente diplomacy was unable to unravel the tangled skein of Balkan politics. In Britain and France the 'Eastern school' was blocked by the addicts to the 'Western Front superstition'.[9] The controversy was unresolved when the Russian Generalissimo's appeal of December 30th arrived.

Briand at once pressed on the French Government the Salonika plan.[10] The November pledges to Nicholas II and his bid for Southern Thrace rankled in Paris. As Lloyd George, after a trip to the Seine, informed Grey, Briand wished 'that France and England should establish a right to a voice in the settlement of the Balkans by having a force there. He does not want Russia to feel that she alone is the

[1] Churchill, *1915*, pp. 29, 33, 39.
[2] The Russian Generalissimo to Churchill, 24 Aug. '14. Churchill, *1915*, p. 39; also 29.
[3] Churchill, *1915*, p. 45.     [4] Dardanelles C. *First Report*, 1.
[5] Churchill, *1915*, p. 47. Dardanelles C. *Supplement to First Report*, 2. The Aga Khan: 'I remember Churchill telling me brusquely that Turkey would be the victor's prize'. *Memoirs*, 90.
[6] Dardanelles C. *Supplement*, 2.
[7] Dardanelles C. *First Report*, 14. The quotation is from the Report.
[8] *ibid.* 48.     [9] Lloyd George, I. 382.
[10] 1 and 7 Jan. '15. Suarez, III. 89. Poincaré, VI. 2–3. Lloyd George, I. 383.

arbiter of . . . the Balkan peoples'.[1] But Joffre, the Supreme Commander, hypnotized by the foe opposing him, would not give up a single man. He was confident of breaking the German lines before long. The expedition, opposed also by the War Minister Millerand and the British Commander in France, General French, was shelved.[2] In London, meantime, the diversion was strongly championed by Lloyd George. Like Briand, and on the same day, he too proposed an operation in Salonika, and 'an attack on Turkey': 'a force of 100,000 should be landed in Syria.[3] And Kitchener, replying to the Russian Generalissimo on January 2nd 1915, promised 'a demonstration against the Turks'.[4]

This demonstration soon developed into a larger enterprise. With the support of 'very weighty opinion',[5] the First Sea Lord, Fisher, wrote to Churchill on January 3rd that a British army should be sent 'against Haifa and Alexandretta, the latter to be a *real* occupation because of its inestimable value as regards the oil fields of the Garden of Eden [Mesopotamia] with which by rail it is in direct communication, and we shove out the Germans now established at Alexandretta. . . .' Simultaneously 'the Greeks [were] to go to Gallipoli . . . and the Bulgarians for Constantinople', whilst the Royal Navy 'forces the Dardanelles'.[6] On January 13th, according to Churchill and the Report of the Dardanelles Commission, the War Council decided that the Admiralty—apart from considering action in the Adriatic—'should also prepare for a naval expedition in February to . . . take the Gallipoli Peninsula, with Constantinople as its objective'.[7] There is no reference in either source to Syria. But Churchill, in a minute to his Department, laid down that 'as soon as the attack on the Dardanelles has begun, the seizure of Alexandretta should take place'.[8] And shortly before, with the approval of Grey, Asquith, Kitchener and Fisher, he had handed the French Naval Attaché this Note:

'The Admiralty have . . . decided to attack the Dardanelles forts, and force . . . a passage into the Sea of Marmora. . . . The Admiralty do not

[1] Lloyd George to Grey, 7 Feb. '15. Lloyd George, I. 409. Also Suarez, III. 96.
[2] Lloyd George, I. 384–5, 405. Churchill, *1915*, p. 174. Poincaré, VI. 8, 13, 31–2. Suarez, III. 116.
[3] 1 Jan. '15. Lloyd George, I. 376–7; also 368–9, 370, 373, 383. Dardanelles C. *First Report*, 48.
[4] Churchill, *1915*, p. 94.   [5] Corbett, II. 79.
[6] Churchill, *1915*, pp. 95–6. (Italics in the original). Kitchener, too, advocated a combined attack on Alexandretta. See Corbett, II. 79; also p. 49, footnote 4 above. The plea for a railway across the Syrian desert to Mesopotamia by Sir W. Willcocks, who had projected Mesopotamian irrigation in 1911, was another indication of British interest in Syria. See *Syria and Palestine*. Foreign Office Handbooks, No. 60, p. 78. *Who was Who*, III. p. 1458.
[7] Churchill, *1915*, p. 111. Dardanelles C. *First Report*, 21. The word 'also' is omitted here.
[8] 20 Jan. '15. Churchill, *1915*, pp. 120–1.

wish... that any change in the local command... [which was British]... should be made.... They hope, however, that the squadron of French battleships... will co-operate under a French rear-admiral.... The War Office also considers it necessary during... February to occupy Alexandretta and the surrounding district... it would be convenient that the disembarkation at Alexandretta and the maintenance of the British force on shore should be covered by British ships....'[1]

## 2
### BRITISH AND FRENCH DIVERGENCIES OVER TURKEY

The reaction in Paris was sharp. Of all the regions under the Sultan's sway none was more important to the French investors than Syria. The supremacy of French culture there was only a graceful offshoot of financial predominance. Behind the numerous missionary and secular schools, the Jesuit colleges, the hospitals, and the press stood the invisible power of the Bourse. Some 1,000,000,000 francs were sunk in the key railway system Damas-Hama et Prolongements, the port, the gas and electricity lighting and waterworks of Beirut, the Tramways Libanais, harbour works at Tripoli and elsewhere, the Tobacco Monopoly, the large export trade of Beirut, especially in silk to Lyons, the big general business of the Établissements Orosdi Back, and practically every other important concession or enterprise. Shortly before the War, a group comprising—apart from certain Oriental Jewish interests—the Ottoman Bank, the Banque Bardac and André Tardieu, the foreign political authority of the *Temps*, was pushing a scheme for a railway which was to compete with the *Bagdadbahn* by connecting the Mediterranean with Baghdad via Syria.[2] After the outbreak of war, sections of the Parisian press were vociferous in their demands for the protection of French 'rights and duties' in Asiatic Turkey. On December 30th 1914, *Le Matin* came out with a call for the 'liquidation' of the Eastern Question, and invited France to 'take up where the Crusades had left off'. Since Britain claimed all the roads leading to India—Syria and Palestine, the paper considered, 'deserved to be joined in one term: France of the Levant'.[3] Feeling was reaching such a pitch that a deputy was soon to proclaim in the Chamber:

'The Axis of French policy is in the Mediterranean. One of its poles is in the West, through Algeria, Tunisia and Morocco. It is necessary that the other pole be in the East with Syria, the Lebanon and Palestine'.

[1] Undated. Churchill, *1915*, pp. 118-9.
[2] Cumming, 9. Hallgarten, II. 132, 134 and *ibid.* footnote, 2; 141, 168. Toynbee, *Turkey P.F.*, 63. Hourani, *Syria and Lebanon*, 153-4. Erzberger, 87. *Syria and Palestine*. Foreign Office Handbooks, No. 60, pp. 69, 74, 79, 84-5, 126, 132, 144.
[3] Cumming, 16.

In the *Revue Hebdomadaire*, the Senator Flandin announced that 'it would be inadmissible that France should not succeed to the Ottoman Empire in Syria and Palestine . . .' and, discussing the Arab movement, he asked:

> 'Shall we leave to a rival Power the means of perhaps one day directing it against us? This consideration . . . bids us . . . not to leave in the hands of any Power other than France the ports of Palestine giving access to the railway which, by way of the Hedjaz, will carry . . . Moslem pilgrims to Medina and Mecca'.[1]

As early as January 13th 1915, the *Giornale d'Italia* stated that

> 'according to most secret information coming from a person well informed of the projects of the English Government, England . . . will try to make . . . a second Egypt out of Syria. . . . The weak side of this project will lie in the energetic opposition of France. . . .'[2]

In this context, Churchill's Note about the contemplated British landing at Alexandretta was received with extreme distaste by the Quai d'Orsay. The insult of non-consultation and a *decision accomplie* was added to the injury of further upsetting the accords of 1912 and August 1914 which reserved the Mediterranean command to France. Already, after Turkey's entry into the War, Egypt and the Dardanelles area had been exempted from French direction, and the Royal Navy patrolled the whole of Syria. The fresh British demands for control of Alexandretta and the entire shore from Mersina to El-Arish (the Egyptian frontier) would result in a complete French removal from the Levant.[3] The rulers of the Third Republic, having earmarked for themselves Palestine, Syria, Cilicia and Alexandretta, suspected those of Britain of using the defence of Egypt as a cloak for their own designs on that port. Majority opinion in the French Cabinet, moreover, opposed a potential weakening of the Western front. On January 23rd 1915, the Minister of Marine, Augagneur, was hastily dispatched to Churchill and, having laid on pressure in their parleys, brought back a compromise. France secured the naval command of the Syrian coast as far as Jaffa—at the cost of definitely leaving the British Fleet in control in the Straits.[4] The Alexandretta landing was dropped by Churchill in return for Augagneur's pledge to take part in the operations at the Dardanelles.[5] 'Expédition bien incertaine', grumbled Poincaré. But the few old warships promised

---

[1] Georges Leygues in the French Chamber, 10 May '15. Pierre Etienne Flandin, 'Nos Droits en Syrie et en Palestine', *La Revue Hebdomadaire*, 6 June '15, pp. 17-32, quoted by Cumming, 17-19.
[2] Cumming, 19.
[3] Corbett, II. 74, 79, 142.
[4] Corbett, II. 142.
[5] Corbett, II. 195.

by the French were a small price to pay for preserving Syria from their friend, especially since the latter would 'bear almost all the risks....'[1] At the same time Greece declined a British invitation to join in the War.[2] The Salonika enterprise, conceived by Briand predominantly as a French bid for power in the Near East, was shelved. France, even though she had 'saved' Syria, suffered a political check. The initiative was seized by Britain.[3]

3

THE POLITICAL BACKGROUND OF THE
NAVAL OPERATION

And so, the wheels turned towards the project which Churchill, on his own admission, 'had always so greatly desired'. Though by no means averse to fruit from 'the Garden of Eden', he had, throughout January 1915, pressed hard for his particular plan.[4] On January 2nd, he heard from Kitchener that 'we have no troops to land anywhere.... We shall not be ready for anything big for some months'.[5] Doubtless aware that the Secretary of War was conserving his men for Alexandretta,[6] he took up Lord Fisher's proposal of January 3rd that, simultaneously with the Alexandretta enterprise, the Royal Navy should force the Dardanelles.[7] On the same day, he inquired of Vice-Admiral Carden, Commander-in-Chief Mediterranean, whether it was a 'a practicable operation to force the Dardanelles by the use of ships alone.... The importance of the results would justify severe loss'.[8] When Carden replied that 'they might be forced by extended operations with a large number of ships', Churchill sent him an encouraging telegram: 'High authorities here concur in your opinion'.[9] Considering that Lord Fisher, the supreme naval authority, stated later that, had he known of this message, he would have objected to its formulation, and that Sir Henry Jackson, another Admiralty chief, could not remember having been consulted, the text of this telegram, in the words of the Dardanelles Commission, 'was certainly open to criticism'.[10]

Thanks to the groundless assumption[11] that no soldiers were

[1] Poincaré, VI. 34; also 29, 30, 33, 80. Corbett, I. 59. II. 121. Bertie, I. 172. Dardanelles C. *First Report*, 23. Adamov, II. 21.
[2] 27 Jan. '15. Corbett, II. 103. [3] Suarez, III. 97, 99, 100.
[4] Churchill, *1915*, pp. 97, 113.
[5] Dardanelles C. *First Report*, 15. According to Fisher, Kitchener (in his letter to Churchill, 2 Jan. '15) suggested the Dardanelles as a target for a 'demonstration'. Fisher, *Memories*, 52, footnote 1; 57.
[6] Corbett, II. 79. [7] Churchill, *1915*, p. 96.
[8] Dardanelles C. *First Report*, 16. [9] Dardanelles C. *First Report*, 16, 17.
[10] ibid. 17.
[11] See Lloyd George, I. 390–1. Dardanelles C. *First Report*, 41.

available, Churchill prevailed over Lloyd George's Salonika scheme by marshalling arguments in favour of purely naval action. The traditional Admiralty axiom deprecating unaided Fleet attacks against forts was disregarded. Recent experience at Port Arthur and Wei-Hai-Wei, showing that ships without military backing are impotent against forts, was countered by reference to the rapid fall of Antwerp and Liège, and the contention that warfare had been revolutionized by aircraft and modern artillery. That the Belgian fortresses had been reduced by howitzers, which are impracticable on a ship, was overlooked. The analogy between these fortresses and the long chain of Straits defences was overdrawn. Turkish resistance was 'greatly underestimated'.[1] Whether the forts of the Narrows had been bought, as was asserted in France,[2] or whether they had not, intelligence reports were adduced in support of the hope of 'a revolution taking place in Constantinople if once the British Fleet appeared in the Sea of Marmora'.[3] An uprising of the Greek and Armenian minorities and a Moslem movement against the Young Turks were expected to force the Porte, as Churchill puts it, to 'negotiate or withdraw to Asia'.[4] Perhaps it was even assumed that Enver would understand Britain's intentions. Lord Fisher and his experts preferred Alexandretta or, if it was to be the Straits, a combined operation. Yet in the War Council of January 13th neither they nor the Chief of the Imperial General Staff, General Murray, voiced any objection. And Churchill, with Kitchener's approval, obtained the adoption, in principle, of his plan.[5]

Principle became practice under the impact of France's veto on Alexandretta, Greece's impossible terms for the Salonika operation,[6] and Russia's victory in the Caucasus. The War Council of January 28th, passing beyond 'preparations', firmly resolved on the Dardanelles attack by sea alone.[7] Before that, the First Sea Lord, Fisher, seeing that what he had accepted as a feint or subsidiary to his Syrian scheme was broadening into an independent offensive, had come out in opposition. Acute differences developed between him and Churchill, who admitted having put 'great and continuous pressure . . . upon the old Admiral'.[8] The Sea Lord set forth his criticism and alternative recommendations in a Memorandum to

[1] Dardanelles C. *First Report*, 29; also 13–14, 24, 25, 30, 41. Lloyd George, I. 388–91, 395–6. For Churchill's views on the subject see *1915*, pp. 103–8, 110.
[2] Bertie, I. 214.
[3] Dardanelles C. *First Report*, 29; also 36, and *Supplement*, 2.
[4] Churchill, *1915*, p. 180; also 179. Adamov, II. 37.
[5] Dardanelles C. *First Report*, 19–22, 26. Churchill, *1915*, pp. 110–11.
[6] 27 Jan. '15. Corbett, II. 103.
[7] Dardanelles C. *First Report*, 28. Actually the designated ships were already on the way. Corbett, II. 104. Also Adamov, II. 38.
[8] Churchill, *1915*, p. 165; also 148. Dardanelles C. *First Report*, 20–1, 26, 28.

the Prime Minister who rejected them. He attempted to resign at the Council meeting but surprisingly allowed himself to be dissuaded by Kitchener.[1] Not only did he stay on, but he and Sir Arthur Wilson, the other Admiralty expert present, refrained from stating their views, and were later rebuked for dereliction of duty by the Dardanelles Commission. On the other hand: ' . . . considering what Mr. Churchill knew of the opinions entertained by Lord Fisher and Sir Arthur Wilson . . . he ought, instead of urging Lord Fisher . . . to give a silent, but manifestly very reluctant assent . . . not merely to have invited Lord Fisher and Sir Arthur Wilson to express their views freely to the Council, but further to have insisted on their doing so, in order that the Ministerial members might be placed in full possession of all the arguments. . . . But . . . he was carried away by his sanguine temperament. . . .'[2] Also, 'the other members of the Council, and more especially the Chairman, should have encouraged the experts . . . to give their opinion . . . in order to allow the matter to be further considered. . . .'[3] Instead, the Prime Minister Asquith backed Churchill to the hilt. 'Lord Kitchener considered the naval attack to be vitally important'. Mr. Balfour said, 'it was difficult to imagine a more helpful operation'. Sir Edward Grey invoked diplomatic arguments in its support. The Government as a whole, in the Home Secretary's words, 'accepted without comment or criticism'.[4] For 'the stress laid upon the unquestionable advantages which would accrue from success was so great that the disadvantages . . . were insufficiently considered'.[5]

### 4
#### EXTENDING THE BRITISH EMPIRE IN THE LEVANT

The advantages were, in the first place, strategic. The piercing of the Straits and the capture of Constantinople would cut Turkey into two, detach her from her Allies and strike the country with the creeping paralysis of defeat. This was more than a mere matter of eliminating the least dangerous of the enemies. Germany, as Churchill was soon to remind the Cabinet, intended to 'break through Serbia, seduce Bulgaria, establish a through route to Constantinople, gain full control of the Turkish Empire . . . and

---

[1] Dardanelles C. *First Report*, 26–7.
[2] *ibid.* 28–9. 'Mr. Churchill failed to present fully to the War Council the opinions of his naval advisers . . . due to his own strong personal opinion in favour of a naval attack'. *ibid.* 59.
[3] *ibid.* 29.      [4] *ibid.* 26, 27, 31.
[5] Dardanelles C. *First Report*, 29; also 59. Lloyd George, I. 395–6. Cf. Churchill, *1915*, pp. 97, 148–66.

open to herself avenues to Persia and India . . . in spite of all pressure of this War . . . the construction of the Baghdad Railway has been hurried forward with German material. . . .'[1] A swift stroke by the British would sever from German imperialism its foremost tentacle. The same blow, it was argued, would break the enemy blockade of Russia, release some 350,000 tons of merchant shipping interned in her Black Sea ports, re-open the flow of Entente arms to her battle-fields and of Ukrainian wheat to the West, restore her falling exchanges, stifle the worst pangs of social discontent, and give strength to this reeling giant at a time when the brunt of the War was moving to the East.[2] 'Russia alone', as Churchill pleaded, 'offers the means of providing the Allies with the very large numerical preponderance which they will require to wear down the armies of the Central Powers. To acquire influence over Russia, to organize and equip her is the most important need. . . .' Success in the Dardanelles will, 'conjoined with our other advantages, confer upon us a far-reaching influence among the Allies, and enable us to ensure their indispensable co-operation . . . it will react on Russia. . . . It will dominate the Balkan situation and cover Italy. . . .'[3]

The second benefit, then, to be reaped at the Golden Horn was diplomatic. For months, the Triple Entente's Foreign Services had laboured in Rome, Athens, Sofia and Bucharest at furtive and futile attempts to promote their cause. By January 1915, Grey discovered that, as he told the Dardanelles Commission later, 'diplomacy was perfectly useless without military success'.[4] At the War Council of January 28th, he affirmed that the attack on the Straits would 'finally settle the attitude of Bulgaria and the whole of the Balkans'.[5] A few days later, Asquith confided to his Diary that the operation was 'all important as a preliminary to our démarche in the Balkans'.[6] Churchill, as he related later, 'expected that if and when the Turkish forts began to fall, the Greeks would join us', that this 'would induce Bulgaria to march on Adrianople', and 'lastly I was sure that Russia . . . would not remain indifferent to the fate of Constantinople and that further reinforcements would be forthcoming from her'.[7]

[1] Memorandum, July '15. Churchill, *1915*, p. 427.
[2] War Council, 28 Jan. '15. Dardanelles C. *First Report*, 49, 53. Churchill, *1915*, pp. 28, 46, 163. Also Corbett, II. 68. Morgenthau, 126.
[3] Memorandum, 18 June '15. Churchill, *1915*, pp. 407-8. Although this Memorandum, like the one of July, was written after the events described here, it can be seen from his book that he already had these arguments in mind in January 1915 and before.
[4] Dardanelles C. *First Report*, 19. See also Grey, II. 154.
[5] Dardanelles C. *First Report*, 27.
[6] 10 Feb. '15. Asquith, *Memories and Reflections*, II. 62.
[7] Churchill, *1915*, pp. 179, 180; also Bertie, I. 217.

This latter point was to bring trouble to the First Lord of the Admiralty. The day was not far off, when the New York *World* could state: 'Russia is England's great future enemy. . . . England's endeavour to conquer the Dardanelles, to take Constantinople and deliver her to England's greatest rival . . . is nothing short of political madness', and Bertie could comment that there was 'a good deal of truth' in these remarks.¹ Yet it was easy to foresee that Nicholas II, even if he helped Britain to complete the job, would lack the power to assert his wishes. British intelligence could not have been ignorant of the depressing news Sazonov was receiving from the Stavka.² The Russian Generalissimo's SOS to Kitchener testified to Tsarist weakness in the Black Sea. The strongest weapon in Russian hands was the Entente's November pledge regarding the Narrows. It could be irresistible unless the West was quick in finding an antidote. The *First Report* of the Dardanelles Commission, discussing the contentions in favour of the operation, refers to 'Churchill documents'. But these are omitted from the text³— presumably because they deal 'with the relations between His Majesty's Government and their Allies which could not, without serious detriment to the public interest, have been published'.⁴ The blank could be filled by the cautious statement that the enterprise 'would have gone far to settle a question which has been a constant source of trouble to Europe for centuries past'.⁵ The Ambassador Bertie, in his Diary, dwelt on 'the advisability of England and France . . . getting to Constantinople before Russia, so that the Muscovite may not have it all his own way in deciding the future of that City and the Straits. . . .'⁶ And this may suggest why the naval experts, despite their misgivings, kept silent or allowed themselves to be overruled; they 'all assumed that the War Council looked upon immediate action as a political necessity. . . .'⁷

The third and greatest advantage anticipated from the Dardanelles operation, therefore, was political.⁸ Whereas Lord Fisher and his Admirals intended to treat it as a subsidiary expedition, a powerful section of the Cabinet, led by Churchill, had long envisaged it as a

---

¹ *The World*, New York, 6 Sept. '15, p. 3. Bertie, I. 232.
² See pp. 75–6 above. Also Adamov, II. p. 38.
³ See Dardanelles C. *First Report*, 14.   ⁴ *ibid.* 2.   ⁵ *ibid.* 19.
⁶ 26 Feb. '15. Bertie, I. 121.
⁷ Dardanelles C. *First Report*, 50–1. Corbett, too, speaks of the 'overwhelming political necessity'. See II. 105; also 106. Lord Fisher, in explaining why he did not resign in Jan. '15, mentions among other considerations that he 'understood that there were overwhelming political reasons why the attempt at least [to force the Dardanelles] should be made'. See Fisher, 72; also 62, 65, 71. Balfour's Memorandum, 24 Feb. '15, too, shows that the Dardanelles enterprise was regarded as a matter of vital political expediency. *ibid.* 68.
⁸ See Dardanelles C. *First Report*, 59. Bertie, I. 138.

major offensive of its own. Their over-all policy was to apply the supremacy of naval power to an extension of the British Empire in the Levant. In this, the safeguarding of Britain's interests in the Narrows and the Constantinople zone was a prime concern. It was useless to hanker after the 'Garden of Eden' if, and so long as, a rival could dominate its flank. The Ambassador Bertie was surely not alone in fearing that, 'with Russia in the Caucasus and on the Bosphorus and commanding the Northern terminus of the Baghdad Railway, England would be at the beck and call of Russia in Mesopotamia'.[1] The first task, it would therefore appear, was to counter by action the effect of the promise given to Sazonov that the fate of that area should be settled 'in agreement with Russia'.[2] The Generalissimo's appeal, although a negligible factor in starting it off, was put forward as the reason for the attack. But basically—according to Russian sources—'the centre of gravity of the whole Dardanelles operation was not in the least to help Russia. It consisted in the acquisition of the Near East by Britain, independently of Russia and ... against Russia ... against the establishment of her mastery in the Straits'.[3]

---

[1] 28 March '15. Bertie, L 135. See also p. 49, footnote 4; and p. 79, footnote 6 above.
[2] See p. 71 above.
[3] Prof. E. Grimm, Introduction to Adamov, II. p. 39; also 16, 17, 21, 38. Miller, 54.

CHAPTER V

# The Diplomatic War Among the Allies

## 1
### RUSSIAN REACTIONS TO CHURCHILL'S PLAN

'IT had always been British policy to keep Russia out of Constantinople and the Straits; we fought for that object in the Crimean War . . . and it was our main policy under Beaconsfield. . . . Britain was now going to occupy Constantinople in order that when Britain and France had been enabled, by Russia's help, to win the War, Russia should not have Constantinople at the peace. If this were not so, why were British forces being sent to the Dardanelles at a time when the French and British armies were being so hard pressed in France that the Russian armies were making unheard of sacrifices to save them?' This summing-up of Russian feeling by Sir Edward Grey[1] could not have been bettered in Petrograd. It was also conveyed by the Italian Envoy Carlotti who cabled to Rome that Great Britain preferred to take the Narrows 'with her own forces'.[2] Enver confided to the U.S. Ambassador: 'I do not believe that England is trying to force the Dardanelles because Russia has asked her to. When I was in England . . . Churchill . . . said that, if we took Germany's side, the British Fleet would . . . capture Constantinople'.[3] The Japanese Military Attaché in Petrograd, in a telegram to Tokio, quoted reports that 'the Dardanelles operations have been undertaken by England and France to prevent the Straits from passing into the power of Russia'.[4] For the Russian Foreign Minister, therefore, this action was a logical sequel to the episode of the *Goeben* and the *Breslau*. The Palmerston-Disraeli tradition was directly and consistently continued by Churchill. And when Buchanan and Paléologue informed Sazonov of the coming expedition, the effect was such that, he recalls, 'I had difficulty in concealing from them how painfully the news had affected me'. 'I intensely disliked the thought that the

---

[1] Grey, II. 180-1.
[2] Carlotti to Sonnino, 26 Feb. '15. Deciphered in the Russian Foreign Ministry. Adamov, I. No. 106, p. 307.
[3] Morgenthau, 135.
[4] Ogadiri to the Japanese Chief of Staff, 3 March '15. Deciphered in the Russian Foreign Ministry. Adamov, I. No. 47, p. 251.

Straits and Constantinople might be taken by our Allies and not by the Russian forces'.[1]

Sazonov was so perturbed that he inquired at once at the Stavka whether 'we are, at present, in a position to give the English the support they request[2] and, in the event of a favourable turn of affairs, to play, in the occupation of the Straits, a part becoming to Russia?' Anticipating a negative answer, he pushed his anxiety far enough to ask 'if it might not be better to request our Allies, in view of the change, in our favour, in the Caucasian situation, still to delay a little the intended actions against the Dardanelles?'[3] Sazonov evidently wished to derive diplomatic advantage from recent events on the Turkish front.

Enver, before crossing the Russian and North-Persian frontiers with a German Chief of Staff in December 1914, had promised General von Sanders to march through Afghanistan to India. His offensive, after an initial advance, was routed by the Russians near Ardahan and Sarakamysh early in January 1915. Retreating under pursuit, driving his troops by forced marches through the mountain snow, he left behind 78,000 men (out of a total of 90,000) killed, frozen, starved, and ravaged by spotted fever. In Constantinople all talk of the extent of the catastrophe was suppressed by vigorous punishment.[4]

But though the situation in the Caucasus had improved, the Stavka refused to heed the Foreign Minister. The British Military Attaché, General Williams, was informed on January 23rd that, whilst 'neither naval nor military support could be promised', the Generalissimo would welcome 'any blow dealt to Turkey'.[5] At the same time Sazonov was told that Russia's position in the Caucasus, despite the victory, was unstable; 'our losses there are immense, and there is nothing to replenish them with'. As the Turks were reinforcing, the Russian Army might soon be in the same critical state as in December. Hence any diversion of Ottoman strength would 'ease our military position not only in the Caucasus . . . but also in Europe, for a Turkish defeat will undoubtedly determine the orientation of the Balkan States. . . .' On the other hand, no troops

---

[1] Sazonov, 255. Aide-Memoire, British Embassy, Petrograd, 20 Jan. '15. Adamov, II. No. 12, pp. 129–30. Churchill to the Grand Duke Nikolai, 19 Jan. '15. Churchill, *1915*, p. 119. Also Trevelyan, 283.

[2] The British Aide-Memoire of 20 Jan. '15 expressed the hope that Russia 'will, by naval operations undertaken at the proper moment at the mouth of the Bosphorus and by holding troops in readiness to seize any advantage that may be gained, co-operate powerfully in the proposed attack'.

[3] Sazonov to Kudashev, 21 Jan. '15. Adamov, II. No. 13, p. 131.

[4] Sanders, 37, 39, 40.

[5] Kudashev to Sazonov, 25 Jan. '15. Adamov, II. No. 14, p. 132. The Generalissimo's reply to Kitchener, *ibid.* 134–5. Churchill, *1915*, pp. 157–8.

could be spared in support of the Anglo-French expedition in the Dardanelles. Nor was it deemed necessary to send any, as the Stavka 'regarded the capture of the Straits by the Allied Navy as difficult, almost impossible to achieve'. The Quartermaster-General Danilov 'absolutely declined to believe' in the success of the 'English undertaking'. For 'even if they succeeded in capturing the Straits, annihilating the Turkish Fleet and intimidating the capital of the Ottoman Empire, they will not be able to take possession of it: no landing force they might be able to send, would be capable of overpowering the Turkish Army. . . .' The attempt, however, would be 'useful to us and, from a military viewpoint, even very desirable', and besides 'we risk nothing by encouraging the English'.[1] In spite of the immense political significance of the question, Russia's attitude was decided by purely military arguments.[2]

## 2
### PETROGRAD DEMANDS CONSTANTINOPLE AND THE STRAITS

The indifference of the generals to diplomatic considerations placed a special duty on the Foreign Minister. The British *fait accompli*[3] forced him to intensify his struggle for Russia's claims. At home, moreover, 'more and more pressure' was being exerted upon him, notably by 'the Duma and the military circles'.[4] Prince Trubetskoi, the Envoy to Serbia, cautioned Sazonov in a telegram that 'the seizure of the Straits [by Britain and France] without us would be really perilous . . . in such an event Constantinople would, in future, become the grave of our present Alliance'.[5] In a letter he gave warning that 'an unsuccessful solution of the problem would have repercussions among us worse than a mere Ministerial crisis. The whole of Russia would demand an account of the purpose for which the blood of our kinsmen is being shed'.[6] This notion that 'Tsargrad' alone could square that account, and that only the glittering prize of conquest would save Tsarist imperialism was an

---

[1] Kudashev to Sazonov, 25 Jan. '15. Adamov, I. No. 14, pp. 132-4; also 136.
[2] Adamov, II. pp. 22-3. The Stavka's consent, received in London on 26 Jan. '15, enabled Churchill to overcome French opposition to the Dardanelles enterprise. 'This fact,' Grey wrote to the First Lord of the Admiralty, 'may be used with Augagneur to show that we must go ahead with it and that failure to do so will disappoint Russia. . . .' By 28 Jan. '15, the day of the crucial War Council, the agreement of Paris had been obtained. Churchill, *1915*, p. 157; also 163.
[3] General Williams told Kudashev that 'the forcing of the Dardanelles has already been decided upon by our Admiralty. . . .' Kudashev to Sazonov, 26 Jan. '15. Adamov, II. No. 14, p. 133.
[4] Sazonov, 252; also 243.
[5] Trubetskoi to Sazonov, 26 Feb. '15. Adamov, I. No. 5, p. 199.
[6] Trubetskoi to Sazonov, 9 March '15. Adamov, I. No. 6, p. 202.

echo of the Navy's earlier plea: 'We must bring back from the War something which speaks plainly to every Russian heart and is, at the same time, really important for the fatherland—or else this monstrous War will produce in Russia not unity but discord'.[1] It was to be reiterated later by Neklyudov, the Minister to Sweden: '... after the enormous sacrifices of the present War ... the whole Russian people will expect the great reward....'[2] For the bourgeoisie, Professor E. N. Trubetskoi, the Liberal, hailed St. Sophia as 'that evangelical jewel for which Russia must be prepared to give up everything', and the Straits as embodying 'the problem of Russian independence'.[3] The leader of the Constitutional Democrats, Milyukov, demanded 'the final solution of the age-old tasks of our Near-Eastern policy ... the complete acquisition of the Bosphorus and the Dardanelles ... together with Constantinople and a sufficient portion of the adjacent shores....'[4] It was in response to this ground-swell of opinion (which, at the same time, he exploited for putting pressure on London) that Sazonov, amid general approbation, announced in the Duma, on February 9th 1915, the approach of

'the solution of the economic and political tasks connected with Russia's exit into the open sea....'[5]

This statement, the Japanese Military Attaché in Petrograd reported to his Chief, 'increased the nervousness in England and France....'[6] London and notably Paris newspapers made pointed references to equal rights of all the Powers in the Narrows. The *Temps* and the *Figaro* campaigned for the neutralization of Constantinople and the Straits.[7] A question was asked in the House of Commons, to which Sir Edward Grey, on February 25th, gave a reply which so paraphrased Sazonov's formula that 'solution' became 'nearer to the realization' and 'exit' was turned into 'access to' (cries of 'hear, hear'), and then described it as

'an aspiration with which we are in entire sympathy. The precise form in which it will be realized will no doubt be settled in the terms of peace.'[8]

---

[1] Aide-Memoire by Nemitz, 14 Dec. '14. Adamov, I. No. 3, p. 185; also 103.
[2] Neklyudov to Sazonov, 16 Sept. '15. Adamov, I. No. 7, p. 204.
[3] *Natsionalny vopros (The National Question)*. Moscow, 1915; and *Russkiye Vedomosti*, 1/14 March '15. Adamov, I. pp. 97 and 283, footnote 1.
[4] P. N. Milyukov, *Chevo zhdet Rossiya ot voiny (What Russia expects of the War)*. Petrograd, 1915, p. 57. Adamov, I. pp. 89–90.
[5] Adamov, I. p. 240, footnote 1. Paléologue, I. 274.
[6] Ogadiri to the Chief of the Japanese General Staff, 3 March '15. Deciphered in the Russian Foreign Ministry. Adamov, I. No. 47, p. 251.
[7] Izvolski to Sazonov, 23 Feb. '15, and Sazonov to Izvolski, 10 March '15. Adamov, I. No. 35, p. 241; No. 71, p. 271. Bertie, I. 119. Poincaré, VI. 80.
[8] *The Parliamentary Debates*. 5th Series. Vol. LXX. Third volume of Session 1914–15. 25 Feb. '15, column 364. Also *The Times*, 26 Feb. '15, p. 10.

Meanwhile, the Dardanelles had been attacked on February 19th. After the bombardment on the 25th, the outer forts were destroyed and the Straits entered. Already on the Chicago Stock Exchange wheat prices fell abruptly. There seemed, as Churchill recollects, 'to be a prospect of Constantinople falling into the hands of the Allies'[1]—without Russian participation. Against this background, Grey's declaration, as Sazonov cabled Benckendorff, 'provoked bewilderment in our press and . . . a not altogether favourable impression in Duma circles'.[2] Paléologue telegraphed to Delcassé that, after the British Foreign Secretary's 'ambiguous words. . . . Russian public opinion is afraid lest England should, in the last moment, wish to impose some solution which would not wholly satisfy Russia's historic aspirations'.[3] For this reason, Sazonov informed the British and French Ambassadors: 'A few weeks ago I could still think that the opening of the Straits did not necessarily involve the definite occupation of Constantinople. To-day, I have to state that the whole country demands that radical solution'.[4]

The counsels of caution, in Petrograd, faded before the menacing advent of the Allies. That the Marmora hinterland would entail unnecessary military burdens; that 'Tsargrad', 'the meeting place of *world* interests', 'cannot become a Russian provincial city'; that its annexation, without giving Russia essential strategic advantages, threatened her 'with the greatest political complications'; that it would antagonize the Great Powers and chill the Balkan peoples whom she wished to combine under her aegis[5]—all this earlier advice from the experts was obliterated by the new reality. On March 4th 1915, in an Aide-Memoire to Paléologue and Buchanan, Sazonov demanded that

'the city of Constantinople, the West coast of the Bosphorus, the Sea of Marmora and the Dardanelles, as well as Southern Thrace as far as the Enos-Midia line . . . the part of the Asiatic shore between the Bosphorus, the river Sakaria and a point to be defined on the coast of Ismid Bay, the islands of the Marmora Sea [and] the islands Imbros and Tenedos'

must be 'finally' included in the Tsarist Empire.[6]

---

[1] Churchill, *1915*, p. 198; also 190, 192-3, 197.
[2] Sazonov to Benckendorff, 1 March '15. Adamov, I. No. 40, p. 224.
[3] End of Feb. '15. Poincaré, VI. 86-7.
[4] Paléologue, I. 295. Poincaré, VI. 87. Sazonov to Benckendorff and Izvolski, 2 March '15. Adamov, I. No. 42, p. 245.
[5] See pp. 70-1 above.
[6] Adamov, I. No. 49, p. 252. Also Poincaré, VI. 165. Sazonov, 256. Sazonov however, gives the wrong date.

## 3
### BRITISH EXPEDIENTS:
### INTERNATIONALIZATION, GREEK INVOLVEMENT, COMPROMISE

The first reaction of the Entente was to cling to the original idea of internationalizing the Narrows and the Ottoman capital. 'Grey said', Bertie had noted in the preceding December, 'that ... Russia shall have free passage for her ships of war between the Black Sea and the Mediterranean ... in time of peace, and that in time of war belligerents shall have equal rights. ... The proper solution [in Bertie's opinion] would be: Constantinople a free city, destruction of all forts on the Bosphorus and at the Dardanelles and the adoption under European guarantee of the Suez Canal rules for the ... Straits'.[1] It must have been with something like this in mind that the Foreign Office and the Quai d'Orsay insisted on 'the freedom of the Straits', that is their demilitarization, neutralization under a 'European Commission', and protection by international guarantees.[2]

But the fate of Belgium had just shown that 'international guarantees', in war time, were like a house of cards in a gale. The scrapping of fortifications, far from ensuring the defence of the

[1] Bertie, I. 78.
[2] Izvolski to Sazonov, 6 March '15. Benckendorff to Sazonov, 7 March '15. Adamov, I. NN 58 and 64, pp. 262, 267-8. On the mood in Paris see Izvolski to Sazonov, 2 and 4 March '15. Adamov, I. NN 43 and 53, pp. 245-6, 255. Bertie, I. 119, 141. Poincaré, V. 80.
   On March 15th 1915, the U.S. Ambassador in Petrograd, supported by an inquiry on the same subject by Buchanan, proposed to Sazonov, 'with the aim of ensuring the safety of the peaceful population', the establishment of neutral zones in Constantinople. This was promptly rejected by Russia. (Aide-Memoire, U.S. Embassy, Petrograd, to Sazonov, 15 March '15. Aide-Memoire, British Embassy, Petrograd, to Sazonov, 17 March '15. Aide-Memoire, Sazonov to Paléologue and Buchanan, 20 March '15. Adamov, II NN 292, 294, 295, pp. 331-2. Memorandum, Russian Foreign Ministry, 11 April '15. *Internationale Beziehungen*, II. 7. II. No. 515, p. 513).
   This American move was a significant assertion of the interests of the United States in the Ottoman Empire. As early as 1910, her capital investments in the Near East were sufficiently large to worry the Russian Foreign Ministry. By 1911, her railway projects in that area had advanced far enough for American diplomats to become perturbed about the ramifications of the promoters of the *Bagdadbahn*. (*Slavonic Review*, Dec. 1932, pp. 179, 183). After the outbreak of War, the Secretary of State Bryan refused to admit the Porte's right to abrogate the Capitulations unilaterally and announced that the step taken could have no effect on the foreign privileges involved. (Bakhmetyev to Sazonov, 17 Sept. '14. *Internationale Beziehungen*, II. 6. I. No. 275, p. 209). Conversely, when U.S. ships were dispatched to Turkey 'for the purpose of giving aid and protection to Christians', the Sultan's Ambassador in Washington issued a public protest, and when President Wilson instructed Bryan to rebuke him, he retorted in a letter to the White House that the Americans had no business to talk of possible massacres of Christians in Turkey so long as they themselves were lynching Negroes and torturing Philippinos. (Bakhmetyev to Sazonov, 8 and 26 Sept. '14. *Internationale Beziehungen*, II. 6. I. No. 320, pp. 245-6, and p. 245, footnote 1).

Black Sea, would facilitate the seizure and closure of its outlets by a navy hostile to Russia. The latter, therefore, would be worse off than if the Straits remained in the weak hands of the Turks. Moreover, as Milyukov demanded, 'the Black Sea must be protected against the entry of foreign vessels. ... whereas Russian warships must have a free exit'.[1] Bazili stated: 'By consenting to the access of foreign navies to the Black Sea we would ourselves renounce the exclusive position in that sea and lose one of the means of applying permanent pressure to Turkey for the purpose of achieving our political aims in the Near East.' Moreover, the presence of 'permanent foreign squadrons could be used by unfriendly Powers as a perpetual threat to us. . . .' Therefore, 'a formal recognition of the international significance of the Straits' would conflict with 'our exclusive interests in the Bosphorus and the Dardanelles.' These two must be made independent of 'an alien will'.[2] Western spokesmen themselves, by putting forward as a model the Suez Statute, destroyed the case of the Entente. The Russians had no difficulty in showing that 'the real master of the Suez Canal is Britain'.[3] Since she dominated both its banks and the seas around, she could at any time block this artery. In fact, it was only because Britain was in effective control that she had accepted its neutralization. Hence, as Sazonov writes, the suggested neutralization of the Straits would have represented 'the worst possible solution from Russia's point of view', for it 'would have been a mere fiction and, in truth, they would have been under the control of the strongest naval Power'.[4] Owing to Russia's marine inferiority such a settlement would, in practice, have opened the Narrows to the British. The only satisfactory guarantee safeguarding Russian interests would be 'the subjection of the entire sea route through the Straits . . . to our power'.[5]

In this situation, Grey—seconded by Delcassé[6]—tried a different approach. The British Embassy informed Sazonov that

'it is solely for the common cause that His Majesty's Government have undertaken the operations in the Dardanelles. Great Britain will derive no direct gain from them; she does not intend herself to establish a footing there; in order to render Turkey useless as an Ally to Germany . . . and in

[1] *Voprosy Mirovoi voiny (Problems of the World War).* Petrograd, 1915, p. 548. The same view was expressed by E. N. Trubetskoi, in 'Konstantinopol i Prolivy', *Russkiye Vedomosti*, 1/14 March '15. Adamov, I. p. 95 and p. 283, footnote 1.
[2] Aide-Memoire, Nov. '14. Adamov, I. No. 2, pp. 162, 169, 170.
[3] *ibid.* p. 168. [4] Sazonov, 253.
[5] Bazili's Aide-Memoire, Nov. '14. Adamov, I. No. 2, p. 158; also 167–8. Trubetskoi to Sazonov, 26 Feb. and 9 March '15. Sazonov to Benckendorff, 7 March '15. Adamov, I. NN 5, 6 and 60, pp. 200, 204, 264; also 95–6. Cf. Headlam-Morley, 250–1.
[6] Izvolski to Sazonov, 6 March '15. Adamov, I. No. 57, pp. 261–2.

order to induce the neutral Balkan States to co-operate with the Allied Powers, His Majesty's Government are risking their soldiers, their sailors and their ships'.

But

'... the military assistance of Greece on the Gallipoli Peninsula might be important and even essential to the complete success of the operations, and in the circumstances it would be unreasonable and impossible to hamper them by refusing that assistance.... The Imperial Government must bear in mind that the failure of the operations in the Dardanelles would entail disastrous consequences. His Majesty's Government have never contemplated the annexation to Greece of any part on the Straits.... His Majesty's Government readily admit that Greece must have no footing on the Straits that would be in conflict with the interests of Russia.'[1]

Diplomatic relations between the Entente capitals and Athens had hitherto run a zig-zag course in which Greek co-operation was first offered and declined in August 1914, then sought but withheld early in 1915.[2] On March 1st, however, when the Anglo-French guns appeared to open up the Straits, the Prime Minister Venizelos proposed to send an army corps to Gallipoli. Grey, accepting with alacrity, asked also for Hellenic ships. But the Tsar's generals, convinced that the available Western strength did not suffice to reach the Golden Horn, were disinclined to sanction an accession of force likely to ensure success. 'The occupation of the Straits by the Allies without Russian troops taking part was dreaded far more than the failure of that operation'.[3] A further and still greater difficulty was that the ruling strata of Greece nursed strong pretensions to the Ottoman capital. The main reason for Venizelos's initiative, as the British Military Attaché cabled, was 'the hope of Greek troops reaching Constantinople'[4] and King Constantine entering it in triumph. The least the Greeks wanted was the internationalization of the city.[5] Such an arrangement would give them a focal position there by virtue of the large, rich, close-knit and zealously Hellenic community of their co-nationals among the local residents. Sazonov was aware of, and frowned on, the Graeco-British negotiations which had preceded Grey's proposal. He was perturbed by their intimacy. And he suspected that the British Foreign Office—seeing itself compelled to yield the Narrows to Nicholas II—was trying to neutralize in advance the effect of the surrender by planting there its trusted

---

[1] Aide-Memoire, 6 March '15. Adamov, I. No. 56, pp. 259–61.
[2] Churchill, *1915*, pp. 176, 178.  [3] Adamov, I. p. 102; also Miller, 54.
[4] 6 March '15. Churchill, *1915*, p. 203. Also Trevelyan, 283.
[5] Venizelos to the Minister in Petrograd, Dragoumis, 28 Feb. '15. Deciphered in the Russian Foreign Ministry. Adamov, II. No. 98, p. 187. Poincaré, VI. 161. Also Einstein, 78.

friends. The Greeks, Bazili had warned his Chief, would, as masters of the Straits, 'be more dangerous to us than Turkey'.[1] The rusty Turkish bolt closing the Dardanelles and the Bosphorus would be replaced by a modern lock the key to which, as Russia saw it, would be held by Britain. Hence, as Asquith had to record in his Diary,

> 'Russia, despite all our representations and remonstrances, declined absolutely to allow the Greeks to have any part in the Dardanelles business or the subsequent advance on Constantinople, and the French appear inclined to agree with her.'[2]

Delcassé might have been expected to welcome a move hampering Russia in a sphere where France had vast interests at stake. But interested Frenchmen viewed with repugnance the prospect of Graeco-British ascendancy in Constantinople. Moreover, Paris was still hoping to enrol Sofia rather than Athens as an ally. London, therefore, was notified that 'progress of the Anglo-French Fleet may be such as to appear before Constantinople without necessity of landing troops. . . . There might consequently not be any occasion for military co-operation with Greece. . . .'[3] Churchill, as he admits, 'acutely distressed' by Tsarist perversity, drafted this letter to Grey:

> 'I beseech you. . . . You must be bold and violent. . . . Our Fleet is forcing the Dardanelles. No armies can reach Constantinople but those which we invite . . . no impediment must be placed in the way of Greek co-operation. . . . I am so afraid of your losing Greece, and yet paying all the future into Russian hands.'[4]

But on March 6th 1915, under the impact of Sazonov's veto, Venizelos fell from power.[5]

Four days later in Downing Street, as Asquith recollects, 'the main question was what we are to demand in return for the recognition of Russia's ultimate claim to Constantinople and the Straits.'[6] Actually Grey—seeking reinsurance against a miscarriage of his stratagems—had previously told the Ambassador Benckendorff that, as the latter reported, 'a territorial increase of Russia would raise . . . the question of partitioning the whole of Turkey, which would whet the appetites of many Powers. . . . England has no designs

---

[1] Aide-Memoire, Nov. '14. Adamov, I. No. 2, p. 168.
[2] 6 March '15. Asquith, *Memories and Reflections*, II. 64. Also Grey, II. 180.
[3] Advice from the French Foreign Ministry, 4 March '15. Churchill, *1915*, p. 202.
[4] Churchill, *1915*, pp. 203–4.
[5] *ibid.* p. 204. Abbott, 31; also 7–16, 21–32. For the diplomatic exchanges on the Greek question see Adamov, II. Documents, pp. 184–200. Trevelyan, 283.
[6] 10 March '15. Asquith, *Memories and Reflections*, II. 65.

whatever on any part of Asia Minor or Syria, except for some points in the region of the Persian Gulf. . . .'[1] Presumably the Foreign Secretary must have given—or Petrograd have obtained in other ways—more information on British and French 'appetites'. For Sazonov hastily attached to the final formulation of Russia's wishes the assurance that the Allies would meet with the sympathy of the Imperial Government 'in fulfilling such plans as emerge among them regarding the other provinces of the Ottoman Empire and other places.'[2] Accordingly, on March 10th 1915, the British Cabinet and the leaders of the Conservative Opposition jointly decided that, in Grey's words, 'the force of circumstances was irresistible. It was agreed that the promise of Constantinople to Russia must be made.'[3] Presumably, too, decisions were reached on what rewards Britain might obtain in return, since on the same day the Foreign Secretary said to Benckendorff that he could make no final comment on Russia's claims until he knew her reaction to British aspirations.[4] No doubt Petrograd was communicative and obliging. And, on March 12th 1915, an Aide-Memoire from Buchanan to Sazonov stated that, while 'Sir Edward Grey is as yet unable to make any definite proposal on any point of the British desiderata', he insisted that, after victory, 'the Mussulman Holy Places and Arabia shall under all circumstances remain under independent Mussulman dominion.' He also requested the inclusion in the orbit of Britain of the neutral zone in Persia which was situated between the Russian and British spheres of influence.[5] Another Aide-Memoire of the same date from Buchanan informed Sazonov:

> 'Subject to the War being . . . brought to a successful conclusion and to the desiderata of Great Britain and France in the Ottoman Empire and elsewhere being realized . . . His Majesty's Government will agree to the Russian Government's Aide-Memoire relative to Constantinople and the Straits . . . communicated . . . on March 4th . . . instant'.[6]

While the Entente guns were pounding at the Dardanelles, Russia reduced the diplomatic forts of Whitehall.

---

[1] Benckendorff to Sazonov, 3 March '15. Adamov, I. No. 46, p. 230.
[2] Aide-Memoire, Sazonov to Buchanan and Paléologue, 4 March '15. Adamov, I. No. 49, p. 252.
[3] Grey, II. 181–2. Also Churchill, *1915*, pp. 198–9. Asquith, *Memories and Reflections*, II. 22, 65.
[4] Benckendorff to Sazonov, 10 March '15. Adamov, I. No. 74, p. 273.
[5] Adamov, I. No. 77, p. 276.
[6] Adamov, I. No. 76, pp. 274–5. Also Churchill, *1915*, p. 199. Sazonov, 259 (wrong date given). To these British demands was added the request (in the other Aide-Memoire of 12 March) for a pledge to establish in Constantinople a free port for the transit of goods exchanged between non-Russian territories, and a guarantee of free navigation in the Narrows. Adamov, I. No. 77, pp. 275–6.

D

## 4
### PARIS AND THE FÂCHEUX INCIDENT.
### THE FRANCO-RUSSIAN BARGAIN

But intricate defences had still to be broken through at the Quai d'Orsay. France was more deeply involved in Constantinople than any other Power. The Turkish capital housed the Ottoman Bank through which Parisian financiers, as majority holders, manipulated the railway, industrial and loan issues of the Porte. It was the seat of the Council of the Ottoman Public Debt in which Paris, again, had the preponderant interest. It was the administrative centre of the monopolies, concerns and concessions most of whose money was French.[1] From it, the Ambassador Bompard—despite his Government's anti-clericalism—guarded a ramified missionary and cultural activity, charities, churches, scholarships, which yielded the Third Republic all the temporal benefits of a Catholic protectorate. In it, a large section of the bourgeoisie were linked through business to the Tricolor. Constantinople, in short, was the heart of an Empire enmeshed by immense French political interests and financial investments amounting to 3,000,000,000 francs.[2]

Therefore, when Nicholas II reached out for it, Delcassé, as Izvolski reported, was 'visibly alarmed'. He was prepared to admit Russia to the Northern shore of the Straits, but the annexation of both coasts (which alone guaranteed effective control) would be opposed by 'the whole of European opinion'.[3] On March 3rd, Poincaré, Delcassé and the Premier Viviani were closeted together over this *'fâcheux incident'*.[4] The President, perhaps the most rabid advocate of France's traditional Eastern policy, was particularly indignant: 'Russia is not yet taking part in the Dardanelles operations. . . . If Constantinople falls, Russia will have no hand in it. . . . Rumania will not allow herself to be bottled up in the Black Sea and . . . the Greeks would rather see the Turks than the Russians in Constantinople. . . . Lastly, if Russia is assured that she will have Constantinople, she will disinterest herself . . . wholly from the War against Germany'.[5] The 'extreme elements' in the French Cabinet, as Iz-

---
[1] See pp. 20–1, 80–1 above.
[2] Aide-Memoire, French Embassy, Petrograd, to Sazonov, 12 March '15. Aide-Memoire, Financial Attaché, Russian Embassy, Paris, to Sazonov, 21 April '15. Izvolski to Sazonov, 28 March '15. Adamov, II. NN 289, 314, pp. 329, 345; I. No. 90, pp. 288–9. Also *ibid.* II. p. 58, footnote 3. Sazonov, 246, 254, 258. Miller, 49. Baster, 90, 101-3, 105, 108–9. Erzberger, 86–7.
[3] Izvolski to Sazonov, 2 March '15. Sazonov to Izvolski, 4 March. Adamov, I. NN 43, 50, pp. 246, 252-3. Benckendorff to Sazonov, 3 March. *ibid.* No. 46, p. 250.
[4] Poincaré, VI. 88; also 96, footnote 1. Adamov, I. p. 289.
[5] Poincaré, VI. 88.

volski reported, 'have altogether little sympathy with Russia'.¹ The Foreign Minister instructed Paléologue to insist in Petrograd on acceptance of the absolute and perpetual freedom of the Bosphorus and the Dardanelles as a preliminary to [and safeguard against] any arrangement on the Ottoman capital. Pending the Straits settlement, Sazonov was asked to refrain from making pronouncements on the latter.²

But on the same day, after luncheon, the Tsar confided to the French Ambassador: '... circumstances compel me ... to speak of Constantinople. ... I should not feel justified in imposing on my people the terrible sacrifices of the present War, without granting them as a reward the fulfilment of their centuries-old dream. I shall adopt the radical solution of the problem of Constantinople and the Straits. ... Constantinople and Southern Thrace must be incorporated in my Empire'. In the ensuing dialogue, the list of Russian requirements was met by a recital of France's 'economic and moral interests, privileges, traditions' at the Golden Horn. Nicholas II invoked King George V's November promise of Constantinople as a 'guarantee of the goodwill of the British Government'. Paléologue's reference to 'the questions which concern France directly' evoked this reply: 'I want France to come out of this War as great and strong as possible. I subscribe in advance to everything your Government may desire. Take the left bank of the Rhine; take Mayence, take Coblenz; go further still if you consider it useful.³

Such generosity compelled a *quid pro quo*. An Aide-Memoire from the French Embassy, March 8th 1915, assured Sazonov that he 'can depend entirely on the favourable disposition of the Government of the Republic in the ... solution of the problem of Constantinople and the Straits'.⁴ But 'the influence exerted on the French Government and the press by the interested financiers'⁵ was obviously so great that a rider was added postponing the settlement until the treaty of peace.⁶ Internationalization was peddled in various shapes and forms.⁷ And Poincaré, violating the Constitutional rules of Presidential abstinence from diplomacy, dispatched an urgent letter to Paléologue inveighing against

---
¹ Izvolski to Sazonov, 14 March '15. Adamov, I. No. 79, p. 279.
² Delcassé's telegram, 3 March '15. Poincaré, VI. 88-9. Izvolski to Sazonov, 4 March. Adamov, I. No. 53, p. 255.
³ 3 March '15. Poincaré, VI. 89-90. Paléologue, I. 297.
⁴ Adamov, I. No. 64, pp. 268-9.
⁵ Izvolski to Sazonov, 28 March '15. Adamov, I. No. 90, pp. 288-9.
⁶ Adamov, I. No. 64, pp. 268-9.
⁷ Izvolski to Sazonov, 2, 4, 9, 10, 14, 28 March '15. Adamov, I. NN 43, 53, 69, 73, 79, 90, pp. 245-6, 270, 272, 277-9, 288-9. Bertie, I. 119, 141.

'the partition of the Ottoman Empire. We have no valid reason to desire this partition. If it is inevitable, we do not intend that it should be at our expense... the possession of Constantinople and environs would not only give Russia a kind of privilege in the succession to the Ottoman Empire. It would bring her, by way of the Mediterranean, into the concert of the Western nations and enable her, through the freedom of the seas, to become a great naval Power. Thus the European balance would be entirely changed. Such an aggrandizement and such an increase of power would not be acceptable to us, unless we ourselves came out of the War with equivalent advantages'.

Russia, therefore, should

'continue the struggle in common, rule out any idea of a separate peace and leave the question of partition for the hour of the final settlement.... I do not doubt that, with a certain firmness, you will lead the Emperor and the Russian Minister [of Foreign Affairs] to a conception which does greater justice to the permanent interests of the Alliance'.[1]

The only effect of that firmness, however, was to exasperate Petrograd. Sazonov—emphasizing that Grey's consent had been given 'in writing' and 'in a more positive wording' than the French declaration—repeatedly and with growing impatience instructed Izvolski to obtain from Delcassé 'more precise statements of French assent to the complete satisfaction of our wishes, just like those made by the British Government'.[2] But late in March 'certain influential circles'[3] in Paris were still campaigning for internationalization. The Foreign Affairs Committee of the Chamber, as the Ambassador Bertie noted, 'showed great signs of dissatisfaction' with any '*engagements formels*' to Russia. 'Many French public men hope', his entry continues, 'that the British and French forces will get to Constantinople before the Russians....'[4] The Compagnie Générale des Eaux pour l'Étranger, which controlled the water system in Constantinople, induced Delcassé to request the Allies not to destroy the pumps if military necessity compelled them to disorganize the city's water supply.[5] The State Councillor Deloncle who, we learn from Bertie's Diary, 'knows what the public says', handed in at the British Embassy a document protesting 'in the name of civilization against such an outrage as the Holy Synod master of Pola and Stamboul.... All the work of England and France in the West would be at an end, there would no longer be a free Mediterranean'.[6] And

[1] 9 March '15. Poincaré, VI. 92–5.
[2] Sazonov to Izvolski, 18 March '15. Adamov, I. No. 81, p. 282. Also 23 March and 3 April '15. *ibid.* NN 88, 95, pp. 287-8, 291. Moukhtar, 294–5.
[3] Izvolski to Sazonov, 28 March '15. Adamov, I. No. 90, p. 288.
[4] 28 March '15. Bertie, I. 134–5; also 132, 141.
[5] Izvolski to Sazonov, 22 March '15. Adamov, II. No. 57, p. 162.
[6] 7 April '15. Bertie, I. 139–40. The quotation given is as summarized by Bertie.

it was not until April 10th 1915 that Sazonov was notified by the French Embassy that 'the Government of the Republic give their consent' to Russia's claims in the Straits and Constantinople

'on condition that the War is brought to a victorious conclusion and . . . that France and Britain accomplish their plans in the East as well as elsewhere'.[1]

5

## FRENCH IMPERIALISM IN THE MIDDLE EAST: CONFLICT WITH BRITAIN

The latter provision explains, in part, the surrender of Delcassé. Even while wrestling with the Russians, he had been murmuring to them about 'the partitioning of Turkey's Asiatic possessions'.[2] Poincaré, in his letter to Paléologue, whilst opposing partition, spoke in the same breath of 'the recognition of our rights to Syria, Alexandretta and the vilayet of Adana'.[3] Bertie, after a conversation (which he dismissed as 'academic') with Delcassé, recorded that 'France would have Mayence, Coblenz, Cologne. . . .'[4] Britain, however, opposed a French advance to the Rhine. Also, as Benckendorff reported to Sazonov, 'Grey is afraid of discussing the question of the partition of the Turkish possessions in Asia because of France and Italy, whereas Delcassé is pushing it into the foreground. . . . Cambon insists particularly on French interests in Asia Minor and Syria'.[5] But Bertie (and doubtless the British Foreign Office) did 'not think it would be advisable to have France on the borders of Egypt'.[6] The Tsar, on the other hand, reafirmed his consent to what Paléologue defined as the 'civilizing work France intends to undertake in Syria, Cilicia, and Palestine'.[7] The Quai d'Orsay, therefore, must have thought it prudent to enlist the diplomatic support of one Ally against the other.

The second reason for Delcassé's pliancy lay in the war situation. Early in March 1915, General Birdwood, the Commander of the Australian and New Zealand forces, had cabled to Kitchener from the Dardanelles that he was 'very doubtful if the Navy can force the passage unassisted'.[8] Under the original plan, at least as far as

[1] Note Verbale, 10 April '15. Adamov, I. No. 99, p. 295. Also Sazonov, 246, 254, 258.
[2] Izvolski to Sazonov, 4 March '15. Adamov, I. No. 53, p. 255.
[3] 9 March '15. Poincaré, VI. 94.   [4] 24 Feb. '15. Bertie, I. 120.
[5] 7 March '15. Adamov, I. No. 62, p. 266. Also Bertie, I. 106, 120.
[6] 25 Jan. '15. Bertie, I. 106. Lloyd George held similar views on this subject. See Asquith, *Memories and Reflections*, II. 59, 66.
[7] 16 March '15. Paléologue, I. 303. According to Poincaré, VI. 118, who gives as the date 18 March, Nicholas attached to this promise the claim for a religious protectorate over Jerusalem, Jordan, Galilee and Tiberias.
[8] 5 and 6 March '15. Dardanelles C. *First Report*, 33.

the naval experts were concerned, the operation was to have ended if the Fleet failed to get through. But on March 13th, the day after Grey's secret agreement with Sazonov, General Hamilton, the Commander of the troops in the East, was told by the War Office that 'there can be no idea of abandoning the scheme'.[1] On the day before that agreement (that is on March 11th, after the British Cabinet had decided to promise Constantinople to Russia) Churchill had wired to Admiral Carden:

'If . . . success cannot be obtained without loss of ships and men, the results to be gained are important enough to justify such loss . . . you will have to press hard for a decision'.[2]

On March 18th, the Anglo-French warships opened fire. According to the new Commander, Vice-Admiral de Robeck, 'everyone thought it was better to have a combined operation, but one was not consulted . . . we were told to bombard these forts—so we did it'.[3] Churchill has described it as a 'spectacle . . . of terrible magnificence'.[4] But out of the sixteen attacking ships, three were sunk and four disabled. Nearly 600 French sailors went down with the dreadnought *Bouvet*. There were over 60 British casualties. The action had to be broken off a second time. What had been intended as a sharp and short offensive threatened to drag on. The goal receded into the distance.[5] And in Paris it was concluded that the risk of a deal with Petrograd was small compared with the gain of diplomatic backing against Whitehall.

'There is an antithesis between the English and French point of view on the future fate of Turkey's Asiatic possessions. . . .', Benckendorff advised Sazonov.[6] This Franco-British difference favoured the Russians all the more in that it extended to Constantinople and the Straits. As far as these two problems could be treated separately, Britain—with her vulnerable maritime and commercial life-lines—was more preoccupied with the Narrows, while France—with her enormous financial stakes in the Sultan's realm—was more concerned with his metropolis. The supremacy of French over British shareholding in the Ottoman Bank and the superiority of the latter to Sir Ernest Cassel's National Bank of Turkey symbolized the relative strength of their interests at the Golden Horn.[7] Hence, London

---

[1] Dardanelles C. *First Report*, 34.
[2] Dardanelles C. *First Report*, 35. Also Corbett, II. 204–5.
[3] Dardanelles C. *First Report*, 36.    [4] Churchill, *1915*, p. 225.
[5] Dardanelles C. *First Report*, 37, 41. Churchill, *1915*, pp. 222, 228. Izvolski to Sazonov, 14 March '15. Adamov, I. No. 79, p. 279.
[6] 7 March '15. Adamov, I. No. 62, p. 266. For the statement of the *Giornale d'Italia* on this subject see p. 81 above.
[7] Prof. E. D. Grimm, Introduction to Adamov, II. p. 32. Sazonov, 253. *Politique Étrangère*, Oct. 1952. No. 4, p. 276. Baster, 102–3, 111–12.

was not averse to checking this preponderance of Paris with Russia's assistance, and King George was the first to tell her that Constantinople 'must be yours'. Churchill's *Drang* to the Dardanelles was a bid for the last link in the British power chain encircling the future Levantine Empire from Cyprus and Suez to Aden and the Persian Gulf. Hence, France was less keen on the operation in the Straits and less opposed to the egress of Russian warships from the Black Sea which, in certain contingencies, could help her to counterbalance the Royal Navy. Thus, although Britain and France had enough in common against the advance of Tsarism to the Narrows, their joint resistance did not prevent each from pursuing her special aims. France preferred Salonika as a base for the sphere of influence she sought in the Balkans, and as the main stage overland to the Golden Horn. General Gallieni said: '. . . through Salonika march on Constantinople'.[1] Britain chose the Straits as her route to the Black Sea. Moreover, having decided to shift the Caliphate to Arabia, she ensured the 'independence' of the Moslem centres for her friend Husain, and—by acquiring the neutral zone in Persia—the defence of the coveted Mesopotamian dominion. And finally, after obtaining Sazonov's pledge of free navigation in the Narrows and a free port in Constantinople, she abandoned the latter to the Tsar.

The loss of Britain's traditional support against Russia in the Near East provoked explosions of anger in France. Already in November 1914, when Paléologue reported Sazonov's pleasure at Grey's promises, Poincaré commented: 'No doubt. But we are not in the least able to share in that satisfaction. We find it hard to see how Britain, without consulting us, could have thus given a blank cheque to Russia in a question of common concern to the Allies'.[2] In February 1915, the Senate Foreign Affairs Commission came down heavily on Viviani and Delcassé for yielding the Dardanelles command to the British.[3] In March, to the accompaniment of thunder against Albion from the Elysée,[4] the Ambassador Bertie noted that in the Chamber there was a 'supposition that England and Russia have been disposing of Constantinople behind the back of France' and that 'the Quai d'Orsay exponents of French policy have been representing that the French Government would have been quite

---

[1] *Gallieni Parle*, quoted by Lloyd George, I. 384.
[2] 17 Nov. '14. Poincaré, V. 440.
[3] Poincaré, VI. 80. In February, too, Churchill's request for a naval offensive in the Adriatic, to be synchronized with the attack in the Straits, was rejected by Augagneur. *ibid.* 99–100.
[4] See Poincaré's biting remark that the British Government 'qui ne perd pas son temps' had obtained Russia's consent to the absorption of the neutral zone in Persia in return for their 'trop complaisante adhésion' to Nicholas's designs on Constantinople and the Straits. 13 March '15. Poincaré, VI. 109; also 25 March. *ibid.* 130. Izvolski to Sazonov, 4 March '15. Adamov, I. No. 52, p. 254.

ready to take a firm line towards Russia if the British Government had shown any disposition to support the French Government, but the former had on the contrary been in a hurry to yield everything to Russia'.¹ And the State Councillor Deloncle urged upon the British Embassy early in April 'that the possession by Russia of Constantinople and the Straits would be the *reductio ad absurdum* of British policy in the past. . . . It would be a strange outcome of the long conflict about the Baghdad Railway, if it had its terminus in Russian territory. . . . Mesopotamia would be of no use to England if Russia was on the Bosphorus as well as in the Caucasus.'²

6

OUTBIDDING GERMANY IN RUSSIA

On the other hand, it was obvious that there would be no Mesopotamia at all for England (nor Syria for France), unless the War was won and obvious, too, that it could not be won without Russia. But if Churchill knew that Russia 'was all the time vital for our hopes of general victory'³—so did Sazonov. And Sazonov was becoming difficult. When Grey and notably Delcassé sent him a pressing invitation to a three-Power meeting in Paris, he blandly declined to make the pilgrimage, insisting on the 'undeferred' acceptance of his demands.⁴ He warned Paléologue that French recalcitrance would lead him to resign, and that this could mean his replacement by an adherent of 'the old system of the Three Emperors' League'.⁵ Nor was it, at this juncture, an idle threat.

At the end of February or early in March 1915, a Russian Court lady, M. A. Vasilchikova—then in Austrian 'captivity'—was visited by 'two Germans and one Austrian—all three more or less influential people' who asked her to submit to her Sovereign a proposal of peace. Reporting this in a letter to Nicholas II on March 10th, she hinted at 'l'Alliance des trois Empereurs' and added that, in reply to her question: 'And the Dardanelles?', the answer was that 'the Russian Tsar has only to express the wish, and the passage will be free'.⁶ The British Foreign Office, according to Corbett, 'well knew' that Germany was endeavouring to sever Russia from the Entente. 'Nothing therefore could so well meet the exigencies of the

¹ 24 March '15. Bertie, I. 132.
² Bertie, I. 140–1. The quotation given is as summarized by Bertie.
³ Churchill, *1915*, p. 198.
⁴ Izvolski to Sazonov, 4 and 9 March '15. Adamov, I. NN 52, 53, 70, pp. 254–5, 270–1. Sazonov to Izvolski, 7 and 8 March '15. *ibid.* NN 60, 65, pp. 264–268.
⁵ Memorandum, Russian Foreign Ministry, 5 March '15. *Internationale Beziehungen*, II. 7. I. No. 312, p. 288.
⁶ Vasilchikova to Nicholas II, 10 March '15. Adamov, II. No. 331, pp. 369–70.

hour as a frank abandonment of our old obstructive policy'.[1] In Paris, Delcassé was 'dazed like a rabbit when hunted by a weazel'.[2] He 'told me ... [Bertie recorded] ... that Germany is making frantic efforts to detach Russia from her Allies.... I notice some nervousness if Russia be not humoured about Constantinople and the Straits by France and England'.[3] It was realized at the Quai d'Orsay that, as Izvolski wrote to Sazonov, 'for us to have the least doubt of French readiness to help us in this business could have the most serious effect on relations among the Allies'.[4] And so, despite their differences, the policies of Britain and France converged. They had, in the first place, to overcome Sazonov's objections to the extortionate demands for Dalmatian territory with which Italy coupled her entry into the War.[5] But the main reason why Constantinople and the Narrows were 'given' to Russia was, it seems certain, that Germany was beginning to outbid the West.

---

[1] Corbett, II. 204. Grey, II. 180, writes that 'the British operations against the Dardanelles came near to impairing our relations with Russia. When ... it was thought that they might succeed, we became aware of a very nasty reaction upon Russian opinion ... we always supposed that, among the variety of influences ... in Petrograd, there were some strings that Germany surreptitiously could pull.' It was clear that there was something dangerous we should have to reckon with diplomatically at Petrograd'. Also p. 181.
[2] 5 March '15. Bertie, I. 125.
[3] 2 March '15. Bertie, I. 124. Also Poincaré, VI. 92. Bréal, 153–4.
[4] Izvolski to Sazonov, 14 March '15. Adamov, I. No. 79, p. 279.
[5] See Part II of the present work.

CHAPTER VI

# The Secret Agreements Between Britain, France and Russia

1

THE POLITICAL CONTEXT OF GALLIPOLI

THE Triple Entente's secret Agreements of March and April 1915 were neither more precise nor freer from escape clauses than the loose commitments of the preceding November. The acquisition of Constantinople and the Straits by Russia was now explicitly conditional upon victory, and on her Allies' accomplishing their own expansionist aims. But the scope of the victory was undefined; the terms of Britain and France—apart from a few concrete points— were left vague, and they had complete latitude to extend them at will. When the War was won, they could, by claiming that their plans had not been realized in full, block Nicholas's 'rights' to his spoils. Even if their own aspirations were clearly satisfied, they were still not pledged to assist him in fulfilling his, but could simply let the exhausted bear (to use Adamov's metaphor) crack his teeth on the 'Turkish nut'. If, nevertheless, he did reach the Golden Horn, the West had valuable safeguards in the free port for foreign commerce in Constantinople, the freedom for merchant shipping in the Narrows, and the guarantee of outlets for Bulgaria and Rumania, which Sazonov had to promise.[1] Only the dependence of Tsarist Russia on the Entente, the threat of the Dardanelles operation, the craving for Constantinople, the fear of losing this city altogether, and the need for the 'Byzantine mirage'—as Paléologue called it— to keep the people in the trenches, can explain why Petrograd accepted this problematic deal.

But it was a deal none the less, and one whose formalization was aggravating to France and Britain. Hence the reaction against what Grey, in the Aide-Memoire to Sazonov of March 12th, described as a 'complete revolution' in Britain's traditional policy. It was a reaction expressed in various ways, including, in particular, fresh developments in the Dardanelles. Even while Churchill had been urging sea operations in the Straits, he had not disguised that these

[1] Adamov, I. p. 123. Aide-Memoire, Sazonov to Buchanan and Paléologue, 22 March '15. *ibid.* No. 83, p. 284, and footnote 1. Grey to Buchanan, 24 Aug. '15. Deciphered in the Russian Foreign Ministry. *ibid.* No. 143, p. 340. Miller, 52. *Diplomaticheski Slovar*, II. 467. Moukhtar, 291–2.

could only be decisive with army support.[1] When the British War Council, in January 1915, resolved on the naval attack, this meant no more than that the land forces which were required for the intended capture of the Ottoman capital[2] should not be those of the Entente. To procure the necessary man-power was one of the aims of the negotiations with Bulgaria and Greece.[3] Their failure made the use of British soldiers inevitable. When the Secretary for War, on February 20th, held up the sailing of a division to Lemnos, Churchill threatened to 'disclaim all responsibility if disaster occurred in Turkey owing to the insufficiency of troops'.[4] Lord Kitchener had wished to retain these for Alexandretta.[5] But the eclipse of his scheme, Sazonov's speech in the Duma on February 9th, and Venizelos's second rebuff to the Entente on the 15th, brought Kitchener to Churchill's side. The dispatch of British forces was decided upon the following day. On February 24th, on the eve of Grey's Parliamentary retort to Russia, Kitchener declared in the War Council that, 'if the Fleet would not get through the Straits unaided, the Army ought to see the business through. The effect of a defeat in the Orient would be very serious'.[6] This applied to an equal degree to Italy and the Balkan States with whom intense and delicate negotiations for intervention were in progress. The setbacks at Neuve Chapelle and in the Champagne, contributing to the stalemate in France, strengthened the Eastern school of strategy. 'And undoubtedly the fear existed that to abandon the enterprise might have a bad effect in Russia'.[7]

This claim, valid where the uninformed Russian masses were concerned, served to obscure the fact that, in reality, to go on with the enterprise was to act against 'Russia'. The chain reaction from the Dardanelles decision to the Constantinople compact and thence to the big naval attack continued. The duress under which the compact was signed by the British, and the setback sustained in the Straits on March 18th, caused greater weight to be thrown into the campaign. On the next day, General Hamilton cabled the warning that the Straits 'are less likely to be forced by battleships than ... seemed probable, and ... if the Army is to participate its operations will not assume the subsidiary form anticipated'. Kitchener's reply was prompt and peremptory: ' ... the passage of the Dardanelles must be forced ... if large military operations on the Gallipoli Peninsula ...

[1] Corbett, II. 107-8.
[2] The decision of 13 Jan. '15 was that 'the Admiralty, in preparing for the bombardment, was to consider "Constantinople as its objective"'. Dardanelles C. *First Report*, 22; also 31-2. *The Final Report*, 9.
[3] See Churchill, *1915*, pp. 179-180.    [4] Dardanelles C. *First Report*, 32.
[5] See Dardanelles C. *Final Report*, 6.
[6] Dardanelles C. *First Report*, 32; also 15-16, 30. Churchill, *1915*, p. 180. Kitchener's view was endorsed by Grey. *Final Report*, 7.
[7] Dardanelles C. *Final Report*, 15.

are necessary... those operations must be undertaken....'¹ Churchill was so impatient that, with the support of Asquith and Balfour, he ordered the Fleet to resume the offensive despite its losses. But he was overruled by his Admirals who insisted on postponement for the purpose of combined action.² Meanwhile, the troop sailings from Britain had been delayed by the futile hope of Greek co-operation. More time was wasted waiting for permission to land in Bulgarian Dedeagach and, it was said, for clement weather.³ The element of surprise was lost. The enemy, forewarned, could man and fortify the beaches.⁴ On the other hand, 'no general plan of operations had been prepared by the War Office'; 'no correct appreciation of the nature and difficulties of the task involved was arrived at'; 'sufficient consideration was not given to the measures necessary to carry out such an expedition with success. . . .'⁵ Already the naval attack, in the judgment of the Dardanelles Commission, had been 'mistaken and ill-advised'.⁶ 'For political reasons the Dardanelles bombardment was hurried on before the military preparations were completed'.⁷ This verdict of Bertie's applied with even greater force to the landing on Gallipoli on April 25th 1915.

'The fighting was so severe . . . and the ground gained so small that by the evening Sir William Birdwood feared that it might be necessary to withdraw. . . . Sir Ian Hamilton directed him to maintain his position at all costs'.⁸ But no amount of gallantry could carry the men beyond a few hundred yards from the shore to the commanding heights. The country was difficult. Its shape protected the defenders against the Navy's guns. The Turks, in great numbers and protected by barbed wire, met the invaders with heavy fire. The battles continued with short breaks. The Entente armies, crowded into isolated and vulnerable positions, were reduced to trench war. By May 12th, the British had nearly 15,000 killed and wounded. The French casualties were over 12,600 out of a total of 22,450 combatants engaged. The General and Admiral commanding advised London that 'the only sound procedure is to hammer away until the enemy gets demoralized'.⁹ It was the same grim story as in the West.

¹ Dardanelles C. *First Report*, 37. *Diplomaticheski Slovar*, II. 467.
² Dardanelles C. *First Report*, 38-9.
³ Churchill, *1915*, pp. 182, 188. Dardanelles C. *First Report*, 33; and *Final Report*, 7 (on the question of Greece), 9, 13. Corbett, II. 297 (on Dedeagach). Bertie, I. 175. Sanders, 58.
⁴ Dardanelles C. *Final Report*, 84.   ⁵ *ibid.* 9, 85, 86.
⁶ Dardanelles C. *First Report*, 42. Cf. Poincaré, VI. 130: 'An ill-conceived venture, not well thought out in London . . . and over-hasty in the attempt, without measuring the military difficulties or the diplomatic repercussions'. 25 March '15.
⁷ 3 April '15. Bertie, I. 138.   ⁸ Dardanelles C. *Final Report*, 20.
⁹ Hamilton to Kitchener, 10 May '15. Dardanelles C. *Final Report*, 22; also 21, 61, 84. Poincaré, VI, 187. Churchill, *1915*, pp. 325, 327-8.

## 2
### IN CONSTANTINOPLE. TURKS AND GREEKS. THE ARMENIAN MASSACRES

In Constantinople, meanwhile, the approach of the Entente forces had driven the women and children into the country. The gold and archives were sent into the interior. Art treasures were buried. Preparations were made to fire the city and dynamite St. Sophia. Wangenheim and the German commanders, too, and the U.S. Ambassador expected the British to break through. Trains with steam up were waiting for the diplomatic corps, the Government, the Court and the Sultan.[1] But no sooner had the first enemy waves dashed themselves into froth, than the aged and ailing Mehmed V was proclaimed a 'Ghazi' (conqueror). Medals were exchanged between him and the Kaiser, and 10,000 cigarettes consigned to the latter. The police saw to the display of flags. While legions of wounded darkened the capital, official communiqués exterminated the invaders, glorified two gendarmes for 'repelling' a French force of 400, described the English as fleeing from their 'own shadow' and listed, among the 'few' Turkish casualties, an occasional camel or 'a mule of Hungarian origin'. Enver busied himself buying up land. 'At the Club,' an American diplomatist noted, 'the men who govern gamble daily. Talaat plays poker and the Grand Vizier billiards'.[2]

The transition from panic to brazen confidence brought paroxysms of spite and cruelty. The opposition, plotting during the crisis, advertised their existence in subversive posters,[3] and were crushed. The local Greeks who, because of their Western loyalties, were an obstacle to German penetration, and the Jews, just for good measure, were ruined by sequestration and expelled.[4] The repulse of the Entente removed the restraint from the hand holding the scimitar over the Armenians' head. The Turks were jealous of a race more agile and culturally and economically more powerful than themselves. They resented its links with Petrograd and Paris, and its refusal to foment insurrection in the Caucasus. They needed scapegoats for the defeat at Sarakamysh in January and the fall of Van late in May, thirsted for revenge for the excesses committed by Armenian contingents within the invading Tsarist armies, and sought an outlet for anti-Christian agitation roused by the 'Holy War'. They wanted to popularize the

---

[1] Feb. and March '15. Morgenthau, 121–3, 127, 130–2, 147–50. Sanders, 53. Moukhtar, 299. Erzberger, 78.
[2] Einstein, 11; also 7, 35, 52–4, 144, 173, 261. Morgenthau, 150. Serafimov to Sazonov, 18 April '15. Adamov, II. No. 197, p. 276.
[3] Morgenthau, 128. Miller, 64.   [4] Einstein, 11, 48, 119, 121.

unpopular War by directing greed and fanaticism to the spoliation and destruction of the largest and richest non-Moslem element. Such were the motives of the Porte in deliberately disturbing the neighbourly peace between the Turks and their victims, and inciting the former to hatred and atrocities. The Triple Entente's threat to hold the Ottoman authorities personally responsible left them cold, except for the Grand Vizier, all of whose property was in Egypt. The others, as an American observer recorded, 'go on with their hangings'.[1] The Government of the Reich, which alone could intercede with effect, was not only unwilling to irritate its Turkish Allies but actually wished them to clear its prospective colony from the most formidable competitors on the spot. The German public learned little and late of what was afoot in Turkey, and Wangenheim's purely formal protests were nothing but an incitement to crime. The dispossessions and deportations—on the pretext of evacuation from the battle zone for 'complicity with the enemy'[2]—the destitution and disease, the road-side and desert deaths, the prison murders, the extermination—all over the country—of hundreds of thousands of people[3] make one of the blackest chapters in the lunatic story of this War.

3

PEACE FEELERS AND THEIR FAILURE

Could it not have been cut short by the peace overtures prompted by the panic in Constantinople? Caught between the foe outside and the tide of internal upheaval, some Young Turk leaders sought an escape in exploiting the dissensions within the Triple Entente over Turkey. Early in April 1915, the former Finance Minister Djavid, a moderate who had friends in France, appeared in Geneva, expecting—according to Swiss press reports—to be approached by the West.[4] On May 21st, Sasonov transmitted to Izvolski a report from a secret source alleging that negotiations were proceeding between the Bey and 'French statesmen' in Lausanne. Delcassé denied that there had been parleys, but admitted that Djavid had asked to meet

[1] Einstein, 126.
[2] The fact that Armenian volunteers with the Russian forces, who had escaped from Turkey, had helped to beat Enver early in 1915, is mentioned *inter alia* by Morgenthau to Lansing, 18 Nov. '15. *The Lansing Papers*, I. 767; also 768.
[3] Einstein, pp. VIII, 37, 68, 88, 117, 119–20, 162, 176, 183, 214, 222, 245, 252–3. Toynbee, *Turkey P.F.*, 21–2, 32, 45, 53. Miller, 63. Max of Baden, *Memoirs*, I. 69, 81.
[4] The Russian Minister in Berne to Sazonov, 9 April '15. Adamov, II. No. 264, pp. 315–16; also 94. Morgenthau, 126, 149–50. Churchill, *1915*, p. 265. Miller, 63. On Djavid see Giers to Sazonov, 14 Aug. and 5 Oct. '14. *Das Zaristische Russland*, pp. 22, 52.

someone from the Quai d'Orsay.[1] In Paris, the writer Pierre Loti, interrupting his output of Turkophil romances for a 'petit rôle d'ambassadeur',[2] informed President Poincaré that Djavid or Talaat were offering a clandestine rendezvous in Switzerland. The immediate reply was that the Young Turk boss could, if he wished, even be got into France.[3] Unfortunately, Loti's agent returned from Lake Geneva with the news that Talaat (no doubt encouraged by the warmth of the Entente's response) preferred to stay at home. The proposition, however, still held good for Djavid. But the latter had no official standing, and his presence at that time in Berlin, where he was soliciting money, evoked suspicion in Paris. Poincaré wrote to the novelist-turned-diplomat that he feared a trap.

'If the Turkish Government seriously intend to make proposals to us, they have only to communicate them to us . . . and we shall then see whether we can enter into relations with Djavid or anyone else expressly empowered for that purpose'.[4]

Such an advance commitment, which would impair the hope of bargain and intrigue, was declined by the Turks.[4] Nor could they have been left ignorant of the enemy's terms. Sazonov, on hearing through Delcassé of their suggestion, stipulated that the Entente negotiators 'should announce to them the irrevocable decision of the Allies to concede to Russia Constantinople and the Straits. . . .'[5] Another obstacle, according to the Ambassador Moukhtar, was the autonomy of the Arab provinces[6] which loomed large among the British and French wishes. The fourth and gravest stumbling-block was the Triple Entente's decision of February 28th 1915 that, until the Central Powers had laid down arms, no separate peace would be concluded with the Porte, but only an armistice. This was to be restricted to the region of Constantinople and the Straits, so that fresh arrangements would have to be made for the other Ottoman fronts. The conditions for it—including the elimination of all the defences of the capital and the Narrows, admission of Allied squadrons and troops, and so forth—were tantamount to a demand for capitulation. Had the Sultan accepted them, he would have been unable to resist any proviso, however harsh, made in the subsequent

---

[1] Sazonov to Izvolski, 21 May '15. Izvolski to Sazonov, 23 May '15. Adamov, II. NN 265, 266, p. 316.
[2] Loti to Poincaré, 2 June '15. Poincaré, VI. 243.
[3] 25, 26, 27 May '15. ibid. 227–31.
[4] 2 June '15. Poincaré, 242; also 240–1.
[5] Sazonov to Izvolski, 30 May '15. Izvolski to Sazonov, 28 May '15. Adamov, II. NN 268, 267, pp. 316–17.
[6] Moukhtar, 299.

armistices.¹ Whether or not such details were broached, the soundings—even though Loti's messenger went as far as Munich for talks with Djavid—led to nothing. The Young Turks could afford to break off negotiations (on June 9th) after their change of fortune in the Dardanelles.²

German control in Constantinople tightened. Sanders and his officers were in command at Gallipoli.³ Munitions were so short that some batteries fired blank to deceive the troops into believing that they had artillery support. Equipment, tools, sandbags were lacking, and 'when a few thousand of them arrived . . . there was danger of their being used . . . for patching . . . uniforms'.⁴ In the rear, food scarcity grew and prices soared, coal rising four, rice six, and dried beans seven times above normal.⁵ Yet the Turkish soldiers, 'often barefooted, ragged, hungry. . . .',⁶ held firm in their trenches. And the Entente had to brace itself for further military and diplomatic exertions.

4

THE BULGARIAN IMBROGLIO

The Gallipoli landing had electrified Petrograd. The complacency with which the preceding naval operations had been played down by the Stavka gave way to sudden anxiety about the possible success of the new venture. These fears were fanned by the Quai d'Orsay which had received with distaste the British decision to send troops

¹ Sazonov to Izvolski and Benckendorff, 28 Feb. '15. Izvolski to Sazonov, 1 March. Yanushkevich to Sazonov, 2 March. The Generalissimo to Nicholas II, 2 March. Sazonov to Yanushkevich, 3 March '15. Adamov, II. NN 256, 257, 260, 261, 262, pp. 312-15.

When Sazonov, Buchanan and Paléologue, on 28 Feb. '15, elaborated a joint response to a hypothetical Turkish request for terms, Russia—anxious to shift her forces from the Caucasus to the Austro-German front and impatient, above all, to acquire Constantinople and the Straits—wanted an immediate peace. But Britain and France, apart from holding strong views about the future of the Ottoman capital and the Narrows, feared lest the Tsar, having obtained his principal prize, should lose interest in the War. Hence their insistence on a mere armistice with the Porte. This made it possible to postpone the final settlement with Russia, and enabled Delcassé to inject into the terms not only the question of 'the future fate of Turkey's Asiatic possessions', but also a clause about the 'joint occupation of Constantinople and its environs'. Moreover, as Turkey was expected to abolish the defences of Constantinople and the Straits, and to admit the Entente squadrons of which those of the Royal Navy were the strongest (the whole force was commanded by Admiral Carden), this would have led to the establishment of British supremacy in the entire area of the Straits. All this was so disadvantageous to Russia that the Stavka became restive. Sazonov, admitting that he had accepted these provisions in order 'to avoid discord with our Allies', drew comfort from the thought that 'the articles of the armistice are so onerous that the Turks will not . . . accept them'. ibid.

² Poincaré, VI. 254. ³ Churchill, *1915*, p. 248. Einstein, p. XV.
⁴ Sanders, 74; also 75. Churchill, *1915*, p. 268. Morgenthau, 148, 152.
⁵ Einstein, 242-3, 247. ⁶ Churchill, *1915*, p. 502.

to the Dardanelles. Already alarmed by Kitchener's recent Alexandretta project, Paris was apprehensive lest, while France was glued to the European front, Britain should establish herself in the Near East. Hence, despite the terrible drain on man-power caused by home defence, a French contingent was added to General Hamilton's force. At the same time, Delcassé repeatedly urged upon Izvolski the need for Russian participation in the operations by sea and land.[1] It was sound strategy that Turkey should be attacked from two sides, and that the Russian Fleet should prevent the escape of German and Turkish warships to neutral Black Sea ports. For that reason Churchill and Grey, too, laboured this point.[2] But more significant was Delcassé's emphasis on the desirability of the simultaneous appearance of the three Allied squadrons before Constantinople—'particularly from the political point of view'.[3] His intention was clearly to employ the Tsarist Fleet as a counter-balance and an irritant to the Royal Navy. The Third Republic's departure from the rigid rule not to divert strength from the German theatre of war revealed to the Russians the depth of the Franco-British dissension, and the opportunity it gave them to profit from it.[4] Sazonov, in his communications to the Generalissimo, resumed the old refrain: '... it is essential that our troops, too, should take part in the entry of Allied forces into Constantinople'. And on March 1st 1915, it was decided to send the Black Sea Fleet and a Russian expeditionary corps to the Bosphorus.[5]

On the following day the Stavka informed the Foreign Minister that, in order to seize the Straits, it was 'utterly indispensable' for Russian warships to coal in Burgas, and requested him 'to do absolutely everything in your power' to obtain Bulgaria's consent.[6] That sheltered and spacious Bulgarian port only a hundred miles from the target was so much safer and closer than the nearest Turkish harbours and so much superior to them that, unless it could be used as a Russian base, a landing—in the opinion of the Black

---

[1] Izvolski to Sazonov, 23, 24 Feb. and 6 April '15. Adamov, I. No. 35, p. 241. II. NN 32, 66, pp. 148, 166; also p. 41.
[2] Benckendorff to Sazonov, 25 Feb. '15. Adamov, II. No. 34, p. 149. Sazonov to Kudashev, 28 Feb., 5 and 10 March, transmitting telegrams from Churchill. *ibid.* NN 36, 44, 48, pp. 150, 154-7. Neratov to Kudashev, 15 March, transmitting a telegram from Churchill. *ibid.* No. 52, p. 159. Kitchener to Hamilton, 13 March '15. Dardanelles C. *Final Report*, 11.
[3] Izvolski to Sazonov, 20 Feb. '15. Adamov, II. No. 29, p. 144.
[4] Kitchener to Churchill, 20 Feb. '15: 'The French are in a great way about so many troops being employed as you told them of. I have just seen Grey and hope we shall not be saddled with a French contingent for the Dardanelles'. Churchill, *1915*, p. 182. Adamov, II. pp. 141-3.
[5] Sazonov to Muravyov, 28 Feb. '15. Muravyov to Sazonov, 1 March. Adamov, II. NN 37, 41, pp. 150, 152-3. I. p. 372, footnote 3.
[6] The Generalissimo to Sazonov, 2. March '15. Adamov, II. No. 217, p. 289.

Sea Commander, Admiral Ebergard—was impossible.[1] But Sazonov, already entangled in intricate parleys with Sofia, found such an approach 'extremely undesirable'. To ask King Ferdinand's permission was to invite large claims for compensation, including one for Rodosto which was uncomfortably near Constantinople. To ask permission and reject the counter-claim would, as Sazonov reported to Nicholas II, be courting a refusal injurious to 'our dignity'. To take Burgas without preliminary agreement would inflame the public and the Government in Bulgaria and could drive her into the arms of Germany.[2] Even if it did not, such high-handed action would place Russia at a disadvantage in Sofia in relation to Britain and France. The only way out appeared to lie in a joint diplomatic démarche. On March 19th, when the Allies, after the Dardanelles defeat the day before, could be presumed to be more amenable, the Foreign Minister was ordered by the Tsar to inquire of the Entente 'what view they would take of our occupying Burgas even in disregard of Bulgaria's dissent', considering that 'they recognize the necessity for our simultaneous co-operation. . . .'[3] But it was one thing to request Russia's help (which was expected to be slight) for the Entente's own purposes, and quite another to help her to a footing in a country over which they were already in disagreement, and whence she had every chance of reaching Constantinople. This prospect seemed all the more real since Sazonov had only just (on March 6th) ruled out the collaboration of Greece. Grey, therefore, expressed his 'objections' to a unilateral Russian step which would be 'a most serious political error'.[4]

This did not, however, prevent the British Foreign Office from contemplating a similar move. As the Tsarist Minister in Athens cabled to Sazonov, the British Military Attaché there broached the idea of disembarking at the Bulgarian port of Dedeagach rather than on heavily defended Gallipoli. He proposed that King Ferdinand should be requested to grant free transit to some 150,000-250,000 Anglo-French troops who would link up with a Russian force. But there was no suggestion as to where it should land.[5] To make matters worse, the Bulgarian Premier Radoslavov told Nicholas's

---

[1] Ebergard to the Minister of the Navy, 4 March '15. Adamov, II. No. 221, pp. 292–3. Yanushkevich to Sazonov, 19 March. *ibid.* No. 231, pp. 298–9.
[2] Sazonov to Nicholas II, 6 March '15. Adamov, II. No. 223, pp. 293–4. Memorandum, Minister of the Navy, 3 March '15. *ibid.* No. 219, p. 290.
[3] Yanushkevich to Sazonov, 19 March '15. Adamov, II. No. 231, p. 299. The word 'soglasiye' (consent) in the original is obviously a misprint of 'nesoglasiye' (dissent).
[4] Sazonov to Kudashev, 23 March '15, transmitting an Aide-Memoire from Buchanan. Adamov, II. No. 233, p. 300.
[5] Demidov to Sazonov, 3 April '15. Adamov, II. No. 239, p. 302; also p. 72.

Envoy that 'there is no need for two landings—one is enough'.[1] This was the time when British ships blockading Turkey were warmly received in Dedeagach,[2] and since Radoslavov was patently hostile to Petrograd his statement could only mean that, while closing his country to the Russians, he would open it to the West. Not only was the Tsar to be kept out of Bulgaria, but she would be used by the Entente as a short-cut to Constantinople, where Ferdinand—whose craving for the Byzantine crown was hardly less violent than that of the Greek King—would, the Russians feared, take the latter's place as the agent of Britain and France.

Therefore Sazonov, who had already accepted London's veto on the Burgas enterprise,[3] needed a means of forcing Bulgaria, in the event of her joining in the march on Constantinople, to moderate her demands. Seizing upon a week-old Bulgaro-Serbian border incident for which Vienna, and not Sofia, was responsible, he informed Buchanan on April 10th and 11th that the Tsar intended to take 'coercive measures against Bulgaria'.[4] That this was another bid for Burgas can be deduced from Benckendorff's telegram stating that the British Foreign Office was 'resolutely against the projected landing of our troops in Burgas as violating [Bulgarian] neutrality . . . the English Government would be placed in a position incompatible with the one they held regarding the breach of Belgian neutrality. . . .'[5] Coming on the heels of their infringement of Greek neutrality in Lemnos, this argument was bound to ring hollow to Sazonov. But he could not ignore 'Grey's strong hope that we shall not adopt that project'.[5] In vain did Nicholas II emphasize that 'we need Burgas as our last stage on the way to the Bosphorus'.[5] The idea of the Russian landing was submerged in the bog of Bulgarian politics.

5

THE RUSSIAN PLAY FOR CONSTANTINOPLE

But the policy underlying it was still going strong. While, at the Dardanelles, men in their thousands came to dust, Tsarism was straining with impatience to add a further quota. The Black Sea Fleet bombarded the Turkish coast in March, April and May. An attack was made on Batum and an advance into Turkish Armenia. The Pacific cruiser *Askold*, which had been included among the

---

[1] Savinski to Sazonov, 9 April '15. Adamov, II. No. 241, p. 303.
[2] Corbett, II. 297.
[3] Yanushkevich to Sazonov, 24 March '15. Adamov, II. No. 235, p. 301. Buchanan to Grey, 24 and 28 March '15. Deciphered in the Russian Foreign Ministry. Adamov, II. NN 234, 238, pp. 300, 302.
[4] See Savinski to Sazonov, 16 April '15. Adamov, II. No. 196, p. 274.
[5] Benkendorff to Sazonov, 14 April '15. Adamov, II. No. 244, pp. 306-7; also 72-4.

French forces off Syria, was attached—upon Russian insistence—to the British squadron in the Straits, and went into action on May 8th. By detaining three armed Ottoman divisions in the Bosphorus, Russia weakened the Turkish defences in the Dardanelles.[1] This was not enough, however, to establish the right to a claim, and Sazonov again harassed the Stavka with warnings that it was 'impossible for Tsargrad, the most valuable acquisition which the present War can get us, to be conquered solely by the efforts of our Allies. . . .'[2] But in May the German-Austrian offensive was sweeping from the Carpathians to the Baltic. The shell-starved Tsarist armies withdrew from North Hungary and retreated in Courland, Lithuania and Galicia. The corps earmarked for the Straits had to be sent to the river San.[3] And as the Foreign Minister was at the same time urging that it was 'extremely undesirable', from a political point of view, to allow the Entente to monopolize the Narrows,[2] the Generalissimo hit upon the device of ordering that some 6,000 men should, by mid-July 1915, be dispatched from Vladivostok.[4]

The notion of shipping so small a force around half the world, and so late that it could not reach the Dardanelles until the end of August, was so bizarre that even Nicholas II was astonished.[5] But the generals had to do something to restore a prestige tarnished by the recent defeats. They had to reckon with influential circles in the Duma, the recall of which was imminent. They found it politic to prove how conscious they were of Russia's 'historic' task in the Bosphorus. And they were afraid that Britain and France might get there, without the Russians being anywhere near. Since it was impossible for them to approach Constantinople from the East, their argument was: ' . . . if we wish to attend the ceremony of taking the city, our troops must come from the South',[6] by way of the Mediterranean. As the state of the War precluded an independent Russian operation in the Straits, the Stavka fell back on a 'symbolic' participation in that of their Allies. The Vladivostok contingent, the Generalissimo assured his Sovereign would have 'moral significance'.[7] Kudashev, writing to Sazonov, was plainer: it would give Russia 'the role of a fly on the horns of a bull'.[6]

---

[1] Corbett, II. 74, 196, 295–7. Adamov, II. p. 154, footnote 1; p. 168, and *ibid.* footnote 1; p. 169, and *ibid.* footnote 1. Sanders, 106–7. Einstein, 55, 60.
[2] Sazonov to Kudashev, 13 May '15. Adamov, II. No. 74, p. 170; also 15 and 29 May '15. *ibid.* NN 77, 79, pp. 173–4.
[3] Adamov, I. p. 106. II. p. 76 and *ibid.* footnote 1; p. 169, footnote 1; pp. 176–7. Talenski, *Pervaya mirovaya voina*, 45–6.
[4] The Generalissimo to Nicholas II, 30 May and 1 June '15. Yanushkevich to Sazonov, 12 June '15. Adamov, II. NN 80, 82, 85, pp. 174–77.
[5] Nicholas II to the Generalissimo, 31 May '15. Adamov, II. No. 81, p. 174.
[6] Kudashev to Sazonov, 22 June '15. Adamov, II. No. 87, p. 180; also 80.
[7] 1 June '15. Adamov, II. No. 82, p. 175.

But Britain, having so far kept the Bear at bay, was irritated by its attempt to break through in the guise of a fly. Although the brunt of the attack fell on herself and France, the simultaneous appearance of Russian units before 'Tsargrad' would lead to claims that its capture was the result of tripartite efforts and enable Nicholas II to carry more weight in the settlement. Lord Kitchener, therefore, expressed strong dislike of the plan.[1] This, in turn, stiffened the Stavka. Kudashev reported of the Quartermaster-General Danilov that he 'says that, as a Russian, he cannot admit the thought that there should be no Russian troops in the capture of Constantinople, and that, even if our detachment should bother the English, this does not matter and need not stop us, as it would simply be because they do not want us to enter Constantinople with them.'[2] Sazonov, too, favoured the assignment of a token force.[3]

In the meantime, however, the Kaiser, trying to make capital of his victories in the East, had released another paper dove: Madame Vasilchikova's second letter. On May 27th 1915, after conversations with the Foreign Minister von Jagow, she wrote from Berlin:

'Everyone here is agreed that peace between Germany and Russia is a vital question for both countries which are united by so many trade interests and in no essential sense divided by political differences. . . . Russia will gain far more by concluding a favourable peace with Germany, even where the problem of the Dardanelles is concerned. . . . People here are convinced that England will insist on having freedom of action in the Black Sea . . . she will want to dominate there . . . England has never been the genuine friend of her Allies. . . . England is striving to obtain predominant influence in Constantinople, and despite all her promises she will never permit Russia to seize that city. . . .'[4]

Considering the whole record of Grey's and Delcassé's diplomacy in this field, these insinuations were bound to fall on fertile soil in Petrograd. The grave military reverses, moreover, must have induced some at least of the Russian rulers to respond to the German overtures. Such a response, if it were made, could hardly have escaped notice in the West; but in any case there were leakages of information[5] for which the Wilhelmstrasse—always trying to divide its enemies—presumably was not without responsibility. That exchanges on this subject had, in fact, taken place between the Entente

---

[1] Sazonov to Kudashev, 25 June '15. Adamov, II. No. 88, pp. 180–1. For Kitchener's technical objections, as transmitted by General Williams's Assistant, see Kudashev to Sazonov, 22 June '15. Adamov, II. No. 87, p. 179.
[2] Kudashev to Sazonov, 22 June '15. Adamov, II. No. 87, p. 179.
[3] Sazonov to Kudashev, 2 June '15. Adamov, II. No. 83, p. 175.
[4] Vasilchikova to Nicholas II, 27 May '15. Adamov, II. No. 332, p. 371.
[5] See Poincaré, VI. 92.

and Russia seems to be borne out by Sazonov's sudden intimation to the Stavka that 'it is necessary, from the political point of view . . . to avoid everything that might cast even a passing shadow on the good relations among the Allies. . . .'[1] It may be that the plan to send a detachment from Vladivostok had, among other reasons, been made because the Tsar, strengthened in his attitude towards Britain and France by the Kaiser's dalliance with Madame Vasilchikova, wished to stake out an indisputable claim to Constantinople. It may be that the reverse is true and that it was a move by pro-Entente circles to stress, in refutation of Jagow's theory, the solidarity of Petrograd and London. The British at any rate took the former view. They saw Nicholas reaching out for the supreme prize, and presumably it was the threat of Sazonov's 'shadow on good relations' which made him withdraw. Perhaps Sazonov had some dark reason for wishing to dispel the mistrust of the Allies (his *volte face* was too rapid to be compatible with a clear conscience in the matter of the German feelers); perhaps he had tied his fortune too closely to the West. In either event he clearly shrank from aggravating Britain. On July 9th 1915, he informed the Entente Governments that the expedition from Vladivostok had been called off.[2]

The last desperate attempt to circumvent the ban came in the context of soundings for a Russo-Japanese alliance. After the press of both countries had aired this theme for some months, the *Russkoye Slovo* of July 2nd (June 20th o.s.) proposed that the Mikado should send his soldiers to the Dardanelles.[3] In view of the rising anti-British tide in Tokio[4] the hope in Petrograd clearly was that Japan, who had no interest in the Straits, would put her weight on Russia's side of the balance and, for a price, cast a vote on her behalf in the settlement. But, on July 15th, the Tsarist Ambassador reported the Deputy Foreign Minister Matsui as saying that under no circumstances would Japan send troops to Europe, and the authoritative *Nichi Nichi* dismissed the Russian suggestion as 'ironical'.[5] From mid-summer 1915, Petrograd found every physical approach to Constantinople blocked.

---

[1] Sazonov to Kudashev, 25 June '15. Adamov, II. No. 88, p. 181.
[2] Sazonov to Benckendorff, 9 July '15. Adamov, II. No. 93, p. 183. Yanushkevich to Sazonov, 7 July. *ibid.* No. 90, p. 182. Also Sazonov to Kudashev, 25 June '15. *ibid.* No. 88, p. 181.
[3] The Ambassador in Tokio to Sazonov, 15 and 29 July '15. Adamov, I. NN 198, 199, pp. 386-8.
[4] Adamov, I. No. 198, p. 385.
[5] Adamov, I. No. 198, p. 386. No. 199, p. 387.

## CHAPTER VII

## *Withdrawal*

### 1

#### THE DRAMA OF GALLIPOLI

THE sultry season brought further fighting and suffering at Gallipoli. It made no difference that there was a new Government in Britain. The Cabinet crisis of May 1915 was caused by the shell-shortage, the vagaries of the War, especially in the Straits, the machinations of Lloyd George and, above all, by resentment among the Tories that the party truce of August 1914 was favouring the Liberal Administration.[1] The break-up of the Ministry was provoked by the resignation of the First Sea Lord, Fisher, who rebelled against both the Dardanelles policy and the strain of working under Churchill. '... W.C. is leading them all straight to ruin.... A very great national disaster is very near us.... W.C. is a bigger danger than the Germans by a long way in what is just now imminent in the Dardanelles....' This letter from Fisher to the Leader of the Opposition, Bonar Law,[2] did more than betray the depth of the old Admiral's quarrel with his Chief, or his grievance that, while Kitchener had a voice in the Cabinet and the War Council, he had none. It underlined the mounting hostility of the Conservatives (except Balfour) to Churchill. He had deserted their ranks and, from the Liberal front bench, turned on his former friends. He had antagonized them over the Irish question. He was responsible for the 'utterly stupid business'[3] of Antwerp, and bore formal liability for the disaster of Coronel and the loss of several big ships. He was the prime author of the campaign in the Straits, into which 'the Government had jumped ... without at all counting the cost'.[4] The Conservatives, writes Law's biographer, suspected that Churchill had 'a ruthless love of power, a passionate determination to reach the summit of English politics....' He inspired 'a profound sense of

---

[1] Blake, *The Unknown Prime Minister*, 237. Churchill, *1915*, p. 365; also 309–12, 350–74. Lloyd George, I. 223–32.
[2] Fisher to Law, 17 May '15. B. Law's Papers, quoted by Blake, 245. Also Churchill, *1915*, pp. 358, 361. Asquith, *Memories and Reflections*, II. 90, 93. Fisher, 73, states that he 'only resigned when the drain it [the Dardanelles operation] was making on the resources of the Navy became so great as to jeopardize the major operations of the Fleet'.
[3] Law's letter, 14 Oct. '14. B. Law's Papers. Blake, 235. For Churchill's account of the loss of a naval brigade, the collapse of Antwerp, and his part in this episode see Churchill, *1914*, pp. 332–59.
[4] Law to Sir H. Wilson, 9 April '15. B. Law's Papers. Blake, 241.

mistrust... felt by no one more deeply than by Bonar Law'.¹ The latter was, on the other hand, intimate with Fisher. The First Sea Lord's tenure at the Admiralty was viewed by the Opposition as a curb on the actions of their *bête noire*,² and when he resigned on May 15th, Law, in agreement with Lord Lansdowne and Austen Chamberlain gave notice to the Prime Minister that

'... we cannot allow the House to adjourn until this fact has been made known and discussed... things cannot go on as they are, and some change in the constitution of the Government seems to us inevitable.... The situation in Italy makes it particularly undesirable to have anything in the nature of a controversial discussion in the House of Commons at present, and if you are prepared to take the necessary steps to secure the object which I have indicated... we shall be ready to keep silence now....'³

The 'object' included as a *sine qua non* the dismissal of Churchill from his post.⁴ He, loth to retire, wrote to the Leader of the Opposition, defending his policy and demanding an inquiry. Undeterred by the 'general condemnation, violent newspaper censures, angry lobbies...', he conveyed to the Premier that he would be 'glad... to be *offered* a position in the new Government'.⁵ He even suggested to Fisher that, if he would return to serve under him, he could have a seat in the Cabinet. But Fisher 'rejected the thirty pieces of silver...'⁶ Asquith, dreading a public attack, aware that the survival of the Liberals depended on a coalition, and certain that this was only possible on Tory terms, sacrificed his contentious colleague.⁷ And Churchill, somewhat appeased by his retention in the War Council, was moved to a minor office.

The question of Gallipoli, however, for all the heat it had engendered, was not affected. Balfour, Churchill's successor, continued his policy.⁸ The new Government introduced themselves on May 26th 1915. Two days later, Lord Kitchener informed the Dardanelles Committee (into which the War Council had been transformed) that 'the difficulties of the enterprise have proved more

¹ Blake, 233; also 232, 234.
² Blake, 236, 242. See also Churchill, *1915*, p. 198.
³ Asquith, *Memories and Reflections*, II. 96. For the critical situation in Italy see pp. 381–6 below.
⁴ Blake, 237, 245, 252. Churchill, *1915*, p. 370. Beaverbrook, *Politicians and the War*, I. 112–13.
⁵ Churchill, *1915*, p. 369. Italics in the original. Also 372.
⁶ Fisher to Law, 17 May '15. B. Law's Papers. Blake, 245; also 252. Cf. Churchill to Fisher, 15 May '15. Churchill, *1915*, p. 361.
⁷ Asquith to the Cabinet, 17 May '15. Asquith, *Memories and Reflections*, II. 95–6. Lloyd George, I. 233–4. Blake, 243, 246.
⁸ Churchill in a private letter, 23 May '15: 'Although I am down, the policy goes on....' Churchill, *1915*, p. 378; also 366.

formidable than was at first anticipated, and that a much greater effort than was originally budgeted for was now required'.¹ The spring offensives in France and Belgium had cost the French 220,000 men and the British 100,000, and gained them about eight miles of strategically useless territory.² Armies and arms, voraciously consumed on the Western front, were hardly available for the Straits. Transportation was precarious. But the Byzantine spell was still working. The old arguments against withdrawal—the 'Muscovite danger', the recruitment of Balkan allies, prestige—were advanced as before. Fresh divisions were sent, 'but did little more than keep pace with the wastage'.³ The battles of May to July achieved no more than that 'broadly speaking, the force remained in the position it had occupied on the day of the landing'.⁴ In one action (on May 19th) the casualties were so heavy that a truce had to be made so as to be able to bury the dead.⁵ In another (on June 21st) the French alone lost 2,500 men. 'We take trenches. We are expelled from them', Poincaré noted on June 29th, 'everything as in Artois'.⁶

Meanwhile, 'the weather had become very hot, and with the heat came swarms of flies . . . there were many unburied bodies, both of men and animals . . . and it was found impossible to keep down the plague of flies. These conveyed a great amount of infection . . . dysentery . . . paratyphoid and other complaints. . . . Apart from reduction in numbers caused by death, the force was seriously weakened by the number of men always ill and the lowering of vitality . . . in those who were still on duty'.⁷ The exhausted, depleted, under-armed troops were under continuous fire. At the end of July, Poincaré learned that the position was becoming untenable.⁸ The Gordian knot was to have been cut in the final furious attacks of August 6th to 10th and 21st. New landings were meant to separate the Turkish defenders from their main forces in the rear. An eyewitness reported from Suvla Bay: '. . . the trenches were being torn to pieces . . . off we dashed . . . we met the Turks . . . we fought hand to hand, we bit and fisted, and used rifles and pistols as clubs'. A Ghurka was hit, 'the place was a mass of blood and limbs and screams. . . .'⁹ The British losses exceeded 45,000, those of the Turks were only 5,000 less.¹⁰ And still Gallipoli remained unscaled, forbidden and defiant.

¹ Dardanelles C. *Final Report*, 25.
² Churchill, *1915*, p. 413.
³ Churchill, *1915*, p. 411. Sanders, 76.
⁴ Poincaré, VI. 294; also 252-3. Dardanelles C. *Final Report*, 61.
⁵ Dardanelles C. *Final Report*, 26; also 95.
⁶ ibid. 28, 85-6. Poincaré, VI. 347.
⁷ Col. C. Allanson, quoted by Churchill, *1915*, p. 442.
⁸ Churchill, *1915*, pp. 402-3.
⁹ Dardanelles C. *Final Report*, 28.
¹⁰ Churchill, *1915*, pp. 451-2; also 269, 443, 452. Dardanelles C. *Final Report*, 24-6, 33, 50-1, 54, 84-5. Sanders, 83, 89, 90. Adamov, II. p. 92.

## 2
### THE DIPLOMATIC WRANGLE OVER HYPOTHETICAL DETAILS

The scene lent a ghastly touch to the continuing combat of the diplomats. Back in March 1915, when the Entente navies appeared to be blasting a passage through the Straits, the French and British directors of the Ottoman Bank, the councillors of the Ottoman Public Debt and the business managers, who had been expelled by the Porte, were packing their trunks for return.[1] Even while Izvolski was urging on Sazonov 'the need [for.Russia] to ensure in advance the activity of those institutions which have an important place in the life of Constantinople',[2] Delcassé, on March 12th, requested the Russian Foreign Minister to recognize, in anticipation of the peace settlement,

'which will permit the establishment of the final régime . . . the interests of each of the Powers of the Triple Alliance, and to admit for that purpose all three Powers to an equal share in the temporary administration of Constantinople. . . . With this aim in view . . . the supreme direction of the administrative authorities will be entrusted to three civil High Commissioners. . . . These Commissioners will . . . in the first place see to the restoration in their pre-war posts of the officials, Ministerial advisers, and officers of their own nationality placed at the head of . . . the Ottoman Debt . . . the Ottoman Bank, the Customs, the gendarmerie and so forth. . . . Taking into account the 3,000,000,000 of French capital invested in Turkey . . . the Government of the Republic is obliged to restore and safeguard these large interests . . . to restore the rights of ownership to the interested persons and holders of Ottoman securities, as well as to order the sequestration of the property of the subjects of the enemy Powers. . . .'.[3]

Presented as it was on the day when Grey conditionally recognized Russia's claims to 'Tsargrad' and the Straits, this Aide-Memoire was aimed at whittling down the British concession. Under the guise of 'temporary administration', the Allies—as Izvolski warned Petrograd —wished to establish themselves 'in extremely favourable conditions compared to ourselves'.[4] Sazonov's task, therefore, was to obtain safeguards just for the transition period. Above all, the threatened

[1] Izvolski to Sazonov, 10 and 26 March '15. Adamov, II. NN 287, 302, pp. 328, 337.
[2] He mentioned specifically the Council of the Ottoman Public Debt, the Tobacco Monopoly and the Ottoman Bank. Izvolski to Sazonov, 10 March '15. Adamov, II. No. 286, p. 327.
[3] Aide-Memoire, French Embassy, Petrograd, to Sazonov, 12 March '15. Adamov, II. No. 289, p. 329.
[4] Izvolski to Sazonov, 10 March '15. Adamov, II. No. 287, p. 328; also p. 97.

tripartite rule must be replaced by one-Power control. On March 13th 1915, in identical Notes to Buchanan and Paléologue, he proposed in exact contradiction to Delcassé's plan: (a) that the three High Commissioners constituting a provisional council for the civil administration of the city should be subordinated to 'the supreme direction' of a military Kommandant, and that (b) that office should be filled 'by the most senior in rank of the officers commanding the occupation armies of the three Allies'.[1] One of the striking features of this reply was that it was addressed not only to the French Foreign Minister. Grey was drawn in so as to deprive Delcassé of the initiative in this matter. Britain, less interested than France in Constantinople and, at the same time, doubtless inclined to curtail the ramifications of French capital there (which may help to explain why 'Tsargrad' was promised to Nicholas II), was to be played off against the other companion in arms. The second significant feature was that in the list of the High Commissioners' functions the protection of religious and national interests, which were a potential source of Russian influence, figured first. The third, and most important, feature was that the holder of supreme power at the Golden Horn was to be appointed on no better grounds than those of extreme seniority. This proposal arose from the intention of selecting a long-retired general of the 1837 vintage, whose more than five decades of service not even Joffre could beat, as Chief of the Russian occupying force. There was no mistaking that, this time, Tsarism was trying to slip into Constantinople at the coat-tails of a museum piece.

For Delcassé, however, this was not the only danger. Since Britain was in charge of the operations in the Straits, she too had to be guarded against. With a firmness, no less effective because it was elegant, he objected to any military commander, 'whatever his personal merits',[2] having supreme jurisdiction in the Ottoman capital. In a Note to Sazonov on March 21st—three days after, and despite, the first heavy defeat in the Dardanelles—he reiterated his demand for 'equality among the three Powers . . . from the moment of occupation until the conclusion of the treaty of peace'. The subordination of the High Commissioners to 'a general of Allied nationality' was rejected. Sazonov, who evidently wanted to treat Constantinople as a future provincial city of Russia, was reminded that, in fact, it was 'the seat of an administration whose activity extends over the whole Ottoman Empire'. The control of Constantinople, therefore, would give Russia 'a mortgage' on all the affairs of the Turkish realm. As

---

[1] Aide-Memoire, Sazonov to Buchanan and Paléologue, 13 March '15. Adamov, II. No. 290, p. 330; also pp. 99–100.
[2] Aide-Memoire, French Embassy, Petrograd, to Sazonov, 12 March '15. Adamov, II. No. 289, p. 329; also 98.

this would be injurious to 'the Allies and especially France', it was necessary that, until its fate was settled, Constantinople should remain the Imperial capital with an administration corresponding not to its future but to its existing status.

By virtue of this 'all-important principle', the subjects of the three Powers 'will enjoy all the rights which they had under Turkish rule'. The management of the Ottoman Public Debt in which France had a predominant interest was to continue, until the peace, in its old form. The French religious, educational and charitable institutions were to resume their former functions and property rights. The validity of contracts concluded between the Third Republic or private French companies and the Porte or other Turkish authorities was to be recognized, including the railway concessions in Eastern Anatolia so obnoxious to Russia. The same treatment was requested for 'companies and establishments which, though under a Turkish name or Turkish administration, are in fact French'. In the sequestration of German and Austro-Hungarian enterprises account was to be taken of 'the special rights' of French holders. Firms nominally Turkish but actually French were not to be sequestrated. The supervision of sequestrated Ottoman companies (such as the Baghdad Railway, the Mersina-Adana-Hedjaz Line, the Deraa-Haifa Railway, the port of Alexandretta and so forth) operating in the zone 'to be conceded to us' was to be entrusted to Frenchmen.[1] Reduced to simple terms, all this went far beyond a mere restoration of France's economic and financial interests. It meant the return to her Catholic protectorate and, in effect, the Capitulations, and opened the door wide, as Prof. Grimm puts it, 'to a fictitious or enforced transfer of . . . the greatest possible proportion of enterprises into the hands of French capital'.[2]

Since in Constantinople, even more than elsewhere, economic and financial control was inseparable from political supremacy,[3] these conditions were bound to prevent Russia from establishing her mastery at the Golden Horn. Nor could she draw comfort from the 'provisional' nature of the proposed arrangement. Once the pretensions of Paris were accepted, it was difficult to imagine that they would be dropped when the 'fate of the Ottoman Empire' was finally decided. Even if some of them were abandoned, the price in compensation would be heavy, and if compensation were paid to France, it could not be refused to Britain. The Western Powers would thus be placed in a position to trade the empty shell of Constantinople

[1] Aide-Memoire, French Embassy, Petrograd, to Sazonov, 21 March '15. Adamov, II. No. 298, pp. 333–5; also 100–1.
[2] E. D. Grimm, Introduction to Adamov, II. p. 102.
[3] The Financial Attaché, Russian Embassy, Paris, to the Russian Foreign Ministry, 21 April '15. Adamov, II. No. 314, p. 346.

for the rich kernel remaining in their hands. They might even, considering the scope of Nicholas's ambitions, hold on to the concessions now extorted until he reduced or gave up his claims to a further share in the Sultan's inheritance. The Quai d'Orsay, while striving to prevent a Russian mortgage on Turkey, was at the same time endeavouring to mortgage the whole of Russia's future in the Balkans and Near East.[1]

Nevertheless, Sazonov capitulated, as he himself put it, 'at every point'.[2] His secret agreement with Britain required French endorsement which was hard to obtain, and certainly not on anything less than Delcassé's terms. Petrograd's diplomatic position was further weakened by the assumption that Constantinople would be taken by the Entente and not by Tsarist troops, by adversity on Russia's European fronts and, above all, by her mounting dependence for money and arms on the Allies. But the surrender dismayed informed opinion. 'The Tsargrad financiers, French and English', the Russian Financial Attaché gave warning from Paris, 'are used to the Turks, to the Capitulations, to lording it as they pleased'. They must not now be left 'in sole command', for 'when the provisional joint occupation has to give place to the historic solution for which all Russia is craving' and 'we suddenly wish to become complete masters ... in Constantinople ... we shall have to dislodge some and bargain with others. ...'.[3] Prince Trubetskoi, the Russian High-Commissioner designate, urged upon the Foreign Minister that

'the transitional state ... [of administration] ... must be preparatory to the final one which, of necessity, will have to take on many features of the temporary position. The latter must consequently be under the direction of that same Power which is destined to establish itself' there.

To recognize, in principle, that the Allies have

'equal rights with us and, in practice, that matters should be determined by their two votes to one Russian, would be the same as preparing to establish in Constantinople not Russia, but the Western Powers'.

Hence,

'the Russian Representative alone ... must embody on the spot the sovereign power which will replace that of Turkey. ... It is unthinkable ... to reconcile the French conditions with Russian interests'.[4]

---

[1] See Grimm, Introduction, Adamov, II. p. 102.
[2] Aide-Memoire, Sazonov to Paléologue, 24 March '15. Adamov, II. No. 301, pp. 336–7.
[3] Aide-Memoire to the Russian Foreign Ministry, 21 April '15. Adamov, II. No. 314, p. 346.
[4] Trubetskoi to Sazonov, 20 April '15. Adamov, II. No. 312, pp. 343–4.

And so Sazonov, although the deal with France had been clinched, returned to the attack. 'Telegrams are exchanged daily between Paris, London and Petrograd. One would think [Poincaré jotted down] that our flags were already flying at the Golden Horn'.[1] The big issue was fought out this time on questions of detail. The Russian Foreign Minister, stressing the transitional rather than the provisional element of the expected situation, endeavoured to introduce maximum changes into the future administration of Constantinople. France and Britain tended to preserve as much as possible of the pre-war *status quo*. While the West wished to turn joint occupation into a form of internationalization, the other side tried to restrict the foreign privileges aimed at limiting, by a new type of Capitulations, the prospective Russian sovereignty in 'Tsargrad'.[2] The differences were sharpened by the intervention of the Vatican. On May 7th 1915, the Cardinal Secretary of State, Gasparri, sent a letter to the French Primate, Cardinal Amette, for transmission to the Quai d'Orsay:

'... If Constantinople were taken and the historic temple of St. Sophia wrested from the Mussulmen, the Holy Father would greatly wish it to be assigned to France and thus restored to Catholic worship. ... I beg Your Eminence to use his good offices with ... M. le Président of the Republic, as with the Ministers MM. Delcassé and Briand'.[3]

And the negotiations were further complicated by Franco-British divergencies. A draft presented by Grey provided for the predominance of military authority over civilian power for the duration of tripartite rule. As General Sir Ian Hamilton was in supreme command in the Straits, the whole temporary administration of Constantinople would come under the control of Britain. Delcassé opposed this as vehemently as, earlier on, he had resisted the proposed elevation of the Russian octogenarian. And Sazonov—despite his continuing disagreements with France over economic and legal clauses—was so shocked by the British bid that he forgot that he had championed a similar scheme and sided in this matter with Paris.[4]

[1] 31 March '15. Poincaré, VI. 140.
[2] See Adamov, II. pp. 97, 103–5.
[3] Tabouis, *The Life of Jules Cambon*, 293–4. As early as 14 March '15, Poincaré recorded that the Pope, through Gasparri, Amette and J. Cambon, had raised this question with the French Government. Poincaré added that St. Sophia, at the time of its fall to the Turks, was not a Catholic but a Greek Orthodox shrine. Poincaré, VI. 111–12.
[4] Sazonov to Izvolski, 26 Aug. and 13 Sept. '15. Adamov, II. NN 321, 328, pp. 360, 363–4. Izvolski to Sazonov, 30 Sept. *ibid*. No. 330, pp. 367–8. Trubetskoi to Izvolski, 2 Sept. '15. Stieve, pp. 201–2.

## 3
### CHURCHILL'S RESIGNATION AND THE ABANDONMENT OF THE DARDANELLES

The diplomatic battles, raging alongside those in the Dardanelles, lasted throughout the summer. On August 26th 1915, after the quiet of defeat had fallen on those blood-soaked beaches, a telegram from Sazonov to Izvolski revealed that the Allies still differed 'in some basic points'.[1] On September 13th, he was still posting his desiderata to the West.[2] To speed up the parleys he even suggested that they should be transferred from Petrograd to Paris. But as late as September 30th, the Russian Envoy there reported that the British Embassy 'had as yet no instructions', and that he had

'repeatedly approached the Foreign Ministry here . . . and each time received the assurance that the matter is not being overlooked . . . but that it is held up by other and more pressing anxieties'.[3]

The point is that Bulgaria, swayed by the pendulum of events on Gallipoli, unimpressed by the wooing of the Triple Entente, and enticed by the German-Austrian blandishments, had joined the Central Powers. Serbia cried out for help. The French Government, believing the hour ripe at last for Balkan undertakings, wound up the obnoxious action in the Straits and, in October 1915, moved their two divisions thence to Salonika.[4] In London, the question of Eastern strategy became acute. The terrible Peninsula was consuming British strength to no purpose. The Army, despite reinforcements, was outnumbered by the Turks. Because of illness and exposure to fire and fatigue the average wastage, even without serious engagements, was 24 per cent a month. The picture of autumn drawn by Churchill was one of 'disease and despondency . . . shortage of ammunition . . . the threatening advent of winter . . . rigorous privations. . . .'[5] In November came 'a blizzard of exceptional severity . . . 280 men were drowned in the trenches . . . and many were frozen to death as they stood. 16,000 cases of frost bite and exposure had to be evacuated'.[6] Nevertheless, Churchill opposed the withdrawal. In Russia's perseverance, he urged upon the Cabinet on October 15th,

---

[1] Adamov, II. No. 321, p. 360.
[2] Sazonov to Izvolski, 13 Sept. '15. Adamov, II. No. 328, pp. 363–4.
[3] Izvolski to Sazonov, 30 Sept. '15. Adamov, II. No. 330, p. 367.
[4] Poincaré, VI. 282. Bertie, I. 175, 190, 221, 235. Dardanelles C. *First Report*, 38. *Final Report*, 53, 61. Adamov, II. No. 66, pp. 166; 389, footnote 1. Lloyd George, I. 496. *Dokumente der Deutschen Politik und Geschichte*, II. pp. 317–20.
[5] Churchill, *1915*, p. 465. Also Dardanelles C. *Final Report*, 51.
[6] Dardanelles C. *Final Report*, 58.

'lies the hope of a successful issue from the War.... With the evacuation that hope dies.... Turkey can be re-equipped by Germany, and the East will be open to her. The Balkan Peninsula will be gone.... *Our interests in Egypt, our forces advancing to Baghdad, the Russians in the Caucasus, will soon feel the weight of the Turkish divisions now nailed precariously to the Gallipoli Peninsula*'.[1]

These Turkish divisions, therefore, should not be released from the Dardanelles. He wanted, he implies, 'further efforts on a great scale'.[2]

But General Monro, the new Commander-in-Chief Mediterranean, wired that

'another attempt to carry the Turkish lines would not offer any hope of success.... On purely military grounds ... I recommend the evacuation....'[3]

Lord Kitchener, after personal investigation on the spot, informed the Prime Minister that, since Germany's advance in Serbia [and Bulgaria's adherence to the Central Powers] had opened a through-road from Berlin to Constantinople, Turkey's Army was no longer immobilized by having to defend the capital. Far from being pinned down by the British, it could now—with German assistance—make their position untenable.[4] On the other hand, it was no doubt argued in London that to abandon the Straits did not entail a retreat from the Near East as these could be approached equally well (and, in French opinion, better) from Salonika.[5] Nor, in particular, would it cause the loss of Turkey to Britain whose troops in Mesopotamia were only waiting for the Indian divisions, already on the way, to accomplish the march on Baghdad.[6]

Among the powerful converts to the Salonika plan was the Conservative Leader Bonar Law, who threatened to resign from the Cabinet unless Gallipoli was abandoned. When the War Committee was reconstituted on November 11th, he was included.[7] Churchill

[1] Churchill, *1915*, pp. 486-7. Italics in the original. Also 488.
[2] Churchill, *1915*, p. 497.
[3] 31 Oct. '15. Dardanelles C. *Final Report*, 53-4.
[4] 15 and 22 Nov. '15. *ibid.* 56-7. Churchill, *1915*, p. 481. Morgenthau, 152. Radoslavov, *Bulgarien und die Weltkrise*, 195. By Nov. and Dec. '15, German and Austrian troops had arrived at the Dardanelles. The defences of the Straits had been modernized, and workmen from Krupp's were making munitions. Einstein, 274-5. Sanders, 96; also 97.
[5] See Churchill, *1915*, p. 503.
[6] Corbett, II. 126. Dardanelles C. *Final Report*, 56. Miller, 48.
[7] Law was supported by such stalwarts of the Conservative Party as A. Chamberlain, Carson, Long and, on the Liberal side, Lloyd George. Blake, 267-8, 270-2, 274.

was left out. After he had had to give up the Admiralty in May 1915, he had stayed on in a sinecure in order, he admits, 'to sustain the Dardanelles enterprise'.¹ In mid-November—'I was out of harmony with the views which were prevailing'²—came his departure from the Government. The decision to evacuate, made not without French pressure, followed as a matter of course.³ The balance sheet was grim. On the credit side was the delay caused in Bulgaria's entry into the War, and Kitchener pleaded that 300,000 enemy troops had been pinned down in the Straits. But to do this, at least 400,000 British (not counting Indian) forces were employed, of whom almost 120,000 became casualties.⁴ The Turkish losses were 218,000 of whom 66,000 were killed.⁵ The sacrifice of money and ships was heavy. 'The booty', Sanders boasts, ' . . . was extraordinary'.⁶ The evacuation was carried out on December 18th to 20th 1915 and January 8th 1916. And what remained were the 'empty trenches . . . bought at so terrible a cost, now silent as the graves with which they were surrounded'.⁷

4

THE RIFT BETWEEN RUSSIA AND HER ALLIES

The great withdrawal, however strong were the military reasons for it, had serious political consequences. Morgenthau, the U.S. Envoy, in his Memoirs, ascribed to the Ambassador Wangenheim and General von der Goltz the view that

'England . . . really had no enthusiasm for this attack, because, in the event of success, she would have had to hand Constantinople over to Russia—something which England really did not intend to do. By publishing the losses . . . England intended Russia to understand that she had made a sincere attempt to gain this great prize . . . and expected her not to insist on further sacrifices'.⁸

On August 21st 1915, the American Ambassador in Rome reported to the Secretary of State that

'while it is said that Russia was promised . . . Constantinople and the Dardanelles . . . none of the other Powers, either among the Allies or in the

---

¹ Churchill, *1915*, p. 496; also 495.
² *ibid.* p. 497; also 498.
³ Churchill, *1915*, p. 503. Dardanelles C. *Final Report*, 58. For the French attitude see Bertie, I. 272.
⁴ Dardanelles C. *Final Report*, 86.
⁵ Sanders, 104.   ⁶ *ibid.* 103.   ⁷ Churchill, *1915*, p. 507.
⁸ Morgenthau, 151-2. The quotation is Morgenthau's summary of the German view.

E

Eastern Mediterranean, have been desirous of such a disposition of this apple of discord. . . .'[1]

Even if enemy agents had not played up this theme among the Russians, it would seem unquestionable that such suspicions must have been rife in Petrograd. They were bound to be fed by a shrewd appraisal of the origins of the campaign in the Straits, the way it was waged, and the diplomatic war accompanying it. And they were upheld by revealing comments made in the West. On September 6th 1915, the New York *World*, in a dispatch from its Berlin correspondent, declared:

'. . . The English really have had luck in meeting failure in the Dardanelles. . . . England has simply gone mad from fear of Germany. This absurd "German madness" . . . has caused the best of English statesmen . . . to lose sight of England's best interests, so causing the English to do that which, if successful, would be the worst possible thing for England's future. Russia is England's great future enemy. . . . So, England's endeavour to conquer the Dardanelles, to take Constantinople and deliver her to England's greatest rival of the future, is nothing short of political madness. . ."[2]

In the second half of October, the clerical *Corriere d'Italia* suggested—obviously under Vatican inspiration—that for the diplomacy of the Triple Entente to succeed in the Balkans it was essential for Russia to renounce her Byzantine dreams.[3] Indeed, on September 15th, the former French Cabinet Minister G. Hanotaux, who was close to Catholic circles, confided to Bertie that he wished Constantinople to be a free city and the Straits internationalized, and His Majesty's Ambassador found this 'very sound'.[4] On October 12th, Izvolski reported a 'growing agitation against Russia . . . in French Parliamentary, press and even Government circles'. The *Journal des Débats* suggested that, unless her forces co-operated in the Balkans, Britain and France would have to revise their attitude in the question of Constantinople and the Straits. Some Paris papers went so far as to propose that she should sacrifice a portion of

---

[1] T. N. Page to Lansing, 21 Aug. '15. *The Lansing Papers*, I. 724.

[2] K. v. Wiegand's article of 5 Sept., quoting 'a Turkish diplomat of high rank'. The *World*, New York, 6 Sept. '15, p. 3. Cf. Bertie, 8 May '15: 'Yes, Russia will be made into a great Mediterranean Power, with the Black Sea as her harbour of refuge, of which she will have the keys to keep others out and lock herself in, coming out into the Mediterranean for any purpose that may suit her, retiring into the safety of the Black Sea whenever she may please, and having the riverains of it under her thumb. She will be quite unattackable for us . . . it is a fatuous policy. . . .' I. 162.

[3] The Russian Minister at the Vatican to Sazonov, 2 Nov. '15. Adamov, I. No. 141, pp. 337–8.

[4] Bertie, I. 236.

Bessarabia for Rumania's benefit. The fall of Delcassé on October 13th—the outcome of a furious campaign against, among other things, his 'pro-Russian' orientation,[1] was interpreted on the Neva as a forecast of atmospheric change.

The evacuation from the Dardanelles, therefore, appeared to stem less from military defeat than from the adoption of alternative policies by Britain and France. The defeat itself served largely as evidence of their lack of interest in the operation. The conviction hardened in Petrograd that, after having to sign away 'Tsargrad' and the Straits to Russia, the British and French had lost every desire to capture them for her. And as for doing it herself, it was more than ever true that, as the Quartermaster-General Danilov thought,

'the conquest of the Bosphorus will require a separate war, and he is extremely doubtful whether Russia will be capable and willing to wage such a separate war'.[2]

In September 1915, if not later, influential Russians were heard pressing—vainly—for a successful conclusion of the enterprise in the Straits.[3]

Its abandonment embarrassed the liberal pro-Western Russian bourgeoisie, heartened the reactionary Germanophils around the Romanov Court, and encouraged the tendency towards an understanding and separate peace with Germany. The basic differences dividing the three Entente Powers, far from being resolved by their temporary Alliance, actually grew sharper under the strains and stresses of the War. The Dardanelles campaign, instead of drawing them closer together, opened a rift between Russia and her Allies.

---

[1] Izvolski to Sazonov, 12 Oct. '15. Adamov, I. No. 100, pp. 295–6.
[2] Kudashev to Sazonov, 25 Jan. '15. Adamov, II. No. 14, p. 134; also Yanushkevich to Sazonov, 25 Dec. '14. *ibid.* No. 2, p. 116.
[3] T. N. Page to Lansing, 1 Sept. '15, quoting the Russian Ambassador in Rome. *The Lansing Papers*, I. 727–8.

# PART TWO

*Italy among the Great Powers*

THE EAST COAST OF THE ADRIATIC IN 1914

CHAPTER VIII

# Before 1914

1

### THE ZIG-ZAG COURSE OF ITALIAN DIPLOMACY

THE Turkish tangle was also a major factor in bringing Italy into the War.

The situation in Rome, in 1914, by contrast with that in Constantinople, appeared to favour the Central Powers. The Italian Kingdom was bound to them by an Alliance which was Bismarck's handiwork. Anticipating the great show-down with France long before it actually happened, the Iron Chancellor had sought reinforcement South of the Alps. Jealous of the Latin neighbour, resenting the loss of territories to Napoleon III, afraid of French Republicanism and the sympathy the Pope's Temporal pretensions evoked in Paris, the Savoy Dynasty was expected to side with Germany against the Third Republic. Indeed, considering the benefits of their previous collusion (the liberation of Venetia was the result of Sadowa, the entry into Rome a consequence of Sedan), the Italians hoped that by rendering fresh services to the Germans they would gain Nice, Corsica and Savoy. When Bismarck, to divert France from Europe, encouraged her to occupy Tunis in 1881, Italy—who was just beginning to cast an eye on North Africa—aligned herself with the Reich.

Their association sprang also from common action in the Austro-Prussian War of 1866. Berlin, however, having reduced the ancient rival Empire to junior partnership, strove to extend this new Alliance by reconciling Vienna with Rome. In Italy, the Habsburgs were a byword for foreign tyranny. Their former domination had left a trail of bitterness among large sections of the populace. Some 800,000 Italians, moreover, were still in the Austro-Hungarian prison-state.[1] So long as they remained in chains, the Risorgimento was incomplete. Every patriot shrank from a compact with the traditional enemy and one which would preclude redeeming the Trentino and other Irredentist parts. But the Government was preoccupied with the threat of French supremacy in the Mediterranean and its own nascent policy of overseas expansion. Italy's new colonialism perfectly suited Bismarck's book. His eager promise to support it was pushing her towards a headlong clash with France and, therefore, into the lean embrace of Austria. The struggle against

[1] Michels, *Italien von Heute*, 107. May, *The Hapsburg Monarchy*, 437.

the Habsburgs was abandoned; hundreds of thousands of Italians were left under the alien yoke; and the Triple Alliance (or Triplice) of 1882 was foisted on the bewildered and indignant people. The supreme national interest was sacrificed for Corsican rocks and African sand.

The Triplice protected Italy from the Austrians, her uncongenial friends, and their desires to recover Venetia and Lombardy. It deprived the Pope of the backing of the Central Powers for his Temporal pretensions. It strengthened the Young Kingdom against popular radicalism and, above all, France. All this, however, was paid for by a ruinous tariff war in which the French discriminated against Italian goods and securities. The colonial programme entailed such expenditure that it was impossible to balance the budget. Nor did the political outcome justify the cost. Italy's military and economic machine was so weak that external adventures could only succeed with effective aid from outside. But the conquest of Tripolitania was vetoed in 1895 by none other than the Central Powers. The expected help in obtaining compensation for Tunis[1] was not forthcoming. The defeat in Abyssinia in 1896 was all the more shattering since it was felt that Bismarck's pledge of 'benevolence' towards Rome's imperial aspirations was strictly circumscribed. Had not the Iron Chancellor's successor, on the eve of the luckless War, uttered the warning that 'the Triple Alliance is . . . not a society for the promotion of acquisitions'?[2] Had not the Germans afterwards taunted her with having been thrashed by 'a semi-barbarian opponent' and said that her services might no longer be required?[3] The anger and disappointment in the eternal city struck at the roots of the Triplice. Irredentism regained its voice. The hatred hitherto felt for Austria spread to the Reich.[4] The Italian colonialists turned for support elsewhere.

On signing the Triplice, Rome had obtained from her reluctant Allies a declaration that 'the stipulations of the Secret Treaty . . . cannot in any case . . . be considered as directed against England'.[5] It was an established tenet that Italy, with her vast and vulnerable coastlines, empty larders and hostile neighbours, required the

---

[1] At the renewal of the Triplice in 1887 Bismarck pledged German backing for Italy's colonial aspirations. This pledge was specified in regard to Africa in 1891. May, 290, 296.

[2] *Die Grosse Politik der Europäischen Kabinette*. Vol. XI, No 2766; also No. 2675, pp. 229–30. Prince Hohenlohe warned Crispi that if Italy, as the result of operations in Abyssinia, was involved in a naval clash with France and Russia, the *casus foederis* would not arise.

[3] See *Alldeutsche Blätter*, 11 Dec. 1898. Yerusalimski, *Vneshnyaya politika i diplomatiya germanskovo imperializma v kontse XIX veka*. 2nd ed., pp. 485, 542.

[4] See, for example. L. Magrioni, *Il pericolo tedesco*. 1907.

[5] Salandra, *Italy and the Great War*, 57.

goodwill of the Power controlling most of the world's resources and the seas. Britain, for her part, valued the young Kingdom as a counterweight to France. Her sympathies for the Risorgimento, therefore, broadened into an institutional inclination to favour and stimulate the ambitions germinating in Rome. This was expressed, above all, by the Mediterranean Alliance concluded with Austria (against Russia) and Italy in 1887. Since Bismarck, for his own reasons, approved of this combination, Italian diplomacy revolved, for a time, between London and Berlin. But it was soon disturbed by the antagonisms dividing the British and the German Empires. The non-renewal of the Mediterranean Entente by Whitehall in 1896, which resulted from these divergencies, weakened the Triplice at its Southern end. The Ethiopian disaster drove home the lesson that Mediterranean status and African conquest depended on the patronage of Britain. At the first rumblings of the European storm, the Roman pilots took a zig-zag course towards the West.

The first move was an announcement by the Italian Premier that he was seeking 'to improve' the Triple Alliance, and that 'friendship with England' represented 'the necessary complement' to it.[1] This followed an attempt on his part to insert into the Treaty a clause releasing Italy from the obligation to fight France if dcing so involved war with Britain. Germany put paid to that. But notice was given—and never formally rescinded—that, in certain contingencies, the Italians might repudiate the *casus foederis*. In 1898, they brought to an end the tariff war with France. In 1900, they recognized her 'rights' in Morocco, in return for French liberality towards their own schemes in Libya. In 1902, the two parties exchanged secret pledges that, if one became 'the object of direct or indirect aggression', the other would observe 'strict neutrality'[2]. This understanding, which in effect nullified Italy's part in the Triplice, was celebrated by a visit from her Sovereign to Paris, and from President Loubet to Rome in 1904. The same year brought an Italo-British accord on their respective 'spheres' in East Africa, and in 1907 Victor Emmanuel III met Edward VII. In 1906, the Italian Government deserted the Germans at Algeciras. In 1909, it doublecrossed the Austrians by welcoming the Tsar to Racconigi, where it was agreed not only to back up one another's designs on Turkey but also to defend in the Balkans the principle of nationality against the hegemony of Vienna. This process, accompanied as it was by Conventions with France on trade, labour, finance and other matters, culminated in 1912 in yet another trans-Mediterranean deal

---

[1] Schulthess, *Europäischer Geschichtskalender*. 1896, p. 241. L. Albertini, *The Origins of the War of 1914*, I. 88.
[2] Pribram, *The Secret Treaties of Austria-Hungary*, I. 227-8.

with the Quai d'Orsay. It was significant that, in 1913, the *Stampa* could question the future of the Germanic block.¹

2

GERMAN INVESTMENTS AND INFLUENCES IN ITALY

Such artfulness on the part of the Ally ruffled the feelings of Berlin. Complaints in the German press of Italian disloyalty were endorsed by diplomatic frowns from the Kaiser. As early as 1902, the Chancellor Prince Bülow had to reassure the Reichstag that, in 'a happy marriage ... the husband need not take it ill if his wife dances an extra waltz with another man'.² Nor was this, at the time, an empty metaphor. The cracks appearing in the Triplice were symptomatic of fundamental differences inside. The ruthless use to which Germany—by far the strongest member—put the coalition in pursuit of her own policies, and the sour grudge which Austria bore Italy for every advance she made, forced the latter to pursue her aims independently of, and in opposition to, her partners. But as the dominant Power, the Germans were still able to keep the fickle 'wife' in line. They could urge, not without reason, that it was the adherence to the Triplice which had earned her the French dividends. They could play off the Vatican against the Quirinal, and Vienna against Rome. And they could manipulate Italian politics by means of their economy and banking.

After the Franco-Italian breach of 1881, Germany had opened to Italy her money markets and stock exchanges. By December 31st 1913, the holdings of German concerns in Italy subject to the capital tax³ were estimated at some 28,000,000 lire. In all their various forms, German investments in the Kingdom came to 40,000,000 lire. This sum was reinforced by approximately 20,000,000 lire belonging to Austro-Hungarian companies, and by that part of the 46,000,000 lire invested by the Swiss which was tied up with money in the Reich.⁴ Moreover, although the Germans had a relatively narrow range of

[1] 28 Oct. '13. Michels, 123.
[2] Croce, *A History of Italy*, 233.
[3] This refers to foreign companies with a capital of over 1,000,000 lire. The Law of 4 July 1897; article 70.
[4] Nitti, *Il capitale straniero in Italia*, 42, 48–50. The financial and economic connections between Germany and Switzerland may be illustrated by the following facts: the Deutsche Bank took part in the establishment of the Bank für Orientalische Eisenbahnen in Zürich; the Dresdner Bank founded the stock company Speyr and Co. in Basle; the Darmstädter Bank financed the Gotthard Railway and participated in the fusion of the Jura-Berne-Lucerne Railway with the Swiss Western Railway; the Berliner Handelsgesellschaft had an important share in the founding of the Schweizerische Bankverein in Basle, the Bank für Elektrische Unternehmungen in Zürich, and the Aluminium-Industrie Aktiengesellschaft in Neuhausen. Riesser, 436, 451–2, 495, 503–4, 543.

permanent commitments and comparatively few enterprises of their own in Italy,[1] they exported industrial machinery and methods to various plants, and participated in many Italian undertakings. Commerce in many Italian ports was under the control of German firms. Numerous Italian companies, including those financed by France and Belgium, were under German management. The Italian agencies of the largest British houses were entrusted to Germans.[2] Such penetration, because it was largely indirect, was all the more effective in establishing private connections that yielded political benefits. This was perhaps most striking where banking was concerned. The Italian banks did not hold large German funds, but Germans directed, or had interests in, many of them.[3] The Deutsche Nationalbank was one of the founders of the Credito Italiano.[4] Three of Germany's four giant 'D' banks,[5] in co-operation with Swiss and Austrian banks, set up in Milan in 1894 the Banca Commerciale Italiana. This latter, with its 33 branches (by 1908), became the financial control tower of the country and a stronghold of the Wilhelmstrasse into the bargain. For, even though at the time of its foundation, the German shareholders were in a minority, they exercised the real power. Even though, on the eve of the War, their assets had declined so that, of the £5,200,000 of the Banca's capital, only £180,000 were in German accounts,[6] its German Director, Joel, until the autumn of 1914, at any rate, carried—in the Premier Salandra's words—'much weight . . . with our Foreign Office'.[7] It was said, too, that Giolitti, for many years Prime Minister of Italy, was associated with it.[8]

[1] The leading German undertakings in Italy, apart from the Hamburg-America, Norddeutscher Lloyd and 'Kosmos' shipping lines and some 21 insurance companies, were the electrical industries of Siemens-Schuckert (Genoa, Naples, Florence, Palermo) and of Siemens & Halske (Umbria, Tuscany a.s.f.), the Badische Anilin und Soda Fabrik, the Anilin Fabrikationen A/G, the 'Helios' electrical company, the Allgemeine Baumaschinenbedarfsgesellschaft, the Deutsche Telephonwerke, the Banca Bavarese, the Continental Cautchouc and Gutta-Percha Company in Milan, the Bayer Dye-Stuffs works (Rome), the gas companies in Ancona and Brescia, the 'Merkur' Mining Company (Abbadia San Salvatore), two mining companies in Florence and Iglesias, constructional engineering plants in Venice and Saronno, a mortgage company in Turin, the Società Forestale (Naples), the Hotel Bellevue and Kurhaus (San Remo), sugar factories (Venetia and Lombardy), import and export firms in Genoa, textile mills (Lombardy and Piedmont) and others. Nitti, 109, 141–3. Hallgarten, I. 260; II. 212, footnote 3.
[2] Nitti, 46–8, 82, 150.   [3] Nitti, 47.   [4] Riesser, 453.
[5] The Deutsche Bank, the Dresdner Bank and the Discontogesellschaft. Riesser, 436, 441, 445, 479, 487, 494. Other big German banks taking part were the Berliner Handelsgesellschaft and the Schaaffhausenscher Bankverein. ibid. 451, 453, 511, 525, 687.
[6] Baster, 27.
[7] Salandra, 169. See also San Giuliano to Salandra, 22 Aug. '14. *I Documenti Diplomatici Italiani*, 5 Serie, Vol. I. No. 391, p. 214.
[8] Henry, *Hitler over Russia*, 86–7. Rossi, *The Rise of Italian Fascism*, 64.

The combination of money and diplomatic pressure propped up the crumbling structure of the Triplice. Contributory factors were first Italy's weakness and isolation, and then the occasional crises in her relations with Paris. Even while they were avowing that, in their actions, 'there is nothing . . . aggressive towards France . . .',[1] or allowing the French press to acclaim the Latin 'Alliance in fact',[2] —the Cabinet in Rome consented to four renewals of the Treaty, the last as late as December 1912. In 1909, the understanding just reached with the Tsar at Racconigi was cancelled out by a new accord with Vienna.[3] In 1913, a Naval Convention was concluded, providing for joint operations, under Austro-Hungarian command, of Italian, German and Austrian squadrons against the French Mediterranean Fleet.[4] Early in 1914, King Victor entertained the Kaiser in Venice, while his Chief of Staff not only entered into 'intimate military agreements' whereby, in the event of war, large forces would be sent to the Rhine, but appeared also to contemplate dispatching Italian troops to the Danube.[5] In April 1914, the Abbazia Conference between the Austrian and Italian Foreign Ministers was applauded in an official communiqué for its decision that

> 'everything possible should be done to foster sympathetic public feeling towards the friendly relations existing between the two Governments'.

And in a telegram to the German Chancellor Bethmann, Berchtold and San Giuliano underlined 'the perfect identity of views between the three Allied Powers'.[6]

---

[1] 1902. Pribram, I. 227–8.
[2] 1904. Croce, 231.
[3] *Diplomaticheski Slovar*, II. 812-13. May, 423.
[4] Tirpitz, *Erinnerungen*, 302–3. Pribram, I. 175, 229.
[5] *Revue des Deux Mondes*, XLI. 1 Oct. 1927, p. 536. Conrad, IV. 111; also 35. The Austro-Hungarian Military Attaché in Rome to Conrad, 16 Feb. '14. Moltke to Conrad, 13 March '14 on the Italo-German military negotiations in Berlin of 10 and 11 March '14. Moltke to Conrad, 12 May '14. Conrad, III. 599, 609, 670. San Giuliano's reference to the 'verbal promise' that Italian forces would be sent to Galicia is not invalidated by Cadorna's illogical assertion that there was no trace of it. See *Documenti Diplomatici Italiani*, 5. I. No. 207, p. 121.
[6] Salandra, 24.

CHAPTER IX

# Italy's Social and Economic Structure

THIS *vagabondaccio* from one camp to another was due to the nature of Italian society and the State. The new Kingdom which had emerged from the national and democratic struggles of the 19th century was neither a strong democracy, nor even an economic or political entity. Since the movement had stopped short of radical (notably agrarian) reform, Italy was unified 'not on the basis of equality, but on that of Northern domination over the South',[1] not on a broad popular foundation, but under the exclusive leadership of the bourgeoisie and landlords.[2] The former, despite their predominance in the ruling block, refrained from tampering with the big feudal properties. It was only by degrees that the landed proprietors adopted capitalist farming methods, and even then they retained many relics from the past. Nor did the bourgeoisie, in founding new estates, break with the old forms of village production. Aristocratic and parvenue landlords combined to enforce the system of *métayage* which took part—generally half—of the tenant's harvest as rent, and was not mitigated by an allowance of stock and seed. Where capitalist agriculture developed, it uprooted, like a giant plough, the independent farmers, turning them into hired workers labouring on a paltry wage. While a handful of latifundia comprised 60-65 per cent of the agrarian area and about 50 per cent of the rural wealth,—some 7,500,000 small-holders possessed a mere 5 per cent of the productive area.[3] Archaic methods, mismanagement, and high tariff dues (for the benefit of industry and shipping) added to the causes of agricultural stagnation, so that output estimates between 1896 and 1910 rose only from 5,000,000 to 7,000,000 lire.[4] Since over half the bread-winners worked on the land,[5] the vast majority of the people were sentenced to lifelong servitude. The destitute, neglected and regimented mass of the peasants contrasted sharply with a small group of immensely rich and politically powerful families. Unorganized revolts by the village poor, farm labour strikes and hunger riots were suppressed. The General Confederation of Agriculture was formed in 1911 by the rural employers to uphold

[1] A. Gramsci, *Il Risorgimento*, 79.
[2] Gramsci, *Lettere dal carcere*.
[3] Sereni, *Agrarny vopros v Italii*, 91-2.
[4] Croce, 228.
[5] Sereni, *La questione agraria nella rinascita nazionale italiana*, 45.

their income and status, and impose their influence on the Government.[1]

This coterie, along with the old-established merchants and bankers, provided part of the money for new enterprise, and so was linked with the rising business world. While the South, under the sway of the local die-hards, remained backward, the North was rapidly industrialized, chiefly by foreign capital. Since the end of the 19th century, French, British and German investment and technique had built huge modern plants in the Milan-Genoa-Turin triangle. The relative level of industrialization was low; its centres were few; 95 per cent of all the undertakings had less than 25 operatives each.[2] But this only magnified the dimensions of colossi like Montecatini (chemicals, ordnance, rayon, metals), Fiat (motor cars, rolling stock, armaments, planes and engines), Ercole Marelli (generators, electrical equipment, motors), Breda (locomotives, ships, aircraft, railway equipment), Ansaldo (metals), Crespi (cotton), Pirelli (rubber), Conti and Volpi (electricity), Vickers Terni (ordnance), Franco Tosi, and others. Raised in the period when industry was becoming concentrated, restrictive and dependent upon the big banks, these corporations developed into high-powered engines of Monopoly Capital. They lost no time in building up a central organization. The Association of Italian Joint Stock Companies came into being as early as 1910.[3] Milan, headquarters of the industrial trusts and the Banca Commerciale Italiana, became, in many ways, the real metropolis. It was the dynamo impelling the conservative 'Liberal' politicians who governed Italy. It made men like Giolitti Presidents of the Council, and Orlando of Vickers-Terni, or Sella who represented textile interests,[4] Cabinet Ministers. It could have been Luigi Einaudi's source of inspiration when, in a book published in 1900, he gave a big business man the title of a *Principe Mercante*.[5]

Indeed, the affairs of these 'princes' were remarkable in their ramifications. The automobile industry, started by Fiat in 1899, had 66 factories in 1906, with a total output of 18,000 vehicles. The cotton spinning and weaving mills expanded from 746,000 spindles

---

[1] Brady, *Business as a System of Power*, 58, 70–1. Croce, 228, 248. Sereni, *Razvitiye kapitalizma v italyanskoi derevnye (1860–1900)*, 152, 193. Also Sereni, *Agrarny vopros v Italii*. Gramsci, *Lettere dal carcere*. Grieco, *Problemi della riforma fondiaria*. Michels, 59, 94. Kirova, 'Massovoye dvizheniye v Italii protiv imperialisticheskoi voiny'. *Voprosy Istorii*, 1953. VI. 68.
[2] Prato, *Il Piemonte e gli effetti della guerra sulla sua vita economica e sociale*, 69.
[3] It was instrumental in the birth of the Confederation of Italian Industries in 1920. Brady, 71.
[4] Michels, 147–8. Salandra, 209.
[5] *A Merchant Prince*. Michels, 148; also 59. Brady, 71–3. Kirova, *Voprosy Istorii*, 1953. VI. 68. Henry, 83, 85–6, 88–9. Nitti, *Peaceless Europe*, 14–15.

and 27,000 looms in 1876 to 2,500,000 spindles and 110,000 looms in 1906. Between 1898 and 1907, steel production was multiplying by four and that of carbonate of lime by six. In 1905, Italy had three of the six largest power plants in Europe. Her merchant tonnage took fifth place. The trade of, for example, Venice grew between 1880 and 1912 from 400,000 to 3,000,000 tons. By 1910, Italy's cotton manufactures and motor cars were able to compete in the world market. The value of her silk exports climbed from 16,746,000 lire in 1871 to 67,109,000 lire in 1900, and the amount of cotton fabric exported from 160 to 12,400 metric tons. In the same year (1900), the sales of her goods in Argentina overtook those of the U.S.A. During the period 1890-1907, her export trade rose by 118 per cent— as against Germany's 92 per cent and Britain's 55 per cent. In 1910, it exceeded 5,325,000,000 lire. A measure of her industrial expansion was in the 71,100,000 tons of coal purchased abroad between 1888 1903.[1]

The Italian economy, nevertheless, rested on cardboard foundations. The survival of vast latifundia, semi-feudal relations in the village and mass poverty, especially among the peasants, crippled the capacity of the internal market. This made industry desperate for exports and riveted inordinate attention on the world outside. Another source of weakness is revealed by the enormous scale of emigration, and yet another by the huge quantity of fuel bought beyond the borders. It was bad enough that, in 1902, only 414,000 tons of coal were produced at home, against 5,373,000 tons obtained overseas, and that by 1907 coal imports had mounted to a total of over 8,300,000 (from 4,947,180 in 1900).[2] What made matters worse was that orders for foreign steel and iron, in a short time, increased ten-fold; that those for cotton, copper, oil and wool, too, went up in a spiral, and that enormous quantities of meat and about one third of the required grain had to be imported.[3] Immense sums— almost two thousand million lire for coal alone between 1888 to 1903[4]—had to be spent in other countries. The scarcity of every vital primary material, except mercury and sulphur, forced up manufacturing costs in many branches of Italy's economy, reduced her capacity to compete, and cut down profits. It made for almost complete dependence on monopolies and markets, stock exchanges and chancelleries abroad. Italy's economic system, nurtured by that of Germany, Britain and France, therefore, made every effort to

[1] Croce, 227-8. Michels, 137-140, 142, 146. Lewin, *The German Road to the East*, 252.
[2] Michels, 137-8. Croce, 228.
[3] Nitti, *Peaceless Europe*, 14-15. Michels, 137-8. T. N. Page, *Italy and the World War*, 184. Averbukh, *Italiya v pervoi i vtoroi mirovykh voinakh*, 7.
[4] Michels, 137-8.

stand on its own feet. It is significant that, on the eve of Italy's plunge into the Great War, Nitti wrote: 'By taking advantage of the situation . . . let us make ourselves economically and industrially independent of foreigners. . . .'[1]

Although, for many years, foreign finance had a dominant position in the Kingdom, Italian capital investments in Italian undertakings grew steadily since 1881.[2] The tendency, in the last ten years before the War, to invest in Russian, Austro-Hungarian, Japanese and Turkish securities (Naples alone had about a 100,000,000 worth)[3] marked the beginnings of independent financial activity. So did, for example, the 8,000 shares held in 1911 by the Terni Steel Co. in the Harvey United Steel Co., the other partners of which were representatives of Vickers, Armstrong, Beardmore, John Brown, the [U.S.] Bethlehem Steel Co., Schneider-Creusot and Krupp.[4] From Minghetti's claim in the 'seventies concerning 'the need of youth to expand'[5] it was a straight road to R. Michels's querulous assertion in 1914 that, after England, Italy 'ought to have been the second colonial Power'.[6]

A network of arsenals, barracks and drill-halls spread over the country at the expense of housing, hospitals and schools. Road building, drainage and other amenities were neglected. In 1907, 27,000,000 lire were spent on agriculture, 85,000,000 on education, and 117,000,000 on public works, whereas naval expenditure amounted to 167,000,000 and army estimates to 376,000,000.[7] Labour protection, wholly unknown before 1902, lagged far behind that of Central and Western Europe. The diffusion of culture was so poor that, in so gifted and artistic a nation, vast multitudes had no knowledge of Verdi, or of the heroes of the Risorgimento.[8] The starvation wage in industry, land hunger and feudal servitude in the village, and chronic unemployment in both, drove (by 1910) over five million of those hard-working people to emigrate to the world's meanest slums, the worst-paid jobs, and the cruel ill-will shown towards the 'macaroni'. The suffrage, hitherto severely limited, was extended in 1911-12 from some 3,500,000 to over 8,000,000 voters, as a safety device against social strain and, since the workers had behaved themselves in the Libyan War, to 'stimulate the proletariat

[1] Nitti, *Il capitale straniero in Italia*, 60.
[2] *ibid.*, 17, 18. The Italian capital invested in limited companies rose from 846,000,000 lire in 1898 to 1,500,000,000 lire in 1903. Croce, 208.
[3] Nitti, *Il capitale straniero in Italia*, 52-3.
[4] Perris, 60. The Harvey Company was wound up in 1912.
[5] Croce, 116.
[6] R. Michels, *L'imperialismo italiano*. Milan, 1914; quoted by Lenin, *Collected Works*, XVIII. 331-32. Also Croce, 231. Bowman, 137.
[7] Croce, 225, 227.
[8] Michels, 164, quoting the results of a questionnaire in 1906.

to continue along this ... road'.[1] But, by agreement with the Vatican, the Catholics were allowed to vote and, in the elections of 1913, 'were held in reserve against them [the workers] and led in serried ranks to the ballot by their priests'.[2] Parliamentary practice was of little benefit to the majority of the population. Essentially, the régime remained what Brady called a juxtaposition of Monopoly Capital and feudal institutions, which 'tended ... to strengthen and unify the forces of anti-democratic reaction'.[3]

---

[1] Michels, *L'imperialismo italiano*, quoted by Lenin, XVIII. 334. Giolitti, *Memoirs of My Life*, p. 244: 'It appeared no longer possible to deny full political rights to those classes which were being asked to give their lives' in the Libyan War.
[2] Rossi, 5-6.
[3] Brady, 58. On p. 73, he describes the General Confederation of Agriculture as the 'most conservative and reactionary and at the same time most highly developed of agricultural employer associations anywhere in the world'.

CHAPTER X

## The Pursuit of Empire

SUCH was the background of Italy's pursuit of empire overseas. As early as 1878, Tunis, 'to which she could lay just claim'[1] was coveted in vain. In 1881, after the opening of the Suez Canal, the Gulf of Assab was acquired from the Rubattino Company. In 1882, the occupation of territory on the Red Sea was contemplated but postponed, for fear of complications with France. In 1885, the port of Massawa was taken with a view to making 'a diversion on Khartoum'.[2] A push into the interior led to war with Abyssinia in 1887 and the first major reverse. After a resumption of the invasion in 1889, a colony was founded in Somaliland, another in Eritrea, and the Negus was prevailed upon to accept an Italian protectorate. The vision of imperial conquests in Ethiopia and North Africa brought dreams of mastery in the Mediterranean, which were soon shattered in the terrible defeat of Adowa (1896). A compensation of sorts was sought in 1899, 'this time in China, in the shape of a foolish attempt to occupy the bay of San Mun ... it was checked'.[3]

More serious and pregnant with consequences were the operations in the Balkans. In Montenegro, Italian concerns developed Antivari, built the railway from there to Virbazar, acquired the tobacco monopoly, obtained the rights to navigate the river Boyana and Lake Scutari, and captured most of the import trade. In Albania, they seized vital positions in maritime shipping, the export and import market, and banking.[4] Money was invested in cement and carbide industries in Dalmatia. Italian commerce was pushing into Macedonia. In 1908, efforts were made, jointly with French, Russian and Serbian bankers, to project a new Trans-Balkan Line. In 1907-8, too, the Banca Commerciale Italiana founded the Banca Commerciale Tunisiana and, in Turkey, the Società Commerciale d'Oriente.[5] In the Red Sea provinces of Arabia, Italians owned the Aden Salt Works, installed the pier and provided plant for a condenser and ice machine at Hodeida, and the merchant firm of Caprozzi was dominant at Sana.[6] In Anatolia, in 1913, Italian bondholders of the Ottoman Public Debt extorted concessions for railways from Adalia and Makri, and increased their hold on the Heraclea coal mines east of Constantinople. In May 1914, under a Convention with Britain, whereby

[1] Croce, 108. [2] Instructions from the Minister of War. Croce, 111.
[3] Croce, 200; also 108-11, 124-5, 174-5, 193. Michels, 168.
[4] See p. 330 below. [5] Riesser, 456-7.
[6] *Arabia*. Foreign Office Handbooks, No. 61, pp. 91-2.

Italy acquired privileges and interests in the vicinity of the Province of Adalia, a step was taken towards capturing the trade in rice, tobacco, cotton, opium and fruit, and access to the lignite, chrome, manganese and timber resources, of that rich Mediterranean region.[1] Meanwhile, Tripolitania, 'conceded' by France to Italy in 1902, was subjected to economic and political penetration. This was consummated by conquest in 1911-12, when the beaten Turks had also to abandon to the aggressor the Dodecanese and coal mines in Heraclea. Liberal historians like Croce explained this War by the 'obvious facts' that Italy 'could not resign herself to the idea of the French, the English, and the Spaniards establishing themselves before her eyes along the African coast . . .' nor 'suffer Tripoli and Cyrenaica to be occupied by another Power'.[2] The Socialist Antonio Labriola, who had advocated the expedition as good business for the bourgeoisie,[3] was more forthright in divulging its predatory nature.

The profit, however, was disproportionate to the cost. The meagre soil and arid climate of distant Eritrea and Somali were poor rewards for the blood spilled, treasure wasted and humiliation endured in Abyssinia. The Chinese venture 'led to the loss of some millions and the lowering of our international reputation'.[4] The 80,000 troops, the large naval forces, the 7,000,000,000 lire involved in Libya brought in a country with inadequate harbours, little water, declining trade, hostile tribes and roadless stretches of the Sahara—in fact what Nitti called 'an immense box of sand'.[5] As markets, fields for investment, sources of raw materials and dumps for emigrants alike, these colonies dashed every hope built on them.

That Italy's Empire remained sterile and artificial was partly due to her tardiness in scrambling for spoils, when most and the best of these already had a claimant. But the main flaw lay in herself. It was with an intrinsically agrarian economy, and one that was backward, that she had reached the stage of imperialism. With feudal survivals cramping the village, a heavy industry so weak that, for example, her production of cast iron, between 1909 and 1914, was one twelfth that of France and almost one fortieth that of Germany,[6] a proletarianized peasantry and pauperized labour, her finest but least remunerative exports made up of human beings, and financial control centred in foreign capitals—Italy lacked the essential basis for expansion.

---

[1] *Internationale Beziehungen*, II. 7. II. p. 606. Bowman, 144, 434. *Anatolia*. Foreign Office Handbooks, No. 59, pp. 56-7, 67.
[2] Croce, 260.　　　　[3] See Croce, 259-60.　　　　[4] Croce, 200.
[5] Nitti, *Peaceless Europe*, 85. The export of goods from Benghazi, for example, dropped in value from over £750,000 in 1905 to less than £50,000 in 1913. Bowman, 143.
[6] Italy's annual average output of smelted steel was only a quarter that of Germany's. Averbukh, 8.

This bitter truth, at first, was stifled by what Croce defined as 'the growth of a plutocratic psychology', 'a spirit marked by violence and cynicism and lust for conquest', and 'frantic craving after power'.[1] Italian letters, for instance, sank from the heights of Manzoni or Verga, and some promising achievements early this century, to the malarial swamps of a D'Annunzio. 'Sensual, ostentatious, riotous, commercialized', he and his disciples were the extravagant expression of 'the irrational and arbitrary tendencies which prevailed'[2] among the ruling strata. In 1908, a whole generation of the more prosperous seemed to thrill with the call in his play *La Nave*: 'Man the prow and sail out into the world'.[3] But the discovery that the pirate ship had run aground, caused a change of tune. The colonial frustrations fostered the conception of Italy as 'the Great Proletarian'.[4] The philosopher Alessandro Chiapelli found that the policy of expansion pertained not only to the bourgeoisie but was 'also and primarily the vital movement of the proletariat'.[5] The 'Socialist' economist and leader of Syndicalism, Arturo Labriola, wrote during the Tripolitanian (Libyan) War that

'... we are fighting not only against the Turks ... but also against the intrigues, the threats .... the money, and the armies of plutocratic Europe, which will not tolerate that small nations should dare to make any gesture ... that would compromise its iron hegemony'.[6]

And E. Corradini, the leading Nationalist, declared:

'Just as Socialism is the means of liberating the proletariat from the bourgeoisie, so nationalism will be, for us Italians, the means of liberation from the French, the Germans, the English, the North and South Americans who, in relation to us, are the bourgeoisie'.[7]

In short, as the Syndicalists prepare for the general strike, so the 'poor' nations arm against the master races, and just as labour fights the employer for better wages and conditions, so must Italy for her national 'rights'.[8] Among a people with disfranchised millions, and torn by social struggles, this was an ingenious argument. Its aim was to achieve domestic reconciliation, internal 'unity' against the external Powers, and Socialist consent to aggression overseas.

[1] Croce, 240, 247.   [2] Croce, 263.
[3] Croce, 247; also 264. P. Togliatti in *Rinascita*, *1946*. No. X, p. 285.
[4] The poet Giovanni Pascoli in *La grande proletaria si è mossa*, p. 25.
[5] *Tribuna*, 7 Dec. 1911. See Michels, 174, footnote 2.
[6] *La Scintilla*, 11 Oct. 1911. Also Arturo Labriola, *La guerra di Tripoli e l'opinione socialista*, p. 22. See Lenin, XVIII. 332. Michels, 174, footnote 2.
[7] E. Corradini, *Il volere d'Italia*. I. c. 55, 135, 206. Michels, 174. Lenin, XVIII. 333.
[8] See Michels, 173–4.

The very circles who denied the fact of the class struggle derived from it a 'theory' of international war.

This reasoning introduced a new element into foreign policy. Pleading the country's poverty, of which they were the authors, the Italian pauper-plutocrats deduced from it a title to imperial pretensions.[1] Slipping a beggar's garb over their tinsel armour, they sought to remedy their own deficiencies by diplomatic machinations and importunity abroad. At root, Corradini's 'patriotismo della povera gente'[2] represented a kind of Lumpen-imperialism.

---

[1] See Lenin, XVIII. 334.
[2] See Corradini, *Il volere d'Italia*.

## CHAPTER XI

## Peace or War

### 1

### THE ITALIAN FRIENDS OF VIENNA AND BERLIN

THIS was the frame of mind which determined the Consulta's[1] actions in 1914. Watching the war to the death between the two giant coalitions, 'we of the Government', as the Prime Minister Salandra recollects,

> 'were agreed that such an opportunity should not be allowed to slip ... for here was the chance of reclaiming the nation's territory, of creating frontiers on land and sea no longer open to invasion, and of raising Italy, in reality, to the status of a Great Power'.[2]

These objects, it might be inferred from the recent renewal of the Triple Alliance, would be sought in conjunction with the Central Powers. But, given the overwhelming 'aversion of the country to any collaboration' with Austria,[3] there was much discussion on whether Italy's aims could be achieved by neutrality. The latter would only be worth her while if adequately paid for by her Allies. To earn the maximum reward, however, her neutrality would have to be benevolent enough to enable them to win. And this raised the question whether such a victory would be desirable for Italy.

There were not wanting in Rome those who advertised the advantages accruing from the Triplice. Under its aegis, they noted, the Kingdom had boosted its manufacture, finance and commerce, gained Balkan and African standing, and captured a place among the Great Powers. Much as the Habsburgs were loathed, Germany was respected for her strength and international credit. Her economic structure, based on producing the means of production, far from conflicting with, was actually supplemented by, the mildly industrial and mainly agrarian Italian economy. There was a keen grasp in Rome of the political motives 'which might make her Italy's Ally in the future, as she had been in the past'.[4] Faith in Germany's invinci-

---

[1] The Italian Foreign Office.
[2] Salandra, 221-2.
[3] Salandra's Report to the King, 30 Sept. '14. Salandra, 135. See Rodd, III. p. 209: '... there would have been revolutionary protests ... against collaboration with Austria'. Avarna to Bollati, 5 Oct. '14: 'There is not a single party in Italy that would agree to go to war in favour of Austria. . . .' '*Il carteggio Avarna-Bollati*. *Rivista Storica Italiana*, Anno LXI. Fascicolo II, p. 264.
[4] T. N. Page, 178.

bility pictured the 'frightening' vengeance she would wreak, if she were crossed.[1] Bollati, the Ambassador in Berlin, warned the Foreign Minister San Giuliano that, even if Austria were defeated, the Hohenzollerns could win and deprive the Italians of their part of Venetia.[2]

The friends of the Reich were in the Army, the universities, and the business and banking world based on Milan. The clients of Vienna were the aristocracy, afraid lest their declining feudal status should be further weakened by a Western triumph; the clerical minority 'of high social condition and connections . . . organized round the Vatican',[3] who feared that Italian co-operation with the Entente 'could be made use of by the Masonic and Francophil parties' for the purpose of founding a republic;[4] and the Curia itself which abhorred the War against the Danubian Empire—the last bastion of Catholic power.

These circles were terrified by the fires of unrest which swept Italy in the first half of 1914 and reached their peak in June. The flames, though beaten down by 'recourse to the military', conscription of strikers, and similar repression,[5] were smouldering unquenched and might, by a call to arms, be fanned into a blaze. A victory dearly bought could be as dangerous as a reverse, 'and provide an occasion for the Republican, Socialist and Anarchist parties to provoke a revolution against the existing order. . . .'.[6] The nonagenarian Count Greppi muttered to Prince Bülow that the War 'will change not only the map of Europe, but the political and social face of the world'.[7] The Queen Mother Margherita anticipated from it 'the possible danger of a serious spread of democracy'.[8] Salandra, too, had to admit that, in the event of a defeat, 'the extreme parties opposed to the War . . . would use it as a valid argument against the . . . Monarchy'.[9]

Another object of concern was Tsarist Russia. Whilst the dream ascribed to her of a huge Panslav realm was a myth,[10] her policy of national unification and independence, within her radius of influence, of the Balkan Slavs was a fact. It stood to reason that Petrograd, in acute conflict over this with Vienna, would not admit Italy to that sphere. Conversely, such an extension of Russian power

[1] Bollati to Avarna, 23 Dec. '14. *Carteggio*, LXI. III. 400.
[2] Bollati to San Giuliano, 31 Aug. '14. *Carteggio*, LXI. II. 254.
[3] Salandra, 311.
[4] Avarna to Bollati, 15 Dec. '14. *Carteggio*, LXI. III 390.
[5] Salandra, 101-3. Rossi, 3-4.
[6] Avarna to Bollati, 15 Dec. '14. *Carteggio*, LXI. III. 390.
[7] Dec. '14. Bülow, *Memoirs* 1904-1919 (Vol. III). 210.
[8] Dec. '14. Bülow, III. 219.
[9] Salandra's Report to the King, 30 Sept. '14. Salandra, 138.
[10] See p. 65 above.

was a threat to Rome's own plans of expansion.[1] To prevent this contingency was precisely one of the purposes of her Alliance with Austria. Therefore, as Avarna, the Ambassador to the Habsburg Court, was to urge upon the Foreign Minister Sonnino:

> 'If Russia were to defeat Austria-Hungary, even though we might obtain part of the unredeemed provinces, we should have to fight . . . with Serbia, a young Power, more to be feared than Austria-Hungary, puffed up with her territorial acquisitions and backed . . . by Russia, who would seek to push her own advantage to our detriment'.[2]

His colleague in Berlin, Bollati, expostulated against

> 'the singular incoherence of those who could find no better way of defending themselves against the perils of a Slav pressure . . . than that of helping the Slavs to establish themselves solidly in the Adriatic by encompassing the destruction of Austria'.[3]

A victory of the Entente, moreover, would involve the Mediterranean. If it brought the collapse of Turkey and the opening of the Straits to Russia, her Fleet, added to the British and French, would tilt the naval balance completely 'to our detriment', whereas the territories obtained by Italy would be 'nothing in comparison' with the likely acquisition of the three colossi.[4] This was the view, in particular, of the colonial faction whose appetite had been whetted by Libya. Italy's African venture, it was argued, disturbed the masters of Tunis and Egypt far more than the Central Powers. Already the tone of the London and Paris press had turned chilly. Already Italians and Frenchmen were struggling over the caravan routes to the markets in the heart of the Black Continent. Already the Italian population in Tunisia was treble that of the French (105,000 against 35,000), but held only 83,000 hectares of land against the latter's 700,000.[5] The two nations were competitors in foreign trade. A victorious France would restrict Italy's movements everywhere between Toulon and Suez. The Duke of Avarna was not alone in deploring that 'we have lost sight of what should be one of our aims—the command of the Mediterranean'.[6] Neither was Bollati in clamouring that, if there were kinsmen in Austria, there was also an Irredenta in Corsica, Nice and Malta.[7] And the Naples papers *Matino* and *Il Giorno*—speaking for Southern groups less concerned

---

[1] See pp. 329–31 below.
[2] Avarna to Bollati, 15 Dec. '14. *Carteggio*, LXI. III. 390.
[3] Bollati to Avarna, 24 Sept. '14. *Carteggio*, LXI. II. 259.
[4] Avarna to Bollati, 15 Dec. '14. *Carteggio*. LXI. III 390–1.
[5] Lenin, XVIII. 334.
[6] Avarna to Bollati, 5 Oct. '14. *Carteggio*, LXI. II. 262–3.
[7] Bollati to Avarna, 24 Sept. '14. *Carteggio*, LXI. II. 259.

with Balkan business than maritime commerce—were soon to assert that Italy's prime interest was the Mediterranean position, which demanded a strong attachment to Germany and Austria.[1]

2

## THE ITALIAN CHAMPIONS OF THE ENTENTE

But it was easy to answer that this position depended not on Italy's Allies, but on Britain and France. As her Fleet was inferior to theirs, they could block with impunity her imports of Cardiff coal,[2] Russian grain, Argentine meat and U.S. cotton, which sustained her economic life. They could cut off, and land forces in, Libya and destroy her ships and ports, 'with dangerous political repercussions throughout the country'.[3] Nor would Italy improve her situation by taking all these risks on behalf of the Triplice. For, as San Giuliano instructed the Ambassadors to Vienna and Berlin:

'It would be superfluous to enumerate the serious state of affairs that would follow on the defeat of the Triple Alliance; but, even if it gained a moderate victory, it would not be in a position to give us adequate compensation; while if a complete victory were achieved, and France and Russia reduced to impotence, it would have neither interest nor desire to compensate us in proportion to our sacrifices'.[3]

A victorious Germany would leave the Italians with their impossible Austrian frontier, exclude them from the Balkans, deny them any part of Turkish Anatolia and, at best, offer them some African scraps which they did not particularly want. A victorious Germany, above all, would not let the French colonies in North Africa fall to Italy. She would take them for herself and, from their shores and from Aegean and Adriatic bases, impose her control over the Mediterranean. Salandra's Memoirs show the awareness of his faction that the rulers of the Reich anticipated

'the decline and ultimate collapse of the Dual Monarchy. . . . But they had every intention of securing by hook or by crook its inheritance . . . across constellations of minor states subject to the dominant Empire. From the wedge of the Trentino . . . from Garda . . . from Trieste . . . the German spirit would have surrounded, penetrated, suffocated us more and more.

---

[1] Macchio, *Wahrheit*, 85.
[2] The machines in the North-Italian factories had been designed for the consumption of the high-class Welsh coal, and Germany's offer of Ruhr coal could not be accepted, as this would have entailed time and money consuming reconstructions. Macchio, 44-5.
[3] San Giuliano to Avarna and Bollati, 3 Aug. '14. Salandra, 79.

And . . . Italy, even if a party to their victory, would have been, at best, but the first of the vassal states of the Empire.'[1]

A triumph of the Entente, on the other hand, would yield tangible advantages. It was also more probable. 'We were not blinded by . . . German might', Salandra wrote later. Apart from the 'formidable . . . weight of Russia . . . we were guided in our . . . decisions by our certainty of England's intervention'. And 'the British Empire . . . possessed practically unlimited resources'.[2] The Premier did not share the extreme Right-wing fear of a revolution bred by war. He saw in a successful war the one means of 'trying to avoid this threat to the dynasty and to our institutions'.[3] At the time of Sarayevo, the country was in a state of emergency. The leftward swing in the elections the year before marked a widespread desire for change. The radicalism of the Socialist meetings, which had been mounting since 1912, exploded in the risings of June 1914 at Ancona, Ravenna and Forli. The 'Red Week', when, in the area of unrest, government broke down and the new Communards took over, struck the ruling classes with apocalyptic dread. The bourgeois parties—not reassured by the return of 'calm'—demanded drastic remedies. Mobilization was one, and Salandra conveyed to the King that, if it came to pass, he would keep in 'the larger towns and certain provinces . . . troops for the maintenance of law and order'.[4] Warned by Avarna that his therapy might worsen the complaint, he retorted 'that the arms we were manufacturing at present were not for use only in a war against Austria-Hungary, but also to prevent internal revolution'.[5] Moreover, it was a traditional device to distract attention from home affairs by martial adventures abroad.

One of the gains expected from joining the Entente was support against the Pope. The Temporal Power for which he was striving would have diminished the authority of the Italian Government. Since Austria's triumph was bound to strengthen the Vatican— and was therefore desired by the Catholic coteries in Rome—the middle-class elements which opposed them sought allies on the other side. Protestant Britain, lay France and Orthodox Russia could be relied on to deny the Curia a voice in the coming peace. Equally tempting was the prospective share in the Ottoman inheritance. Germany's policy of propping up the Porte[6] might lead to an Islamic rising in Libya, interference with navigation to Eritrea and Somaliland via Suez, the closure of the Dardanelles to Italy's

[1] Salandra, 55.   [2] Salandra, 57, 182.
[3] Avarna to Bollati, 15 Dec. '14. *Carteggio*, LXI. III. 390.
[4] Salandra, 138.
[5] Avarna to Bollati, 15 Dec. '14. *Carteggio*, LXI. III. 390.
[6] See pp. 31–2 above.

Black Sea trade, the loss of the Dodecanese and the Sporades Islands seized in 1911-12, and expulsion from Adalia. The desire to avoid these dangers, combined with growing preoccupations with Levantine commerce and concern for the incipient colonial zone in Anatolia, gave Italian imperialism a close interest in the question of partitioning Turkey. Grey's, Delcassé's and Sazonov's projects in this direction,[1] which could not have remained altogether secret, drew the Consulta like so many magnets. Last but not least, indeed first and foremost—the Roman hypothesis of Mediterranean domination was overridden by the far more real and vital prospect nearer home. As Salandra stated later:

> 'Italy had never been able to reconcile herself to the results of the inglorious War of '66 ... we had regained possession of fine and flourishing provinces, but ... defence on the Eastern frontier was negatived by the wedge-like Trentino. ... For us the Adriatic provided not a single naval base between Brindisi and Venice; while to others it afforded every facility ... along the shore or within the Dalmatian Archipelago. ... Italy felt herself incomplete ... each of us carried in his heart a spark of the Irredentist spirit. ...'[2]

Such aspirations, of course, raised squarely the issue of relations with Austria-Hungary.

### 3
### ITALY'S CONFLICTS WITH HER AUSTRIAN ALLY

The four extensions of the Triplice Treaty did not arrest the progressive deterioration in Rome's intercourse with Vienna. The flame of Irredentism was burning in the Peninsula and beyond the Isonzo. Though curbed by successive Italian Governments, it flared up none the less at every crisis between the two 'Allies'. A special law, passed in Rome, bestowed on everyone of Italian speech the Kingdom's citizenship. The 'Alighieri' Society saw to the maintenance of cultural—and other—ties with these elements abroad. School-books in Italy described the Tyrol and Istria as 'wrongfully possessed by Austria'. Victor Emmanuel, reviewing troops in the North, was greeted by Triestinos with banners of mourning. Marcora, the President of the Chamber, spoke in 1905 of 'our Trieste and our Trentino.' In 1909, General Bernezzo, a veteran of Custozza (1866), declaimed about 'the unredeemed territories awaiting the

---

[1] See pp. 92, 97, 101 above.
[2] Salandra, 25–6. In a telegram to Avarna, 3 Aug. '14, San Giuliano showed himself 'greatly preoccupied with the Adriatic and Balkan equilibrium in the event of Austria's victory'. *Documenti Diplomatici*, 5. I. p. 11, footnote 2.

hour of their deliverance'.[1] Save for the Catholic clergy and for business men trading with the Danube region,[2] all the Habsburg Italians desired unification. Their masters retaliated with heavy (including capital) punishments, expulsions and discrimination in favour of the Slovenes,[3] which provoked the two subject races to street fighting and bloodshed in May 1914. In reply, Austro-Hungarian consulates and flags in Naples, Rome and Venice were insulted. Demands for apology were refused. Each incident, despite half-hearted settlement, was like salt rubbed into a wound.

The infection was aggravated by constant friction from rival expansionist designs. When Italy seized Massawa in 1885, the Austrians endeavoured to put a term to the occupation. When the Italians sought colonies in Turkey, they found Austria defending Ottoman integrity. Conversely Vienna, striving to obtain from the Porte a sphere in Adalia in 1913-14, was forestalled by Rome. The Austrian quest for compensation in the form of railways and harbours around Alaya was hampered by Italian insistence that the extent of these concessions should correspond to the size of the zone which they themselves would acquire.[4]

But the Oriental imbroglio was just a side-show compared with their quarrel in the Balkans. In 1887, the Dual Monarchy was compelled by Italo-German pressure to recognize Italy's 'rights' as a Near-Eastern Power. A special Convention, which later became the notorious Article VII of the Triplice, laid down that, if Austria made Balkan gains, the Italians would be entitled to corresponding benefits. The diplomat von Szilassy's subsequent complaint that this compromise was 'without the slightest *quid pro quo*'[5] shows how deeply it rankled. King Victor's marriage to a Montenegrin princess was resented in Vienna, both for its political implications and because of the dowry of business favours she brought to her adopted land.[6] In Montenegro, Macedonia and elsewhere the trade of the two countries was in competition. The plan of Italian financiers to extend their Antivari Line to the Danube intensified Austrian objections to the Italian incursion into 'their' domain.[7] As early as 1901, the Austro-Hungarian Foreign Minister announced that Vienna would stop any Balkan changes 'prejudicial to her vital

[1] Croce, 235. May, 389–90.       [2] May, 188.
[3] In Istria. In Dalmatia, where the Slavs were in a majority, the Italians were favoured.
[4] Conrad, III. 569–70. Szilassy, 256. May, 299.
[5] Szilassy, 118.
[6] In August 1910, the King and Queen of Italy, accompanied by an Italian squadron, visited Montenegro. Steed, *The Hapsburg Monarchy*, 256. For the Italian business enterprises in Montenegro see p. 330 below.
[7] Szilassy, 118, 120, 124. Croce, 234. Salandra, 23. May, 290–1, 296, 390–2, 303, 414.

interests'.¹ In 1907, Conrad, the Chief of Staff, declared to the Emperor: 'Our future lies in the Balkans, our obstacle is Italy, it is Italy with whom accounts must be settled first'.² The Dual Monarchy's dreadnought programme (1909) and the fortification of the Trentino frontier and the coast were obviously directed against the Kingdom.³ Conversely, the annexation of Bosnia-Herzegovina in 1908—the Habsburgs' first stride in the march down the Balkans— 'gravely affected Italy'.⁴ Mass protests outside the Austrian Embassy in Rome and outbursts of Irredentism accompanied an ex-Premier's warning that a situation might arise in which 'we must war against an Allied Power.'⁵ Before long, the Italians were demanding a 'two-Power standard' for their Fleet in the Adriatic, and the Navy League publicized its claims to that sea in its mouthpiece *Mare Nostro*.⁶ During the Libyan War (1911-12) Vienna thwarted Italian operations against Turkey in the Adriatic, the Aegean, and the Dardanelles, and claimed compensation for Italy's seizure of the Dodecanese. In 1913, the Kingdom prevented Austria-Hungary from hurling herself first on Montenegro, then Serbia. In May 1914, a storm on the Danube was caused by reports that the Montenegrins had received from Rome money and arms to fortify the Lovchen which towered above the Habsburg naval base of Cattaro. The Dual Monarchy, as Salandra has recorded,

'... in Balkan politics, saw in us an obstacle to ... territorial aggrandizement, or ... its hegemony. We, on the contrary ... could not permit Austrian predominance to increase; and could not see Valona or Southern Albania pass into other hands'.⁷

## 4

### THE ALBANIAN AND THE SERBIAN COCKPITS

Albania, in fact, was the main theatre of this conflict.⁸ More than once (1897 and 1901), the two inimical Allies had induced each other

¹ May, 391.
² Conrad, IV. 171. At the time of the earthquake in Messina (1909) and the Libyan War, he urged an attack on the 'Ally whom I have always regarded as an enemy in disguise'. *ibid.* III. 598; also 755. Conrad to Berchtold, 19 Dec. '12. Pribram, *The Secret Treaties of Austria-Hungary*, II. 175. Croce, 271.
³ May, 451-2. Conrad, III. 560, 771.   ⁴ Croce, 234.
⁵ May, 416. Steed, 276.   ⁶ Szilassy, 113. May, 390.
⁷ Salandra, 35; also 234-5. Cf. Conrad to the Emperor, Memorandum, 16 Jan. '14: '... the conflicts of interest ... between Italy and the [Dual] Monarchy ... are increased by the Albanian question. ...' Conrad, III. 779; also 665. Pribram, *The Secret Treaties of Austria-Hungary*, II. 176-7. Macchio, 21, 23. Szilassy, 212. Giolitti, 330. T. N. Page, 143-4, 177, 220. Croce, 234, 271. May 423-4.
⁸ Hoyos, *Der deutsch-englische Gegensatz und sein Einfluss auf die Balkanpolitik Österreich-Ungarns*, 64. For the respective commercial and financial interests of Austria-Hungary and Italy in Albania see pp. 257, 330 below.

to agree that, if the disintegrating Turkish Empire lost that Province, it was to become an autonomous unit, in which their reciprocal interests would be reconciled on the basis of parity. The Albanian people were not consulted. When they gained liberty in the Balkan War of 1912, a Conference of Ambassadors fashioned an 'independent' State with truncated frontiers, and gave it a musical comedy Prince who neither cared about, nor knew, the life and language, the needs and desires of his subjects. And since that potentate from the German House of Wied was friendly to Vienna and, therefore, much disliked in Rome, his rule became a farce. His rugged realm—abysmally neglected and torn by clan feuds—had fertile plains, mineral wealth and untapped markets, but its chief value in the power game was strategic. The Austrians envisaged it, according to Conrad, the Chief of Staff, 'in close economic, cultural and political relations with the [Dual] Monarchy and also in alliance with her'[1]. It was to serve 'as a counterweight'[2] not only to Serbia and Montenegro (that is Russia), but also to Italy. While blocking the Slavs' exit to the Adriatic, it was to keep the Italians from the Eastern shore of that sea. These, on the other hand, saw in Albania precisely the keypoint for entering the Balkans and, at the same time, closing the Straits of Otranto. From Valona it would be as easy to push military and commercial railways in all directions, as to turn its splendid harbour—a mere sixty miles from the opposite coast—into a new Gibraltar, and the Adriatic into an Italian lake. But Austria-Hungary clung to her mountain-prey. Moreover, 'he who took Albania from us, would lock us up as in a cage. If this was done by Italy . . . we should cease to be a Great Power'.[3] As Macchio, one of the Heads of the Vienna Foreign Office, emphasized, 'the Freedom of the Adriatic was vital for us as our only maritime access to world trade'.[4] The two Allies, therefore, through their respective agents, business men, naval and military missions and especially their diplomatic Envoys 'disputed every inch of ground in acquiring local influence'.[5]

Such was the setting in which Wilhelm von Wied—braced by an international loan of £3,000,000 and a visit to the Danube—arrived in March 1914 to claim his throne. His coming was a success for the Austrians who, as the formal guardians of the local minority of 200,000 Catholics, sought to reinforce his authority by combatants in cassocks.[6] Rome, meanwhile, had chosen her warriors among the Moslems who could not square a Christian Prince with Allah, and

[1] Conrad, III. 676; also 677, 587.
[2] Conrad, III. 585.
[3] Szilassy, 121.
[4] Macchio, 23.
[5] Salandra, 34. Also Conrad, III. 589, 681.
[6] See May, 188, 391, 473.

whose foremost leader, Essad, as Salandra admits, 'declared himself Italy's friend'.¹ The Pasha, though War Minister in the Government, was conducting an agitation against Wied.² This was taken as proof that 'the new Sovereign was in immediate need of protection'. The only question was: 'Which of the two Ministers—the Austrian or the Italian—was to direct the wavering policy of the poor Prince?'³ In April 1914, at Abbazia, the Foreign Ministers Berchtold and San Giuliano, with mutual vows of fidelity, appeared to have come to terms over Albania. In May, however, Essad rose up in revolt—or at least was said to have done so,⁴ and was arrested by orders of Wied. The Italians at once ascribed this to the influence of Francis Joseph's Envoy. The Prince, unnerved by the rebellion, took refuge on an Italian yacht. The Austrians promptly accused Victor Emmanuel's Minister of trying to engineer his abdication. The putsch was suppressed. The royal fugitive returned, Essad found shelter in Italy, and in the Italian Chamber San Giuliano declared that his exchanges with Berchtold had been

'permeated by that mutual trust and complete loyalty which have always constituted, constitute and will constitute, the firm foundation of our cordial and close relations'.⁵

But *Il Matino*⁶ and kindred papers were increasing their barrage on Vienna's Albanian policy. The Italian Minister in Durazzo continued to rock the shaky throne, while every request from the Central Powers for his recall met with refusal from Rome. On June 26th, the Austro-Hungarian Ambassador Merey read to San Giuliano a telegram from Berchtold, charging him, in effect, with disloyalty in planning to set up a kind of Adriatic Morocco. The démarche ended with the threat 'of a bold step which would cause the most painful surprise in Italy'.⁷ And on July 8th, the Ambassador Bollati reported to his Chief that

'appearances would lead one to assume an absolute want of good faith on both sides.... If it were only the question of Albania! But there are so many other grounds for disagreement... the Lovchen question; possible strife between Austria and Serbia; the alarming problem of a union between Serbia and Montenegro... to say nothing of... the possession

---

[1] Salandra, 34. Also T. N. Page, 173.
[2] See Conrad's information, 17 Jan. '14, and the Austro-Hungarian Military Attaché in Rome to Conrad, 25 Feb. '14. Conrad, III. 539, 592.
[3] Salandra, 33–4. Also May, 473.
[4] Conrad, III. 692, 683.
[5] 26 May '14. Aldrovandi Marescotti, *Guerre diplomatique*, 23.
[6] 21 and 22 May '14. Conrad, III. 690.
[7] L. Albertini, II. 218. Aldrovandi Marescotti, 21–2.

by Austria of provinces racially and linguistically Italian.... In fact, there is, perhaps, not a single question where the interests of Italy coincide with those of Austria....'[1]

Salandra went further by speaking, as he did later, of 'the inevitable clash of interests and aspirations' between the two nominal Allies.[2] 'The blunt, inescapable fact was that Habsburg and Italian interests and ambitions ... were irreconcilable'.[3]

Therefore, when Austria-Hungary, after Sarayevo, turned on Belgrade and so resumed her march on the Balkans,[4] Italy finally decided to put her own Balkan policy before her Mediterranean plans.[5] Since, as San Giuliano admonished Bülow, she had

'always watched with suspicion Austria's territorial ambitions in the Balkans and the Adriatic ... she considers the real independence and territorial integrity of Serbia as a bulwark and an element of balance which her interests require....'[6]

Hence, in Salandra's words,

'the reduction of Serbia ... to a state of impotence and vassalage signified Austria's hegemony ... throughout the Balkan Peninsula, while for us it meant the loss of every possibility of expansion, and the loss of the Adriatic both commercially and strategically.'[7]

It was something, the Foreign Minister San Giuliano told the German Envoy, 'which Italy could not tolerate'.[8] Even so staunch a supporter of the Triplice as Avarna had to concede that an Austrian victory

'must always be an irreparable disaster for Italy and fatal to her very existence'.[9]

In the circumstances, for Italy to join the Central Powers would have meant fighting for causes ruinous to her own. The programme of Italian imperialism could, on the contrary, only be accomplished

[1] Salandra, 38. *Carteggio*, LXI. II. 250.
[2] Salandra, 25.
[3] May, 392. The same view is expressed by Pribram, II. 176.
[4] See pp. 165–6 below.
[5] See Corradini, 'Il nostro dovere'. *L'Idea Nazionale*, 13 Aug. '14. IV. 33. Michels, 186.
[6] 31 Aug. '14. Macchio, 31.
[7] Salandra, 54–5.
[8] 14 July '14. Flotow to Jagow, 15 July '14. *Die Deutschen Dokumente zum Kriegsausbruch*, I. No. 51, p. 77.
[9] Avarna to Bollati, 22 Oct. '14. *Carteggio*, LXI. II. 267. Also L. Albertini, II. 218, 237, 314.

by a collision with Austria-Hungary. With the latter immersed in war, Russia apparently diverted from the Balkans, Albania open, Rumania friendly, the Serbs in need of allies against the Habsburgs, the West grateful for an access of strength—here was the chance to oust the age-long rival from South-Eastern Europe. Rather than help the Austrians to an aggrandizement that would be her undoing, Italy's very interests required their defeat.

CHAPTER XII

## The Crisis in the Triple Alliance

1

A *FAIT ACCOMPLI* AND AN INTRIGUE

THIS goes far to explain Vienna's attitude to Rome during the Sarayevo crisis. Under Article VII of the Triplice, the two Allies undertook

> 'to use their influence to prevent any territorial change prejudicial to the interests of either of the contracting Powers. They agree to interchange all information throwing light on their own dispositions. . . . If, however, events should occur rendering the maintenance of the *status quo* impossible in the region of the Balkans, or the coasts and Ottoman islands of the Adriatic and the Aegean Sea . . . and Austria-Hungary or Italy should be compelled to alter it by a temporary or permanent occupation on their part, such occupation shall not take place without previous agreement between the two Powers. . . .'[1]

Italy, therefore, was entitled to be consulted beforehand on a step so momentous as the ultimatum to Belgrade. But she had, as the Austrians argued, 'quite plainly blossomed forth as our rival in the whole Balkan area'.[2] While no one 'ever counted on this Ally as a fellow combatant',[3] everyone remembered how San Giuliano the year before, on being notified of Habsburg intentions, had staved off their attack on Serbia.[4] Now, in July 1914, the Foreign Minister Berchtold was sure that this would happen again. He was afraid 'that the slightest hint to Italy would at once be passed on to Russia and used for counter-moves. . . .'[5] And he dreaded, above all, lest the Consulta should exploit the additional clause in Article VII, whereby the stipulated 'previous agreement' on expansion in the Balkans was to be

> 'based on the principle of reciprocal compensation for every advantage, territorial or otherwise, which either of them should obtain. . . .'[1]

The Austro-Hungarian Ambassador in Rome, Merey, sent several warnings that Italy would invoke this right to compensation in support of a policy of sweeping blackmail.[6] According to Berchtold's

---
[1] Salandra, 53. Pribram, I. 249, 251.  [2] Burián, 21.
[3] Burián, 17. Hoyos, 64.  [4] Giolitti, 379–80.
[5] Tschirsky to Jagow, 20 July '14. *Deutsche Dokumente*, I. No. 94, p. 120.
[6] Macchio, 24. Merey to Berchtold, 16 July '14. *Österreich-Ungarns Aussenpolitik*, VIII, p. 463.

adviser Hoyos, it was expected that she would ask for the Trentino, and as this had to be refused, 'the outcome would have been a conflict driving Italy to join our enemies much earlier'.[1] To counter this danger and avoid, at the same time, having to pay ransom for Austria's aggrandizement, Berchtold decided 'to confront the Italian Government with a *fait accompli*'.[2]

Following the old Viennese maxim that the Italians were 'dominated by the most Italian of all emotions—fear',[3] it was believed in Vienna that the awkward Ally could be bullied and stunned into acquiescence. The Austro-Hungarian Military Attaché reported from Rome that 'Italy is financially and militarily feeble, the revolutionary excesses in Ancona, Ravenna and so forth have revealed fresh elements of weakness'.[4] Berchtold assumed that 'Italy, as a result of the Libyan campaign, is in no fighting mood'.[5] Nor would she have time enough to build up sufficient strength, since, in those days, 'nobody here thought of a long war'.[6] A quick Austrian victory—all the more probable with German help—would, it was believed, soon silence the '*lazzaroni*'. Meanwhile, the Dual Monarchy, as Berchtold declared to the German Ambassador Tschirsky, 'asks neither for co-operation nor for support, but merely for [Italy's] abstention from hostile acts against her Ally'.[7] And if, in consequence of Vienna's policy, their relations 'for years to come ... will be extremely bad',—*tant pis* for Rome. 'One does not [in Merey's offhand phrase] make an omelette without breaking eggs'.[8]

But such flippancy was deprecated in Berlin. The Germans relied no more on active Italian belligerency than the Austrians. What they did expect after their old partnership was an unequivocal and benevolent neutrality.[9] They counted, in their operational plans, on General Pollio's pledges[10] that he would enable the Habsburgs to denude the Trentino frontier, and immobilize several French army corps in the Alps.[11] As the Chancellor Bethmann informed Tschirsky, 'the [German] Chief of Staff regards it as urgently necessary for Italy to be kept firmly with the Triplice. An understanding

[1] Hoyos, 65–6. L. Albertini, II. 220–1.
[2] The German Embassy Councillor Stolberg to Jagow, 18 July '14. *Deutsche Dokumente*, I. No. 87, p. 113. Hoyos, 65.
[3] Conrad, II. 225. L. Albertini, II. 237.
[4] The Military Attaché to Conrad, 2 July '14. Conrad, IV. 25.
[5] Berchtold to Tschirsky, 20 July '14. *Österreich-Ungarns Aussenpolitik*, VIII, pp. 521–2.
[6] Berchtold's letter to Albertini, 23 Nov. 1933. Albertini, II. 221. Also Macchio, 39.
[7] Tschirsky to Bethmann, 20 July '14. *Deutsche Dokumente*, I. No. 94, p. 119.
[8] French in the original. Merey to Berchtold, 16 July '14. *Österreich-Ungarns Aussenpolitik*, VIII, p. 454.
[9] Helfferich, II. 64.
[10] Conrad, III. 598.
[11] Helfferich, II. 65.

between Vienna and Rome is, therefore, required'.[1] Since Berchtold's lips were sealed and San Giuliano, for reasons soon to become clear, showed no curiosity, the Foreign Minister Jagow instructed the German Ambassador in Italy, Flotow, to confide to the Consulta 'that it would hardly be possible for Austria-Hungary to take such [Serbian] provocations quietly'.[2] The Envoy, after a talk with San Giuliano, reported back 'that Italy would not be able to support the Austrian claims . . . the Italian Government could never take a stand against the principle of nationality. He is apparently preparing us for his not remaining by the side of Austria. . . .'[3] Jagow therefore—apart from ordering Flotow to 'do what you can to influence the Italian press'[4] —directed the Ambassador Tschirsky in Vienna 'to make the Italian attitude the subject of a detailed confidential conversation with Count Berchtold, and possibly to touch on the question of compensation'.[5]

The Count, however, knew from Merey that 'the German Ambassador has been . . . confiding to the Italian Foreign Minister our intentions concerning Serbia',[6] and was ready to meet the attack. So, in his discussions with the Germans, he 'displayed great optimism and thought that Italy could surely not be so perfidious an Ally as to turn against the [Dual] Monarchy'.[7] He maintained that, in Vienna, 'it had been decided to refrain from any permanent acquisition of foreign territory. Thus there would be no valid reason for Italy to claim compensation. . . .'[8] He rejected the German suggestion to buy her off with Valona. And he made a point of rubbing in how 'very regrettable it was that Italy, judging by all appearances, had already got wind of our intended proceedings against Serbia. . . . Herr von Tschirsky's assertions that no information on the subject had come from German quarters I countered with the remark that Flotow had probably told some tales on his own. Such confidences towards Italy . . . seemed to me highly questionable, and I had grounds for assuming that she was bent on countering our action. That is why I could not bring myself as yet to an exchange of views . . . with the Italian Government'.[9]

The mainspring of the assurance evinced by Berchtold was an

[1] *Deutsche Dokumente*, I. No. 202, p. 205.
[2] Jagow to Flotow, 11 July '14. *Deutsche Dokumente*, I. No. 33, p. 55.
[3] Flotow to the Wilhelmstrasse, 14 July '14. *Deutsche Dokumente*, I. No. 42, p. 67.
[4] 14 July '14. *Deutsche Dokumente*, I. No. 44, p. 69.
[5] Jagow to Tschirsky, 15 July '14. *Deutsche Dokumente*, I. No. 46, p. 72.
[6] Merey to Berchtold, 18 July '14. *Diplomatische Aktenstücke*, I, p. 60.
[7] The German Embassy Councillor to Jagow, 18 July '14. *Deutsche Dokumente*, I. No. 87, p. 114.
[8] Tschirsky to Bethmann, 20 July '14. *Deutsche Dokumente*, I. No. 94, p. 119.
[9] Berchtold's Account, 20 July '14. *Österreich-Ungarns Aussenpolitik*, VIII, pp. 521–2.

Austrian understanding with none other than—the Reich. The German rulers, in prodding the Habsburgs into starting the War, ought to have made their pledge of 'Nibelungen loyalty' conditional on Vienna's coming to terms with Rome. But it was clearly impossible for them to put restrictions in advance on the principal Ally. After the question of German backing for the attack on Serbia had been raised in Berlin by Count Hoyos, the Austro-Hungarian Ambassador Szögyény, as early as July 6th 1914, was able to inform his Chief that the Chancellor Bethmann 'is in complete agreement with our not informing either Italy or Rumania in advance of any action we may take against Serbia'.[1] On the 11th, Jagow telegraphed Flotow: 'We have left it to the Austro-Hungarian Government to take the steps they deem suitable, and promised them . . . our support. . . .'[2] And two days after directing Tschirsky to goad the Dual Monarchy into negotiations with Italy, the German Foreign Minister had to caution him to be careful 'not to give the impression that we mean . . . to hinder Austria's actions or lay down certain limits or objectives for her'.[3]

Hence, Berchtold could continue to play blind-man's-buff with San Giuliano. On July 20th, he instructed the Ambassador Szögyény 'to defend our viewpoint with sufficient emphasis in the Wilhelmstrasse'.[4] On the 21st, he requested Merey, the Envoy in Rome—in case the Italians should raise, and prove obdurate over, Article VII—'to evade a further discussion of this subject'.[5] In fact, the Ambassador, at the Consulta, 'strictly avoided the Serbian affair'.[6] The only relevant message from Vienna to Rome was an arrogant telegram, dispatched immediately after Tschirsky's offensive: '. . . we are convinced that we can count on Italy's loyalty as an Ally in the clarification of our relations with Serbia . . . it is to Italy's interest to come out openly on our side'.[7] And it was only 'as a sop to Italy, so that the Note does not first become known there through the press'[8]—that she was apprised of the ultimatum, though not until almost the hour when it was presented. A Memorandum, delivered at the Consulta by a junior Austrian diplomatist, stated laconically that the Austro-Hungarian Minister in Belgrade

[1] *Osterreich-Ungarns Aussenpolitik*, VIII, p. 320. Also Conrad, IV. 80, 44. L. Albertini, II. 234–5.
[2] *Deutsche Dokumente*, I. No. 33, p. 55.
[3] Jagow to Tschirsky, 17 July '14. *Deutsche Dokumente*. I. No. 61, p. 88.
[4] *Österreich-Ungarns Aussenpolitik*, VIII, p. 540.
[5] *Diplomatische Aktenstücke*, I, p. 113.
[6] Tschirsky to Bethmann, 20 July '14. *Deutsche Dokumente*, I. No. 94, pp. 119–20.
[7] Berchtold to Merey, 20 July '14. *Österreich-Ungarns Aussenpolitik*, VIII, p. 539.
[8] Tschirsky to Bethmann, 20 July '14. *Deutsche Dokumente*, I. No. 94, p. 120.

'on Thursday 23rd July in the afternoon . . . will hand to the Serbian Government a Note containing a certain number of requests. . . .'[1]

The text of the démarche was not transmitted to Salandra and San Giuliano until the following day.[2] According to Salandra, 'all the colour left our faces. We had a foreboding of impending catastrophe'.[3]

2

'DO YOU THINK IT USEFUL TO KNOW THE TRUTH?'

It was a case of diplomatic pallor—as this moment had long been expected and prepared for. As far back as January 1914, Aldrovandi Marescotti, the Chargé d'Affaires in Vienna, had signalled that the clouds of war were gathering on the horizon.[4] On March 1st, the Austrian Emperor had said to Avarna that 'the general situation in Europe at present is such that . . . it is capable of eventually leading to a conflict'.[5] In April, at Abbazia, San Giuliano learned from Berchtold 'that, in the near future, there may be fresh territorial changes in the Balkan Peninsula. . . .'[6] On the 28th, Marescotti sent this warning: 'It would appear probable that Austria-Hungary, having suffered disappointments and setbacks in connection with the recent Balkan crisis, desires revenge'.[7] On May 17th, Flotow mentioned to the Rumanian Minister in Rome, who was close to the Consulta, the possibility of an open clash between the Dual Monarchy and Serbia.[8] Early in June, the Italian Envoy wired from Bucharest that, according to his Austrian colleague, Czernin, the Habsburgs 'would not be disinclined . . . if the opportunity arose', to resort to arms.[9] After the Sarayevo crime, therefore, the Consulta could be in no doubt that the Austro-Hungarian Empire would seize the occasion to deal summarily with Belgrade.[10]

The Italian Ambassador Avarna, as Marescotti recollects, 'was a meticulous informant'. He was in the habit of visiting the Austrian Foreign Office every day and, at times, even twice.[11] Through him, Italy 'could have . . . compelled her Ally, in conformity with the . . . Triplice Alliance, to keep her informed about Austria's inten-

---

[1] Salandra, *La neutralità italiana*, 74. L. Albertini, II. 312.
[2] L. Albertini, II. 313. Aldrovandi Marescotti, 2.
[3] Salandra, *Italy and the Great War*, 49.
[4] Aldrovandi Marescotti, 7.   [5] *ibid.*
[6] San Giuliano to the Italian Embassy in Vienna, 30 April '14. Aldrovandi Marescotti, 10.
[7] Aldrovandi Marescotti to San Giuliano, 28 April '14. *ibid.* 8.
[8] *Revue des Deux Mondes*, XLI. 1 Oct. 1927, p. 537.
[9] Aldrovandi Marescotti, 10.
[10] See L. Albertini, II. 241.   [11] Aldrovandi Marescotti, 2.

## THE CRISIS IN THE TRIPLE ALLIANCE 167

tions in these very grave circumstances'.[1] But as it was also his custom 'never to exceed the precise instructions he had received', he asked no questions about what was afoot.[2] No less peculiar was Bollati's conduct in Berlin. As early as March, he quoted Jagow as having stated that, while Germany would do her best to avoid a war, she would always be ready to meet it, and 'better to-day than tomorrow'.[3] In another telegram, the Ambassador reported that 'the balance remains unstable: a minor occurrence would be enough to disturb it'.[4] After it had, in fact, been disturbed by Sarayevo—'to all the questions with which I daily plied Jagow about the plans of Austria-Hungary, he answered always that he had no information; that he knew Austria-Hungary meant to make stiff demands . . . but that . . . in any case no serious complications were likely to ensue'.[5] Bollati inquired of Jagow whether, in his opinion, he could safely go for a cure of some weeks. The Foreign Minister, obviously unable to betray German-Austrian secrets, was trapped into an affirmative reply—at the height of the crisis, and after all his attempts to open Italian eyes. On July 20th, Bollati actually left Berlin.[6] He must have been of one mind with Avarna who, early that summer, had said to Marescotti: 'Do you think it useful to know the truth?'[7]

The truth, in this instance, would certainly have been damaging to the Consulta's plans. Official knowledge of Vienna's intentions would either have forced Italy into open opposition as in 1913, with the risk of having to take responsibility for a break, or it would have committed her to supporting the Dual Monarchy—a course so contrary to her interests that no compensation, even if any were forthcoming, could make up for it. In 1913, San Giuliano had restrained Austria-Hungary because Germany, too, was then doing so, which meant that there would be no general conflagration. In 1914, the Reich—far from holding back the Habsburgs—was actually encouraging them to strike.[8] A great war was imminent, and Italy strove for freedom of action for 'the diplomatic gamble now beginning'.[9] While the rulers of the Dual Monarchy were trying to

---
[1] Aldrovandi Marescotti, 3.
[2] ibid. 2. 'The Austrian documents show no trace of conversations between Avarna and Berchtold in the period from 18 July to 24 July'. L. Albertini, II. 240.
[3] A telegram re-transmitted from Rome to Avarna, 6 March '14. Aldrovandi Marescotti, 13; 18, footnote 1.
[4] Transmitted from Rome to Avarna, 19 March '14. Aldrovandi Marescotti, 18, footnote 1.
[5] Bollati's telegram to Rome, 5 Aug. '14. Aldrovandi Marescotti (Ital. edit.), 23–4.
[6] Aldrovandi Marescotti, *Guerre diplomatique*, 3–4.
[7] ibid. 3.
[8] See Szögyény's telegram to Berchtold, 6 July '14. *Österreich-Ungarns Aussenpolitik*, VIII, pp. 319–20.
[9] L. Albertini, II. 248.

dodge the compensation article of the Alliance, those of Italy were seeking a smooth way of escaping from the Triplice altogether.

This appears to be borne out by the Italian reaction to the Ambassador Flotow's indiscretions. These indicate that the Wilhelmstrasse saw through the Consulta's game and was trying to spoil it. But on July 16th, Flotow had to write to Berlin that in the 'emphatic' view of Rome, 'Austria has no right to make claims on Belgrade. . . . The murder of the Heir to the Throne . . . was not committed by a Serbian subject. . . . If Austria intended to suppress Serbian national aspirations . . . no Italian Government could follow her along this road; the whole tradition of the idea of nationality and the liberal principle would force Italy to keep aloof. . . .'[1] On the 20th, San Giuliano requested the Ambassador Bollati to inform the German Foreign Minister Jagow that 'Italy is not obliged to join against Serbia, if the War is provoked by Austria's aggressive action and condemned by the whole civilized world'.[2] Neither San Giuliano nor Salandra could have had any illusions about the efficacy of appeals to the 'civilized world' while they were copying its practices. To invoke 'the idea of nationality' and the 'liberal principle', after trampling underfoot the one in Libya (as Berchtold was not slow to point out[3]), and the other during 'Red Week,' was to tread on slippery ground. But the Consulta needed a legal case permitting Italy to claim that she 'had been deliberately kept in ignorance of an action prepared by her Allies. . . .'[4]—that is that Austria had violated the Triplice. As Berchtold, by his silence, was doing precisely this, San Giuliano had only to give him sufficient rope.

'What an ignominious standpoint to take at so grave and critical a moment', the Liberal historian L. Albertini lamented later. 'This whole policy . . . revealed a total absence of all sense of horror at the tragedy that was about to be enacted and did not raise a finger to avert it'.[5] But, quite apart from the question of whether Italy's strength and international prestige were adequate for such a move, the Consulta found it expedient to play the deaf-mute in Vienna and Berlin. On July 15th, the German Ambassador in Constantinople told the Italian Envoy: 'Nous sommes à la guerre'.[6] Whether or not the latter reported this at once to the Consulta[7]—San Giuliano, on the 16th, telegraphed to Avarna and Bollati that, from his conversation with

[1] Flotow to Bethmann, 16 July '14. *Deutsche Dokumente*, I. No. 64, pp. 91–2.
[2] Salandra, 48–9.   [3] *Deutsche Dokumente*, I. No. 94, p. 119.
[4] Aldrovandi Marescotti, 4.   [5] L. Albertini, II. 252.
[6] *ibid.* II. 225.
[7] Though there is no record in the Archives, Garroni claimed to have done so on July 16th, and it is hardly conceivable that he should have suppressed such vital information. See L. Albertini, II. 225. Also *Revue des Deux Mondes*. XLI. 539.

Flotow, he 'had drawn the conclusion that the Austro-Serbian conflict would be inevitable. . . .'¹ On July 18th, he was warned by Avarna that the Austro-Serbian situation may 'render a war imminent'.² Yet, as Flotow cabled to Jagow, although San Giuliano 'regards the situation as serious . . . he . . . avoids . . . detailed discussions with me on this question'.³ A telegram from Merey to Berchtold of July 21st shows the Italian Foreign Minister 'as very preoccupied with our pending démarche in Belgrade', but still refraining from asking for advance information (under Article VII) about its terms.⁴ Salandra, in his Memoirs, tries to excuse such inaction by saying that 'the Italian Government, concentrated on internal unrest, had its attention diverted from the much weightier tasks Fate had in store for it'. Despite all the danger warnings he and the Foreign Minister had received, he invites posterity to believe that they 'relied on the pacific spirit of the [Austrian] Emperor', and 'that the War was at hand no Chancery in those early days . . . was prescient enough to perceive'.⁵

3

THE DISPUTE OVER ARTICLE VII

But no sooner had Vienna's ultimatum become public, than Rome's diplomatic time bomb went off. The first reaction on the Tiber 'was a general relief that Italy, not having been consulted,

¹ Salandra, *La neutralità italiana*, 119. Albertini, II. 225.
² Salandra, *Italy and the Great War*, 47.
³ Flotow to Jagow, 19 July '14. *Deutsche Dokumente*, I. No. 78, p. 104.
⁴ *Diplomatische Aktenstücke*, I, pp. 114–16. L. Albertini, mentioning the 'ambiguous attitude of San Giuliano' (II. 243), remarks that, in the July crisis, 'he remained inactive, nor were the Italian Ambassadors less inactive than he'. (II. 240). 'Not a single diplomatic document of the Central Powers shows San Giuliano speaking before the ultimatum [of 1914] as he had spoken in 1913'. (II. 243). Nor could it have been by accident that San Giuliano's support for the various peace moves was tardy and conditional, and that his own proposal to London 'that discussions should begin at once' (Gooch and Temperley, XI. 231) was not made until July 28th, that is about the time when Sir R. Rodd reported to Grey that the Italian Foreign Minister 'now thinks moment is past for any further discussion'. (Gooch and Temperley, XI. 268). L. Albertini writes that 'to avail himself of Italian rights and Austrian obligations' should have been San Giuliano's 'sole aim if he did not mean to have war'. (II. 319). But it would seem that, in Rome, the abhorrence of war was about as strong—or as weak—as in the other capitals. Having encouraged its partners, by repeated treaty renewals and strategic agreements, to commit aggression, the Consulta was evidently preparing to exploit the situation for its own ends. In judging San Giuliano's motives and actions in July 1914, L. Albertini (II. 241-253) seems to do less than justice to his astuteness in serving the needs of Italian imperialism. Cf. Croce, 272: 'Italy . . . found it convenient, for the sake of having her hands free, not to pay any attention to the information which must have reached her'. Also Pryce, 'Italy and the Outbreak of the First World War'. *Cambridge Historical Journal*, 1954. XI. No. 2, p. 224.
⁵ Salandra, 46–7; also 45.

F*

was left free in her action'.¹ The next was to telegraph at once to Avarna and Bollati, for use in the Central capitals,

> 'that Austria had no right, according to ... the Triple Alliance, to undertake a démarche such as she has made at Belgrade without previous agreement with her Allies ... Austria has plainly shown that she means to provoke a war ... in view of this behaviour on the part of Austria and of the defensive and conservative nature of ... the Triple Alliance, Italy is under no obligation to go to the help of Austria if ... she finds herself at war with Russia....'²

This was a plain intimation that Rome would not recognize the *casus foederis*. Since the Dual Monarchy must have known that her move would bring in Russia and hence Germany and France, and since unconsulted Italy could not be expected to plunge into a major war, this point was sound. 'However', San Giuliano went on to say,

> 'the fact that we are under no obligation does not exclude the possibility that it may suit us to take part in the eventual War, if this were to conform to our vital interests ... any such participation by us would in no case be possible if the Government could not give the country beforehand the certitude of an advantage commensurate with the risks ... it is not possible for the Royal Government to lay down its line of conduct ... without first knowing whether our Allies concur in our interpretation of Article VII....'³

In Salandra's interpretation of Article VII, whether or not Italy joined her Ally, 'any occupation of Serbian territory ... or any other advantage Austria's position in the Balkans might derive from the War would give us the right to compensation....'⁴ San Giuliano, therefore, through Avarna, warned the Habsburgs that,

> 'if Austria-Hungary should proceed to territorial occupation ... without our preliminary consent, she would violate Article VII ... and that, in consequence, we should make every reservation concerning our liberty of action and the safeguarding of our rights and interests'.⁵

As such consent was not to be had for nothing, this was the formal bid for the stipulated *quid pro quo*. At one and the same time Italy contrived to repudiate her commitments under the Treaty and to claim the benefits arising from it.⁶

---

¹ T. N. Page, 106.
² San Giuliano to Avarna and Bollati, 24 July '14. Salandra, *La neutralità italiana*, 76–8. Salandra, *Italy and the Great War*, 50–1.
³ *ibid.* Cf. Avarna to San Giuliano, 2 Aug. '14. *Documenti Diplomatici*, 5. I. No. 11, pp. 7–8.
⁴ Salandra, 54.
⁵ 24 July '14. Aldrovandi Marescotti, 15. Burián, 25.
⁶ See Salandra, 63. Helfferich, II. 65.

These diplomatic gymnastics were met with nonchalance on the Danube. On July 20th, Berchtold had mentioned to his Envoys in Rome and Berlin 'the possibility . . . that the Royal Italian Government, in the event of war between ourselves and Serbia, will attempt to interpret Article VII . . . in a sense acceptable to itself and raise the question of compensation'. 'Your Excellency [Merey was told] may . . . as a personal opinion express your conviction that . . . the Vienna Cabinet does not contemplate a campaign of conquest'.[1] The Ambassador accordingly assured San Giuliano 'that we did not aim at annexation'. But 'I answered in the negative his question whether he could use this in the press, and I even stressed the fact that this confidential communication was in the nature of a sincere intention . . . but not of a pledge'.[2] On July 21st, Merey was even instructed, in case the Italians were obdurate, 'to avoid further discussion of this subject'.[3] Nor were the Austrians discomfited when they learned Rome's reaction to the ultimatum. Berchtold remarked drily that 'Italy probably wished to make a deal'.[4] Meanwhile, as the Dual Monarchy mobilized against Serbia on July 25th, a reserve force was provided to cope, if it came to that, with the Italians.[5]

By now, however, Flotow's summary of Salandra's and San Giuliano's response to the ultimatum had reached Berlin. 'Italy will hold on to this possibility of slipping out. . . . A directly hostile attitude of Italy towards Austria could . . . be averted by a clever policy on Austria's part'.[6] The Kaiser might well annotate the Ambassador's report with the remark that 'the little thief must always get his bit to gobble up as well'—the fact remained 'that the only means of holding Italy was by a timely promise of compensation. . . .'[7] Despite Flotow's repeated exhortations that he should declare for the Allies, San Giuliano contended, as late as July 31st (the day of Germany's ultimatum to Russia and France), that, unless he obtained immediate satisfaction, the Triple Alliance was dead.[8] And since the Habsburgs, by issuing the ultimatum, had already burned their boats, the Wilhelmstrasse could safely intercede in Vienna on behalf of the

---

[1] *Österreich-Ungarns Aussenpolitik*, VIII, p. 539.
[2] Merey to Berchtold, 21 July '14. *Diplomatische Aktenstücke*, I, p. 115.
[3] *Österreich-Ungarns Aussenpolitik*, VIII, p. 564.
[4] 26 July '14. Conrad, IV. 131. See also Minutes of the Conference between Stürgkh, Tisza, Berchtold, Burián, Conrad and the War Minister, 31 July '14. Conrad, IV. 154–5; also Salandra, 62.
[5] Conrad, IV. 123.
[6] Flotow to Bethmann, 25 July '14. *Deutsche Dokumente*. I. No. 244, pp. 239–40.
[7] Flotow's telegram, 25 July '14. *Deutsche Dokumente*, I. No. 168, p. 182.
[8] See Avarna to San Giuliano, 2 Aug. '14. *Documenti Diplomatici*, 5. I. No. 11, p. 7. Salandra, 60–1 67. Bülow, III. 184. Conrad, IV. 153–4.

trouble-makers in the South. It was this German pressure[1] which extorted from Berchtold, on August 1st, the statement that

'I accept the interpretation given to Article VII by Italy and Germany on condition that Italy observes a friendly attitude towards the military operations in progress between Austria-Hungary and Serbia, and, should the present conflict lead to a general conflagration, fulfils her duty as an Ally.'[2]

But Moses could not have been more intent on the Seventh Commandment than was the Marquis di San Giuliano on the Seventh Article of the Triplice. He retorted that its 'interpretation cannot be made dependent on any condition whatever'. For the Alliance to endure 'in absolute harmony ... we must be completely reassured over the interpretation of Article VII ... even if we take no part in the War'.[3] Meanwhile, Francis Joseph had written to the King of Italy:

'Russia ... is menacing the peace of Europe. ... In agreement with Germany, I have decided to defend the rights of the Triple Alliance ... I am happy, at this solemn moment, to be able to count on the co-operation of my Allies....'[4]

Victor Emmanuel replied:

'Italy who has made every possible effort to assure the maintenance of peace ... will preserve an attitude of cordial friendship towards her Allies in conformity with ... the Triplice, her sincere sentiments and the great interests which she has to safeguard.'[5]

William II, on receipt of a similar message:

'Right from the beginning, my Government has informed yours and the Austro-Hungarian that, since the *casus foederis* provided for in the Triple Alliance does not apply at present, it will exert its whole diplomatic activity to defend the legitimate interests of our Allies and our own,'

put 'scoundrel' against the name of his fellow Sovereign.[6] Meanwhile, too, the Austrian Chief of Staff requested his Italian counterpart 'to continue the oral discussions I had conducted personally

[1] Salandra, 62. Conrad, IV. 131
[2] Salandra, 64. Burián, 26. Avarna to San Giuliano, 2 Aug. '14. *Documenti Diplomatici*, 5. I. No. 11, p. 8.
[3] San Giuliano to Merey, 2 Aug. '14. Salandra, 64-5.
[4] Conrad, IV. 169.
[5] 2 Aug. '14. Conrad, IV. 169-70.
[6] The King of Italy to the Kaiser. 3 Aug. '14. *Deutsche Dokumente*, IV. No. 755, p. 12.

in strict confidence with the late Excellency Pollio. It has been envisaged that Italy, apart from the forces she is to send . . . in direct support of Germany, will place further troops at the disposal . . . of Austria-Hungary. I beg your Excellency to favour me with the information as to what forces would be allocated, when and where. . . .'¹ General Cadorna answered: 'Conferences purposeless. . . . If Austria-Hungary refrains from . . . disturbing the balance of power in the Adriatic, Italy will never march against her'.² Italian neutrality—decided upon on August 1st 1914 after receiving Berchtold's procrastinating dispatch—was formally announced on the 3rd.³ The stock exchanges were closed, a moratorium was declared, and exports were forbidden.⁴ In Vienna everyone, except the privileged few, was weighed down by the 'oppressive atmosphere of uneasy expectation and sombre doubt'.⁵ The men destined for the Serbian front were marched to the railway station at night to avoid anti-war demonstrations. They were accompanied by weeping women.⁶ At the Foreign Ministry, Berchtold stormed at the Ambassador Avarna that Rome's policy was a 'rash one' and might be regretted 'very bitterly'.⁷ The friendly manifestations by the unsuspecting populace outside the Italian Embassy were called off. In the coffee-houses, the playing of the *Marcia Reale* was stopped by the baton of—the police.⁸

---

[1] 1 Aug. '14. Conrad, IV. 158. Pollio was the former Italian Commander-in-Chief.
[2] Received 4 Aug. '14. Conrad, IV. 176. See also *Documenti Diplomatici*, 5. I. No. 207, p. 121.
[3] Salandra, 65, 67.
[4] T. N. Page, 160-1.
[5] Macchio, 7; also 8. Aldrovandi Marescotti, 13.
[6] Dumaine, *La dernière ambassade de France en Autriche*, 146, 151-2. Redlich, *Das politische Tagebuch*, I. 241.
[7] Bülow, III. 185.
[8] The Italian Anthem. Macchio, 11-12. Aldrovandi Marescotti, 14.

CHAPTER XIII

# *Neutrality*

## 1

### THE EPHEMERAL NEUTRALITY

IN Rome, 'the declaration of neutrality counted', as Croce has recognized, '... for nothing more than freedom to deal with the situation'.[1] '... prudence, reserve, secrecy', San Giuliano whispered to Salandra. He wanted Italy to 'maintain good relations with all the belligerents' until the outcome of the War could be foreseen and, meanwhile, pursue 'silent and rapid military preparations'.[2] Baron von Macchio, Merey's successor as Ambassador to the Quirinal, advised Vienna as late as December 1914 that it was Italy's 'ideal... to make the maximum possible territorial gains without attacking, by using the striking power of her Army as a threat'.[3] He credited the Consulta with planning, in the event of a German-Austrian defeat, to seize the Irredentist regions on the pretext (to be advanced in London and Paris) of stemming the westward tide of the Slavs, or—if the Entente lost—to ascribe this to the non-intervention of Rome, and claim rewards from the Central Powers. Indeed, some Italians like Bollati urged that, in case of a genuine Italian neutrality, 'our Allies would not only harbour no ill will against us, but would even be disposed as victors to take into account, at least in a certain measure, our legitimate aspirations'. Moreover, if Italy was not involved, she could, by acting as peace mediator, acquire 'the right to make her own voice heard in an authoritative and effective manner on behalf of her own interests....'[4]

But it could not be gainsaid that, for all practical purposes, Rome's defection, which released French forces for the Rhine and so tied down three German divisions earmarked for the East, was a hostile act. 'History will avenge Italy's felony', Moltke, the German Chief of Staff, wrote to Conrad, 'God grant you victory now, so that you can square accounts with these scoundrels later'.[5] The Austrian Liaison Officer with the Hohenzollern High Command informed Vienna on the authority of the Kaiser and Moltke that, 'once the

---

[1] Croce, 272.
[2] San Giuliano to Salandra, 4, 7 and 13 Aug. '14. *Documenti Diplomatici*, 5. I. NN 54, 117, 119, 230, pp. 30, 64–5, 124.
[3] Promemoria, before Christmas '14. Macchio, 65.
[4] Bollati to San Giuliano, 31 Aug. '14. *Carteggio*, LXI. II. 255. Also *Das Zaristische Russland im Weltkriege*, p. 279.
[5] 5 Aug. '14. Conrad, IV. 194.

War with Russia is over, we can challenge Italy, and Germany will be sure to stand by us'.[1] And Conrad suggested to his senior officers that, 'repaying perfidy with perfidy', any concessions now made could 'be recovered from the blackmailer' after victory.[2] The gist of these utterances at once trickled through to the Consulta. The Ambassador Imperiali wired from London that German Embassy officials, before leaving Britain, had threatened that, if Germany and Austria were victorious, they would immediately attack Italy. Similar warnings came via Bucharest.[3] If, as San Giuliano said, Italy would get little from the Central Powers as a co-belligerent,[4] she could certainly expect nothing but evil from them as a neutral.

Nor was the prospect brighter on the other side. Whilst, for the moment, the Entente was promising to keep Greece out of the Epirus and Valona,[5] who could tell the fate of these areas or of the Dodecanese, if Italy looked on with folded arms? Or what would happen if Turkey was thrown on the dissecting board, and Italy was not present, knife in hand? Still more alarming was the danger that, if she stayed out, her large sphere of Adriatic interests would fall either to a greater Austria-Hungary, or to a Russian-orientated Serbia. As early as August 7th 1914, when the Italian Commercial Attaché in Paris intimated to Poincaré that his country, in return for neutrality, 'must naturally be promised certain advantages', the President replied that inaction established no title to benefits.[6] From London, the Ambassador Imperiali gave warning on August 14th that, 'if we persist to the last in our neutrality, Italy will be exposed . . . to the indifference of the Entente. If the Entente wins, our position in the Adriatic, in the Balkans and on the Mediterranean will remain as it is, certainly not be improved. . . .'[7] The same cold wind blew from Petrograd: 'Sazonov believes that the future conference will be substantially a ratification of the positions occupied by the victors, and that important gains will be made only by those States which have taken part in the War. . . .[8] As for the idea of earning something by waving the olive branch rather than brandishing the sword—early in November the Ambassadors Carlotti in

[1] 8 and 9 Aug. '14. Conrad, IV. 197.
[2] 7 Aug. '14. Conrad, IV. 185.
[3] Imperiali to San Giuliano, 7 Aug. '14. *Documenti Diplomatici*, 5. I. No. 115, pp. 62–3. Fasciotti to San Giuliano, 8 Aug. *ibid.* No. 127, p. 68.
[4] San Giuliano to Avarna and Bollati, 3 Aug. '14. Salandra, 79. See also p. 153 above.
[5] Avarna to Bollati, 19 Sept. '14. *Carteggio*, LXI. II. 257.
[6] Poincaré, V. 30–1.
[7] Salandra, 82.
[8] Carlotti to San Giuliano, 14 Sept. '14. *Documenti Diplomatici*, 5. I. No. 674, p. 391. See also *Internationale Beziehungen*, II. 6. I. No. 257, p. 195.

Russia and Tittoni in France inquired how mediation proposals would be received.[1] The answers were sternly negative, and Sazonov wired to his Envoys in Rome, London and Paris that, 'if Italy should make fresh attempts, it would be desirable to deprive her at once of any hope. . . .'[2]

To wait passively, then, until the conflict had burned out, was tantamount to self-exclusion from the peace settlement. It was no less clear that the Kingdom would not be strong enough to assert its 'interests' by force of arms against the victors, however exhausted they might be.[3] In order to establish in good time a right to claims, and to make them effective, Italy—as Sazonov reminded San Giuliano—must go to war.[4] As early as August, therefore, King Victor and his Foreign Minister refused to discount the possibility that she might attack the Dual Monarchy.[5] Even the more neutrally minded Italian imperialists were determined not to be left empty-handed at the re-division of the world.[6]

However, it was not a foregone conclusion that the enemy would be Austria. Salandra has written: '. . . had we believed the victory of the Central Powers to be inevitable, we should have been obliged to stifle our feelings and . . . accept . . . the facile interpretation given by the two Emperors to the Treaty. . . .'[7] The Foreign Minister conveyed to Avarna and Bollati that 'one could perhaps . . . drag the country into a war which does not correspond to popular sentiment, if . . . there were advantages to be gained'.[8] It was to provide for this contingency that the Consulta had coupled the repudiation of the *casus foederis* with the intimation that it might be resurrected on certain terms. To say, as San Giuliano did in the declaration of neutrality, that 'we hope opportunities will occur of proving our friendly feeling towards our Allies. . . .'[9]—was something more than a farewell courtesy. Like his earlier statement: '. . . nor can we take

---

[1] The move was made in collusion with Germany and the U.S.A. *Carteggio*, LXI. II. 255. Stieve, p. 123.

[2] Sazonov to Benckendorff and Izvolski, 6 Nov. '14. *Internationale Beziehungen*, II. 6. II. No. 470, p. 412. Krupenski made a statement in this sense to the Consulta, adding that any such step might be damaging to Italy. Krupenski to Sazonov, 7 Nov. '14. *ibid.* II. 6. II. No. 480, p. 418. For Delcassé's reply to Tittoni see Izvolski to Sazonov, 7 Nov. '14. *ibid.* II. 6. II. No. 477, p. 417.

[3] Avarna to Bollati, 19 Sept. '14. *Carteggio*, LXI. II. 257.

[4] Carlotti to San Giuliano, 14 Sept. '14. Deciphered in the Russian Foreign Ministry. *Internationale Beziehungen*, II. 6. I. No. 257, p. 195.

[5] San Giuliano to Salandra, 9 and 15 Aug. '14. *Documenti Diplomatici*, 5. I. NN 151, 260, pp. 83, 149. Bollati to Avarna, 24 Sept. '14. *Carteggio*, LXI. II. 258.

[6] See Avarna to Bollati, 15 Dec. '14. *Carteggio*, LXI. III. 389. Michels, 180; and Avarna to Bollati, 19 Sept. '14. *Carteggio*, LXI. II. 156.

[7] Salandra, 57.

[8] 3 Aug. '14. Salandra, 78-9.

[9] San Giuliano to Merey, 2 Aug. '14. Salandra, 65.

any step favourable to Austria-Hungary . . . until the question of compensation has been settled',[1] it was carefully designed to leave the door ajar.

As long as the invasion of Belgium and Germany's victories in France strengthened the widespread belief in a rapid triumph of the Kaiser,[2] Italian preparations could be turned against the Entente. If his luck had held, Rome presumably would have discovered that this was a crusade of European civilization against Russian barbarism and French wickedness. But the Imperial war-lord stumbled at the Marne. That battle, Salandra recollects, 'had a more or less decisive influence on my point of view'[3]; ' . . . the Government . . . were convinced . . . that, as the plan of crushing France had failed, the War would be prolonged and thereby the chance of success for the Entente increased, as they were so much better off in men and material. . . . We were now convinced that . . . our intervention was inevitable. . . .'[4] The Germans might temporarily, and even greatly, improve their fortunes. That staunch advocate of the Triplice, Avarna, might walk in and out of the Austrian Foreign Office, begging: 'Donnez-nous des victoires. . . .'[5] He might write to the like-minded Bollati that 'only a German victory can prevent the final disgrace of Italy'.[6] But already on September 30th, in a report to the King, the Prime Minister, discussing as the only alternatives 'the maintenance of neutrality or participation in the War on the side of the Triple Entente',[7] came down heavily in favour of the latter, with the proviso that this be 'put off . . . until the spring'.[8]

---

[1] San Giuliano to Bolleti, 20 July '14. L. Albertini, II. 240; also 320, 322, 244. For San Giuliano's statement to the Habsburg Ambassador that Italy's neutrality decision was not final, and his instructions to the Minister in Albania that it was desirable 'to preserve, and demonstrate to Austria, a loyal and friendly attitude. . . .' See Avarna to San Giuliano, 2 Aug. '14, and San Giuliano to Aliotti, 4 Aug. *Documenti Diplomatici*, 5. I. NN 15, 46, pp. 11, 25.
[2] The Austro-Hungarian Naval Attaché in Rome to War Ministry, Vienna, 2 Sept. '14. The Austro-Hungarian Military Attaché in Rome to Conrad, 2 Sept. '14. Conrad, IV, 683, 677. San Giuliano to Salandra, 13 Aug. '14, mentions 'the probability that Germany and Austria may win. . . .' *Documenti Diplomatici*, 5. I. No. 234, p. 137.
[3] Salandra, 94. See also San Giuliano's telegram of 13 Sept. '14. *Documenti Diplomatici*, 5. I. No. 670, p. 388.
[4] Salandra, 96.
[5] Macchio, 36.
[6] 5 Oct. '14. *Carteggio*, LXI. II. 262.
[7] Salandra, 135.
[8] Salandra, 137. Although invoking the opinion of the Army, he adduced several reasons of his own for delay. For the whole report see pp. 134–40. Also *Internationale Beziehungen*, II. 6. I. No. 332, p. 256. *Carteggio*, LXI. II. 257. A letter from Avarna to Bollati, 22 Oct. '14, shows that the Italian Government was meditating action against Austria-Hungary. *Carteggio*, LXI. II. 267.

## 2
### THE REASONS FOR MARKING TIME

The reasons for delay were the same as those which prompted the neutrality decision in August 1914: '... fear of Italian public opinion ... the consciousness of military weakness ... the desire to turn the occasion to good account' in the diplomatic field,[1] and the wish to wait on events in order (according to a Frenchman's cruel jibe) 'to fly to the succour of the victor'.[2] To take the second point first, there were serious 'deficiencies in mobilization assets' and 'disorder ... in the depots'. The 'supplies lacking amounted to the sum of 35,000,000 lire'.[3] On August 2nd, the Chief of Staff, Cadorna, reported on the bad state of the cadres, 'the lack of training and the scarcity of equipment and transport'. On September 3rd, he listed the shortage of 'clothing and arms ... transport and various materials'.[4] They were short of some 13,500 officers, while those with the colours had 'degraded' the service 'to a ... bread-winning career'. Economies had cut the number of troops; conscripts had been sent home half trained; and the rank and file were affected by 'subversive elements'.[5] Salandra may have overdrawn the picture to justify his procrastinations and to indict his predecessor (and rival) Giolitti. The latter's denial that he had left Italy's forces unprepared[6] may not be entirely self-exculpatory. But foreign observers, too, agreed that the country was still exhausted from the Libyan War.[7] Governmental ineptitude, Parliamentary intrigue, budget deficits, the 'subterfuges and ambiguities of the official departments', 'the vultures hovering around the millions so lavishly poured out'[8], reduced still further the level of preparedness. In this state of affairs, the call-up of several classes, the secret troop movements, often unknown to the families involved, the purchase at great cost of horses from America, the imports of grain, oil, coal, steel, guns and ammunition and the allocation of 50,000,000 lire,[9] were but the first steps towards mobilization. 'On September 24th, 31,000,000 having been already spent ... the Commander-in-

---
[1] Flotow to Bethmann, 25 July '14. *Deutsche Dokumente*, I. No. 244, p. 239.
[2] T. N. Page, 217. The Russian Military Attaché in Rome reported that, since the Italians were convinced that the winter would put an almost complete stop to military operations, they could use the time for preparation in order, thereafter, to 'secure with the least risk the profound gratitude of the victors'. Telegram, 29 Sept. 14. *Internationale Beziehungen*, II. 6. I. No. 333, pp. 256-7.
[3] Salandra, 123, 125, 128.     [4] *ibid.* 121, 124.
[5] Salandra to the King, 30 Sept. '14. Salandra, 136; also 132. Rodd, III. 218-19.
[6] Giolitti, 388-90.
[7] See Rodd, III. 218-19. T. N. Page, 150. Burián, 41. Conrad, V. 307.
[8] Salandra, 124-5.
[9] Salandra, 120, 131. T. N. Page, 165. Conrad, IV. 676. V. 331.

## NEUTRALITY

Chief considered that we were not in a condition to take the field'. 'November, the earliest date possible [he said], would have been too late for beginning serious operations'.¹ 'The absolute want of winter equipment' precluded, as the Premier informed the King, 'a campaign from November to March'.² For most of 1914, Italy, in the American Ambassador's pithy summing-up, suffered from 'want of every conceivable necessary of war, save men'.³

But here was another difficulty: the 'men' had no taste for carnage. Whilst a handful of well-to-do youths, infected by Libya, were running a martial temperature, the sacrifices of that expedition had only strengthened the people's healthy pacifism. According to San Giuliano, 'except for an infinitely small minority, the nation has shown itself unanimous against participation in a war. . . .'⁴ The Austrophil aristocracy and clericals, the sections of industry and finance which had German affiliations, and big business eager to exploit the possibilities of contraband trade,⁵ favoured neutrality. The Catholic and the red sections of the peasantry and, above all, the workers supplied the mass support for the partisans of peace.

### 3
#### THE ITALIAN SOCIALIST PARTY AND WAR

Of these, the Socialist Party, as Salandra has confirmed, was 'the most powerful political leaven in Italy at that time'.⁶ Its birth in 1892 had been accompanied by revolutionary ferment and demonstrations, such as tearing up railway lines to stop the troop trains for Abyssinia in 1896. The trade unions and peasant associations, despite the Government's recourse to the soldiery and the resulting bloodshed,⁷ were on the offensive. With labour stoppages mounting from 642 in 1899-1900 to 1,852 in 1901-2 (and those of farm labour from 36 to 856), the Kingdom, by 1903, was fourth from the top in international strike statistics.⁸ By 1909, four general strikes had swept the country. Another was called in 1911 in protest against the Libyan War. The chronic discord, provoked by abuse and repression

---

¹ Salandra, 128, 142.
² 30 Sept. '14. Salandra, 136. See also Avarna to Bollati, 22 Oct. '14. *Carteggio*, LXI. II. 267.
³ T. N. Page, 178.
⁴ San Giuliano to Avarna and Bollati, 3 Aug. '14. Salandra, 78. Although the reference here is to a war on Austria's side, there is ample evidence that this sentiment was against war in general. See the Austro-Hungarian Military Attaché in Rome to Conrad, 2 Sept. '14. Conrad, IV. 675, 677; and Avarna to Bollati, 22 Oct. '14. *Carteggio*, LXI. II. 267; also T. N. Page, 143. Salandra, 135, 307. Michels, 194–5.
⁵ Rodd, III. 218.   ⁶ Salandra, 74.   ⁷ Croce, 219–20.
⁸ Croce, 227. Michels, 149.

came to a head in June 1914, when a general strike throughout Italy, unrest in Rome, Milan, Florence and Ancona, provincial uprisings, the proclamation of a republic in the Marches, and the shaping of a new social order in Emilia and Romagna, went down in history as 'Red Week'.[1]

The radicalism of the masses was sharpened by the fact that Italy's economic system, unlike Britain's or Germany's, was too poor and politically immature to nurture more than a sprinkling of labour aristocrats. This narrowed and weakened, inside the movement, the basis for collaboration with other classes. The Socialist leadership, for 20 years, was almost solely reformist. The Marxist Antonio Labriola could propagate bourgeois prosperity as a precondition of Socialism and, from 1902 onwards, advocate the seizure of Tripolitania as 'una nuova patria' of the Italian proletariat. His 'comrade' Arturo Labriola could, in 1911-12, call for war against the Turks on the grounds that it was really a struggle with 'plutocratic Europe'.[2] Some Left-wing writers could go so far as to say that such an enterprise would entail the submission of the military power to the cause of the workers. But this defence of empire-building under the guise of national 'socialism' cut little ice in Italy. So strong was the opposition to war and colonial policy among the rank and file of the workers that only Leonida Bissolati and Ivanoe Bonomi, with their Right-wing faction, dared openly to support the Libyan campaign, and were promptly expelled from the Socialist Party in 1912.[3]

This was the mood in which the Italian labour movement had built up its strength by 1914. It had a powerful organization with a far-flung network of local branches. The Socialist trade unions were affiliated to the *Confederazione Generale del Lavoro* which had some 321,000 members,[4] and the peasant associations to the *Federazione dei Lavorotari della Terra* numbering about 200,000. The Socialist Party, 50,000 strong, had (together with the trade

[1] Colombi, *Pagine di storia del movimento operaio*, 97. Sereni, *La questione agraria nella rinascita nazionale italiana*, 37-8. Nenni, *The Years of Tyranny in Italy*, 38. Megaro, *Mussolini in the Making*, 253. Michels, 150, 152. Croce, 220-1, 325. Salandra, 17, 45. Rossi, 1. T. N. Page, 145.

[2] Antonio Labriola, *Scritti vari di filosofia e politica*, 432-41. Arturo Labriola, *La guerra di Tripoli e l'opinione socialista*. Lenin, XVIII. 332. Michels, 174, footnote 2. Croce, 259-60.

[3] The other offences for which they were punished were uninhibited reformism, obsequiousness before the Monarchy, and a *penchant* for office in bourgeois Cabinets. Megaro, 224, 282, 288-9, 304. Croce, 219, 226. Salandra, 75. Lenin, XVIII. 417. Balabanoff, *Erinnerungen und Erlebnisse*, 39. *Encyclopaedia Britannica*, 1929. XVI. 29.

[4] The Catholic Confederation of Labour had a membership of about 103,000, and the Syndicalist Union approximately 100,000. Brady, 66. Salvemini, *The Fascist Dictatorship in Italy*, I. 26, footnote 1.

unions) over 200 newspapers, substantial support among the teachers, the youths and in the Army, and a dominant position in almost 400 municipalities, including such centres as Bologna and Milan. In the 1913 elections, it polled nearly 1,000,000 votes[1] and captured 52 Parliamentary seats. In almost permanent opposition in the Chamber, notably against military expenditures, its influence was all the greater since, by that time, it had overcome much of its interfactional strife. Purged of the Syndicalists by 1908, Italian Socialism had still retained three divisions, of which the reformists of Turati and Treves had formed the middle-of-the-road majority, and Bissolati's group the extreme Right. The eviction of the latter at the Congress of 1912 was the achievement of the 'Maximalists', a small but fiery band of the Left led by Constanto Lazzari and Serrati who simultaneously gained control of the Executive and of *Avanti*, the official organ of the Party. The reformists shrank to a minority. The mounting nation-wide ferment, impatience inside the movement with compromise, and the rapid growth of the revolutionary forces, promoted by the Libyan ordeal, led to the victory of the Left wing exactly two years before the Great War.[2]

The Italian Socialist Party, therefore, as Lenin wrote in 1914, 'was an exception to the rule . . . of the Second International'.[3] Unlike most of the other constituent parties of the latter, it did not set about popularizing the War among its followers. As early as July 28th 1914, it appealed to

'the proletariat of all nations to impede, circumscribe and limit as much as possible the armed conflict which is useful only for the triumph of militarism and the parasitical business affairs of the bourgeoisie. You, the proletariat of Italy . . . must . . . not let Italy go down into the abyss of this terrible adventure'.[4]

On the same day, *Avanti* gave warning:

'If the Government does not heed unanimous public opinion but enters into the new adventure, the "armed truce" declared by us at the close of Red Week will be ended'.[5]

On August 2nd, in joint session with the *Confederazione Generale del Lavoro*, the autonomous Railwaymen's Union and the Seamen's

---

[1] Salandra, 74–5.
[2] Croce, 220. Salandra, 17–18. Kirova, *Voprosy Istorii*, 1953. VI. 70–1. Megaro, 282, 289, 301, 304–5, 312. Balabanoff, 39–40, 61, 76. Michels, 165.
[3] 'And Now What?' *Sotsial-Demokrat*, No. 36, Berne, 23 Dec, '14, Lenin, XVIII. 107.
[4] Seldes, *Sawdust Caesar*, 44.
[5] 28 July '14, Seldes, 44.

Federation, a resolution was passed, urging labour to 'be on its guard', and to insist on Italy's neutrality. Notice was served on the ruling classes that, if they departed from it, they would be faced with 'direct action on the part of the working class'.[1] On September 22nd, a Manifesto was issued summoning the workers to demonstrate against those who were clamouring for intervention. The Socialist press exposed the propaganda of the belligerents, the nature of the imperialist struggle and its consequences for the masses. Meetings throughout the country carried the torch of resistance among the people. And steps were taken to resuscitate the shattered International. A conference of representatives of the Italian and the Swiss Social-Democratic Parties, held on the initiative of the former in Lugano in September 1914, adopted a motion which, in part, incorporated Lenin's recent 'Theses on the War' and advocated both the urgent recall of the Socialist Bureau and the fight of the international proletariat for peace.[2]

Such action, in the eyes of the bellicose sections of the Italian bourgeoisie, called for counter-measures. A slanderous press campaign was unleashed against the Socialists. After Lugano, the *Secolo* accused them of taking bribes from Berlin, and serving as agents of the Kaiser. Blame for the coming of a German Social-Democrat (Dr. Südekum) to plead his country's cause was laid at their door.[3] Nor did it take long to resort to the old device of splitting the Left.[4] How was the Government to know that the Socialist Party, for all the radicalism of its language, would, as Lenin considered possible, not 'remain perfectly solid in case Italy enters the War'?[5] It was impossible to mistake the pacifist mood of the masses, or fail to see that the stand of the Maximalists Serrati and Lazzari was different from that of, say, Scheidemann or Vandervelde. Hence it was politically expedient to cultivate the latter's Italian counterparts. First among these was L. Bissolati, Chief of the new Italian Reformist Socialist Party, who already in 1911 had been offered a Cabinet post and granted an audience by the King.[6] In 1914, he exerted himself, as Salandra says with approval, for intervention 'with all his might'.[7] So did Syndicalists like F. Corridoni,

---

[1] Lenin, XVIII. 418.
[2] Lenin, XVIII. 85, 418, 409. Kirova, *Voprosy Istorii*, 1553. VI. 70–1. Balabanoff, 66–9, 58. Salandra, 109.
[3] Balabanoff, 60, 68, 74.
[4] See Sir Charles Petrie, *Mussolini*, 24. Seldes, 1.
[5] 'And Now What?' *Sotsial-Demokrat*, No. 36. 23 Dec. '14. Lenin, XVIII. 107.
[6] Croce, 219, 266.
[7] Salandra, 75, footnote 1. On 2 Aug. '14 Bissolati conveyed to his friend Bonomi that 'one must prepare the soul of the proletariat for war against the militaristic forces'. Sforza, *Makers of Modern Europe*, 287.

the Secretary of the Milan organization of the Italian Syndicalist Union, and A. De Ambris who, on October 5th, signed the interventionist appeal of the *Fasci d'Azione Rivoluzionaria*.[1]

## 4

### THE GENESIS OF MUSSOLINI

But the latest and, to date, most notorious recruit from the Left was the Editor of *Avanti*. Not long before, he had fulminated against the 'old *cliché* of the fatherland in danger' with which 'the blood has been pumped from the poverty-stricken proletariat for the past 30 years'.[2] He had denounced the national flag as 'a rag to be planted on a dunghill',[3] and upbraided 'international militarism' for 'its orgies of destruction and death'.[4] On July 27th 1914, he demanded that 'our neutrality must be absolute'.[5] In August, he uttered the warning: 'Workers . . . the people who are inciting you to war are betraying you'.[6] On September 8th, he scoffed: 'We are invited to weep over martyred Belgium. We are witnessing a sentimental farce staged by France and Belgium. All the belligerent Powers are equally guilty. . . .'[7] But by October 19th he had promoted the 'farce' to a 'grand and tragic drama' of which 'it is impossible for Socialists to remain spectators',[8] and become one of the principal trumpeters of the Entente.[9] The name of the man was Benito Mussolini.

'Chi paga?' This question travelled as fast as sound through cafés, newspaper offices and party branches.[10] Soon it was rumoured and reported that the future Duce's metamorphosis was due to French gold.[11] What was not known at the time was that he was in touch with Filippo Naldi, the publisher of *Il Resto del Carlino* which, two years previously, Mussolini had scornfully labelled as 'the reactionary landlords' ' organ, and which was now campaigning for an entente with the West.[12] That paper, in an article written by a man who later became a prominent fascist, suddenly asserted that

---

[1] This attitude was not universal among the Syndicalists. At the Congress of the Italian Syndicalist Union in mid-September, De Ambris's bellicose resolution was challenged by a motion opposing the War and summoning the workers of all countries to revolutionary action against the bourgeois states weakened by the European crisis. The majority vote in favour of this motion brought about the resignation of the Central Committee. Rosmer, *Le Mouvement ouvrier pendant la guerre*, 126, 134. Monelli, *Mussolini*, 65, 68.
[2] At the Socialist Congress, Oct. 1910. Megaro, 229.
[3] *La Lotta di Classe*, 2 July 1910. Megaro, 229.
[4] June 1912. Megaro, 272.   [5] *Avanti*. Seldes, 1.   [6] Monelli, 64.
[7] *Avanti*, 8 Sept. '14. Salvemini, *Mussolini diplomate*, 11–12. Rossi, 3.
[8] Party Executive meeting, Bologna, 19 Oct. '14. Rosmer, 328.
[9] Rodd, III. 249.   [10] 'Who is paying?' Seldes, 4.
[11] Monelli, 274. Rosmer, 328. Seldes, 46.   [12] Megaro, 240. Monelli, 66.

the opposition of the Socialists was not serious, and that, according to 'a very influential Socialist leader', the Party 'would assume quite a different position if it were a matter of war . . . against the Central Powers'.¹ This lightning-stroke was followed by the thunder-clap of Mussolini's *Avanti* editorial 'From Absolute to Armed Neutrality' (October 18th) engineered, it has been suggested, by Naldi. The Party Executive, incensed by this muted call for war, dismissed Mussolini from his editorial post.²

According to one of his biographers, it was Naldi who proposed that, if this came to pass, Mussolini should found a new 'Socialist' daily, and that its title *Il Popolo d'Italia* should strike a war-like note among the workers.³ Another student of his career thinks 'that venality was not the motivating force' of Mussolini's somersault, but that, impelled by megalomania, he was simply 'exploiting every opportunity . . . that would advance his . . . personal power'.⁴ He was aware, writes Pietro Nenni, 'that the Socialist Party would not submit to being bent and moulded at will'.⁵ And in Monelli's view, it was the fear that the bellicose Syndicalists might steal a march on him, which drove him into the open.⁶ A generation in Italy was indoctrinated with the notion that, in order to start his martial sheet, 'he raised a small subscription among his friends'.⁷ 'A contract for some advertisements, and . . . 4,000 lire obtained on a bill of exchange was all the capital available'.⁸ Actually, there is weighty evidence that—egocentric ambitions apart—Mussolini was heavily financed from Paris.⁹ And it has been stated for a fact that Naldi had promised to provide money,¹⁰ and that Naldi 'was in the confidence' of the Foreign Minister San Giuliano.¹¹

A variety of reasons operated in favour of picking Mussolini for a blackleg among those who struck for peace. The paper he was editing had a daily circulation of 94,000.¹² In preparing for war, as

---

¹ Balabanoff, 90. Rossi, 3. Rosmer, 328. Megaro, 236.
² The dismissal took effect as from 20 Oct. '14. Salvemini, *The Fascist Dictatorship in Italy*, I. 55. Nenni, 42. Balabanoff, 90–2. Seldes, 46–7. Rosmer, 328. Monelli, 64–5.
³ Monelli, 67. Rossi, 3.      ⁴ Megaro, 191, 326–7.
⁵ Nenni, 42.      ⁶ Monelli, 68–70.
⁷ L. Villari, *Italy*. London, 1929, p. 139. This author is an unhesitating defender of the fascist régime.
⁸ V. Jeanne Bordeux, *Benito Mussolini—the Man*. Preface by Prince Potenziani, Governor of Rome. London, 1927, p. 117.
⁹ See p. 230 below.
¹⁰ Monelli, 67. Mussolini's *Autobiography*, London, 1928, p. 48, says: 'I needed a daily paper. . . . When money alone is concerned I am anything but a wizard. When it is a question of . . . capital . . . to finance a newspaper, I grasp only . . . the political value. . . .' Although this book has been described by an expert as a 'shameless literary fraud' (Megaro, 244–5), the above is nevertheless a valuable admission, since it was written on Mussolini's authority.
¹¹ Monelli, 66.      ¹² By Oct. '14. Megaro, 317.

Sir Charles Petrie noted, 'it was clear that the Government could take no step in this direction unless it could be assured of Socialist support, and as to that the word of the Editor of *Avanti* would be decisive'.[1] Mussolini, it appears, had for some time already been watched with care. His violence and fulminations against the capitalist order were treated, where it was deemed necessary, with a dose of prison—for instance for resisting the Libyan War. But little disapprobation and, perhaps, more than a touch of interest were contained in such verdicts as that of the *Corriere della Sera* that he 'speaks explosively', in the *Secolo*'s reference to the 'novel Romagnuole agitator', or in the discovery by the reactionary *Momento* that 'there is nothing terrible about him: only a deep bass voice'.[2] Mussolini's usefulness, moreover, was enhanced by his record as a refractory member of the Party. From 1910 to 1912, in his provincial weekly *La Lotta di Classe*, he had vented his wrath against the official movement.[3] Having broken with it in April 1911, he rejoined the year after, when he could see his opportunity in the sharpening social struggles. Exploits such as those leading to his expulsion from Austria, or his call, during the Libyan War, to dynamite the railway lines, gave him a name. The radical wave which, at the 1912 Socialist Congress, established Left-wing leadership, swept him on to the Executive Committee. A series of accidents brought him the editorship of *Avanti*. Intuition enabled him in his editorials to strike the popular note. Essentially, however, Mussolini's 'Socialism'—a hotch-potch of scraps from Sorel, Bergson, Nietzsche and Pareto—was only a vehicle to satisfy his personal ambitions.[4] No effort, therefore, was required to exchange it for a different doctrine, if it was made worth his while. And it would seem that it paid those working for Italian belligerency to provide the inducements. Indeed, who but one known to be a vainglorious demagogue and rabble-rouser[5] could, in a pacific country, help the weather-makers to raise a storm? A 'plebeian', as he described himself,[6] was needed to mislead the proletariat. The unsocial Socialist was to disrupt the Socialist opposition to war.

It was in keeping with this that the front page of the *Popolo d'Italia* should have featured Blanqui's dictum 'he who has steel has bread', and Napoleon's 'Revolution is an idea that has found bayonets'[7]; that Mussolini should have claimed this to be a 'peoples' war' which would inaugurate Socialism; and that in the first issue of his paper (November 15th) he should have uttered 'with a loud

[1] Petrie, 24; also 25.      [2] 1910. Megaro, 301.
[3] See Megaro, 33, 288, 296, 298, 301.
[4] Megaro, 243–4, 293, 303, 305–7, 309, 311, 315–16, 323, 327. Nenni, 36, 38. Balabanoff, 77–8. Croce, 266.
[5] Megaro, 319–20.      [6] Megaro, 296.      [7] Rossi, 10–1. Rosmer, 331.

voice ... without restraint ... a terrible and fascinating word: Guerra!'¹ The renegade was tried at a Party meeting of the Milan division on November 24th. The public hurled copper coins at the defendant: 'Judas, here is your blood money!'² The sentence was expulsion and political death. Mussolini retorted: 'If you imagine you can shut me out of political life, you are very much mistaken. You will have to face me ... alive and implacable'.³ And in the press: 'The Mussolini case is not over yet. ... It is just beginning. ... I am openly raising the flag of schism. ...'⁴ His war cries against the Central Powers blended with malignant attacks on the Socialists he had deserted. He was forsaken and branded by all save a few of his comrades, and abandoned by the masses. The slippery slope led him into new company.⁵

This was the time when the future 'Duce' took up his fatal association with the *Fasci d'Azione Rivoluzionaria* whose gangs were formed for interventionist agitation.⁶ He joined up with the bellicose Syndicalists of De Ambris and F. Corridoni whom, for some months, he had decried as 'subversive traitors'.⁷ He rallied to D'Annunzio, and to Marinetti's Futurists who quenched their protests against bourgeois society in enthusiasm for its War. And he made common cause with the Nationalists whom, previously, he had termed bluffers, dandies, pimps and—as recently as August 1914—victims of *'delirium tremens'*.⁸

Monarchical, clerical, militarist, the Nationalist Party was the most reactionary force in the country. Though numerically small, it carried great weight in politics owing to the support of sections of the nobility and the industrialists, and electoral co-operation with the Catholics. It stood for what Croce described as 'the establishment of an autocratic régime ... rooted in modern plutocracy',⁹ war and imperialist expansion in North Africa, Malta, Nice, Corsica and Savoy. Mediterranean ambition and clerical conservatism alike made it a rabid enemy of France and champion of the Triplice. At a

¹ Salandra, 110. Monelli, 69. Rosmer, 328–9. Croce, 327. Salvemini, *Mussolini diplomate*, 72. Megaro, 293. Rossi, 3, 10–11. If Italy, Mussolini said, promoted the victory of the Entente, 'more liberty would exist in Europe, and the proletariat would have better opportunities to develop its class capacities ... if Prussian reaction triumphed ... the level of human civilization would be lowered'. *Encyclopaedia Britannica*, 1947. XVI. 29.
² Monelli, 69.   ³ Nenni, 43.   ⁴ Seldes, 8.
⁵ Salandra, 110. Nenni, 43. Balabanoff, 95. Megaro, 289, 307. Petrie, 27. Monelli, 69. Rossi, 3.
⁶ Megaro, 172. Petrie, 28. Rosmer, 336. *Encyclopaedia Britannica*, 1947. XVI. 29.
⁷ Monelli, 68.   ⁸ Megaro, 241. Seldes, 2.
⁹ Croce, 280; also 265. The leader of the Nationalist Party Enrico Corradini propounded the theory that nationalism recognized no human rights, but only absolute submission of the individual to the national entity. See 'Stato liberale e stato nazionale' in *Manifesti del Nazionalismo Italiano*, p. 102. ff. Michels, 168, 170. Also Salvemini, *The Fascist Dictatorship*, 118.

meeting on July 28th 1914, the Party inveighed against 'Austrophobia' and 'Philoserbism'. Its mouthpiece *L'Idea Nazionale* accompanied the outbreak of the conflict with adulations of the Reich. Plans were in hand to foment Italian Irredentism in Tunis and Malta. The demand went up for common action with Germany and Austria. But no sooner was it recognized in Rome that this was no paying proposition, than (to use a contemporary Austrian epithet) 'this abortion of old Italian phrase-mongering and the new Italian *mania-grandiosa*'[1] discovered that virtue was on the side of the Entente.[2] The *Idea Nazionale* and D'Annunzio appealed to the more solid or intellectual bourgeoisie; the bellicose Syndicalists to the Anarchist element in the factories; Mussolini addressed himself to the immature workers, the petty bourgeoisie and the uneducated; the *Fasci* activated the mob.[3] Those who were soon to coalesce in the morass of Fascism met for the first time together as drum-beaters of the fratricidal War.[4]

5

PROPAGANDA AND THE ROLE OF THE PRESS

The other *guerrafondai*[5] were the pro-French Radicals, Republicans, Freemasons, Irredentists, some Christian Democrats and, above all, the governing Right wing of the Liberal Party.[6] Apart from some petty-bourgeois groups, therefore, the middle classes, as Salandra recollects, 'were amongst the most ardent supporters of immediate intervention'.[7] Anxious to stem the tide, the Socialists (and, for opposite reasons, some Republicans) pressed for the recall of Parliament. But the Prime Minister reported to the King that 'the country does not expect any useful result from the Chamber, and the Government at present can do without it'.[8] Indeed, since the

[1] The Austro-Hungarian Naval Attaché in Rome to Naval Section, War Ministry, Vienna, 2 Sept. '14. Conrad, IV. 683.
[2] See E. Corradini, 'Il nostro dovere'. *L'Idea Nazionale*, IV. No. 33. 13 Aug. '14. Michels, 186.
[3] Petrie, 27. *Encyclopaedia Britannica*, 1929. XVI. 29. Croce, 248, 265, 280. Salandra, 75–6, Megaro, 241. Giolitti, 384, Rossi, 2. Michels, 170, 172–3, 184–5, 189, 193, 196. Conrad, IV. 675, 683. Salvatorelli. *A Concise History of Italy*, 616.
[4] The Italian Nationalists, of whom Corradini, Federzoni, Dino Alfieri and others held high posts under Mussolini, have been described as the spiritual precursors of Fascism. Among the Syndicalists actively associated with it were Alceste and Amilcare De Ambris, Arturo Labriola and Cesare Rossi. See Megaro, 241, 235, 250, 276. Balabanoff, 61. Monelli, 64.
[5] Italian for war-mongers. See Bülow, III. 220. Salandra, 135.
[6] Salandra, 308, 76, 111, 214. T. N. Page, 188–9. Rodd, III, 219. Conrad, IV. 675, 683. May, 438. Michels, 186–7. Renouvin, *La Crise européenne et la Grande guerre (1914–1918)*, 270.
[7] Salandra, 308.
[8] 30 Sept. '14. Salandra, 138.

Italian people were at first almost unanimous in their desire for peace,[1] and the deputies were bound to reflect this sentiment, it was preferable that they should remain dispersed. As Victor Emmanuel was informed, the 'assertions of those ready to face every sacrifice', sincere in some cases, were 'in others . . . merely rhetorical, while from the lower classes they are not heard at all'.[2] But, as they composed the majority of the nation, it was just the 'lower classes' who had to be conditioned for blood and toil. Neutrality, as Salandra records, had been acclaimed out of 'the satisfaction of not having to take part in . . . war. . . . With a clear insight into the future, I . . . had to prepare the country for the renunciation of this . . . cause of contentment'.[3] This, as well as mobilization of men and material, seems to be implied in his statement that 'our work from August 1914 to May 1915 consisted in "preparation for intervention".'[4]

Since Italy was not invaded (unfortunately, as Clemenceau was to say), there could be no 'defence of the fatherland'. So it was claimed that this would be a campaign to liberate the kinsmen beyond the border and free the Kingdom finally from Austrian pressure. The anti-Habsburg spirit of the Risorgimento was invoked and Garibaldi's call for Italy's 'inevitable war . . . against Austria' thrown in. A brigade bearing his name was formed to make another Expedition of the Thousand; but, since it was too early for a breach with Vienna, it repaired to the Rhine. Pleas that national unification should be crowned by the inclusion of the Trentino and Trieste mixed with forecasts of the democratic changes which would result in Italy from the victory of the West. Promises were made that the struggle would be short. An itinerant orator from Belgium appealed to the population's tears. Postcards, caricaturing William II and Francis Joseph, added the sting of ridicule. D'Annunzio, from Paris, sent a frenzied ode to war. The Mayor of Rome, Prince P. Colonna, went so far as to tell the Italians that 'the nation, conscious of its strength, solemnly affirms its readiness to face every contingency'. And the King, in a public telegram, expressed his 'faith in the prosperity and greatness of the country'.[5]

The press, meanwhile, accompanied these voices with its cacophony. The moderate *Secolo* (Milan), the *Messagero*, the *Stampa* (Turin) which was patronized by Fiat,[6] and the *Giornale d'Italia* which was connected with the Montecatini trust, and of which

---

[1] See Salandra, 307.
[2] Salandra to the King, 30 Sept. '14. Salandra, 137.
[3] Salandra, 107.
[4] Salandra, 98. See also 122.
[5] 20 Sept. '14. Salandra, 108; also 43–4. T. N. Page, 281. Michels, 196. Conrad, V. 240. Aldrovandi Marescotti, 28.
[6] Henry, 87. Conrad, IV. 831. *Carteggio*, LXI. II. 265. Rosmer, 331.

the Prime Minister Salandra was an important, and the new Foreign Minister Sonnino 'the largest and most authoritative shareholder',[1] were all for the Entente. Perhaps the biggest guns were those of the Right-wing Liberal *Corriere della Sera* (Milan) which was controlled by Benigno Crespi, the cotton magnate, Ernesto de Angeli, the head of the huge cotton-dyeing concern, and G. B. Pirelli—banker and rubber king who had a world-wide network of enterprises, including plantations in Malaya.[2] With a circulation approaching 600,000 and its reputation of being the leading national paper, this organ of big business in Lombardy was so powerful that, as Bollati said, it 'rules Italy'.[3] On August 21st 1914, as the Russian Ambassador reported, L. Albertini, the Editor of the *Corriere della Sera*, had told him that he intended to start a campaign in favour of joining the Entente, that he wished to know whether Italy would be granted hegemony in the Adriatic, and he, Krupenski, had 'reassured' him.[4] Promptly, on August 27th, the paper came out against indefinite neutrality. On September 22nd, it announced: '... we cannot, we must not remain silent. The public conscience must be made clear to those who govern....'[5] On October 9th, noting the mounting war fever at home, Bollati wrote to Avarna that 'this alleged public opinion can be reduced ... to a hundred or so journalists'. If the authorities 'really wanted', they could make them 'use reasonable language'.[6] But then, as Salandra has confessed since, 'without the newspapers Italy's intervention could not have been achieved'.[7]

---

[1] Salandra, 112; also Henry, 87.
[2] A. Albertini, *Vita di Luigi Albertini*, 53–55. The Chief Editor and Director of the *Corriere*, the Parliamentary Deputy Luigi Albertini owed his appointment to de Angeli. See A. Albertini, 55, 60, 69–70.
[3] Bollati to Avarna, 26 Oct. '14. *Carteggio*, LXI. II. 271. Also Salandra, 108, 112, 168, 196, 200. A. Albertini, 56, 115, 141, 165–6. The reading public of the *Corriere della Sera* was greatly increased by the publication of the illustrated weekly *Domenica del Corriere* which had large sales (*ibid.* 61-2). Evidence of the inter-relations between Italy's leading newspapers may be gleaned from the fact that Antonio Albertini, a brother of Luigi's (and in later years a Director of the Pirelli company) joined the editorial board of the *Corriere* after a period of apprenticeship in the *Giornale d'Italia*. Torre, for a time Chief Editor of the latter, became a prominent contributor to the *Corriere*. On the other hand, Luigi Albertini's one-time Secretary, Alberto Bergamini, became the Editor of the *Giornale*. V. Banzatti of the *Stampa* came also from the senior staff of the *Corriere*. See A. Albertini, 6, footnote; 108–9, 123–4. Salandra, 113.
[4] Krupenski to Sazonov, 21 Aug. '14. *Internationale Beziehungen*, II. 6. I. p. 116, footnote 3.
[5] *Documenti Diplomatici*, 5. I. p. 264, footnote 3. Salandra, 108.
[6] *Carteggio*, LXI. II. 265.
[7] Salandra, 112.

CHAPTER XIV

## The Diplomatic Duel Between Italy and Austria-Hungary

AGAINST this background, the Consulta was busily reconnoitring the diplomatic front.

When San Giuliano denied Rome's obligation to join Austria-Hungary, he was careful not to preclude the possibility of doing so. To say, as he did to the Ambassador Merey on August 2nd 1914, that 'even without our intervention we hope that opportunities will occur of proving our friendly feeling towards our Allies', served the purpose of avoiding a break. To add 'we therefore count upon an agreement . . . to reconcile our respective interests',[1] was plainly an offer of negotiations.

In Vienna, meanwhile, the light-headed confidence in Italy's pliancy had turned into resentful spite. Her declaration of neutrality was appraised as equivalent to abandoning the Alliance.[2] A sudden crop of cartoons displayed two soldiers of the *Dreibund* (Triplice) —a German and an Austrian—linked in a *Zweibund* and a lonely Bersaglieri as *Vagabund*.[3] Count Forgách, one of the Chiefs of the Foreign Ministry, expressed to Aldrovandi Marescotti his nostalgia for the vanished ambassadorial residences at Naples and Florence— a threat of dismemberment of the Kingdom, to which the Chargé d'Affaires retorted by owning to a similar sentiment regarding Warsaw.[4] The official attitude, however, was correct and, as Marescotti reported, 'extremely courteous'. Apart from the total absence of recriminations, the aggrieved partners went out of their way to satisfy 'the various demands addressed to them by us'.[5] Assurances were given regarding the security of Mount Lovchen which the Italians considered to be strategically vital to their position in the Adriatic. An indemnity was promised for the destruction of the radio station at Antivari (Montenegro) owned by an Italian company. The press was told to hold its peace. There were no public demonstrations.[6] Merey's idea of expelling the truant from the Alliance was

[1] Letter, 2 Aug. '14. Salandra, 65. L. Albertini, II. 251–2.
[2] Bollati to San Giuliano, 4 Aug. '14, quoting the Austrian Envoy in Berlin. *Documenti Diplomatici*, 5. I. No. 41, p. 23.
[3] Aldrovandi Marescotti, 14.
[4] *ibid.* 29, footnote 1. This reference to a restoration of Poland implied the loss of Galicia by Austria.
[5] Aldrovandi Marescotti to San Giuliano, 11 Aug. '14. Aldrovandi Marescotti, 17.
[6] Salandra, 90–1. Aldrovandi Marescotti, 17–18. Conrad, IV. 478. *Documenti Diplomatici*, 5. I. NN 49, 332, pp. 26, 182.

rejected. Berchtold was clearly anxious not to imperil a situation of such delicacy. And when Avarna, after a short absence, unexpectedly returned to the Danube, it was decided to send a new Envoy to the Quirinal.[1]

Merey, hectoring and insolent, was unpopular with his hosts. He was said to be seriously ill. Even if he was not, his record and the part he had played (so well from Vienna's standpoint) made him unfit to deal with this fresh and decisive stage in Italo-Austrian relations. Baron von Macchio, his successor, was Berchtold's right-hand man and supposed to possess the requisite polite and patient firmness.[2] The Emperor's words of farewell contained the hope that 'you will be able to deter the Italians from hostile steps'.[3] Ladies from the Red Cross added 'a little ovation' by way of patriotic encouragement.[4] The Foreign Ministry, as Macchio recollects, packed into his 'diplomatic bag . . . the extremely meagre wish. . . .: May God help us on!'[5] On August 15th, he called on San Giuliano who raised at once the issue of Article VII, claiming that any change in the *status quo* anywhere in the Balkans by the Dual Monarchy, including temporary occupation, entitled Rome to an equivalent benefit. Berchtold, in reply, asked the Italians to believe that Austria-Hungary had no thought of disturbing the equilibrium in the Balkans and the Adriatic. She did not seek territorial gains, and there was, therefore, no question of compensation. If perchance such designs should later on mature, she would not fail in loyal regard for her Ally's interests.[6] But the Italian demand was re-stated with such vigour that the Austrians, submitting to German pressure, accepted San Giuliano's interpretation on August 26th 1914. The condition hitherto insisted upon that such a reward must depend on Italy's honouring the Triplice Treaty was waived and the concession applied explicitly to the whole region of the Balkans.[7] This gave the Consulta, as Macchio reflected mournfully, 'a screw without an end . . . with which it could, as it pleased, make each phase of our

[1] Aldrovandi Marescotti's report, 11 Aug. '14. Aldrovandi Marescotti, 18; also 20. Salandra, 90.
[2] Salandra, 90-1. *Documenti Diplomatici*, 5. I. No. 459. pp. 248-9.
[3] 11 Aug. '14. Macchio, 26.
[4] Macchio, 29.       [5] Macchio, 27.
[6] Avarna to San Giuliano, 17 Aug. '14. *Documenti Diplomatici*, 5. I. No. 300, p. 169; also 12, 20 and 24 Aug. *ibid*. NN 209, 352, 423, pp. 121-2, 194, 229.
[7] San Giuliano to Avarna, 26 Aug. '14. *Documenti Diplomatici*, 5. I. No. 448, pp. 242-3. Also Macchio, 30, 38. Burián, 26. Salandra, 91, 219. Pribram, *Secret Treaties of Austria-Hungary*, II. 179. As the Habsburg Ambassador in Constantinople informed his Italian colleague, Italy's co-belligerency was no longer counted upon, but she was expected to preserve a benevolent neutrality. Garroni to San Giuliano, 26 Aug. *Documenti Diplomatici*, 5. I. No. 457, pp. 247-8. Pallavicini to Berchtold, 27 Aug. Deciphered in the Russian Foreign Ministry. *Internationale Beziehungen*, II. 6. I. p. 147, footnote 2.

military operations in Serbia the object of parleys on . . . compensation'.[1]

The first turn of the screw came inside a week in the shape of this telegram to Bollati:

> 'Numerous meetings have taken place in various parts of Italy . . . to bring pressure to bear on the Royal Government and to urge it into a war with Austria-Hungary. . . . The Royal Government will not be able to remain insensitive to the agitation of public opinion and . . . foresees that it will find it difficult . . . to continue its policy of neutrality. . . . It would, therefore, be appropriate for the Italian Government to give some satisfaction to Italian public opinion, at least . . . until public agitation quietens down, for example in regard to the Adriatic question. For this purpose, we could . . . occupy the island of Saseno[2] . . . and I . . . empower you to state everywhere that we do not thereby aim at territorial extension.'[3]

The Ambassador was instructed to ask Zimmermann, the Under-Secretary in the Wilhelmstrasse,

> 'to put this plan . . . before Count Berchtold in a favourable light as far as the German Government is concerned. . . .'[3]

This sortie caused no undue dismay in Vienna, since Macchio had already been striving to divert San Giuliano's attention to Albania.[4] Barely two months before, during the Sarayevo crisis, Berchtold had ruled out any compromise in this direction. Until late in August, the Dual Monarchy was still sending arms to that country.[5] But by now it had become advantageous to oblige, and simultaneously tie down, the wayward Ally in a region which, for the time being, was of secondary importance to Austria-Hungary. As Berchtold was soon to enlighten General Conrad,

> 'considering that an Albanian action by Italy is, after all, more opportune for us than any other exercise of her expansionist proclivities, and since it seems by no means ruled out that, in view of the pan-Islam movement in Albania, the latter will cause the Italians more bother than is apparently believed in Rome, there is no reason for Austria-Hungary, so long as the War lasts, to oppose Italy, while the oft-used phrases about preserving the accord . . . are quite sufficient to safeguard . . . our rights *pro futuro*. . . .'[6]

---

[1] Macchio, 38.
[2] Saseno dominates the entrance to the Bay of Valona.
[3] San Giuliano to Bollati, 4 Sept. '14. *Documenti Diplomatici*, 5. I. No. 576, p. 324. Cf. *Internationale Beziehungen*, II. 6. I. No. 219. p. 166. Salandra, 155.
[4] Macchio, 38.
[5] Berchtold to Tschirsky. *Österreich-Ungarns Aussenpolitik*, VIII, p. 278. Conrad, IV. 478.
[6] Memorandum from the Austro-Hungarian Foreign Office to Conrad, mid-Oct. '14. Conrad, V. 156. Cf. also *Documenti Diplomatici*, 5. I. No. 582, p. 333.

Hence, in reply to the demand of September 4th, Berlin, as Salandra states, 'raised no difficulty; Berchtold consented to discussion'.[1] The German Ambassador said at the Consulta: 'Why shouldn't you go to Valona? Who would prevent you? Everybody occupies something nowadays, why shouldn't you?'[2] Or, as Conrad put it: 'If they want to make for Albania, let them. I do not believe they will have much joy there'.[3] But no sooner had the Central Empires been forthcoming, than the Italians began a cat-and-mouse game, disclaiming interest in what was conceded, raising a different point (Valona), implying action, then hesitating.[4] No doubt, they had to tread warily lest they be tricked into misunderstandings with the Entente or, worse still—co-operation with their Allies.[5] Nor could they trust Vienna to be sincere in making this concession. Essentially, however, Albania was for them at this juncture only a pretext for starting negotiations. But care was taken to avoid the risk of their becoming an entanglement. For the Consulta had bigger fish to fry.

As early as July 27th 1914, Berchtold had received notice that 'the only territorial compensation we were prepared to accept would be the cession of a portion of the Italian provinces under Austria. . . .'[6] Even if the German Envoy, in a dispatch from Rome, had not mentioned it by name, this was an obvious reference to the Trentino.[7] In August, Berchtold told Conrad that Italy demanded that pearl of the Habsburg crown, without so much as contemplating co-belligerency. The General's comment was: 'impossible'. When the Foreign Minister asked him whether it would be worth while buying Italian co-operation by ceding the province, 'I replied that this was out of the question'. Rome should be 'kept waiting' while Austria improved her position by gaining Balkan Allies.[8] This being endorsed by the Emperor and the Hungarian Premier Tisza, San Giuliano was given to understand that the matter was tabu.[9]

Such obstinacy derived, *inter alia*, from what Macchio later defined as his 'cool appraisal of the situation which was as yet far from

---

[1] Salandra, 155. Also Bollati to San Giuliano, 5 and 8 Sept. '14. *Documenti Diplomatici*, 5. I. NN 589, 613, pp. 338-9, 353-4. Avarna to San Giuliano, 10 Sept. ibid. No. 640, pp. 371-2. Avarna to Bollati, 5 Oct. '14. *Carteggio*, LXI. II. 264.
[2] Salandra, 158-9. Cf. San Giuliano to Avarna, Bollati etc., 2 Oct. '14. *Documenti Diplomatici*, 5. I. No. 866, p. 514.
[3] Letter to Berchtold, 19 Oct. '14. Conrad, V. 206.
[4] San Giuliano to Bollati and Avarna, 10 Sept. '14. *Documenti Diplomatici*, 5 I. No. 642, p. 372. Also Salandra, 155-6, 158. Macchio, 38.
[5] See Salandra, 159-60.
[6] Salandra, 62.
[7] Letter to the Chancellor, 25 July '14. *Deutsche Dokumente*, I. No. 244, p. 239. Italy had asked for the Trentino as far back as 1878. Croce, 108.
[8] 6 and 7 Aug. '14. Conrad, IV. 182, 186, 185.
[9] Salandra, 62, 90. Cf. Avarna to San Giuliano, 2 Aug. '14. *Documenti Diplomatici*, 5. I. No. 11, p. 8.

G

having ripened'.¹ The Consulta was still directed by San Giuliano, 'a thoroughly conservative statesman' whose opposition to the restless pro-Entente radicals at home was expected by the Ambassador to produce a temporary identity of interests with the Habsburgs.² Italy was still presumed to be affected by 'her rivalry with France in North Africa and the Mediterranean',³ and to prefer as a neighbour an Austria-Hungary 'satiated in the Italian direction' to an avid Greater Serbia.⁴ She was still unready so that, if she were to take the field, this would not endanger the Dual Monarchy. It was unlikely, too, that the West would pay well enough for her assistance, of such negligible value. Also, Rome was known still to be waiting on developments.⁵ Drawing on 'confidential information', Berchtold could wire to his Envoys in Bucharest and Constantinople: 'There is no cause at all to believe that Italy, particularly in view of the present war position, will very soon abandon her neutrality. . . .'⁶ This view was confirmed as 'certain' by the Austro-Hungarian Military Attaché in Rome.⁷ On September 14th, the Vienna Foreign Office wrote to the Ambassador Macchio that 'the calm estimate . . . of the present situation . . . which you have given in your reports since your arrival in Rome has proved perfectly correct. . . . The rest naturally depends . . . on events at the fronts'.⁸

Not even the Marne disaster, or Avarna's growing despondency could shake the optimism of the Habsburg ruling set. Considering— —rightly—'that the war position . . . was the decisive factor in the game of Italian policy',⁹ they hoped that their anticipated victories would drive the prodigal back to the fold. Meanwhile, von Macchio was fighting in the shadows. Since the bigger of the Kingdom's accessible dailies were, as he asserted later, serving France and Britain, 'I . . . could only give attention to the provincial press'.¹⁰ Whilst the German Embassy founded and financed the *Victoria* and the *Concordia* and installed a news agency which 'blossomed in secret',¹⁰—he patronized the publishers of the leading Naples paper *Matino*, and of *Il Giorno*. The result was that the Southern Italians, every morning, were lectured on how much less important the Trentino was than Italy's Mediterranean status, which only

¹ Macchio, 57; also 40.   ² Macchio, 49.
³ Conrad to Berchtold, 28 July '14. Conrad, IV. 135. See also Conrad's Memorandum to Francis Joseph, Jan. '14. Conrad, III. 759.
⁴ See Conrad, III. 598.   ⁵ Burián, 59. Macchio, 65.
⁶ Berchtold to Pallavicini, 27 Aug. '14. Deciphered in the Russian Foreign Ministry. *Internationale Beziehungen*, II. 6. I. No. 169, p. 126. Also Berchtold to Conrad, 26 Aug. '14. Conrad, IV. 537.
⁷ Report to Conrad, 2 Sept. '14. Conrad, IV. 677.
⁸ Macchio, 39.
⁹ Macchio, 36. Also the Austro-Hungarian Military Attaché in Rome to Conrad, 12 Aug. '14. Conrad, IV. 204.
¹⁰ Macchio, 42; also 109.

the Triplice could shield against the French.¹ Some hitherto anti-Austrian sheets, moreover, were paid to change their tune. Large sums went on gaining the favours of politicians and deputies who, according to Conrad's Diary, 'promised to work on our behalf for a percentage commission'.² Industrialists were won by substantial orders, including deliveries worth 2,500,000 crowns for the Austro-Hungarian Ministry of War. Macchio had many dealings with 'firms and traders who did not scorn profitable business'.³ The Ambassador also reported a visit from the well-known Christian-Social Member for South Tyrol in the Austrian Parliament, Dr. Degasperi⁴ who was 'absolutely loyal to the Empire' and who, 'having many an acquaintance here, especially among the Catholic press, might on my repeated promptings ... by explaining the real state of affairs in South Tyrol, exert a soothing influence in Rome'.⁵

While this was going on, it was Berchtold's job to hold the diplomatic fort. With Austria-Hungary deeply engaged in Serbia and Galicia, it was vital not to provoke fresh enmities. Since the General Staff reckoned on victory by the summer of 1915 at the latest, the Foreign Minister had to play for time. This was to be gained by concessions without commitment. Hence the diversion to Albania which barely concealed a trap. Hence the offer that Italy should have 'primacy among the Latin peoples'.⁶ Hence the recognition of the principle of compensation, with the mental reservation that principles are frequent casualties in politics. And hence the firm avoidance of any discussion on the surrender of Austrian territory.⁷ 'Our flirtation with San Giuliano is delightful', the Hungarian Premier Tisza wrote to Berchtold, 'only one thing may not be promised: that we will give part of our own body'.⁸

In this, paradoxically, Berchtold was aided by the attitude of the Consulta. Avarna had warned San Giuliano that the Habsburgs would not abandon any part of their patrimony.⁹ Early in August, the Russians learned from Italian sources that 'there is little hope of

¹ Macchio, 85. Salandra, 205.
² 2 Nov. '14. Conrad, V. 369.
³ Macchio, 43. Conrad, V. 397; also 369.
⁴ Evidently the subsequent Prime Minister of the Republic of Italy, A. de Gasperri. See *Chi È*, 5th edit., p. 307.
⁵ Macchio to Berchtold, 6 Oct. '14. Conrad, V. 112–13.
⁶ Avarna to San Giuliano, 12 Aug. '14. *Documenti Diplomatici*, 5. I. No. 209, p. 122.
⁷ Andrassy, *Diplomacy and the War*, 127. Salandra, 91. Conrad, V. 331. Macchio, 39. Cf. Avarna to San Giuliano, 12 Aug. '14. *Documenti Diplomatici*, 5. I. No. 212, p. 125.
⁸ Tisza to Berchtold, 24 Aug. '14. Tisza, I. 60.
⁹ Avarna to San Giuliano, 2 Aug. '14. *Documenti Diplomatici*, 5. I. No. 11, p. 8. Avarna to Bollati, 5 Oct. '14. *Carteggio*, LXI II. 263.

obtaining what is desired from Germany and Austria'.[1] An official request for the Trentino, therefore, could only result in a formal refusal. This, in turn, would carry the risk of a breach which was undesirable at this stage of Italy's preparations.[2] In consequence, although the claim was pressed in various shapes and forms, it was never put forward directly, but always so as to leave scope for disavowal. The most favoured channel of transmission was Berlin.[3] Hints would also be dropped in Constantinople. Or Victor Emmanuel's Minister in Bucharest would tell King Carol, a loyal friend of William and Francis Joseph, that Italy would join the Central Alliance, if she obtained the main object of her desires.[4] But, as the Ambassador Avarna—the only person, apart from his Chief, qualified to raise the matter—wrote to Bollati as late as October 5th 1914, 'with regard to the eventual cession of the Trentino, I was never charged with the task of exploring the possibility here in Vienna'.[5]

Such reticence allowed Berchtold to imply No without saying it, and so to maintain, without fear of rupture, a negative attitude. Nor did this ruffle the waters of the Tiber. For, like their Austrian antagonists, the Italians, too, wanted as yet no Rubicon to cross. Like them, they welcomed the interval in the exchanges occasioned by San Giuliano's confinement to his death-bed.[6] As it was evident that any conceivable compromise on the Trentino would be too much for the Dual Monarchy and not nearly enough for the Kingdom,[7] it would seem that Italy could neither have expected nor wished to strike a bargain with Austria-Hungary.

But why spend all that ingenuity and trouble negotiating claims, 'even while convinced [as Salandra confessed later] they would not be accepted'?[8] It was prudent to provide for the off-chance that the Central Powers might after all be victorious. It was advisable to confuse and distract the men on the Danube, lest they disturb Italy's preparations by a preventive military move. It was necessary to

---

[1] Sazonov to Izvolski, 4 Aug. '14. *Das Zaristische Russland*, p. 263.
[2] Salandra, 219.
[3] Avarna to Bollati, 5 Oct. '14. *Carteggio*, LXI. II. 263.
[4] The Austro-Hungarian Military Attaché in Rumania to Conrad, 7 Aug. '14. Conrad, IV. 185.
[5] *Carteggio*, LXI. II. 263.
[6] See San Giuliano to Avarna, 11 Oct. '14. *Documenti Diplomatici*, 5. I. No. 934, p. 559. Avarna to San Giuliano, 13 Oct. *ibid.* No. 939, p. 563. Also Macchio, 39, 45.
[7] 'It would be impossible to hope for any sufficiently precise declaration such as would satisfy adequately our national aspirations'. Avarna to Bollati, 5 Oct. '14. *Carteggio*, LXI. II. 264. As early as Aug. '14, San Giuliano told Avarna that, even if the Trentino were ceded, Italy would not march with Austria-Hungary. *Documenti Diplomatici*, 5. I. No. 212, p. 125.
[8] Salandra, 264.

be able to convince the pacific majority of the nation that the War, when it came, was the fault of the enemy.[1] It was expedient to gain time so as to be able to choose the best moment for attack. And it was, above all, imperative to help on—by parleys with the Central Powers—the discussions conducted simultaneously with the Entente.

Salandra, 264. Croce, 273.

CHAPTER XV

## Italy and the Triple Entente

1

SOUNDINGS IN PETROGRAD AND LONDON

THE Consulta had thrown out feelers to both sides from the first days of the War. Even while coupling its neutrality declaration with assurances to the German Envoy that Italy might consider assisting her Allies, it conveyed to the Russian Foreign Minister 'in strict confidence' that, as he wired to the Ambassador Izvolski, 'Italy could enter with us into an exchange of views. . . .'[1] Carlotti, the Ambassador in Petrograd, intimated to Sazonov the conditions on which his country would join the Entente: ' . . . apart from acquiring the Trentino, Italy wishes to secure predominance in the Adriatic and . . . to obtain Valona. . . . Invoking the lack of mutual confidence which still distinguishes Franco-Italian relations, the Ambassador suggested that the negotiations . . . should proceed by our good offices'.[1] Considering Poincaré's opinion that Rome should be won by the offer of a free hand in Albania,[2] Sazonov consented to the demand for Valona in addition to the Trentino. Izvolski was instructed to consult the Quai d'Orsay. 'I assume that, if the French Government should agree . . . we could enter into very confidential negotiations with Italy'.[3]

The warm response of Russia was due to the expectation that the Galician and Serbian fronts would benefit at once if Austria were diverted by an attack from the South-West. Italy's adherence moreover was almost certain to entail that of Rumania.[4] France, too, stood to gain from an Italian Alliance; it would lead to the uncontested mastery of the Mediterranean, safe transport for her African Army, security of her Alpine frontier, the release of forces immobilized there, and the end of Germany's strategic and numerical superiority on the Rhine.[5] Poincaré found fault with the 'rather ominous' Russian proposition. For 'this singularly premature guarantee' to Italy would enable her, after victory, to push her claims before the restitution of Alsace-Lorraine to the French.[6]

[1] Sazonov to Izvolski, 4 Aug. '14. *Das Zaristische Russland*, pp. 263–4.
[2] Izvolski to Sazonov, 1 Aug. '14. *Das Zaristische Russland*, p. 263, footnote 1.
[3] Sazonov to Izvolski, 4 Aug. '14. *Das Zatistische Russland*, p. 263. Cf. Carlotti to San Giuliano, 5 Aug. '14. *Documenti Diplomatici*, 5. I. No. 65, p. 37. This dispatch implies that the initiative was Sazonov's; but it is printed with a significant footnote-reference to the above telegram from Sazonov to Izvolski of 4 Aug.
[4] Poklevski to Sazonov, 27 Aug. '14. Stieve, p. 86.
[5] Tirpitz, 250. Noël, *Camille Barrère*, 92.   [6] Poincaré, V. 15.

ITALY AND THE TRIPLE ENTENTE 199

The advantages, however, were so great that, on August 5th, the Foreign Minister Doumergue accepted the cession of the Trentino and Valona—'without prejudice to our national revendications',[1] and agreed 'that the negotiations are conducted through the medium of Russia. . . .'[2] He also informed Britain of the move. A telegram from Benckendorff shows that 'Grey attaches extraordinary importance to it. He thinks that it is absolutely necessary to add Trieste . . . which . . . more than anthing else will satisfy public opinion in Italy'.[3] Paris raised no objections to this increment.[4] London not only agreed to, but insisted on, the talks being held in Petrograd.[5] And on August 7th, Sazonov could inform the Ambassador in Rome, Krupenski, of the Entente's offer of the Trentino, Trieste, Valona and Adriatic supremacy (linked with territorial extensions for Serbia and Greece), 'on condition that Italy . . . on some suitable pretext immediately declared war on Austria'. In Russia's view, 'time is short and Italy must decide quickly, or else her help will become less valuable to us. . . . You should . . . speak in this sense to the [Italian] Foreign Minister. . . . If he is agreeable . . . the negotiations on detail . . . could be entrusted to the four-Power representatives in Petrograd. . . .'[6] At the same time, Izvolski and Benkendorff were instructed to get France and Britain to make identical declarations and to press for speed in Rome.[7]

For the Consulta was hesitating, and not only because Italy was not ready. Salandra later summed up his reactions by the revealing comment that the Russians 'made us generous offers of Austrian territory—to be won, *bien entendu*, by our arms'.[8] He does not say whether he expected the others to do the fighting for him. But it is clear that the promised rewards were insufficient for the Italian imperialists. They wanted spoils not only from their prospective enemies but also from their future Allies.[9] Sazonov was the first to

[1] Poincaré, V. 16. *Das Zaristische Russland*, p. 264.
[2] Izvolski to Sazonov, 5 Aug. '14. *Das Zaristische Russland*, p. 264.
[3] Benckendorff to Sazonov, 6 Aug. '14. *Das Zaristische Russland*, pp. 264–5.
[4] Izvolski to Sazonov, 6 Aug. '14. *Das Zaristische Russland*, p. 265.
[5] Izvolski to Sazonov, 7 Aug. '14. Stieve, p. 27. Sazonov to Krupenski, 7 Aug. '14. *Das Zaristische Russland*, p. 266.
[6] Sazonov to Krupenski, 7 Aug. '14. *Das Zaristische Russland*, pp. 265–6. Carlotti to San Giuliano, 7 and 8 Aug. '14. *Documenti Diplomatici*, 5. I. NN 120, 133, pp. 65, 71.
[7] Sazonov to Benckendorff and Izvolski, 7 and 10 Aug. '14. *Des Zaristische Russland*, pp. 266–8. Carlotti to San Giuliano, 11 Aug. '14. *Documenti Diplomatici*, 5. I. No. 179, p. 101. Salandra, 87.
[8] Salandra, 87.
[9] 'M. Sazonov said that, judging by conversations with the Italian Ambassador here, the Italian claims were growing rapidly in every direction and that they were aspiring after territories in which both England and France are very interested'. Buchanan to Grey, 7 Oct. '14. Deciphered in the Russian Foreign Ministry. Retranslated from a translation of the original. *Internationale Beziehungen*, II. 6. I. No. 368, pp. 290–1.

be approached because at this juncture Russia, anticipating more direct relief from Italian belligerency than Britain and France, could be expected to intercede with the latter, particularly as she would not yet have to pay for it out of her own pocket. Essentially San Giuliano used Petrograd as the sounding board of the Entente and, having struck a satisfactory response,[1] soon tried another tune. According to a dispatch from Grey to Sir Rennell Rodd,

'to-day, the Italian Ambassador, having impressed absolute secrecy on me, made a communication to me. . . . Italy desired to be neutral . . . but she felt the danger of a change of equilibrium being brought about, especially in the Adriatic and Mediterranean; she felt the danger to herself from the animosity that Germany and Austria had towards her . . . and she sympathized very much with the idea . . . that we were fighting to put an end to a military domination in the West of Europe. Italy might, therefore, be brought to side with us in this War. If so, certain conditions would be necessary. . . .
1. The British, French and Russian Governments to agree not to conclude peace separately from Italy. 2. The British and French Fleets to unite . . . with the Italian Fleet . . . and then together destroy the Austrian Fleet. 3. . . . Italy to have the Trentino up to the Alpine watershed and Trieste. . . . 4. Valona with the region near it, to be . . . neutralized . . . made autonomous and internationalized . . . with all Adriatic Powers, including Italy, taking part in its administration. 5. . . . if Turkish integrity is not preserved, Italy to have her part in the provinces on the Mediterranean. 6. The Italian concessions at Adalia to be maintained. 7. . . . some functionaries . . . might be left by Italy on the Aegean islands at present occupied by her. 8. Italy to have a share of the war indemnity. . . . 9. The four Powers, Britain, France, Russia and Italy, to pledge themselves to maintain and defend the settlement and equilibrium resulting from the War. . . .
I said that . . . if Italy became our Ally . . . we would, subject to the discussion of details, give a general assent to these conditions, and to some of them, such as the acquisition of the Trentino and Trieste . . . we would consent absolutely; but we could not pledge ourselves to any of these things till Italy stated definitely that she was prepared to join us'.[2]

The measured courtesy of Grey's reply revealed the distance dividing Whitehall from the Consulta, despite the mutual desire

[1] See Carlotti to San Giuliano, 11 Aug. '14. *Documenti Diplomatici*, 5. I. No. 194, pp. 109–10.
[2] Grey to Rodd, 12 Aug. '14. Trevelyan, 291–2. Cf. San Giuliano to Imperiali, 11 Aug. '14. *Documenti Diplomatici*, 5. I. No. 201, pp. 114–16, where the same communication is given more fully and with slight verbal modifications. For Grey's reply, expressing general agreement with eight of the nine points submitted by Italy, see Imperiali to San Giuliano, 12 and 15 Aug. *ibid.* NN 223, 269, pp. 130, 154. It was presumably to amplify point 2 that San Giuliano on 20 Aug. demanded a guarantee that Britain and France would see the War against Austria through to the end. *ibid.* No. 355, p. 196.

for co-operation. The British regarded Trieste, the Trentino and Valona as inducements which were both necessary and adequate. But, as San Giuliano instructed Imperiali, 'neither Trent nor Trieste could be considered in the light of cessions made to us by the Triple Entente.... Italy's chief interest... is in the Adriatic. Austria-Hungary and not Germany is our adversary. On the other hand, the principal aim of the Triple Entente is to crush Germany, while the Adriatic question is of secondary importance to it. It follows that we have need of distinct pledges and most adequate assistance against Austria-Hungary'.[1] The first of these pledges was the ban on a separate peace whereby the future Allies might come to terms with the Reich and leave Italy to cope with Vienna as best she might. This point was soon accepted by Grey.[2] But joint operations of the British, French and Italian Navies to 'destroy' the Habsburg Fleet was another matter, for it touched a sensitive spot in Britain's traditional policy.

2

LONDON, VIENNA AND THE BALANCE OF POWER

When Berchtold requested Mensdorff, the Ambassador in London, to acquaint Grey, on July 23rd 1914, with the ultimatum to Belgrade, he was instructed to remind the Foreign Secretary of the important role the Dual Monarchy was playing among the Powers.[3] This was a bid to turn to his Government's advantage the ingrained British notion that the Danubian Empire was essential for the European balance. Although, as an Ally of the Reich, Austria-Hungary had long stood in the rival camp, her relations with Britain were friendly. Their paths hardly crossed overseas, and despite commercial competition in the Balkans they were drawn together by common antagonisms.[4] If the Dual Monarchy had not existed, it would (to adapt a famous saying) have had to be invented by Whitehall as a counterpoise to Germany and Russia.

So, on July 30th, Mensdorff could telegraph that Grey was doing

[1] San Giuliano to Imperiali, 16 Sept. '14. Salandra, 266–7.
[2] Izvolski to Sazonov, 25 Aug. '14, on Grey's instructions to Rodd. *Das Zaristische Russland*, pp. 275–6. Also Krupenski to Sazonov, 29 Aug. '14. *Internationale Beziehungen*, II. 6. I. No. 186, p. 141.
[3] Pribram, *Austria-Hungary and Great Britain*, 229.
[4] ibid. 216, 218. May, 92. Jonescu, 96. A leading article in *The Times*, 30 Aug. 1909, expressed 'the wish that relations with Austria-Hungary may regain their former cordiality... it is eminently desirable to know whether, in their relations with Austria-Hungary, British statesmen will have to reckon with a Power conscious of its own individuality or with a Power that...will feel bound, over and above its obligations as an Ally, to identify itself with another Power....' Steed, 264–5.

his utmost to obtain from Serbia complete satisfaction and guarantees for Vienna.¹ On the day when Britain took up arms, Grey wired to Rodd: 'I do not suppose we shall declare war upon Austria unless some direct provocation is given'.² About the same time, the Austrian Ambassador reported an assurance from the Foreign Secretary that there was no cause for conflict between their respective countries.³ The *Westminster Gazette*, which was close to the Foreign Office, wrote during the Sarayevo crisis that 'Austria-Hungary had a *prima facie* case....' The *Daily Chronicle* described the ultimatum as 'reasonable self-defence'. The *Manchester Guardian* saw in the Tsar's warning of armed intervention 'a piece of sheer brutality'. *John Bull* later summarized these widespread sentiments in the slogan: 'To Hell with Serbia!'⁴ After Britain, too, was involved, new considerations reinforced the old sympathy restraining her from taking up arms against the Habsburgs. These were the strategic situation in the Mediterranean, where the *Goeben* and the *Breslau* were at large, and the unwillingness to give Austria a legal case for soliciting Italian co-operation under the Triplice.

But in order to enrol Italy, the Entente had to be in a position to offer her the prizes she coveted most, and these were held by Francis Joseph. Also, Russia began to resent the Western tenderness towards her principal enemy,⁵ and it was necessary to reassure her. The British and French declaration of war (on August 12th 1914) therefore was unavoidable. However, as Franckenstein, at the time Commercial Counsellor in London, recollects, 'in the early days many people, both in Austria and England . . . believed that, thanks to geography, the British declaration of war . . . was more or less formal, and would not lead to serious hostilities. . . . Many friends of Count Mensdorff . . . came to the Embassy. . . . The Ambassador several times saw Sir Edward Grey and Lord Haldane. He was also received kindly, but unofficially, by King George and Queen Mary. . . .'⁶ According to the Russian Ambassador's 'private conversations with Ministers and influential Conservatives', their programme of severing from the Danubian Monarchy her Polish and Ukrainian provinces, the Bukovina, Transylvania, Bosnia-Herzego-

---

¹ Pribram, *Austria-Hungary and Great Britain*, 256.
² Grey to Rodd, 4 Aug. '14. Gooch and Temperley, Vol. XI. No. 591, p. 313.
³ Conrad, IV. 179.
⁴ Pribram, *Austria-Hungary and Great Britain*, 222–23, 234. 'Servia' in the original. The *Daily Telegraph*, the *Pall Mall Gazette* and the *Standard* were also pro-Austrian. The *Times* and the *Morning Post* led the opposite camp. *ibid*. 234, 240.
⁵ Poincaré, V. 56. For San Giuliano's complaint that 'England, whilst urging us to take part in the War . . . is not yet at war with Austria. . . .' See his telegram to Imperiali, 11 Aug. '14. *Documenti Diplomatici*, 5. I. No. 201, p. 116.
⁶ Franckenstein, *Facts and Features of My Life*, 160–1.

vina, the Trentino and the Adriatic coast was coupled 'with a certain regret, since Austria is fairly generally regarded as . . . a fictim of Germany'.[1] Izvolski, reporting to his Chief on 'the indubitable French sympathies' for Austria-Hungary, emphasized that they 'are still stronger in England'.[2] A memorandum from a high Russian Consular official mentions that 'some anxieties regarding Hungary's future' were apparent in the West, that already Magyar agents were able to busy themselves in London, and that the tendency to accord them a good reception came from 'the fear of too strong an advance of the Slavs to the Mediterranean'.[3]

3
BRITAIN'S RESPONSE TO ITALY

In the circumstances, it could be argued that Whitehall did not wish to aggravate the inevitable diminution of Austria-Hungary's power by the destruction of her Fleet, which the Consulta was demanding. Since the expected victory was certain to result in an extension of Italy, Britain must, on the contrary, have had an added motive for wishing to preserve a viable Central European State— including, it was presumed, Austria-Hungary, the Czech and Slovak lands, Slovenia and Croatia—to balance not only Germany (however reduced) and a much enlarged Russia, but also the expanding Italian Kingdom. The Habsburg naval forces, in particular, could serve as a useful check on the Mediterranean ambitions of Rome.

Salandra was to write later that 'from the very first months of the War we considered . . . that, notwithstanding our . . . unpreparedness, in the case of a serious offensive by the Anglo-French Fleet in the Adriatic . . . our immediate participation was inevitable. We could not . . . have left it to the Serbs and Montenegrins; but there was nothing more than . . . a bombardment of Cattaro. . . .'[4] Time and again the Ambassador Imperiali was instructed to underline in London 'the great influence a more decisive action of the Anglo-French Fleet in the Adriatic would have upon our decisions'.[5] His colleague Tittoni said at the Quai d'Orsay that Italy, 'may be, will end up by marching with you . . . if you and England decide to

---

[1] Benckendorff to Sazonov, 28 Sept. '14. *Internationale Beziehungen*, II. 6. I. No. 329, pp. 253–4. Some of these terms, of course, depended on Italian and Rumanian belligerency.
[2] Izvolski to Sazonov, 13 Oct. '14. *Internationale Beziehungen*, II. 6. I. No. 386, p. 305.
[3] Izvolski to Sazonov, 14 Dec. '14. Stieve, pp. 136, 159.
[4] Salandra, 266.
[5] The quotation is from Salandra, 267. See also San Giuliano to Imperiali, 12, 24, 28 Aug., 16, 19, 21 Sept. '14. *Documenti Diplomatici*, 5. I. NN 205, 421, 474, 703, 740, 764, pp. 120, 228, 261–2, 412, 435, 451.

render the Austrian Navy innocuous!'[1] Yet, as late as October 24th 1914, Admiral Haus, the Commander-in-Chief of the Austro-Hungarian Marine, could state that French warships had appeared in Dalmatian waters only eight times, and a solitary British cruiser once, to convoy food and arms to Antivari. The French conducted only minor operations. 'For the rest, they content themselves with blockading the Straits of Otranto'.[2] Grey was said to have stated to the Consulta that, if Italy joined the Entente, her Navy would co-operate with those of the Allies. But this was far from a pledge to destroy the Habsburg flotillas. San Giuliano complained, not without reason, that 'the inaction of the Anglo-French Fleet . . . increases the suspicion that the Triple Entente wants to spare Austria-Hungary. . . .'[3]

Nor is there evidence of Britain's readiness to guarantee 'the settlement . . . resulting from the War'.[4] It is more likely that she did not care to perpetuate terms which, by tradition, she was bound to regret. This was all the more true since Italy's pretensions transcended the continental sphere. Points 5 and 6 in San Giuliano's list were claims for a share in the Ottoman inheritance. A telegram from San Giuliano to the Ambassador in Russia mentions—apart from 'Austria's Italian provinces', Valona and the Dodecanese—also an extension of the Italian zone in Turkey from Adalia to Mersina, plus 'diplomatic support in the event of difficulties on the part of Abyssinia' and 'concessions in Africa' as compensation for what Britain and France would gain in the German colonies.[5]

Even if such requests were not specified in August, Grey could not have been unaware that Rome's aspirations overseas could, unless they were checked, become a challenge to British imperial interests some day. Far from contemplating a wider radius of activity for the Italian Navy, the Foreign Secretary, on August 8th, implied to Benckendorff that it would be well occupied [that is tied down] in the

---

[1] 12 Aug. '14. Poincaré, V. 79. See also San Giuliano to Tittoni, 12 and 30 Aug. and 22 Sept. '14. *Documenti Diplomatici*, 5. I. NN 206, 503, 775, pp. 12, 278, 457.

[2] Memorandum, 24 Oct. '14. Conrad, V. 303–4. Considering the Franco-Italian rivalry in the Mediterranean, it would seem that the French interest in preserving the Austro-Hungarian Fleet as a counterweight to that of Italy was even greater than Britain's.

[3] San Giuliano to Imperiali, 17 Sept. '14. *Documenti Diplomatici*, 5. I. No. 726, p. 426. For Grey's statement see Izvolski to Sazonov, 25 Aug. '14. *Das Zaristische Russland*, p. 275–6. Krupenski to Sazonov, 29 Aug. *Internationale Beziehungen*, II. 6. I. No. 186, p. 141.

[4] See p. 200 above.

[5] San Giuliano to Carlotti, 25 Sept. '14. Deciphered in the Russian Foreign Ministry. *Internationale Beziehungen*, II. 6. I. No. 313, pp. 239–40. Also Imperiali to San Giuliano, 28 Aug. '14. San Giuliano to Imperiali, 29 Aug. *Documenti Diplomatici*, 5. I. NN 474, 497, pp. 260–1, 275.

Adriatic.[1] Sir Francis Bertie's question: 'How soon will the Italians think the time propitious for selling themselves?'[2] reflected more than personal irritation with the rapaciousness of the Consulta. Churchill, in an interview granted to the *Giornale d'Italia*, gave scant encouragement to Rome's claims in the Mediterranean and elsewhere.[3] Even if such sentiments were not vocal earlier, they must have been forming in August, especially since little help could, at this stage, be expected from an Ally so little prepared. Japan's entry into the War on August 15th 1914 relieved the Royal Navy (at least in the Pacific and Indian Oceans) sufficiently to dispense with whatever assistance might otherwise have been required from the Italian. In 1914, therefore, the service Rome could render appeared to Britain as altogether out of proportion to the computed costs. And what made these wholly unacceptable was the demand for an advance commitment, without which 'it would not be possible for Italy to come into agreement with us'.[4] The Consulta's purpose was to use such a preliminary understanding as a means of getting a higher price in Vienna, then to blackmail the Entente with it, and treat each side alternatively to a spiral of extortions. Hence, Grey refused altogether to negotiate so long as the Italians adhered to 'hypothetical eventualities'.[5] He 'does not wish to embarrass the Italian Government by insistence and importune solicitations, but rather desires to leave it complete freedom to make decisions. . . .'[6] In short, he would do nothing until the Italians had communicated to him their decision to abandon neutrality.[7] And this meant that, once having burnt her boats, Italy would have to accept what she was given.

As a result of this policy, Sazonov found that Grey, backed by Doumergue, opposed the urgent démarche which he desired to be made in Rome. The Russian Ambassador there reported on August 12th that 'my instructions do not tally' with those of the British and French Envoys. Rodd was only authorized to hint to San Giuliano that 'Great Britain will certainly consider herself fortunate if Italy should adhere to the Triple Entente, but that this is Italy's own

---

[1] Benckendorff to Sazonov, 8 Aug. '14. *Das Zaristische Russland*, p. 273.
[2] 18 Sept. '14. Bertie, L. 34.
[3] Imperiali to San Giuliano, 24 and 25 Sept. '14. *Documenti Diplomatici*, 5. I. No. 802, p. 474 and *ibid.*, footnote 2. Buchanan to Grey, 7 Oct. '14. Deciphered in the Russian Foreign Ministry. *Internationale Beziehungen*, II. 6. I. No. 368, pp. 290–1.
[4] Grey to Rodd, 12 Aug. '14. Trevelyan, 291. Cf. Salandra, 165: Italy could never 'have been induced to intervene without previous agreements'.
[5] Imperiali to San Giuliano, 18 Aug. '14. *Documenti Diplomatici*, 5. I. No. 317, p. 175. Also 24 Aug. *ibid.* No. 434, p. 235.
[6] Imperiali to San Giuliano, 15 Aug. '14. *Documenti Diplomatici*, 5. I. No. 256, p. 147.
[7] Salandra, 265–6. Also Poincaré, V. 127. *Carteggio*, LXI. III. 394.

concern, and that it is not for Britain to make such a proposition'.[1] Barrère was enjoined to confine himself to 'discreet' intimations. As for himself, Krupenski added that, owing to their attitude, he had postponed making his own representations. Izvolski and Benckendorff wired that Doumergue and Grey maintained their veto on any official steps lest 'they should render more difficult Italy's complete *volte face*'.[2] So there was nothing left to Sazonov but to tell Krupenski:

'You may, after the example of the English and French Ambassadors, confine yourself for the time being to expressing to the [Italian] Foreign Minister your gratification about Italy's ... neutrality. You may add that, if Italy should be willing to pursue the road of co-ordinating her policy with the views of the ... Triple Entente, she would meet with ... the readiness to satisfy her national desires in a far-reaching way....'[3]

But when Rodd, apart from endorsing the promises made by Sazonov, presented to Salandra, on August 13th, the prescribed generalities, he was reminded that Italy's neutrality was in keeping with her duties as an Ally of the Central Powers.[4] This notice that she was as yet by no means on the side of the angels was coupled with the rejoinder that, things being what they were, it was 'better at present to refrain from any action which might compel Italy to deny her co-operation to the Triple Entente, and perhaps impede the success of further discussions'.[5] On the 16th, the Ambassador Imperiali was instructed to inform Britain that 'it is not possible at present to take a definite decision, and we shall not be able to do so later without knowing whether our just and moderate conditions are accepted.... Grey might expound them to Russia and France as his ideas ... and then make us concrete proposals'. Italy would not abandon neutrality unless detailed agreements had first been concluded with the three Allied Powers to be negotiated with the utmost secrecy by Grey and Imperiali only, and exclusively in London. The Foreign Secretary was to ensure that neither Barrère

---

[1] Krupenski to Sazonov, 12 Aug. '14. The quotation is translated from a translation of the French original. *Internationale Beziehungen*, II. 6. I. No. 80, pp. 55–6. Salandra to San Giuliano, 13 Aug. '14. *Documenti Diplomatici*, 5. I. No. 232, p. 135.
[2] Benckendorff to Sazonov, 12 Aug. '14. *Internationale Beziehungen*, II. 6. I. No. 77, p. 54. Izvolski to Sazonov, 11 Aug. Stieve, p. 43. Also Imperiali to San Giuliano, 22 Aug. '14. *Documenti Diplomatici*, 5. I. No. 397, p. 216.
[3] Sazonov to Krupenski, 13 Aug. '14. *Internationale Beziehungen*, II. 6. I. No. 86, p. 60.
[4] Benckendorff to Sazonov, 14 Aug. '14. *Internationale Beziehungen*, II. 6. I. p. 53, footnote 2.
[5] Krupenski to Sazonov, 13 Aug. '14. *Internationale Beziehungen*, II. 6. I. No. 91, p. 62. Salandra to San Giuliano, 13 Aug. *Documenti Diplomatici*, 5. I. No. 232, p. 135. Also Poincaré, V. 88–9.

nor Krupenski mentioned the subject to San Giuliano.¹ Diverse excuses were offered for shifting the scene of the parleys. The French were told that Izvolski was not trusted, the British that their discretion was much preferred, the Russians that Germany and Austria might become suspicious if talks were held in Rome.²

But this was not why the Consulta shunned the diplomacy of the revolving door which admits one set of negotiators as the other is leaving. One reason was the sudden obduracy of Sazonov. He had had a dispatch from the Ambassador Giers reporting—after a reference to 'members of the Italian Embassy in Constantinople'— that 'I have received in a round-about way a map showing ... the outlines of a possible boundary between Italy and Serbia. According to the competent authority who handed me the map, it is said to be necessary to fix the frontiers now', allocating to the Italians Istria, the Southern portion of Croatia and a part of Dalmatia, with the islands facing these shores. 'They do not deny that, in some places, they aspire to areas where Slavs are in the majority'.³ Next day, the Russian Foreign Ministry deciphered a telegram from San Giuliano to Carlotti which mentioned a border-line 'following the watershed of the Alps as far as the Quarnero. This would require that we should march into Dalmatia'.⁴ These messages were dated September 24th and 25th. But already by August 11th Sazonov had heard from Carlotti that Italy had pretensions to the Dalmatian littoral.⁵ On August 17th, he cabled to Benckendorff that 'we have drawn the Italian Ambassador's attention to the danger for Italy of creating an Irredentism as the outcome of the War ... we cannot consent to such an aim'. And on August 24th: 'Since Serbia has pressing need of an outlet to the sea ... I consider it necessary, in the negotiations with Italy, carefully to avoid premature promises regarding the Dalmatian coast. ...'⁶

San Giuliano, therefore, playing on Russo-British rivalries in the

¹ San Giuliano to Imperiali, 16 Aug. '14. *Documenti Diplomatici*, 5. I. No. 276, p. 157. Also 19 and 24 Aug. *ibid.* NN 334, 422, pp. 183, 229. San Giuliano to Carlotti, 16 Aug. '14. *ibid.* No. 279, pp. 158–9. Poincaré, V. 113. Salandra, 88. Macchio, 40.
² Sazonov to Krupenski, 18 Aug. '14. *Das Zaristische Russland*, p. 272. Poincaré, V. 113.
³ Giers to Sazonov, 24 Sept. '14. *Internationale Beziehungen*, II. 6. I. No. 310, pp. 237–8. Also Poklevski to Sazonov, 10 Sept. '14, on Fasciotti's request for the Adriatic coast, including Istria. Stieve, p. 110.
⁴ San Giuliano to Carlotti, 25 Sept. '14. *Internationale Beziehungen*, II. 6. I. No. 313, pp. 239–40.
⁵ Paléologue to Doumergue, 11 Aug. '14. Poincaré, V. 72. Poklevski to Sazonov, 17 Aug. '14, mentions also Istria. Stieve, p. 61.
⁶ Sazonov to Benckendorff, 17 and 24 Aug. '14. *Das Zaristische Russland*, pp. 271–2, 274–5. This would seem to contradict Carlotti's assertion (telegram to San Giuliano, 11 Aug. *Documenti Diplomatici*, 5. I. No. 194, p. 110) that Russia had granted to Italy Dalmatia from Zara to Ragusa.

Near East, sought backing in Whitehall against Petrograd. The Russian stand, moreover, was reinforced by M. Doumergue.[1] Considering the difficulties San Giuliano was having in Paris,[2] he hoped to defeat the French, too, on the Thames. 'Italo-English friendship . . . given the common interests of the two Governments to maintain a stable equilibrium . . . will allow us to count always on British help should this equilibrium be threatened by a victorious and emboldened France'.[3] However, the main cause for this concentration on London was Britain herself. There was no sense in parleying with the lesser partner, if the doyen of the coalition rejected Italy's most crucial terms. So it was Imperiali's task to out-manoeuvre and out-fight Grey. The lead in the discussions with the Consulta passed from Russia to Britain.

Meanwhile Sazonov, unabashed by his own refusal to gratify Rome's Dalmatian desires, was 'continuously telling Carlotti that the more quickly Italy joined us, the more valuable to us would be her co-operation'.[4] He reminded the Consulta that the Dual Monarchy's main force was in Serbia and Galicia, leaving only one army corps on the Italian frontier. 'It is now in Italy's interest to hasten the capture of the Tyrol'.[5] His constant refrain was that 'no one could get anything for nothing' and that peace terms would be dictated sword in hand.[6] At the same time, he urged in London and Paris that, even if a démarche in Rome was avoided, there should be other means of 'pulling Italy into the War with Austria, for example by some action of the Anglo-French Navy in the Adriatic'. And: 'One should have thought that, with its superiority over the Austrian Fleet . . . it could still undertake something on the Dalmatian coast. . . .'[7] In fact, San Giuliano stated explicitly to Krupenski that naval operations by the Entente would speed Italy's decision.[8] But so far as the British and French Admiralties were concerned, the Adriatic might have been *mare incognito*.[9] As for their Foreign Ministries, Grey, far from giving Rodd new instructions, actually

[1] Izvolski to Sazonov, 25 Aug. '14. Stieve, p. 77.
[2] See pp. 211–23 below.
[3] Imperiali to San Giuliano, 14 Aug. '14. *Documenti Diplomatici*, 5. I. No. 242, p. 140. Similar ideas were expressed by Salandra in an interview with Rodd. Salandra to San Giuliano, 13 Aug. *ibid.* No. 232, p. 136.
[4] Sazonov to Benckendorff, 18 Aug. '14. *Internationale Beziehungen*, II. 6. I. No. 123, pp. 91–2.
[5] Sazonov to Krupenski, 26 Aug. '14. *Das Zaristische Russland*, p. 276.
[6] Krupenski to Sazonov, 29 Aug. '14. *Internationale Beziehungen*, II. 6. I. No. 186, p. 141. Carlotti to San Giuliano, 14 Sept. '14. *Documenti Diplomatici*, 5. I. No. 674, pp. 391–3; and *Internationale Beziehungen*, II. 6. I. No. 257, pp. 195–6.
[7] Sazonov to Benckendorff and Izvolski, 29 Aug. and 20 Sept. '14. *Das Zaristische Russland*, pp. 277–80.
[8] Krupenski to Sazonov, 22 Aug. '14. *Das Zaristische Russland*, p. 274. For Imperiali's and Tittoni's statements in the same sense, see pp. 203–4 above.
[9] See p. 204 above.

directed him not to broach any more the question of Italian belligerency. And in a telegram to Buchanan—seconded by one from Doumergue to Paléologue—he expressed the hope that Krupenski would be told to take the same course.[1]

If, as is possible, the Central Powers guessed what was afoot, Austria's compromise in accepting the principle of compensation on August 26th[2], was shrewdly designed to widen the gulf between London and Rome. Combined with the Allied defeats in France, it stiffened San Giuliano. On the 28th, he informed Imperiali: 'Austria and Germany have . . . assured us that, despite our neutrality, they intend to maintain good relations with us. . . .' Already on the 27th, the French and Russian Ambassadors had reported his statement that 'the likelihood of Italy's departure from neutrality had been reduced to a minimum'.[3] Thereupon Rodd, Barrère and Krupenski agreed that 'in view of the present political mood of the Italian Government', it was best to leave it alone.[4] From mid-September, Imperiali detected in London increasing signs of 'a certain indifference towards our interests. . . .'[5]

### 4
### PARIS—VIENNA

Nor were proceedings easier in Paris. The Quai d'Orsay matched Anglo-Saxon reticence by Gallic circumspection. This was not mitigated by the Chamber's cheers for Italian neutrality, or the congratulations of Briand, Barthou, Bourgeois, Deschanel and other big politicians at the Embassy.[6] In the first place, Austria had long served as a field for the investment of French capital. The great Banque de Paris et des Pays Bas controlled the Allgemeine Österreichische Bodenkreditanstalt and the Österreichische Bodenkreditbank whose board included representatives of Skoda and of the Steyr armaments works. The Chairman of the Société Générale,

---

[1] Grey to Buchanan, 18 Aug. '14. Deciphered in the Russian Foreign Ministry. Krupenski to Sazonov, 29 Aug. '14. *Internationale Beziehungen*, II. 6. I. No. 186, p. 141, and *ibid.* footnote 1. Doumergue to Paléologue, 24 Aug. Deciphered in the Russian Foreign Ministry. *Das Zaristische Russland*, p. 275. See also Salandra, 87: 'Pressing invitations did not actually reach us from Paris or London during that first month of the War'.
[2] See p. 191 above.
[3] Izvolski to Sazonov, 28 Aug. '14. *Internationale Beziehungen*, II. 6. I. p. 138, footnote 4. San Giuliano to Imperiali, 28 Aug. *Documenti Diplomatici*, 5. I. No. 478, p. 264. Barrère to Delcassé, 27 Aug. Poincaré, V. 194–5. Krupenski to Sazonov, 27 Aug. *Das Zaristische Russland*, p. 277.
[4] Krupenski to Sazonov, 29 Aug. '14. *Internationale Beziehungen*, II. 6. I. No. 186, pp. 140–1.
[5] Imperiali to San Giuliano, 17 Sept. '14. *Documenti Diplomatici*, 5. I. No. 710, p. 418; also 25 Sept., 2 Oct. *ibid.* NN 802, 863, pp. 474, 515–16.
[6] Salandra, 86.

Baron d'Oissel, was a Director of the Wiener Bankverein (which had fostered Skoda), and another of its tycoons, Monsieur von Adler, had, by 1914, acquired immense influence over Vienna's financial policy.[1] Moreover, the Foreign Minister Doumergue, like Grey, hesitated to break with the Dual Monarchy for whom 'the French indubitably have certain sympathies . . . based on an utterly wrongheaded conception of an alleged Austrian striving for independence from Germany'.[2] While Britain saw in Vienna a balancing force against the Reich and Russia, Paléologue wrote that, 'so long as there is a Germany and an Italy, we shall have an interest in the preservation of Austria'.[3] It was as part of this balance-of-power policy that Michael Karolyi and other members of the Hungarian Independence Party, who opposed the Triple Alliance and, before the War, had come to Paris to seek a rapprochement with the Entente, were released from short internment and given passports for Spain.[4]

But like Grey, Doumergue had to think of Petrograd[5] and Rome. Early in August 1914, San Giuliano had already expressed to Barrère his painful surprise that the Third Republic was not yet at war with the Danubian Monarchy.[6] Seeing that the Consulta might strike a bargain with Berchtold, 'our abstention [Poincaré noted] entails the risk of encouraging such dealings'.[7] Austria, however, wanting a *casus belli* wherewith to confound the Italians, perversely left the onus of taking up arms to France.[8] Another snag, according to the President, was 'what reason . . . should be given to justify this declaration.?'[9]

Happily, it was reported that Francis Joseph was marching some regiments to the Rhine. Doumergue's eager inquiries elicited three strenuous denials from Vienna.[10] Berchtold, adopting the formula

[1] Hallgarten, II. 290, footnote 8; 368–9. It is also noteworthy that, for a time, a relative of Clemenceau's was the Chief Editor of the big Vienna paper *Neue Freie Presse*, ibid. 191.
[2] Izvolski to Sazonov, 13 Oct. '14. *Internationale Beziehungen*, II. 6. I. No. 386, p. 305.
[3] Poincaré, VI. 5–6. Also May, 92.
[4] Poincaré, V. 290. Karolyi, *Memoirs*, 43, 48–9, 53–5. Before the outbreak of hostilities Karolyi negotiated with Poincaré, Caillaux, Tardieu (the Foreign Editor of the *Temps*) and Clemenceau. He and his friends were arrested as enemy aliens in Aug. '14 and released in Sept. During his internment Karolyi was in correspondence with Poincaré and Caillaux and was financially supported by his relative de Polignac.
[5] Poincaré, V. 63–4; also 56.
[6] Barrère to Doumergue, 9 Aug. '14. Poincaré, V. 50.
[7] 11 Aug. '14. Poincaré, V. 63.
[8] Dumaine, 153. Poincaré, V. 36–7. Also Izvolski to Sazonov, 5 Aug. '14. Stieve, p. 21.
[9] 11 Aug. '14. Poincaré, V. 64. Also Dumaine, 153.
[10] Poincaré, V. 36, 49, 55, 56. Doumergue to Dumaine, 9 and 10 Aug. '14. Dumaine, 154. Conrad, IV. 192, 197. Izvolski to Sazonov, 9 Aug. '14. Stieve, p. 34.

demanded by the French, declared in writing 'that no Austro-Hungarian troops had been transported to the West outside Austrian territory'.[1] Dumaine, the French Ambassador, cabled this to Paris on August 10th. 'Où est la vérité?' At any rate, it was politic to regard Berchtold's protestations of innocence as 'very suspect'.[2] So, the same day, Dumaine received instructions (formulated long before the arrival of his telegram) that the Habsburg denials were contradicted by information from Germany, and that he was to leave Vienna.[3] On the same day, too, the Foreign Minister Doumergue told the Austro-Hungarian Envoy that he was not reassured and that, even if the Austrians were not sending men to the West, they were helping Germany to do so, and anyhow they were assisting France's enemies against her Allies. In the circumstances, 'I do not know how I could, in the long run, guarantee Your Excellency's safety'. As Count Czeczen still made no move, Doumergue added that he was 'forced to recall M. Dumaine', whereupon the Ambassador asked for his passports[4]. But 'neither side mentioned the word "war" '.[5] The hope of the Quai d'Orsay that a diplomatic rupture might suffice, faded before Britain's realistic insistence on something more drastic.[6] Though there was still 'much uncertainty'[7] about the troop-transport story, the Cabinet—acting without Parliamentary approval—devised the ingenious formula that Austria-Hungary,

'having... been the first to initiate hostilities in Europe... has, without any provocation on the part of the Government of the Republic, placed herself in a state of war with France'.[8]

5

ITALY EXPLORES POSSIBILITIES IN PARIS:
NICE, CORSICA, SAVOY AND TUNIS

This Note of August 13th gave little comfort to San Giuliano. For, having gone so far, Paris was even less willing than London to expose herself to the extortions of the Consulta. Two days previously, Doumergue had impressed on Izvolski that, while agreeing with the need to enrol the Kingdom, he thought it 'dangerous to take too definite steps in Rome.... Italy's neutrality in itself [was] a great success'.[9] On the eve of the plunge, he instructed Paléologue

[1] Dumaine, 154.      [2] Poincaré, V. 56 and 55.
[3] Dumaine, 154–5.      [4] Poincaré, V. 57.
[5] Izvolski to Sazonov, 10 Aug. '14. Stieve, p. 37.
[6] Poincaré, V. 63, 76. Benckendorff to Sazonov, 13 Aug. '14. *Internationale Beziehungen*, II. 6. I. p. 61, footnote 2.
[7] Poincaré, V. 76.
[8] Poincaré, V. 76–7. Izvolski to Sazonov, 13 Aug. '14. Stieve, p. 49.
[9] Izvolski to Sazonov, 11 Aug. '14. *Internationale Beziehungen*, II. 6. I. p. 54 footnote 1. Poincaré V. 49.

'to recommend this method to M. Sazonov. . . .' The Italians ought to be 'thanked' for their attitude and 'informed that we do not wish to exert pressure on them . . . but that we should be prepared . . . to grant them notable advantages'—'since these advantages [as he said in the same telegram] could be granted without detriment to our own national interests'.[1]

The word 'since' here was an obvious euphemism for 'so long as'. France had only to recall the Nationalist agitation South of the Alps[2] to be aware of the extent to which Roman pretensions were directed precisely against her 'own national interests'. Whereas the bill Italy presented in Petrograd could formally at least be debited to the enemy, and the demands raised in Whitehall were a potential rather than immediate irritant, the claims which the Consulta had against the Quai d'Orsay went so near the bone that a special approach was required. For the Ambassador Tittoni to ask the French for what was theirs meant courting a rebuff, discrediting his Government, and undoing, before its inception, the coveted Alliance. There could, therefore, be no question of a frontal diplomatic assault in which the attacker would risk not only political death, but the ruin of his cause. This was a case for scouting, intelligence, and resting the defences, for fire from the flank and the silent ambush, in which—if it came to the worst—only an unknown soldier, denied and disowned, would be left in no-man's land. If Tittoni had not been on a holiday cruise, he would have had to be sent on one—to make room for Count Sabini.

Sabini, as Commercial Attaché, was a comparatively minor official of the Italian Embassy in Paris. But he was linked with high society in Rome. He was a former university student of, and a favourite with, Salandra, who knew his family.[3] He was a confidant of the Deputy A. Torre, the Ententophil Colonial Minister Ferdinando Martini, the Minister of the Royal Household Posqualini and, above all, of Bergamini who edited Sonnino's interventionist *Giornale d'Italia* and was one of the close friends of the Premier.[4] It was with this background that he took—as he asserts in his Diary—'on my own initiative and personal responsibility . . . the first steps to associate France and Italy in the War'.[5] He was, without doubt, the right man for the errand. He was so well disposed towards France that he

---

[1] Doumergue to Paléologue, 12 Aug. '14. Deciphered in the Russian Foreign Ministry. *Internationale Beziehungen*, II. 6. I. No. 79, pp. 54–5. This telegram went also to Barrère in Rome. On 24 Aug. Doumergue informed Paléologue that official three-Power démarches in Rome must be avoided. Deciphered in the Russian Foreign Ministry. *Das Zaristische Russland*, p. 275.
[2] See p. 186 above.    [3] Sabini, *Le Fond d'une querelle*, 106–7.
[4] Sabini, 13, 14, 103, 105.    [5] Sabini, 14–15, 103.

'always considered [her] as his second motherland'.[1] He had 'old and cordial relations with the most eminent French politicians'.[2] And he was intimate with Clemenceau[3] who—being out of office—could lend himself more easily, and without compromising the Cabinet, to this delicate approach. The 'Tiger', moreover, had long wanted an Italian Alliance. He had proposed it during his first premiership. He had helped to dispel some of the friction between the two countries. He had said to Sabini as recently as April 1914: 'In three months we shall have war. Will Italy be against us?'[4] Hence, on the day of the German ultimatum to France (on August 1st), the Count, rushing back from home leave, sent him a wire requesting an interview.[5]

They met on August 6th and embraced 'with effusion'.[6] Sabini recalled to Clemenceau his earlier offers of co-operation. Having decided 'to inaugurate the necessary démarches . . . we were seized with vehement emotion',[7] from which the Italian, at any rate, recovered sufficiently to table, on the 7th, a massive list of terms. Italy, being unready, he said, would postpone intervention. Meanwhile, 'we need guarantees, either financial or of other kinds. France must give us monetary advances, furnish us with arms and munitions . . . she must help us so that our civilian population is able to work and live. Everything must be pooled: the blood and the money. Italy is poor, all she can give is men; it is for France to provide the rest'.[8] The Frenchman asked, in effect, what was the price of 'the blood'. The answer was: a defensive and offensive Alliance, reimbursement of costs, the 'Italian Adriatic', the Trentino, Trieste and 'all the Italian territories', the Dodecanese, an extension of the sphere of influence in Asia Minor, advantages in Abyssinia, a Mediterranean condominium, a customs and economic entente with France.[9]

Clemenceau took the visitor to Poincaré, and introduced him as having 'no official assignment whatever . . . he acts on his own initiative'. They agreed, as Sabini recollects, to 'chat as ordinary private persons and solely in the interest of our respective countries'.[10] The President was given a recital of the terms,[11] and—he noted—'to my great surprise, M. Clemenceau did not recoil'.[12] Poincaré reminded his guest that, having signed the 1902 Agreements, Italy

[1] Sabini, 21, 30, 192.      [2] Sabini to Salandra, 22 Sept. '14. Sabini, 113.
[3] Sabini, 37; also 33–4.      [4] Sabini, 37; also 26, 38.
[5] Sabini, 30, 37.      [6] Sabini, 38.      [7] Sabini, 39.
[8] Sabini, 43; also 41–2.      [9] Sabini, 47. Poincaré, V. 30.
[10] 7 Aug. '14. Sabini, 54; also 51. Poincaré, V. 30.      [11] Sabini, 55.
[12] Poincaré, V. 30. Poincaré's assertion that the above advantages were claimed as compensation for neutrality (V. 30) is hardly credible. It seems that Italy must have demanded them in return for eventual belligerency.

could not march with France's enemies. 'Ah,' said Sabini, 'the Agreements of 1902! They have not the contractual force of the Triplice'.¹ The next question was who should officially initiate the negotiations. Tittoni being absent, and Prince Ruspoli, the Chargé d'Affaires—as Sabini implied—unwilling, Clemenceau proposed that the Commercial Attaché should go to Rome. Sabini declined on the grounds that he was 'too modest a figure' for such a task. In the end, it was decided that the French Ambassador Barrère would broach the matter with San Giuliano, and that the actual conditions would, in Sabini's words, 'be settled in the greatest spirit of conciliation in the final pourparlers'.² When he brought these tidings to Ruspoli, he was charged with obtaining what he described as 'a vague allusion to my démarches in order to establish a little official contact'.³ On the 9th, thanks to Clemenceau's efforts, the Chargé d'Affaires received the desired 'few lines on a visiting card' from the Director of Political Affairs at the Quai d'Orsay.⁴

By accident or design, this was the date of the Italian Ambassador Tittoni's return to Paris. Whether or not he regarded the scene as well enough set, he welcomed at once Clemenceau who—in 'an ultra-cordial interview'⁵—spoke openly with the President's consent of Italy's intervention and the benefits she would derive from it.⁶ Tittoni then called on the Foreign Minister Doumergue, but remained in Poincaré's words, 'impenetrable, hermetically sealed and silent as the tomb, whilst the Minister mentioned to him, with prudent circumlocution, the certain advantages of common action'.⁷ This was partly the normal reflex action of a neutral Envoy, and partly (or largely) pique at what he must have considered the circumlocutory excesses of the French. For Doumergue and Poincaré, like Grey, were determined 'to promise Italy nothing unless she offers us positive co-operation'.⁸ And as she would offer nothing without receiving the promises required, Tittoni and Sabini agreed that the spadework must go on. While Ruspoli maintained the official contact with the Quai d'Orsay, the Alliance would be shaped informally by Sabini and Clemenceau.⁹

The two conspirators brought in statesmen of stature like Briand,

---

¹ Poincaré, V. 30.  ² Sabini, 56–8.  ³ Sabini, 59–60.
⁴ Sabini, 62, 64. On the same day, a telegram from Ruspoli quoted Clemenceau as saying that Italy had a unique opportunity to realize her aspirations. *Documenti Diplomatici*, 5. I. No. 147, p. 80.
⁵ Clemenceau to Poincaré, 9 Aug. '14. Poincaré, V. 50.
⁶ Tittoni to San Giuliano, 10 Aug. '14. *Documenti Diplomatici*, 5. I. No. 169, pp. 95–6. Sabini, 62, 64.
⁷ Poincaré, V. 60. Tittoni to San Giuliano, 10 Aug. '14. *Documenti Diplomatici*, 5. I. No. 169, p. 96.
⁸ Poincaré, V. 31.
⁹ 10 Aug. '14. Sabini, 57, 64–5.

Bourgeois and Deschanel, and got them together with Tittoni.[1] The latter saw the Premier, 'who was extremely courteous ...', and drove to the Elysée where he heard from the President that the War might put an end to Austria-Hungary. 'Italy has national aspirations. The hour is decisive....'[2] 'Europe will be constructed on new foundations and Italy must have the place which is her due'.[3] It was a dual operation which involved thawing the surface of French reserve and softening the rigidity of the Italians. By August 14th, Sabini must have advanced far enough to draft, under Tittoni's watchful gaze, a report for the Minister of Agriculture Cavasola, a close associate of Salandra's. Quoting 'very high-ranking politicians' in Paris, but expressly refraining from setting forth 'the territorial and political advantages' envisaged by them for Italy, he stated that he was

'authorized to affirm officially that, if we decided to intervene against Austria, they would be disposed here to furnish us with the financial aid required for the War. Thereupon, in the event of victory, apart from the war indemnity ... France is disposed to grant us a loan of several thousand millions on the best terms; she would also undertake to conclude with us a commercial agreement assuring us special customs terms, and to improve the present Treaty of Labour in favour of our workers. The benefits which Italian commerce, industry, finance and emigration would derive therefrom are evident.... I have telegraphed this ... having [obtained] the certain guarantee of the French Government'.[4]

Endorsed by Clemenceau, the text was submitted to Poincaré. His comment was: 'personally I approve', but pleading that he had no Constitutional powers to sanction it, he advised the Attaché, 'or rather ... Tittoni', to see the Foreign Minister.[5]

The latter confirmed to Sabini the Entente's offer of the Trentino, Trieste and Adriatic territory, sanctioned the financial and economic items in Sabini's draft, and 'assured me that, if we became Allies, France would assist in the development of a greater and stronger Italy'.[6] Sabini hastened to Tittoni—only to find him in a quandary. The Ambassador was not to be lured by Poincaré's advice into going to the Foreign Minister. He had instructions not to commit himself.[7] He was influenced by the French military reverses. He noticed, above all, the explicit exclusion of political and

---
[1] Sabini, 65–6, 75–8. Tittoni to San Giuliano, 12 and 15 Aug. '14. *Documenti Diplomatici*, 5. I. NN 220, 250, pp. 128, 144.
[2] Poincaré, V. 80.
[3] Salandra, 87. Tittoni to San Giuliano, 11 and 12 Aug. '14. *Documenti Diplomatici*, 5. I. NN 177, 221, 222, pp. 101, 128–9.
[4] Sabini, 79–81.       [5] 14 Aug. '14. Poincaré, V. 94. Sabini, 83; also 81.
[6] 14 Aug. '14. Sabini, 84.       [7] See Sabini, 87; also 85.

territorial questions from the message addressed to Rome. He 'would like [as Sabini recorded] to keep in touch with France and, at the same time, to preserve complete liberty of action'.[1] He therefore vetoed the dispatch. The author quickly secured Briand's intervention. Clemencau uttered the warning that the refusal could be interpreted as a sign of unfriendliness to France. Tittoni, under pressure, withdrew his objections, provided that Sabini himself posted, and paid for, the telegram, so that it did not figure in the Embassy books, and on condition that, if questioned by San Giuliano, he could plead ignorance. The report was sent on August 15th.[2] But, at the same time, Tittoni cabled that 'premature negotiations with the Triple Entente would not be opportune'. The three Powers were ready 'to accept cordially any overture by Italy . . . but not to make other overtures beyond those already known. . . .'[3]

What happened in the next few weeks is shrouded in mystery, relieved intermittently by a statement in the *Temps* thanking Italy for her neutrality, and saying 'we are asking nothing more . . .'[4]; by interviews given to the *Giornale d'Italia* and the *Corriere della Sera* by Delcassé, Clemenceau and other leaders of the Third Republic;[5] by San Giuliano's boast of the assurances received from Austria and Germany, which caused Poincaré to sigh about 'that temple of prudence and wisdom calling itself the Consulta'[6]; and by a visit from the Ambassador Tittoni to the President significantly synchronized with news from the Marne.[7] Then, suddenly, on September 17th, Sabini appeared in Rome. He informed the Editor Bergamini and the Deputy Nava (another intimate of Salandra's) of the French concessions.[8] Finding the Premier's door closed on the grounds that their conversation would be compromising, he wrote him a letter, recapitulating his activities in Paris, outlining the terms envisaged for the Alliance (with Pola and an Adriatic region thrown in) and its economic benefits, and asserting that he had the blessings of Poincaré, Doumergue, Clemenceau, Briand and Delcassé.[9] Thereupon he learned from D'Atri, Salandra's *Chef du Cabinet*, that the Premier was inclined to give him a note to Tittoni empowering Sabini to undertake,

---

[1] 14 Aug. '14. Sabini, 85.
[2] Sabini, 85–7. Cavasola's reply to Sabini, expressing the desire that, 'to avoid possible equivocations', the French should address themselves to Tittoni (16 Aug. '14. Sabini, 88), was a significant attempt to obtain a commitment from the Quai d'Orsay.
[3] Tittoni to San Giuliano, 15 and 20 Aug. '14. *Documenti Diplomatici*, 5. I. NN 251, 345, pp. 145, 190.
[4] 19 Aug. '14. A similar assertion was made by the *Figaro* on the following day. *Documenti Diplomatici*, 5. I. No. 345, pp. 190–1.
[5] 17, 22, 23 Aug. '14. Sabini, 94, 99.
[6] 27 Aug. '14. Poincaré, V. 195.
[7] 10 Sept. '14. Poincaré, V. 275.
[8] Sabini, 104–5.   [9] 22 Sept. '14. Sabini, 108–10; also 105–6, 118.

in his own words, 'a secret action with the French Government, press and politicians'.[1] Sabini decided to forgo the credentials lest they should hamper the Consulta's freedom to manoeuvre. It was agreed that he would communicate with D'Atri by code. Returning to his post, he wrote to the French Ambassador Barrère that 'the personal effort which I have imposed upon myself . . . has already yielded the best results. . . . I am leaving tonight. . . . M. Delcassé . . . will be interested to hear me'.[2]

But no sooner had the modern Mercury arrived in Bordeaux[3] (on September 30th), no sooner had he informed his slow-footed Chief 'of the policy which Signor Salandra proposes to pursue, and of the understanding arrived at . . . between D'Atri and myself . . .',[4] than 'small indications made me fear that French enthusiasm on our behalf might have cooled somewhat'.[5] It is certain that the sweep of the German invasion had forced Doumergue to compromise. The concessions listed in Sabini's telegram of August 15th must have been real, for the Foreign Minister transmitted them to Barrère.[6] But the men at the Quai d'Orsay drew confidence from the Marne. They were (and could now afford to appear) irritated by San Giuliano's evident determination to wait for the highest bidder.[7] They were increasingly finding Sabini's 'intentions as obscure as they were complicated'[8]—especially as, even after his trip to Rome, he worked on 'without committing either the Embassy . . . or the Government of Italy'.[9] But what, in particular, put them on guard was the accumulating evidence that the intention was to despoil France.

As early as August 9th 1914, San Giuliano impressed upon Salandra that, in the event of a French victory, 'our position in the Mediterranean might become extremely perilous. . . .'[10] The need to counter this danger by aggrandizement combined well with the plain urge for expansion. On August 11th, the Ambassador Carlotti confided to Sazonov that the Central Powers were promising the Italians Savoy, Nice, Corsica and Tunis.[11] A few days later, his colleague in Constantinople was telling the Russian Ambassador Giers that Italy's waverings would cease if, in addition to the Trentino, Trieste, Valona and Rhodes, she 'could count on the possibility of considerable improvement of her frontier in Tunis'.[12]

[1] 25 Sept. '14. Sabini, 112, 115.
[2] Sabini, 116-18.
[3] The temporal capital.
[4] 1 Oct. '14. Sabini, 122.
[5] Sabini to D'Atri, 3 Oct. '14. Sabini, 130.
[6] Sabini, 88, 89.
[7] Barrère to Sabini, 17 Sept. '14. Sabini, 104.
[8] 20 Sept. '14. Poincaré, V. 317. Also 14 Aug. '14. Poincaré, V. 94.
[9] 1 Oct. '14. Sabini, 122.
[10] *Documenti Diplomatici*, 5. I. No. 151, p. 83.
[11] Paléologue to Doumergue, 11 Aug. '14. Poincaré, V. 72.
[12] Giers to Sazonov and Izvolski, 17 Aug. '14. Stieve, p. 60.

The Kaiser's advance on Paris led to a tightening of the Roman screw. Alleging that Austria was willing to pay for Italian neutrality by substantial border rectifications in the Trentino and the abandonment of Albania, 'an Italian source' notified Giers on August 30th that, as he wired to Sazonov, 'in such circumstances, only a positive French sacrifice in Tunis, particularly the cession of that city . . . could constitute a counterweight. . . .'[1] When France's fate hung in the balance, the Minister in Bucharest, Fasciotti—in conversation with Poklevski, Russia's Envoy—raised the price to include 'the county of Nice up to the river Var and . . . Corsica' which latter 'could later on be bartered for a part of Tunis'.[2] The events on the Marne curbed the Consulta's fancies. By September 21st, Fasciotti was saying to Poklevski that the French could now forget about Nice, but should offer whatever they were prepared to give.[3] Sabini, meanwhile, made clear to Barrère that this new-found modesty did not extend to Tunis.[4] Poincaré put it mildly when he noted that this was 'a frame of mind which we shall be careful not to encourage'.[5] And the *Echo de Paris* referred pointedly to 'the political acumen of the Italians who will not allow the minarets of Gabes to drive from their minds the gleaming cupolas of Pola' and to 'the spirit of the French who do not at all want to drag Italy into a war'.[6]

This must have been why Sabini was not this time greeted 'with effusion' by Clemenceau. The 'Tiger' told the Attaché (as the latter reported to Rome) 'events tended to prove: 1. that France and Britain are in themselves sufficient to contain Germany . . .; 2. that the Russian successes have reduced Austria militarily . . .; 3. that Italian action to-day would no longer have enough value to justify the important political and territorial concessions which we are claiming; that France, bearing in mind our neutrality, could contemplate with pleasure at most our occupation of the Trentino and Trieste; 4. that, as for Trieste, we should have to take an immediate

---

[1] Giers to Sazonov, 30 Aug. '14. *Das Zaristische Russland*, p. 278.
[2] Poklevski to Izvolski, 10 Sept. '14. Stieve, p. 110. 11 Sept. in *Das Zaristische Russland*, pp. 176–177.
[3] Poklevski to Sazonov, 21 Sept. '14. Stieve, p. 115.
[4] 20 Sept. '14. Poincaré, V. 317. For the claim to cessions in Tunis made by the *Resto del Carlino* see Tittoni to San Giuliano, 3 and 5 Oct. '14. *Documenti Diplomatici*, 5. I. NN 879, 890, pp. 523, 532.
[5] 12 Sept. '14. Poincaré, V. 286. The French Minister in Bucharest who had reported Fasciotti's proposals regarding Nice and Tunis received the 'very categorical reply' from France that they were inadmissible. (Izvolski to Sazonov, 4 Oct. '14. *Internationale Beziehungen*, II. 6. I. No. 357, p. 282). On 28 Sept. '14 Tittoni reported to San Giuliano the 'unofficial' French view 'that it was not possible to reach an understanding with Italy because she was asking too much'. *Documenti Diplomatici*, 5. I. No. 838, p. 497.
[6] Tittoni to San Giuliano, 5 Oct. '14. *Documenti Diplomatici*, 5. I. No. 890, p. 532.

decision, otherwise Russia, having to take account . . . of Slav aspirations, might change her attitude'.[1] Here was a red light before which it would have been wise to stop. The points conceded to Sabini on August 15th were probably the logical maximum. Whatever additional concessions might have been wrung from France if the German invasion had spread, there was nothing to be hoped for once it had been checked. Italian diplomacy no less than the Kaiser's armies had been defeated on the Marne.

But precisely the outcome of that battle, making as it did wellnigh inevitable Italy's adherence to the Entente, forced her onwards. Time seemed to be running short. Only so long as the Western front was still fluid and French confidence not yet hardened was there a chance for blackmail. The benefits already extracted engendered a false sense of security. The recent compromise by the Central Powers served as a stimulant. The freedom allowed him by Salandra, and his incognito, led Sabini to overplay his hand. In a talk with the Prime Minister Viviani, on October 2nd, 'I told him that the proposals envisaged last August by the President of the Republic and myself, did not appear to satisfy Italy . . . by intervening with a magnificent Fleet and a million soldiers, Italy would immediately reduce the effort for the Allies. . . . Moreover, Italian intervention would bring France the following advantages: 1. the absolute certainty of final victory. . . . 2. the shortening of the present War. 3. an enormous economy in men and money. . . . Then I added: "Do not the advantages France would derive therefrom, and the sacrifices this would entail for Italy, justify Italian public sentiment in demanding some recompense from France?" M. Viviani replied: "The Trentino and Trieste are the recompense due to Italy. France will lend Italy diplomatic and military aid in this enterprise". I answered: ". . . the Trentino and Trieste do not belong to France; the Trentino and Trieste redeemed by us, with our money and our blood, [will] be but the fruit of our sacrifices, and not the recompense you owe us. In 1859, you have received Nice and Savoy, two Italian provinces, and in addition 200 millions, to reward your intervention. Besides, the question of the Adriatic is neither the only nor the most important of the international questions which are of interest to Italy. . . . What interests Italy above all is the Mediterranean; it is in regard to the Mediterranean that Italy expects from France a precise agreement designed to improve the present political and military situation, by rectifying our frontiers and removing the menace of Bizerta. . . ." '[2]

[1] Sabini to D'Atri for Salandra, 3 Oct. '14. Sabini, 129, 131; also 121. Sabini, in his book, always speaks of 'Trente', but means of course 'the Trentino'.
[2] Sabini to Salandra, 3 Oct. '14. The report was read by Tittoni before dispatch. Sabini, 125-9; also 122.

Had they been private individuals discussing personal matters, this might have been a case for showing the visitor the door, or calling the police. A statesman steeped in traditional diplomacy keeps to the rules of the game. 'M. Viviani, courteous as ever, replied: "This has to be thought over. Go and see M. Delcassé".'[1] The new French Foreign Minister, in the past, had made those agreements with Italy which Bulow had dubbed 'extra waltz'.[2] Shortly before his return to the Quai d'Orsay, he had openly wooed Italy in an interview granted to the *Corriere della Sera*: 'Germany who has an intense longing for access to the Adriatic . . . stands across your path' while, in the Entente, Italy 'sees a group of Powers able to help her to obtain what she desires'. But the strict limitation of his offers to the Trentino, Trieste and Valona, and his warning that 'the distribution of the war gains will be proportionate to the sacrifice made by each State',[3] being the same as Doumergue's, were ominous for Sabini.

Hence, prior to bearding the lion in his den, the Italian appealed to other members of the Cabinet. He found Thomson, the Minister for Industry and Commerce, dodging every important point. He found the Vice-Premier Briand admitting that 'intervention would cost Italy several thousand millions and the flower of her youth. I brought up again the need for a reward. M. Briand replied: "That is right, the Trentino and Trieste will be yours: we shall help you". I repeated the arguments I had put before M. Viviani. . . . But M. Briand interrupted me: ". . . What is Italy's indisputable interest? The crushing of Austria. . . . But it is necessary for Italy to take part in it. She runs plenty of risks by neutrality . . . it is almost a confession of impotence. . . . For, if she did not intervene, she would come out of the War in a diminished state. It is necessary that she should play her part as a Great Power in world politics; unless she does, Italy . . . becomes a second-rate Power. . . . It is on the battlefield that one must forge one's rights. . . . All those who will have taken part in the War will have a very large share. . . . The questions of detail. . . ."—"The questions of detail", I said, "have a certain importance; that of the Mediterranean, for example. . . ." M. Briand did not let me finish: ". . . . the questions of detail are not of very great importance in so vast a problem. Go and see M. Delcassé. . . ."'[4]

But Delcassé would not see him. Sabini's repeated requests for an interview with the Foreign Minister were refused. On October 10th,

---

[1] Sabini to Salandra, 3 Oct. '14. Sabini, 129.
[2] Sabini, 94. See also p. 138 above. Delcassé had previously been Foreign Minister from 1898 to 1908.
[3] *Corriere della Sera*, reprinted at length in *Le Temps*, 24 Aug. '14. Porter 326–7.
[4] Sabini to Salandra, 5 Oct. '14. Sabini, 134–9.

the politician de Monzie told him that 'there is nothing personal against you in the delay. . . . It was felt that a postponement was advisable'.[1] On the 14th, Sabini, still without word from the Quai d'Orsay, went to Clemenceau, Ribot and Briand. The latter advised him 'to think of the Italian Embassy when making investigations'.[2] Clemenceau said: 'All your Tittoni can do is to make a b—y mess of things. You can't make a silk purse out of a sow's ear'.[3] The Attaché, too, subsequently blamed the Ambassador for his misfortunes. He accused him of double-dealing, professional jealousy and rank partiality for Germany.[4] Even if this had been so, Tittoni at this juncture did not make policy. His views in themselves counted no more than those of the champions of the Triplice Avarna and Bollati. In reality, he had been one of the first Italians to insist that the Alliance with the Central Powers was 'no longer applicable'.[5] He was in close touch and agreement with Sabini's enterprise,[6] communicated continuously with the Consulta, especially during the crucial first fortnight in October,[7] and of course obeyed its directives. These were that he must not commit Italy.[8] Judging by Briand's and Ribot's confidences, Delcassé tackled the Ambassador about Sabini.[9] Indeed, he was bound to probe deeper into the latter's mission. But, at the same time clearly, he avoided comitting France, since Tittoni drew further into his shell. On September 28th, the Ambassador sent a scathing report on 'Sabini who often sees Clemenceau and equally often indulges in idle chatter'. On October 2nd, he assured San Giuliano that 'no one here has ever seriously thought, or now thinks, of allowing France to give up Tunisia to Italy in exchange for her co-operation in the War . . . therefore any request by us for a concession by France ought to be put forward by Imperiali to Grey.'[10] Meanwhile, all he himself did in his interview with the French Foreign Minister was to 'allude to the strictly official . . . declarations which were to be made to M. Delcassé. . . . I have spoken to M. Delcassé only once . . . and following the instructions from Rome, I informed him that, if there had been any departure from neutrality, the Italian Government would have made their declarations in London, and not Paris'.[11] According to

---

[1] Sabini, 143; also 141–2.
[2] Sabini, 144; also 143.
[3] 15 Oct. '14. Sabini, 144–5.
[4] Sabini, 153–4, 158.
[5] Tittoni to San Giuliano, 26 July '14. *Revue des Deux Mondes*, XLI. 1 Oct. 1927, p. 542.
[6] See Sabini, 64, 85, 123–4, 147, 153.
[7] Sabini, 61, 65, 82, 153–5.
[8] Sabini, 140. As Salandra wrote later, 'our line of conduct' was 'to intervene in the spring but not to compromise ourselves in the meantime'. Salandra, 159.
[9] Sabini, 145.
[10] Tittoni to San Giuliano, 28 Sept. and 2 Oct. '14. *Documenti Diplomatici*, 5. I.NN 838, 870, pp. 497, 517.
[11] Tittoni to Sabini. Sabini, 146–7.

the French, Tittoni even asked the Foreign Minister to deal only with him.[1] Considering how Sabini's importunities must have outraged the Quai d'Orsay, nothing could have suited them better. Sabini, meanwhile, set siege to Delcassé: 'Does the fact that, since August, M. Tittoni has known of all my démarches, the fact that the [Italian] Government, having heard what I had to say, has sent me back to Bordeaux, convey nothing to a mind as shrewd as yours?' Whereas the Ambassador was prevented by Italy's formal neutrality from intervening, 'it is I who can and must do so. Do have confidence and talk with me ... in a purely private capacity. ... I shall submit to you my dispatches ... so that you can correct them as you think fit. ... You can disavow me, if you wish, but do not refuse me a talk. It is indispensable that we should talk as friends, frankly ... looking one another straight in the eye'.[2] Shortly before, he had written to Salandra (via D'Atri) that the Quai d'Orsay was beginning to inspire press comments that Trieste was a Slav city which, with Pola, Fiume and Dalmatia, should go to the Serbs. He complained bitterly about the 'Machiavellian instructions of the Consulta', and urged for official negotiations in Bordeaux.[3]

If Sabini had been able to weaken France's defences, discussions would in fact have started, and Tittoni would have stepped in with a conqueror's mien. But precisely their double game of greed and caution allowed Delcassé to beat off the attack, without injuring

---

[1] Sabini, 145. Sabini's story is given a somewhat different version in Izvolski's information from 'a private but very reliable source' that Tittoni 'had been instructed to ascertain whether France would consent to cede a part of Tunis to Italy in return for her armed co-operation'. It is possible, however, that Izvolski, or his informant, has misunderstood the nature of Tittoni's instructions. In the light of Franco-Italian relations at the time, Sabini's narrative seems more credible. It is, moreover, confirmed in the second part of Izvolski's dispatch: 'Since Tittoni was fully aware that such an inquiry had no prospect of success and would only offend France, he decided not to take this step. On his instructions, some private persons attempted to enter into discussions on this subject with officials of the French Foreign Ministry, but naturally without success'. (Izvolski to Sazonov, 4 Oct. '14. *Internationale Beziehungen*, II. 6. I. No. 357, p. 282.)

According to Tittoni, Clemenceau, when the fall of Paris seemed imminent, touched upon sessions in Tunis, but the French Government dismissed the idea. (Tittoni to San Giuliano, 28 Sept. '14. *Documenti Diplomatici*, 5. I. No. 838, p. 457). Bollati, in a letter to Avarna, 9 Oct. '14, mentions a 'vague' French promise to dismantle the fortifications at Bizerta and to agree to some minor frontier rectifications in the interior of Tunis. (*Carteggio*, LXI, II. 265). Even if this has substance, it could not have satisfied the Italians. At any rate, Tittoni, after his conversation with Delcassé, which must have been the purely formal one referred to above, advised the Consulta to maintain its waiting attitude. See Carlotti's telegram to San Giuliano, 1 Oct. '14, deciphered in the Russian Foreign Ministry and reported by Sazonov to Izvolski, 5 Oct. '14. *Internationale Beziehungen*, II. 6. I. No. 361, p. 284, and *ibid*, footnote 3.

[2] Sabini to Delcassé, 16 Oct. '14. Sabini, 147–51.
[3] Sabini to D'Atri, 6 Oct. '14. Sabini, 139–41.

the aggressor. The Quai d'Orsay's cold acknowledgement, without compliance,¹ of Sabini's desperate last letter did not involve the Ambassador. He could still come forward without loss of face, on France's terms.

The Consulta, however, at the first sign of resistance, drew back —abandoning its unknown soldier to his own grievances and wounds. A curt note from D'Atri informed Sabini that 'the President [of the Council] . . . is absolutely unwilling to authorize any démarches which have not already been authorized by his Excellency Tittoni'.²

---

[1] 18 Oct. '14. Sabini, 151-2.
[2] D'Atri to Sabini, 15 Oct. '14. Sabini, 152-3. The dates suggest that this note was the direct consequence of Tittoni's telegram of 13 Oct. about 'the vain mirage of a total or partial cession of Tunisia. . . .' *Documenti Diplomatici*, 5. I. No. 942, p. 563.

CHAPTER XVI

# Extra-Diplomatic Factors

1

BRITISH, FRENCH AND BELGIAN INVESTMENTS
IN ITALY

THE asperity of this communication reflected the depth of Italian feeling against the Entente. For the Allied Powers, while rejecting Italy's claims, left no stone unturned to inveigle her into the War on terms of their own.

These efforts may, perhaps, be better understood, if account is taken of the wide infiltration, by 1913-14, of the Italian economy by Western business.

The sixty or so British enterprises in the Peninsula included the subsidiaries of Vickers—the naval dockyards and arsenals of Vickers-Terni, Odero (Genoa) and Orlando (Leghorn); the subsidiaries of Armstrong—the Armstrong-Pozzuoli Co. (in the Bay of Naples) and the Armstrong-Ansaldo Co. (Genoa); the waterworks in Naples, Genoa and district; gas companies in Milan, Messina, Prato, Trapani; railways (Lombardy, Sicily, Carrara-Versilia); copper, gold, zinc, sulphur, talc, asbestos and asphalt mines; granite and marble quarries; lead-smelting and glass works; warehouses in Genoa; petroleum, oil, rubber, tyre and engineering concerns; exporting firms; the power station in San Remo; a hotel syndicate; the Tuscan Wine Co.; the branches of 16 insurance companies and of the big shipping Lines (Cunard, White Star). The total amount of British capital involved was estimated to be at least 110,000,000 lire.[1] Some fifty Belgian concerns owned the tramways in no less than eleven cities[2] and seven provinces,[3] some inter-provincial lines,[4] and railways in various parts of the country[5]; electricity companies in Milan and Barletta; gas and waterworks; some of the biggest mining and metallurgical companies in Sardinia and Tuscany, and

[1] Nitti, *Il capitale straniero in Italia*, 42, 45. For a detailed list of British enterprises in Italy, too long to be given here, see *ibid.* 112–18, 131–6. Also Perris, 61–2.
[2] Turin, Bologna, Florence, Verona, Mantua, Forli, Leghorn, Naples, Capodimonte, Palermo and Messina.
[3] Naples, Salerno, Verona, Alessandria, Vincenze, Piedmont, Sicily.
[4] Milan-Bergamo-Cremona, Treviso-Venice-Padua.
[5] Nostra Signora della Guardia (Genoa), Naples-Nola-Baiano, North Rome, Bari-Barletta, Catania, Rome-Milan-Bologna, Rome-Civita Castellana-Viterbo, and the General Goods Line (Turin).

in Iglesias, Rome and Turin; sugar refineries; the Hermes Automobile Co. in Rome; the C-ie Internationale des Wagons Lits, and many others. The total Belgian capital thus invested has been computed at well above 180,000,000 lire.[1] About eighty French undertakings controlled a vast railway network[2]; gas companies in Genoa, Naples, Turin, Venice, Florence, Verona and Cazerta, waterworks in Ancona and Venice; mining concerns[3]; sulphur, talc, asphalt and bitumen mines; marble quarries; chemical and explosives factories, including 'Dynamite Nobel'; the Gnome Motor Co. in Turin; silk and textile factories; petrol companies; lignite enterprise; industrial plants (Milan, Turin, Cagliari); banks in Florence and Bordighera, the Banque Populaire de Menton and the Caisse de Crédit de Nice, the Causemille-Roche match factory; steamship lines in Naples and Genoa, and the C-ie Générale Transatlantique; 37 insurance branch offices; a mortgage society and the Municipal Casino in San Remo, and so forth. The aggregate capital of French enterprise in the Kingdom was put at nearly 150,000,000 lire.[4]

These French, Belgian and British private investments, which totalled at least 440,000,000 lire, reduced to relative insignificance the approximate amount of 60,000,000 lire of German and Austrian capital privately invested in Italy. As for the Italian national debt, the portion owed to German interests appears to have been completely dwarfed by that due to Western creditors.[5] Such, at any rate, would be the conclusions derived from Nitti's figures. In the financial year 1892-93, of the 162,000,000 lire of public money the Italians paid abroad on account of foreign investments, 95,000,000 went to France alone.[6] There were times, above all in 1889-90 and 1893-4, when it seemed that Germany would take the place of the French in absorbing Italian consolidated stock. But from then on the income she was drawing from Italy diminished steadily. Thus, the German investors, in 1891-2, received 72,000,000 lire as interest on Italian consols (as against 78,000,000 lire drawn that year by France). But having been compelled by the slump in the Reich between 1900

---

[1] Nitti, 42–3, 48–9. For details see *ibid.* 97–101, 137–40.
[2] The South-Italian, Tuscan, Franco-Swiss, Naples Metropolitan, Naples Central, and Castellamare-Sorrento rail and tramway companies, and the C-ie Internationale des Transports Économiques.
[3] In Malfidano, Aragona, Crottacalda, Gallitano, Liguria, Rome and Genoa.
[4] Nitti, 42, 45. For details see *ibid.* 94–131.
[5] On the Entente side, neither Belgian nor British interests held many Italian State bonds. Belgium, although she had the largest amount of capital invested permanently in Italy, had only some 20,000,000 lire worth of Italian State bonds. The total of Italian securities in British hands was well below 50–60,000,000 lire. The largest packet of Italian securities was held by France. See Nitti, 44, 45, 48–9, 51.
[6] Nitti, 44.

H

and 1902[1] to withdraw a large part of their foreign holdings, they received only 4,200,000 lire in 1903-4, and in 1913-14 that amount dropped to a mere 1,300,000.[2] France, by contrast, took up 40,500,000 out of the total of 43,300,000 lire[3] paid abroad in the same year on account of foreign investments in public undertakings—a far greater proportion of the whole than in the 'nineties.[4] It is significant, too, that, some time previously, a large amount of stock in the Banca Commerciale Italiana had been acquired by a French banking group.[5]

Considering that loans and investments abroad tend to give the capital exporters and their Governments positions of advantage in the recipient countries,[6] this rise and fall in the respective holdings of France and Germany could be taken to indicate the relative strength of their political influence in Rome. Since the French loans to Russia late in the 'eighties (when Russian securities were boycotted by the Berlin stock exchange and the banks) enabled the Quai d'Orsay to accomplish the rapprochement and eventual Alliance between the two Powers, it might be presumed that a similar process was at work in Italy. It has been argued that 'the beginning of better political relations between France and Italy [was] brought on primarily through financial reconciliation'.[7] Nor could it have been purely accidental that it was in 1900 and 1902—that is precisely when the economic crisis in the Reich opened the Italian markets to French money—that Paris and Rome struck their first colonial bargain and that Italy undertook not to fight France if the latter were at war with the Central Empires.[8] It may be too much to say, as some scholars do, that the enormous financial penetration by France predetermined Italy's ultimate transition to the Entente.[9] But if (despite its decline in Italy) German business, in 1914, could still carry 'much weight' with the Consulta through such persons as the Director of the Banca Commerciale Italiana,[10] then it would seem that the large preponderance of British, Belgian and notably French investments in the Kingdom was bound to give the three Govern-

---

[1] Riesser, 86-7.  [2] Nitti, 45-6.
[3] The reduction in the total Italian national debt may have been due to the fact that, between the years 1907-08 and 1909-10, the Italian market had absorbed almost all the consolidated stock. After 1910 large amounts of stock were again sold abroad, especially in France. See Nitti. 51-2.
[4] Nitti, 44.  [5] Riesser, 543-4.
[6] For example, Turkey; see Part I. The German financial expert and scholar Riesser, p. 543, writes 'that industrial contracts, commercial enterprises, and ... investments are conveying from one country to another not only capital ... but also political influence'.
[7] Riesser, 543.
[8] See p. 137 above.
[9] *Diplomaticheski Slovar*, I. 584-5.
[10] See p. 139 above.

ments concerned proportionately greater power to mould Italian policy by means of anonymous agents.[1]

## 2
### INFORMAL CONTACTS; CREATING A WAR ATMOSPHERE; THE USES OF MONEY

Indeed, what were the connections, one may wonder, of people like the Belgian Catholic Deputy A. Melot who arrived in Italy to confer with the Pope and address a gathering of Vatican supporters; or of his Liberal colleague Georges Lorand who came to campaign among broader strata for 'Belgium and the Rights of Man'; or of their Socialist fellow M.P. Jules Destrée who joined in this public agitation?[2] Why did Destrée, who had in Rome 'des amis bien informés',[3] make a point of seeing such diverse individuals as the veteran statesman Luzzati (political patron of the Editor of the interventionist *Corriere della Sera*) and Mussolini?[4] Why was it Luchaire, the Director of the French Institute in Milan, who was asked by Mussolini for a 'loan' of 30,000 lire?[5] Was it just a coincidence that it was the Anglo-French gas company in Milan whose workers were led by the bellicose Syndicalist F. Corridoni?[6] And, above all, who was 'the important personage in financial circles' who offered his services to Imperiali 'to act as an intermediary with Asquith'?[7] Is there room for doubt that it was Alfred de Rothschild who called more than once on the Ambassador to invoke the 'goodwill' which his House had acquired in Italy, and entice her into the War?[8]

Men such as these, whatever their intentions, served to strengthen the diplomacy of the Entente in Rome. It was certainly an exaggeration to represent, as the Berlin *Ulk* did, the British Ambassador, in tweeds, riding the horse of Marcus Aurelius on the Capitol, and Victor Emmanuel's Ministers, in similar garments, dejectedly

---

[1] If Sir R. Rodd, III. 244, 229, could say that, with the co-operation of the Banca Commerciale Italiana, 'strong influence could be brought to bear on senators and deputies connected with the many industrial enterprises it controlled' —could this not also be said of the strongholds of Western business and finance in Italy?
[2] Destrée, *En Italie avant la guerre*, pp. IX, X, 2, 11.   [3] Destrée, 40.
[4] Nov. '14. Destrée, 21, 24, 35. Luzzati, in conjunction with the big industrialist de Angeli, had been responsible for Albertini's appointment to the *Corriere della Sera*. See A. Albertini, 60.
[5] Salvemini, 'Mussolini e l'oro francese'. *Il Mondo*, 7 Jan. 1950, reproduced in the 1952 edition of *Mussolini diplomatico*. Monelli, 275.
[6] Rosmer, 335–6.   [7] Salandra, 265.
[8] Imperiali to San Giuliano, 6 and 9 Aug. '14. *Documenti Diplomatici*, 5. I. NN 85, 155, pp. 48–9, 86. On 21 Aug. Imperiali reported that 'a fellow countryman of ours, who works in the City', had come with an offer of a £20,000,000 loan from a British group. *ibid*. No. 370, p. 203.

climbing the hill in a chain-gang.[1] But even while Grey carefully avoided courting the Italians, even while the Consulta entrenched itself behind the ramparts of neutrality, there were those who, as Sir Rennell Rodd has admitted since, 'were working most actively in support of the Allies'.[2] As for 'the part I played in . . . 1914-15 before Italy became our Ally . . . I worked unceasingly to encourage the zealots, to put heart into the hesitating, and to remain in close and constant touch with men of every class and denomination. But I carefully refrained from appearing to exercise any pressure'.[3] Discretion gave potency to proceedings arising from Rodd's belief that, in another diplomat's words, 'in the end, public opinion will compel the [Italian] Government to declare war on Austria'.[4]

The Russian Foreign Ministry was less reticent. As early as August 1914, Sazonov intimated to his Ambassador how 'very desirable' it would be for the Italian press 'to exert pressure on the Government'.[5] Krupenski replied that the abstention from official parleys 'will not prevent us from continuing to influence' the papers and the people.[6] These efforts culminated in a *tour de force* aimed at 'arousing enthusiasm' in Rome and increasing her strife with Vienna.[7] Krupenski was instructed to transmit to Salandra an offer from Nicholas II to release Austro-Hungarian army prisoners of Italian nationality against a formal guarantee that they would not be allowed to regain their units.[8] 'Our ardent patriots', Bollati wrote grimly, 'will no doubt be highly enthusiastic at the magnanimity of the Tsar's Government which is such a great protector, as we all know, of subject nationalities. . . .'[9] In point of fact, when Krupenski, on the day before its delivery, handed the communication to the *Stefani* news agency, the Cabinet vetoed publication, only to find that it was passed on privately to certain editors. Salandra, gravely embarrassed, declined the Russian proposition, on the peculiar grounds that its application would infringe personal liberty. Carlotti, in Petrograd, accused Sazonov of plotting 'to evoke a sympathetic echo' in the Peninsula. The Foreign Minister retorted that 'after the victories of Russian arms . . . Italian action against Austria [was becoming] increasingly a matter of indifference to us', and

[1] Rodd, III. 258.   [2] Rodd, III. 219.   [3] Rodd, III. 258.
[4] Krupenski to Sazonov, 29 Aug. '14. *Internationale Beziehungen*, II. 6. I. No. 186, p. 141.
[5] Sazonov to Krupenski, 22 and 26 Aug. '14. *Das Zaristische Russland*, pp. 273, 276.
[6] Krupenski to Sazonov, 29 Aug. '14. *Internationale Beziehungen*, II. 6. I. No. 186, p. 141.
[7] Krupenski to Sazonov, 23 Sept. '14. Sazonov to Nicholas II, 28 Sept. '14. *Internationale Beziehungen*, II. 6. I. No. 328, p. 252, and *ibid.* footnote 3.
[8] Sazonov to Krupenski, 22 Oct. '14. *Internationale Beziehungen*, II. 6. I. p. 252, footote 4.
[9] Bollati to Avarna, 26 Oct. '14. *Carteggio*, LXI. II. 270.

hinted at possible impediments 'to the realization of certain Italian wishes, especially regarding Trieste and the Dodecanese'.[1] None of which helped to improve the negative impression left by this episode in Rome.

The French Ambassador Barrère, meanwhile, vied with, and surpassed, his British and Russian colleagues. The Envoy of the country which was the most unyielding toiled hardest to recruit Italy. He was, as Salandra recollects, 'in continuous and active relations with San Giuliano and with me' when her neutrality was decided.[2] Thereafter, says his biographer, 'he deployed an extraordinary activity' in conjuring up the martial spirit of Rome. Like Rodd, he 'knew how to sustain usefully the Italian interventionists....' and 'set everything in motion to enlighten Italian opinion'.[3] Then, the ex-Ambassador Cambon, fresh from his failure to avert war in Berlin, came to add fuel to the rising flames on the Tiber. Officially, his purpose was to visit Benedict XV on his elevation to the Papacy. In private, he asked San Giuliano whether Italy would not 'express in action . . . the very real sympathy she felt towards the cause of the Allies'.[4] Received in audience by the King, he voiced the hope that 'the Italian and French peoples would shortly find themselves comrades in battle again, as in 1859'. 'Victor Emmanuel [according to the diplomat's chronicler] smiled without replying, but taking Jules Cambon's hand . . . betrayed the depth of his feelings'.[5]

Simultaneously attempts were made to mobilize the feelings of the crowd. If Bülow is to be believed, Belgian propaganda was responsible for street sales of small statues of the Madonna with a kneeling child whose hands had been cut off. Raising its bleeding stumps it prayed: 'Holy Mother, make my hands grow again, which the barbarous Germans have taken from me'.[6] Daily from September 13th to the 20th, some thousands of demonstrators tried to break through to the Austro-Hungarian Embassy. Macchio's story that, on one occasion, the ringleaders inadvertently went for their pay to the German Mission and were thence sent to the French,[7] is probably too good to be true. He also asserts that Barrère hired the rabble to make bad blood between Vienna and Rome, force Salandra's hand, and manifest the 'will' of the Italian people.[8] Indeed, it may not have been quite without significance that the *Bataille Syndicaliste*,

---

[1] Krupenski to Sazonov, 23 Oct. '14, and Memorandum of the Russian Foreign Ministry, 26 Oct. '14. *Internationale Beziehungen*, II. 6. I. p. 252, footnote 4. *Carteggio*, LXI. II. 270.
[2] Salandra, 69.  [3] Noël, 92, 94.
[4] Tabouis, 282. Cf. San Giuliano to Bollati and Avarna, 10 Oct. '14. *Documenti Diplomatici*, 5. I. No. 928, p. 555.
[5] Oct. '14. Tabouis, 284.  [6] Bülow, III. 217.
[7] Macchio, 41.  [8] Macchio, 40.

which was summoning the French trade-unionists to the trenches, asked Italy whether she would 'remain deaf to the *vox populi*'.[1] On November 15th, in that paper, Mussolini was eulogized for having 'freed his conscience. Let us wish that this beautiful example may find followers'.[2]

The piquancy of this utterance lies in the evidence that the future Duce's transmogrification was largely due to monetary magic from Paris. According to one source, his political god-father Naldi, whose *Resto del Carlino* was being publicly charged with receiving subsidies from France, 'knew where the French funds were'.[3] Others name Barrère as the paymaster.[4] At any rate, it has been stated on high authority that the Quai d'Orsay was greatly concerned over the pacifism of the Italian Socialists. It was decided to subvert one of their leaders, and those French Socialists who had put on war paint acted as intermediaries. 'The first sum paid to Mussolini was 15,000 francs, after which a monthly payment of 10,000 francs was agreed upon. The first sum was handed over by M. Dumas, Secretary of the [Socialist] Minister, M. Guesde. Thus the *Popolo d'Italia* was launched. . . .'[5] On one occasion, Jules Guesde was reported to have handed a group of Italians an envelope: 'Give this to Mussolini. It is the monthly contribution for his paper from the French comrades to help the interventionist campaign'.[6]

[1] 24 Sept. '14. Rosmer, 135.     [2] Rosmer, 138.
[3] Seldes, 47; also 46, 48. He adds that the promise of these funds induced Mussolini to write the *Avanti* article which led to his dismissal from the editorship of that paper. Monelli, p. 275, however does not think that Naldi's money came from French sources. According to C. Rossi, French money came later. See Monelli, 274.
[4] Rossi, 28. *Encyclopaedia Britannica*, 1947. XVI. 29.
[5] Maître Torrès, Interview, published in the leaflet *Guerra di Classe*, Paris, March 1925. The statement adds: 'This genuine account . . . no one dares to deny, for fear of even more crushing documents'. The celebrated Attorney, at the spectacular trial of Bonomini at the Paris Court of Assizes (March 1925), repeated the charge that Mussolini, in 1914, had 'trafficked' with the French Government. The Milanese weekly *L'Italia del Popolo*, 3 May 1919, accused Mussolini of 'having cashed patriotic cheques from the French Government' and challenged him to take legal action, concluding: 'We hold proof of all that we have said and written'. The French Socialist Deputy Renaudel wrote in *Le Quotidien*, 9 Nov. 1926: ' . . . the first issues of the *Popolo d'Italia* were published thanks to French money'. All the above is quoted from Salvemini, *The Fascist Dictatorship in Italy*, I. 23, footnote 2. Also Seldes, 50. Another French Deputy, Paul Faure, recollects in *Le Populaire*, 9 Jan. 1928, that 'Jules Guesde . . . confided to me . . . that we had there a man of our own: Mussolini; we had sent him a first bill (appoint) for 100,000 francs to launch his paper'. See *Mussolini diplomate*, p. 20, by Salvemini who explains this divergence in the amount 'by a lapse of memory of M. Faure after ten years, whereas Maître Torrès refers to documents'. Also Nenni, 42. Rosmer, 327–9.
[6] Monelli, 275, quoting Salvemini, 'Mussolini e l'oro francese'. *Il Mondo*, 7 Jan. 1950. Salandra, discussing in a letter to Sonnino one of the attempts to provoke Italy into war with Austria, said: 'It is easy to guess who is finding the money'. Salandra, 113.

CHAPTER XVII

# 'Sacred Egoism'

1

THE GOVERNMENT OF *SACRO EGOISMO*

THESE machinations of the Entente, countered and provoked as they were by those of the Central Powers,[1] this wrestling of the two giant coalitions over Italy, stiffened the determination of her rulers to defend and promote their own interests. What must have been a long-smouldering and widespread sentiment was soon to explode in these words of Nitti's: 'Italy's political activity has not manifested itself with sufficient effectiveness along diplomatic lines because it has been invaded by foreign diplomatic activity which went hand in hand with banking activity'.[2] The desire to exploit the war situation for the purpose of making Italian imperialism independent would seem to account for the complexion of the reconstituted Cabinet.

The reconstruction, occasioned by the death of San Giuliano (October 16th 1914), left at the helm Salandra and the Right who called themselves Liberals since, 'after the Risorgimento . . . , no group was disposed to accept the label of Conservative'.[3] He and his friends constituted the far smaller wing of the dominant Liberal Party, the larger section of which was led by Giolitti. Salandra had formed his first Government after the latter's resignation from the premiership in March 1914, and resorted to such ruthless repression of the strike and revolutionary movement that the Labour Confederation denounced his 'reactionary system . . . injurious to Democracy', and the Socialists protested against the 'Draconian sentences' imposed on the workers.[4] Facing a Chamber in which he had no majority, and which—on his own later admission—was 'partly hostile and partly suspicious'[5] where his predilections were concerned, and overwhelmingly in favour of neutrality, he leaned on 'the interventionists, the Nationalists, the Fascists . . . who were most in touch with my intentions'.[6]

This shaped the composition of Salandra's second Ministry. Rubini, the Head of the Treasury who suffered, in Salandra's view, 'from excessive scruple', was dropped because he objected, on account of the budget deficit, to 'increasing the army estimates by

---

[1] See pp. 194–5 above.    [2] Nitti, *Il capitale straniero in Italia*, 58.
[3] Rodd in his Foreword to Salandra's *Italy and the Great War*, 9.
[4] Salandra, 46; also 10. 101–4, 106. See also p. 151 above.
[5] Salandra, 103. Also *The Lansing Papers*, I. 734.    [6] Salandra, 297.

231

many hundreds of millions' and would not condone mobilization except for defence.¹ The War Minister Grandi, under fire from the bellicose press for the country's unpreparedness, was replaced by General Zupelli—the tool and nominee of the Chief of Staff, Cadorna, who was widely reputed to be Francophil.² Such also was the orientation of Carcano, the new Director of the Treasury, and of Ferdinando Martini, the Minister for Colonies, described by Macchio as the driving spirit of the war party, 'who every morning called on Sir Rennell Rodd for instructions'.³

The strongest member of the new Cabinet, however, was Baron Sonnino, the *de facto* chief of the Right, whose inability to get on with Parliament made it politic to give the titular leadership to the more subtle and flexible Salandra.⁴ The son of a banker, whose family fortune derived from investment and speculation in Egypt, and principal shareholder of the *Giornale d'Italia*, Sonnino had previously headed two Administrations, each lasting a hundred days.⁵ But having, unlike Napoleon, suffered no political St. Helena, he exercised such back-stage influence that, as Salandra has written, 'more than any of my colleagues he had been constantly informed of all military and diplomatic affairs of a confidential nature'.⁶ A forerunner of Fascism at home—he had been an early advocate of the 'union of national parties' above classes, serving 'the higher ends of the nation as a whole'⁷—he was an extreme imperialist abroad.⁸ The French seizure of Tunis (in 1881) drew from him the declaration that 'friendship with Austria is for us an indispensable condition for a conclusive and effective policy'.⁹ As late as July 1914, he led the Nationalists in demanding that Italy should join the War on the side of the Central Powers.¹⁰ On August 1st, he wrote to Salandra: 'I have great doubts as to the wisdom of the decision for neutrality. The probability is that Austria and Germany will conquer on land. And what will become of us . . . in future? . . . . from now on we shall be debarred from world politics'.¹¹ As late as November,

¹ Salandra, 141, 146; also 148.
² Macchio to Berchtold, 13 Oct. '14. Conrad, V. 306–7, 308. Krupenski to Sazonov, 15 Oct. '14. *Internationale Beziehungen*, II. 6. I. p. 316, footnote 3; 390. Also Macchio, 58. Salandra, 140, 142–3. Rodd, III, 218–19, 227.
³ Macchio to Burián, 15 May '15. Tisza, I. 213. The Austro-Hungarian Naval Attaché in Rome to War Ministry, Vienna, 2 Sept. '14. Conrad, IV. 683. Also Macchio, 113–4. Rodd, III, 227.
⁴ Rodd, Foreword to Salandra, 10. Giolitti, 378. T. N. Page, 168.
⁵ A. Albertini, 157. Albrecht-Carrié, *Italy at the Paris Peace Conference*, 19. Salandra, 145, 147. T. N. Page, 167–8.
⁶ Salandra, 147; also 146, 73. Aldrovandi Marescotti, 29. Rodd, III. 227.
⁷ *Nuova Antologia*, Sept. 1900. Croce, 217. Sforza, 283.
⁸ T. N. Page, 300. ⁹ May, 279.
¹⁰ Giolitti, 384. Bülow, III. 183. Rossi, 3–4. *Carteggio*, LXI. III. 386.
¹¹ Salandra, 73.

Avarna could express the hope that the Baron 'would never consent to Italy's becoming guilty of the supreme shame' of letting down her Allies.[1] Britain's intervention, however, had changed Sonnino's views.[2] By November, certainly, he was 'considered to be pro-British'.[3] As such, no doubt, he assumed the key post of Foreign Affairs. But this meant no more than that he would seek to extract from co-operation with the Entente the utmost advantage to further Italy's aims. For the diplomatic *leitmotif* of Salandra's second Cabinet, which was presented to the public on November 5th, was the one sounded by the Prime Minister himself during his temporary tenure at the Consulta. On October 18th (the day when Sabini received his *coup de grâce*), Salandra announced that Italian policy

'will require immense firmness, a serene vision of the true interests of our country . . . coupled, when needful, with prompt action. We must be bold in deeds . . . without prejudice and preconceptions, and uninfluenced by any sentiment but that of an exclusive, unlimited devotion to our country, a sacred egoism for Italy.'[4]

Something akin to a hush of horror enveloped Europe's chancelleries.[5] The 'cynical phrase of the *sacro egoismo*', as Austria was soon to brand it,[6] came as as shock on two accounts. Frankness, uncommon in diplomacy's normal usage, was in war time more dangerous than a secret weapon. The implication that, as Salandra put it later, the 'cause of democracy against militarism . . . the liberty of oppressed peoples' was, or at least might be, 'windy, nebulous stuff',[7] struck at the roots of the belligerents' propaganda everywhere. His rejection of 'a romantic sense of national honour'[8] in favour of what Rodd has criticised as 'purely selfish national motives'[9] threatened to puncture the conceptions for which the peoples were asked to die. That, ten years after, the British Ambassador, in his Memoirs, could still chide Salandra for asserting 'that the War was not fought for the sake of humanity, for justice, for democracy',[10] testifies to the sharpness of the grudge felt abroad.

---

[1] Avarna to Bollati, 6 Nov. '14. *Carteggio*, LXI. II. 274.
[2] Salandra, 73.
[3] Krupenski to Sazonov. 4 Nov. '14. *Das Zaristische Russland*, p. 283.
[4] Salandra, 153. Rodd, III. 224.
[5] See Rodd, III. 224. C. R. M. Crutwell, in his standard *History o the Great War 1914-1918*, p. 133, has criticized Salandra's statement for its 'repellent and naked form'. Salandra's phrase was all the more unwelcome since the policy underlying it was not confined to Italy. Much the same view was expressed in Viviani's reply to the German ultimatum: 'France will consult her own interests'. *ibid.* 133.
[6] Salandra, 154.   [7] Salandra, 287.
[8] Salandra, 81-2. This formulation is given in his book.
[9] Rodd, III. 224.   [10] Rodd, III. 225.

Moreover, while inside the other countries the *sacro egoismo* could be glossed over or dismissed as typically 'Italian',[1] it remained the overriding factor in the relations of the Powers with Rome. The 'underlying meaning', according to its author was this: 'Pressure of all kinds, open and secret, was exerted to influence Italy's action ... the Italian Government desired to preserve complete liberty of initiative and movement'.[2] Formally and ostensibly, the warning was addressed to both sides. But in Berlin and Vienna it lacked the flavour of novelty. For the Austrians, in particular, *sacro egoismo* was only a *forte* variation on a well-worn theme. It was in Petrograd, Paris and London that it had, and was meant to have, the effect of a sudden and shrill disharmony. This beatification of national selfishness must be read in conjunction with the Western orientation of the new Cabinet. Salandra and Sonnino and their colleagues 'were agreed as to intervention in the spring'[3]; 'we planned, desired, prepared and initiated the ... War'.[4] This, in the circumstances, had to be preceded by a diplomatic war with the Entente. As the sword was unsheathed for the future enemy, *sacro egoismo* was reserved for the prospective Allies.

2

THE 'PROTECTION' OF ALBANIA

The road to the latter led, as before, through Vienna and Berlin. Twice at the end of October 1914, when the Porte's belligerency grew imminent, Carlotti inquired in Petrograd, 'as it were in passing', whether the moment was not ripe for Russia to settle the issue of the Straits. The non-committal reply that this was not the time for diplomatic measures foiled Italy's 'hope to tie up with this the solution of those questions in Turkey in which she is herself most interested'.[5] In the same way, the Ambassador Paléologue stated at the Russian Foreign Ministry, and the French presumably intimated directly to the Italians, that Paris did not desire Italian action against the Ottoman Empire. 'France is afraid that Italy might make full use of the difficult position of the Entente in the European War

---

[1] Salandra, 154, quotes a French newspaper appraising it 'in the light of the past! Is not the House of Savoy a case in point?'
[2] Salandra, 154.
[3] Salandra, 147. On 26 Oct. '14, Bollati wrote to Avarna: 'Indications are piling up to the effect that the decision to depart from neutrality has been taken'. *Carteggio*, LXI. II. 269.
[4] Salandra, 151.
[5] Memorandum, Russian Foreign Ministry, 31 Oct. '14, and Note, Russian Foreign Ministry, about 25 Oct. '14. *Internationale Beziehungen*, II. 6. I. No. 440, p. 352, No. 410, p. 327.

'SACRED EGOISM' 235

to settle her affairs with Turkey'.[1] The Entente, clearly, would not pay Italy's price, unless and until it saw that her stock stood high in the Central capitals.

It followed that there must be no room for secondary concessions such as those Germany and Austria, after their Marne and Galician defeats, were ready to make in Albania. Ever since Essad Pasha's Italian-sponsored movement had ousted the pathetic Prince of Wied, Rome had its eyes fixed on this prey.[2] The parleys conducted, from September 4th, over the projected Italian landing on Saseno revealed that Jagow's and Berchtold's acquiescence[3] was coupled with strong Austrian reservations. According to a Memorandum from Berchtold to Conrad,

'an Italian occupation of Valona [certain to follow that of Saseno], no matter how much it may suit us for the moment, would, nevertheless, 1. contradict our pre-war policy, 2. affect our political, military, maritime and economic interests in the Adriatic, and ought therefore . . . to be accompanied by guarantees. . . .: 1. the safeguarding of the Freedom of the Adriatic for our Navy and Merchant Fleet; 2. the establishment of a . . . . land connection between the [Dual] Monarchy and Albania. . . .; 3. . . . the acquisition of the Lovchen; 4. limitations by international law to be imposed on Italy regarding the use of the Bay of Valona as a naval base'.[4]

Although there was no intention to uphold 'these desiderata . . . against Italy, as long as the War lasts',[4] they must at least have been mentioned to the Consulta, for the Ambassador Page recollects that 'Austria's consent . . . contained an inconvenient condition'.[5] At any rate, her continuous insistence on Italian adherence to the decisions of the Ambassadors' Conference on Albania[6] was quite enough to nullify the compromise.

Another obstacle to agreement was that the Entente, whilst ready to 'give' the Italians Valona, objected to its being 'given' to

[1] Memorandum, Russian Foreign Ministry, 2 Nov. '14. *Internationale Beziehungen*, II. 6. I. p. 352, footnote 2. The same point is made in a Memorandum of the Russian Foreign Ministry, 30 Oct. '14, on a conversation with the French Embassy Councillor. *Internationale Beziehungen*, II. 6. I. No. 428, p. 342.
[2] The Prince left Albania on 31 Aug. '14. Salandra, 155. T. N. Page, 173–4.
[3] See p. 193 above; also Salandra, 155, 158–9. Bollati to San Giuliano, 3 and 5 Oct. '14. *Documenti Diplomatici*, 5. I. NN 872, 886, pp. 518, 527.
[4] Mid-Oct. '14. Conrad, V. 156–7. For Austria-Hungary's relentless struggle with Italy in and over Albania in the first half of 1914 see Conrad, III. 588–9, 678, 701. On 22 June '14 Conrad, in a letter to Berchtold, insisted that occupation by any other State should be resisted—if necessary by war. Conrad, III. 696. As late as 3 Aug. the Ambassador in Rome affirmed Austria's interest in that country. *Documenti Diplomatici*, 5. I. No. 35, p. 20.
[5] T. N. Page, 175.
[6] Conrad, V. 156–7. The reference is to the London Conference of Oct. and Nov. 1913.

them by the Central Powers. Already news of these parleys had leaked out in Paris,[1] and Sazonov was telling Carlotti 'that Russia, France and England would have been willing to leave Valona to Italy on account of her action against Austria. But if she should occupy Valona with Austrian assent, the matter would assume quite a different aspect'.[2] Salandra, scandalized by the brisk Russian formula of 'nothing for nothing',[3] reckoned that Britain would not object if Italy established a counterpoise to Slavdom in the Balkans. He sent Imperiali a telegram saying that 'the occupation of Valona ... must be considered as the preface to other engagements which we hoped to conclude, but these would be more difficult of accomplishment if the nation gained the impression that we had been thwarted by the ... Triple Entente'. He impressed upon the Ambassador

'the importance of obtaining Grey's ... consent. I ... hope that he will not encourage the tendency shown by Sazonov ... to exercise pressure upon us.... public opinion in Italy is far from being represented by a few noisy demonstrations.... All they have achieved is a reaction in favour of ... neutrality.... If the Government is to act in another sense (as we hope), it will need a kind of prestige which could only result from the occupation of Valona'.[4]

Two days later, Grey cabled to Buchanan that, according to Imperiali, Albanian and Epirote bands threatened to seize Valona, and the Italian Government, therefore, wished to take over that port as a 'temporary' measure. Britain was asked to acquiesce and intercede with Russia and France. 'If we should oppose this step', the Foreign Secretary went on, 'we shall evidently reduce altogether the possibility of Italy's joining us ... I hope that M. Sazonov is not against my ... giving an affirmative reply'.[5] But while differing from Sazonov regarding the Albanian *carte blanche* for Italy, Grey seems to have shared his opinion that she must not negotiate with the Central Powers. For, already after their first talk, Imperiali warned Salandra about 'the absolute necessity of avoiding any subsequent confidential exchange of views with Berlin and Vienna—for such a

---

[1] Salandra, 159. *Documenti Diplomatici*, 5. I. No. 873, p. 520.
[2] Sazonov to Benckendorff and Izvolski, 19 Sept. '14. *Das Zaristische Russland*, p. 279.
[3] See p. 208 above. Also San Giuliano to Imperiali, 4 Oct. '14. *Documenti Diplomatici*, 5. I. No. 880, p. 524. Salandra, 159.
[4] 2 Oct. '14. *Documenti Diplomatici*, 5. I. p. 518, footnote 2. Salandra, 159–60.
[5] Grey to Buchanan, 4 Oct. '14. Deciphered in the Russian Foreign Ministry. Retranslated from a translation of the original. *Das Zaristische Russland*, p. 281. An Aide-Memoire with an identical content was sent by the British Embassy to Sazonov the same day. *Internationale Beziehungen*, II, 6, I. No. 355, pp. 280–1. Also Salandra, 160.

thing ... might definitely alienate Grey's confidence to the injury of our present and future interests'.¹ In consequence, the Consulta dropped the idea of discussing Valona with Austria and Germany.² This was the reason Sazonov gave for his consent which, like Delcassé's, was due, as Imperiali reported, 'to Grey's insistence both in Paris and St. Petersburg'.³ At the same time Britain, anxious to balance Italy's imminent leap across the Adriatic, secured an accord between Rome and Athens, whereby the former approved the Greek occupation of the Epirus, in return for a free hand in Valona.⁴ On October 29th 1914, an 'Italian Sanitary Mission' was landed there under naval cover 'in aid', as Salandra claims, 'of the refugees from ... Epirote bands ... notorious for their murders and robberies'.⁵ The Admiral in command enlarged on the humanitarian nature of his task by stating: 'At present peace is undisturbed. ... If there are disturbances later, Italy will be compelled to intervene'.⁶ As there were none, Saseno was occupied by marines the following day 'for the protection of Albania's neutrality'.⁷

This sample of *sacro egoismo* stemmed from a variety of motives. Albania, according to Salandra's subsequent apologia, was 'in a chaotic state, an easy prey' to other Powers, which was contrary to 'our vital interests and historical rights to a dominant position in the Adriatic'.⁸ Whatever the outcome of the War, there would be, as Tittoni urged, a territorial re-distribution in the Balkans and the certain partition of Albania. Hence, Italy's aspirations to Valona must be secured in advance.⁹ In control of that key point, she 'could view more calmly what went on in the North of the ... Peninsula'.¹⁰ At the very least, this would foil Sazonov's scheme for dividing Albania between the Serbs and Greeks.¹¹ The adventure had also

¹ Imperiali to Salandra, 3 Oct. '14. Salandra, 150.
² San Giuliano to Imperiali, 6 Oct. '14. *Documenti Diplomatici*, 5. I. No. 903, p. 540. Salandra, 161. According to a Communication from the Serbian Legation in Petrograd to Sazonov, 31 Oct. '14, Italy had failed to reach an agreement with Austria on Albania. *Internationale Beziehungen*, II. 6. I. No. 438, p. 351, and *ibid*. footnote 2.
³ Imperiali to Salandra, 6 Oct. '14. Salandra, 160–1. Also Sazonov to Krupenski, 4 Oct. *Das Zaristische Russland*, p. 282. Izvolski to Sazonov, 5 Oct. *Internationale Beziehungen*, II. 6. I. p. 281, footnote 1. Carlotti, Imperiali and Tittoni to San Giuliano, 6 Oct. *Documenti Diplomatici*, 5. I. NN 892, 896, 904, pp. 533–5, 540.
⁴ Demidov to Sazonov, 23 Oct. '14. *Das Zaristische Russland*, p. 282. Also T. N. Page, 175.
⁵ Salandra, 161. Some sources give 26 Oct. as the landing date. See *Internationale Beziehungen*, II. 6. I. p. 351, and T. N. Page, 175.
⁶ Salandra, 161.     ⁷ T. N. Page, 175. Salandra, 161.
⁸ Salandra, 155.     ⁹ Salandra, 156.
¹⁰ Merey to Berchtold, 16 July '14. *Österreich-Ungarns Aussenpolitik*, VIII, p. 464.
¹¹ See Aide-Memoire, Russian Foreign Ministry to Paléologue and Buchanan, 5 Nov '14. *Internationale Beziehungen*, II. 6. II. No. 466, p. 409. 30 Nov. '14. Poincaré, V. 470.

its domestic uses by 'distracting people's thoughts from so many other dangerous questions and giving the Government the opportunity of arranging a more serious and general action in March'.[1] Over and above this, the Consulta wanted international 'prestige',[2] an assertion of independence vis-à-vis the tabus of the Entente, a cheap victory, snatching unconditionally that which the three Powers could not withhold, but wished to attach strings to. The most crucial aspect of the affair, however, was its impact on Vienna. By the seizure of Valona and Saseno, as Sonnino reasoned, 'an easier ultimate solution of foreign questions would be provided for us, in so far as we could claim to possess [already] an important guarantee for our action in the Trentino'. The Secretary-General of the Consulta, urging the need for a démarche in the Central capitals, said that, as a compensation for Austria's gains, Italy might be given Saseno and ought, therefore, to forestall such a proposition by an immediate occupation of the island.[3] This argument applied with still greater force to Valona. The Italian incursion into Albania was to deprive Austria-Hungary of the means of offering, under Article VII, something which (under German pressure)[4] she might decide to forgo. Indeed, the occupation of Valona caused great displeasure on the Danube.[5] For, having taken this trinket from the Habsburgs, Italian imperialism could now demand their life.

### 3
### ITALY'S DIPLOMATIC OFFENSIVE IN VIENNA

'The Italian Government holds it necessary to proceed without further delay to an exchange of views, and then to concrete negotiations, with the Royal and Imperial Government concerning the complex situation which has a close bearing upon the vital interests, both political and economic, of Italy'.

This was the Note which the new Foreign Minister Sonnino dispatched to Berchtold on December 9th 1914,[6] while thousands of millions were being spent on military preparations 'and hardly a

[1] Sonnino to Salandra, 26 Sept. '14. Salandra, 156.   [2] Salandra, 159.
[3] Sonnino to Salandra, 26 Sept. '14. Salandra, 157. De Martino to San Giuliano, 4 Sept. *Documenti Diplomatici*, 5. I. No. 581, pp. 330–1.
[4] On 26 Oct. '14, Bollati wrote to Avarna that 'they so readily agreed in Berlin' to the Italian occupation of Valona that he gathered Vienna would also consent. *Carteggio*, LXI. II. 269.
[5] Krupenski to Sazonov, 31 Dec. '14. *Internationale Beziehungen*, II. 6. II. p. 600, footnote 2. The Austrian Consul was reported as having tried to persuade the authorities of Valona to avoid giving any pretext for Italy's intervention. *Documenti Diplomatici*, 5. I. No. 837, p. 520.
[6] Bollati to Avarna, 10 Dec. '14. *Carteggio*, LXI. III. 389, and *ibid*. footnote 1. Giolitti, 392. Musulin, *Das Haus am Ballplatz*, 254.

cabin was left in Italy without a man away in camp—"for training" . . .'[1] Though the great majority in the country desired neutrality, and food shortage and unemployment were already serious enough to provoke disturbances,[2] the Consulta, re-opening the question of Article VII of the Triplice, took the step which led towards war.[3]

The communication hit Vienna at a moment of deepest gloom. On December 2nd, William II and Conrad had drunk a toast to the fall of Belgrade. But the Serbian counter-attack brought Austria 'a surprising catastrophe'.[4] On the 10th, the Chief of Staff muttered to his intimates: 'We have lost our position in the Balkans'.[5] In Rome, this rout and retreat, as Macchio reported, 'was looked upon as the beginning of the collapse of the [Dual] Monarchy'.[6] In Vienna, it cracked the polished surface of the 'cool do-nothing attitude'[7] which Berchtold had hitherto maintained towards the cantankerous Ally.

His stubborn optimism had been fed by a secret report that 'Italy was working to a plan preparing for action against Austria-Hungary, said to be envisaged for the spring 1915'.[8] Until then, it was thought, much would happen to put presumption in its place. Not even Sonnino's advent caused alarm, for he passed as a staunch supporter of the Triplice, Berchtold only expressing the hope 'that he has not changed opinion with advancing years, adopting the turbulent ideas of youth'.[9] As late as November 21st, the Austrian Foreign Minister, replying to the Ambassador Macchio's query on the Trentino, sent him instructions expressly 'endorsing the negative attitude you have maintained hitherto, and which is to be continued in the future'.[10] But the Dual Monarchy's Eastern campaign—despite monstrous losses from fighting, cholera and desertion—remained indecisive.[11] Belgrade was evacuated on December 14th, and Conrad, noting an 'undeniable defeat', had nightmares of what might happen to Syrmia, the Banat, and even Budapest or Vienna.[12] Sonnino, far from displaying the 'wisdom' expected of his age, was only beginning to sow his wild oats. And the appointment of Prince Bülow as Germany's new Envoy to Rome imposed an additional strain.

[1] T. N. Page, 218. Also Salandra, 172.
[2] Avarna to Bollati, 15 Dec. '14. *Carteggio*, LXI. III. 389. Salandra, 172.
[3] Bollati wrote to Avarna, 23 Dec. '14, that war against the Central Powers had become 'inevitable'. *Carteggio*, LXI. III. 397.
[4] Conrad, V. 713; and 658. [5] Conrad, V. 714; also 685.
[6] Macchio to Berchtold, 6 Jan. '15. Macchio, 74.
[7] Macchio, 40.
[8] Berchtold to Macchio, 25 Nov. '14. Macchio, 56.
[9] Berchtold to Macchio, 6 Nov. '14. Macchio, 51; also 52.
[10] Macchio, 54.
[11] Conrad, V. 913, 942. 969-70, 982-3.
[12] Conrad's Memorandum to the Government, 14 Dec. '14. Conrad, V. 748-9; also 723.

## 4
### GERMAN PRESSURE IN VIENNA

The coming of the Allied Ambassador, whose task was to restrain the Consulta, would not have worried the Austrians had not Berlin persistently endeavoured to buy Italian moderation at their expense. The German indiscretions at the Consulta prior to the Sarayevo ultimatum[1] were kept fresh in their minds by direct and continuous pressure from the Wilhelmstrasse.

As far back as July 1914, no sooner had the Foreign Minister von Jagow learned that San Giuliano had mentioned 'a cession of territory in the Trentino',[2] than he telegraphed to Tschirsky, the German Envoy in Vienna, that 'Italy has a right to compensation' and that 'the only compensation regarded as adequate in Italy would be the acquisition of the Trentino'.[3] On July 17th, the German Embassy Councillor discussed 'the diocese of Trento' with Berchtold's *Chef du Cabinet*.[4] On the 31st, the Kaiser asked Francis Joseph 'to do all you can to induce Italy to co-operate by meeting [her views] as much as possible'.[5] In August, Moltke, the Reich's Chief of Staff, seconded by his Imperial master, pressed Austria, 'for a start, to fill the gob of the hungry beast of prey' with the Trentino.[6] Conrad, for his part, notified him that—since Italy, 'that perfidious State . . . compels us to take certain military precautions', and these were reduced to 'a minimum' by the need to send all his available forces against Russia (as Germany desired)—'it would be of the utmost value for us to receive help from Germany'.[7] But the answer was so discouraging[8] that the Austrian later ruminated bitterly on 'Germany's hesitant and often negative attitude regarding every decisive and energetic step against Italy'.[9] The Hungarian Premier Tisza, 'painfully affected by the repeated German suggestions that we should hold out to Italy certain prospects about the Trentino', invited Berchtold to speak to Berlin 'in a very friendly yet very serious manner, and to exclude this topic from all further conversations'.[10] But Vienna's

---

[1] See p. 164 above.
[2] Flotow to Jagow, 10 July '14. L. Albertini, II. 231.
[3] Jagow to Tschirsky, 15 July, 14. *Deutsche Dokumente*, I. No. 46, pp. 71–2.
[4] Stolberg to Jagow, 18 July '14. *Deutsche Dokumente*, I. No. 87, p. 114.
[5] William II to Francis Joseph, 31 July '14. Conrad, IV. 156.
[6] Moltke to Conrad, 9 Aug. '14. Conrad, IV. 203. At the same time, Tschirsky raised this question with Berchtold. See Avarna to San Giuliano, 12 Aug. *Documenti Diplomatici*, 5. I. No. 212, p. 125.
[7] Conrad to Moltke, 8 Aug. '14. Conrad, IV. 352–3.
[8] Moltke to Conrad, 9 Aug. '14. Conrad, IV. 203. Conrad to Berchtold, 11 Aug. '14. Conrad, IV. 200.
[9] Conrad, IV. 353.
[10] Tisza to Berchtold, 26 Aug. '14. Tisza, I. 61–2.

# 'SACRED EGOISM'

resistance availed as little as its surrender 'in principle' on August 26th.[1] After the Marne retreat, Jagow increased his exertions. The cynical injunction that Austria-Hungary should forgo 'that scrap of South Tyrol'[2] was in profound accord, as Macchio recollects, 'with Berlin's notions with which we were served in every shape, and from a hundred sources'.[3]

This intermezzo between the two Allies—though camouflaged by lavish exchanges of regimental honours and highest decorations[4] —did not escape the notice of the Consulta. As early as August 9th, San Giuliano mentioned that the German Ambassador 'believes the cession of the Trentino is possible'. Bollati soon wrote that the Germans 'continue to tell me that . . . it would not, in certain circumstances, be absolutely impossible to obtain the consent of Austria to such a proposition'.[5] Avarna counselled Rome to take up the matter with Berlin[6] in order either to secure the cession with the help of the latter or, failing that, divide the Central Powers and isolate the Habsburgs. This line was assiduously pursued by the Italians.[7] Hence, Jagow was at once informed of Sonnino's communication to Berchtold of December 9th.[8] To this was added the warning that

'the flow of public opinion in favour of neutrality does not signify the renunciation of Italian interests in the Balkans and the Adriatic, or of national aspirations, but the conviction that these will be properly safeguarded even if neutrality be maintained. If this conviction were disturbed, the reaction in public opinion would be very serious'.[9]

It is clear from a letter by Avarna to Bollati what Sonnino and Salandra expected. They 'hope that, as a consequence of your step [at the Wilhelmstrasse], the Berlin Cabinet will bring pressure to bear on Vienna for Count Berchtold to discuss with us the question, or to open the way for the cession, of the Trentino and rectification of the Isonzo frontier. They are confirmed in this hope by the imminent arrival of Bülow'.[10] It is equally plain that the Aus-

---

[1] See *Deutsche Dokumente*, I. No. 94, p. 119. Bülow, III. 183, 185; and p. 191 above.
[2] Tschirsky to Macchio. Macchio, 26.
[3] Macchio, 30. For Jagow's exertions see Erzberger, 38, Bülow, III. 205–6.
[4] Conrad, V. 658–9.
[5] San Giuliano to Salandra, 9 Aug. '14. *Documenti Diplomatici*, 5. I. No. 152, p. 84. Bollati to Avarna, 24 Sept. '14. *Carteggio*, LXI. II. 260.
[6] Avarna to San Giuliano, 12 Aug. '14. *Documenti Diplomatici*, 5. I. No. 212, p. 125. Avarna to Bollati, 5 Oct. '14. *Carteggio*, LXI. II. 263.
[7] San Giuliano to Salandra, 4 Aug., and to Bollati, 31 Aug. '14. *Documenti Diplomatici*, 5. I. NN. 55, 518, pp. 31, 288.
[8] Bollati to Avarna, 10 Dec. '14. *Carteggio*, LXI. III. 388–9. Also p. 238 above.
[9] Salandra, 219. Burián, 27.
[10] Avarna to Bollati, 15 Dec. '14. *Carteggio*, LXI. III. 392.

trians could not have been ignorant of these calculations. Even if unaware that, over three months ago, San Giuliano had solicited the Prince's visit to Rome—'when I shall tell you a good deal about the reasons for our neutrality, which I cannot put in writing'[1]— they were bound to connect with his coming Sonnino's peremptory Note.[2]

'We have packed the Trentino in Prince von Bülow's trunk', Jagow remarked to the Empress. That, as the new Ambassador was to say, 'was a lie'. For he had received no mandate from the owners of the province.[3] But quite obviously the success of his mission depended on his obtaining it. Only some weeks before, the German diplomat Count Monts had come to sound Vienna on this question, and the staff of Tschirsky's Embassy canvassed it through every social channel.[4] As Macchio reflected, it was easy to see 'how little understanding and assistance in this business we could find just where it would have been most desirable'.[5] Berchtold, faced once again with the fatal Article VII, sought to escape in the contention that, the occupation of Serbian districts being a 'momentary' measure, no compensation was due. Avarna had no difficulty in reminding him that he had himself refused to concede this point to Italy in the Libyan War, and that the seizure of Bosnia-Herzegovina had also been 'temporary'.[6] But what, apart from the loss of Belgrade, really defeated the Austro-Hungarian Foreign Minister was his dread of Bülow's 'trunk'. To negotiate seemed the only means of filling it with something less costly than the Trentino. Yielding to heavy German pressure, Berchtold on December 15th 1914 consented to an exchange of ideas on Article VII with Italy.[7]

Sonnino put his foot squarely in the opening door. 'From the point of view of legality', as Salandra has confessed, 'we could raise no other question than the execution of Article VII'.[8] It was also a fact that (as the Minister Burián recollects), 'in accordance with the obvious meaning' of the latter,[9] claims could only be made in the Balkans. But, Salandra goes on to say, 'we . . . did not . . . restrict

[1] San Giuliano to Bülow, 31 Aug. '14. Macchio, 32.
[2] The Ambassador T. N. Page, p. 191, states: 'In anticipation of the arrival in Rome of . . . Bülow . . .' the Italian Government sent its Note to Vienna on December 9th 1914.
[3] Bülow, III. 191.
[4] Macchio, 61. Avarna, on the contrary, asserts that Monts had been sent by circles hostile to Bülow in order to frustrate his mission. Avarna to Bollati, 15 Dec. '14. *Carteggio*, LXI. III. 393.
[5] Macchio, 27.
[6] Salandra, 219–20. T. N. Page, 192. Avarna to Bollati, 15 and 20 Dec. '14. *Carteggio*, LXI. III. 392, 395. Szilassy, 212.
[7] Tschirsky-Berchtold interview, 13 Dec. '14. Avarna to Bollati, 7 Jan. '15. *Carteggio*, LXI. III. 401. Also Salandra, 220. T. N. Page, 192.
[8] Salandra, 221–2.      [9] Burián, 27. Also Helfferich, II. 67.

ourselves to such aims as the maintenance of the . . . equilibrium in the Balkan Peninsula . . . for here was the chance of reclaiming the nation's territory, of creating frontiers on land and sea no longer open to invasion, and of raising Italy, in reality, to the status of a Great Power; ambitions . . . very different from those of acquiring a modest scrap of territory. . . .'[1]

The first step, then, was to complete the conquest of Valona, partly also because Sazonov wished to partition Albania between the Serbs and the Greeks, and threatened Italy that, if she remained obstreperous, the Entente might change its views on the fate of that port.[2] The 'Sanitary Mission' placed there in October,[3] had donned the humanitarian garb so as not to provoke Austria-Hungary unduly.[4] Such tact having become superfluous after Berchtold's surrender, the Mission suddenly discovered that it required bayonets. On December 20th, at Durazzo, the Government of Essad, Rome's old protégé, was said to have asked Sonnino for intervention. On Christmas Day, 'rifle shots' were heard in Valona, the Italian Consul called for warships, and marines and Carabinieri were landed for 'the preservation of order and the protection of Italian citizens'.[5] And now that it was finally impossible for the Central Powers to offer minor benefits, the Consulta was ready for a major move. On January 12th 1915, the Ambassador Avarna raised with Berchtold the issue of an 'eventual cession' of Austrian territory.[6]

5

THE FALL OF THE AUSTRO-HUNGARIAN FOREIGN MINISTER

Vienna, meanwhile, was 'depressed, sombre, shaken in its faith in the future'.[7] It is not likely that Berchtold, one of the archcriminals of the War, was appalled by what, at the time, the British Premier described as 'an enormous waste of life and money day after day with no appreciable progress'.[8] Berchtold's attitude was best summed up by himself: 'For goodness' sake, shut up about the War; it bores me stiff. . . . I know, the Russians will come to Buchlowitz and . . . burn it down, but then I have another castle in

---

[1] Salandra, 221-2.
[2] Sazonov to Benckendorff and Izvolski, 10 Dec. '14. *Das Zaristische Russland*, p. 285.
[3] See p. 237 above.
[4] The Serbian Legation, Petrograd, to Sazonov, 31 Oct. '14. *Internationale Beziehungen*, II. 6. I. No. 438, p. 351.
[5] T. N. Page, 176.
[6] Burián, 27-8, 39. Tisza, I. 148, 263-4. Rodd, III. 247. Pribram, *The Secret Treaties of Austria-Hungary*, II. 179.
[7] Dec. '14. Macchio, 68. Also Redlich, I. 273, 275.
[8] 29 Dec. '14. Asquith, *Memories and Reflections*, II. 52.

Salzburg, and I'll live there'.¹ But Czernin, the Minister in Bucharest, believed that if Rome was bought off, the Rumanian threat, too, would be averted.² Macchio, reporting signs of the gathering storm in Italy, wondered 'whether by making a momentary smaller sacrifice to this robber State much larger interests would not be saved'.³ Even Conrad, admitting to Czernin that the outcome of all the fighting was a stalemate, found that 'diplomatic action should be started now in order to reach some result. Our military forces would not be strong enough if Italy and Rumania joined our enemies'.⁴ It became obvious that, as Macchio pleaded, 'vague Albanian prospects and perhaps the Dodecanese [both already in Italian hands]... will make little impression' on the Consulta.⁵ And Berchtold, arguing that 'Italy would not lightly depart from the Triple Alliance, since after all she could achieve something without war', suggested the cession of South Tyrol.⁶

But had not already Francis I said: 'My realm resembles a worm-eaten house. If one part is removed one cannot tell how much will fall?'⁷ To satisfy Italian Irredentism was tantamount to adding dynamite to the restiveness of the Czechs, Slovaks, Poles, Croats, Slovenes and other subject races.⁸ To abandon imperial territory would be creating a precedent for Rumania's claims on Transylvania. This prospect was so abhorrent to the Magyar oligarchs that, as early as October 2nd 1914, the Premier Tisza had instructed Czernin 'to emphasize categorically that we shall give away nothing that is ours.... So long as I have a say, anyone marching into our country will be fired at'.⁹ Moreover, it was known in Vienna that the Entente had made sweeping promises to the Consulta.¹⁰ Berchtold himself had ascertained through 'secret channels' that Rome would not content herself with the Trentino. Austria's capitulation, therefore, would only strengthen 'in Italy... the belief in our weakness and war-weariness' and become 'the starting point of murderous blackmail regarding the extent of the cession.... which could not but... become fatal for us'.¹¹ As Burián showed later, 'there was

¹ Redlich, I. 274.
² 26 Dec. '14. Conrad, V. 910.
³ Macchio to Berchtold, 6 Jan. '15. Macchio, 74–5.
⁴ 26 Dec. '14. Conrad, V. 911.
⁵ Macchio to Berchtold, 6 Jan. '15. Macchio, 76.
⁶ 30 Dec. '14, at General Headquarters. Conrad, V. 957. Cf. Redlich, II. 8.
⁷ May, 22.
⁸ Berchtold to Macchio, 21 Nov. '14. Macchio, 53–4. Also Burián, 28.
⁹ Tisza, I. 87. Also Conrad to Berchtold, 6 Aug. '14. Conrad, IV. 182. Erzberger, 130.
¹⁰ Aug. '14. Conrad, IV. 198; also 187.
¹¹ Berchtold to Macchio, 21 Nov. '14. Macchio, 53–4. See also Burián, 48: 'If we once begin to surrender territory, it would be the first step of a steep path from which there was no turning back'.

'SACRED EGOISM' 245

no question' of the Danubian Monarchy being able to buy a free hand by an agreement on compensation. 'Italy was determined to make use of the World War to achieve, as far as she possibly could, her Irredentist, Adriatic and Near Eastern ambitions'.[1] Sonnino had only just lifted the lid of the cauldron roaring with nationalist and imperialist agitation. 'Whatever we may throw . . . to Italy to-day', Burián wrote to Tisza, ' . . . this good friend of ours will have digested by March 1st . . . and will then demand fresh sacrifices at bayonet point'.[2] 'From the moment when Italy committed her breach of the Treaty', Conrad 'did not doubt . . . that henceforth she would pursue unscrupulously her far-reaching aims against Austria-Hungary, and that she would not be deterred by signs of friendliness . . . from proceeding to overt hostility'.[3] No compromise therefore, it was argued, could guarantee Italian neutrality.[4]

Indeed, even if Rome's motives were as pure as the water of her fountains, she could still not remain neutral, for she would have to distrust Austria-Hungary. The latter was bound, as Conrad suggested, to 'repay perfidy with perfidy'.[5] The very victory achieved through Italy's abstention could be exploited against the Italians. They 'must conclude', as Burián intimated to the Habsburg Ambassador in Berlin, 'that . . . we would presumably make such far-reaching concessions only with the mental reservation that we should reconquer, at the next opportunity, what we have ceded . . . that we shall be dominated in future . . . by the idea of revenge . . .'[6] The faithless Ally was threatened and abused in the clubs and salons of Budapest and Vienna, and Tisza had to admonish the officers of the Navy 'to avoid most carefully every utterance from which she [Italy] could deduce that she would have to pay the bill when the [Dual] Monarchy has emerged more powerful from the great trial of strength'.[7] In support of his plea that, having enforced the concession, Italy would have all the more reason to go to war, the Hungarian Premier was soon to remind the Emperor of the 'old Italian recipe . . . kill those whom you have insulted or injured, for the dead wreak no vengeance'.[8]

In the circumstances, to hand over the Trentino would have enabled the prospective enemy, as Conrad wrote later, to 'take possession, without a fight, of our fortified territory, from which she could afterwards continue her easy incursion'.[9] Far from intend-

[1] Burián, 28.
[2] Burián to Tisza, probably 5 Jan. '15. Tisza, I. 143. Also Burián, 34–35.
[3] Conrad, V. 59–60.  [4] See Burián, 59. Redlich, II. 19.
[5] Conrad, IV. 185; also 377.
[6] Burián to Hohenlohe, 1 May '15. Tisza, I. 203–4. Also Andrassy, 132.
[7] Tisza to Capt. Horthy, 14 March '15. Tisza, I. 174; and 195.
[8] Tisza's Memorandum, 1 May '15, Tisza, I. 193–9.
[9] Conrad, IV. 183.

ing to surrender 'in advance the strongest protection of our frontier', the Austrians were determined to menace from South Tyrol the Italian flank in the event of an invasion via Venetia.[1] In any case, as Macchio stressed, fears of Italy's belligerency, at that time, were premature.[2] It was known that she 'has timed all her war preparations for March 1st'. 'Since . . . we still have two months ahead of us, it is not necessary to discuss things that need not happen'.[3] Such were the arguments of the Court, some leaders of the Christian-Social Party, and notably Conrad and Tisza.[4] The latter, on January 10th 1915, arrived in Vienna 'with the intention of raising the matter' with Francis Joseph and taking a stand against Berchtold. On January 14th, two days after his last interview with the Italian Ambassador, the Foreign Minister was dismissed.[5]

The fall of the senior member of the Cabinet—Knight of the Golden Fleece, kinsman of three Emperors, and a *grand seigneur* noted for his estates, racing-stable and glittering receptions[6]— revealed a crisis far deeper than could have been caused by this particular issue. It marked a turning point in Austro-Hungarian foreign policy.

---

[1] Burián, 35. Conrad, IV. 183.
[2] Macchio, Promemoria, before Christmas '14. Macchio, 64.
[3] Conrad to Berchtold, 21 Dec. '14. Conrad to Czernin, 26 Dec. Conrad, V. 854, 910.
[4] Macchio, 83. Erzberger, 44.
[5] Tisza, I. 150–2, 263.
[6] Bülow, III. 175. May, 458. Szilassy, 182, 202. Dumaine, 22, 221.

CHAPTER XVIII

# *Austria-Hungary*

1

THE SOCIAL SCENE

THAT foreign policy begins at home would be a commonplace, were it not so grotesquely over-emphasized by the example of the Danubian Monarchy. Austria, as Alexander Herzen wrote back in 1859, 'is not a nation, Austria is a police measure, a summary administration . . . the biggest historical spectre that ever was. Everything here is a lie. . . . Only when she has been abolished will people really be amazed that there could have been such an absurdity, sewn together from scraps by congresses, and consolidated by deep diplomatic considerations'.[1] By 1914, even such a traditionist as the French Ambassador recognized that the Empire's much vaunted charm, elegance and gaiety were mere 'façades d'une splendeur postiche'.[2]

In Austria, near-universal manhood suffrage[3] had produced a Parliament debased by corruption, strife and intrigue to the level of a political café. The Cabinet, hand-picked by the Emperor, purchased majorities by concessions to pressure groups behind the parties, favours to protégés, and secret subventions to the press. From March 1914, when the Reichsrat was dispersed, the ultra-conservative clerical Premier Stürgkh governed by decree. The Chamber in Budapest, unmoved by fisticuffs and pistol shots, remained an exclusive club. The general ballot was vetoed because it would have ended not only the supremacy of the Magyar ruling classes but also Magyar national predominance in Hungary. Materially nothing had changed since 1901, when nearly a third of the M.P's. were returned by constituencies with less than a hundred, and over nine tenths by constituencies with under 1,500, voters. Elections were fought by bribery and terrorism involving heavy casualties. In 1912, having gagged the debates and employed gendarmes against Opposition deputies, Tisza became the dictator of the Hungarian Kingdom.[4] The Empire of Waltz and Czardas, on

---

[1] 12 Jan. 1859. *Za Pyatj Let*. Volnaya Russkaya Tipografiya. London, 1860, p. 130.
[2] 'Façades of false splendour'. Dumaine, 19.
[3] It had been withheld until 1907, when Socialist unrest at home and Revolution in Russia made it a matter of expediency. May 337–8.
[4] May, 440, 506.

inspection, turned out to be a tyranny exercised by the officers' caste, the arbitrary bureaucracy, the Argus-eyed police, the Jesuit colleges, and the Catholic hierarchy 'whose close-knit organization reached into every urban district and almost every hamlet'.[1] The consequence was a twin State, in which a minority of Austro-Germans and Magyars, abetted by Polish landlords and prelates, misruled a majority of nine subject nations, and where the common people even of the 'master races' were outside the pale. The unbearable food prices and housing conditions of the Austrian workers provoked Socialist demonstrations of such magnitude (in 1911) that they were quenched in blood.[2] Hungarian industrial labour—sweated and dwelling in 'disease-breeding pest holes'[3]—was only prevented from exploding by the persecution of the trade unions and of Social-Democracy. The agricultural scene in Austria ranged between comfortable farmsteads, tenancies surrendering two-thirds of their output, and holdings unable to sustain a family. The village poor—housed in hovels, down-trodden, debt-ridden and drink-sodden—touched rock-bottom in Galicia with its 'strikes, rioting and home-burnings'.[4] In the Magyar Kingdom, where 'rural destitution prevailed on a large scale', waves of agrarian unrest throughout the 'nineties and from 1905 to 1907 were broken 'with whip and gun', blacklegs and laws reminiscent of medieval codes.[5]

By contrast, vast latifundia were owned by an aristocracy 'gripped by moral indolence and without . . . sense of public responsibility . . . ignorant and narrow-minded . . . pompous, futile'.[6] The House of Esterházy had 695,000 acres, Schönborn—300,000, Károlyi—218,000. The Starhembergs and the Lichtensteins possessed scores of castles. Over a quarter of the territory of Bohemia, where the Schwarzenbergs had above 500,000 acres, was in the hands of less than two per cent of the landowners; in Moravia, a third was controlled by fewer than one per cent. In Galicia, three-fifths of the productive land was occupied by large estates.[7] The great magnates included churchmen of whom, in Hungary, most bishops had over 35,000 and some more than 100,000 acres, so that, with the monasteries, the ecclesiastical domains in 1914 totalled 2,250,000 acres.[8] The Austrian branch of Roman Catholicism with its princely properties and incomes—the Archbishop of Olmütz's annual revenue reached £60,000[9]—

[1] May, 182.
[2] May, 428.
[3] May, 246; also 247, 371–2.
[4] May, 168; also 165–9.
[5] May, 373; also 232–3, 372–4.
[6] May, 162.
[7] May, 159, 167, 501. Count M. Karolyi, pp. 16, 31, 46–7, states that he alone owned 60,000 acres of land, several country estates and shooting-boxes, a spa, a coal mine, a glass factory, a mansion with 72 rooms and several houses in Budapest, and the lucrative terrain in five suburbs.
[8] May, 247.
[9] Steed, 118.

was probably the most opulent in Europe. The dean of the landlords was His Apostolic Majesty Francis Joseph, who figured among the landed grandees in the electoral register of most of the provinces, and whose dynastic motto has been aptly summarized as 'more acres'.[1] 'Irresponsible', above the law, claiming divine appointment, and yet a prisoner of his position, his personal bigotry and his dread of the summer lightning witnessed in 1848; callous and cold about the sufferings of 'his' peoples; and having outlived his wife, son, brother, heirs and time, the octogenarian drifted like a stubborn ghost through the halls of Schönbrunn, murmuring: 'Everyone dies, only I cannot . . .'[2]—and yet would not relax the grip of the régime, nor even the stiff Spanish ceremonial of the Court.

But while the traditions of Maria-Theresa still draped the throne; while Prince Montenuovo, the grandson of the Empress Marie-Louise, enforced etiquette *suaviter in modo*,[3] the upstart hosts of Mammon invaded the baroque palaces and council chambers. Trade, industry and finance produced the new power of the bourgeoisie. At the time when many old nobles went into banking, insurance, the stock-market and business or, like the Schwarzenbergs, built sugar refineries, distilleries and paper mills; when even the monasteries extended their activities beyond wine cellars and inns to factories and banks, the middle class threw up its barons of monopoly. Liebig became a multi-millionaire. The steel and armaments maker Skoda ruled like a king. Bata was building an empire of shoes and leather. The steel rails, textiles, chemicals, arms, glass, paper, sugar and brewing cartels dominated economic life and enhanced the weight of the Vienna financiers who controlled them.[4] Rothschild's Kreditanstalt was connected with the Skoda company. The S.M. von Rothschild bank financed the Witkowitz Coal, Steel and Iron Works and the Floridsdorf Engineering Plant. The great Resita Iron and Steel Combine in Southern Hungary was owned by Viennese finance. The arms factory in Steyr was one of the

---

[1] Steed, 25, 40.  [2] Conrad, IV. 37.
[3] Dumaine, 94, 137, 217. May, 161.
[4] May, 200–1, 223. The growth of monopoly, by 1913, is described by W. Steed, pp. 142–3: 'In Austria-Hungary . . . the bureaucratization of financial and industrial undertakings is proceeding apace. . . . Smaller firms tend . . . to seek the support of the larger banks, and some industrial enterprises of respectable dimensions have of late been converted into mere dividend-earning departments of what were originally purely financial institutes. A few men . . . find remunerative positions as business or technical managers of these amalgamated undertakings but the rank and file of business men are gradually drifting into the position of salaried officials in the employ of vast soulless machines'. As for 'the relationships between the heads of such undertakings and the State . . . the difficulty lies . . . in maintaining a line of demarcation between the industrial and financial bureaucracy and the bureaucracy of the State'. In fact, there are many 'points of subterranean contact between the bureaucracy and the private enterprises'. *ibid.* 89–90.

enterprises of the Bodenkreditanstalt.¹ In a society where the peak of ambition was to be 'hoffähig',² and—quoting a current quip— no one lower than a 'von' was human, these conquistadors injected themselves into the aristocracy. It was not fortuitous that Count Tisza, the chief of the Magyar gentry, was the chairman of a Budapest bank, that the Foreign Minister with the sonorous name of Count Alois Lexa von Aehrenthal was the grandson of a grain merchant from Prague, and that Princess Pauline Metternich consorted with the Rothschilds.³

2

THE DUAL MONARCHY AND THE YUGOSLAVS

This union of blue blood and gilt-edged had a profound effect on foreign policy. The dynamics of capitalist expansion intensified the aggressiveness of Austro-Hungarian feudal militarism. But this was not what the tortured peoples at home and the public abroad were led to believe. The manufacturers and merchants of opinion in Vienna and Budapest—the press, pulpit, politicians and professors—depicted the War of 1914 as one of defence not only against the external but also the internal enemy. The story was a perversion arising from the Habsburgs' mistreatment of their subject nations. That some, at least, of the latter were kept in semi-colonial bondage was openly admitted by Tisza in 1910: 'Our non-Magyar fellow citizens must . . . reconcile themselves to the fact that they belong to a national State which is not a conglomerate of different races, but which one nation has conquered'.⁴ The oligarchs of Hungary bartered a measure of their support to the Crown in army and diplomatic affairs for untrammelled domestic authority. Magyarization and discrimination struck millions of Slovaks, Ukrainians, Serbs, Croats, Rumanians and Germans like a blight. The masters of Austria safeguarded themselves by a suffrage law (1907) which gave the 35·8 per cent Germans in the population 45·1 per cent of the Parliamentary seats, as against, for example, a 6·3 per cent representation for the Ukrainians who, as even the garbled statistics admitted, formed 13·2 per cent of the populace.⁵ In parts of Hungary, 'Slovak rustics . . . lived in caves in dire degradation. The Ruthenian [Ukrainian] peasantry existed on even lower and more sordid

¹ May, 65, 246, 452. Conrad, V. 890. L. de Rothschild's obituary, *The Times*, 17 Jan. 1955.
² Presentable at Court.
³ May, 161, 396, 508. Jonescu, 167. The connection between the Austro-Hungarian aristocracy and international finance was symbolized by the marriage of Count Szechenyi to Miss Gladys Vanderbilt. Karolyi, 36.
⁴ May, 440.          ⁵ May, 506.

levels'.[1] In Bosnia-Herzegovina, the Christian tenant farmers were left at the mercy of the Turkish landlords and peasant proprietors, and 'the great bulk of the Bosniak land workers remained in chains'.[2] A rule of this kind was made possible only by dividing the victims and fomenting their animosities. The result was paralysis of local diets, financial chaos, rural risings and students' battles in Galicia, Irredentism in the Tyrol and Transylvania, Polish ferment, Czech and German struggles, bloodshed in Slovakia, Slovene-Italian, Italian-German and German-Slovene clashes, a smouldering revolt in Croatia and, in 1910, a peasant rebellion in Bosnia-Herzegovina. The Sokol and kindred organizations had freedom written on their flags. The growing Yugoslav[3] cohesion was loaded with dynamite.

The disintegration of the Dual Monarchy appeared all the more certain since the breakaway elements inside had friends beyond the borders. Blind to the calendar and clock (as are those systems whom history has condemned to death), Austria-Hungary had centred her diplomacy in the Balkans on conserving Turkey[4] as a bulwark against Russia, the Yugoslavs and Italy. The Balkan Wars of 1912-13, which shattered that tradition, raised up a Serbia greatly enlarged in size, power and self-confidence. On the eve of that contest, a Yugoslav had written that, if it 'succeeds, the [Dual] Monarchy will cease to be a Great Power'.[5] On the morrow of victory, the Serbian Prime Minister Pashich declared: 'The first round is won; now we must prepare for the second—against Austria'.[6] Serbia's march into Albania, attempted fusion with Montenegro, and Alliance with Greece and Rumania were distasteful to the Ballplatz.[7] Moreover, 'behind Serbia stood Russia', whom Panslav agitation and Tsarism's 'far-reaching plans of conquest at our expense',[8] it was claimed, had made 'the principal adversary' of Austria-Hungary.[9] The tension was increased by the fact that the Serbian Kingdom was rapidly becoming 'the Piedmont of the Yugoslavs'.[10]

Roused by the wine of national liberation, the Serbs of all classes extended their hand to the shackled brethren next door. Doubtless they worked—as was their historic task—for a common State. Doubtless their organizations included terrorist groups without respect for frontiers. But even if the dominant groups and parties

[1] May, 234.      [2] May, 408; also 406–9.
[3] The term Yugoslav stands throughout for South-Slav.
[4] Hoyos, 36.      [5] Steed, 282.      [6] May, 466.
[7] See Conrad, III. 574, 631, 661. Hoyos, 39, 46. May, 469. The 'Ballplatz' was the current designation of the Austro-Hungarian Foreign Ministry.
[8] Hoyos, 76, 83. Also Macchio, 7.
[9] Conrad to Francis Joseph, Jan. '14. Conrad, III. 776; also 661.
[10] Hoyos, 73; also 34.

had not made a 'Greater Serbia' the pivot of policy,[1] the young Kingdom could not fail to become a magnet and a beacon to the seven million Croats, Slovenes and Serbs under the Habsburgs. The reshaping—despite Vienna's vetoes—of the Balkans and, notably, the rise of Serbia killed the last vestige of the Empire's prestige among its reluctant subjects. Their rulers, meanwhile, were misled by fear and resentment to intensify the ill-treatment of the Slav provinces. The middle class, slowly developing here with its businesses and banks, found that 'economic suffocation . . . [was] added to . . . political oppression'.[2] It was tempting to compare its lot to the advances made by the kinsmen who were free. It was natural for the Bosnian tenant farmer, forced as he was to surrender to the Government one tenth of his crop, and to the landlord a third of the remainder, to reflect that in Serbia the land was owned by the peasants.[3]

In the summer of 1913, a high Ballplatz official reported, after a stay in Croatia, such an ascendancy among the local intelligentsia of 'the idea of Yugoslavia under Serbian leadership' that it was 'frightening to an Austro-Hungarian patriot'.[4] Unwilling to see that the gathering revolt was a product of their own régime, the 'patriots' pressed for counter-measures.[5] The lesson of Piedmont, the loss of Lombardy and Venetia was wasted on a set of rulers bent on maintaining a racial and social supremacy from which they drew privileges and profit. 'Trialism'[6] was rejected by the Magyars who would not accept a new partner likely to weaken their influence in the Dual State. They would no more allow the Croats to block the road to the Adriatic than the Austrians would grant this freedom to the Slovenes and Dalmatians. Both 'master' races were loth to establish a precedent for the Czechs and others. Above all, the oligarchs of Vienna and Budapest were not going to free 'their' peasants, give scope to a competitive bourgeoisie, and loosen their hold on lands containing their great estates,[7] huge economic resources and strategic possibilities. Concessions, it was contended, could only end in chaos, so long as nothing was done against 'the insidious agitation' from Belgrade.[8]

The general view was expressed by Macchio's later assertion

[1] Hoyos, 44–5. Conrad, III. 574, 617, 661.
[2] Steed, 287; also 283, 285. Musulin, 204. Hoyos, 74. The Hungarian Government dismissed all the plans for railways to connect the Croatian and Dalmatian ports with their natural hinterland. The railways were built so as to serve the Magyar Kingdom. May, 87.
[3] May, 407–8. Hoyos, 74.   [4] Musulin, 208; also 203–4.
[5] See Musulin, 208–9.
[6] The creation of a Triple Empire of Austria, Hungary and Yugoslavia.
[7] A relative of the Tiszas, for example, owned enormous estates in Bosnia.
[8] Hoyos, 76. See also Conrad, IV. 46.

that 'the mole-like activity of the Serbian Irredenta—the almost undisguised furtherance of which by official Serbia was known to us—had reached a degree in 1914 which would have made it the duty of any Government to intervene . . . unless it was prepared to leave the integrity of the Empire altogether in jeopardy'.[1] Hoyos, Berchtold's *Chef du Cabinet*, has written that the outcome of the Balkan Wars had produced 'untenable conditions on our South-Eastern frontier'.[2] The Minister in Belgrade, Giesl, dwelt on the 'well-known axiom that Serbia's policy is based on the severance of the Yugoslav territories and, subsequently, the destruction of the [Dual] Monarchy as a Great Power'.[3] According to Conrad, the Serbian Kingdom was 'the never resting mortal enemy of Austria-Hungary' and—he urged upon Francis Joseph—'can only be treated as such'.[4] The Ballplatz, especially its press office (misnamed 'literary bureau'), spread fumes of hate conditioning the public for what Hoyos called a 'surgical intervention against the cause of the disease'.[5] The flight from reform led to ascribing all the trouble to outside irritants. It transformed a predominantly domestic problem into an external crisis. The misconduct of internal policy made for aggressive war.

This was not, however, the only reason. The War with Serbia had been in the offing since 1903, when her new dynasty ended Belgrade's vassalage to the Habsburgs. In 1904, the Austrians frustrated her plans for a customs union with Bulgaria. In 1906, they struck at the neighbour's principal staples—corn, prunes and swine, which were dependent on the markets and railways in the North.[6] The 'pig policy' was dictated partly by the objection of the agrarians in the Dual Monarchy to the competition of the cheaper Serbian products, partly by the desire to coerce her into buying armaments from Skoda rather than at Creusot's, and mainly by the intention to enforce, through commercial pressure, her return to the Habsburg fold. The annexation of Bosnia-Herzegovina in 1908 was another blow from the same adversary. The Treaty of 1911 enabled Austria to re-invade the Kingdom with her manufactures, yet to maintain the tabu on the unwelcome hogs. To escape this economic stranglehold, the purpose of which was to cripple Belgrade politically, Pashich strove for an Adriatic outlet. After the first

---

[1] Macchio, 8–9. Also Hoyos, 74. Conrad, IV. 91.   [2] Hoyos, 73.
[3] Giesl to Berchtold, 21 July '14. Conrad, IV. 102–3.
[4] Conrad to Francis Joseph, Jan. '14. Conrad, III. 753; also 631. This was also Tisza's view. See May, 439.
[5] Hoyos, 75. Also Dumaine, 77.
[6] Trade discrimination reduced Serbia's exports to Austria-Hungary from 90 per cent of her total to 15 per cent, and her imports from 70 per cent to 36 per cent of all her purchases abroad, May, 402, 508.

Balkan War he sought Berchtold's consent to Serbian sovereignty over an Albanian port with a connecting railway corridor, in return for military guarantees and mercantile advantages. But, although his compatriots had cleared parts of Albania of the Turks, he had to look on while Berchtold (and San Giuliano) fashioned the 'independent' realm of Wied. After Serbia's triumph in the second Balkan War, the Habsburg Empire was only just stopped by Germany and Italy from hurling itself at the 'mortal enemy'.[1] The Chief of Staff, however, continued to press for 'the seizure of Serbia and Montenegro'.[2] The 'decisive problem of the [Dual] Monarchy is in the Balkans and, above all, in the solution of the Yugoslav (or more precisely, the Serbian) question'.[3] And Berchtold 'had no longer any doubts that our settlement of accounts with Serbia must come'.[4]

3

SARAYEVO AND WAR WITH SERBIA

In the circumstances, Sarayevo was a godsend, or rather a gift from Mars. It 'has . . . created for us a fortunate moral position', Giesl, the Minister in Belgrade, impressed upon Berchtold.[5] This was a 'shining' moment for starting the War.[6] The assassination of the unloved Crown Prince and his morganatic consort left the Austro-Hungarian peoples cold. No one in Vienna, especially among those who mattered, shed a tear for them.[7] It would have remained an operetta turned melodrama, had not those in control been bent on tragedy. A high-ranking Ballplatz investigator wired from the scene of the outrage that there was 'no proof of the complicity of the Serbian Government in . . . the attempt or its preparation. . . .'[8] No one in Vienna was able to lay the blame directly at the neighbour's door. Hoyos admitted subsequently that he had 'never believed that the murder . . . had been prepared or even

---

[1] Szilassy, 217. Dumaine, 45. May, 461–5.
[2] Conrad's Memorandum to the Emperor, 16 Jan. '14. Conrad, III. 755.
[3] Conrad to Berchtold, 22 June '14. Conrad, III. 694; also 661.
[4] See Berchtold to Macchio, Jan. '15. Macchio, 80. For the same opinion see also Czernin to Berchtold, 11 March '14. Conrad, III. 782, and Tisza's conversation with Szilassy late in 1913. Szilassy, 259.
[5] Giesl to Berchtold, 21 July '14. Conrad, IV. 105.
[6] Giesl's interview with Conrad, 8 July '14. Conrad, IV. 57.
[7] Dumaine, 135. Redlich, I. 235.
[8] Wiesner to Berchtold, 13 July '14. Conrad, IV. 81. See also Bülow, III. 136. Lewin, 228: '. . . the removal of the Archduke was far more a German, a Magyar, even a [Habsburg] Court interest than it was in the interests of Serbia'. Also Redlich, I. 235, 237. Lewin, 229–30, quotes W. Steed's articles in the *Edinburgh Review*, Oct. '15, and *Nineteenth Century*, Feb. '16, to show the Austrian authorship of the crime. General Potiorek's accusations against Serbia (Conrad, IV. 83) are so absurd that they defeat their own purpose.

# AUSTRIA-HUNGARY 255

desired by the authorities in Belgrade'.[1] But it was convenient to distinguish between legal and political responsibility.[2] The press clamoured for vengeance and coercion.[3] For Berchtold the crime was 'the culmination in the process of dissolution' at work in the subject provinces.[4] Conrad argued that the Bosnian pistol shots had been directed not at an individual but at the heart of the Danubian Empire. This was, he insisted later, 'Serbia's declaration of war on Austria-Hungary. The only possible reply was war'.[5]

The word actually used was 'punitive expedition'. It was ostensibly to put down the foreign 'trouble-makers', and sober the hot-heads at home. The world was assured that no conquest was intended.[6] Indeed, neither the Austrian nor the Magyar rulers had, as Czernin put it, 'an appetite for more Serbs in the [Dual] Monarchy'. But the question could not be treated 'solely from the viewpoint of consumption . . . no one allows his appendix to be cut out for gastronomic considerations'.[7] Tisza's idea was that 'Serbia would have to be diminished by ceding to Bulgaria, Greece and Albania the districts she had conquered [in 1912-13], while we should demand for ourselves at most certain strategically important frontier readjustments. To be sure, we should have claims for a restitution of the war costs, which would give us the means of retaining Serbia for a long time firmly in our hands'.[8] The Austrian Premier Stürgkh added that, even if territory was not taken, 'it will still be possible to bring Serbia to a state of dependence . . . by deposing the dynasty, a military convention and other appropriate measures'.[9] Berchtold foresaw 'the possibility that, at the end of the War . . . it will no longer be practicable for us not to annex anything'.[9] Conrad demanded 'Belgrade and Shabats with adjacent districts'.[10] In the first days of the War, Finance—in the person of the Chairman of the Bodenkreditanstalt—called on the Chief of Staff, 'and gave his views on what . . . ought to be done in the economic respect' with

---

[1] Hoyos, 77. Also Dumaine, 139. Musulin, 220.     [2] Musulin, 220.
[3] Pribram, *Austria-Hungary and Great Britain*, 218-19, 221. The Serbs were charged with having, in addition to the official Cabinet, a military shadow government. Both centres of authority patronized, it was alleged, the 'Narodna Obrana' which was implicated, and Serb officers on active service, having fomented subversive propaganda in Bosnia, were said to have been partners to the crime. See Conrad, IV. 82-3. Musulin, 219. Dumaine, 139.
[4] Hoyos, 78. The quotation is from Hoyos.
[5] Conrad, IV. 18, 39. Also Francis Joseph to William II, 2 July '14. Dumaine, 139.
[6] Hoyos, 82; also 78. Conrad, IV. 31-2, 60, 91, 310. Musulin, 219.
[7] Czernin to Berchtold, 11 March '14. Conrad, III. 782.
[8] Tisza to Francis Joseph, 8 July '14. Conrad, IV. 60. The same view concerning the diminution of Serbia was expressed by Czernin to Berchtold in the Ministerial Council, 19 July '14. Conrad, IV. 90.
[9] Ministerial Council, 19 July '14. Minutes. Conrad, IV. 90-1.
[10] Conference with the Emperor and Berchtold, 30 July '14. Conrad, IV. 150.

Serbia.¹ Less than a fortnight later, 'in the dining car of the special train' at the disposal of the Supreme Command, the new Heir to the Throne and Conrad 'discussed Serbia. I described the country as beautiful and productive; capable of high development under Austria-Hungary, hence a desirable acquisition'.²

4

HABSBURG IMPERIALISM IN THE BALKANS

Nor was it a matter of 'acquiring' merely a limited space. The little Kingdom was one of the main lines of approach to the Near East whither Habsburg imperialism was pushing its ramifications. The growth of Austria's big industry, railway enterprise and banking in the late 'sixties and early 'seventies had been so rapid and the resulting slump of 1873 so catastrophic, that business looked for salvation to accelerated monopolization.³ The cartels sought (and found at the end of the decade) recovery from the crisis by turning up the virgin soil of Balkan trade. Concessions were snatched from the Porte for railroad building in European Turkey. The great artery connecting Vienna and Budapest with the Ottoman capital and the Aegean ports, which was completed in 1888, was designed to combine commerce with strategy. Money was heavily invested in Turkey proper. In 1913-14, Berchtold exerted himself to obtain from the Sultan a port and a sphere of influence in South Anatolia. Shortly before Sarayevo, the Vienna Bodenkreditanstalt and the Ungarische Bank- und Handelsgesellschaft formed, with the German Discontogesellschaft, a banking association to take over the construction of the Gemlik-Brusa-Simav railway.⁴ When Conrad subsequently wrote that Austria-Hungary, 'more than any other State, would have been destined by her geographical position to have a momentous say in the Orient', he was but echoing Crown Prince Rudolph's early pledge to his wife in Constantinople: 'You will be Empress here!'⁵

At the end of the 19th century, the Dual Monarchy was reported as coveting a portion of the Chinese coast. Two firms, some missionaries, a small amount of commerce and shipping betokened Austria's 'interests' in China, and the black and yellow flag mingled with those of the international army which broke the Boxer rising.⁶ But funds to sustain overseas expansion were lacking. The Magyar agrarians, well-nigh indifferent to business outside Europe, opposed an increase of naval forces. Instead, both ruling sections of Austria-Hungary preferred to rely on their big land armies, the advantages

¹ 5 Aug. '14. Conrad, IV. 332, 954.　　² 16 Aug. '14. Conrad, IV. 406–7.
³ May, 65–7, 223, 335. Steed, 142–3.
⁴ May, 87, 102, 113, 222, 234, 419. Conrad, III. 569–70, 655, 660.
⁵ Conrad, III, 571. Steed, 212.　　⁶ May, 405.

of proximity and the untapped resources around them, for colonialism nearer home. Schemes were pursued, with the active support of the Uniate Church,¹ for a puppet 'Greater Ukraine' to consist of East Galicia, a portion of Bukovina, and the Ukrainian parts of Russia, after the latter had, with German help, been dismembered.² This blended with eager 'Austro-Polish' dreams. As early as August 6th 1914, the Finance Minister Bilinski spoke to Conrad of the desire to include Congress-Poland in the Dual Monarchy.³ On the 12th, at the Foreign Ministry, 'the question was raised how Poland's boundaries were to be defined, whether the Ukraine should be . . . extended to the East'.⁴ On the 16th, the Heir to the Throne asked Conrad 'which Russian districts . . . could be considered for us . . . and what would be done with Poland. I replied that Poland was a very rich country capable of [high] cultural development'.⁵

Nothing, however, could compare with the concentration on the Balkans. Ever since the Railway Conventions, the Alliance and the Trade Pact signed with Belgrade between 1880 and 1883 gave the Habsburgs predominance in the Western part of the Peninsula; ever since the Commercial Agreements of 1875 and 1883 opened Rumania to Austrian exports and scrambles for railroad and Danube traffic, the Balkans had been treated as 'our very own market',⁶ especially for the cheaper Viennese, Bohemian and other wares. Austro-Hungarian interests had in Albania first place in the import and export business and a strong banking position. The Austrian Lloyd and the Fiume Obotti Co. carried most of Albania's seaborne trade. The Austrian Lloyd had steamships plying on the Boyana, and another group held, until 1913, the petrol monopoly in Montenegro.⁷ The onset of Serb resistance and Italian competition only intensified the southward drive. As early as 1897, Count Julius Andrassy rejected 'a situation in which we should be entirely on an equality with our Southern neighbours . . . Hungary is the natural guardian . . . of these Southern States'. By 1907, it was openly admitted that this policy combined home-political and downright imperialist motives.⁸ Indeed, the annexation of Bosnia-Herzegovina in 1908 was an act of manifest colonialism. The 4,300 miles of new,

---

¹ Roman Catholic in doctrine, Orthodox in rite.
² Steed, 290–1, 293. Barán, 130.   ³ Conrad, IV. 184.
⁴ Conrad, IV. 206. Also Redlich, I. 246.
⁵ Conrad, IV. 407. See also Steed, 293–4.
⁶ Szilassy, 120. Also Hoyos, 34. Macchio, 7 May. 200, 272–3, 281, 283, 306, 348, 401, 508. The Railway Conventions provided for a line across Serbia and Bulgaria to link up with the line to Constantinople.
⁷ *Albania*. Foreign Office Handbooks, No. 17, pp. 79, 91–2. *Montenegro*. Foreign Office Handbooks, No. 19, pp. 41, 72.
⁸ L. von Chlumecky, *Österreich-Ungarn und Italien*, mentioned by Lewin, 226. For the quotation from Andrassy's book see Lewin, 222.

mainly strategic, roads and railways, the heavy garrisons, the foreign bureaucracy, the industrial imports (ruinous to the local crafts) emphasized the character of the province as an Austro-Hungarian Egypt.[1] In the same year, the Foreign Minister announced that, under a concession obtained from the Turks, a railway was to be built across Novibazar, and that it would 'constitute a new and important route from Central Europe to Egypt and India'.[2] Although the scheme was dropped under Russian and Italian pressure, it revealed Vienna's designs in the Lower Balkans and the intention to approach the Aegean.[3]

For the Empire's economy was rapidly expanding. In 1912, Austria's high-tariff-protected factory output 'was reported about 50 per cent ahead of that a decade earlier'.[4] By 1913, the tonnage in Trieste 'had doubled over 1900. ... Shipbuilding ... and shipping companies expanded their operations; the Austrian Lloyd ... handled traffic to Adriatic ports and to the Near East and Asia. Smaller companies carried on business with the Latin countries and the Americas ... and an Austro-American Company was organized to share in the profitable emigrant traffic'.[5] Already Trieste competed with Hamburg and Genoa. Fiume, too, raised its turnover of goods by half between 1900 and 1912.[6] The statistical spiral demonstrated, at the same time, the perils of potential imprisonment in the Adriatic. The mounting challenge of Italy in that very sea (and Tsarist ambitions for Constantinople) sharpened the craving of Austro-Hungarian imperialism for unimpeded outlets. The most obvious of these was Salonika. The latter, as early as 1907, was proclaimed by a spokesman of Francis Ferdinand to be 'the most advanced gateway in the South East for the commerce of Southern Austria and Hungary. Salonika is our hope for the future'.[7] Despite all self-exculpatory denials, this notion was so strong that even in the Dardanelles crisis, when Greece was wavering in the balance, the Ballhaus was instinctively unwilling to give her stronger assurances than that 'Austria-Hungary pursues no selfish aims' in that port.[8]

But the road to Salonika, as Berchtold said, went via Serbia. The Habsburg General staff urged that the best line of advance to that port was along the Morava valley right through the heart of the Kingdom.[9] The march was only possible if the Yugoslavs sub-

---

[1] May, 404–6, 410. Steed, 211–12.      [2] Steed, 235.
[3] Steed, 235–6. May, 403, 412. Lewin, 213–14.
[4] May, 336.      [5] May, 335.      [6] May, 335, 371.
[7] *Österreich-Ungarn und Italien* (p. 63) by L. von Chlumecky, quoted by Lewin, 226. Also Steed, 207, 275. May, 298. Yerusalimski, 251. Jonescu, 26. Marcovich, *Serbia and Europe*, 161. Salandra, 42.
[8] Szilassy, 273. For the denials see, for example, Hoyos, 35, 42.
[9] May, 466. Steed, 236.

AUSTRIA-HUNGARY 259

mitted, and as they resisted, they were condemned to subjugation.

The War with the Serbs, therefore, did not—as was asserted—'arise, above all, from considerations of internal policy',[1] or from the need 'to put a thorough stop to the Greater-Serbian agitation'.[2] It was not (despite Panslavism and Russian support for Belgrade) essentially 'the struggle for the existence of the [Dual] Monarchy'.[3] The plaintive story of a venerable Empire disturbed in its 'peaceful evolution'[4] and 'conservative . . . foreign policy[5] and forced into self-defence against the 'danger threatening from "below"',[6] is shown up in the light of fact as a fabrication. The vast armaments, the preparatory mobilizations of men and money lend more reality to Hoyos's boast that 'in 1914 . . . there was as yet no anaemia in our system'.[7]

The War with the Serbs, in the main, was a bid to fill the 'vacuum' left after the collapse of European Turkey, lest the resurgent peoples should take their rightful place. It was the application of Conrad's reiterated motto 'that the future of the [Dual] Monarchy lies in the Balkans'.[8] It was a major step of imperialist aggression designed to establish Austro-Hungarian hegemony in South-Eastern Europe.[9]

---

[1] Hoyos, 78. Also Musulin, 219. Conrad, IV. 48–9.
[2] Potiorek to Conrad, 16 July '14. Conrad, IV. 92.
[3] Musulin 252; also 228. Giesl to Berchtold, 21 July '14. Conrad, IV. 105, 31. Hoyos, 36, 87. Pribram, *Austria-Hungary and Great Britain*, 259.
[4] Macchio, 7.     [5] Hoyos, 73.
[6] Musulin, 233, 234. Conrad, IV. 9, 31–2.
[7] Hoyos, 86–7. For the war preparations see Jonescu, 24–5. Conrad, III. 618, 711.
[8] Conrad's Memorandum to the Emperor, Jan. 1914. Conrad, III. 755. Also the article by C. Stere in *Viata Romaneasca*, 1913, approvingly quoted by Conrad, III. 710–11.
[9] See T. N. Page, 155. Szilassy, 215.

CHAPTER XIX

## Tension Between Austria-Hungary and Germany

1

*MITTELEUROPA,* THE ADRIATIC AND THE ROAD TO BAGHDAD

BUT when the Habsburgs pounced on the victim, they found themselves trapped by the chronic differences dividing them from their principal Ally. It was not only that Berlin had long deprecated each independent move by Vienna, while the latter had made several attempts[1] to steer a freer course; nor yet that they had diverged after the Second Balkan War, and had fought several tariff duels; or that the Deutsche Bank and the German General Staff foiled Berchtold's endeavours in 1913-14 to obtain from Turkey a sphere of influence with port and railway concessions in Southern Anatolia.[2] Such differences, one might say, occurred by tradition in the best international families. What was extraordinary, in this case, was the indecent frankness with which the younger prepared for the demise of the older relative.

Since Bismarck's departure, everyone in the Reich viewed the disintegrating Empire as a prospective 'corpse'. Every scheme of the Junker and bourgeois Pan-German League—such as the Customs Union with Austria-Hungary, *Mitteleuropa,* or 'Greater Germany' —implied the economic and, subsequently, political absorption of Austria, and the domination of her subject lands.[3] Pan-German spokesmen dismissed Hungary as 'a bundle of impossibilities', and declared that 'the Germanization of Austria, quite apart from the question of the political use of Austria as a German colony, is, from the standpoint of the Foreign Ministry, "a vital question"'.[4] A Munich pamphlet announced that the Herrenvolk had 'lent ten millions of their countrymen to Austria' as an 'investment . . . in the Austrian joint-stock company' to cement her amalgamation with

---

[1] At Algericas, 1906, and during the Bosnian and Morocco crises, 1908, 1911.
[2] Conrad, III. 569–71, Szilassy, 253, 255–7. Hoyos, 26–8, 33, 36, 59. Steed, 261, 265–6. Yerusalimski, 179. May, 255, 295, 387–8, 454–5, 466–7, 472–3, 510.
[3] May, 331. Yerusalimski, 288–90, 559. Lewin, 225. May, 505, quotes a Pan-German pamphlet published at the turn of the century in Munich, stating that the Habsburg crown should be transferred to the Hohenzollerns, Austria Germanized and the Czech area converted into a kind of huge concentration camp.
[4] Prof. P. de Lagarde, *Deutsche Schriften,* 1903, pp. 112, 391, quoted by Lewin, 199–200.

the Reich.¹ R. Tannenberg's much-read book *Grossdeutschland* envisaged the division of the Habsburg Empire among Prussia, Bavaria, Saxony and Baden, while 'every insult offered to a German student at Prague, every popular riot at Laibach [Lyublyana], is an affront to German honour and a sufficient . . . reason for us to occupy the territories in question'.²

Nor were these individual hallucinations. For German imperialism, the Dual Monarchy was the land-bridge to the Balkans, the Near and Middle East. Vienna and Budapest were the key points of the railway to Constantinople and Baghdad. As this route involved long and costly transport through restless countries, Trieste was earmarked, as early as 1895, for 'the commercial door opening on the Orient and the Suez Canal. Trieste should, therefore, become a German port'.³ This was related to the idea that 'the Austrian littoral, with the Southern portion of Dalmatia, Ragusa, Cattaro, Trieste and Pola, should constitute, as Alsace-Lorraine, a Reichsland . . . which would serve as a base for the maritime power of Germany in the Adriatic and Mediterranean'.⁴ The Crown Prince Francis Ferdinand was anathema to the Hohenzollerns because 'Trialism', by means of which he sought to prevent the dissolution of his future legacy, 'might have succeeded [it has been suggested] in checking the inordinate ambitions of German statesmen. . . .' His elimination, therefore, was far more a German than it was a Serbian interest. 'Whatever may be the inner history of the Sarayevo affair . . . the Archduke's death directly removed the most formidable obstacle to the realization of German plans'.⁵ At any rate, it cast a sinister light on an early Pan-German propaganda postcard on which the Habsburg crest was mauled by the Prussian eagle.⁶

2

FINANCIAL, ECONOMIC AND
POLITICAL DEPENDENCE ON GERMANY

That, nevertheless, the two Allies kept, and after Sarayevo fought, together was due, in the first place, to the fact that the Reich pro-

---

¹ Dr. v. Winterstetten, Munich, 1913. See Lewin, 219.
² Richard Tannenberg, *Grossdeutschland*, 1911. Lewin, 216–18.
³ Dr. E. Hasse, Reichstag's Deputy and Director of Statistics at Leipzig, one of the principal Pan-German leaders, quoted by Lewin, 250; also 198.
⁴ From *Österreichs Zusammenbruch und Wiederaufbau* by a Pan-German author. Munich, 1899. The same fate was also envisaged for Slovenia—the direct avenue to Trieste. Lewin, 250, 255; also 202, 217. Yerusalimski, 158. Chéradame, *L'Europe et la question d'Autriche au seuil du XX-e siècle*, 101.
⁵ Lewin, 225, 228, 230.
⁶ Issued by the Evangelical Odin Society, Munich, at the end of the 19th century. May, 188.

vided the market for at least half the Dual Monarchy's exports, especially those of the powerful Magyar agrarians.[1] Still more crucial was Austria-Hungary's financial dependence on Germany. By 1890 already, the two billion French francs placed in Austro-Hungarian railways, banks, manufactures and Government securities were overwhelmed by the invasion of the mark. Since the Franco-Russian Entente of 1893 stopped the monetary flow from Paris, the Empire's needs were covered by German capital, especially in public bonds and banking and industrial enterprise. Thus the Deutsche Bank founded the German-Austrian Mannesmann Tube Works and also organized a group of German and Austrian banks in order to gain a footing in Austrian and Hungarian undertakings. The Dresdner Bank promoted German business in the Dual Monarchy by close co-operation with several Viennese banks, and played an important role in forming the Central Bank for Railway Securities, which handled Austro-Hungarian railway securities. The Discontogesellschaft and the Darmstädter Bank, both members of the Rothschild Syndicate, took part in a great many Austro-Hungarian State, railway and other financial transactions. The Discontogesellschaft, moreover, acquired an interest in the blast furnaces at the Iron Gate in Hungary, while the Darmstädter Bank set up the Ungarische Escompte-und Wechslerbank in Budapest and was closely allied to the Wechselstuben A/G 'Merkur' in Vienna. Led by the four giant D-banks, the German investments in the Danubian Empire, by 1914, were at least 50 per cent greater than those from France.[2] This could not but stimulate the growth of the Austro-German *Anschluss* faction which would have resisted any attempts by the governing Catholic party, which stood for Habsburg independence, to effect a divorce from Berlin. The achievement of independence, moreover, was conditional on Austria's increasing her strength through imperialist expansion, and this demanded co-operation with the Reich. Hence, Vienna's involvements in the Balkans and the resulting tensions with Russia enabled the Wilhelmstrasse to take virtual control of Austria-Hungary's foreign policy.[3]

By January 1914, the ties had grown strong enough for Conrad to tell the Emperor that 'Germany must always be retained as an Ally . . . a defeated Germany would spell the ruin of the [Dual] Monarchy'.[4] After Sarayevo, every eye in the Ballplatz was turned to the North. If Hoyos can be believed, 'Berchtold . . . would have been prepared to set aside all those . . . reasons which made for the

[1] May, 255.
[2] May, 221–2. Riesser, 439, 445, 449, 476, 483, 494–5, 501–4, 506.
[3] See Steed, 293–4.
[4] Conrad's Memorandum to Francis Joseph, Jan. '14. Conrad, III. 759.

War... if such a policy had been recommended to him upon inquiry in Berlin'.¹ But the Kaiser and the Chancellor not only 'assured us with all emphasis of Germany's unqualified support'.² Hoyos, who had been sent to them for special soundings, recorded his own and the Ambassador Szögyény's 'impression that the German Government was biased in favour of our taking immediate action against Serbia, although it clearly recognized the danger that a world war could arise therefrom'.³ This, the Prime Minister Stürgkh ruled, 'ought to have a very great effect on our decision'.⁴ According to the French Envoy, the Austro-Hungarian Cabinet was under heavy pressure from the Ambassador Tschirsky.⁵ Yet there is no sign whatsoever of reluctance to be prodded. Although it suited the Ballplatz to shift most of the war-guilt on to its Allies, Berchtold actually defined their attitude as 'very gratifying'.⁶ Their help was appraised as a factor of prime importance in the design for conquests in Russia and the Balkans. And 'if the War ends in victory, then [Conrad thought at the height of the struggle] Austria-Hungary will be so much strengthened that she will be able to face Germany as an equal.'⁷

The Reich, on the contrary, used the Ally as a mere tool in its *Drang* for domination. When the Dual Monarchy, despite urgent exhortations, delayed taking up arms against France and Britain,⁸ the *Bund* of Berne and the *Nouvelles de Basle*—said to be susceptible to German inspiration—produced those reports of Austrian troop movements to Alsace, which enabled Grey and Doumergue to bring about the rupture Vienna had wished to postpone.⁹ The victory at Namur was so monopolized by the Germans to the detriment of Austria-Hungary's anonymously participating batteries, that—in order to assert herself—she sent Belgium (with whom she had no real quarrel) a declaration of war.¹⁰ Shortly before, William II had forced her to join in the hostilities against Japan, despite Conrad's anxious protest that, 'in consequence, [Russia's] East-Asian, and even Japanese, troops could be drawn to Europe'.¹¹ Conversely,

¹ Hoyos, 79.
² Berchtold at the Ministerial Council, 7 July '14. Minutes. Conrad, IV. 43–4.
³ Hoyos, 80. Conrad, too, states that Germany advised them 'to strike'. Conrad, IV. 42.
⁴ Ministerial Council, 7 July '14. Minutes. Conrad, IV. 47. The Emperor was of the same opinion. See Berchtold's statement to Conrad, 10 July '14. Conrad, IV. 70.
⁵ Dumaine, 133.
⁶ Ministerial Council, 7 July '14. Minutes. Conrad, IV. 43.
⁷ 8 Oct. '14. Conrad, V. 79. ⁸ See pp. 202, 210–11 above.
⁹ 6, 7 ff. Aug. '14. Dumaine, 153; also 156, quoting *Le Temps*, 23 Feb. '15. Conrad, IV. 178–9, 181–2, 189–90. Pribram, *Austria-Hungary and Great Britain*, 258.
¹⁰ 27 Aug. '14. Conrad, IV. 554–5.
¹¹ Conrad to Berchtold, 26 Aug. '14. Conrad, IV. 538–9.

although the Austrian Chief of Staff considered it 'of the greatest importance for our military position vis-à-vis Serbia and Montenegro that Bulgaria should . . . intervene as soon as possible',¹ Berlin held back in Sofia, preferring Rumanian collaboration which was bound to be costly to the Dual Monarchy.

3

DIFFERENCES OVER STRATEGY

The differences among the two Allies were still more pronounced in strategy. Under their joint plan of operations, Germany deployed almost her entire might in the West, where—Moltke, the German Chief of Staff, had assured Conrad—'we hope to have finished with France in six weeks . . . or at least sufficiently to be in a position to shift our main forces against the East'.² Pending the day of common reckoning with the Tsar, Austria-Hungary undertook to mount a large offensive against Russia which she expected to be synchronized with, and supported by, a German push into Poland.³ When the War was unleashed, Moltke had 'the fullest confidence, everything splendid, in Germany the mood as not even in 1870'.⁴ Conrad was requested to be guided 'in everything' by 'the one aim . . . of putting down Russia . . . . Serbia [Austria-Hungary's particular enemy] will have to be held off with slender forces'.⁵ This only amplified the Kaiser's dictum that 'Austria should employ her main forces against Russia . . . . in the gigantic struggle . . . Serbia plays a completely secondary part'.⁶ Vienna, agreeing that 'the decision in the North is the principal objective', nevertheless, found that 'the situation presses for the quickest possible successful blow in the Balkans'.⁷ But neither the 'violent fighting' and 'heavy losses',⁸ nor the official frenzy—'our own population hostile, towns and villages burnt down, inhabitants fired on'⁹—nor the hasty display of trophies: 'the so-called Serbian prisoners—peasants, women and children'¹⁰—could prevent this campaign from ending in total

---

¹ Conrad to Berchtold, 4 Aug. '14. Conrad, IV. 175.
² 12 May '14. Conrad, III. 673.
³ Towards Siedlce. Hindenburg, *Out of My Life*, 100. Conrad, III. 613. IV. 252. V. 977–8.
⁴ Moltke's telegram to Conrad, 2 Aug. '14. Conrad, IV. 317.
⁵ Moltke to Conrad, 2 Aug. '14. Conrad, IV. 319; also 5 Aug. Conrad, IV. 195.
⁶ William to Francis Joseph, 31 July '14. Conrad, IV. 156.
⁷ Conrad to Moltke, 10 Aug. '14. Conrad, IV. 195; also 324.
⁸ Report, 15 Aug. '14. Conrad, IV. 405; also 397–8, 406, 432, 470, 550, 553.
⁹ Résumé of operations by 16 Aug. '14. Conrad, IV. 408.
¹⁰ The Chief of the Emperor's Military Chancellery, Bolfras, to Conrad, 24 Aug. '14. Conrad, IV. 550.

failure. Considerable portions of the Army intended for the Russian front were seriously involved.¹

The Eastern theatre, meanwhile, produced grave inter-Allied strains. The extent of German support for the Dual Monarchy depended on Italian co-belligerency against France, which would have released German troops.² It was for military, as well as diplomatic, reasons that Berlin, in the spring and summer of 1914, had laboured to tighten the links with Rome.³ Since Vienna, despite German exhortations, made it easier for Italy to default, the Reich had to withhold the divisions which were to have gone East.⁴ If Austria-Hungary, none the less, struck in Galicia, it was partly for strategic and largely for political considerations. It was advisable not to leave all the laurels to the *Waffenbruder* and necessary to fulfil her part of the bargain, if he was to be kept to the arrangement of shifting his armies against Russia after what was expected to be a bigger and better Sedan. But what, in fact, came was the Marne.

Conrad at once, as he recollects, wished the Germans to recognize that, 'for the time being, nothing could be achieved in the West . . . the decision . . . must be sought in the East'.⁵ The Dual Monarchy 'had taken the offensive against Russia with inferior forces to tie down that enemy until victory was decided in France'. The defeat sustained there 'must not be made the occasion to drop the agreed plan, and to abandon . . . the Ally to his fate'. It required, on the contrary, that—confining the struggle with the French and British to temporary defence—the promised legions should be sent to Austria's aid. 'The German bill of exchange was now due'.⁶ However, 'I strove vainly . . . to drive this idea home to General Falkenhayn'.⁷ Moltke's successor 'was always of the opinion that France was the principal opponent, and that, therefore, she must be dealt the decisive blow'. Already the first crisis of the War produced a divergence of views between the two High Commands. The 'substantial' German forces expected by Austria-Hungary continued to pursue purely German aims in the West.⁸

The gulf was widened by 'a strong difference' over the Russian front.⁹ 'The German Army of the East', Conrad wrote to Berchtold, 'has undertaken an operation contrary to our agreements . . . render-

---

¹ Conrad, IV. 439, 441, 467.
² Conrad to Francis Joseph, 16 Jan. '14. Conrad, III, 759; also 613, 668.
³ Moltke to Conrad, 31 July '14, and the Austro-Hungarian Military Attaché in Berlin, 31 July, quoting Moltke's demand for concessions to Italy. Conrad, IV. 152; also III, 666, 671. IV. 35.
⁴ Conrad, IV. 295, 607. V. 979.     ⁵ Conrad, V. 310; also 79.
⁶ Conrad, IV. 907, 916–17, 786. V. 22.     ⁷ Conrad, V. 310.
⁸ Conrad, V. 208, 310. Also Andrassy, 196.
⁹ The Austro-Hungarian Liaison Officer at the German High Command to Conrad, 10 Sept. '14. Conrad, IV. 746–7.

ing our own position more difficult'.[1] That not even the few divisions available in Prussia fought by Austria's side was due to the Russian invasion of that province. The thud of Cossack horses trampling the soil of the Fatherland, the looming threat to Berlin, the dread of losing the spring-board to the Baltic lands halted the march into Poland before it could start.[2] Hindenburg, recalled from somnolent retirement because he knew the terrain, and Ludendorff, fresh from the fighting at Liège, directed 'the murderous combat'[3] of Tannenberg, which turned the tide. Two German armies, drawn from, and draining, those that were to brave the Marne, were switched to the Masurian Lakes.[4] This meant that even now, as Conrad grumbled, 'the Germans are winning their victories at our expense . . . . untroubled by our heavy struggle at Lublin they go on in East Prussia, probably to protect the studs of Trakehnen and the deer hunts in Rominten'.[5]

The Habsburgs argued that East Galicia, which they had abandoned to Russia, was 'at least as valuable to us as East Prussia to Germany'.[6] The Austro-Hungarian Commander-in-Chief appealed to the Kaiser to honour his pledge by ordering 'an energetic . . . offensive' in Poland.[7] But William's generals—wishing, above all, to clear East Prussia, and reasoning that, so long as the Russians stayed there, they could cut off a force moving South—refused.[8] It was not until their 'pet province'[9] was free that they conceded direct co-operation with the Ally. But even then it was not up to Conrad's expectations.[10]

Meanwhile, as the Germans were 'pocketing their triumphs', Conrad reported grimly that the Austro-Hungarians were 'bleeding to death at Lublin . . . great losses of our troops and . . . material'.[11] Vienna was crowded with 'swarms of wounded'.[12] Behind the lines,

---

[1] Conrad to Berchtold, 24 Aug. '14. Conrad, IV. 511; also 455.
[2] Conrad, IV. 390, 467, 522.   [3] Hindenburg, 94.
[4] Conrad, IV. 608, 625. Hindenburg, 99–100.
[5] Conrad to Bolfras, 5 Sept. '14. Conrad, IV. 647; also 658–9. V. 958. Rominten was William II's favourite haunt.
[6] Conrad to his Liaison Officer with the German Army of the East, 7 Sept. '14. Conrad, IV. 670.
[7] The Archduke Frederick to William II, 2 Sept. '14. Conrad, IV. 626. As early as 4 Aug. '14, and then again on the 14 and 15, Conrad had requested Moltke that he should leave the defence of East Prussia to reserve divisions and the *Landwehr*, and send the bulk of the German Army of the East into Poland in order to link up with the Austro-Hungarian armies. The German refusal to do so caused sharp irritation in Austria. Conrad, IV. 388, 390–4.
[8] Moltke to Frederick, 4 Sept. '14. Conrad, IV. 656; also 748. Hindenburg, 99–101.
[9] The Austro-Hungarian Liaison Officer with the German Army of the East to Conrad, 2 Sept. '14. Conrad, IV. 624. Also Talenski, 30–1.
[10] Conrad, IV. 563, 607, 783; also 751. Redlich, I. 270.
[11] Conrad to Bolfras, 5 Sept. '14. Conrad, IV. 647–8.
[12] Bolfras to Conrad, 5 Sept. '14. Conrad, IV. 671.

trains dripping blood carried loads of human wreckage unattended by doctors; the hospitals were so packed that operations had to be performed without anaesthetics.[1] At the front, the Chief of Staff met with 'convoys, transports of casualties, war prisoner columns, everything in thick dust . . . the roar of the battlefield'. A town he went through, 'was partly burnt down. The bodies of six of the inhabitants . . . were hanging from the trees. . . .'[2] Despite all the 'sanguinary sacrifices',[3] the Galician fighting ended in wholesale retreat. The reverse was blamed on Germany's refusal to play her part. Recriminations were coupled with the demand for 'at least three German corps'.[4] The Habsburg Ambassador in Berlin warned the Foreign Under-Secretary, as he wired to Berchtold, 'very seriously that the responsibility for a failure of the entire campaign falls on Germany who is leaving us . . . in the lurch. . . . If . . . they can or will not help us, then . . . we are exposed to being crushed by Russia, the immediate result of which must be the incursion of Russian troops into Prussian Silesia'.[5]

The recipients of these tidings had watched the events in Poland 'with great anxiety'[6] and certainly without admiration. Writing in retrospect, Hindenburg could still reprove his Allies for 'making a hazardous attack'.[7] Ludendorff—oblivious of the Marne—rubbed in that their Army 'was unfortunately . . . completely defeated'.[8] But the mere thought of a threat to 'fertile Silesia, with its highly developed coal mines and great industrial areas',[9] worked like magic. The Austro-Hungarian Ambassador recounted that, of all his arguments, 'only my reference to the devastation of Prussian Silesia by the Russians has made a visible impression on the Under-Secretary'.[10] Nor would it do to let the one and only Ally 'be annihilated'.[11] A new German force was established, with Hindenburg in command and Ludendorff as his Chief of Staff. Their orders were to give direct support to the Dual Monarchy, but to deploy in such a way 'that the fact that we were German reinforcements for Austria-Hungary . . . should be more obvious'.[12] Conrad, to shield Hungary and prevent too deep a withdrawal, desired these reinforcements to

[1] 4, 5 Sept. '14. Redlich, I. 266–8.  [2] Conrad, IV. 690.
[3] Conrad, IV. 709; also 704. Talenski, 32–3.
[4] Conrad to Berchtold, 8 Sept. '14. Conrad, IV. 681; also 608, 660, 670. Conrad to Moltke, 11 Sept. '14. Conrad, IV. 703; and 9 Sept. ibid. 689.
[5] Hohenlohe to Berchtold, 13 Sept. '14. Conrad, IV. 810–11.
[6] Hindenburg, 110.  [7] Hindenburg, 101.
[8] Ludendorff, *My War Memories*, I. 71.
[9] Hindenburg, 122. Also Talenski, 33.
[10] Hohenlohe to Berchtold, 13 Sept. '14. Conrad, IV. 811. See also Ludendorff, I. 71, on the need to protect Upper Silesia and Moravia.
[11] Ludendorff, I. 71.
[12] The German High Command to Hindenburg, 16 Sept. '14. Ludendorff, I. 74, Conrad, IV. 776, 751, Hindenburg, 111.

be joined to the Austro-Hungarian forces near Cracow. William's generals—anxious to retain their operational freedom, and bent mainly on protecting not only Silesia but also the approach to Berlin—assembled them, despite Conrad's protests, East of Breslau.[1] Conrad requested that the field-greys should be placed under the Habsburg High Command. The Kaiser's reply that Hindenburg would act 'in concord' with the Ally, but that 'the Supreme Command over . . . Hindenburg I have reserved for myself'[2] was a plain rebuff. The conflict, serious enough to send Ludendorff to Conrad, was solved 'in accordance with German requirements'.[3] For the Dual Monarchy had, after its costly fiasco against Russia, become wholly dependent on the Reich.[4]

The Austro-Hungarian defeat was followed by weeks of falling back along blocked or impassable roads, under enemy pressure, in ceaseless rain. Discipline crumbled. The magnitude of the losses (some regiments having melted to 1,400, 800 or even 400 men) compelled new comb-outs and a quicker recall of the lighter casualties.[5] Berchtold inquired how soon a Russian advance on Budapest and Vienna was to be expected.[6] From the capital, the Chief of the Emperor's Military Chancellery signalled that, 'apart from cartridges, we are also in need of a great deal of morale'.[7] After dysentery came cholera—another 'evil guest',[8] devouring thousands more victims. Troops, affected by the epidemic, were 'dragged from Galicia . . . by train . . . leaving hundreds of sick and dead on the route', to new duties at the front.[7] And this was the time when Tisza could write that 'one of the most elevating phenomena of this War . . . is that it brings hearts closer together and opens souls to mutual love and . . . trust'.[9]

'Trusting in Germany's help', as Ludendorff has crudely put it,[10] the Austro-Hungarian rulers hurled their subjects into fresh holocausts.[11] But the Germans, claiming to help the Austrians, used them for their own benefit. This, and the attempted self-assertion of the latter, could not but further the failure of their joint campaign. And when the disaster broke (at Warsaw-Ivangorod), their mutual

---

[1] Conrad, IV. 651, 751, 761–2, 775–7. Hindenburg, 111. Ludendorff, I. 74.
[2] The Archduke Frederick to William II, 15 Sept. '14. William II to Frederick, 17 Sept. Conrad, IV. 763, 785–6; also 759.
[3] 18 Sept. '14. Ludendorff, I. 78; also 74. Conrad, IV. 759.
[4] See Conrad, IV. 257. Talenski, 34.   [5] Conrad, IV. 487, 874.
[6] Berchtold to Conrad, 22 Sept. '14. Conrad, IV. 864.
[7] Bolfras to Conrad, 28 Sept. '14. Conrad, IV. 899; also 900. V. 37. Redlich, I. 272–3.
[8] Conrad, IV. 874; also V. 38, 256. Redlich, I. 273, 279.
[9] Letter, 27 Sept. '14. Tisza, I. 83.   [10] Ludendorff, I. 76.
[11] At the end of Sept. and early in Oct. '14. Ludendorff, I. 81. Conrad, IV. 905. Talenski, 34.

accusations rivalled in vehemence the roar of the cannon. Conrad denounced the Germans' 'competitive race to the Vistula and . . . Warsaw'.[1] And Hindenburg protested that the uncovering of his flank by a beaten Habsburg army had sealed the doom of the entire operation.[2]

Against this background, the continued pressure of Conrad's refrain that 'in the East . . . a rapid employment of strong German forces . . . would bring a favourable and lasting decision'[3] maddened the Hohenzollern like the proverbial red rag the bull. German imperialism, still in the stage of acute obsession with the need to knock out Britain and France, was just then pawing the ground of Ypres. Nothing was worse, therefore, than to hear that the Reich 'could calmly devote itself to the War in the West' after the victory in Russia.[4] Falkenhayn's reply to his Austro-Hungarian colleague was an 'urgent' summons to a discussion. 'Propose . . . meeting Berlin'. Conrad—aware that, within the rich man's gates, the beggar was at a double disadvantage—answered: 'Even my brief absence from here, alas, out of the question. Direct oral exchanges, therefore, possible only here'. Falkenhayn declined and repeated his invitation with greater emphasis. Conrad wired back his 'most cordial thanks', but sent his Aide instead.[5] That officer was told that 'the German victory must take precedence; in the East, meanwhile, there must be delay'. In these words, as Conrad ruminates bitterly, 'lay the unbridgeable difference of basic views between General Falkenhayn and myself . . . the cold admission that . . . the Ally, who had bled himself white . . . in the certain expectation of success in the West, would still be left to his fate'.[6]

### 4
### POLITICAL DIVERGENCIES

This war behind the War was aggravated by blackmail. The day when Conrad refused to go to Berlin, he raised the strength of the reinforcements solicited to 'at least 30 . . . divisions' and threatened that, unless these came 'at once', his armies might have to retire

---

[1] Conrad to Bolfras, 17 Oct. and 8 Nov. '14. Conrad, V. 178, 427.
[2] Conrad, V. 265–8, 249–50, 370, 542, 969. Hindenburg, 115, 117, 119, 120–22. Ludendorff, I. 88–93. Talenski, 34–5.
[3] Conrad to Supreme German Headquarters, 27 Oct. '14. Conrad, V. 300; also 301, 309. Ludendorff, I. 95.
[4] Conrad to the German Liaison Officer at the Habsburg High Command, 28 Oct. '14. Conrad, V. 309.
[5] Falkenhayn to Conrad, 28 Oct. '14. Conrad to Falkenhayn, 28 Oct. '14. Falkenhayn to Conrad, 29 Oct. '14. Conrad to Falkenhayn, 29 Oct. '14. Conrad, V. 312–13, 323–4.
[6] Conrad, V. 340–1.

to 'the Danube line Vienna-Budapest'.[1] The prospect of Austria-Hungary's withdrawal to self-defence, exposing the heart of the Reich to the Russian thrust, and certain (as Conrad could not forbear to point out) to have a disastrous effect on wavering neutrals,[2] loomed up at a moment which Ludendorff has admitted to have been 'highly critical. . . . We had now to expect . . . the probable invasion of Posen, Silesia and Moravia'. 'From the frontier provinces, the youths capable of bearing arms were removed. . . . The mines in several districts . . . had already been rendered unworkable. . . . Terror . . . spread through the province'.[3]

The preparations against the enemy, however, only made sense if something drastic was done to get the Ally under control. When the field at Warsaw was abandoned to the Russians, Francis Joseph was requested by William II 'to subordinate forthwith to General Hindenburg the Austrian 1st Army' which operated in close touch with the Germans.[4] Coming so soon after the Kaiser's blunt refusal to place Hindenburg under Austro-Hungarian orders, this was a stinging insult to Habsburg pride. Combined with his reluctance to relieve the Eastern front by reinforcements from the Rhine, it was a glaring proof 'that the interests of the Ally were given second place. . . . It was all the more imperative for him to hold together his own forces, and not to play into alien hands'.[5] Francis Joseph notified his fellow Sovereign that the 1st Army had been told to act 'in complete concord' with Hindenburg.[6] The very term wherewith the Hohenzollern had recently rebuffed Austro-Hungarian presumption was now thrown back to repudiate his demand.

But to think that German imperialism would accept the snub was to mistake its mood born of exasperation with defeat and the obstreperousness of the Ally.[7] On November 1st 1914, Hindenburg was appointed Commander-in-Chief of all the forces in the East, and Ludendorff his Chief of Staff. On the 4th, Conrad was informed that the Foreign Minister von Jagow had hinted to the Austro-Hungarian Ambassador in Berlin at the desirability of establishing a Supreme Command of the Central Powers on the Russian front. It was proposed to vest the highest authority in the Archduke Frederick, to give him Ludendorff as Chief of the new General Staff, and to put Conrad in charge of the Habsburg armies in the Eastern theatre.

[1] Conrad to Falkenhayn, 28 Oct. '14. Conrad, IV. 313–14.
[2] Conrad to Falkenhayn, 3 Nov. '14. Conrad, V. 373.
[3] Ludendorff, I. 93, 97–8.
[4] William II to Francis Joseph, 18 Oct. '14. Conrad, V. 180–1.
[5] Conrad, V. 182. The Archduke Frederick to Francis Joseph, 18 Oct. '14. Conrad, V. 181–2; also 209.
[6] Francis Joseph to William II, 19 Oct. '14. Conrad, V. 189.
[7] See Conrad, V. 382, 425.

But, as the intention was to attach to Ludendorff a German staff,[1] the honour paid to Vienna was clearly nominal and the aim, Conrad retorted, to place 'the operative direction entirely into ... Ludendorff's hands'.[2] It was a plain attempt to determine, through an agent 'of an alien, even though Allied Power', the very 'fate of the [Dual] Monarchy'.[3] For the loss of military independence would make it impotent to resist Berlin's diplomatic encroachments, especially on behalf of Italy and Rumania. Conrad was so outraged personally and politically that he threatened to resign'.[3] And the Emperor, assuring him of his 'fullest confidence', shelved the scheme.[4]

The Reich had to submit because at Ypres blood was flowing in vain, and the sands were running out. It had also to yield to Austria-Hungary's persistent importunities for men.[5] The new battles in Poland brought 'rapid changes from attack to defence, enveloping to being enveloped, breaking through to being broken through'.[6] Conrad—lamenting that his country had thrown three armies into the common pool, abandoned Galicia, exposed the Carpathian passes, and supplied 26 divisions to protect Germany from invasion —threatened to divert the bulk of his forces to the defence of the Dual Monarchy.[7] Since the fighting in the West, meanwhile, had become static,[8] it was both possible and urgent to send five German divisions to the East, and even to incorporate one into the Habsburg Army. But they were too few and too late to decide the struggle[9] and—to fill the cup of Austrian bitterness to overflowing—were alleged to have come in response to Conrad's plea 'that the soil of the Allied Monarchy should, as quickly as possible, be cleared of the enemy'.[10] Years after, Conrad still waxed 'indignant that Falkenhayn should have represented each troop dispatch to the East as a support for Austria-Hungary, instead of viewing it from the standpoint of common action on equal terms. . . . He overlooked the fact that these troop dispatches were but a repayment in instalments of a great debt which we had unselfishly allowed Germany to incur for her enterprise in France . . . . the instalment repayments were made out to be a disturbing and troublesome act of charity for the weaker brother'.[11]

[1] Bolfras to Conrad, 4 Nov. '14. Conrad, V. 382 and 610.
[2] Conrad to Bolfras, 5 Nov. '14. Conrad, V. 393.
[3] Conrad, V. 393–4. See also Conrad to Bolfras, 8 Nov. '14. Conrad, V. 427.
[4] Francis Joseph to Conrad and Frederick, 6 Nov. '14. Conrad, V. 408.
[5] Conrad to Falkenhayn, 16 and 17 Nov. '14. Conrad to the German Supreme Command, 22 Nov. Conrad, V. 506, 514–16, 569.
[6] Hindenburg, 127. Also Conrad, V. 569, 582.
[7] Conrad to Falkenhayn, 17 Nov. '14. Conrad, V. 515.
[8] Talenski, 29.  [9] Conrad, V. 541, 576, 591, 807, 984.
[10] Falkenhayn to Conrad, 18 Nov. '14. Conrad, V. 540–1.
[11] Conrad, V. 543. See also Conrad to Bolfras, 19 Nov. '14. ibid.

All this recalled the homeric laughter at the old cartoon in the Berlin *Simplicissimus* depicting the Habsburg soldiers with heads of lions, the officers with heads of donkeys, and the generals with no heads at all.[1] To emphasize their own prowess and to disguise or gloss over their own failures, the Germans scattered sarcasms belittling the efforts and sacrifices of their Ally.[2] The early reverses in Prussia were ascribed to Vienna's failure to provide relief against the Russians.[3] The frustration in France was explained away by the need to send reinforcements to the 'puffed out Austrians'.[4] The latter's claim to have protected Silesia was countered by the rejoinder that, as Ludendorff has it, 'in reality they were defending their own homes'. When Conrad, after his first defeat in Poland, launched another attack, 'he would [again according to Ludendorff] never have done it without German support'.[5]

Nor was there a lack of method in such malice. It strengthened the arguments in which the rulers of the Reich dwelt, as does Hindenburg, on 'the contrast between Austria-Hungary's political aims and her domestic and military resources'.[6] It emboldened Ludendorff to affirm in his book that the Dual Monarchy 'has always looked after its own interests in a measure which is not justified by its military achievements'.[7] Self-glorification and disparagement of the *Waffenbruder* were weapons of the Wilhelmstrasse in the diplomatic duel with the Ballplatz over the fruits of the War. If, as Conrad says, in Berlin 'our dead were valued less than the German',[8] it was to gain priority for Germany's imperialist designs.

5

RIVAL DESIGNS IN POLAND AND RUSSIA. SEEKING A DECISION: EAST OR WEST?

What the Reich wanted, among other things, was Russian Poland. And since the Habsburgs desired the 'Austro-Polish solution', this opened, from the day the frontier was crossed, 'the ticklish question of delimitating the German and Austro-Hungarian spheres'.[9] Vienna, quick to designate a Governor for the invaded territories, endeavoured to obtain Jagow's consent to Austro-Hungarian rule in the districts taken by the Germans, including a 'permanent'

[1] Dumaine, 76.
[2] Conrad, IV. 257. V. 522, 544, 984, 986. Cf. Ludendorff, I. 92, 117, 137.
[3] Hohenlohe to Berchtold, 27 Aug. '14. Conrad, IV. 554.
[4] Conrad, V. 753; also 807.
[5] Ludendorff, I. 120; also 75. Conrad, IV. 715.
[6] Hindenburg, 78–9.   [7] Ludendorff, I. 78.   [8] Conrad, V. 544.
[9] Conrad, IV. 479. Also Redlich (5, 6, 10 Aug. '14), I. 243, 245–6. On 9 Aug. '14, Conrad issued a proclamation announcing Poland's 'liberation from the Muscovite yoke'.

administration in Warsaw, 'as soon as she is occupied by Germany'. The request was forestalled by the appointment of German officials, and all Berchtold could do was entreat his Allies to make a public disclaimer of annexationist intentions.[1] This appears to have been labour lost, for—according to Conrad's Memoirs—here were 'the shoots of the subsequent differences in the Polish question' between the Central Powers. As early as October 16th 1914, he noted on that score 'difficulties encountered in the political field'.[2]

The race to be first in the capital was intense. Each side sought backing among different social strata. The Germans irritated the Ballplatz by entrusting much of the local government to Polish collaborators.[3] Berlin's idea of an 'independent'—in reality a puppet —Russian Poland, which would have drawn Galicia away from the Habsburgs, caused Berchtold to lodge objections at the Wilhelmstrasse.[4] Another conflict exploded at a meeting of Conrad and Falkenhayn on December 19th 1914 when the latter proposed a demarcation line assigning to his Government, *inter alia*, the rich coal-bearing areas of Bendzhin and Czestokhowa and the Kalisz province —on which, according to the Austrian's subsequent angry comment, 'Germany had hastened to lay hands right at the start of the War'. Conrad's expostulations were met with the riposte that 'only we can exploit these industrial districts. For you this is impossible now'.[5] All his counter-claims proved unavailing. Germany 'resisted stiffly any larger territorial acquisitions by Austria-Hungary in Russian Poland'.[6]

This controversy was not only galling—it was futile. While the cartels like Skoda were making astronomical profits, and Hungarian grain speculators were holding the country to ransom,[7] hundreds of thousands died in vain. 'The colossal block we tried to roll back to the East only moved a short stretch, then lay still, and nothing could shift it. Our energies flagged. . . . The approach of winter laid its paralysing hand on the activity of friend and foe alike. The line which had already become rigid in battle was now covered with snow and ice'.[8] The season brought thick clouds of rumour and suspicion. On December 14th, Conrad learned from his Liaison Officer at Hindenburg's Command that Hindenburg had impressed on the Chancellor the impossibility of achieving a decision in the East. In the words of the informant, 'the offensive power of the 9th Army[9] is

---

[1] Aug. '14. Conrad, IV. 478–82.  [2] Conrad, IV. 482. V. 165.
[3] See Berchtold to Conrad, 14 Oct. '14. Conrad to Bolfras, 17 Oct. Conrad, V. 166, 178; also 167–8.
[4] Conrad, V. 166, 217.  [5] Conrad, V. 822–3.
[6] Conrad, V. 812; also 823, 856.  [7] Conrad, V. 396–7, 890.
[8] Hindenburg, 128; also 129. Conrad, V. 969–70, 982–3. Talenski, 35–6. Ludendorff, I. 112–13.
[9] The German Army in Poland.

dwindling. . . . They reckon on perhaps being able to push the Russians behind the Vistula, and . . . when this success has been achieved, they will send two corps to East Prussia,[1] to make a clean sweep there. They want to bring about a possible situation—no enemy on German soil—for ushering in negotiations. I do not know whether something is not already afoot'. Conrad asked: 'But surely not before we have cleared East Galicia. . . .' The reply was that the Germans 'regard this matter very coolly. . . . They want to come to an understanding with the Russians'. 'So they want to make peace and leave us in a hole?'[2]

Indeed, it was believed in Berlin that the Tsar, once his armies had been forced over the Vistula, might agree to separate talks.[3] But these, in the view of Berchtold (whom Conrad had summoned to make an 'immediate diplomatic intervention'[4]) would not be sought by way of 'parting from us and coming to terms with Russia at our expense'. The Foreign Minister's information was that the Germans contemplated 'an arrangement between Germany and Austria-Hungary on the one hand and Russia on the other'.[5] The Habsburg Ambassador in Berlin reported that it was 'completely out of the question that Germany should, at present, be thinking of a separate agreement with Russia, of which we would have to pay the price by renouncing East Galicia'.[6] But he seems to have ignored the contingency of losing that province under a tripartite deal. Admiral Tirpitz, William's powerful Minister of Marine, was soon to write in a letter that a bargain with Nicholas II 'will seem possible to me, if

---

[1] Re-invaded by Russia in the middle of Nov. '14. Ludendorff, I. 104.
[2] Conrad, V. 752-3. Worse still was the secrecy of these and similar German proceedings. It was not until 10 Jan. '15 that the Austro-Hungarian Ambassador in Constantinople heard from his American colleague that, some six weeks previously, the German Envoy Wangenheim—without telling him a word—had intimated to Morgenthau that 'they are not averse in Germany . . . to the idea of peace'. (This is confirmed by Morgenthau, 117 ff.). It was not until 12 Jan. that Pallavicini could cable to Vienna that Wangenheim had at last reported to him the conversation with Morgenthau. Pallavicini to Berchtold, 10 and 12 Jan. '15. Deciphered in the Russian Foreign Ministry. *Internationale Beziehungen*, II. 6. II. No. 752, pp. 643–4, and p. 644, footnote 1.
[3] Conrad, V. 753. 'They speak with emphasis here of the tendency towards peace said to manifest itself at the Imperial Court of Petrograd'. (The Italian Ambassador in Berlin to Sonnino. See Sonnino to Carlotti, 8 Dec. '14. Deciphered in the Russian Foreign Ministry. *Internationale Beziehungen*, II. 6. I. No. 623, p. 531). It may not be without interest, in this connection, that Count Witte, in a Memorandum on Tsarist aspirations in Turkey, wrote that, if these were satisfied and the Germans withdrew from Poland, Petrograd and Berlin could make peace. Under this arrangement, Russia would obtain Galicia and a part of Bukovina and consent, in return, to the incorporation of several Austrian provinces in the Reich. Carlotti to Sonnino, 19 Jan. '15. Deciphered in the Russian Foreign Ministry. *Internationale Beziehungen*, II. 7. I. No. 37, pp. 34–5.
[4] Conrad to Berchtold, 14 Dec. '14. Conrad, V. 754–6.
[5] Berchtold to Conrad, 19 Dec. '14. Conrad, V. 848.
[6] Hohenlohe to Berchtold, about 23 Dec. '14. Conrad, V. 898.

Austria is not obstinate',[1] and his Memoirs show that what he had in mind was, in fact, an offer of East-Galician territory to the Russians.[2] This was at a time when, as Berchtold had to admit, 'we are still far from having achieved the minimum of what was to have been won by war against Russia. This minimum success . . . must consist in proving that Russia is not in a position to protect Serbia against an effective assertion of our will. . . . A decisive military success against Serbia is indispensable for our position among the Yugoslavs and in the Balkans generally, and without that premise a termination of the conflict with Russia, no matter how advantageous the conditions may be in other respects, is not to be thought of'.[3]

Yet termination was just what Falkenhayn suggested to Conrad on December 19th 1914. He said : ' . . . we can be content, when the Russians are pushed behind the Vistula'. Conrad insisted that they must be beaten first and, 'if necessary', followed beyond that river. He desired a return to 'the same situation as at the beginning of the War, and the operation as planned for the start of the campaign'. The German, however, was thinking of 'the resistance of France'. Conrad considered 'Russia . . . as the main pillar of this War. . . . When Russia crumbles, France will collapse too'. Falkenhayn replied: 'I do not believe that, because England will not give in'. He wished to release the largest possible force for the West. 'We want to open our offensive in France early in February'. Hence, 'when the Russians are thrown over the Vistula . . . we shall erect a Chinese wall in Poland'.[4] The Under-Secretary Zimmermann suggested to the Austrian Ambassador that the Central Powers, in addition to receiving war damages, might be content with all the land to the left of the Vistula'.[5] Now, assuming that all this was achieved, the Reich would be in a strong position, but not so the Dual Monarchy. For Germany, after she had freed East Prussia and seized—besides Belgium— some choice portions of Poland, peace would be a substantial victory. For Austria-Hungary—chased out of Galicia and beaten at Belgrade —it would spell defeat. At this juncture, to entertain, as Berlin did, the notion of a compromise with Petrograd, even in co-operation with Vienna, was to commit a hostile act against the Ally.[6]

---

[1] 20 Jan. '15. Tirpitz, 441.   [2] Tirpitz, 270.
[3] Berchtold to Conrad, 19 Dec. '14. Conrad, V. 849. The Austro-Hungarian Ambassador in Constantinople told his American colleague that in his 'personal opinion . . . the Austrian Government could not think of peace until it had settled accounts with Serbia'. Pallavicini to Berchtold, 10 Jan. '15. Deciphered in the Russian Foreign Ministry. *Internationale Beziehungen*, II. 6. II. No. 752, p. 644.
[4] Meeting at Oppeln, 19 Dec. '14. Conrad, V. 817-20.
[5] Berchtold to Conrad, about 23 Dec. '14. Conrad, V. 900.
[6] Conrad opposed the idea of a separate peace with Russia in a telegram to Falkenhayn, 27 Dec. '14. Conrad, V. 915.

The Habsburgs wanted 'a decisive success against Russia', because it would free their territory occupied by her and rescue it from becoming an object of diplomatic barter. It would clear Russian Poland and parts, at least, of the Ukraine. It would deprive the Balkans of the Slav protector and deliver them up to the Dual Monarchy. It would paralyse Italy and offer the one effective means of saving the Trentino.[1] It would stop the progressive deterioration of the internal situation. These aims could be achieved only by making use of the huge military machine of the Reich. The one means of doing so was to harp on one's own dwindling strength, play on the joint antagonism to Russia, and present each German contingent clamoured for as a contribution to 'the common interests' of 'the war situation as a whole'.[2]

But a common antagonism, as the only cement of imperialist alliances, is a brittle bond. For the rulers of Germany, 'the war situation as a whole' was far from limited to the Eastern front. The latter, in fact, was then greatly subordinate to the Western theatre of war. Not the least reason for this was that victory over Russia (even if it was not offset by the risk of disaster in France[3]) would, at this stage, have been the consummation of the Dual Monarchy's policy, allowing her to desert the Ally. It was known in Berlin that Vienna, though frowning on German soundings in Petrograd, was simultaneously testing peace possibilities in the enemy capitals.[4] Hence, the denial of large reinforcements to Conrad, while primarily dictated by the concentration on France and Britain, was at the same time a device to involve Austria-Hungary deeper in the fighting, to drain her strength, and tighten her dependence on Germany.

When 1914 drew to a close, not only had, as Conrad recollects, 'all my proposals to carry to a decision the War in the East been dropped',[5] but Falkenhayn even thought of transferring troops from Poland to the Rhine.[6] Moreover, the Habsburg Army was told by William II that it must 'stake everything on tying down its adversary .... in no circumstances must the pressure be relaxed'.[7] By the close of 1914, too, the Germans, as they hammered home to Conrad, were 'already stronger' than the Austro-Hungarians in the Russian theatre.

[1] Conrad to Falkenhayn, at Oppeln, 19 Dec. '14. Conrad, V. 819–20. Conrad to Berchtold, 14 Dec. '14. Conrad, V. 756. '... if the intervention of neutrals ... is to be forestalled' there must be 'the speediest employment of new German forces' in the East. Conrad to Falkenhayn, 27 Dec. '14. Conrad, V. 915.
[2] Conrad, V. 541. Conrad to Falkenhayn, 27 Dec. '14. Conrad, V. 915. Hindenburg, 135–6.
[3] William II's statement at Breslau, 2 Dec. '14. Conrad, V. 651.
[4] See pp. 296–7 below.    [5] Conrad, V. 652.
[6] The German Liaison Officer at Austro-Hungarian Headquarters to Conrad, 26 Dec. '14. Conrad, V. 918–19. Also Breslau meeting, 2 Dec. '14. Conrad, V. 656; and 341, 649, 651–2, 820.
[7] Breslau meeting, 2 Dec. '14. Minutes. Conrad, V. 651.

It was no use being able to retort: 'Because, at the beginning, we bled ourselves white'.[1] This was the very reason why, as he meditated later, 'I had no choice but to submit'.[2] 'It was our evil fate' that the Germans 'mixed operational requirements with their postwar aims: territorial expansion, economic and political hegemony over their own Allies'.[3] Austria-Hungary, far from reaching her own goal, had to supply the cannon-fodder to achieve Germany's. Not only did she not advance into the Balkans, she was diverted from them. Instead of holding Italy at bay, she was expected to give her the Trentino.

6

CANCELLING OUT THE ALLY'S PROSPECTIVE GAINS

But could the Wilhelmstrasse seriously believe that this sacrifice would satisfy the Consulta? Could it ignore the symptoms 'of a completely independent development of Italian policy?' The Ambassador Macchio cannot have been the only leading Austrian to ask this question.[4] The declaration of neutrality was so obvious a sign of Italy's defection that, as the Foreign Minister Jagow stated to the Ambassador Bollati, it made 'a most painful impression' in Berlin.[5] The last illusions regarding the Southern Ally must have been torn to shreds at the Marne. Early in October 1914, the German Envoy in Vienna expressed his conviction to Avarna that Rome, even if she were granted the Trentino, would not honour the Alliance.[6] At the end of the month, Bollati told Zimmermann, the Under-Secretary of State, that the Trentino 'had been the cause of many evils. He answered: "If you are prepared to march with us, you can have it". I replied that the offer was already too late, and that it should have been made before the declaration of war and in that case perhaps (and under my breath I said to myself, only perhaps, more probably not) we would have been able to go with them'.[7] On November 11th, the Under-Secretary 'insisted once more, and with much heat, that Italy should intervene in the War'. But

[1] Conrad and the German Liaison Officer, conversation, 26 Dec. '14. Conrad, V. 918; also 541, 650. Newspapers close to the Vienna Government were attributing Austria-Hungary's failures to the German General Staff. The Serbian Legation, Petrograd, to Sazonov, 19 Dec. '14. *Internationale Beziehungen*, II. 6. II. No. 688, pp. 566–7.
[2] Conrad, V. 374; also 652, 489.
[3] Conrad, IV. 256; also 786. V. 78. Tisza, I. 6.    [4] Macchio, 24, 27.
[5] Salandra, 89; also 90. Bollati to San Giuliano, 5 and 8 Aug. '14. *Documenti Diplomatici*, 5. I. NN 74, 130, pp. 43, 69–70.
[6] Avarna to Bollati, 5 Oct. '14. *Carteggio*, LXI. II. 253. That this opinion was widespread in Germany is confirmed by Bollati to San Giulano, 10 Oct. '14. *Documenti Diplomatici*, 5. I. No. 931, p. 557.
[7] Bollati to Avarna, 26 Oct. '14. *Carteggio*, LXI. II. 271.

'to believe still that there is a possibility of our entering the War at the side of Austria is plain foolishness, and I did not hesitate to tell Zimmermann so. . . . He however . . . continued to enumerate the advantages which we would obtain . . . and he ended by saying that, even concerning the Trentino, a "geheime Zusicherung" could be given. . . . I immediately told him that this would not be enough, and that what was wanted was a public undertaking, to which he replied that perhaps even this could be had—but then I added that, even with this, it was now too late'.[1] By the end of the year, Italy's position had crystallized enough for Bollati to report that the Germans knew she was only seeking a pretext for the break.[2]

It seems astonishing, therefore, that, as Macchio mused in retrospect, 'while in official Vienna', ever since August 1914, 'no one any longer considered as a possibility Italy's departure from neutrality in favour of her Allies, Berlin . . . should have hit upon the idea that giving away the "bit" of Trentino . . . ought to suffice to still her voracious appetite'.[3] It is equally surprising that Germany, even though she was steadily increasing her pressure for the surrender of that province, should have refused every Austro-Hungarian request to 'show the spiked helmet on our Italian frontier',[4] which alone could have acted as a deterrent to Rome. And odder still is the sustained encouragement which, right from July 1914, the Wilhelmstrasse was giving the Consulta.[5]

One of the pieces in this jig-saw puzzle must have been the desire to complete, with Italian help, the strategic encirclement of France, and circumvent the economic blockade imposed by the Entente. Another and more likely piece was the inveterate German expectation that the Dual Monarchy would dissolve. Hindenburg, looking back on the time in question, remembered 'the signs, even then quite distinguishable, of the disintegration of the [Habsburg] State and loss of confidence in a favourable termination of the War'.[6] Zimmermann admitted to Bollati that sooner or later this outcome was inevitable.[7] The Ambassador Dumaine quotes a German diplomatist as saying: '. . . if that misfortune happens . . . we shall be ready to

---

[1] Bollati to Avarna, 11 Nov. '14. *Carteggio*, LXI. III. 388. 'Geheime Zusicherung' —a 'secret assurance'.
[2] Bollati to Avarna, 23 Dec. '14. *Carteggio*, LXI. III. 398.
[3] Macchio, 24. Also p. 241 above.
[4] Tisza to Conrad and Berchtold, 10 Aug. '14. Conrad to Moltke, 13 and 15 Aug. Moltke to Conrad, 9 Aug. Conrad, IV. 199, 209, 212–13, 203. Bollati to Avarna, 26 Oct. '14. *Carteggio*, LXI. II. 271.
[5] See pp. 164, 240–1 above. Also Huldermann, *Alfred Ballin*, 242. Macchio, 30.
[6] Hindenburg, 135–6.
[7] Bollati to Avarna, 11 Nov. '14. *Carteggio*, LXI. III. 387. Already in Sept. '14, 'well-informed' Germans in Rome were talking of a possible settlement of the War at the expense of Austria. San Giuliano to Avarna and Bollati, 11 Sept. *Documenti Diplomatici*, 5. I. No. 652, p. 377.

scoop up the biggest lot'.¹ And as this crime required aiders and abettors (against Tsarism for example), it was hardly far-fetched for the Russian Minister in Serbia to discuss the possibility that 'Germany is already making preparations for the moment, when she can drop her present Ally, unless she were left in the lurch first. In that case, Germany would probably magnanimously offer to Italy Austria's place in the Balkans'.² In fact, the Italian Minister in Bucharest, Fasciotti, who was close to the Consulta, expressed to his Russian colleague the conviction that Berlin, if need be, would abandon Austria-Hungary and come to a separate agreement with Rome.³

The jig-saw piece which completes the picture appears to be contained in the fact that the Reich, of course, counted on victory. This would entail an automatic aggrandizement of the Dual Monarchy. The task of the Wilhelmstrasse, in consequence, was to neutralize or curtail this contingency by reducing the Habsburgs elsewhere. Tirpitz, in effect, threw out the idea that Vienna, if 'in case of necessity' she acquired Albania and Novibazar, should forfeit East Galicia.⁴ As a logical corollary the German Ambassador in Rome suggested that the anticipated subjection of Serbia to the Austrians could well be balanced by depriving them of the Trentino.⁵ The latter, unlike Slovenia or Trieste, did not bestride the road from Berlin to the Adriatic, and a contemporary observer wrote correctly that 'no direct Pan-German interests would be affected by the return of this district to . . . Italy'.⁶ On the contrary, these interests would be superbly served by what Tisza described as a '*capitis diminutio*' of the Danubian Monarchy, and Zimmermann admitted to be a 'vivisection'.⁷ The Serbian Minister in Athens, quoting information

¹ Dumaine, 159.
² Trubetskoi to Sazonov, 9 Dec. '14, on his conversation with the Rumanian Foreign Minister Porumbaru. *Internationale Beziehungen*, II. 6. II. No. 629, p. 536.
³ Poklevski to Sazonov, 15 Jan. '15. *Internationale Beziehungen*, II. 7. I. No. 14, p. 15. Count Witte, in his Memorandum on a separate peace between Germany and Russia (see p. 274 above, footnote 3) also envisaged the break-up of the Dual Monarchy. Under his plan, Hungary, Bohemia and Yugoslavia would be set up as independent Kingdoms, leaving an Austrian dwarf State of six million inhabitants. The Trentino and Western Istria were to go to Italy. Carlotti to Sonnino, 19 Jan. '15. Deciphered in the Russian Foreign Ministry. *Internationale Beziehungen*, II. 7. I. No. 37, pp. 34–5.
⁴ Letter, 20 Jan. '15. Tirpitz, 442; also 270–271.
⁵ San Giuliano to Bollati and Avarna, 10 Aug. '14. *Documenti Diplomatici*, 5. I. No. 172, p. 98. Flotow also envisaged the surrender by Austria of some of her other Italian territories, always excepting Trieste. This was, moreover, bound to be followed by the cession of at least part of Transylvania to Rumania. Nor would Austria-Hungary, even if victorious, be able to dream of reconquering Northern Italy, once she had lost the Trentino. See Lewin, 258.
⁶ Lewin, 258.
⁷ Tisza, I. 61. Bollati to Avarna, 26 Oct. '14. *Carteggio*, LXI. II. 271.

apparently received there from the Greek Envoy to the Habsburgs, reported the prevailing 'conviction in Vienna that Germany was shaping Austria-Hungary's future in conformity with her own plans . . . . they are clearly aware in Vienna that Germany is doing everything to pull out of the War as cheaply as possible, at the expense of Austria-Hungary. It is still being asserted here that negotiations in this sense are in progress between Berlin and Rome'.[1]

This, it would seem, was the context in which the Ballplatz was bound to see Germany's diplomatic assault on the Trentino. It was all part of the internecine political struggle of the two imperialist systems. Whilst, in July, it was impracticable to restrict an Austria who was to set the world ablaze, she was weakened and battered enough in December. The War in which they were Allies was exploited by the upstart Power to defeat its ageing junior partner.

CHAPTER XX

# Three Craftsmen of Diplomacy

1

## IMPLICATIONS OF THE APPOINTMENT OF A NEW FOREIGN MINISTER

IN these circumstances, Berchtold's willingness to compromise on the Trentino[1] assumed the proportions of a major surrender to Berlin. To some extent, his new tactic towards Italy was to secure Austria's rear for an all-out effort against the Serbs—if necessary, with German help.[2] This, in his opinion, would not only achieve the required 'minimum' object of the War, but also serve to enlist Rumania and Bulgaria. Conrad, however, argued that all this would be attained, if Russia were beaten. Above all, he wanted no Germans in the Balkans.[3] He wished every Allied division obtainable to be sent to the Eastern front. Hence, 'Berchtold's sundry desires, still one-sidedly set upon Serbia . . . and aimed at having the centre of gravity of the operation shifted there, as if Russia were a negligible quantity, convinced me that the Minister lacked that clear picture of the situation which the conduct of policy required in this difficult time'.[4]

Actually their divergencies went far beyond questions of strategy. That Berchtold was ready to admit the field-greys to the Balkans seemed to fit in with earlier signs of his pliancy vis-à-vis the Wilhelmstrasse. In July 1914, he was the principal transmitter in the Austro-Hungarian Cabinet of the Kaiser's and the Chancellor's pressure for war.[5] He allowed the Ambassador Tschirsky to take a hand in formulating the Sarayevo ultimatum.[6] According to Conrad, he was inclined, 'in the spirit of Germany's wishes', to win Rome by conciliation.[7] And, whatever his subsequent diplomatic acrobatics with the Consulta, his reasoning, in December 1914, that the Italians might

---

[1] See p. 244 above.
[2] Berchtold to Conrad, 19 Dec. '14. Conrad, V. 849. Berchtold's and Hohenlohe's discussions with Conrad, 30 Dec. Conrad, V. 956; also 911.
[3] See Conrad to his Chief of Operations, 18 Dec. '14. Conrad, V. 810; also 956.
[4] 21 Dec. '14. Conrad, V. 851; also IV. 879.
[5] See pp. 262–3 above. Also Pribram, *Austria-Hungary and Great Britain*, 220, 223, 291.
[6] Dumaine, 140.
[7] 31 July '14. Conrad, IV. 154. In the pre-War years, at any rate, Berchtold appears to have taken the line that there was sufficient scope for the interests of the three partners inside the Triplice, and that Italy could derive special benefits from it in the Mediterranean. See Hoyos, 63.

be content to 'gain something' without war[1] chimed in with that of the pro-Germans on the Tiber.[2] A well-informed Austrian noted at the time that Berchtold changed his policy on the Trentino because he was 'willing to yield to the pressure of . . . the German Reich'.[3]

This tendency of the Foreign Minister, as Tisza noted, became intolerable 'with the beginning of Bülow's intrigues'. Henceforth 'the vital interests of the [Dual] Monarchy demanded that the conduct of our external affairs should be put into stronger hands'.[4] These words reflected the will of Austria-Hungary's rulers to resist what was, to date, the worst encroachment by the Reich. In the light they shed, one might read Hoyos's subsequent phrase that 'there was no organic necessity for . . . Germany to dominate not only Europe, but the world'.[5] They were certainly in line with the Hungarian Premier's injunction to Berchtold: 'We must not . . . for a moment appear as the weak and timid protégé, for then we should have to bear, along with complete German protection, also the whole burden of that protectorate'.[6] This argument stiffened the opposition which Tisza and Conrad led against a cession of territory to Italy.[7] And Prince von Bülow's mission to Rome brought matters to a head.

The Ambassador Avarna testified to the depth of the suspicions which this appointment provoked on the Danube.[8] Tisza, in particular, was exercised by this threat to Austro-Hungarian imperialism and even more by the fear of the Magyar oligarchs that a surrender over the Trentino would establish a precedent for Rumanian claims in Transylvania. He subjected Berchtold's conciliatory line to withering criticism. He came to Vienna and 'worked upon' the German Ambassador Tschirsky 'to convince him of the erroneousness and danger of Bülow's tactics'. He went in person to the Emperor and demanded, on January 10th 1915, the dismissal of the Foreign Minister. 'I communicated to his Majesty . . . my views on the tactics to be pursued in regard to the Italians and the Germans, adding that

[1] Berchtold's and Hohenlohe's conversation with Conrad. 30 Dec. '14. Conrad, V. 957.
[2] See p. 294 below.
[3] 14 Jan. '15. Redlich, II. 8. Also Renouvin, *La Crise européenne et la Grande guerre*, 272.
[4] 'Notes on Count Berchtold's Resignation', 18 Jan. '15. Tisza, I. 150–1. Also Macchio, 79.
[5] Hoyos, 92.
[6] Tisza to Berchtold, 3 Sept. '14. Tisza, I. 71.
[7] Conrad's conversations with Berchtold, 6 Aug. and 30 Dec. '14. Conrad, IV. 182. V. 957. Tisza to Berchtold, 26 Aug. '14. Tisza, I. 61–2.
[8] Avarna to Bollati, 19 Feb. '15. *Carteggio*, LXII. I. 71. Also Andrassy, 134. Wedel, 'Fürst Bülow und Österreich'. *Süddeutsche Monatshefte*, March 1931, pp. 407–8.

the game was difficult . . . but it could be won, only it must be played well'.[1]

As the Hungarian Premier had, since Sarayevo, been in *de facto* control of the Ballplatz, Francis Joseph now offered him the portfolio. This, some of his counsellors felt, would substantially increase 'the weight of the action'[2] for which Habsburg diplomacy was sharpening its blade. But, as the senior office-holder in the Dual Monarchy, Tisza would have been unable to continue his narrow policy of Magyar predominance. He might even have had to subordinate the interests of the magnate class he represented to those of the Empire as a whole. Nor did Hungarian reaction want to lose his iron fist, now more than ever needed to stifle democracy at home.[3] Hence, Tisza refused to leave Budapest. It was 'essential', however, 'that the Hungarian nation should retain the directing influence on the conduct of foreign affairs'.[4] It was apparently still more important 'to have, from my present position, the possibility of exerting influence on external affairs'.[5] All that was needed was a tool. So he insisted on the candidature of Count Burián who, Tisza assured the Sovereign, 'agrees with me in all important questions and is on such close and friendly terms with me as to ensure a trustful and harmonious co-operation'.[6] Burián, as the Representative of the Hungarian Government in Vienna, had strongly supported Tizsa's attack on Berchtold's policy. His appointment as Foreign Minister (on January 14th 1915) was plainly a demonstration of intransigence.[7] Burián was Austria-Hungary's answer not only to Sonnino, but also to Bülow.

2

PRINCE BÜLOW'S MISSION AND THE BANCA COMMERCIALE ITALIANA

Prince Bülow, according to the French Ambassador in Rome, headed the secret Berlin committee directing 'all Austro-Hungarian matters'.[8] If this were true, he was a formidable figure for Habsburg

[1] 'Notes on Berchtold's Resignation', Tisza, I. 151. Also Macchio, 83. Redlich, II. 8-9. The fact that Tisza was an admirer and supporter of Germany (Tisza, I. 31, 133) had the effect of engendering, not submissiveness, but a desire that the Dual Monarchy, and notably Hungary, should imitate and emulate the Reich.
[2] *ibid.* Tisza, I. 152.   [3] See Tisza, I. 22-3, 90.
[4] Tisza to Burián, 11 Aug. '14. Tisza, I. 53. Also Macchio, 79.
[5] 'Notes on Berchtold's Resignation', Tisza, I. 152.
[6] *ibid.*
[7] Macchio, 79; also 83. Tisza, I. 31, 42, 150-53, 258, Musulin, 254. Hoyos, 69-70. Andrassy, 128. Redlich, II. 19. Renouvin, 272.
[8] Delcassé to Paléologue, 7 Dec. '14, quoting a telegram from Barrère. Deciphered in the Russian Foreign Ministry. *Internationale Beziehungen*, II. 6. II. p. 530, footnote 2.

diplomacy to contend with in the Eternal City. He had, moreover, every attribute for success. A former Chancellor, Foreign Minister, and Ambassador to the Quirinal, he had firmly upheld the Triplice and rendered important services to Italy. A Knight of the Collar of the Annunziata, he was one of the twelve elect entitled to style themselves cousins of King Victor. A friend of the shipping magnate Albert von Ballin and other captains of German monopoly,[1] he was in touch with Italian business and high finance, senators and deputies who had risen through economic connections with Germany, and he 'had been for a number of years on the best of terms with Sonnino'.[2] As the husband of 'an Italian lady of high birth',[3] he spent almost every winter in Rome among the roses of Villa Malta, keeping his fingers on the social and political pulse of the capital. 'Need I add, my dear Prince, that you, with all your intimate knowledge of Roman life, your position in Roman society and many close relationships in Rome, seem eminently suitable for the post?'[4]

This bouquet from the Chancellor Bethmann was mere ostentation, for he, like Jagow and the Kaiser, abhorred this appointment. They feared, not without reason, that the ambitious beneficiary would use it to engineer his return to power.[5] But Salandra's speech in the Chamber on December 3rd 1914—heralding an 'alert and armed neutrality'[6]—caused enough alarm in Berlin to make Bülow indispensable. Two days later, he was given the Embassy he had demanded. A large fund was deposited to his credit at the Banca Commerciale Italiana. Joel, its German director, sent him a message of welcome when he arrived in Rome on December 17th.[7] The Turkish Ambassador was among those greeting him at the station. The Austrian, Macchio, however, was absent—'mindful', he proudly recollects, 'to preserve my independence and dignity as Representative of my Emperor'.[8] Undaunted (or spurred) by this portent, the Prince and Princess set going a brilliant cascade of entertainment for a constant stream of illustrious guests. Their residence, as Salandra has testified, 'became of great importance in Italian politics'.[9] The

---

[1] Bülow's connections included Schwabach, the owner of the bank S. Bleichröder. Bülow, III. 135, 139, 174, 190, 192, 206, 238. Huldermann, 241. T. N. Page, 169. Hallgarten, II. 471.
[2] Bülow, III. 213. Also Suarez, III. 110, 236. Macchio, 93.
[3] Salandra, 92.
[4] Bethmann-Hollweg to Bülow, 30 Nov. '14. Bülow, III. 188.
[5] Bollati to Avarna, 23 Dec. '14. *Carteggio*, LXI. III. 400. Wedel, 'Die Daily Telegraph Affaire—Bülows römische Mission'. *Süddeutsche Monatshefte*, March 1931, p. 398. Flotow, 'Um Bülows römische Mission'. *ibid.* 403. Also Salandra, 175.
[6] See p. 292 below.
[7] Delcassé to Paléologue, 7 Dec. '14, quoting Barrère. *Internationale Beziehungen*, II. 6. II. p. 530, footnote 2. Bülow, III. 144, 209. *Carteggio*, LXI. III. 400. Salandra, 178, 220.
[8] Macchio, 61.      [9] Salandra, 177.

British Ambassador's wife, in Rodd's rueful words, 'felt reluctantly obliged to follow the example of the Villa Malta. The attendance at such receptions . . . acted as a barometric register of the rise and fall of our respective stock in social circles'.[1]

This battle of the balls, this duel by dinner invitations provided the background for Bülow's contest with the Envoys of the Entente. His task—since there was no longer any hope of enlisting Italian co-belligerency—was 'to make a last effort to keep Italy from declaring war on our Austrian Ally'.[2] He 'found the situation here worse than all the pessimistic information had led me to foresee. I would not have believed that we could lose so much ground in a few months'.[3] It was also discouraging to hear from Victor Emmanuel that Germany, by giving free rein to Austria and taking up arms against Russia and France, had herself violated the Triplice.[4]

The first thing, therefore, he must have done was to repeat the earlier promises made to the Consulta. Already on October 28th 1914 (and later) his predecessor Flotow had assured Salandra that, if the Kingdom remained friendly, account would be taken of its interests and advantages in the Mediterranean, the Balkans and North Africa.[5] French sources claimed that Bülow 'is going to offer, or has already offered . . . Egypt'.[6] Before very long he was to add 'a concession . . . in Asia Minor (Adalia)'[7] at the expense of his Turkish Allies. These proposals were interspersed with German hints that it was also Rome's concern to support the Dual Monarchy—obviously against Russia—and, alternatively, that the Habsburg Empire might collapse,[8] in which case Italy would need the Reich to keep in check

---

[1] Rodd, III. 245.   [2] Bülow, III. 187; also 192. Salandra, 176.
[3] Bülow to Erzberger, 24 Dec. '14. Erzberger, 40.
[4] Bülow, III. 218.
[5] Salandra, 163. Also Avarna to Bollati, 6 Nov. '14. *Carteggio*, LXI. II. 272. Bülow himself, as far back as August—i.e. several months before his appointment—had written to San Giuliano that, if Italy co-operated in the War, she would be in a position to fulfil her 'constant dream in regard to the coast of Africa and the Mediterranean'. (Salandra, 93). On 11 Nov. '14, Bollati wrote to Avarna that the Under-Secretary Zimmermann had offered Italy, for her belligerency, advantages in 'North Africa and Albania . . . and all that we could seize from France'. (*Carteggio*, LXI. III. 387-8). In the early days of the War, there were hints and reports that the Central Powers were, or intended, promising her Nice, Corsica and Tunis. Fasciotti to San Giuliano, 2 Aug. '14. Garroni to San Giuliano, 19 Aug. *Documenti Diplomatici*, 5. I. p. 20, footnote 2, and No. 338, p. 186. Also Bréal, 137.
[6] Mme. Bulteau to Briand, Dec. '14. Suarez, III. 110. Informal German offers to Italy of Egypt and Malta were mentioned by Bollati to San Giuliano as early as 31 Aug. '14. *Carteggio*, LXI. II. 254.
[7] Memorandum from the Duke d'Andria to Salandra, quoting an assurance given by Bülow, 15 April '15. Salandra, 202.
[8] Zimmermann's statement. Bollati to Avarna, 11 Nov. '14. *Carteggio*, LXI. III. 387-8. Salandra, 177.

the Slavs. Nor would it be surprising if Bülow had emphasized that the victory of the Entente would destroy the continental balance, and establish French hegemony in the Mediterranean.[1]

3

### THE TUSSLE OVER TRIESTE

But his 'instinct' told him that what really mattered in Rome was 'giving Italian statesmen the speediest possible guarantee that Austria would acknowledge, without *arrière pensée*, the minimum at least of Italian aspirations. . . .'[2] That these coincided with Berlin's anti-Viennese schemes could only lend special vigour to his exertions. And so, while the Ballplatz went on talking blithely of Albanian concessions, Bülow, upon arrival, conceded discussions on the Trentino.[3]

Baron Sonnino, however, in their very first interview, spoke also of Trieste.[4] This must have irritated the Ambassador more than he cared to convey. Since the trade route from Hamburg was longer and more costly in time of peace, and liable to be cut by the British and French Navies in war, the Adriatic became 'the principal commerical avenue leading from Central Europe to the Middle and Far East'.[5] One of the German objects in penetrating the Danubian Empire was to acquire 'command of the route to Trieste and . . . the Mediterranean.'[6] In 1909, a new railway to Trieste was inaugurated to serve the markets of Southern Germany. The port itself was sufficiently enlarged to compete, among others, with Genoa.[7] On the eve of the War, Wickham Steed wrote that 'the Adriatic . . . is in process of becoming not an Italian nor a Slav, but a German sea. German shipping companies, scarcely disguised under Italian names, already challenge the supremacy of the Austrian Lloyd at Trieste; German banks, bearing Viennese and Italian names, are gradually absorbing the commerce and controlling the interests of the port'.[8] The latter, in short, 'assumed an importance with regard to the Fatherland that can only be likened to the position of Hamburg in the commercial system of modern Germany'.[9] In the early summer of 1914, the French Ambassador in Austria-Hungary heard rumours of plans hatched in Berlin to reorganize the Dual Monarchy with a view to incorporating German Austria and Trieste.[10] Even if this was invention, and the Kaiser for a time still willing to leave the city to his

---

[1] See Bülow, III. 216.     [2] Bülow, III. 216.
[3] Salandra, 220–1; also 177.
[4] Bülow, III. 214. *Carteggio*, LXI. IV. 555.     [5] Lewin, 251.
[6] Steed, 294.     [7] May, 335.     [8] Steed, 281.
[9] Lewin, 251. Also Michels, 189.     [10] Dumaine. 127.

Habsburg satellite, he was certainly not prepared to lose it to the Italians.[1]

This is why Bülow, as Sonnino reported, impressed on him 'the absolute necessity, if we wished to arrive at a result, of restricting our requests to the Trentino alone. In Vienna, Trieste is regarded as the "lung of the Empire", and rather than talk of ceding it they would prefer . . . war'.[2] To judge from his Memoirs, the utmost he seems to have contemplated for the contested port was 'autonomy'.[3] Moreover, 'he even disputed the boundaries of the Trentino. . . .' Salandra, in stating this in his Recollections, went to the length of quoting a presumably private letter from the Prince 'to an intimate German friend', saying that all the Italians ought to get was 'a relatively small and impoverished territory'.[4] Was the Ambassador really so niggardly over the disputed Province, or was he deliberately bidding low to have bargaining scope? Was the Italian Premier indulging in post-factum denigrations of the offer so as to excuse the denunciation of the Alliance? At any rate, Rome was far from satisfied with what Salandra has termed 'moderate concessions'.[5] On January 14th 1915, Sonnino told Bülow 'that no lasting state of concord between Austria and Italy could be achieved, except by the complete elimination of the Irredentist formula "Trento e Trieste" '.[6]

But the Ambassador, foreseeing the rebuff, had realized on (or before) his arrival in the Kingdom that 'a current of opinion must be created which should lead the Italian Government to prefer the pacific realization of its ambitions'.[7] This obviously was a euphemism for bringing the Consulta to accept a curtailment of its aims. It is equally clear that he was too shrewd to rely for this simply on the sedative of his soirées or the polemics of a purchased press.[8] He was bound to realize that what the Wilhelmstrasse required in Rome was not just a 'current' but a Cabinet to suit Germany's purpose, and that Salandra and Sonnino were not the men to lead it. It follows that he had to look for support among personalities and politicians close to German business and finance in Italy.[9] The British Envoy mentions 'one of the principal industrial banks . . . administered by

---

[1] Fasciotti to San Giuliano, 17 Sept. '14, quoting King Carol I. *Documenti Diplomatici*, 5. I. No. 721, p. 424. Avarna to Bollati, quoting Prince Wedel, 20 Jan. '15. *Carteggio*, LXI. IV. 555. Also Rodd, III. 239. Yerusalimski, 158. Steed, 294. Michels, 189.
[2] Sonnino to Salandra, about 30 Dec. '14. Salandra, 221. Also Bollati to Avarna, 27 Jan. '15. *Carteggio*, LXI. IV. 558.
[3] Bülow, III. 205.  [4] Salandra, 230.  [5] Salandra, 223.
[6] Bollati to Avarna, 27 Jan. '15, referring to a telegram from Sonnino of 15 Jan. *Carteggio*, LXI. IV. 558. Also Salandra, 230.
[7] Bülow, III. 216.
[8] See Macchio, 109, on the German controlled papers *Victoria* and *Concordia*.
[9] See pp. 138–9 above. Also T. N. Page, 145, 182, 210, 216.

a triumvirate which had tap-roots in Berlin, and the considerable influence which it exercised on the [Italian] commercial community'. With its 'co-operation . . . strong influence could be brought to bear on senators and deputies connected with the many industrial enterprises which it controlled'.[1] This is a reference to the Banca Commerciale Italiana, whose 'all-too-powerful' German Director, Joel, was 'much attached to Bülow'.[2] The Milanese Banca, at the same time, was interwoven with formidable elements of the Liberal Party, several of whose Ministries had been headed by Giovanni Giolitti.[3]

4

'THE MINISTER OF THE UNDERWORLD' AND HIS PROGRAMME

Giolitti, from the turn of the century onwards, had been the key figure in the politics of the Kingdom. Having held the premiership for nearly eight years, he wielded control in or out of office. Able to muster some three-fifths of the deputies, he dominated the Chamber and, by virtue of patronage and favours (protective tariffs for the industrial North), commanded a widespread coterie among senators, prefects, press men, public servants and the professions. Denounced as 'the Minister of the Underworld',[4] he had high repute as a master of manipulations, opportunism and intrigue. A skilful champion of the industrial and financial bourgeoisie, he could—according to circumstances—fight the Socialists in 1904, penalize strikers in 1908, wage the imperialist War in Libya in 1911-12, read the writing on the wall well enough to authorize public works and pass the electoral law of 1912 which introduced almost universal manhood suffrage, yet offset the increased representation of the Left by a pact with the Vatican resulting in the emergence of Catholic M.P's. One of his favourite methods was to retire from, and return to, the conduct of affairs more or less at will. Thus, in March 1914, having obtained a huge vote of confidence approving his colonial adventure, he suddenly resigned. Ostensibly this was due to the desertion of the governing Coalition by the Radicals. Actually—since Italy faced a railway strike and a grave budget deficit from the African War—Giolitti preferred someone else to suppress the workers and pay for his Libyan laurels. It appeared certain that the strong majority he had won in the post-reform elections of 1913

[1] Rodd, III. 229, 244.
[2] Salandra, 205; also 169. Bülow, III. 209.
[3] Henry, 86-7, 89. Rossi, 64.
[4] G. Salvemini, *Il Ministro della Malavita*, 1910. Megaro, 285-6.

would, as on previous occasions, enable him to resume in a few months the Presidency of the Council.¹

When Giolitti's Administration of mainly moderate Liberals withdrew, it was up to the Right wing of the Party to take the reins. Their leader Sonnino, however, was disliked by Parliament and in bitter feud with Giolitti. Twice already the latter's followers had overthrown his Cabinet. The choice, therefore, fell on Salandra, 'always... a friend of Sonnino' and one who 'had always fought on different sides' from Giolitti,² but was presumably so insignificant a rival that the veteran statesman did not hesitate to recommend him to the King and—to underline the continuity of foreign policy— leave San Giuliano in the Government. Yet, as the new Premier was to write fretfully, 'he would give me none of his lieutenants in the Chamber, for which reason he remained... arbiter of the situation'.²

For a time indeed, Salandra's position was precarious. But the violence used in suppressing the 'Red Week' in June 1914, the popularity of the neutrality declaration, and the exploitation of the European crisis for the enforcement of internal discipline, increased, as he has admitted, his 'possibilities of resistance'³ to Giolitti. With opportunity came the taste for power—both personal and on behalf of the section of Italian imperialism served by the 'Liberals of the Right'. The officially inspired press seized on the country's unpreparedness to raise a hue and cry against the ex-Prime Minister. The Cabinet reshuffle in disregard of the Giolittian majority and the open advent of Sonnino, in November 1914, betokened Salandra's growing ascendancy.⁴ The caretaker was taking care in a way not anticipated by Giolitti. It would be surprising if this had not fired the latter's resolve to climb back to office.⁵ All he required, it seemed, was the means.

No special insight was needed to see that each step the Government took towards intervention only increased the widespread revulsion against war. The pacifism of the Socialists was echoed by a motley chorus. The Catholics anathematized any assault on the Habsburg pillar of the Church. The adherents of the Triplice preferred the lesser evil of non-belligerency to collaboration with the Entente. The Conservatives inveighed against the martial disorder of the Freemasons, Radicals and Republicans. Broad strata of the bourgeoisie

¹ Lenin, XVIII. 334. Giolitti, 247, 378. Croce, 216, 221, 227, 257. Averbukh, 12–3. Megaro, 283. Salandra, 17, 194, 317. T. N. Page, 149–50, 186. Rodd, III, 239–40. Rossi, 1, 5–6. A. Albertini, 154–5.
² Salandra, 194; also 147, 186. Giolitti, 378. T. N. Page, 168.
³ Salandra, 195.
⁴ Giolitti, 388. Salandra, 150. T. N. Page, 189. Bollati, writing to Avarna, 10 Nov. '14, reported Giolitti as being against Sonnino's appointment. *Carteggio*, LXI. III. 386.
⁵ See Salandra, 190.

K

clung to their German business connections, chafed against the British blockade and dreaded the tolls and taxes of the Armageddon.[1] The great mass of the Italian people, wanting to stay neutral,[2] waited for a statesman to implement this desire. Even those who opposed him on other grounds would back him in order to avoid the War. Giolitti would have been unworthy of his rank and reputation as a politician if he had been insensitive to the prospects inherent in this groundswell of opinion. Experience and acumen could not but tell him that by adopting neutrality—the one popular alternative to Salandra's and Sonnino's line of involvement—he could displace his rivals and return to the helm.[3]

The additional logic of such a course was in its conformity to that taken by the Banca Commerciale Italiana and the German interests wherewith it and the Giolitti faction were connected. However, apart from personal opportunism and political subservience to a foreign Power, this orientation had yet another and deeper cause. Giolitti, like Salandra, acted for Italian imperialism, but each represented a particular section thereof. Each section had, within the wider frame, its own peculiar interests and needs which shaped and varied the tactics of its agents. The neutralist paper *Italia Nostra*, which first appeared on December 6th 1914, announced: 'We stand neither for the Central Powers nor for the Triple Entente; nor are we, *a priori*, for peace or for war. We stand for . . . Italy'.[4] With this, not even Salandra and Sonnino could have quarrelled. Giolitti, for his part, had shown himself in Libya as an inveterate expansionist. In August 1914, he not only agreed with the Government that Italy was not obliged to side with the Central Powers, but found, like Salandra and—later on—Sonnino, 'that the ends Austria has in view are . . . not in keeping with our interests'. Like them, he believed that 'a conflict between Italy and England is out of the question . . . now more than ever, we should keep on good terms with England'.[5] On August 10th, in a public speech, he stressed the need for 'assuring to Italy the place that should be hers in the world'.[6]

But the specific setting of 1914, encouraging as it did maximum predatoriness among the 'Liberals of the Right', brought out the

---
[1] Macchio, 64. Croce, 275, 284. Salandra, 110, 317–8. Rodd, III. 229. Giolitti, 393.
[2] Avarna to Bollati, 7 Jan. '15, quoting a report from Rome. *Carteggio*, LXI. III. 403. Salandra, 310–11, 313.
[3] See Salandra, 195, 318.   [4] Croce, 327.
[5] Giolitti to Ruspoli, 1 Aug. '14. Giolitti, 379–80. Ruspoli to San Giuliano, 2 Aug. *Documenti Diplomatici*, 5. I. No. 6, p. 5. San Giuliano and Salandra to Giolitti, 3 Aug., confirming that the latter was 'in harmony with our interpretation of the Triple Alliance Treaty'. Giolitti to San Giuliano, 5 Aug. Giolitti, 380–82. Salandra, 72.
[6] Salandra, 72.

comparative caution and temperance of Giolitti's party. He favoured, of course, the policy of exploiting the European crisis for Italian aggrandizement. Had his rivals stood up for neutrality, his personal and political ambitions might possibly have led him to come out for war. But in the situation in which he found himself, and with his Germanophil associations, 'it was my conviction . . . that the War would take at least three years' and 'entail great sacrifices, which would weigh especially heavily on a country such as ours, where capital was scarce and taxation maintained at a high pressure'. 'As for the Italian front, its difficulties . . . were formidable'. On the other hand, 'I believed that the Austro-Hungarian Empire . . . was destined by fate to break up; in which case the Italian portion would be peaceably united to Italy'. And if this did not come to pass, then 'in view of the very grave reasons which Austria had for avoiding war with Italy . . . there was every reason to suppose that well-conducted negotiations would lead to a favourable result'.[1] This appeared all the more likely since, according to Lloyd George, Giolitti 'believed that adequate concessions might be secured from Austria under German pressure'.[2] Above all, Giolitti perceived that 'the War was becoming a struggle for world hegemony between the two chief belligerents, while it was to Italy's interest that the balance of European power be maintained, to which she could only contribute by keeping all her forces intact'.[1]

This argument, before Sonnino's advent, was axiomatic in the Consulta. Italy's weak and penurious imperialism abhorred the preponderance of a single State or a group of nations to which, even if co-victorious, it would have to submit. It throve on the differences of antagonistic coalitions. And it was sure to flourish if, while the two warring camps were exhausting each other, it kept and developed its own strength. The moderates in Rome were moderate in the sense only that they intended to wait for the end of the fighting to present Italy's demands at bayonet point. The Trentino, and perhaps even Trieste, were to be acquired for nothing, either from Germany or from the Entente, at a moment when neither side would want, or be able, to oppose the lusty neutral.[3]

Such were the personal and political motives which led Giolitti, as early as August 1st 1914, to propound the policy of neutrality.[4] Aware

---
[1] Giolitti, 386–7. Also Croce, 275. Nenni, 41–2.
[2] Lloyd George, *The Truth about the Peace Treaties*, II. 761–2. Also T. N. Page, 207.
[3] Trubetskoi to Sazonov, 15 Feb. '15, quoting the opinion of the Government and of diplomatic circles in Serbia. *Internationale Beziehungen*, II. 7. I. No. 203, p. 186. Also: an intelligence report for Conrad from Baron 'C', 2 Nov. '14. Conrad, V. 369.
[4] See p. 290, footnote 5 above,

presumably of the Consulta's soundings in the Entente capitals, he urged, in a letter destined for the Premier's eyes, that 'every act should be avoided which is likely to give the impression of a departure' from it.[1] He pressed his views on the deputies in the Parliamentary lobbies.[2] And when the Chamber reconvened on December 3rd 1914, he must have been discomfited enough both by the ascendancy of Sonnino and the obvious trend of the reconstructed Cabinet to launch an overt attack. Salandra was applauded for announcing that 'our neutrality . . . is not sufficient to safeguard us from the consequences of the immense upheaval. . . . On the continent of Europe . . . Italy has vital interests to protect and just aspirations . . . to uphold. . . . Our neutrality must be . . . alert and active, not impotent, but strongly armed and ready'.[3] But Giolitti, not content with insisting on nonintervention, disclosed that, in the summer of 1913, when Austria-Hungary was about to strike at the Serbs, he had, as Prime Minister, instructed San Giuliano to warn her that, if she committed the aggression, Rome would not be bound by the Alliance. He had joined with Berlin in restraining Vienna, and his stand had not affected Italy's relations with the Central Powers.[4]

This revelation was a blow to the Government on more than one account. It was, to say the least, a hint that Salandra—if he had acted in 1914 as his predecessor did the year before—might have restrained the Habsburgs and averted the War. It was certainly an attempt 'to claim credit for having discovered and vindicated Italy's right to remain neutral before Salandra did so'[5] and thereby to dim the Premier's political merits. It was an implied promise that the friendship with Germany would not suffer, if the course Giolitti had mapped out was pursued. It was designed to, and did, earn him the cheers of the entire House. And, as the American Ambassador in Rome recollects, it 'was considered by many as a step in an intrigue to weaken the existing Cabinet and secure the reins of power in the interest of the Central Empires'.[6]

Whether or not this Parliamentary performance was concerted with Bülow, it is certain that the latter could not but appreciate the value of Giolitti's policy. As Italy's co-belligerency was clearly unrealizable, her neutrality was much desired by the Wilhelmstrasse.

[1] 23 Aug. '14. Salandra, 111.   [2] Giolitti, 385.
[3] Fedele, *Why Italy is at War*, 16. Salandra, 172–3. T. N. Page, 186.
[4] 5 Dec. '14. Salandra, 173. L. Albertini, II. 246. *Internationale Beziehungen*, II. 6. II. p. 531.
[5] Salandra's statement to Albertini. L. Albertini, II. 246. Also Krupenski to Sazonov, 8 Dec. '14. *Internationale Beziehungen*, II. 6. II. No. 622, p. 531.
[6] T. N. Page, 187; also 186. Bollati, too, had received information that Giolitti was engaged in an underground campaign to undermine the Government. Bollati to Avarna, 27 Jan. '15. *Carteggio*, LXI. IV. 559; and 11 Feb. '15. *ibid.* LXII. I. 68.

The veteran statesman, on the other hand, could only hope to return to power and implement his programme, if he obtained tangible concessions, and these depended on the Reich. In Lloyd George's account, Giolitti 'was able to induce Germany to exert... pressure on her Austrian confederates, and von Bülow was dispatched to Rome'.[1] According to the Ambassador Bollati, Giolitti's stand and the corresponding attitude of his paper *La Stampa* (Turin) were believed to be due to the Prince, 'who, in fact, told me that he intended to bring pressure to bear on him'.[2] The Memoirs of one of the two chief actors are significantly silent on this subject—except for the admission that Giolitti was 'our best and surest Italian friend'.[3] In the words of the other, 'I have known Prince von Bülow for many years. ... When he was living in Rome as a private citizen, he used often to come to see me. Now that he has come to Rome as Ambassador ... we met casually in the Piazza Tritone, on which occasion he told me he was coming to see me. I replied that ... I would come to see him, which I did the next day. Our conversation turned in a general way on the great events of the day, but I was careful to avoid discussing what Italy's attitude should be. To do so would have been a breach of duty on my part, nor did Prince von Bülow ... raise this question. A few days later he returned my call. As I was out, he left his card and I have not seen him since.'[4] But the U.S. Envoy quotes allegations 'that his visit to the German Ambassador took place on ... the day after the latter arrived in Rome and the day before he [Bülow] had his first conversation with ... Salandra and ... Sonnino'.[5] His British colleague recalls 'many rumours ... regarding visits exchanged between Bülow and Giolitti'.[6] And if these were untrue, then, as Salandra suggests, 'that does not exclude the possibility' that his associates 'did not avoid direct or indirect contact with Villa Malta'.[7] Before long, the Russian Minister in Bucharest was to report 'from a trustworthy source that Bülow had entered into negotiations with Giolitti'.[8]

In fact, Giolitti himself gave the game away. For how—unless he was in touch with the Prince—could he propound the profitability of neutrality?[9] Nor could he avoid an indirect confession of his plot. He had to answer his enemies who were beginning to charge him with

---

[1] Lloyd George, *The Truth about the Peace Treaties*, II. 762.
[2] Bollati to Avarna, 12 Jan. '15. *Carteggio*, LXI. IV. 551-2.
[3] Bülow, III. 165. See also 221-2.
[4] Giolitti to Peano, 24 Jan. '15. Giolitti, 391. In his *Memoirs*, 338, he adds: '... nor did I come into any further contact with him, either directly or indirectly'.
[5] T. N. Page, 187.   [6] Rodd, III. 240.   [7] Salandra, 192.
[8] Poklevski to Sazonov, 5 March '15. *Internationale Beziehungen*, II. 7. I. No. 318, p. 292.
[9] Rodd, III. 240, writes that he had 'always presumed that Giolitti ... was ... kept fully informed throughout of Bülow's activities and proposals'.

something akin to betrayal of national interests.[1] He had to act, before the country was swamped by the bellicose preparations and propaganda. The feverish military and economic precautions[2] were irrevocably committing it to the explosion. The mounting internal tension was not diverted by the earthquake in the Abruzzi on January 13th 1915, which struck 54 communes, killing 20,000 people, leaving 100,000 without a home or food in the frosty, snow-swept mountains, and crowding the capital with its victims. Even the relief-work was exploited for political intrigue and diplomatic demonstrations. Salandra not only declined a hypocritical Austrian offer of assistance, but hastened, as he recollects, 'to dispel the impression that, impoverished and discouraged by this cruel blow, Italy had abandoned her international ambitions'.[3] These latter were served, too, by plagiarizing Louis Philippe's earlier attempt to rouse popular emotions by moving Napoleon's ashes from St. Helena to the Dôme des Invalides. The body of Bruno Garibaldi (the grandson of the hero), who had fallen in France fighting in the Garibaldi Legion, was brought for burial to Rome, and—despite the dangerous republican associations of the name—the huge funeral procession was turned into a manifestation mixing patriotism with pro-Entente sentiments.[4] A meeting of Fascists gave Mussolini the occasion to demand the immediate abrogation of the Triplice—'Either war, or erasure from the roll of the Great Powers!'—and to denounce the endeavours to unseat Salandra for the benefit of Giolitti.[5]

Clearly, for the latter it was high time to hit back. He was encouraged by the knowledge that he had Socialist, Catholic and large middle-class support. In January 1915, his followers were sounding with other Opposition groups the possibilities of an alternative administration.[6] And on February 2nd, Giolitti came before the public by having his letter of January 24th to the Deputy Peano printed in the much-read *Tribuna*, his Roman mouthpiece. In this, he denied the 'legends' of 'my alleged relations with . . . Bülow' and of

'my being in favour of neutrality at all costs. It is certainly true that, unlike the Nationalists, I do not look on war as desirable. . . . Given the actual conditions in Europe, it is my belief that much [parecchio] may be obtained without going to war'.[7]

[1] See Giolitti, 388, 390–1. Salandra, 191.
[2] Benckendorff to Sazonov, 16 Dec. '14, quoting Imperiali. *Internationale Beziehungen*, II. 6. II. No. 651, p. 554.
[3] Salandra, 187; also 183–4. Macchio, 60, 77–8.
[4] Jan. '15. Macchio, 94.   [5] Milan, 24 Jan. '15. Salandra, 197.
[6] Salandra, 191. According to Bollati, the Giolitti faction intended to overthrow the Government at the reopening of Parliament. Bollati to Avarna, 11 Feb. '15. *Carteggio*, LXII. I. 68.
[7] Giolitti to Peano, 24 Jan. '15. Published in the *Tribuna*, 2 Feb. '15. Giolitti, 391–2. Also Salandra, 191–2, 334.

something akin to betrayal of national interests.[1] He had to act, before the country was swamped by the bellicose preparations and propaganda. The feverish military and economic precautions[2] were irrevocably committing it to the explosion. The mounting internal tension was not diverted by the earthquake in the Abruzzi on January 13th 1915, which struck 54 communes, killing 20,000 people, leaving 100,000 without a home or food in the frosty, snow-swept mountains, and crowding the capital with its victims. Even the relief-work was exploited for political intrigue and diplomatic demonstrations. Salandra not only declined a hypocritical Austrian offer of assistance, but hastened, as he recollects, 'to dispel the impression that, impoverished and discouraged by this cruel blow, Italy had abandoned her international ambitions'.[3] These latter were served, too, by plagiarizing Louis Philippe's earlier attempt to rouse popular emotions by moving Napoleon's ashes from St. Helena to the Dôme des Invalides. The body of Bruno Garibaldi (the grandson of the hero), who had fallen in France fighting in the Garibaldi Legion, was brought for burial to Rome, and—despite the dangerous republican associations of the name—the huge funeral procession was turned into a manifestation mixing patriotism with pro-Entente sentiments.[4] A meeting of Fascists gave Mussolini the occasion to demand the immediate abrogation of the Triplice—'Either war, or erasure from the roll of the Great Powers!'—and to denounce the endeavours to unseat Salandra for the benefit of Giolitti.[5]

Clearly, for the latter it was high time to hit back. He was encouraged by the knowledge that he had Socialist, Catholic and large middle-class support. In January 1915, his followers were sounding with other Opposition groups the possibilities of an alternative administration.[6] And on February 2nd, Giolitti came before the public by having his letter of January 24th to the Deputy Peano printed in the much-read *Tribuna*, his Roman mouthpiece. In this, he denied the 'legends' of 'my alleged relations with . . . Bülow' and of

'my being in favour of neutrality at all costs. It is certainly true that, unlike the Nationalists, I do not look on war as desirable. . . . Given the actual conditions in Europe, it is my belief that much [parecchio] may be obtained without going to war'.[7]

[1] See Giolitti, 388, 390–1. Salandra, 191.
[2] Benckendorff to Sazonov, 16 Dec. '14, quoting Imperiali. *Internationale Beziehungen*, II. 6. II. No. 651, p. 554.
[3] Salandra, 187; also 183–4. Macchio, 60, 77–8.
[4] Jan. '15. Macchio, 94.   [5] Milan, 24 Jan. '15. Salandra, 197.
[6] Salandra, 191. According to Bollati, the Giolitti faction intended to overthrow the Government at the reopening of Parliament. Bollati to Avarna, 11 Feb. '15. *Carteggio*, LXII. I. 68.
[7] Giolitti to Peano, 24 Jan. '15. Published in the *Tribuna*, 2 Feb. '15. Giolitti, 391–2. Also Salandra, 191–2, 334.

CHAPTER XXI

# A Diplomatic Triangle: Rome-Berlin-Vienna

## 1
### A SEPARATE PEACE BETWEEN AUSTRIA AND RUSSIA?

THE efficacy of the *parecchio*, needless to say, depended on the disposition of Vienna. German diplomacy, therefore, coupled its support of Giolitti with intensified pressure on the Austrians. In their first interview Bülow told Macchio: 'We must win Italy's co-operation; there is no way of getting it without your sacrificing territory'.[1]

But was there really no way out of this predicament for the Dual Monarchy? Could it not, for example, make a separate peace with Russia? As a matter of fact, the War was barely six weeks old, when the Italian Foreign Minister determined that the Italian envoys abroad should pay close attention to this possibility.[2] In November 1914, Salandra, in a telegram to Carlotti, returned to this hypothesis.[3] And when the Ambassador sounded the Petrograd Foreign Ministry in this matter, he was told that 'Russia would be guided solely by her personal interests'.[4] Soon afterwards, Prince Trubetskoi warned the Italian Representative in Bucharest that all the Consulta's 'petty calculations' might be completely upset if the Ballplatz offered Russia and Serbia acceptable terms.[5] At about the same time Sonnino learned from Bordeaux that the King of Spain was said to have explored what British and French reactions would be, if the Habsburgs held out an olive branch.[6] Bollati, quoting German opinion, cabled that Alphonso may have been urged on by his Austrian mother, and that 'a peace between Austria and England and France would still be no solution, as the War between these Powers was not serious ... King of Spain would rather have a

---

[1] Macchio, 61–2. Also Hoyos, 68. Helfferich, II. 68. Tirpitz, 438. Burián, 59. Tisza, I. 143.
[2] San Giuliano to Imperiali, Tittoni, Avarna, Bollati and Carlotti, 13 Sept.'14. *Documenti Diplomatici*, 5. I. No. 670, pp. 388–9. Cf. *Internationale Beziehungen*, II. 6. II. p. 499, footnote 3.
[3] 3 Nov. '14. Deciphered in the Russian Foreign Ministry. *Internationale Beziehungen*, II. 6. II. No. 456, p. 400.
[4] Memorandum, Russian Foreign Ministry, 20 Nov. '14. *Internationale Beziehungen*, II. 6. II. No. 541, p. 465.
[5] Trubetskoi to Sazonov, 9 Dec. '14. *Internationale Beziehungen*, II. 6. II. No. 629, p. 535.
[6] Sonnino to Carlotti, 30 Nov. '14. Deciphered in the Russian Foreign Ministry. *Internationale Beziehungen*, II. 6. II. p. 499, footnote 2.

peace between Austria and Russia'.¹ This chimed in with a report from Berne stating, on good authority, that Vienna was alleged to have requested Madrid to mediate with Petrograd.² Meanwhile, Carlotti read to Sazonov, presumably to test his intentions, a communication from the Italian Chargé d'Affaires in Vienna. It said that Count Forgách, one of Berchtold's right-hand men—emphasizing that the struggle had become one basically between Germany and Britain—had suggested the time had come to sheathe the sword.³

The question arose whether this was a genuine feeler from the Ballplatz or part of a wider German scheme to divide and confuse the Entente. But the Greek Minister to the Habsburg Court sent word in mid-December, in effect, that 'there is in Vienna, and notably in Budapest, an ever-growing inclination that Austria-Hungary should make peace with the . . . Triple Entente, independently of Germany and even against her'.⁴ And Izvolski wired from Paris that, according to 'stubborn rumours', Berchtold had invited the prominent Austro-French financier Adler,⁵ at the time resident in Switzerland, to initiate negotiations. The Ambassador inquired of his Chief whether Russia would 'insist on the complete fragmentation of the Dual Monarchy . . . or . . . prefer to isolate Germany by a separate peace with Austria'.⁶

This, obviously, was something the British and French Governments also wished to know. The reasons they had had for being reluctant to fight Francis Joseph were such as to make them all the more eager for a reconciliation. Paléologue gave a succinct formulation of Western policy in recalling to Delcassé 'the unquestionable advantage to France of the preservation of a great political system in the Danube basin'.⁷ As early as December 2nd 1914, Sir Edward Grey broached to the Russian Ambassador the notion of a direct deal with Austria-Hungary. The Foreign Secretary 'told me [Benckendorff reported] that he spoke to me about it . . .

---

¹ Sonnino to Carlotti, 2 Dec. '14, transmitting a telegram from Bollati. Deciphered in the Russian Foreign Ministry. *Internationale Beziehungen*, II. 6. II. No. 586, p. 499.
² Poklevski to Sazonov, 11 Dec. '14. *Internationale Beziehungen*, II. 5. II. No. 638, p. 545. Sazonov replied, 13 Dec.: 'Similar information has also arrived here'. *ibid.*
³ Memorandum, Russian Foreign Ministry, 8 Dec. '14. *Internationale Beziehungen*, II. 6. II. No. 620, p. 528.
⁴ The Serbian Legation in Petrograd to Sazonov, 19 Dec. '14, transmitting a telegram from the Serbian Minister in Athens of 17 Dec. The quotation is from this telegram. *Internationale Beziehungen*, II. 6. II. No. 668, p. 566; also p. 567.
⁵ See p. 210 above.
⁶ Izvolski to Sazonov, 16 Dec. '14. *Internationale Beziehungen*, II. 6. II. No. 656, pp. 557–8. According to a telegram from Sazonov to Izvolski, 19 Dec. '14, Russia, too, had information about a possible Austro-Hungarian attempt to conclude a separate peace, but these reports were described as very uncertain. *Internationale Beziehungen*, II. 6. II. No. 669, p. 567.
⁷ Paléologue to Sazonov, 1 Jan. '15. Paléologue, I. 236.

because Serbia's catastrophe appears to him an exceedingly grave matter . . . and Russia is in this case in honour bound as England has pledged her honour for Belgium, that there is a complete parallel here, and that the other Austro-Russian questions concern more especially Russia . . . Grey did not pursue the exchange of ideas'.[1] Why, the Russians may have wondered, did Sir Edward stop short? Did he hesitate to imply more clearly that the acute threat to Belgrade should make Sazonov more amenable, that Britain sympathized with, and supported, Russia's efforts on Serbia's behalf, but was far less interested in (if not opposed to) her further aims, and that these should not be allowed to block a compromise? At any rate, he argued that—since the matter mainly affected Petrograd—Britain and France would not object to a peace with Vienna, if she proposed terms acceptable to Sazonov.[2]

The French, however, were more explicit. On New Year's Day 1915, the Ambassador Paléologue, in the presence of his British colleague, said to Sazonov: 'As the German block is such a hard nut to crack, we should endeavour to detach Austria-Hungary. . . . Quite between ourselves, my dear Minister, if the Vienna Cabinet agreed to cede Galicia to you, and Bosnia-Herzegovina to Serbia, would not that seem to you an adequate return for making a separate peace with Austria-Hungary?' Sazonov interjected: 'What about Bohemia? And Croatia? Would you leave them under the present system?' Paléologue retorted: ' . . . in this terrible hour of trial for France, the Czech and Yugoslav problems seem to me secondary'. Sazonov replied: 'No. Austria-Hungary must be dismembered'. The Ambassador persisted. 'I showed that . . . it was our obvious interest and plain duty to concentrate the whole of our offensive power . . . against Germany, and that if the Vienna Cabinet offered us reasonable terms . . . we should commit a grave error if we rejected them *a priori*'.[3]

But Sazonov was as well aware of the role of the Habsburg system in the international power balance as were Whitehall and the Quai d'Orsay.[4] Since they sought to preserve as much as possible of that system,[5] it was his chief purpose to destroy it. Whereas the main enemy of the West was the Hohenzollern Empire, that of Russia was the Dual Monarchy. In Petrograd, therefore, the immediate

[1] Benckendorff to Sazonov, 3 Dec. '14. *Internationale Beziehungen*, II. 6. II. No. 594, p. 506.
[2] Grey to Buchanan, 29 Dec. '14. Deciphered in the Russian Foreign Ministry. *Internationale Beziehungen*, II. 6. II. p. 567, footnote 3.
[3] Paléologue, I. 235-6.   [4] See pp. 201, 210 above.
[5] According to a statement by the Russian Minister in Serbia, 'the dissolution of Austria in itself is hardly the aim of our Allies; in many business and financial circles there is no enthusiasm for this perspective'. Trubetskoi to Sazonov, 3. Feb. '15. *Internationale Beziehungen*, II. 7. I. p. 115, footnote 2.

advantage of isolating Germany counted for less than the prospect of eliminating the principal rival in South-Eastern Europe. Hence, Tsarist diplomacy embroidered Sazonov's list of sacrifices in store for Francis Joseph by the addition of the Bukovina, Transylvania, the Italian provinces, and an independent Bohemia.[1] And Britain and France were so much in need of the Russian steamroller, and so anxious not to offend those directing it, that Delcassé, in answer to Paléologue's telegram outlining his talk with Sazonov, gave the Ambassador what the latter felt were 'strict orders not to say a word which might lead the Russian Government to think that we do not hand over Austria-Hungary to Russia *in toto*'.[2]

Tsarist intransigence was matched by that of the Habsburgs. True, there were in Vienna, notably among the feudal aristocrats, those who sought in a deal with Nicholas II a weapon against Rome.[3] News of his armies being short of equipment and weakened by battle was lapped up on the Danube.[4] The hope that revolution would undermine his power of resistance throve like evergreen on its banks. Italy's encroachments on the Balkans, it was thought, might make him more amenable. The diplomat Czernin was not the only one to wonder whether a peace with Russia could be bought with a slice of East Galicia, in which case 'the anxieties over Italy and Rumania would lapse of their own accord'.[5] December 25th 1914, when the big Russian offensive began in the Carpathians, was defined by Conrad as 'a day of heavy crisis'.[6] Yet, on the 26th, discussing peace prospects, he contemplated no more than bartering East Galicia for a corresponding slice of Russian Poland.[7] Far from admitting the thought of a territorial sacrifice, or the defraying of war costs,[8] he did not seem to have dropped his designs on Warsaw, Radom, Petrokov, Ivangorod, Kielce, that is some of the richest and most important parts of the country. Since these were to be paid for by ceding a province whose Russophilism only made it a liability, and of which, moreover, the San and Dnyestr oil wells and the key

[1] Paléologue to Delcassé, 22 Nov. '14, on his conversation with Nicholas II. Deciphered in the Russian Foreign Ministry. *Internationale Beziehungen*, II. 6. II. No. 546, pp. 468–9. Benckendorff to Sazonov, 3 Dec. '14. *ibid*. II. 6. II. No. 594, p. 506. Aide-Memoire, Russian Foreign Ministry to Buchanan, 23 Jan. '15. *ibid*. II. 7. I. No. 67, pp. 61–2.
[2] 9 Jan. '15. Paléologue, I. 246.   [3] Salandra, 223. Redlich, II. 22.
[4] A report to this effect in the London *Economist* of 17 Sept. '14 had reached Vienna by 23 Oct. Conrad, V. 360.
[5] Czernin in conversation with Conrad, 26 Dec. '14. Conrad, V. 910. Redlich, II. 22.
[6] Conrad, V. 883.
[7] Conrad in conversation with Czernin, 26 Dec. '14. Conrad, V. 911. Also Redlich, II. 7.
[8] Conrad, V. 911. Among the Austrian bourgeoisie there was firm opposition to the 'absurd' idea of abandoning East Galicia—'the most important domestic market for our industries'. Redlich, II. 22,

fortress Przemysl were to be retained by Austria, all the advantages of such a deal would have accrued to the Dual Monarchy.

Small wonder, then, that the 'peril' of a separate Austro-Russian peace—as Avarna informed Rome—appeared unlikely and that, by February 11th 1915, Bollati diagnozed it as 'well-nigh impossible'.[1] And it must have been on the same grounds that Erzberger, at about the same time, assured his Government that 'there is no reason to fear that, if Germany exerted too much pressure on Vienna, the latter would conceive the design of a separate peace with Russia'.[2] Austria-Hungary had very largely herself to blame that Germany and Italy could, with impunity, hold her in diplomatic pincers.

2

BERLIN AND VIENNA

This is why it was safe for Bülow, right from their first interview, to urge upon Macchio the surrender of the Trentino. He also imparted (as the Austrian Envoy reported home) his views to the Italians. He mobilized his Turkish and Bulgarian colleagues against the Habsburg Envoy. He paraded a pessimism about the outlook, which caused panic among the Austrian colony in Rome and 'grave tension' between it and the Germans. He resorted to 'systematic intimidation . . . to make the Imperial and Royal Government tractable'.[3] He bombarded leading citizens of the Dual Monarchy with spates of private letters, directed in the *Victoria*, *Concordia* and other papers in his pay a campaign for a compromise by Francis Joseph, and announced in the *Frankfurter Zeitung* that the Reich would support border changes affecting the Trentino and Isonzo.[4] 'Bülow's conduct', a high Ballplatz official wrote to Macchio, 'is *incredible*'.[5] 'Bülow', so Burián decided, 'must be rendered altogether innocuous'.[6]

But the Prince was not, of course, just following his own inclinations. 'The Trentino policy,' according to an expert's testimonial, 'was . . . pursued by Berlin'.[7] The shipping magnate Ballin confided

[1] Avarna to Bollati, 20 Jan. '15. *Carteggio*, LXI. IV. 555. Bollati to Avarna, 27 Jan. and 11 Feb. '15. *Carteggio*, LXI. IV. 559-60. XLII. I. 69.
[2] Erzberger, 43.
[3] Macchio to Berchtold, 6 Jan. '15. Macchio, 73, 108-9. See also p. 296 above.
[4] Bollati to Avarna, 11 Feb. '15. *Carteggio*, LXII. I. 68. Tisza, I. 145. Macchio, 109.
[5] Forgách to Macchio, 21 Jan. '15. Macchio, 82. Italics in the original.
[6] Burián to Macchio, 1 Feb. '15. Macchio, 81.
[7] Count B. Wedel, 'Fürst Bülow und Österreich'. *Süddeutsche Monatshefte*, March 1931, p. 405. Wedel, at that time, was *Personalreferent* in the German Foreign Office. *ibid.* p. 398. Bollati confirms that it was the Wilhelmstrasse which was endeavouring to get Austria 'to give way', and that Zimmermann's views on this subject were supported in 'high places'. Bollati to Avarna, 12 Jan. '15. *Carteggio*, LXI. IV. 552; also 27 Jan. *ibid.* LXI. IV. 557.

## A DIPLOMATIC TRIANGLE: ROME-BERLIN-VIENNA  301

to the High Command that 'no pressure is ... too strong' to enforce Austrian compliance.[1] As one of the prime authors of Bülow's Roman mission, he wrote to the new tenant of Villa Malta: 'I ... intend to advise Zimmermann most urgently to get all energy used in Vienna'.[2] To reinforce the diplomatic dynamos brought into action by the Ambassador Tschirsky, a delegation from German Headquarters led by Prince Wedel was sent to persuade the Emperor to part with the Trentino. On January 16th 1915, barely two days after taking office, Burián, the Foreign Minister, was presented by Wedel with a 'suggestion ... expressing ... Bülow's attempts at ... mediation'.[3] Early in February, Matthias Erzberger, a prominent member of the Catholic Centre Party, appeared in Rome, seconding Bülow's efforts, hob-nobbing with a 'Germanophil deputy'[4] and other pro-Triplice politicians and, according to Berlin press reports, prepossessing 'the Vatican in Germany's favour'.[5] When, at that time, the Papal Nuncio intervened with Francis Joseph, rumour had it that this was due to Bülow's and Erzberger's machinations.[6] Nor could Austria-Hungary have been ignorant of the latter's argument that 'Vienna's resistance can be defeated all the more easily as it may be hoped that the Holy See will make its influence prevail'.[7]

The Emperor's blunt *non possumus* to Wedel and the Prelate, his threat to abdicate rather than relinquish his possession, showed the vexation mounting among the rulers of the Dual Monarchy.[8] They felt that, as Conrad put it, 'the Germans have had us' in military matters by failing to win in the West and letting Austria down in the East, and in diplomacy by misjudging Britain's position.[9] Tisza expressed the view that Berlin was partly responsible for Italy's attitude by provoking the English declaration of war'.[10] The Wilhelmstrasse, therefore, was 'in honour bound' to sustain the Ballplatz against the Consulta.[11] Instead, it grew ever more obvious that Bülow's 'behaviour incites and encourages the Italians'.[12] What made things worse was his collusion with Giolitti. Not even the most arrant

[1] Huldermann, 241.  [2] Ballin to Bülow. Bülow, III. 206.
[3] Burián, 30, 33, 35. Also Macchio, 83.  [4] Erzberger, 41.
[5] Salandra, 206, quoting Bollati.  [6] Salandra, 232. Cf. Bülow, III. 203–4.
[7] Erzberger to his Government. Erzberger, 43. Also Wedel, 'Fürst Bülow und Österreich'. *Süddeutsche Monatshefte*, 1931, p. 406. Bülow, III. 202–4. Salandra, 207. See also p. 376 below.
[8] Avarna to Bollati, 5 Feb. '15. *Carteggio*, LXI. IV. 562; also 20 Jan. *ibid.* LXI. IV. 554–5. Bollati to Avarna, 11 Feb. *ibid.* LXII. I. 67. Salandra, 232. Burián, 30. Redlich, II. 20.
[9] Conrad to Berchtold, 30 Dec. '14. Conrad, V. 957.
[10] Tisza to Conrad, 10 Aug. '14. Conrad, IV. 199. Also Tisza, I. 48. In Hoyos's opinion, Germany's clash with Great Britain 'shook all the premises of the [Triple] Alliance' in Rome. Hoyos, 54–5; also 29–30.
[11] Tisza to Burián, 15 Jan. '15. Tisza, I. 149. See also Tisza to Berchtold, 10 Aug. '14. Tisza, I. 48.
[12] Tisza to Berchtold, 6 Jan. '15. Tisza. I. 145.

imperialists North of the frontier could expect the Habsburg Empire to submit to the *sacro egoismo*. But it was different with the *parecchio* appeal. As Hoyos was to write later, Vienna's 'position vis-à-vis the German Government would have been far stronger if it had emerged ... that Italy was not prepared to commit herself ... even to maintaining neutrality until the end of the War'.[1] Unfortunately, this was just what the Liberal leader was offering to do, and a high official of the Austrian Foreign Ministry commented glumly on 'this notable sally by Giolitti, who may well before long overthrow Salandra .... Giolitti ... will probably be less ready than ... Salandra to decide on *war*. But the diplomatic blackmail will probably be still more intensified, and Giolitti and Bülow, who understand one another very well, will work hand in glove over it'.[2]

Hence, it was certainly with an eye on Germany no less than Italy that Conrad pronounced himself 'against any voluntary cessions'.[3] The Hungarian Premier instructed Burián that, while Sonnino was to be fobbed off with 'general terms', 'the Germans ... must be told roundly the handing over of our own territory is not a matter for discussion'.[4] The Ballplatz was invited to 'speak ... very seriously ... in Berlin ... about Bülow's activity'.[5] 'Indeed, even more important than our [diplomatic] skill [in Rome] is German support, and the most important part of our action is to convince the German political leaders of this in the quickest and most emphatic manner'.[6]

The new Foreign Minister responded with such alacrity to these injunctions that one of his intimates informed Macchio: 'A keener wind will blow now, especially ... in the Trentino affair! ... Burián is going to the German High Command. He wants to speak to the Germans very clearly and firmly'.[7] According to a Ballplatz dispatch, 'he hoped to *force* Bülow and the Germans to a complete change of front'.[8] He saw the Kaiser, the Chancellor, the Secretary of State and the Chief of Staff on January 23rd 1915. 'The Italian question', he recollected later, 'was the central point both of political and military interest. ... Exhaustive conversations ... gave me the opportunity of countering their constantly reiterated suggestion that Italian neutrality should be secured by territorial concessions. ...'[9]

[1] Hoyos, 70.
[2] Merey to Macchio, 1 Feb. '15. Macchio, 96–7. Italics in the original.
[3] Conrad to Tisza, 19 Jan. '15. Tisza, I. 160.
[4] Tisza to Burián, 5 Jan. '15. Tisza, I. 141.
[5] Tisza to the Ballhaus, 5 Jan. '15. Tisza, I. 145. Also Tisza to Conrad, 16 Jan. Tisza, I. 156.
[6] Tisza to Burián, 15 Jan. '15. Tisza, I. 149.
[7] Forgách to Macchio, 21 Jan. '15. Macchio, 82.
[8] The Ballhaus to Macchio, 24 Feb. '15. Macchio, 99. Italics in the original.
[9] Burián, 36.

As Macchio was informed, Burián 'spent hours trying to impress the gentlemen with his views . . . . neither convinced the other on the issue of compensation'. But 'they promised to put a stop to Bülow's doings'.[1]

What were the arguments he marshalled against the Germans? Did he echo Tisza's warning about 'the immeasurable damage they would cause to their own interests' unless they curbed Italy's greed?[2] Did he repeat Conrad's earlier retort that they should point the way by making concessions to France?[3] He must have made much of the big offensive beginning in the last week of January for the reconquest of Galicia. All Vienna, like Conrad, expected that it would have 'a decisive bearing on the entire situation'.[4] There was no denying that a resounding victory, rather than sacrifices or 'sweet reasoning', would contain the 'open robber policy' of the Consulta, and that, until then, common sense dictated a waiting attitude.[5] Burián will surely also have contended, as he did in writing afterwards, that 'there was no danger in delay'. Italy 'was only just at the beginning of her game'.[6] She was still too far from agreement with the Entente to take up arms. Even if she wished to do so, her fighting machine was unready. The Ballplatz knew from Conrad that she had timed her war preparations for March 1st.[7] So there need be no 'hasty surrender of things the weight and value of which will be augmented by the delay in granting them'. It was never too late for a climb-down as 'the price of our defeat'. At all events, the Dual Monarchy had at least a month to win a much-needed victory.[8] Soon after his encounter with the Germans, Burián expressed the hope 'that, in the end, we shall get over this difficult episode of *brigantaggio* with trifling loss'.[9]

[1] Merey to Macchio, 1 Feb. '15. Macchio, 96. Burián to Macchio, 1 Feb. '15: 'Bülow is no longer authorized to suggest to the Italians that Germany counsels a cession of Austro-Hungarian territory'. Macchio, 81. The Kaiser's claim that Burián had not pleaded with him against the surrender of the Trentino is hardly credible. There is, moreover, what seems to be a deliberate ambiguity in his statement which refers merely to Burián's 'Antrittsbesuch', that is the first visit paid to him by the new Austro-Hungarian Foreign Minister. See Helfferich, II. 68.
[2] Tisza to Berchtold and Burián, 6 Jan. '15. Tisza, I. 146.
[3] Conrad to Tisza, 19 Jan. '15. Tisza, I. 161.
[4] Conrad to Tisza, 19 Jan. '15. Tisza, I. 159. Also Hindenburg, 135. Conrad, V. 910. Macchio, 81-2. Hoyos, 69-70. Andrassy, 128.
[5] Forgách to Macchio, 21 Jan. '15. Macchio, 82. Conrad to Tisza, 19 Jan. Tisza, I. 159.
[6] Burián, 44, 28.
[7] Conrad to Berchtold, 21 Dec. '14. Conrad, V. 852. Burián to Tisza, probably 5 Jan. '15. Tisza, I. 142. Also Burián, 44. Conrad, V. 913. Macchio, 71.
[8] Burián to Tisza, probably 5 Jan. '15. Tisza, I. 143. Conrad to Tisza, 19 Jan. '15. Tisza, I. 159.
[9] Burián to Macchio, 1 Feb. '15. Macchio, 81. The Austro-Hungarian Crown Prince, during this visit to German Headquarters, informed the Kaiser of Francis Joseph's reluctance to satisfy Italy's pretensions. Helfferich, II. 68. Redlich, II. 12.

## 3
### VIENNA AND ROME

Meanwhile, having (as he believed) held Berlin at bay, he played for time in Rome. 'We shall not sever the thread, but seek to protract the negotiations, without engaging ourselves'.[1] His first task was to reply to the Italian communication of January 12th 1915.[2] But his immediate concern was to exclude Bülow from the ensuing parleys. Macchio was instructed to refrain from supporting his German colleague, to do no more than 'observe and listen' and—by outshining the Prince in dinner attendances and invitations—to manifest Austria-Hungary's self-confidence and loyalty.[3] The talks themselves were concentrated in Vienna.[4]

On January 17th 1915, Burián explained to the Ambassador Avarna that, whereas 'Italy had a preference for securing a portion of the territory of the [Dual] Monarchy . . . we suggested that the compensation should be found elsewhere'.[5] This obvious reference to Valona and the Dodecanese—'both already in our power, though we had not yet established our legal title to them'[6]—was scorned by the Consulta. Accompanied as it was by hostile rumblings in the Empire—officers at their club in Pola were drinking to the earthquake in the Abruzzi[7]—it was clearly a rejection of the main demand.[8] On January 28th, therefore, Avarna was told to warn Burián, in effect, 'that Italy would consider only territorial concessions from Austria-Hungary's possessions, and that nothing else could be discussed'.[9] And on February 1st, Sonnino said to Bülow that, unless Vienna complied, he might ask for 'the Trentino, Trieste, Istria, or any other territory . . . . further delay could only result in increased demands.'[10]

The case was unique in diplomatic annals. An Ally repudiating a compact, yet claiming its benefits. Extortions, not (as was usual in imperialist practice) at the expense of an extraneous party, but of the

[1] Tisza to Conrad, 16 Jan. '15. Tisza, I. 154. Also Tisza to Burián, 15 Jan. Tisza, I. 149. Macchio, 84, 96. Burián, 45. Musulin, 254.
[2] See p. 243 above.
[3] Macchio, 92; also 61–3. Burián to Macchio, 14 Jan. '15. Salandra, 227. Tisza, I. 145.
[4] Forgách to Macchio, 21 Jan. '15. Macchio, 82, 84. Tisza to the Ballhaus, 5 Jan. '15. Tisza, I. 144. Salandra, 231.
[5] Burián, 44 and 42. The quotation is from Burián's book. Also Tisza, I. 161.
[6] Salandra, 220; also 228. Tisza, I. 160.
[7] Salandra, 187.
[8] Avarna to Bollati, 20 Jan. '15. *Carteggio*, LXI. IV. 554. Bollati to Avarna, 27 Jan. *Carteggio*, LXI. IV. 556–7; also 561. Salandra, 228–9.
[9] Burián, 44. Also Salandra, 233.
[10] Sonnino to Bollati, 2 Feb. '15. *The Italian Green Book*, No. 17, p. 1236. Burián, 29, 30. Macchio, 83. *Carteggio*, LXI. IV. 558.

partner to the Treaty which, as Burián expostulated, was 'directed towards the maintenance of the territorial integrity of the Allies'. A request for 'definite compensation in advance for the bare possibility of future gains of ours'[1] which, at the time at least, were quite uncertain. It was no longer any use to say, as Tisza did to the Italian Consul-General in Budapest: 'If Italy's friends gain advantages, they will be able to contrive that she shall have a share'.[2] It became pointless 'to caution them very seriously' that it was 'a vital interest' for the Italians 'to find in Austria-Hungary a real backing for their Mediterranean policy', and that 'the Trentino would not outweigh the evil consequences of its enforced surrender; even if they achieved their present aim, they would thereby compromise the future benefits ... of our friendship'.[3] It was no longer the hour for supercilious or patronizing attitudes.[4] The enormity of the exaction called for a display of energy. On February 9th, Avarna was notified that, under the much-quoted Article VII of the Triplice, the Italian occupation of the Dodecanese in 1912 and of Valona in December 1914 entitled the Danubian Empire to a *quid pro quo*. This, Burián averred, should have been the subject of a preliminary agreement. Spurred by his recent 'victory' over the Germans, he demanded that his 'obvious counter-claim' should be discussed simultaneously with Sonnino's claim, 'and thus everything be settled at once'.[5]

But the diversion was too clever to succeed. Designed to draw out and bedevil the proceedings, it only provoked the Consulta which regarded 'any prolonged conversations with Vienna as gravely damaging to our interests'.[6] Already the British and French squadrons were steaming towards the Dardanelles,[7] leaving Sonnino dancing with impatience lest Italy should miss the boat. He saw, on the other hand, Austria-Hungary's bargaining position weakened by the plodding steps of her Army in Galicia.[8] He was encouraged by the impression that, as Macchio complained, 'the Italians have Germany on their side, and only us to deal with, which ... must make them still more exacting'.[9] And so, 'not having [as Burián has emphasized] any reasonable arguments against our similar claims

---

[1] Burián, 43, 45.      [2] 5 Jan. '15. Tisza, I. 139.
[3] Tisza's instructions to Burián, 15 Jan. '15. Tisza, I. 148–9.
[4] On 12 Jan. '15, Bollati wrote to Avarna that, two days previously, he had had a conversation on the Trentino with the Austro-Hungarian Ambassador in Berlin, who at once started to 'monter sur ses grands chevaux' (*sic*). *Carteggio*, LXI. IV. 552.
[5] Burián, 45. Bollati to Avarna, 11 Feb. '15. *Carteggio*, LXII. I. 66. Macchio, 96. Salandra, 233.
[6] Bollati to Avarna, 12 Jan. '15. *Carteggio*, LXI. IV. 553.
[7] See p. 92 above.      [8] Macchio, 98. Talerski, 45.
[9] Macchio to Berchtold, 6 Jan. '15. Macchio, 73. Also Andrassy, 128.

under Article VII',[1] the Italians, on February 15th, opened this broadside against the Ballplatz:

'Two months and more have passed since we put to the Austro-Hungarian Government the question of Article VII . . . . we have never succeeded in getting an answer, not even to the first important question: "Would the Imperial and Royal Government agree to accept a discussion on the basis of a cession of territory at present in the possession of Austria-Hungary?" Instead, while on one hand they are proposing new questions and arguments . . . with the obvious intention of avoiding every discussion of the subject . . . on the other they are preparing new military measures in the Balkans. Taking this consistently dilatory attitude into consideration, we can no longer cherish any illusions as to the practical outcome of the negotiations. Therefore, the Royal Government is obliged, in order to safeguard its own dignity, to withdraw all proposals . . . for discussion, and to entrench itself behind the simple wording of Article VII, declaring that it considers any military operations whatever that Austria-Hungary may undertake in the Balkans . . . to be an infringement of the Article in question unless so undertaken by a preliminary agreement as required by Article VII . . . . if the Austro-Hungarian Monarchy shows no desire to observe the Pact, serious consequences may ensue'.[2]

Burián—surprised but outwardly calm as ever[3]—consented to honour the ill-starred Article as soon as the Balkan campaign was reopened. But, for the moment, he would make no *accord préalable* on any military operations (except for their 'preliminary stages'), since 'their results could not be measured beforehand, nor could an "adequate" compensation be arrived at'.[4] Concurring that negotiations on the subject could be started, he did not think they need be completed before Austria-Hungary was allowed to move.[5] Sonnino, doubtless annoyed by such immaculate logic, retorted on February 22nd with a veto on any Habsburg offensive against Serbia or Montenegro, unless Italy's recompense was firmly agreed upon in advance. That deal must not merely be drawn up, but clinched. A deviation from this principle by Vienna would be regarded in Rome as a breach of the Alliance and enable the Italians to 'hold ourselves fully justified in resuming our liberty of action for the protection of our interests'.[6]

This effort to place on the Dual Monarchy the onus of wrecking the Triplice seems to have irked Berlin. It was one thing for the Wilhelmstrasse to weaken and hamstring its Danubian Ally, it was

[1] Burián, 45–6.
[2] Salandra, 233–4. *Carteggio*, LXII. I. 70. Burián, 46. Macchio, 98.
[3] Avarna to Bollati, 19 Feb. '15. *Carteggio*, LXII. I. 70.
[4] Burián, 46.
[5] Salandra, 235. Avarna to Bollati, 19 Feb. '15. *Carteggio*, LXII. I. 72.
[6] Salandra, 235. Burián, 46–7.

another to let Italy get out of control. Bülow had all along combined his sponsorship of the Trentino cession with suave pressure intended to restrain the Consulta's worst excesses.[1] That he should have chosen this sultry period in the Austro-Italian exchanges (of which he was kept aware) to broach to Sonnino an alternative compensation in Albania or elswhere[2], could easily have implied that, in certain circumstances, German support of the Irredenta's aspirations might lapse. The Under-Secretary Zimmermann's proposal to Bollati for a three-Power meeting in Berlin was so obvious a German bid to act as 'intermediary and protector',[3] that it was opposed not only by Burián but also, and even more hotly, by the Italian partner. When the Ambassador threatened the Foreign Minister von Jagow with the 'grave complications' likely to flow from Viennese procrastinations, the answer was 'vogue la galère!'[4] The warning was underlined by an article in the *Kölnische Zeitung* openly accusing Italy of war-like intentions against her Allies.[5] Amidst these trends and portents, the parleys were entering the realm of the ludicrous, where notions such as 'a graduated series of hypotheses, a sort of sliding scale'[6] of benefits competed feebly with a staggering geometrical progression of Italian demands. For more reasons than one it was advisable for Sonnino to cut the Gordian knot. On March 4th 1915, he wired to Vienna that 'there is nothing to be hoped for in prolonging the discussions with Baron Burián'. And, declining to 'admit any discussions as to compensation from us for the occupation of the Dodecanese and Valona', he presented, virtually on a take-it-or-leave-it basis, the following 'fixed points':

'1. That no military action by Austria-Hungary in the Balkans ought to be started before an agreement has been arrived at as to compensation....

2. That any infringement of the above will be considered by us as an open violation of the Treaty, justifying Italy in resuming her full liberty of action....

3. That no proposal . . . of compensation can lead to an agreement unless it provides for the cession of territory in the possession of Austria-Hungary.

4. That . . . we claim compensation through the very fact of the initiation of military action by Austria-Hungary in the Balkans, independently of any results arising from such action; without prejudice, however, to our right to claim further compensation . . . in proportion to the advantages which Austria-Hungary may actually succeed in obtaining.

[1] See p. 287 above. Also Macchio, 83.    [2] Salandra, 235.    [3] Salandra, 229.
[4] 'It is too late to do anything about it'. Bollati to Avarna, 27 Feb. '15. *Carteggio*, LXII. I. 73. Salandra, 229.
[5] 26 Feb. '15. *Carteggio*, LXII. I. 73. The *Kölnische Zeitung* was generally used by the German Foreign Office to send up diplomatic trial balloons.
[6] Salandra, 236. Burián, 47.

5. That this fixed quota of compensation, due upon the initiation of military action, independent of results, should, instead of being kept secret, be carried into effect by the immediate transfer of the ceded territories and their immediate occupation by Italy'.[1]

One might wonder how much heart-burning this communication caused in Vienna. Since the beginning of 1915, Macchio had been reporting a steady drop in Austria-Hungary's political stock in Rome. As early as January 6th, he cautioned his rulers not to wait 'until . . . the right moment for safeguarding ourselves in this direction had irrevocably passed'.[2] As far back as the preceding December, he realized that talks 'on the basis of our vague Albanian concessions had become an impossibility'.[3] The Austro-Hungarians in January, as he admitted later, 'should have made the appearance of entering into [Italy's] blackmailing Note . . . to the extent of authorizing me to accept, *in principle*, the cession of our own territory as a basis of negotiations, instead of maintaining the rigidly negative attitude represented by Tisza and Burián'. But the latter, despite all evidence to the contrary, persisted in his 'imperturbable optimism'.[4] Basing his whole diplomatic strategy on the brittle premise of 'decisive military successes and a complete change of front on the part of . . . the Germans', he was 'so convinced of the correctness of his arguments and theories' that, according to a dejected letter from the Ballplatz, he was 'losing the sense of reality'. The result was that Burián, 'in six weeks has brought matters to such a pass that the . . . thread has snapped, and the Italians *au fond* have presented us with a kind of ultimatum'.[5] By mid-February a high Viennese Foreign Ministry official made this reference to his Chief: 'So far he has been pettifogging, but now he must find practical . . . ways' of coping with Sonnino.[6] Yet, as another colleague wrote to Macchio, 'Burián does not dream of handing over the Trentino even in the event of a direct threat of Italian aggression'.[7] Nothing shows up more starkly the Bourbon blindness of this servant of lost causes than his remark that 'we shall . . ."shoot at the Italians"'.[7]

This makes it doubtful whether Vienna's obduracy would have been shaken by Sonnino's cutting short the talks, if his latest Note had not been synchronized with other hammer-blows. The winter war had stained the mountains crimson. Decimated by fighting, frostbite and fatigue, the Habsburg armies and the reinforcements at

[1] Salandra, 237. *Carteggio*, LXII. I. 80–1.
[2] Macchio to Berchtold, 6 Jan. '15. Macchio, 74–5, 99.
[3] Macchio, 71.   [4] Macchio, 71, 81, 83. Italics in the original.
[5] The Ballhaus to Macchio, received 24 Feb. '15. Macchio, 99. Italics in the original.
[6] Forgách to Macchio. Macchio, 98.
[7] Merey to Macchio, 16 Feb. '15. Macchio, 97.

long last obtained from Hindenburg were unable to break what the latter has called 'the fearful and continuous tension ... in the Carpathians'.¹ The Russians were battling for the ridges, tightening their ring around the key fortress of Przemysl, and driving towards the Hungarian plain.² In this situation, Rumania had to be watched with lynx-eyed attention. Since August 1914, the Ballplatz had been aware of Italy's efforts to deter her from joining the Central Powers.³ On September 23rd, Rome and Bucharest signed a Convention providing for consultation and common action in the event of abandoning neutrality.⁴ Vienna must at least have had an inkling of this partnership for, in December, Conrad mentioned it to Berchtold.⁵ Early in February 1915, Tisza and Burián learned from intercepted documents of the conclusion of a fresh Italo-Rumanian Treaty which, in the former's words, 'could easily constitute the starting point for further aggressive arrangements'.⁶ In the beginning of March, it was revealed from the same source that the Consulta, upon inquiry, had been informed of the new friend's readiness for a joint attack on Austria-Hungary at the latest by the end of the next month.⁷ On March 3rd, the Magyar Premier noted the 'formidable danger of an agreement between Italy, Rumania and Russia',⁸ and he entreated the Foreign Minister: 'For heaven's sake, be on your guard, and do not, on any account, let the two brigands link up for robbery in common'.⁹

Tisza's descent from arrogance to anguish was accelerated by the dread of disaster in the Dardanelles. On March 5th and 6th 1915, came the news (via Berlin) of the utter precariousness of Turkey's defences. Constantinople seemed bound to fall. The Entente would resume its Black Sea-Mediterranean communications, chase Germany from the Near East¹⁰ and, with the bait of Ottoman spoils, win the adherence of the Balkans. Already Bulgaria seemed to be swerving to the West, Rumania became intransigent, and the Athens press, heralding the passage of the Anglo-French fleets through the Straits, announced that Greece would support them.¹¹ The only means of

¹ Hindenburg, 139.
² Hindenburg, 138–9. Ludendorff, I. 113–4, 120, 129, 138. Talenski, 44–5. *Carteggio*, LXII. I. 79. Macchio, 84. Tisza, I. 170.
³ Berchtold to Pallavicini, 27 Aug. '14. Deciphered in the Russian Foreign Ministry. *Internationale Beziehungen*, II. 6. I. No. 169, p. 126.
⁴ *Carteggio*, LXI. IV. 558. Poincaré, V. 346.
⁵ Conrad to Berchtold, 21 Dec. '14. Conrad, V. 852.
⁶ Tisza to Burián, 7 Feb. '15. Burián to Tisza, 12 Feb. '15. Tisza, I. 166–7, 264. The Treaty was concluded on 6 Feb. '15. *Carteggio*, LXI. IV. 558.
⁷ Merey to Macchio, 2 March '15. Macchio, 100.    ⁸ Tisza, I. 170.
⁹ Tisza to Burián, 3 March '15. Tisza, I. 171. Also Macchio, 101.
¹⁰ See p. 85 above.
¹¹ T. N. Page to the U.S. Secretary of State, 17 March '15. *The Lansing Papers*, I. 720.

brightening the prospects of the Central coalition was to pour arms and munitions into the Golden Horn. This required a speedy restoration of the Orient Express, which was impossible without an immediate offensive against Serbia. Since Italy, with her pretensions in Anatolia, had every incentive to prevent any aid reaching the Sultan, such an offensive could only precipitate her desertion. The mere fact of the Dardanelles expedition had a magnetic effect in Rome. So it was vital to keep the Consulta negotiating. As Bethmann-Hollweg warned the Austro-Hungarian Ambassador on March 5th, it was now zero hour for the concession demanded by Sonnino.[1]

The Chancellor's was but the final shot in a continuous barrage from Berlin. The assurances Burián had—or believed himself to have—received from his main Allies, were illusory.[2] Even while threatening Italy, through Bülow, that they would no longer champion her interests against the Ballplatz, the Germans continued to press the latter to give up the Trentino. Even while the *Kölnische Zeitung* asked in so many words whether Italy wanted war, the *Frankfurter Zeitung* clamoured for Burián to accept the principle of sacrificing Habsburg property. Some papers laboured this theme so hard that Austria was forced to remonstrate.[3] From Ludendorff's subsequent complaint: 'Had the Austro-Hungarian Army accomplished even half of what could properly have been expected . . . German troops need not have been brought in such masses to reinforce their fronts',[4] it may be presumed that military superiority was exploited for diplomatic blackmail. Recourse was had to confidential go-betweens ranging from the shipping magnate Ballin, who had 'old-established [business] relations with Vienna'[5], to Frau Schratt, the aged actress to whom the Emperor was still attached.[6] Some of the strongest opposition came from Sieghart, the Governor of the Bodenkreditanstalt, who was described as 'a kind of co-regent' of Francis Joseph, and whom Ballin—acting, it was said, also for the Deutsche Bank—had specially to appease.[7] 'Not knowing what Saint to turn to, they thought of the Pope' who 'showed great alacrity'.[8] The German Catholic Deputy Erzberger was sent to

[1] Macchio, 101-2. Also Salandra, 238. Poincaré, VI. 108. Tisza, I. 171. *Carteggio*, LXII. I. 76.
[2] Merey to Macchio, 1 Feb. '15. Macchio, 96.
[3] Krupenski to Sazonov, 3 March '15. Adamov, I. No. 107, p. 308. Bollati to Avarna, 27 Jan., 27 Feb. and 9 March '15. *Carteggio*, LXI. IV. 557. LXII. I. 74, 79. Burián, 35, 59. Erzberger, 43-4. Hoyos, 68. Tirpitz, 438. Helfferich, II. 68.
[4] Ludendorff, I. 116.
[5] Huldermann, 242; also 243. Ballin saw the Austrian Premier on 8 March '15. Redlich, II. 30.
[6] Avarna to Bollati, 7 March '15. *Carteggio*, LXII. I. 76.
[7] Redlich, II. 23, 390.
[8] Princess Radziwill from Berlin to J. Cambon, 28 March '15. Tabouis, 289-90, Redlich, II. 23.

the Danube in order, as he claims, 'to defeat the opposition of the [governing] Christian-Social Party'.¹

Erzberger was the author of the scheme whereby Germany, 'in exchange for the concessions to be made to Italy' by Austria-Hungary, would grant the latter the benefits of navigation on the Elbe free of dues, and cede her the Polish coal-basin of Sosnowice.² Although evidence of a formal proposal in that sense having been made to Vienna is lacking, it is very likely that both the strength of the Habsburg resistance and the gravity of the Constantinople crisis constrained the Wilhelmstrasse to lessen the sacrifice³ which the Dual Monarchy was expected to bear. In fact, Erzberger asserts that 'the compensation that I had advised Germany should make finally broke the ice'.⁴ On March 8th 1915, the Crown Council, attended by Francis Joseph, Tisza and Conrad, decided to bow to the force of circumstances and German blandishments. And on the 9th, Burián informed the Ambassador Avarna that he accepted Italy's demand to discuss compensation on the basis of surrendering Austrian territory.⁵

This might have been a step forward, if Sonnino had not five days previously entered into formal negotiations with the other camp.⁶

---

[1] Erzberger, 44; also 139-40. *Carteggio*, LXII. I. 76. Macchio, 112.

[2] Erzberger, 43. Tisza, L 252. Avarna, writing to Bollati, 13 March '15 (*Carteggio*, LXII. I. 84), mentions a possible cession of a part of Prussian Silesia to Austria-Hungary. Bollati refers to continuous talk in Berlin of German territorial cessions to Austria-Hungary, in particular that of Berchtesgaden by Bavaria, who would be indemnified by a portion of Alsace. Bollati to Avarna, 14 April '15. *Carteggio*, LXII. III. 381.

[3] See Avarna to Bollati, 7 March '15. *Carteggio*, LXII. I. 76. Macchio, 112. Bollati to Avarna, 24 March '15. *Carteggio*, LXII. I. 85.

[4] Erzberger, 44. Bollati confirms that the Austro-Hungarian decision was taken under the impetus of the Reich. See Bollati to Avarna, 9 March '15. *Carteggio*, LXII. I. 79. Also Macchio, 102.

[5] Burián, 50-1. *Carteggio*, LXII. I. 77. Salandra, 239. Macchio, 102-3, 112.

[6] Macchio, 130-1.

CHAPTER XXII

# The Secret Treaty of London

## 1
### ITALY AND TURKEY

THE Entente, since December 1914, had kept an eye on the Consulta. In December, as Italy's soundings in London and Paris had been of no avail, Salandra proclaimed 'a watchful and active neutrality'[1] —'watchful [the Foreign Minister enlightened the Russian Envoy] regarding our interests . . . and active in that we are arming to be ready for all eventualities'. In December, too, Bülow appeared in Rome, and Krupenski, having suggested that the Prince's purpose was to tie Italy's hands, was told by Sonnino: 'Rome is not Constantinople . . . we . . . shall preserve full freedom of action'.[2]

This self-assurance came from a careful survey of the tortured European scene. After six months of fighting, everyone was agreed, as the Ambassador Tittoni reported from France, 'that an almost perfect equilibrium has been established by the belligerent forces on the two main fronts . . . . So they are calling for a new intervention against Germany and Austria to end the War. . . .'[3] 'Hence', as Salandra was to say later, 'on all sides, the anxious and sometimes fantastic search for new political combinations and new military projects. . . .' And 'hence the growing importance of the neutrals, among whom, in Europe, Italy ranked first'.[4] Her Representative in Bucharest imparted to his Russian colleague what the latter defined as the 'pretty cynical view' that, since the Italian Alliance would tilt the balance in favour of either party, it could be sold 'at the highest possible price'.[5] As late as February 6th 1915, Tittoni, according to Poincaré's Diary, still wore his 'enigmatic smile'.[6]

In no time, however, the aspect of the Consulta darkened. Sonnino had cause to regret his reference to Constantinople, for he discovered that sovereign Italy—although more mistress of her fate, of course, than semi-colonial Turkey—was nevertheless tossed by the currents of imperialism and torn, sooner than she could have wished,

---
[1] In the Chamber, 3 Dec. '14. Salandra, 173. *Das Zaristische Russland*, p. 287.
[2] Krupenski to Sazonov, 8 Dec. '14. *Das Zaristische Russland*, pp. 284-5.
[3] Salandra, 181-2.   [4] Salandra, 182 and 180.
[5] Poklevski to Sazonov, 15 Jan. '15. *Internationale Beziehungen*, II. 7. I. No. 14, p. 15.
[6] Poincaré, VI. 48.

from her waiting and weighing attitude. On February 9th, Sazonov in the Duma heralded Russia's approaching access to the open sea, and the leader of the bourgeois Liberals, Milyukov, among other deputies, demanded 'the acquisition' of the Ottoman capital and the Straits.[1] A few days later, the Anglo-French fleets were on the way to the Dardanelles. It was not long before the Greek Minister in Petrograd wired that the Ambassador Carlotti 'told me very categorically . . . the settlement of the question of Constantinople and the Narrows by the Entente alone would signify the exclusive predominance of these three Powers in the basin of the Eastern Mediterranean, which was by no means in accordance with Italy's interests'.[2]

The point is that, as far back as 1895, Rome had begun to apply for a portion of the Sultan's legacy.[3] She snatched Libya from his grasp in 1911-12. By 1914, a foothold was gained (by agreement with Britain) in South Anatolia,[4] and a Convention signed by the Italian Commercial, Industrial and Financial Corporation with the British-owned Ottoman Railway Company Smyrna-Aidin about their respective lines in Asia Minor.[5] The expansion of Italian business in Turkey was exemplified by the ramifications of the Società Commerciale d'Oriente.[6] And the seizure, in the Libyan War, of the Dodecanese and the Sporades islands, including Rhodes, was clearly a step towards annexations on the nearby mainland. Foiled in Tunis, and having to build on sand in Libya, the colonial school in Italy craved for the fabulous fertility and untapped wealth of Asia Minor. Therefore, 'if the whole Turkish Empire [in Churchill's words] was to be cast on to the board . . . with all its rich provinces and immense Italian interests perhaps an easy prey, could Italy afford to remain indifferent?'[7] The Russian Ambassador in Rome noted a growing fear lest she should be omitted from the share-out after the liquidation of that vast estate.[8] If, furthermore, Greece or Bulgaria joined in the scramble for Turkish spoils, they would acquire

---

[1] See p. 91 above.
[2] Dragoumis to Zaimis, 7 March '15. Deciphered in the Russian Foreign Ministry. *Internationale Beziehungen*, II. 7. I. No. 328, p. 300. Carlotti made the same statement to the Rumanian Minister. Diamandi to Porumbaru, 6 March '15. Deciphered in the Russian Foreign Ministry. Adamov, I. No. 182, p. 372. Also Avarna to Bollati, 7 March '15. *Carteggio*, LXII. I. 78.
[3] Yerusalimski, 157.
[4] March '14. Conrad, III. 570.
[5] May '14 Aldrovandi Marescotti, 9. *Internationale Beziehungen*, II. 7. II. No. 612, p. 606, and *ibid.* footnote 1.
[6] Adamov, II. p. 353. Also Albrecht-Carrié, 206; and pp. 146-7 above.
[7] Churchill, *1915*, p. 112. The same view was expressed by Imperiali to San Giuliano, 5 Sept. '14. *Documenti Diplomatici*, 5. I. No. 592, p. 341.
[8] Krupenski to Sazonov, 3 March '15. Adamov, I. No. 107, p. 309.

a position strong enough to undo or curtail Italy's Balkan ambitions. Last but not least, if Russia gained egress through the Straits, Slav pressure would make itself felt in the Eastern Mediterranean and the Adriatic.[1] To balance this triple danger, it was imperative to share with the Entente in the solution of the Oriental problems, and it was 'well understood in Rome that, short of intervention, Italy would get nothing'.[2]

Yet while, as Churchill has put it, 'the Dardanelles and Turkey were the real "motor muscles" of Italian resolve',[3] they were not its main objectives. Though, without the shock of the campaign for Constantinople, Salandra and Sonnino would have lingered on in the diplomatic alleys and by-ways—once they were pushed on to the highroad of war, they had to remember that Adalia and the Dodecanese were only a 'supplementary satisfaction'.[4] Had they contented themselves with this, it would have been easy to gain admission into the Entente. But they were still hampered by desires affecting at least two of their prospective Allies.

2

ITALY TRIES TO DIVIDE FRANCE AND RUSSIA

The questions Sabini had raised in Paris were further than ever from solution, and in the Eastern Adriatic fresh obstacles were erected by Russia. Back in November 1914, Sazonov had proposed to Britain and France that Albania should be partitioned between Serbia and Greece.[5] Grey declined the suggestion as certain to antagonize Rome.[6] In fact, the Ambassador Carlotti reminded Sazonov more than once that substantial Italian interests were at stake in Albania. The Foreign Minister, far from impressed, said that, if the Serbs obtained a portion of the latter, this would not reduce their rights to Dalmatian territory. Carlotti brought up the mainly Moslem-inhabited area of Albania which tended towards

[1] Avarna to Bollati, 7 March '15. *Carteggio*, LXII. I. 78. Macchio, 101.
[2] The Bulgarian Minister in London, Khadzhimishev (quoting Lloyd George), to Radoslavov, 4 March '15. Adamov, II. No. 183, p. 258. Also Krupenski to Sazonov, 3 and 10 March. *ibid.* I. NN 107, 115, pp. 309, 315. Diamandi (quoting Carlotti) to Porumbaru, 7 March. *ibid.* I. No. 183, p. 373. Dragoumis (quoting Carlotti) to Zaimis, 7 March. *Internationale Beziehungen*, II. 7. I. No. 328, p. 300. All these telegrams have been deciphered in the Russian Foreign Ministry.
[3] Churchill, *1915*, p. 111. Also Rodd, III. 228.
[4] Salandra to the King, 30 Sept. '14. Salandra, 135. San Giuliano to Imperiali, 16 Sept. '14: 'Italy's main interest... is in the Adriatic'. *Documenti Diplomatici*, 5. I. No. 703, p. 412.
[5] Sazonov to Benckendorff and Izvolski, 27 Nov. '14. *Internationale Beziehungen*, II. 6. II. No. 561, p. 481.
[6] Aide-Memoire, British Embassy in Petrograd, to Sazonov, 3 Dec. '14. *Internationale Beziehungen*, II. 6. II. No. 590, p. 503.

Valona. Sazonov stated 'firmly' that, even if that port were given to Italy, she could not expect an important hinterland to be added to it. 'Russia, at any rate, would never recognize a far-reaching seizure of Albania by Italy ... not even in the form of an Italian protectorate'.[1]

It was in defiance of this ruling that the Italians, having occupied Valona late in December 1914,[2] spread into its environs and, exploiting the turmoil in the country, prepared to lay hands on Durazzo.[3] Sazonov, meanwhile, not only persisted with his partition plan[4] which was to bar the march of Rome; but, on hearing from Carlotti that the Consulta 'had found itself forced to send a warship to Durazzo' for the relief of foreign residents, he replied: 'I sympathize fully with the love of humanity which induces the Italian Government to assist the departure of the Europeans. ... However, I cannot in any circumstances agree to a landing of Italian troops, for it could later on compel the Italians to entrench themselves more permanently in that district'.[5] And his opposition was strong enough to make them desist.[6]

By a coincidence so curious that it looked like design, the prominent Italian financier Volpi was busying himself in Paris about that time. Allegedly, he was concerned with private business matters, including the Heraclea mines which were controlled by Franco-Italian capital. Actually, he was close enough to the Consulta—he had attended several international conferences before the War—to rank as its secret emissary. Conversing with the Russian Embassy Counsellor, he made acidly hostile references to France, demanded that she should concede parity in the Mediterranean and guarantees against the annexation of Tunis (as Britain should regarding Egypt), and complained, in particular, about certain French writers' inciting Serbia to extravagant expansion, evidently with the aim of establishing a strong competitor to Italy. Confessing that Rome's main aspiration was Adriatic hegemony, based on possession of a lengthy line on the Eastern shore, he emphasized that the only Power whose interference with this question Sonnino would brook was Russia.

---

[1] Memorandum, Russian Foreign Ministry, 15 Dec. '14. *Internationale Beziehungen*, II. 6. II. No. 648, p. 552. Also Sazonov to Benckendorff and Izvolski, 10 Dec. '14. *Das Zaristische Russland*, p. 285.
[2] See p. 243 above.
[3] Demidov from Athens to Sazonov, 8 Jan. '15. Trubetskoi to Sazonov, 8 Jan. *Internationale Beziehungen*, II. 6. II. NN 737, 738, pp. 632-3.
[4] Trubetskoi to Sazonov, 11 Jan. '15. *ibid.* II. 6. II. No. 758, p. 651.
[5] Sazonov to Izvolski and Benckendorff, 7 Jan. '15. *ibid.* II. 6. II. No. 730, pp. 625-6.
[6] Sazonov to Demidov, 12 Jan. '15. *ibid.* II. 6. II. No. 761, p. 653. Also Delcassé (quoting Tittoni) to Paléologue, 14 Jan. Deciphered in the Russian Foreign Ministry. *ibid.* II. 7. I. p. 24, footnote 1.

No other State would be admitted to the discussion, especially not France. The negotiations with Petrograd, moreover, should also cover the dismemberment of Turkey, on which, too, Sonnino wanted an understanding with Sazonov.[1]

Giuseppe Volpi was presumably the man referred to as President of the Compagnia di Antivari and a director of the Società Commerciale d'Oriente, both of which had large interests in Montenegro.[2] If so, this would explain why he attempted to reach a Balkan agreement with Russia, and why the Consulta considered him an appropriate go-between. His object, clearly, was to buy this agreement by offering Rome's support for Petrograd's claims to Constantinople and the Straits, and to seek Sazonov's backing for Italy's Mediterranean schemes, which were directed against the Western Powers. However, this bid to separate the Allies was a failure. The Counsellor's reply that his Government would remain loyal to, and take no decisions by-passing, the Quai d'Orsay,[3] could only widen the distance between Neva and Tiber. Sazonov surely was not unconscious of what he did, when, on January 31st 1915, he reiterated his veto on further Italian operations along the Albanian coast.[4] At the same time, Volpi's confidences on his country's claims to Nice, Corsica and Tunis, and the retort they drew,[5] revealed the depth of the gulf dividing Rome from Paris.

[1] Izvolski to Sazonov, 20 Jan. '15. *Internationale Beziehungen*, II. 7. I. No. 47, pp. 45–6.
   On 16 Feb. '15, General Garibaldi assured Benckendorff in London that Italy desired neither Dalmatia nor territorial extensions beyond Valona, but that the Mediterranean should be neutralized. Whatever effect this was intended to have on Petrograd was nullified by his statement that, while Russia should expand in Armenia and Asia Minor, the Straits should be free, and Constantinople given to Greece. Benckendorff retorted that any resistance to Russian wishes in this respect would 'provoke the greatest complications'. Benckendorff to Sazonov, 17 Feb. '15. Adamov, I. No. 105, pp. 305–6.
[2] *Montenegro*. Foreign Office Handbooks, No. 19, p. 65; see p. 330 below. Also *Internationale Beziehungen*, II. 7. I. p. 402.
[3] *Internationale Beziehungen*, II. 7. I. No. 47, p. 46.
[4] Aide-Memoire, Russian Foreign Ministry, to Paléologue and Buchanan, 26 Jan. '15. Sazonov to Krupenski, 31 Jan. '15. *Internationale Beziehungen*, II. 7. I. No. 80, p. 71, and *ibid.* footnote 3.
[5] *Internationale Beziehungen*, II. 7. I. No. 47, p. 46. Despite, or because of, Sabini's failure, the Consulta—through Fasciotti—continued to press for French territorial concessions. (Poklevski to the Russian Foreign Ministry, 23 Nov. '14. *ibid.* II. 6. II. No. 553, p. 474). As late as 1 March '15, Fasciotti in Bucharest was still talking to Poklevski of 'a rectification of the frontier between Tripolitania and Tunisia in Italy's favour . . . or any other concession of this kind by France'. Poklevski to Sazonov, 1 March '15. *ibid.* II. 7. I. No. 275, p. 262.

## 3
### THE ORIGINS OF THE ITALO-BRITISH PARTNERSHIP

These in themselves would have been ample reasons to solicit the support of Britain against the future associates, if Britain, for her part, had not provided even more solid grounds.

Grey, plainly, was worried by the *parecchio* appeal. In his opinion, if Giolitti had concluded a bargain with Vienna and Berlin, 'Italy would have been unable to maintain a real neutrality. She would have been told . . . that her neutrality must be such as to satisfy German and Austrian needs, or else the advantages promised would be withdrawn; and Italy would have been forced into an attitude unfriendly to us. . . .'[1] Conversely, her military co-operation was regarded in Whitehall as important and would, it was believed, lead to the intervention of Rumania, Greece and possibly Bulgaria. It was the common aim of the Entente 'to finish this War as quickly as possible on satisfactory terms. The participation on our side of Italy and the Balkan States would enormously facilitate this object'.[2] On the other hand there was, in those years, nothing important to come between London and Rome. Victor Emmanuel's Fleet was no challenge to the Royal Navy. Italy's enterprise could not match British business. Having collaborated with her in Turkey as far back as 1896, Whitehall did not grudge her a modest slice of Adalia whence, moreover, she could help to counter the French. Sonnino's readiness to 'guarantee the independence' of the Yemen, to leave the Moslem Holy Places 'in free hands', to disclaim any designs on Western Arabia, and to be satisfied with an 'appropriate share' in the event of the partial or total 'dismemberment . . . of the Ottoman Empire' or with a 'modification of the present zones of interest of the . . . Powers', went far to reassure the British Cabinet. In the one field where they could have clashed, the Consulta proved its astuteness by mentioning but vaguely 'African colonies' and demanding—in the event of the others' increasing their possessions there at Germany's expense—no more than 'a corresponding and equitable compensation', especially on the Somali, Eritrean and Libyan borders[3] where London in any case was much less involved than Paris.

Italy's policy in Britain was the application of an older lesson

---

[1] Grey to Rodd, 25 May '15. Trevelyan, 293.
[2] Grey to Bertie, 4 March '15. Grey, II. 207. See Benckendorff to Sazonov, 6 April '15, on the desire of the British War Office and the Admiralty for the Italian Alliance. *Internationale Beziehungen*, II. 7. II. No. 492, p. 494. On the question of Rumania see Aide-Memoire, Buchanan to Sazonov, 26 March '15. *Das Zaristische Russland*, p. 296.
[3] Salandra, 270. *Internationale Beziehungen*, II. 7. I. No. 348, p. 315. II. 7. II. No. 417, pp. 430–1. Poincaré, VI. 107.

brought up to date. It was easy to see that the traditional Franco-British rivalry in the Eastern Mediterranean and Asia Minor was being sharpened by the grindstones of war. It was not hard to guess the drift of remarks made by Rodd and Tyrrel about France.[1] The emphasis laid by Sonnino's *Giornale d'Italia* on the tension which the Syrian question had produced between the two Western Powers may well have indicated an intention to exploit the situation for the Consulta's benefit.[2] As late as March 21st 1915, Poincaré had to warn Marshal Joffre that 'we have reason to believe that Italy is increasingly turning to England, and preparing to conclude a Mediterranean alliance with her for the future'.[3] It was still more evident that the old Russo-British conflict in the Near East would be brought to a head by Turkey's belligerency. As early as December 1914, the Ambassador Avarna was hopeful that 'the long-standing differences between Russia and Britain would once more arise in the future'.[4] After the start of the campaign in the Straits, there was an obvious implication in telegrams, such as Carlotti's, that Grey and Sazonòv were said to be discussing the Ottoman problem, but that 'Great Britain would prefer to draw out these negotiations and take the Dardanelles with her own forces'.[5] These preoccupations of the British Foreign Office were aggravated by Russia's sponsorship of her kindred races in the Balkans.[6] The inevitable enlargement of Serbia was bound to extend Tsarist influence in Europe. One way of preventing this was to circumscribe the growth of the little Kingdom. This was done by adding Trieste to Italy's bag, opposing the designs of the Serbs in Albania, and restricting them to commercial, as distinct from naval, ports.[7] The other and more effective means lay in the hands of Italy. 'For us [Bertie was soon to record] it would be better that she should be the mistress of the Adriatic than that the Slavs, through Serbia, should have a strong position there, with Russia to back them up. . . .'[8] 'It was then still an accepted doctrine that Russia', as Rodd, the Envoy to Rome, recollects, 'would some day become a naval factor in the Mediterranean'.[9] Her two-pronged

[1] See Salandra to San Giuliano, 13 Aug. '14. Imperiali to San Giuliano, 4 Sept. *Documenti Diplomatici*, 5 I. NN 232, 571, pp. 136, 321. For the Franco-British rivalries see pp. 80-1, 102-4 above.
[2] *Giornale d'Italia*, 13. Jan. '15. See p. 81 above.
[3] Poincaré, VI. 124.
[4] Avarna to Bollati, 15 Dec. '14. *Carteggio*, LXI. III. 391.
[5] Carlotti to Sonnino, 26 Feb. '15. Deciphered in the Russian Foreign Ministry. Adamov, I. No. 106, pp. 306-7.
[6] See Rodd, III. 242.
[7] Benckendorff to Sazonov, 6 Aug. '14. *Das Zaristische Russland*, pp. 264-5. Aide-Memoires, Buchanan to Sazonov, 24 and 30 March '15, *Internationale Beziehungen*, II. 7. II. NN 417, 446, pp. 429-30, 457.
[8] 11 April '15. Bertie, I. 143.
[9] Rodd, III. 242.

move westward via the Dardanelles and Belgrade, therefore, started off the British machinery for check and balance. This gained additional momentum from Britain's own quests in the Middle East. The struggle over Constantinople and the Straits had its corollary in Grey's boosting Italian imperialism in the Balkans.[1]

Such would seem to have been the genesis of one of the fateful diplomatic partnerships of this War. In London, the Ambassador Imperiali, so Grey wired to Rodd, 'pointed out that we were now Allies with France and Russia; but time brought changes, and the securing of the substantial interests of Italy in Mediterranean questions might be desirable from our point of view'.[2] In Rome, while the French and Russian Envoys were still hesitant in their forecasts, their British colleague thought that Italy would come in 'irresistibly in the end'. 'Sir Rennell Rodd . . . has telegraphed to Sir Edward Grey that . . . a serious and urgent inquiry should now be addressed to the Rome Cabinet about its intentions, and a more definite exchange of views entered into'.[3] And Lloyd George, the then Chancellor of the Exchequer, has stated that 'Sonnino . . . responded to the advances made to him by the British Government through the Marquis Imperiali, the tactful and dexterous Italian Ambassador. . . .'[4]

4
LONDON AND PETROGRAD

The day of decision—whatever the date of the advances—was February 16th 1915. Twenty-four hours after sending his first note of warning to Vienna,[5] and having learned from the General Staff that they would be 'militarily sufficiently well prepared towards mid-April'—the Italian Foreign Minister sent Imperiali the minimum terms 'on the acceptance of which by the Entente', his Government would be disposed to give a 'precise undertaking to join in the War on its side'. But the Consulta was so addicted to prevarication that the conditions were not to be presented until the Ambassador had received further orders.[6] The intention, apparently, was to wait

[1] See Adamov, I. p. 127. Albrecht-Carrié, 201. It would seem to be in line with Grey's policy that 'Asquith has reported it to be his firm conviction that Italy should have predominance in the Adriatic. . . .' (A telegram from Imperiali, 6 April '15. Salandra, 280). An increase of Italian strength in the Balkans was certain to have the 'direct effect' of prejudicing Russia's influence there. See Trubetskoi to Sazonov, 27 April '15. *Internationale Beziehungen*, II. 7. II. No. 627, p. 619.
[2] Grey to Rodd, 8 March '15, reporting an earlier conversation with Imperiali. Trevelyan, 296. Similar thoughts were expressed by Salandra to Rodd as far back as Aug. '14. *Documenti Diplomatici*, 5. I. No. 232, p. 136.
[3] Krupenski to Sazonov, 3 March '15. Adamov, I. No. 107, pp. 309–10.
[4] Lloyd George, *The Truth about the Peace Treaties*, II. 763. The last date given prior to this statement is 15 Jan. '15.
[5] See p. 306 above.  [6] Aldrovandi Marescotti, 36. Salandra, 263.

for the first concrete move to come from the other side and, at the same time, to soften up the strongpoint of resistance. For, on March 1st, Fasciotti in Bucharest spoke to the Russian Minister 'in far more exact and pressing accents. He considered it extremely desirable that the Powers of the Triple Entente should open negotiations now' about Italy's intervention and her future Adriatic, Turkish and Tunisian acquisitions. With an Army of 1,800,000 to be ready in four weeks, she would not limit herself to her own objective, but play her full part by 'marching straight' on the Austrian capital.[1] But to Sazonov the prospect of Bersaglieri bivouacs was even less attractive on the Danube than in Dalmatia. Worse still, if Italy joined the Entente, she would reinforce the front of anti-Russian Powers in the Straits. Some months previously the Ambassador in Rome had reported: 'Since our rupture with Turkey, the Consulta is watching the course of events even more closely'.[2] Quite recently, General Garibaldi had suggested that Constantinople should become Greek.[3] When, in the first days of the War, Russia had sought Italian co-operation, it was for a quick bilateral thrust against the full might of Austria-Hungary. Now that the latter was much weakened and Italy's potential contribution had, therefore, become 'pretty well a matter of indifference to us', Sazonov did not want a new Ally to intrude on whatever agreements on the Ottoman Empire were reached with Britain and France.[4] A Memorandum of the Russian Foreign Ministry of March 2nd 1915, expressing itself against the resumption of discussions with Italy, laid down that any step in this direction must, 'at all events', emanate from her.[5] And on the 3rd, Grey was notified by Buchanan that

'M. Sazonov said to-day he would not regard without misgivings entrance of Italy upon scene at a moment when her naval and military co-operation has lost much of its value. Any fresh collaboration would complicate peace negotiations. Intimacy and confidence existing between the three Allies was essence of their strength, and if a fourth Power attached

[1] Poklevski to Sazonov, 1 March '15. *Internationale Beziehungen*, II. 7. I. No. 275, p. 262. This report, except for the mention of Tunisia, is confirmed by a telegram from the British Minister in Bucharest to Grey, 2 March '15. Churchill, *1915*, pp. 199–200. A Memorandum, Russian Foreign Ministry, 2 March, says that proposals that the Entente should negotiate with Italy came from several sources. *Internationale Beziehungen*, II. 7. I. No. 281, p. 265.
[2] Krupenski to Sazonov, 30 Nov. '14. *ibid.* II. 6. II. p. 426, footnote 1.
[3] Benckendorff to Sazonov, 17 Feb. '15. Adamov, I. No. 105, p. 305.
[4] This view was propounded, as early as 8 Nov. '14, by the Director of the Chancellery of the Russian Foreign Ministry, who wrote to the Grand Duke Nikolai Mikhailovich that the Entente 'would now perhaps have reason to prefer that Italy should preserve her neutrality'. *Internationale Beziehungen*, II. 6. II. No. 482, p. 420. Also *Das Zaristische Russland*, p. XXX. Adamov, I. pp. 126–7. Stieve, p. 236.
[5] *Internationale Beziehungen*, II. 7. I. No. 281, pp. 265–6.

itself to their concert there might be danger of its trying to disunite them for its own personal profit. M. Sazonov is accordingly of opinion that, if Italian Government offer their help, Powers should evade giving a definite answer, while giving a most friendly form to the discussion'.[1]

Was the news of Russian obstruction flashed to Sonnino through some secret channel? Or did the tidings that, after the bombardment on February 25th, the door of the Dardanelles was open, suffice to decide him? Clearly, he had to clinch the deal with the Entente before Italy's bargaining position had been weakened by the anticipated success of the expedition. On March 3rd, the eve of his ultimatum to Austria, he instructed Imperiali to proceed on the lines of his communication of February 16th.[2] On March 4th, the Ambassador conveyed this to Grey:

'On the one hand . . . as Italy was neither attacked nor provoked by anyone, nothing forces her . . . to encounter the immense risks and responsibilities of a war except the desire to free her brothers from a foreign yoke and to satisfy certain fundamental and legitimate national aspirations. On the other, if we take part in the War, we must do so side by side with certain companions-at-arms, no doubt entirely estimable, but who in some respects have interests and political ideals in opposition to our own. It is our duty, therefore, to consider . . . what is the minimum of cessions in our favour which . . . would suffice to guarantee that our hopes, once the War had come to a favourable end, would not be frustrated through pressure brought to bear by those same companions at whose side we had fought'.[3]

There followed a recital of the terms. And, in their next interview, on March 8th, as the Foreign Secretary cabled to Rodd, 'the Ambassador pressed me very much for my personal view. I observed that the conditions went beyond those suggested last August, and that some of them seemed to me excessive from the general point of view; but . . . there were none to which I need take objection purely from the point of view of British interests. . . .'[4]

It is understandable, therefore, that the Russian notion of repelling 'the Italian overture' seemed to Grey 'the height of folly'.[5] On March 5th, Churchill had 'minuted to Sir Edward Grey: "The attitude of Italy is remarkable. If she can be induced to join with us, the Austrian

---

[1] Grey, II. 206. The text of the corresponding Russian Aide-Memoire to Buchanan and Paléologue, which tallies with the above, is in *Internationale Beziehungen*, II. 7. I. No. 276, pp. 262-3. See also Poincaré, VI. 96.
[2] Aldrovandi Marescotti, 37.
[3] Salandra, 267-8; also 263. For Italy's terms see Salandra, 268-70.
[4] Grey to Rodd, 8 March '15. Trevelyan, 296. Aldrovandi Marescotti, p. 37, reproduces the above statement of Grey's in the entry of 10 March. Salandra, p. 273, quotes it under 9 March.
[5] Grey, II. 207. Also Asquith, *Memories and Reflections*, II. 65. 6 March '15.

L

Fleet would be powerless and the Mediterranean as safe as an English lake".... The Foreign Secretary replied.... "I will neglect no opportunity".[1] Indeed, the day before he had already, in a telegram to Bertie referring to Sazonov's objections, invited the Ambassador to 'inform the [French] Minister for Foreign Affairs that I cannot share this view. ... If Italy or any other Power demanded, as price of co-operation, conditions that appeared to Russia likely to impair a settlement in her favour of question of Constantinople and Straits, Great Britain and, I presume, France also, would support Russia in resisting such conditions. ... It must also be remembered that if co-operation of any other Power is offered to and refused by the three Allies, the Power refused may go to Germany....'[2]

Swayed by the latter argument, Delcassé asked Paléologue to persuade Sazonov 'to say nothing from which Italy could deduce that the Triple Entente attributes no importance to her military co-operation....'[3] The joint pressure from her Allies, coupled with Britain's assurance regarding Constantinople and the Straits, brought Russia to accept the principle of parleys with Sonnino. On March 5th, Sazonov told Buchanan and Paléologue that he would reconcile himself to Italy's collaboration, provided it did not extend to the region of the Narrows, and was not rewarded with the South-Dalmatian shore.[4] But he put up another hurdle by demanding that her partnership against the Porte should be entirely conditional on 'effective and simultaneous participation in the War against Austria-Hungary', and insisting that, since the expected help would be slight, it was 'necessary to revise the promises the Powers had been disposed to make to Italy six months ago'.[5] And only when Delcassé —while sympathizing with Sazonov's above-mentioned stipulations concerning Turkey—refused to allow any tampering with their promise of the Trentino (which he knew to have been offered to Rome by Bülow), Trieste and Valona,[6] was, it appears, the field clear for the final contest.

[1] Churchill, *1915*, p. 200.
[2] Grey to Bertie, 4 March '15. Grey, II. 207. The text of this telegram, repeated to Buchanan on the same day, and deciphered in the Russian Foreign Ministry, is also in Adamov, I. No. 109, pp. 311–12.
[3] Delcassé's telegram to Paléologue, received by Grey from Paris and transmitted by him to Buchanan, 5 March '15. Deciphered in the Russian Foreign Ministry. *Internationale Beziehungen*, II. 7. I. p. 263, footnote 1. A telegram from Izvolski to Sazonov, 4 March, quotes Delcassé as having underlined 'with great insistence' the danger of repelling Italy at this moment. Adamov, I. No. 108, p. 311. Also Izvolski to Sazonov, 6 March. *ibid.* I. No. 58, p. 262. Poincaré. VI. 96, 105. Asquith, II. 65. Grey, II. 206.
[4] Buchanan to Grey, 5 March '15. Deciphered in the Russian Foreign Ministry. Adamov, I. No. 110, p. 312. Also Grey, II. 207.
[5] Aide-Memoire, Sazonov to Paléologue and Buchanan, 7 March '15. Adamov, I. No. 112, p. 313.
[6] Izvolski to Sazonov, 10 March '15. Adamov, I. No. 116, p. 317.

5

FRANCO-ITALIAN RIVALRY IN THE BALKANS. ANGLO-FRENCH
INTERESTS IN THE MEDITERRANEAN AND AFRICA

Anyhow, it was not until March 10th that Grey, after another meeting with Imperiali, conveyed to the French and Russian Ambassadors Sonnino's wishes.[1]

In Paris, Poincaré's immediate comment was: 'C'est beaucoup'.[2] Though Nice and Corsica were not alluded to, the pretensions to colonial compensation—for potential British and French gains in Africa—on the Eritrean, Somali and Libyan borders affected Tunisia and the French port of Djibouti. What made it worse was that Grey, in his first communication through Bertie, had suppressed this point which (as Cambon reported) 'appeared to him secondary', but at the same time considered it 'very difficult to make concessions involving Somaliland'.[3] 'Secondary', chafed the President, 'that is all very well, but as far as Eritrea and Libya are concerned, France would have to foot the bill, and she has no valid reason for allowing herself to be imposed upon'.[4] There was ground for 'serious reservations' also in the Italian postulates on Dalmatia, the neutralization of the territory to be transferred to the Serbs and Montenegrins, and the formation of a Moslem Albanian State obviously under Italian control.[5] The Quai d'Orsay saw in the Balkans a market for business and finance, a causeway to the Ottoman Empire, and the base of French power in the Eastern Mediterranean. It wooed Bulgaria, supported an extension of Serbia and Greece in Albania, showed an active interest in Durazzo and aspired, 'to a certain extent' at least, to 'the role of protector of the Montenegrins'.[6] Far from favouring Italy's expansion beyond, and supremacy in, the Adriatic, which could only upset the

---

[1] Benckendorff to Sazonov, 10 March '15. *Das Zaristische Russland*, pp. 290–1. This telegram arrived in Petrograd on 11 March, and on the same day Italy's conditions were transmitted by Buchanan in an Aide-Memoire to Sazonov. Memorandum, Russian Foreign Ministry, 11 March, 15. *Internationale Beziehungen*, II. 7. I. No. 349, p. 316. Aldrovandi Marescotti, 37. Salandra, 273. Poincaré, VI. 103.
[2] 11 March '15. Poincaré, VI. 104.
[3] Cambon to Delcassé, 13 March '15. Poincaré, VI. 107. Bertie to Delcassé, 12 March. Poincaré, VI. 105.
[4] 13 March '15. Poincaré, VI. 107.
[5] Poincaré, VI. 105. For P. Cambon's and Delcassé's objections in March '15 see *Das Zaristische Russland*, pp. 291–2, and those of Doumergue in Aug. '14—*Das Zaristische Russland*, pp. 275–6. Also Sonnino to Carlotti, 11 Jan. '15. Deciphered in the Russian Foreign Ministry. *Internationale Beziehungen*, II. 6. II. No. 755, p. 647.
[6] The Russian Chargé d'Affaires in Tsetinye to Sazonov, 28 Sept. '14, quoting the French Minister there. *Internationale Beziehungen*, II. 6. I. No. 331, p. 256. For French policy in Albania see Izvolski to Sazonov, 5 Aug. '14. *Das Zaristische Russland*, p. 264. Trubetskoi to Sazonov, 8 Jan. '15. *Internationale Beziehungen*, II. 6. II. No. 738, p. 633.

relation of forces between the two Latin Powers, Paris was inclined to use the fancies of Belgrade and Athens as a curb on those of Rome. Hence Poincaré's frigid aside: 'To encourage Italy, nothing could be better, but do not let us dishearten Serbia. . . .'[1] Moreover, contrary to Britain, the French Government were 'afraid that Italy may exploit the difficult situation of the Entente in the European War to settle her affairs with Turkey'.[2] Delcassé, certainly, was in no doubt 'that Italy's co-operation will increase the difficulties in fixing the terms of peace. . . .'[3]

But the French war losses were such that, in local attacks between December 17th 1914 and January 17th 1915 alone, some 80,000 were wounded, 18,000 missing and 26,000 killed. By March 12th, 25,000 more men were wasted in the Champagne.[4] The rear of the army was ravaged by diphtheria, typhoid, scarlet fever and meningitis. 'Magnificent soldiers', wrote Poincaré, 'how will France ever be able to thank you for your patriotism and devotion?'[5] The answer seemed to be: buy fresh lives wherever they can be got. 'Italy put a pistol to our heads', Delcassé was soon to confide to a visitor. 'Within a month there will be a million Italian bayonets . . . and shortly afterwards 600,000 Rumanians. Reinforcements as large as that may be worth some sacrifice. . . .'[6] The Habsburg Crown Council's decision of March 8th on territorial concessions to Rome was soon known in Paris,[7] and presently the British Ambassador Bertie gathered 'that the apprehension here (the Government) is that Italy may accept the Trentino as a bribe from Austria, and at the end of the War attempt to blackmail France, whose troops would be exhausted, into making other concessions to Italian ambition. . . .'[8] So it was well to ensure Italy's future exhaustion by drawing her into the holocaust. This seemed all the more advisable since the entanglement in the Balkans would divert her attention from the Western Mediterranean. Delcassé, according to Izvolski, openly stressed the fact that 'her intentions are now, to all appearances, wholly directed towards the East'.[9] Nor did French jealousy of the Consulta's trespass upon Anatolia compare to the alarm raised in Paris by the Tsar's

[1] 12 March '15. Poincaré, VI. 105.
[2] Memorandum, Russian Foreign Ministry, 2 Nov. '14, recording a conversation with Paléologue. *Internationale Beziehungen*, II. 6. I. p. 352, footnote 2. There seems no reason to assume that the French attitude had changed before March '15.
[3] Delcassé's telegram to Paléologue, received by Grey from Paris and transmitted by him to Buchanan, 5 March '15. Deciphered in the Russian Foreign Ministry. *Internationale Beziehungen*, II. 7. I. p. 263, footnote 1.
[4] Poincaré, VI. 26, 105–6, 109.   [5] 12 March '15. Poincaré, VI. 107.
[6] Interview with Wickham Steed, 1 May '15. Steed, *Through Thirty Years*, II. 66. Also Izvolski to Sazonov, 4 March '15. Adamov, I. No. 108, p. 311.
[7] 13 March '15. Poincaré, VI. 108.   [8] 7 April '15. Bertie, I. 141.
[9] Izvolski to Sazonov, 6 March '15. Adamov, I. No. 57, p. 262.

demand for the city of St. Sophia.[1] On the day when Sazonov served his Allies with the claim to Constantinople and the Straits,[2] the French Foreign Minister pressed for Italy's 'inclusion in the Allied operations against Turkey'[3]—doubtless in order to restrain the Russians.

On the only two points directly injurious to French imperialism—African colonies and naval status—which also impinged upon the concerns of Britain, the Quai d'Orsay found backing in Whitehall. This was expressed by the 'prudent and dilatory reservations in the French and British replies'.[4] In the first Memorandum on Italy's 'interest . . . in the equilibrium of the Mediterranean' and her expectations, as Salandra has put it, of 'an eventual partition of territories and zones of influence in the Ottoman Empire', the vague formula was accepted. But, he complained bitterly in retrospect, 'when . . . we asked permission to word the clause a little more precisely, we met with a categorical refusal from Grey. He said that no discussion had taken place on this thorny subject with France and Russia, and to start one now would be inopportune. . . . We tried again but in vain. Indeed, Grey showed vexation at our insistence—to the point of reminding us of the great sacrifices sustained by France and England without our co-operation. We were obliged to content ourselves with the assurance that, "if Italy becomes an Ally, it is clear she must participate when the discussions are initiated".'[5] In the end, though it was recognized 'in a general way' that she was 'interested in the maintenance of the balance of power in the Mediterranean' and that, if the Turkish Empire were dismembered, 'she must obtain an appropriate share of the Mediterranean region adjacent to the province of Adalia', the portion was not specified, but was left to be defined 'at the proper time' and not without due 'account being taken of the existing interests of France and Great Britain'. Equally so, the 'equitable compensation' in Africa was cut down from a pledge to the principle that she 'might' claim 'some just' *quid pro quo* amounting to what the Italians considered to be mere 'rectifications of our colonial frontiers'.[6]

It was futile to lament, as Salandra did later, that Grey and Delcassé 'should have given us the right to greater consideration'.[7] Sonnino, spokesman of by far the weaker country, simply had to yield when and wherever he came up against the preponderant force of the two Western Powers acting in unison. Yielding, however, was rendered easy by admission to their anti-Russian diplomatic front.

---

[1] See pp. 98–9 above.   [2] See p. 92 above.
[3] Izvolski to Sazonov, 4 March '15. Adamov, I. No. 108, p. 311.
[4] Suarez, III. 111.   [5] Salandra, 283; also 291.
[6] Salandra, 291. Treaty text in *Internationale Beziehungen*, II. 7. II. No. 612, pp. 606–7. Also Albrecht-Carrié, 201–2. Michels, 193.
[7] Salandra, 291.

British and French benevolence gave Italy a voice, utterly out of proportion to her real strength, in the Adriatic and the Balkans.¹

6

## ITALIAN IMPERIALISM IN THE BALKANS AND THE YUGOSLAVS

These were the circumstances in which Sazonov, on March 11th 1915, was assured by Grey 'that the Italian Government, unsolicited and without any suggestion on his part, made this overture [for an Alliance] entirely on their own initiative'. This was preceded by the list of Sonnino's principal terms, and accompanied by the request that, since 'considerable offers have been made to Italy by Prince Bülow . . . the conditions proposed by the Italian Government should not be rejected, but should, where excessive, be met either by a counter-proposal or with criticism'.² There was no need to probe deeply into these desiderata to perceive how the imperialists behind the Consulta were making the most of their opportunity. Salandra admitted later that 'it was not merely sentimental or historical motives —such as Irredentism and the traditions of the Risorgimento—which decided the Government's course'.³ Their demand, *inter alia*, for

'. . . Trieste and the whole of Istria as far as the Quarnero including Volosca as well as the Istrian Islands . . . the Province of Dalmatia as far South as the River Narenta . . . the Peninsula of Sabbioncello and all the islands situated North and West of Dalmatia . . . full sovereignty [over] Valona and . . . Saseno with . . . territory . . . from the river Voyusa on the North and East approximately as far as Khimara to the South',

combined with the stipulation that

the coast from Khimara to Cape Stylos, and from the mouth of the Voyusa to, and including, the Bocche di Cattaro should be neutralized, and Durazzo allotted to a new 'independent' Moslem State in Central Albania [obviously to be controlled from Rome],⁴

was frankly designed to establish 'our military predominance in the Adriatic'. That sea, Salandra has pleaded, 'was too narrow for joint possession by two Powers who were bound to become rivals

¹ See Trubetskoi to Sazonov, 27 April '15. Benckendorff to Sazonov, 28 April. *Internationale Beziehungen*, II. 7. II. NN 627, 633, pp. 617, 624.
² Aide-Memoire, British Embassy, Petrograd to Sazonov. *Internationale Beziehungen*, II. 7. I. No. 348, p. 316.
³ Salandra, 54.
⁴ Aide-Memoire, British Embassy, Petrograd, to Sazonov, 11 March '15. *Internationale Beziehungen*, II. 7. I. No. 348, p. 315. Sonnino also desired that the fate of the coast from the Narenta to the Drin and from the Bay of Volosca to the Northern frontier of Dalmatia should be left 'to the decision of Europe . . . at the end of the War'.

and potential enemies.... With an amount of coast disproportionate to the size of her territory, Italy was forced to employ forces disproportionate to her means'. By lessening, through the desired acquisitions, the extent of her long and vulnerable sea frontiers, she hoped both to reduce her strategic expenditure and to obtain that 'absolute security in the East', which came only from 'complete domination'. That formula, it was claimed, implied no more than the defensive striving 'to exclude any possibility of another maritime Power taking possession of the Austrian shore'.[1]

Even while Serbia, by her stand against Vienna, inspired Italian sympathy, that sentiment was poisoned by suspicions of the pull she had on the Slav subjects of Francis Joseph, and of her schemes in Albania and Montenegro.[2] Already before 1914, San Giuliano had actively denied her an access to the sea. And when the growing solidarity of Croats, Slovenes and Serbs brought visions of the Yugoslavia to come, the Ambassador Carlotti implied in Petrograd that the emergence of such a State would 'hardly be acceptable' to Italy, all the more since it could 'easily' become Russia's 'outpost in the Adriatic'.[3] According to Churchill, who negotiated the Naval Convention with them, the Italians were apprehensive that, if Russia gained Constantinople, and Serbia expanded towards the sea, these two Slav States would build a great naval base in the Dalmatian littoral.[4] In Rome, as the British Ambassador recollects, 'Slavism had always been regarded as a potential danger', and if Italy was to side with the Russians and the Serbs, she wished to ensure 'that she was not going to fight for... her own ultimate disadvantage'.[5] These considerations revived the shadow of earlier Italo-Russian rivalry in the Balkans. It seemed to have been halted in 1909 by the Racconigi Agreement which was the fruit of their common antagonism to the penetration of that region by the Habsburgs. But the very object uniting them contained the seed of inevitable conflict. Since the eclipse of the Dual Monarchy was coming into sight, the question of who was to succeed it in the South-East European power game became acute. As early as September 1914, the Consulta decided that 'we cannot possibly change over from the incubus of the Austrian menace to the incubus of the Slav menace, and that is why we require solid guarantees'.[6]

[1] Salandra, 292–3. The Adriatic, Tittoni said to Delcassé, 'is for us what the Western Mediterranean is for France'. 17 Dec. '14. Poincaré, V. 511.
[2] T. N. Page, 143.
[3] Memorandum, Russian Foreign Ministry, 12 March '15. *Internationale Beziehungen*, II. 7. I. No. 354, p. 322.
[4] Churchill, *1915*, p. 331.                 [5] Rodd, III, 242.
[6] San Giuliano to Imperiali, 16 Sept. '14. Salandra, 266. *Documenti Diplomatici*, 5. I. No. 703, p. 412. Imperiali to Grey, 8 March '15. Trevelyan, 296. Sonnino to Imperiali, after 21 March '15. Salandra, 275.

That these 'guarantees' violated the principle of national self-determination of which Italy, in Salandra's words, claimed 'to be the chief champion',[1] did not perturb her rulers. The Dalmatian population of some 633,000 included no more than 18,000 Italians. Except for Zara, there was no town with an Italian majority, and none where they numbered over 10 per cent of the inhabitants. As in Gorizia and Istria, they lived, amidst a huge preponderance of Slav peasants, as urban dwellers monopolizing commerce, and subsisting on an imported culture. The cities were economically inseparable from the hinterland. To subject these territories to Rome meant tearing the ethnical and racial affinities of the Slavs to shreds. The islands, such as Lagosta, whose grape and fishing industries were dependent on trade with the adjacent mainland, could only expect ruin from the threatening annexation.[2] But the would-be conquerors asserted that the weakness of the Latin element in the Province was due to Austria's deliberate policy of causing a large Slav influx; that until 1866 Dalmatia had been Italian in character; and that anyhow for six hundred years she had belonged to Venice. An additional argument advanced by the Consulta was that Northern Dalmatia was essential for the protection of Pola and that, altogether, Italy had to 'rid herself once and for all of the unbearable position of inferiority in the Adriatic . . . forced upon her by the geographical configuration of the two shores'. If the rocky, deep-water Dalmatian littoral with its many ports and islands was turned by another Power into an impregnable shelter for destroyers and submarines, the flat and virtually harbourless coast between Brindisi and Venice would become indefensible.[3]

But, as Sazonov pointed out, the possession (in addition to Venice, Trięste, Taranto and Ancona) of Istria with the naval base of Pola, and of Valona which dominates the Adriatic gates, was bound to transform that sea into an Italian lake where Serbia would not be in a position to make trouble.[4] Even though some Yugoslavs were

---

[1] Salandra, 293.
[2] Bowman, 261-2, 264, 268. Michels, 128-9. Steed, *The Hapsburg Monarchy*, 125-6. Rodd, III. 243.
[3] Imperiali to Grey. See Aide-Memoires, British Embassy, Petrograd, to Sazonov, 21 and 24 March '15. *Internationale Beziehungen*, II. 7. I. No. 402, pp. 374-5. II. 7. II. No. 418, p. 431. Sonnino to Imperiali, after 21 March. Salandra, 275. Also *Internationale Beziehungen*, II. 7. II. pp. 433, 447, 457. Rodd, III, 242. Albrecht-Carrié, 30-1. It was in line with Italy's claims that the Nationalist *Lega Nazionale*, even before the War, had displayed on propaganda postcards the 'old-historic' frontier running nearly as far as the Slovene capital Lyublyana. Michels, 130.
[4] Aide-Memoire, Russian Foreign Ministry to Paléologue and Buchanan, 25 March '15. *Internationale Beziehungen*, II. 7. II. No. 423, pp. 436-7. Sazonov also asked why, if Italy was really afraid of submarine bases, she consented to let Serbia have Ragusa. See also Sazonov, 263.

painting her future on the Adriatic 'with rich commercial harbours, with a "Riviera" of her own at Ragusa . . . perhaps with naval ports, where the population were born sailors. . . .'[1]—the alleged Serb danger to Rome, as others emphasized, was vastly overdrawn. After the War, a much enlarged Italy, with 50 million people and strong armed forces, would have little to fear even from a united Yugoslavia of barely 12 million, a State ravaged by neglect, persecution and invasion, with a small Army and a non-existent Fleet, painfully struggling to fuse its diversities into an integral whole.[2] If ever it tended to menace its Western neighbour, or in particular helped to project Tsarist influence into the Mediterranean, Italy would soon find Allies in Britain and France.

Viewed in this light, Italy's *Drang* to Dalmatia could not have been dictated by defensive strategy alone. In conjunction with the demand for Istria, it looked very much like an attempt to deprive Serbia of her natural maritime outlets. If the Narenta were the new frontier, it would paralyse nearby Metkovich—the only Dalmatian harbour with a railway connection to the interior of Bosnia—especially as that railway, running along the right bank of the river, would be in Italian hands.[3] Considering that on the shore to be left to Serbia, the mountains drop so abruptly into the sea as almost to preclude the development of large ports, that a treacherous wind endangers shipping in the narrow passages, that Buccari is encircled by stiff cliffs, that Porto Re was too small, that Spalato—despite good harbourage—was cut off in winter from the interior, and that Ragusa and Castelnuovo had each only a precarious narrow-gauge line inland, while Cattaro had no railway link at all,[4] the annexation of the Northern half of Dalmatia by Italy would seem to have been a design to cripple the future Yugoslav State at birth. The alleged fear of a hypothetical Serb Fleet betrayed, as Sazonov protested, the intention of leaving Serbia's unfortified shore at the mercy of the powerful Italian Navy 'already in being'.[5] And this was in keeping with the policy—advocated by the *Secolo*—of splitting 'the imperialist Serbian block . . . . it is better to have two small States as neighbours than one which includes them both. With an Albania, anti-Slav *par excellence* on the one side, and a Catholic anti-Serbian Croatia on the other, we would establish an advantageous equilibrium in the Eastern Adriatic'.[6]

Moreover, added to Istria and the Valona district, Dalmatia was envisaged as another bridgehead to the East. An early telegram

[1] Trubetskoi to Sazonov, 15 Feb. '15, on Supilo's statements. *Internationale Beziehungen*, II. 7. I. No. 202, p. 185.
[2] Marcovich, 275. [3] *Internationale Beziehungen*, II. 7. II. p. 436.
[4] Bowman, 266. [5] *Internationale Beziehungen*, II. 7. II. p. 449.
[6] *Secolo*, 8 May '15. Marcovich, 265. Italics in the original.

from the Ambassador Carlotti shows Italian diplomacy to have been aware that Adriatic hegemony would ensure Italy's economic penetration of the Balkans.[1] Italy (after Austria-Hungary) was the principal importer and exporter in Albania, accounting for 25 per cent of the goods leaving Scutari and 30 per cent of those from the Albanian South. The Servizi Marittimi carried her mails; the Puglia Line served the North Albanian ports. Italian financial houses operated in Durazzo and Valona, and in the latter the Società Commerciale d'Oriente ranked as the official bank. In Montenegro, the Compagnia di Antivari, which was financed by the Banca Commerciale Italiana, had built the harbour, the power station and a large hotel in Antivari. It had constructed, and was working, the railway from that port to Virbazar, and held the steamship concession on Lake Scutari. The vessels of the Puglia Line plied on the river Boyana. The firm of Bravi, Massini, Plata & Co. was draining the marshes between the latter and Dulcigno. The Regia Co-interessata dei Tabacchi del Montenegro had an almost complete monopoly in the country. The growing import business of the Società Commerciale d'Oriente (food-stuffs, oils, candles, soap), the Italo-American Petroleum Company and other undertakings contributed to a state of affairs in which 'commercially Montenegro became almost an Italian colony. . . .'[2]

These enterprises were tokens of Italy's long-standing preoccupation with the Balkans. Proximity, low transport costs and familiarity with local tastes made that area an 'ideal' market for her comparatively cheap manufactures. It appeared to offer unlimited employment to her surplus labour in skilled trades. Its untouched wealth and technical backwardness were considered to be inviting the investing capitalist. It lent itself, in Francesco Nitti's opinion, more easily to Italian financial penetration than to that of other countries. 'The Balkan peoples see in Italy an indication of the road traced for them by destiny'.[3] It was significant that Durazzo, which the Italians desired, was eminently suited to serve as the starting point for a Trans-Balkan railway.[4] In Yugoslav circles, Italy was likened to Napoleonic France who occupied Dalmatia in order to subjugate the whole Peninsula and, by capturing the road to Constantinople, solve to her advantage the Eastern Question.[5] If the parallel was exaggerated, it was certainly true that, by 1895, the veteran statesman Crispi

[1] Carlotti to San Giuliano, 4 Oct. '14. *Documenti Diplomatici*, 5. I. No. 883, p. 526.
[2] *Montenegro*. Foreign Office Handbooks, No. 19, p. 31; also 32, 41, 43–4, 47, 49–50, 53, 62, 65, 72. *Albania*. Foreign Office Handbooks, No. 17, pp. 65, 79, 91–2.
[3] Written in the spring of 1915. Nitti, *Il capitale straniero in Italia*, 22, 23.
[4] *Internationale Beziehungen*, II. 6. II. p. 650.
[5] Marcovich, 272.

saw in the Western Balkans the future colonial reservoir of Italian imperialism.¹ By the time the World War was under way, the U.S. Ambassador in Rome reported to Washington that Italy wanted 'an abiding foothold on the Eastern shore of the Adriatic'.²

7

THE STRUGGLE BETWEEN ITALY AND
RUSSIA OVER THE BALKANS

It is easy to see how this affected Sazonov. He put it mildly in saying later that Sonnino's 'demands seemed to me exaggerated'.³ If the Consulta objected to substituting for the Habsburg hegemony in South-Eastern Europe that of Russia, Russia was even less willing to shoulder the burdens of the War merely to drive out Austria-Hungary for the benefit of Italy. Tsarist diplomacy was quick to spot 'the tendency of the Rome Cabinet to take Austria's place in the Balkans'.⁴ Italy was expanding in Albania, conniving with Rumania, inciting Bulgaria against the Serbs, sowing dissensions between them and Montenegro, and browbeating Greece. If she were now to spread out not only in Istria, but also in Dalmatia, then—as a senior expert advised Sazonov—'the present War will contain the seeds of an inevitable future clash between Italy and the enlarged Serbia', and it will be 'very difficult for Russia to hold back from such a struggle'.⁵ For the expected acquisition of Constantinople—if it was to fulfil its basic purpose—was not 'the end', but a beginning of Russian expansion.⁶ Given the imperialist nature of Tsarist foreign policy, it would be only the first step into the Mediterranean forum, and engender further quests for security and power, above all, in the Eastern Mediterranean.⁷ It was revealing, for example, that the Generalissimo, the Grand Duke Nikolai, could say that 'Cattaro is very important as a harbour, where our Fleet may lie and on which it may be based'.⁸

The same considerations underlay Petrograd's preoccupations with Serbia and her approach to the sea. The future gains, 'the

¹ Crispi, *Questioni internazionali*, 144. Yerusalimski, 157. May, 290.
² T. N. Page to Lansing, 4 Dec. '15. *Lansing Papers*, I. 731. Also Suarez, III. 110–1. Marcovich, 296–7. Salandra, p. 293, admits that 'we were obliged to subordinate . . . ethnical considerations to strategic and commercial ones'.
³ Sazonov, 263.
⁴ Trubetskoi to Sazonov, 11 Jan. '15. Savinski to Sazonov, 11 Jan. *Internationale Beziehungen*, II. 6. II. No. 756, p. 648; No. 758, p. 650.
⁵ Trubetskoi to Sazonov, 15 Feb. '15. *Internationale Beziehungen*, II. 7. I. No. 203, p. 187. See also pp. 64–5, 207 above.
⁶ See p. 66 above.
⁷ Adamov, I. p. 127.
⁸ The Generalissimo to Sazonov, 6 April '15. *Internationale Beziehungen*, II. 7. II. No. 493, p. 495.

realization of the national ideal . . . of the Kingdom'[1] so closely tied up with them was worth its weight in gold to the politicians and strategists on the Neva. Originally, Sazonov had not contemplated the attachment of the Catholic Croats and Slovenes to the Orthodox Serbs. This would have entailed the risk of the latter's coming under Vatican influence, or of Belgrade, as the centre of the new federation, emancipating herself from her old protector, and turning into a rival focus of attraction in the Balkans. But leading Yugoslavs were increasingly worried by evidence of Italy's Adriatic predilections. As early as October 1914, the Serbian Premier Pashich informed Sazonov that Dalmatia would resist Rome by force of arms. She 'wishes to join Serbia . . . this is . . . the constant desire of the entire Serbo-Croat people'.[2] By mid-January 1915, Fasciotti in Bucharest was telling his Russian colleague that the Consulta wanted about half of the Dalmatian coast.[3] Such news must have spurred Franco Supilo, the ex-Deputy for Ragusa in the Hungarian Parliament, to leave his temporary abode on the Tiber for Nish and Petrograd. His aim was 'to reach agreement with the Serbs on the basis of their political unification with the Croats and Slovenes', and to enlist Tsarist patronage for it. Three deputies of the Zagreb Diet, now members of the Yugoslav Committee abroad, requested the Russian Government through the Ambassador in Rome 'to regard Supilo as the plenipotentiary of all the Serbo-Croat emigrés. . . .' They added that 'Pashich, too, has fully approved of Supilo's programme'.[4]

Inevitably, this and, more than anything, the shock of Italy's Eastern ambitions,[5] modified Russian views on the Yugoslavs. In the autumn of 1914, Izvolski in France, campaigning for 'a unified strong Serbo-Croat State, including Istria and Dalmatia', introduced Supilo to Delcassé.[6] On January 1st 1915, Sazonov startled Paléologue by refusing to leave Croatia 'under the present system'.[7] By March, he must have gone far enough to prompt Carlotti's inquiry concerning 'some symptoms . . . that the idea of the necessity of a political fusion between Serbs and Croats was gradually maturing in Russia'. The reply the Ambassador received was that, if the two peoples concerned wished to unite, 'Russia could only

[1] Trubetskoi to Sazonov, 15 Feb. '15. *ibid.* II. 7. I. No. 202, p. 183.
[2] Aide-Memoire, Serbian Legation, Petrograd, to Sazonov, 3 Oct. '14. *ibid.* II. 6. I. No. 352, p. 275.
[3] Poklevski to Sazonov, 15 Jan. '15. *ibid.* II. 7. I. No. 14, p. 15.
[4] Krupenski and Giers to Sazonov, 26 Jan. '15. Trubetskoi to Sazonov, 15 Feb. Krupenski to Sazonov, 10 March '15. *Internationale Beziehungen*, II. 7. I. No. 202, p. 183, and *ibid.* footnote 1.
[5] As early as 11 Aug. '14, Carlotti had spoken to Sazonov of the Dalmatian littoral. Poincaré, V. 72.
[6] Izvolski to Sazonov, 13 Oct. '14. *Internationale Beziehungen*, II. 6. I. No. 386, p. 305.
[7] Paléologne, I. 236.

sympathize'.[1] Indeed, as one of his top-ranking advisers wrote to Sazonov,

> 'Russia's interest in the fate of the South-Western Slavs cannot be determined solely by a natural sympathy with the liberation of our brothers'. It 'is at the same time the expression of a correct political instinct.... this attitude of ours to the Slavs establishes ... Russia's position in Europe ... which we cannot renounce without forfeiting our status as a Great Power'.[2]

But just because it was mainly a matter of 'political instinct', the Tsar's new-found zeal for national self-determination was vitiated by his striving to violate this principle elsewhere. 'Our status as a Great Power' after the War depended primarily on incorporating Constantinople and the Straits. And this issue, by an astute piece of British timing, was tied into a knot with that of the Balkans. It was no coincidence that Sir George Buchanan's Aide-Memoire containing Sonnino's terms, and Grey's statement consenting to the coming realization of Russia's desires in Turkey were delivered to Sazonov, on March 11th 1915, within a few hours of each other.[3]

Britain's double move was certainly not unconnected with Vienna's decision of March 9th and German press reports that Rome was to obtain the Trentino.[4] Sazonov, therefore, was left in no doubt that the Consulta might slip through the meshes of the Entente, and that —in return for gaining his prize in Ottoman waters—he was expected to prevent this. Basically, it was imperative for Russian policy 'to erect a barrier ... against Italy's endeavours on the Adriatic coast'. But, he confessed to Nicholas II, 'in the quarrel over this question, we cannot count on firm support from our Allies'.[5] He did not say, but may have reflected, that (unless they were prepared to lose Russia) the Allies would have had to back him against Sonnino, if he had not weakened himself by his claims on the Porte. At any rate, he must have been aware that Grey's generosity at Turkey's expense compelled a *quid pro quo* even though it was to the detriment of the Slavs, for he prepared his Sovereign for the need to com-

---

[1] Memorandum, Russian Foreign Ministry, 12 March '15. *Internationale Beziehungen*, II. 7. I. No. 354, p. 322.
[2] Trubetskoi to Sazonov, 15 Feb. '15. *Internationale Beziehungen*, II. 7. I. No. 202, pp. 183–4.
[3] Memorandum, Russian Foreign Ministry, 11 March '15. *Internationale Beziehungen*, II. 7. I. No. 349, p. 316. It states, *inter alia*, that Buchanan read to Sazonov Grey's telegram on Constantinople and the Straits at 10.30 p.m. The formal British notification on this subject was made on 12 March. See p. 97 above.
[4] *Deutsche Tageszeitung*, 9 March '15. *Internationale Beziehungen*, II. 7. I. No. 349, pp. 316, 419–20. Also p. 311 above.
[5] Sazonov to Nicholas II, 15 March '15. *Internationale Beziehungen*, II. 7. I. No. 373, p. 342.

promise. To obtain the Straits and Constantinople, Tsarist imperialism was ready to sacrifice Yugoslav rights and aspirations.[1] Serbo-Croat-Slovene unification went by the board. Slovene and Croat territories were abandoned. Since an agreement with Italy would otherwise be quite impossible, Russia was reconciled to her acquiring Trieste, the whole of Istria with the islands in the Quarnero and, 'if it is absolutely necessary', Northern Dalmatia as far as the river Krka, with the adjacent islands and the towns of Zara and Sebenico. 'Our chief task, in this case, is to safeguard to the largest possible extent the interests of the Serbian Kingdom'. Hence, the main effort was to secure for it and Montenegro the coast and islands from the mouth of the Krka to the then frontier of the latter, while the littoral from Zara to Volosca was to go to Croatia, irrespective of her political fate. As for Italy's insistence on neutralization, this could be applied to the shore from Khimara to Stylos in Greece, and the waters of 'independent' Albania, but 'in no case' to the Bocche di Cattaro or the rest of the shore earmarked for Montenegro.[2] A telegram to this effect, without mentioning, however, the possibility of concessions in North Dalmatia, was sent to London and Paris on March 15th 1915.[3]

8

BRITAIN AND FRANCE VERSUS RUSSIA

But the military offensive in the Champagne had cost the French, between February 26th and March 15th 1915, well over 37,000 casualties.[4] The British lost the Battle of Neuve Chapelle on March 10th-12th. In Rome, Sonnino—while denying that he was conducting 'negotiations properly speaking' with Vienna—admitted to the Ambassador Barrère that 'we have received offers and naturally must ... examine them'.[5] He was still more playful with the Russian

---

[1] Miller, 52. On 5 April '15, Sazonov, in a telegram to the Russian Chief of Staff, General Yanushkevich, spoke of the need to sacrifice Croat and Slovene interests. *Internationale Beziehungen*, II. 7. II. No. 485, p. 490. Cf. Sazonov, 264: 'It cost me a great effort to sacrifice to ... the Italian Alliance the interest of the Serbian people'.

[2] Sazonov to Nicholas II, 15 March '15. *Internationale Beziehungen*, II. 7. I. No. 373, p. 342.

[3] Sazonov to Benckendorff and Izvolski, 15 March '15, and Sazonov's Aide-Memoire to Buchanan and Paléologue, 17 March. *ibid.* II. 7. I. p. 341, footnote 2. Full text in *Das Zaristische Russland*, pp. 292-4, where it is erroneously given as a telegram to Rome. Italy's demands for the Trentino and Tyrol (up to the Alpine frontier), Trieste, Istria and the Quarnero, Valona, Adalia, Moslem Albania with Durazzo, and the annexation of the Dodecanese were accepted, and so were her requests for a military convention with Russia, a pledge against a separate peace, and the exclusion of the Pope from the peace settlement. Italy was requested to attack by 1 April '15.

[4] Poincaré, VI. 117.   [5] 20 March '15. Poincaré, VI. 120.

Envoy. 'We are prepared to enter into negotiations with anyone, with Berlin, with Vienna, with the . . . Triple Entente, even with Mexico (the Minister added with a laugh) but that does not yet mean that such negotiations are bound to be crowned with success. . . . We are committed by nothing and to nobody . . . although, of course, this situation may change'.[1] In the meantime, the French Representative in Stockholm heard from the Swedish Foreign Minister that an Italo-Austrian agreement was thought to be imminent. Poincaré wondered whether this was true or whether 'it is not Italy who is spreading this rumour to get increased advantages from us?'[2] At any rate, it was wiser to err on the side of caution. And Declassé, suppressing his own doubts about the desirability of, among other things, an 'independent'—that is Italian controlled—Albania, urged upon Izvolski that Russia should soften her objections. Attributing as he did a 'colossal importance' to the Italian Alliance, he would not be responsible for delaying it 'even by ten minutes'. And to accelerate the proceedings, he was 'ready to agree in advance to every point on which an understanding is reached between Petrograd and London'.[3]

Grey, too, gave signs of impatience by proposing to Russia the kind of reply that should be given to Sonnino.[4] Sazonov, meanwhile, heard from the Ambassador Krupenski that 'the Rome Cabinet, in its last communication to Vienna, has . . . gone much further than hitherto'.[5] On the other hand, he found from Buchanan's draft that the British—obviously mindful of the repercussions of this question in Belgrade—were not inclined to give Italy a *carte blanche* in the Adriatic.[6] So, once more pushing his claims in Serbia's favour, the Russian Foreign Minister notified his Allies that, provided the Consulta dropped its Albanian pretensions outside the Valona district (so that the rest of that country could be divided between Serbs and Greeks), Russia would grant Italy the Dalmatian ports of Zara and Sebenico with the connecting coastline and nearby islands.[7] And on

---

[1] Krupenski to Sazonov, 17 March '15, quoting a statement from Sonnino on 10 March. *Internationale Beziehungen*, II. 7. I. No. 389, p. 363.
[2] 17 March '15. Poincaré, VI. 114.
[3] Izvolski to Sazonov, 17 and 19 March '15. *Internationale Beziehungen*, II. 7. I. No. 388, pp. 360–1 and p. 361, footnote 1.
[4] Aide-Memoire, Buchanan to Sazonov, 18 March '15. On 20 March, Benckendorff telegraphed that Delcassé had approved the British draft. *ibid.* II. 7. I. p. 367, footnote 2.
[5] Krupenski to Sazonov, 11 March '15. *ibid.* II. 7. I. No. 389, p. 362.
[6] Memorandum, Russian Foreign Ministry, 18 March '15. *ibid.* II. 7. I. No. 394, p. 368. Also II. 7. I. p. 367, footnote 2; No. 402, p. 374. See Grey, II. p. 208: 'We did not want to dishearten Serbia. . . .' Poincaré, VI. 121. Aldrovandi Marescotti, 37.
[7] Memorandum, Russian Foreign Ministry, 18 March '15. Sazonov to Benckendorff, 18 March, transmitting Sazonov's Aide-Memoire to Buchanan and Paléologue of the same date. *Internationale Beziehungen*, II. 7. I. NN 393, 394, pp. 367–8.

March 20th, Grey presented to the Ambassador Imperiali this Memorandum:

'The three Powers are prepared to take the Italian proposals into their most favourable consideration and have little doubt that an agreement could quickly be reached on the points of detail. . . . There is, however, one important question on which . . . the Italian proposals give rise to some difficulty. The Italian demand for Dalmatia, joined to the proposal to neutralize a large portion of the East-Adriatic coast and claim to the islands of Quarnero, leaves to Serbia very restricted opportunities . . . for her outlet to the sea; and it shuts in the Yugoslav provinces which have with reason looked to this War to secure for them the legitimate aspirations of expansion and development . . . . the three Powers would ask the Italian Government to review their claims in this direction and if possible to find some means of ascertaining the desiderata of the Yugoslav leaders. In other respects the three Powers accept generally the Italian proposals subject to agreement on points of detail'.[1]

As Imperiali, 'with great emphasis', stressed the Consulta's Dalmatian desires, the Foreign Secretary brought out Sazonov's concession regarding the Zara-Sebenico line, and mentioned 'the coast nearest Herzegovina and that bounding Spalato' as a necessity for Serbia and the Yugoslavs.[1]

But something quite obviously happened in Whitehall in the next few days. Presumably it was not unconnected, on the one hand, with Sonnino's compromise on Africa and the Middle East[2] and, on the other, with the fall of the Carpathian fortress Przemysl on March 22nd, which brought nearer Russia's westward advance on the ruins of Austria-Hungary. For, on March 24th, Buchanan transmitted to Sazonov three Aide-Memoires. The first contained a draft agreement with Italy elaborated in London. Under its terms, Rome was to receive, *inter alia*, not only Trieste, Gorizia and Gradisca, 'the whole of Istria as far as the Quarnero, including Volosca' and the Istrian islands, the Valona disctrict with Saseno and the 'independent' Moslem Albanian State with Durazzo, but also 'the Province of Dalmatia corresponding to the present administrative frontier . . . as far as the Narenta river in the South, furthermore the Peninsula of Sabbioncello, and all the islands lying to the North and West of Dalmatia. . . .'[3] This covered all the Consulta's Adriatic desiderata.

[1] Aide-Memoire, Buchanan to Sazonov, 21 March '15. *Internationale Beziehungen*, II. 7. I. No. 402, pp. 374–5. Cf. the text of Grey's Memorandum with slight verbal modifications in Salandra, 274, according to whom the Entente requested Italy to find means of 'satisfying Yugoslav aspirations'. See also Aldrovandi Marescotti, 38.
[2] See p. 325 above. Also Aide-Memoire, Buchanan to Sazonov, 24 March '15. *Internationale Beziehungen*, II. 7. II. No. 417, pp. 430–1.
[3] Aide-Memoire, Buchanan to Sazonov, 24 March '15. *ibid.* II. 7. II. No. 417, pp. 429–30. Retranslated from a translation of the English original.

The second Aide-Memoire, reproducing Imperiali's reply to Grey's Memorandum of March 21st, stated among other things that, while Serbia and Montenegro would get the shore between the mouths of the Narenta and the Drin, 'Italy must . . . insist on the neutralization of the coast from Cattaro down to the Voyusa'.[1] And the third emphasized that 'Italy will not be content with less than will give her effective control of the Adriatic. We must, therefore, decide either to admit the Italian claim or forgo the prospect of Italian co-operation. Italian co-operation . . . will be the turning point of the War'. Grey, like the British Military authorities and the Cabinet, was 'absolutely of the view that we should accept Italy's terms' on certain conditions.[2]

Sazonov, however, was elated with the victory at Przemysl, and reassured by his Envoys in Rome and Bucharest that the Consulta 'will not be satisfied with the trivial concessions Germany is said to contemplate'.[3] So he retorted that 'the present situation of the Allies is not such as to warrant a capitulation . . . before all Italy's claims'. 'If the Powers want the future peace to last, then they cannot allow that . . . Serbia and Montenegro should, for lack of a sufficient position on the coast, be wholly delivered up to Italy's annexationist designs'. It was 'indispensable to accord Serbia a larger share of Dalmatia, and not to rob Montenegro of the possibility of defending her coast by adopting its neutralization from Cattaro to the Voyusa'.[4] As he wired to Benckendorff, 'the accomplishment of an agreement is no less important for Italy than it is for us, for . . . if Germany and Austria learn that the agreement with the Entente has not materialized, they will hardly think it necessary to consent to territorial concessions in Italy's favour'.[5] But this flow of common sense must have been suddenly cut short by the vision of Constantinople, and Sazonov, applying once more the scissors to the map, announced that, as the 'utmost concession', Italy's slice of Dalmatia might be extended to Cape Planka.[6]

---

[1] Aide-Memoire, Buchanan to Sazonov, 24 March '15. *ibid*. II. 7. II. No. 418, pp. 431–2. Retranslated from a translation of the English original. Sonnino's telegram to Imperiali, Tittoni and Carlotti. Salandra, 275–6.

[2] Aide-Memoire, Buchanan to Sazonov, 24 March '15. *Internationale Beziehungen*, II. 7. II. No. 419, pp. 432–3. The contents is the same as in Grey's instructions to Buchanan, 22 March '15. Trevelyan, 296–7.

[3] Krupenski to Sazonov, 17 March '15. *Internationale Beziehungen*, II. 7. I. No. 389, p. 363. Poklevski to Sazonov, 17 March '15. Adamov, I. No. 117, pp. 317–18.

[4] Aide-Memoire, Russian Foreign Ministry to Buchanan and Paléologue, 25 March '15. *Internationale Beziehungen*, II. 7. II. No. 423, p. 436.

[5] Sazonov to Benckendorff, 25 March '15. *Das Zaristische Russland*, pp. 295–6.

[6] Aide-Memoire, Russian Foreign Ministry to Buchanan and Paléologue, 25 March '15. *Internationale Beziehungen*, II. 7. II. No. 423, p. 437. Sazonov also agreed that Italy should have the Moslem Albanian State, provided Greece and Serbia obtained a common frontier in Albania.

Thereupon Grey produced what was claimed to be a compromise. Rome would receive the territory and islands from Zara to Spalato, while the latter, and the coast to the South of it, was to go to the Serbs. This was to give them 'an unrestricted commercial approach to the Adriatic', but no more—for an unlimited control of these maritime outlets by Belgrade 'could constitute a strategic danger for Italy [and her protectors] if in future a strong Slav State should gain the mastery of that coast'. Hence Britain, like Italy, wished the whole littoral from Spalato to the Voyusa to be neutralized.[1] Moreover, as Benckendorff reported, Grey suggested to Imperiali that, if Dalmatia up to Spalato was abandoned to the Serbs, Italy could have the islands opposite the shore'.[2] This provoked a furious outburst from Sazonov: 'In insisting that Serbia should obtain the coast from the future Montenegrin frontier up to Cape Planka, I have, of course, also in mind the adjacent islands which are inseparable from it, as, without them, the possession of the coast would be illusory. . . . Grey's idea of ceding the islands to Italy is, therefore, unacceptable'.[3] The icy answer was that 'the negotiations between His Majesty's Government and Italy might be broken off as soon as the views of the Russian Government were communicated to the Italian Government, unless the Russian Government find it possible to modify them'.[4]

9

STRIFE

The British Foreign Secretary was all the more annoyed since he was doing well in Rome. Having proposed his compromise to Imperiali, he had added on March 26th that, feeling tired, he intended to leave London for a short rest. The Italian Ambassador wired to

---

[1] Aide-Memoire, Buchanan to Sazonov, 26 March '15. *Das Zaristische Russland*, p. 297. Izvolski to Sazonov, 27 March '15. Stieve, p. 180. Aldrovandi Marescotti, 39–40. Salandra, 277. For Britain's view on Serbia's approach to the Adriatic see Aide-Memoire, Buchanan to Sazonov, 24 March '15. *Internationale Beziehungen*, II. 7. II. No. 419, p. 433.

[2] Benckendorff to Sazonov, 25 March '15. *ibid*. II. 7. II. p. 442, footnote 3. In his Aide-Memoire of 26 March to Sazonov, Buchanan indicated that Italy would demand the coastal islands, while Grey thought they should be neutralized and left to Serbia. (*Das Zaristische Russland*, p. 297). But whether Grey had changed his mind or whether he had all along wished to strengthen the Adriatic barrier against Russia, the real position seems to have been as reported by Benckendorff, for this is borne out by Sazonov's attitude, the subsequent exchanges, and by Italian reactions—see Salandra, 277. Moreover, Aldrovandi Marescotti, 39–40, states that it was a question 'of leaving Spalato to the Serbs, and apportioning to us Zara and Sebenico, with the islands indispensable for our defence'. See also Izvolski to Sazonov, 27 March '15. Stieve, p. 180.

[3] Sazonov to Benckendorff, 26 March '15. *Internationale Beziehungen*, II. 7. II. No. 430, p. 442.

[4] Aide-Memoire, Buchanan to Sazonov, 28 March '15. *ibid*. II. 7. II. No. 438, p. 447. Retranslated from a translation of the English original.

Sonnino that 'we are at the culminating point of the discussions'.[1] If, as it could be, the 'fatigue' of the chief Entente spokesman was diplomatic, it was a warning not to reject his proffered hand. Already Imperiali telegraphed that the three Powers, 'while strongly desirous of our co-operation, had had to envisage ... the possibility of renouncing it'.[2] Then there was the improvement in Russia's bargaining position due to her capture of Przemysl, and the Consulta realized, as Salandra says, 'that it would not do to arrive too late'.[3] To crown it all, Madame Vasilchikova's letter, sounding the Tsar on a separate peace with Vienna and Berlin, had arrived in Petrograd.[4] Sazonov, although not attributing 'much importance' to the offer and leaving it unanswered, decided nevertheless to use it as a weapon against Sonnino. On March 28th, a high official of the Russian Foreign Ministry, having 'met the Italian Ambassador at dinner in the Yachting Club, related to him the attempt to initiate peace parleys with us, which had just been made by Austria. . . . This communication made a visible impression on the Ambassador. "That is very serious," he said. . . . "Did this person speak in the name of the Government?" . . . . "In the name of people whose voice carries authority in Austria." After a brief silence, the Ambassador, not without emotion, started hurriedly to say that Italy must quickly conclude an agreement with us, lest she should fall between two stools ... in his opinion Spalato ought to be left to Serbia without discussion'.[5]

Salandra lamented in retrospect that 'it was hard to abandon Spalato, home of our glorious Latin civilization and object of our fervid patriotism'.[6] Yet there was nothing to do but 'restrict our demands to Cape Planka'.[6] And on March 29th, Imperiali informed Grey that the Consulta would concede to Serbia and Montenegro the coast from Cape Planka to the Voyusa, including Spalato and five islands in close proximity to that port—provided that this entire littoral was neutralized and that Rome acquired, apart from all the other adjacent islands, also the Curzolari, with the neighbouring Peninsula of Sabbioncello.[7] 'The Italians', the Prime Minister Asquith

---

[1] Aldrovandi Marescotti, 40.
[2] Aldrovandi Marescotti, 40. A. M.'s formulation.
[3] Salandra, 277.      [4] See p. 104 above.
[5] Memorandum, Russian Foreign Ministry, 28 March '15. *Internationale Beziehungen*, II. 7. II. No. 441, pp. 450–1.
[6] Salandra, 277.
[7] Aide-Memoire, British Embassy, Petrograd, to Sazonov, 30 March '15, quoting Imperiali's Aide-Memoire to Grey of the preceding day. *Internationale Beziehungen*, II. 7. II. No. 448, p. 456. Salandra, 277, and Aldrovandi, 40, give 27. March as the date when Sonnino instructed Imperiali to communicate this to the British Foreign Secretary. If this date is correct, it would seem to destroy the causal connection between the Italian decision on Spalato and Vasilchikova's letter. But the fact that Imperiali did not hand this urgent Aide-Memoire to Grey until 29 March may be an indication that the relevant instructions were sent to

noted contentedly, 'are slightly contracting the orifice of their gullet'.[1]

But the Russians, he added, 'are still on the haggle'.[1] Sazonov could not fail to see that the Consulta, although apparently accepting the Dalmatian pattern he had designed for Serbia, had disturbed it by demanding all the islands—including now also the Curzolari —which dominate the entire land and sea scape. He remembered that the key port of Metkovich would have its marine exit blocked and, as Grey had admitted, completely lose its strategic, as distinct from commercial, value if Italy seized Sabbioncello.[2] He knew, as well as Churchill, that the Canal of Sabbioncello with its 'good anchorage for the largest vessels . . . out of gunfire from the shore . . . presented . . . every ideal condition for an Italian naval base'.[3] He was aware that this was true also of the Curzolari islands. And he reflected that, whereas there had, at first, been no question of neutralizing the stretch from Cattaro to the Narenta, Grey and Sonnino now combined their endeavours to extend that principle to all the sea outlets which Serbia was to have.[4]

On the other hand, Sazonov was much refreshed by Madame Vasilchikova's tonic. So, on March 28th, he notified Grey that, since he 'has reason to believe that Italy is even more interested than the Allied Powers in reaching an understanding . . . he has no apprehensions that the result of the London negotiations would be . . . compromised if certain exaggerated demands of the Italian Government were resisted with greater energy'. He suggested therefore this transaction: the North-Dalmatian coast and islands down to Cape Planka to Italy; the Southern portion of the Province with all the adjacent islands to Serbia. Complying with the British-Italian request, he granted that Cattaro should not be fortified, but raised,

him later, that is after Carlotti had reported the Vasilchikova affair in the evening of 28 March. Significantly, it was on the 29th that Sazonov wired to Benckendorff 'that, according to the Italian Ambassador [who, as Salandra says on p. 277, was given the same instructions as Imperiali and at the same time], they have realized in Rome the necessity of giving in on the question of the Dalmatian coast'. (*Internationale Beziehungen*, II. 7. II. p. 458, footnote 5. *Das Zaristische Russland*, p. 299; the date given here as 19 March is obviously an error and must read 29 March). It is hardly likely that either Sazonov or Carlotti would have withheld information of this nature had they had it earlier. Nor was it until 30 March that Delcassé received this information from London. See Izvolski to Sazonov, 30 March. *Internationale Beziehungen*, II. 7. II. No. 453, p. 460. Asquith's apposite comment is dated 29 March '15.

[1] 29 March '15. Asquith, II. 69.
[2] Aide-Memoire, Russian Foreign Ministry to Buchanan and Paléologue, 25 March '15. *Internationale Beziehungen*, II. 7. II. No. 423, p. 436. Aide-Memoire, British Embassy, Petrograd, to Sazonov, 30 March. *ibid.* II. 7. II. No. 448, p. 456.
[3] Churchill, *1915*, p. 331. Also Rodd, III. 242-3.
[4] Aide-Memoire, Russian Foreign Ministry to Buchanan, 28 March '15 *Internationale Beziehungen*, II. 7. II. No. 440. pp. 448-9.

at the same time, the question of neutralizing the entire line from Zara to the Narenta—that is only a part of the future Serbian, but practically the whole of the future Italian shore.[1] On the 29th— since, 'according to the Italian Ambassador, they have realised in Rome the necessity of giving in on the question of the Dalmatian coast'—he objected altogether to the idea of fixing 'the minute details' of Italy's future acquisitions 'at the present moment'.[2] On the 30th, he rejected Grey's proposal to grant Sonnino the neutralization of the coast and the possession of Sabbioncello and the islands, provided the Consulta compromised by leaving the latter and the Peninsula unfortified.[3] Sazonov simply stated that, 'to his great regret, it is quite impossible for him to admit that the islands lying off the coast which Serbia is to receive, and above all the Sabbioncello Peninsula, are ceded to Italy'.[4]

But on the same day, the Russian Ambassador wired from London that 'Grey doubts whether Serbia can complain about insufficient support by the Powers who have ensured her a three-fold increase of territory and ... a broad access to the sea for her trade.... the Italian Alliance would shorten the War by many months; consequently the Powers would prolong it solely in order to secure Serbia another limited coastal strip, and because of the islands and the problems of neutralization.... Posed in this way, the question of prolonging the War becomes one of such extraordinary gravity for England that the Cabinet... cannot shoulder the risk.... the opinion of the French Government is wholly fixed in the sense that we must clinch [the deal] with Italy forthwith.... Thus we are faced with the unalterable opinion of the English and French Governments ... that we cannot compel them substantially to prolong this War solely in the interests of Serbia'.[5]

This hint that arms might have to be laid down before Constantinople was taken was barely offset by Grey's offers to console Serbia by gains in the Banat.[6] Coming on the heels of the naval failure in the Dardanelles,[7] it acquired the weight of a threat. It was futile to argue, as Sazonov tried to, that Rome, having extorted almost every imaginable advantage from the Entente, would not jeopardize

---
[1] *ibid.*
[2] Sazonov to Benckendorff, 29 March '15. *Das Zaristische Russland,* p. 229. (The date here is an obvious error. See *Internationale Beziehungen,* II. 7. II. p. 458, footnote 5). Aide-Memoire, Russian Foreign Ministry to Buchanan and Paléologue, 29 March '15. *Internationale Beziehungen,* II. 7. II. No. 444, p. 453.
[3] Two Aide-Memoires from the British Embassy, Petrograd, to Sazonov, 30 March '15. *Internationale Beziehungen,* II. 7. II. No. 448, pp. 456-7, and p. 457, footnote 1.
[4] Aide-Memoire, Sazonov to Buchanan, 30 March '15. See *ibid.* II. 7. II. No. 450, p. 458.
[5] Benckendorff to Sazonov, 30 March '15. *ibid.* II. 7. II. No. 451, pp. 458-9.
[6] *ibid.* [7] See p. 102 above.

them because of a few Adriatic rocks.[1] It was no good ruminating, as he must have done, that when Grey spoke of 'trumping Germany's last cards',[2] he really meant those of Tsarist Russia. It was useless for Nicholas II to decree: 'Let England and France accept Italy's demands. We have reached the utmost limit of our concessions'.[3] On March 31st, Sazonov, 'because of the repeated representations' of his Allies, made another: four of the islands lying off the littoral to be allotted to Serbia could go to Italy; if Belgrade received Dalmatia from Cape Planka to Montenegro, including Sabbioncello and all (except four of) the adjacent islands, then all the islands, Sabbioncello and the Cattaro estuary could, like the coast from Zara to the Narenta, be neutralized.[4] But he could not refrain from underlining

'the very negative aspect of the ... situation. Among Italy's demands there are many which, like those affecting Asia Minor or the African colonies, call for no opposition at all from Russia. Nevertheless, since they ... involve the interests of our Allies, I considered myself obliged to support, in this respect, the viewpoint of the latter in every way. Grey, however, who has seen fit to repudiate out of hand Italy's claims to territories in which England and France take a closer interest, has not only manifested an unusual indulgence in those spheres where we were concerned with restricting the Italian demands, but he has apparently not even concealed from the Italian Ambassador that Russia alone is the obstacle to an understanding ... I told Buchanan ... that, if I had been able to foresee that Grey would conduct the negotiations in this fashion, I would never have consented for them to be held in London. ... As it is, all the concessions made to Italy at Slovene and Croat expense will be met with loud disapproval in Russia; the limitations now imposed on Serbia ... will be received with even greater indignation. But if it is known that we have been forced to make these concessions not only for lack of timely support ... but by downright pressure from Grey, who suddenly appeared as the defender of indivisible Italian predominance in the Adriatic, then Russian public opinion will doubtless turn against England'.[5]

---

[1] Sazonov to Benckendorff, 30 March '15. *Internationale Beziehungen*, II. 7. II. No. 450, p. 458.
[2] Benckendorff to Sazonov, 30 March '15. *ibid.* II. 7. II. No. 451, p. 459.
[3] 1 April '15. *ibid.* II. 7. II. No. 452, p. 460.
[4] Aide-Memoire, Russian Foreign Ministry to Buchanan and Paléologue, 31 March '15. *ibid.* II. 7. II. No. 455, pp. 462–3. Sazonov's proposal meant, of course, the neutralization of most of the coast which was to be allotted to Italy.
[5] Sazonov to Benckendorff, 31 March '15. *Internationale Beziehungen*, II. 7. II. No. 456, pp. 463–4. The point regarding Sazonov's defence of British and French interests, and the argument that Sonnino's intransigence was due to Grey's lack of firmness were stated more than once. See Sazonov's Aide-Memoire to Buchanan and Paléologue, 29 March '15, and his telegram to Benckendorff, 28 March. *ibid.* II. 7. II. No. 444, pp. 453–4 and p. 449, footnote 2.

Sir Edward's reply, all the more devastating because it was indirect, was contained in this message to Buchanan:

'There seems no chance now of coming to an agreement with Italy for some days and perhaps not at all if the Russian Minister for Foreign Affairs adheres to the line taken. . . . It is essential that I should have some rest and I am therefore going away for a few days. The Prime Minister . . . will personally take charge of the negotiations with Italy . . . and make whatever progress . . . the Russian Minister for Foreign Affairs renders possible'.[1]

Increasing blindness and insomnia, it was said, sent Grey on holiday over Easter-week. But Sazonov, for one, must have wondered whether this illness, at such a juncture, was not predominantly diplomatic. Already he was cautioned by Izvolski that Delcassé saw in Grey's departure, on March 31st, a sign 'that the parleys with Italy have been finally broken off. . . .'[2] Even if this was not so, it was certainly a warning of a potential crisis for which—judging by the tenor of the British communication—Russia would be held wholly responsible. Grey was one of the chief architects of the Entente, and he and Sazonov 'personally trusted one another'.[3] If Sazonov now caused him to resign—how would he stand with a new Foreign Secretary? Above all, it was Grey who had promised him spoils in Turkey, and even his temporary absence was a threat that his eventual successor might, in the circumstances, wish to revise the understanding arrived at. Already Petrograd was being reminded by Buchanan that,

'by the accord with France and Great Britain, the Russian Government has secured its future position regarding the Straits and Constantinople; and if the objections of the Russian Government to minor points affecting the Adriatic should deprive France and Great Britain of Italy's valuable aid, they will be very disappointed . . . Sir Edward Grey is very disheartened and he fears that he might forfeit Italian co-operation, which will have highly unfortunate consequences for us'.[4]

The French Envoy, meanwhile, had 'another lively discussion' with Sazonov. 'Italy's claims', Sazonov said, 'are a challenge to the Slav conscience!' Paléologue 'replied somewhat sharply: "We have taken up arms to save Serbia . . . but we are not fighting to realize the chimeric dreams of Slavism. The sacrifice of Constantinople is quite enough!"'.[5]

[1] Grey to Buchanan, 31 March '15. Trevelyan, 297; also 295.
[2] Izvolski to Sazonov, 1 April '15. *Internationale Beziehungen*, II. 7. II. No. 463, p. 471.
[3] Trevelyan, 297.
[4] Aide-Memoire, British Embassy, Petrograd, to Sazonov, 1 April '15. Retranslated from a translation of the English original. *Internationale Beziehungen*, II. 7. II. No. 461, p. 469.
[5] 31 March '15. Paléologue, I. 316.

So the defender of Dalmatia had to retreat another step. On April 1st, he learned through Buchanan that Sonnino had scorned the latest Russian idea of neutralizing the coast and islands coveted by Italy. The Consulta also persisted in its demand for Sabbioncello, conceding however that the latter could remain unfortified, if that restriction was applied also to the future Serbian shore. Buchanan, making the most of this 'final' Italian compromise, urged upon the Russian Foreign Minister 'not to make difficulties' over that Peninsula.[1] And Sazonov notified the Ambassador that, whilst declining to make any new concessions (the Curzolari), and upholding 'in particular' his demand for the allocation of Sabbioncello to Serbia, he was abandoning his contention that the littoral allotted to Italy should be neutralized.[2]

## 10
### DIFFICULTIES BETWEEN BRITAIN AND ITALY

Meanwhile, Asquith—deputizing for Grey—offered to Italy, on April 1st, the four islands granted earlier by Sazonov (Lissa, Busi, Cazza, Lagosta) plus Pelagosa which he added off his own bat, and the Adriatic coast with the adjoining islands from the Northern frontier of Dalmatia to Cape Planka. The rest of the Dalmatian shore from Cape Planka to the Montenegrin frontier, including Sabbioncello, with all the neighbouring islands—except the above five—would go to Serbia. All the islands along the coast, the coast from Zara to the mouth of the Narenta, and the Bay of Cattaro were to be neutralized.[3] These terms—not to speak of the denial of Sabbioncello—would withhold the Curzolari group from Italy. 'They would', as Salandra and Sonnino were quick to see and as the former has recorded, 'result in the neutralization of the greater part of our [sic] coast . . . while the stretch of Serbian coast which included the Peninsula of Sabbioncello would *not* be neutralized . . . . they would deprive us of the more strategically important islands'. Asquith's

[1] Aide-Memoire, British Embassy, Petrograd, toサzonov, 1 April '15. Retranslated from a translation of the English original. *Internationale Beziehungen*, II. 7. II. No. 461, pp. 468–9.
[2] Aide-Memoire, Sazonov to Buchanan, 1 April '15. *ibid.* II. 7. II. p. 469, footnote 1.
[3] Asquith to Imperiali, 1 April '15. See Aide-Memoire, British Embassy, Petrograd, to Sazonov, 3 April '15. *Internationale Beziehungen*, II. 7. II. p. 479, footnote 3. The summary of Asquith's terms given here makes no mention of neutralizing the coast from Zara to the mouth of the Narenta. But Salandra, 277, and Aldrovandi Marescotti, 41, in their rendering of these terms, explicitly refer to that coastline, and so does Rodd as quoted in the above footnote. Also Benckendorff to Sazonov, 2 April '15. *Das Zaristische Russland*, p. 303. Aldrovandi Marescotti, 40–41. Salandra, 277–8. Asquith's proposals were made on the basis of Sazonov's Note of 31 March '15. See *Internationale Beziehungen*, II. 7. II. p. 463, footnote 1.

solution, in short, 'completely prejudiced that military supremacy' in the Adriatic,[1] which Italian imperialism considered as its due. Grey's rest-cure suddenly proved to be a weapon aimed not only at Petrograd, but also at Rome. Assuming, perhaps, that Whitehall was not disinclined to keep Italian aspirations within certain bounds, even while it sponsored them, Sazonov hastened to express his 'sincere gratification' with the 'firm tone' adopted by the British Premier.[2]

But Sonnino at once instructed Imperiali to explain in London, 'why, if the three Powers maintain their emendation, we are compelled ... to withdraw our proposals....'[3] He also spoke, as Salandra says, 'very plainly and firmly' to the Ambassador Rodd.[4] Recalling that 'Russia, if she obtained control over Constantinople, might become in future the leading naval Power in the Mediterranean', he insisted on the ownership of the Curzolari, underlined that, 'unless the Serbian coast is neutralized, the greater part of the Italian coast will have no more reliable security guarantee than it has at present', and emphasized that, as 'considerable claims' had 'already been booked by other Powers' elsewhere, Italy had 'a vital interest in the maintenance of the balance of power in the Eastern Mediterranean. Hence, the prospect of obtaining absolute security in the Adriatic ... is the only point an Italian statesman could advance as a motive for his country to go to war'. Buchanan, in transmitting this to Sazonov, quoted Rodd's opinion that the Entente could 'gain Italy's immediate co-operation' by giving her Sabbioncello (which, like the Serbian coast, was not to be fortified) and the Curzolari islands, and exempting her future acquisitions from neutralization while applying it wholesale to those of Serbia. Failing that, they would 'face an issue which can only be regarded as critical'.[5] Simultaneously, the Ambassador Carlotti, in a heated conversation, confirmed in Petrograd Sonnino's threat to suspend negotiations. And no sooner had Sazonov declared that Italy's claim to Sabbioncello and the Curzolari was 'unacceptable'[6], than Buchanan brought him 'another urgent request' for accommodation.[7]

[1] Salandra, 278. Italics in the original.
[2] Sazonov to Benckendorff, 4 April '15. *Das Zaristische Russland*, p. 304.
[3] 3 April '15. Salandra, 278. Aldrovandi Marescotti, 41.
[4] Salandra, 279.
[5] Aide-Memoire, British Embassy, Petrograd, to Sazonov, 4 April '15. Retranslated from a translation of the English original. *Internationale Beziehungen*, II. 7. II. No. 475, pp. 480–2. Salandra, 279.
[6] Aldrovandi Marescotti, 42.
[7] Memorandum, Russian Foreign Ministry, 4 April '15. *Internationale Beziehungen*, II. 7. II. No. 479, pp. 484–5. According to Imperiali, Asquith 'has not failed to inform the Petrograd Cabinet ... in a very decided manner' that Italy 'should have predominance in the Adriatic'. A telegram from Imperiali to Rome, 6 April '15. Salandra, 280.

## 11
### FRANCE TABLES A FORMULA

The emergency suddenly activized Delcassé. In Paris, the attitude to Italy had fluctuated with the strains and stresses experienced by French imperialism. Poincaré noted that 'Tittoni who, the day following the first attack on the Dardanelles, was all fire and flame, joyfully announcing the imminent intervention of Italy, and never leaving Delcassé's study, suddenly cooled off after the loss of the *Bouvet*.' Listing the offers made to Rome, the President ruminated that 'Italy, who had experienced none of the initial difficulties of the War, will thus reap victory's finest fruits'.[1] Moreover, France had so far no agreement with Britain and Russia on the gains she expected to make in this War. 'If we consent to-day to give up or assign lands to Italy, we are undertaking to guarantee her the districts she aims at. Then, should Italy feel incapable of conquering them herself, she would be able to oppose any peace negotiations until we had put her in possession....'[2] The Government, therefore, 'desired that, henceforth at least, no excessive promises are made either in the Adriatic or Asia Minor', and, on March 23rd, the Foreign Minister was charged with keeping the Consulta's pretensions within stricter bounds.[3] He must have acted promptly enough, for, two days later, he received a Note from Grey pressing for immediate acceptance of Sonnino's terms, and the French Cabinet, not without serious hesitation, 'resigns itself to bearing them'.[4] Thereafter the Quai d'Orsay seconded faithfully Whitehall's efforts in Petrograd, and Delcassé was as eloquent and 'anxious and sombre'[5] as the occasion seemed to require.

This mood was deepened by the 'lugubrious monotony' of the army communiqués. 'Days of fog and rain', wrote Poincaré. 'We take or lose a trench ... that is all. But men fall, and death pitilessly pursues her fatal errand'.[6] Since December 1914, 'the military picture has hardly changed.... The isolated engagements which ... have cost them prodigious sacrifices have, nevertheless, not led to the piercing of the German lines. In the last fighting of this kind ... the French have lost over 30,000 men.... France ... is placing four million soldiers, that is ten per cent of her population, under arms. The fact that ten of her richest departments are occupied by the enemy is making itself felt economically, as well as in the quality

---

[1] 23 March '15. Poincaré, VI. 126–7.    [2] Poincaré, VI. 148–9.
[3] Poincaré, VI. 127. The quotation is from Poincaré.
[4] 25 March '14. Poincaré, VI. 130.
[5] Izvolski to Sazonov, 1 April '15. *Internationale Beziehungen*, II. 7. II. No. 463, p. 471. Also 25, 27 and 30 March '15. Stieve, p. 180. *Int. Bez.*, II. 7. II. NN 426, 453, pp. 438, 460–1.
[6] 7 April '15. Poincaré, VI. 147.

and numbers of the enlisted . . . contingents. All the troops fit for service are already with the colours. . . . In these circumstances, the prospect of a second winter campaign may produce a sudden . . . fit of despair . . . . events can only be speeded up, if some new element joins in, namely Italy's belligerency. . . .'[1] The latter was also required by diplomatic strategy. As Britain had just 'given' Constantinople and the Straits for the steamroller of the Tsar, France could not lag behind long. But Paris, like London, would only sanction Russia's advance into the Mediterranean after ensuring that Italy moved into the Balkans. This depended on a *détente* between Petrograd and Rome. On April 5th 1915—five days before making his Turkish present to Sazonov—Delcassé, having learned of the 'categorical' rejection of Asquith's proposals by Sonnino, tabled a compromise solution: Sabbioncello to be neutralized and allocated to Serbia, the nearby islands of Curzola, Meleda and Lesina, not neutralized, to fall to the Italians.[2]

Did Delcassé know that Salandra, meanwhile, had decided that Sabbioncello was 'not . . . indispensable?'[3] The Consulta was too well steeped in international politics not to see that the very stiffness of Asquith's terms was both a means of pressure and an invitation to bargain. The Italian threat 'to break off negotiations'[4] was, therefore, simply an exercise in retaliation, with a concession up the negotiator's sleeve. The rapid surrender in this instance was prompted, moreover, by the recurrent rumours that Vienna might seek to escape from her quandaries by a separate peace. On April 3rd, a high official of the Russian Foreign Ministry made a point of representing to the Italian Ambassador the arrival in Petrograd of an emissary from the Stavka (High Command) 'as being connected with the question recently raised by Austria'. On the 4th, referring to Rome's intransigence, the official declared: 'Rest assured that we shall take care not to fall between two stools'. Three days later, when Carlotti—alluding to the departure of the Premier Goremykin for Headquarters—voiced the hope that the Russians had not written off his country, he was told that this would depend primarily on the Consulta.[5] In Berlin, the Chancellor was sufficiently disquietened by Austria's intentions to endeavour—without much success—to persuade the Ambassador Bollati of Francis Joseph's loyalty to

---

[1] Izvolski to Sazonov, 20 April '15. *Internationale Beziehungen*, II. 7. II. No. 568, pp. 568–9.
[2] Izvolski to Sazonov, 5 April '15. *Internationale Beziehungen*, II. 7. II. No. 486, pp. 490–1. Poincaré, VI. 147. Suarez, III. 112. See also p. 101 above.
[3] Salandra to Sonnino, presumably 1 or 2 April '15. Salandra, 279.
[4] Salandra, 279.
[5] Memoranda, Russian Foreign Ministry, 3, 4 and 7 April '15. *Internationale Beziehungen*, II. 7. II. NN 469, 479, 494, pp. 475, 485, 496.

William.[1] Even from London, there came indications of a possible arrangement with the Ballplatz.[2] Sonnino did not have to wait for his Envoys' telegrams from Nish and Sophia to know that an Austro-Russian peace would not only cost him all his prizes, but leave the Habsburgs 'free to deal with Italy'.[3]

## 12
### RUSSIA AND THE YUGOSLAVS

In the meantime, Sazonov was beset by conflicting influences. Since the beginning of the year, the Russian High Command had been stressing the need for Italian co-belligerency. Although its military benefits were rated low, the contention was that the Alliance would close the enemies' contraband gap in the Mediterranean, impress wavering neutrals in the Balkans, and have 'an immense moral effect' on flagging spirits in the field.[4] In the heyday of Przemysl, Victor Emmanuel's Army was treated with indifference by the Russians. But their attempt—despite the shell shortage—to cross the Carpathians brought operations, as the Generalissimo wired to Sazonov, 'to such a stage that, at this very moment, Italy's intervention would be of particular importance'.[5] The Tsar was so unnerved that, in Sazonov's words, 'His Majesty was pleased to command me to inform the British Government that we consent to Delcassé's proposal to concede to Italy the contested islands, but continue to insist that Sabbioncello should be assigned to Serbia. In case an understanding should not be attainable on this basis, His Majesty was pleased to authorize me, as a last resort, to make one more concession . . . that Sabbioncello should be ceded to Italy, if it is neutralized and Italy pledges herself to attack Austria by the end of April . . . at the latest'.[6] This echoed the view of the Generalissimo that 'Serbia, in whose defence we have started the War, could make some sacrifices'.[7]

[1] Memorandum, Russian Foreign Ministry, 7 April. *ibid.* II. 7. II. No. 494, p. 495, on Bollati's report to Rome about his conversation with Bethmann-Hollweg.
[2] Aldrovandi Marescotti, 41.
[3] Cucchi to Sonnino, 13 April '15, No. 68. Squitti to Sonnino, 10 April. No. 66. *The Italian Green Book*, pp. 1303–4. Also Aldrovandi Marescotti, 35. Giolitti, 386.
[4] Kudashev to Sazonov, 21 Jan. '15, quoting General Danilov. *Internationale Beziehungen*, II. 7. I. p. 22, footnote 1. Sazonov to Benckendorff and Izvolski, 8 March '15. Adamov, I. No. 114, p. 314. Memoranda, Russian Foreign Ministry, 15, 16 March '15, quoting the Generalissimo. *Int. Bez.*, II. 7. I. No. 378, p. 347; No. 381, p. 351. Sazonov, 264.
[5] 6 April '15. *Internationale Beziehungen*, II. 7. II. No. 493, p. 495. Talenski, 45.
[6] Sazonov to the Generalissimo, 6 April '15. *Das Zaristische Russland*, pp. 305–6. Also the Generalissimo to Sazonov, 6 April '15. *Internationale Beziehungen*, II. 7. II. No. 493, p. 495.
[7] Secretary, Diplomatic Chancellery at the Stavka, to Sazonov, 3 April '15. *ibid.* II. 7. II. No. 471, p. 477.

The Yugoslavs, however, suspected the altruism of Petrograd. Even supposing they had not perceived the real reasons why Tsarist imperialism had drawn the sword, they understood only too well the implication of statements such as Sazonov's to the Dalmatian Supilo to the effect that many a hope of theirs would have to be slain on the Roman altar,[1] or of a leading Russian press man in Rome that his Government was ready 'to recognize the justification of some of Italy's territorial claims, even though they are not based on the national principle'.[2] Supilo, clearly, did not believe that, in Russia, he was merely forcing his way 'through an open door', for —disregarding the advice received that he should go to Paris and London—he asked for an audience with Nicholas II.[3] The Serbian Crown Prince, not content with expressing to the Russian Envoy his 'grave concern' about the Consulta's pretensions, wished to send the Prime Minister Pashich on a mission to the Neva.[4] The first Croato-Slovene Congress, endorsing the programme of Yugoslav unification under Serbia's aegis, resolved on resisting, 'by force if necessary', any move 'to exchange their present servitude . . . for death under final Italian domination'.[5] And Pashich coupled his warnings that their future relations with Rome would resemble those prevailing then between the latter and Vienna with an appeal to the Russian Foreign Ministry 'that the Yugoslav provinces should not become an object of barter. . . .'[6] But Sazonov vetoed the Premier's visit. He invited the Stavka not to rouse 'unrealizable expectations' in Supilo, who went to plead with the generals.[7] And the Powers continued to deal in lands, islands and human beings.

## 13

### DEALING IN LANDS AND PEOPLE

The acceptance by both Rome and Petrograd of Delcassé's formula (Sabbioncello to Serbia, the Curzolari to the Italians) did not ex-

[1] Memorandum, Russian Foreign Ministry, 25 March '15. *ibid*. II. 7. II. No. 425, pp. 437–8.
[2] Statement by the Representative of the Petrograd Telegraph Agency in Rome, published in the Italian press (*Il Messagero*) in the first days of April. Krupenski to Sazonov, 3 April '15. *Internationale Beziehungen*, II. 7. II. No. 470, p. 476, and *ibid*. footnote 2.
[3] Memoranda, Russian Foreign Ministry, 27 and 29 March '15. *Internationale Beziehungen*, II. 7. II. No. 434, p. 445; No. 445, pp. 454–5.
[4] Trubetskoi to Sazonov, 31 March '15. *ibid*. II. 7. II. No. 460, pp. 467–8.
[5] 11 April '15 in Trieste. The Russian Chargé d'Affaires in Rome to Sazonov, 19 April '15. *ibid*. II. 7. II. No. 560, pp. 559–60.
[6] Telegram, 6 April '15, transmitted by the Serbian Legation, Petrograd, to the Russian Foreign Ministry, 9 April '15. *ibid*. II. 7. II. No. 501, pp. 502–4. Trubetskoi to Sazonov, 29 March. *ibid*. II. 7. II. No. 446, p. 455.
[7] Sazonov to Trubetskoi, 3 April '15. *ibid*. II. 7. II. No. 468, p. 475. Sazonov to Kudashev, 11 April. *ibid*. II. 7. II. No. 514, pp. 512–13.

haust the quarrel. Sazonov suggested that these three islands should not be fortified, but this was declined by the Consulta.[1] Asquith and Rodd, evidently at one with Sonnino, proposed the neutralization of the entire coast assigned to Serbia, but the Russian Foreign Minister —having adopted that principle for the future Serbian coast from Cape Planka to the Narenta, the adjacent islands, Sabbioncello and the Bocche di Cattaro—demanded, in return for consenting to lift all restrictions from Italy's portion of Dalmatia, that she should allow the same freedom to the Serbo-Montenegrin shore from Sabbioncello to the Albanian frontier.[2] The British Prime Minister, while holding with Rome that the three Curzolari islands were not to be neutralized, offered the Slavs a coastal strip between Sabbioncello and Castelnuovo on the same condition.[3] Although this was less than Sazonov asked for, Sonnino reduced it further by substituting for Castelnuovo: 'a point ten miles South of Ragusa', on the grounds that Castelnuovo was too near Cattaro. As a *quid pro quo* for this concession, he requested that Italy be entrusted with the diplomatic representation of Moslem Albania. Grey (whose recovery and return, on April 14th, coincided with the final Dalmatian bargain between Rome and Petrograd[4]) consented—with the proviso that 'the hinterland of that State should be demarcated with a view to giving Serbia and Greece a territorial connection'.[5] The Consulta—suspecting no doubt that its Whitehall friends were trying to bar further Italian penetration in the Central Balkans—desired that this border should be left undefined.[6] The Foreign Secretary, 'somewhat nettled',[7] retorted that, to avoid delay, he had refrained from introducing some very desirable modifications. But if Italy now stuck to her guns he would insist on equal vagueness regarding the inland frontiers of her portion of Dalmatia.[8] Sonnino, needless to say, had to give in.[9]

---

[1] Sazonov to Benckendorff, 6 April '15. *ibid.* II. 7. II. No. 490, p. 493. Aldrovandi Marescotti, 42.

[2] Aide-Memoire, Buchanan to Sazonov, 4 April '15. Aide-Memoire, Russian Foreign Ministry to Buchanan and Paléologue, 4 April '15. *Internationale Beziehungen*, II. 7. II. No. 474, pp. 479–80 and p. 479, footnote 3. Sazonov to Benckendorff, 6 April '15. *ibid.* II. 7. II. No. 490, p. 493. Aldrovandi Marescotti, 42.

[3] 9 April '15. Aldrovandi Marescotti, 43. Aide-Memoire, Buchanan to Sazonov, 10 April '15. *Das Zaristische Russland*, p. 307.

[4] Trevelyan, 295. Salandra, 280.

[5] Aide-Memoire, British Embassy, Petrograd, to Sazonov, 15 April '15. Retranslated from a translation of the English original. *Internationale Beziehungen*, II. 7. II. No. 535, pp. 535–6. Aldrovandi Marescotti, 43.

[6] Aide-Memoire, Russian Foreign Ministry to Buchanan and Paléologue, 18 April '15. *Internationale Beziehungen*, II. 7. II. No. 550, p. 552.

[7] Imperiali's telegram, 21 April '15. Aldrovandi Marescotti, 44; also 45.

[8] Aide-Memoire, British Embassy, Petrograd, to Sazonov, 22 April '15. *Internationale Beziehungen*, II. 7. II. No. 581, p. 581. Benckendorff to Sazonov, 22 April. *ibid.* II. 7. II. No. 586, p. 585.

[9] Treaty Text. *Internationale Beziehungen*, II. 7. II. No. 612, p. 606.

Sazonov, for his part, whilst agreeing to the Asquith plan of April 10th, the Sonnino line for the non-neutralized Serbian shore, and Grey's Albanian stipulations, strenuously resisted Italy's suddenly expressed intention not to march until a month after the signature of the contemplated Treaty.[1] This fresh procrastination, according to Salandra, came from the desire to have 'more time for military preparations', to depart 'in a fitting manner' from the Triple Alliance, and to wear down the neutralist opposition at home.[2] Another reason doubtless was the wish to browbeat Russia into making more rapid concessions. At the root of it all, however, lay the Consulta's calculated distaste for irrevocable steps, 'reserving to itself [Salandra has confessed] as long as possible a change of route in case a mistake had been made'.[3] Sazonov, on the other hand, was preoccupied with the Carpathian battle and the need for diverting the enemy. So he protested angrily that the only purpose of all his compromises had been 'to secure Italy's immediate intervention'. Her belligerency had been authoritatively foreshadowed for the end of April. If Rome, 'having by her intransigence drawn out the negotiations and obtained important advantages, is now trying to postpone the fulfilment of the reciprocal obligations, Russia will be compelled to revoke the concessions. The prospective understanding, therefore, will have to be considered as lapsed, unless Italy has entered the War at the latest by May 1st.'[4] The French Commander-in-Chief, as Poincaré recorded, confirmed that Italian intervention, 'to be really effective, should take place in the first days of May. Failing that, the Russian offensive in the Carpathians might be stopped. . . . According to Joffre, it is indispensable that Austria should be immobilized in the Trentino and the Trieste region . . . . Otherwise, if Russia is . . . beaten or paralysed, Germany will be able to withdraw several army corps from the Eastern front and lead them back to France'.[5] But Delcassé and Grey were so bent on the Italian Alliance that they pressed for 'top-speed' signature.[6] Sazonov was ready to accept May 15th as the dead-line on condition that, to boost the morale of the Russian Army in the Carpathians, 'the fact that understanding

---

[1] Aide-Memoire, Russian Foreign Ministry to Buchanan and Paléologue, 16 April '15. *ibid.* II. 7. II. No. 537, pp. 538–9. Aldrovandi Marescotti, 43. Sazonov to Benckendorff, 15 April '15. *Das Zaristische Russland,* pp. 309–10.
[2] Salandra, 281.
[3] Salandra, 208.
[4] Aide-Memoire, Russian Foreign Ministry to Buchanan and Paléologue, 16 April '15. *Internationale Beziehungen,* II. 7. II. No. 537, p. 539. Sazonov to Benckendorff, 15 April '15. *Das Zaristische Russland,* pp 309–10. Aldrovandi Marescotti, 43. Poincaré, VI. 165–6.
[5] Poincaré, VI. 163–4.
[6] Izvolski to Sazonov, 16 April '15. *Internationale Beziehungen,* II. 7. II. p. 544, footnote 2. Benckendorff to Sazonov, 17 April '15. *Das Zaristische Russland,* p. 313.

has been reached is made public not later than May 1st. . . .'¹ Grey and Delcassé, however, not only stood their ground² but raised fresh difficulties.

The modified Treaty draft, as transmitted from London, laid down that the neutralization provided for the future Serbian coast (except from Sabbioncello to a point ten kilometres below Ragusa Vecchia) and the islands not falling to Italy should be extended as far as the river Voyusa.³ This, as Sazonov at once protested, implied new restrictions for the shore already possessed by Montenegro, so that the latter would, 'after a victorious war, lose sovereign rights'.⁴ That country, meantime, was racked by famine exploding in hunger rioting by women.⁵ The snail's pace of the relief which was attempted contrasted starkly with the speed at which the wheels of diplomacy were revolving. Sazonov pounced on the chance to embarrass his Allies by a great show of moral indignation 'that England and France, in their hurry to sign the Treaty, could so forget international law as to conclude a Treaty at the expense of a third, independent and, moreover, Allied State'.⁶ He also criticized the retention of Sonnino's original formula whereby the destiny of the littoral not apportioned to Italy would simply be 'left to the decision of Europe after the termination of the War'.⁷ He wished, on the contrary, that the future Slav acquisitions should be explicitly fixed in the Agreement, by listing those of Serbia and Montenegro, and specifying that, in the Upper Adriatic, the whole area from the Bay of Volosca and Istria to Northern Dalmatia, with Fiume and the other ports, and five contiguous islands should be assigned to Croatia 'whatever will be the fate of the latter'.⁸ When Grey reluctantly and Delcassé readily assented to leaving the existing Montenegrin shore without new restrictions, Sonnino was prevailed upon to accept

¹ Sazonov to Benckendorff and Izvolski, 17 April '15. *Internationale Beziehungen*, II. 7. II. No. 545, p. 544.
² Izvolski to Sazonov, 18 April '15. Benckendorff to Sazonov, 19 April. Sazonov to Kudashev, 19 April. *ibid.* II. 7. II. p. 545, footnote 1; No. 558, p. 558. Poincaré, VI. 166.
³ Benckendorff to Sazonov, 16 April '15. Buchanan to Sazonov, 17 April. *Internationale Beziehungen*, II. 7. II. p. 548, footnote 3; p. 549, footnote 8.
⁴ Aide-Memoire, Russian Foreign Ministry to Buchanan and Paléologue, 18 April '15. *ibid.* II. 7. II. No. 550, p. 550.
⁵ The Russian Chargé d'Affaires in Tsetinye to the Russian Assistant Foreign Minister, 22 April 15. *Internationale Beziehungen*, II. 7. II. No. 591, p. 589; also 2 May '15. *ibid.* p. 589, footnote 2.
⁶ Sazonov to Izvolski, 21 April '15. *Internationale Beziehungen*, II. 7. II. No. 573, pp. 573–4. Also Sazonov to Benckendorff, 23 April. *ibid.* II. 7. II. No. 594, p. 592.
⁷ See British Embassy, Petrograd, to Sazonov, 24 March '15. *ibid.* II. 7. II. No. 417, p. 430. Salandra, 294.
⁸ Aide-Memoire, Russian Foreign Ministry to Buchanan and Paléologue, 18 April '15. *Internationale Beziehungen*, II. 7. II. No. 550, pp. 550–1. Aldrovandi Marescotti, 45.

this.¹ But the British Foreign Secretary found fault with the idea of determining at this moment the question of the territories to go to Serbia, Croatia and Montenegro.² This attitude was related to the fact that, in 1915, none of the Powers expected, and few desired, the complete collapse of the Habsburg structure. The utmost aim was 'a sensible diminution of its strength'.³ Certainly, Britain appeared disinclined to exclude Austria-Hungary wholly from the Adriatic lest this should 'push her into the embrace of Germany' or 'leave her at the mercy of Russia', for, instead of a direct maritime outlet, she 'would have only the Danube approach to the Black Sea, or the road through Germany to the Baltic and North Sea'. The Ambassador Bertie, for one, thought it 'a very mistaken policy' to make Italy 'supreme in the Adriatic'.⁴ Paradoxically, Italy herself counted on the survival of her mortal enemy. An Austria thoroughly curbed and castigated was necessary to her as a counterweight to Anglo-French hegemony in the Mediterranean, Yugoslav unification and Russian influence in the Balkans.⁵ So, not to demand the Hungarian-Croatian coast, at this juncture, was useful both as an inducement to Vienna if it came to deserting Berlin, and a pledge of 'friendship' to come. Alternatively, there were Hungary and Croatia—the one known, the other presumed to be, anti-Serb. Both or either, it was supposed, might be rallied to Rome and mobilized against Belgrade at the price of leaving them the 'purely commercial'⁶ gateway of Fiume.

In the spring of 1915, a secret emissary from the Hungarian Independence Party made several calls on Sonnino and brought him Karolyi's message that the Hungarian people did not desire Germany's victory, as it would make them her vassals. 'An independent Hungary was a first-class Italian interest . . . Hungary was neither Slav nor Teuton. She was not strong enough to harbour territorial ambitions—for instance in the Balkans—but she could oppose a barrier to the territorial ambitions of other States'. The agent 'also mentioned the indispensability of a sea coast for Hungary'. Sonnino, according to Karolyi, gave the assurance that he would abandon his claim to Fiume and the adjacent shores.⁷ With the prospect of having in her hands Trieste, Pola, Northern Dalmatia and Valona, Italy felt able to afford a 'sacrifice' which would, moreover, embroil the Magyars with the Slavs, or the Croats with the Serbs, and so

---

¹ Izvolski to Sazonov, 21 April '15. Benckendorff to Sazonov, 22 April. *Internationale Beziehungen*, II. 7. II. NN 577, 586, pp. 577, 585. Sonnino to Imperiali, 22 April '15. Aldrovandi Marescotti, 44–5.
² See *Internationale Beziehungen*, II. 7. II. p. 551, footnote 1.
³ Rodd, III. 243.   ⁴ 2 April '15. Bertie, I. 137.
⁵ Bollati to Avarna, 14 April '15. *Carteggio*, LXII. III. 380.
⁶ Salandra, 295.   ⁷ Karolyi, 71–2. The quotation is from Karolyi's book.

set the seal on her 'military predominance in the Adriatic'.[1] To leave the future of that region vague meant to preserve freedom of manoeuvre for the Consulta.

But the scheme was too clever to find favour with the Quai d'Orsay. Even though France, like Britain, valued the Danubian Empire as a guarantee against a Greater Germany and Tsarist Russia, she shared the latter's dislike of Italy's South-Eastern expansion, and hence became interested in a solid Slav buffer in the Balkans. This would seem to be why Paul Cambon, the Ambassador in London, who (in Italian opinion) was 'not very well disposed towards us', and who was charged with making the French translation of the terms of agreement, turned simple interpreting into what Aldrovandi Marescotti acidly describes as the 'skilful probe of a negotiator'.[2] For—to the delight of Sazonov—'Europe', whom Sonnino had chosen to dispose of the lands he had not laid his hands on, was stripped of her role of Lady Bountiful, and the operative clause suddenly read that, at the peace, the four Entente Powers would distribute these territories among Croatia, Serbia and Montenegro.[3] The change was accepted in Rome[4] with a rapidity which would have been surprising were it not for the imminence of the attack on Gallipoli.[5] Lest a successful landing should wipe out the value of the Italian Alliance, it was imperative to rush the conclusion of the Treaty.

14

AGREEMENT OVER CONSTANTINOPLE AND COMPROMISE OVER ITALY

The hot winds of impatience blew also in other capitals. 'Mon cher et grand ami', President Poincaré wired to Nicholas II,

'will Your Majesty permit me to say how dangerous it appears to me to delay the adherence of the Allies to the Italian Memorandum. General Joffre desires Italy's speediest entry into the War.... Better that she should intervene late rather than never. Your Majesty, who has so high and en-

---

[1] Salandra, 295; also 294, 297. Rodd, III. 243.
[2] Aldrovandi Marescotti, 35.
[3] The wording made plain that, while Serbia and Montenegro were to receive the coasts and islands already allotted to them in the present negotiations, the area between Istria and Dalmatia, with Fiume, would go to Croatia. Treaty Text. *Internationale Beziehungen*, II. 7. II. No. 612, pp. 605–6. Imperiali to Sonnino, 21 April '15. Aldrovandi Marescotti, 45; also 34. Salandra, 294–5. Benckendorff to Sazonov, 22 April '15. *Int. Bez.*, II. 7. II. No. 586, p. 585; and again 22 April, mentioning Cambon's translation. *ibid.* II. 7. II. No. 587, p. 586. Imperiali to Sonnino, 16 April '15, on the same subject. Aldrovandi Marescotti, 43–4. Salandra, 280.
[4] Sonnino to Imperiali, 22 April '15. Aldrovandi Marescotti, 45.
[5] See p. 108 above.

lightened an awareness of the interests of the Allied countries, will surely not hesitate to ward off a rupture which could have the gravest consequences'.[1]

King George V telegraphed to the Tsar in the same sense.[2] Lord Kitchener, as Benckendorff reported, urged that 'a prompt understanding was necessary from the military and naval point of view'.[3] The fighting on the Eastern front, it was feared, 'might end in an overwhelming defeat' and deter the Italians from staking their fortune on the Entente.[4] In the West, the second battle of Ypres was in train, with poison gas, panic and such casualties that those of the British alone touched 50,000. Grey and Delcassé felt justified in taking up stronger weapons. The Foreign Secretary cabled to Petrograd:

'Having shown our readiness to meet the Russian wishes concerning Constantinople, it does not strike me as very sensible for M. Sazonov to insist that the negotiations should be broken off . . . unless Italy's assistance can be ensured earlier than a month after signature. . . . From Russia's standpoint, Italy's assistance may perhaps be a matter of indifference, but to us . . . Italian co-operation and its effects on the neutral Powers are of the very greatest importance'.[5]

On the same day, Izvolski reported from Paris that,

'if the London discussions should miscarry at the last moment, this could produce here a profound feeling of disappointment. It is absolutely essential to bear in mind that the French think they have made Russia a concession of immense value on the question of Constantinople and the Straits, and that, of all the Allies, France will derive the least material gain from the War. If, moreover, they should now get the notion that, owing to our negative attitude, France has forgone Italy's military assistance, and that the War has thereby been considerably prolonged, this can have the most harmful consequences for our relations with France'.[6]

And, as a result, as Benckendorff had warned, 'our interests would certainly have to suffer heavily'.[7]

All this was bound to bring home to Sazonov Benckendorff's reflection that 'between England and France on the one hand, and

---

[1] 19 April '15. Poincaré, VI. 166–7. *Das Zaristische Russland*, p. 315.
[2] Poincaré, VI. 171.
[3] Benckendorff to Sazonov, 20 April '15. *Das Zaristische Russland*, p. 316.
[4] Lloyd George, *The Truth about the Peace Treaties*, II. 764.
[5] Aide-Memoire, British Embassy, Petrograd, to Sazonov, 20 April '15, transmitting a telegram from Grey. Retranslated from a translation of the English original. *Internationale Beziehungen*, II. 7. II. No. 563, pp. 563–4.
[6] Izvolski to Sazonov, 20 April '15. *ibid*. II. 7. II. No. 568, pp. 568–9.
[7] Benckendorff to Sazonov, 1 April '15. *ibid*. II. 7. II. No. 462, pp. 470–1.

Russia on the other, the match is not equal'.¹ The Tsarist Empire's dependence on the West for money and munitions was aggravated, from mid-April 1915, by military failure in the Carpathians, where Nicholas's exhausted, shell-starved troops were reduced to the defensive.² The resulting weakness caused, and was in turn sharply increased by, Petrograd's foreign political subservience to the Allies. The weapon of a separate peace, which alone could have redressed the diplomatic power balance between them, was thrown away in Turkey.³ By 'granting', in that area, Russia's principal aspiration, Britain and France acquired the whip-hand over her elsewhere. Sazonov's victories concerning Spalato, Sabbioncello and Montenegro were puny compared to his defeat on the main Adriatic issues. But his overriding consideration was that 'we must guarantee Russia the fruits of this gigantic War through the . . . solution of the Constantinople question, which has so far been regarded as insoluble'.⁴ Sazonov could well complain that 'this Treaty, unsatisfactory in content, is unsatisfactory also in form'.⁵ He could write to Benckendorff:

'I cannot . . . disguise the disheartening impression . . . left on me by the manner in which Grey has conducted the negotiations. . . . He has never met Imperiali's demands with the immediate resistance they called for . . . he has even strengthened the latter's stubbornness. . . . The only firmness Grey displayed was when he tried to convince me that it was necessary to conclude the Agreement as soon as possible even at the price of conceding everything to Italy. He and Cambon have between them drawn up the articles of the Treaty, without our participation, and communicated them to me as finally adopted without, in most cases, having made the slightest attempt to press the Rome Cabinet to accept my modifications'.⁶

But this was the eve of Gallipoli.⁷ The landing was expected to make the British and French masters of the entire region of the Straits. Grey's and Delcassés hints at a worsening of their future intercourse with Russia, therefore, meant that any further obstruction of the Italian Alliance would mar her prospects of possessing Byzantium. So, 'yielding to the urgent requests of our Allies, I am compelled

---

¹ Benckendorff to Sazonov, 1 April '15. *ibid.* II. 7. II. No. 462, pp. 470-1.
² Talenski, 45.   ³ See pp. 97, 101, 104–5 above.
⁴ Benckendorff to Sazonov, 22 April '15. *Internationale Beziehungen*, II. 7. II No. 587, p. 586; also 1 April '15. *ibid.* No. 462, p. 470.
⁵ Sazonov to Benckendorff, 20 April '15. *ibid.* II. 7. II. No. 564, p. 565. Also Aide-Memoire, Sazonov to Buchanan and Paléologue, 21 April '15. Adamov, I. No. 126, pp. 326–7.
⁶ Sazonov to Benckendorff, 21 April '15. *Internationale Beziehungen*, II. 7. II. No. 575, p. 575. Cf. Salandra, p. 283: 'Sazonov's bitter comment that Grey had condescended excessively to the pretensions contested by Russia . . . appears to have been justified.'
⁷ See p. 108 above.

to agree that the Treaty with Italy be signed in the . . . highly unsatisfactory form in which England and France are in a hurry to sign it'.[1]

The surrender was qualified by the reservation that 'all decisions concerning the future peace on which an understanding was already reached, before Italy's adherence, by Russia, France and England, must remain in force'.[2] Sazonov wished a statement to this effect to be signed by the Italians simultaneously with that of their attachment to the Entente.[3] The British Foreign Office, however, was worried, as Benckendorff cabled, that, in such a case, 'Italy, before signing, would probably inquire what Agreements have already been entered into by the Powers. She would be thus initiated into the secret'.[4] Having palmed off Sonnino with the vaguest of promises regarding the Middle East, it was clearly not desirable to give him a pretext for reopening the subject and raising concrete claims. 'Nicolson's personal opinion is that all the Agreements among the Powers, including that on Constantinople and the Straits, which have been concluded before Italy's accession, are not Italy's business. . . . When peace is made, we need not trouble about Italy's objections. . . .'[5] Delcassé, according to Izvolski, shared this view and thought that it would be 'imprudent' to communicate their compact to Sonnino lest he should wish 'to discuss it'.[6] This obviously appealed to Sazonov. As for his French and British colleagues, having achieved their purpose by paltering with their recent pledges, they had to reaffirm them lest Tsarist imperialism should lose its will to war. Grey, expressing to the Russian Foreign Minister 'how highly he appreciates the sacrifice' made by the latter in the Adriatic, reassured him that he would not broach the topic of the Straits and Constantinople again.[7] A way was also found to calm Petrograd's apprehension that

---

[1] Sazonov to Benckendorff, 20 April '15. *Internationale Beziehungen*, II. 7. II. No. 564, pp. 564–5.

[2] *ibid*, and Sazonov to Benckendorff, 19 April '15. Adamov, I. No. 121, p. 322. Sazonov's two other reservations, dealing with Montenegro and the allocation to Croatia, Serbia and Montenegro 'in any event' of those parts of the East-Adriatic coast not ceded to Italy, have been dealt with above.

[3] See Aide-Memoire, British Embassy, Petrograd, to Sazonov, 22 April '15. *Internationale Beziehungen*, II. 7. II. No. 580, p. 580.

[4] Benckendorff to Sazonov, 20 April '15. *ibid*. II. 7. II. No. 566, p. 566.

[5] *ibid*. Grey, deeming it 'wiser to let this matter rest', suggested that Italy, after her adherence to the Entente, should be told that she must accept the question of Constantinople and the Straits as a 'chose reglée'. Aide-Memoire, British Embassy, Petrograd, to Sazonov, 22 April '15. Retranslated from a translation of the original. *Internationale Beziehungen*, II. 7. II. No. 580, p. 580. Sir Arthur Nicolson was the Permanent Under-Secretary in the Foreign Office.

[6] Izvolski to Sazonov, 21 April '15. *Internationale Beziehungen*, II. 7. II. No. 577, p. 577.

[7] Aide-Memoire, British Embassy, Petrograd, 22 April '15. *ibid*. II. 7. II. No. 579, pp. 578–80.

Rome, not having been informed of the previous deal, might later demand its revision and be supported therein by London and Paris. This was effected by means of Notes containing Sazonov's reservation, and exchanged—while the ink on the new Treaty was still fresh —behind the back of the new Ally.[1] The Treaty itself[2] was signed secretly in London on April 26th 1915. Friendly co-belligerents were ignored. In each of the four countries concerned, Parliament was by-passed, the press was told nothing, the public remained in the dark. The men who, the day before, had landed in Gallipoli, or those tied down on the other Allied fronts, and those presently to be thrown into the holocaust, did not know that, henceforth, they were fighting to put more than 600,000 Slavs,[3] 230,000 Germans[4] and no one had counted how many Albanians, Africans and Turks—none of whom had been consulted —under the sway of Italian imperialism. Among the Governments involved, the Russian was not the only one to have heart-burning and misgivings. President Poincaré, too, admitted (at least to his Diary) that the stipulations of the Alliance were 'not such as to give us complete satisfaction.... Italy's participation ... looks as though it would be very costly'.[5] The terms, as Lloyd George was to write later, 'were undoubtedly in contravention of the principles upon which we entered the War....' But 'we were only too well pleased to secure ... another Ally to scrutinize closely the ... conditions of the bargain'.[6] And Salandra, having won his pound of flesh, prayed in a letter to his confederate Sonnino: 'May God help us'.[7]

---

[1] Aide-Memoires, Sazonov to Buchanan and Paléologue, 22 April '15; British Embassy, Petrograd, to Sazonov, 23 April; French Embassy, Petrograd, to Sazonov, 24 April. Adamov, I. NN 130, 131, 132, pp. 331–2. For the Notes exchanged between Benckendorff and Grey, Grey and Benckendorff, Benckendorff and Cambon, Cambon and Benckendorff, on 26 April '15 see *Internationale Beziehungen*, II. 7. II. NN 615, 616, 617, pp. 609–10 and 609, footnote 1. Benckendorff to Sazonov, 28 April '15. Adamov, I. No. 135, pp. 334–5; also 128. The Notes, though exchanged on the 27th, were dated April 26th 1915.
[2] More correctly: the Memorandum of Italy's Rights and Obligations, and a Declaration against a Separate Peace. *Internationale Beziehungen*, II. 7. II. NN 612, 613, 614, pp. 604–9.
[3] *Italy*. Edit. J. Buchan, p. 190.
[4] Albrecht-Carrié, 414.
[5] 19 April '15. Poincaré, VI. 168–9.
[6] Lloyd George, *The Truth about the Peace Treaties*, II, 763, 765. Asquith subsequently defended 'every one of the conditions as being justified by ethnological, historical or strategic considerations'. *ibid.* 767.
[7] 26 April '15. Aldrovandi Marescotti, 47.

CHAPTER XXIII

# The Final Struggle

1

## INSIDE ITALY

INDEED, the two principal Italian protagonists needed all the help they could get for the last act of the drama. From the beginning of the year, the country was plunged more and more deeply into crisis. The bad harvest of 1914, the faulty system of distribution, and the growing requirements of the Army forced up the demand for wheat. Imports, however, were restricted by the closure of the Dardanelles, the commandeering of transport by the belligerents, and the difficulties of payment caused by the interruption of international trade and credit. The scarcity was increased because private concerns withheld their ships from war-risk zones such as Sicily, Sardinia and the Adriatic ports. The shortage of money and raw materials, the stoppage of emigration and exports, and the armaments drive, dislocated industry. The price of food, and especially bread, soared. The growing stress led to serious strikes and unrest, particularly in Southern Italy and the East-coast provinces. Even the elements were ranged against them, for, after the earthquake in the Abbruzzi, came the disastrous Tiber floods of February 15th 1915.[1]

The temper of the public was conveyed in what the Premier later called 'the insidious currents around me' in Parliament. In the Senate, among 'the immense majority', he was informed, there was 'a universal and ardent desire to avert a conflict....' The Lower Chamber was restive over the failings of the Government, the incompetence in relieving the stricken, the general dearth of necessities and, above all, the great issue of war and peace.[2] Already in December 1914, Salandra had met the widespread anxiety about unpreparedness with evasive demagogy: 'I have nothing to say.... he who ... desires to make inquiries as to the facts sins against his country'.[3] In March 1915, when a deputy, referring to 'rumours of diplomatic negotiations', asked for information, the answer was that there would be none.[4] Throughout the session, the Government's only real concern was to gag opposition. The new Bill 'for the economic and military

---

[1] *Carteggio*, LXII. I. 82. Salandra, 188. T. N. Page, 198. Rossi, 5. Adamov, I. No. 107, p. 309. Macchio, 97.
[2] Memorandum from the Duke d'Andria to Salandra, 17 April '15. Salandra, 203; also 184, 185, 189–90. Giolitti, 393.
[3] Statement in the Chamber. Salandra, 130; also 128–9.
[4] 11 March '15. Salandra, 239.

defence of the State' was propounded by the Privy Seal Orlando, the Director of Vickers-Terni, with these words: 'If . . . I were obliged to choose between liberty and the safety of my country . . . I should sacrifice liberty'.[1] In passing this Bill against the solitary votes of the Socialist Party, the House virtually abandoned its prerogatives. A week later, Salandra could calmly prorogue it, as he recollects, for 'rather longer Easter holidays than usual'. Armed with a motion of confidence giving him 'freedom of action to safeguard the nation's legitimate interests',[2] he assumed such stringent powers that even the die-hard Ambassador Krupenski was struck by the extent to which they infringed the Italian Constitution.[3]

By March 1915, Salandra and Sonnino had travelled far from the days when interventionist manifestations were forbidden, the *Marseillaise* was banned from the performance of *André Chenier* in Rome, and the puppet show *Attila* in Milan was suspended lest its allusions should offend the Kaiser.[4] Now that the Consulta had involved the Entente in serious negotiations, the fiction of neutrality could be suffered to wear thin. The armed preparations which cost thousands of millions 'were made quietly without asking from Parliament authorization for the outlay'.[5] But the recall of officers in reserve, including non-commissioned, and the steady mobilization could not escape notice. The voices of the *Corriere della Sera*, the *Idea Nazionale* and the *Secolo* grew shrill. Mussolini's *Popolo d'Italia*, displaying a regular column 'Movimento Fascista', screamed for 'war against Austria and Germany'. 'Comrades of France, the people of Italy are with you in your aspirations and your hopes; they will soon be with you in action'.[6] And the Premier, according to his Reminiscences, used 'every occasion for dwelling on the gravity of the situation and . . . the civic duties it imposed'.[7] Inevitably, all this drum-beating alerted the defenders of peace. Interventionist demonstrations provoked counter-demonstrations. Press differences became feuds. Polemics degenerated into street fighting and bloodshed. The Cabinet seized upon this pretext to abrogate the right of assembly and expression. On March 7th 1915, Avarna wrote to Bollati: 'The disorders show once more that the country on the whole does not want war'. But, as Salandra has since admitted, 'there could be no halting on the road we had chosen'.[8]

[1] 14 March '15. Salandra, 210; also 209, 211.
[2] Salandra's statement in the Chamber, 22 March '15. Salandra, 199.
[3] Krupenski to Sazonov, 3 March '15. Adamov, I. No. 107, p. 309.
[4] Destrée, 40. Conrad, IV. 677.  [5] Salandra, 209.
[6] 9 and 11 Feb. '15. Rosmer, 340-1.  [7] Salandra, 211.
[8] *Carteggio*, LXII. I. 78. Salandra, 313. Cf. p. 308: 'It cannot be claimed that the majority of the people were converted'. Also 195-198, 211. Giolitti, 395. Rossi, 5-6. Adamov, I. 309. Macchio, 86-7, 89. *Carteggio*, LXII. I. 82.

2

ENGINEERING A BREAK

In these circumstances, Austria-Hungary's offer of March 9th 1915[1] would have been an embarrassment, if it had not been for such an adept in power politics as Sonnino. Having at last obtained Burián's consent to negotiate the cession of Habsburg territory, he promptly set up another obstacle to agreement by demanding more. Besides, he was well aware that Vienna's compliance, coupled as it was with the proviso that it should be publicized in the Italian Chamber, was intended to check the interventionists and strengthen the neutralist elements in the Kingdom. As well as warding off the collision with the Dual Monarchy and ruling out parleys with the Entente, such a vindication of the *parecchio* would greatly enhance Giolitti's prestige and enable him, if Salandra remained obdurate, to unseat the Government. Sonnino, therefore, in his reply of March 12th, insisted on 'absolute secrecy' as a condition of continuing the discussions and added, out of the blue, the crucial stipulation that 'when the agreement is concluded it should immediately be given effect'.[2] To justify this last extraordinary point, the Italians argued that 'the mere announcement of an agreement to be executed at an indefinite time and under conditions then unknown' was not enough, and that, while Italy would by the end of the War have fulfilled her obligation of neutrality, the cession of Habsburg territories 'would still be subject to the future ratification of the Austro-Hungarian Chambers'.[3] Sonnino told Bülow plainly that 'at the end of the War, if the [Austro-Hungarian] Parliament were to withhold its sanction of the cessions accorded, nothing could then be done. . . .'[4] For, as Salandra says, 'were the Central Powers victorious, we should have no means of compelling them to fulfil their engagements. . . .'[5]

These apprehensions were not out of place. It was just then that Conrad wrote: 'If we wish to keep Italy . . . out of the War, we must immediately offer her the Trentino. . . . This opinion is shared by Count Tisza. . . . He justly observes that if we win the War, we

[1] See p. 311 above.
[2] Avarna to Sonnino, 9 March '15. Sonnino to Avarna, 10 March. *The Italian Green Book*, NN 41, 42, pp. 1270–2. This was communicated to Burián on the 12th. Also Bollati to Avarna, 9 March '15. *Carteggio*, LXII. I. 80, 83. Salandra, 239–240. Burián, 51. T. N. Page, 197. Macchio, 103.
[3] Salandra, 240–1. Vienna had consented that such an announcement should be made. See Sonnino to Avarna and Bollati, 17 March '15. *Italian Green Book*, No. 46, p. 1279.
[4] Sonnino to Avarna and Bollati, 17 March '15. ibid. No. 46, p. 1280.
[5] Salandra, 241.

M*

shall be strong enough to insist upon the revision of our promises and to punish the Treaty-breakers'.[1] Even though at the time that letter was unknown to the Consulta, the sentiments underlying it were not. For Italy to be content with a scrap of paper would have meant 'that we should have engaged our liberty of action against insecure promises of problematic advantages'.[2] No one in Rome could doubt Vienna's unalterable objection to sacrificing her domains. Hence, 'the immediate occupation of these on the part of Italy'[3] was the only solid guarantee.

For Austria-Hungary, however, this would have been an irrevocable step incompatible with Conrad's and Tisza's revisionist designs. Quite apart from that, it would have been an unprecedented occurrence for a Great Power to dispossess itself of a vital province in the midst of war, to expose itself to further blackmail by denuding its defences, and to disorganize its Army by the release on all fronts of troops native to the abandoned areas. It would have been a blow to the stability of the Empire, provoking internal upheaval; a confession of weakness, encouraging the pretensions of Rumania and others.[4] Burián rightly reminded the Ambassador Avarna that, as the latter reported, 'if Article VII provided that the agreement should be anticipatory, it did not . . . provide that its fulfilment should also be anticipatory'. On the contrary, 'the realization of the compensation by one of the contracting parties would be simultaneous with the advantages of which the other party would have assured itself'.[5] As Vienna, so far, had assured herself of none, she was in effect asked to reward the rival for her own reverses. As the future was uncertain, she would—by a sacrifice in the Trentino—help Italy to an effortless victory in advance of her own possible defeat. Even if the March offer of the Ballplatz had been sincere—which, clearly, it was not—Sonnino's clause, as Burián recalls, was 'an impossibility which we must refuse point-blank'.[6] And since Sonnino must have known this, his purpose could only have been to prevent the parleys from succeeding.

But he seems to have overlooked Prince Bülow. The Ambassador 'came to see me on the 15th', the Italian Foreign Minister cabled

---

[1] Conrad to L. Chlumecky, Publisher of the *Österreichische Rundschau*, 10 March '15. Salandra, 243, quoting from *Pesti Hirlap*, July 1929.
[2] Salandra, 242.
[3] Avarna to Sonnino, 13 March '15, reporting his conversation with Burián. *Italian Green Book*, No. 43, p. 1274.
[4] Avarna to Sonnino, 16 March '15. Sonnino to Avarna and Bollati, 17 March. *ibid.* NN 45, 46, pp. 1277, 1279. Salandra, 240. Burián, 51. Macchio, 103.
[5] Avarna to Sonnino, 13 and 16 March '15. *Italian Green Book*, NN 43, 45, pp. 1273, 1277.
[6] Burián, 51. Avarna to Bollati, 13 March '15. *Carteggio*, XLII. I. 84. Macchio, 103.

to Avarna and Bollati, 'and appeared deeply concerned by ... the state of our negotiations with Vienna'. He cavilled at the demand for 'immediate execution' of the terms to be arrived at. 'Once the agreement was concluded we should have every guarantee of Germany as mediator....'[1] Had Italy, then, as Salandra wondered in retrospect, 'any reason to doubt?'[2] But what confidence could be placed in the word of a Power which had just broken faith in Belgium? How could the Consulta—busily engaged in treaty-breaking—not query the value of international pledges? Finding the Foreign Minister perverse, Bülow 'proposed in the end that, for the present, the discussion on this question ... should be put aside.... He was convinced that in this way it would still be possible to arrive at a conclusion, "unless", he added, "you should already have made up your minds for war in March".'[1] Here, suddenly, was a threat not to be ignored. Salandra and his friends had, indeed, 'decided on war unless we obtained all that we asked and this we believed to be impossible; but as for war in March—no! At General Headquarters, Cadorna and Zupelli[3] ... had informed us that the Army would not be ready before the end of April'.[4] The domestic battle was not yet won. Above all, the Entente was still far from being committed to Italy's terms. So 'we must avoid the risk of a sudden rupture'.[4] Sonnino, therefore, accepted the German proposition that the question of the territories to be ceded should be thrashed out first. 'I told Prince Bülow that I had no wish to precipitate matters, but that I would no longer undertake the initiative ... that if the Austro-Hungarian Government desired to arrive at any conclusion, it could submit its proposals clearly....'[5]

Though three months had passed since the Consulta formally broached the subject, each side—anxious not to commit itself— had refrained from defining either its demand or offer. As the initiative was his, it was really for Sonnino to be specific. But his compromise enabled him to pass the buck to the Viennese. Now that 'immediate execution' was dropped, they could, and—by way of a *quid pro quo* had to—make a concrete suggestion. The need was the greater because the fall of Przemysl on March 22nd and the Russian advance in the Carpathians had deepened the depression in the Dual Monarchy. 'Public opinion', Avarna wrote, 'already considers the War as lost'.[6] For military reasons, as well as those of internal policy,

---

[1] Sonnino to Avarna and Bollati, 17 March '15. *Italian Green Book*, No. 46, pp. 1279–80.
[2] Salandra, 241.
[3] The Commander-in-Chief and the Minister of War.   [4] Salandra, 244.
[5] Sonnino to Avarna and Bollati, 17 and 20 March '15. *Italian Green Book*, NN 48, 50, pp. 1282–4. Also Salandra, 244–5.
[6] Avarna to Bollati, 31 March '15. *Carteggio*, LXII. III. 377.

it was imperative to appease the Roman wolf. And finally, there was the ceaseless German pressure.[1] The mere fact of Berlin's 'full and complete guarantee that the agreement to be concluded between Italy and Austria-Hungary should be faithfully . . . given effect as soon as peace should be concluded'[2] indicated the determination of the Wilhelmstrasse. Hence, on March 27th 1915, Burián informed the Italian Ambassador that, if Italy

'should undertake to observe until the end of the present War a friendly neutrality' and 'engage herself for the whole duration of the present War to leave Austria-Hungary . . . complete freedom of action in the Balkans [except Albania], and to renounce in advance any fresh compensation for the advantages . . . that might eventually accrue to Austria-Hungary . . .',

then the latter would

'be prepared to make a cession of territory in Southern Tyrol comprising the city of Trent' and demarcated 'in such a manner as to take into account both the strategic exigencies which a new frontier would create for the the [Dual] Monarchy, and for the economic needs of the population'.[3]

And as Sonnino dismissed these proposals as 'too vague . . . indefinite, and . . . absolutely inadequate . . . I cannot understand what it really is that the Imperial and Royal Government intends to offer us . . .'[4]—the Ballplatz expressed itself as disposed to cede to Italy

'all the districts forming what is commonly known as the Trentino'.[5]

This Easter gift was vexing on two counts. First, it was poor—there was, as Salandra deplored, no thought of yielding up the fortified Alpine heights dominating the open valleys of the Province, nor even the slightest reference to the Adriatic;[6] and second, it required a clear-cut answer. Silence would have implied acceptance, while a reply was bound to contain demands leading to a break which—since Sonnino was just then contending with Asquith and Sazonov—would have been definitely premature. There was an obvious touch of *Schadenfreude* in Burián's smart request to Sonnino 'to make known, in your turn, what were your own proposals'.[7]

[1] *ibid.* Also Avarna to Sonnino, 24 March '15. *Italian Green Book*, NN 54, 55, pp. 1289–91. Salandra, 245, 271.
[2] Sonnino to Avarna and Bollati, 20 March '15, on the statement made to him by Bülow. *Italian Green Book*, No. 49, p. 1283.
[3] Avarna to Sonnino, 27 March '15. *ibid.* No. 56, pp. 1291–2. Also Burián, 51–2. Salandra, 245. Regarding Albania, Italy was to observe both the old Agreement existing between herself and Austria-Hungary, and the decisions of the London Conference of 1913.
[4] Sonnino to Avarna, 31 March '15. *Italian Green Book*, No. 58, pp. 1293–5.
[5] Avarna to Sonnino, 2 April '15. *ibid.* No. 60, p. 1297.
[6] Salandra, 245, 323.
[7] Avarna to Sonnino, 6 April '15. *Italian Green Book*, No. 62, p. 1298.

Berlin strongly supported this invitation, but made it plain 'that Trieste [perpetually claimed by the Italians] be not included'.[1] And as 'without Trieste no *parecchio* was worth having',[2] the Consulta's quandary was so complete that Salandra—to account for Italian indecision—left the capital, like Grey, for 'a little rest'. But 'the truth is that we ... had long discussions over the form of our counterproposals, particularly in connection with Trieste, its abandonment to Austria being impossible. Nor could we ask for its complete and immediate cession without the danger of a prompt rupture'.[3] So it was not until April 8th that the following terms were dispatched to Vienna:

'I. The cession of the Trentino. . . .

II. Italy's Eastern frontier to be corrected in her favour, so as to bring ... Gradisca and Gorizia within the ceded territory. . . .

III. The city of Trieste with its territory ... to be constituted an autonomous and independent State ... and Austria-Hungary shall renounce all sovereignty over it. . . .

IV. Austria-Hungary cedes to Italy the archipelago of Curzola including Lissa... Busi, Lesina ... Curzola, Lagosta ... Cazza, Meleda and Pelagosa.

V. Italy should immediately occupy the ceded territories. . . .

VI. Austria-Hungary is to recognize Italy's full sovereignty over Valona and ... Saseno, together with ... the hinterland. . . .

VII. Austria-Hungary is to cease completely to interest herself in Albania. . . .'[4]

The reaction to this catalogue may be judged by that of the Italian Ambassador Bollati, who was 'simply horrified' by 'such an accumulation of pretensions, each more exaggerated, more humiliating and more offensive than the next. It is a bunch of the sort of conditions which, after a long war, a victor might impose upon a completely prostrate enemy, and we are putting them up as the price

---

[1] Jagow's statement. Salandra, 213.
[2] Salandra, 213. The reason for this view was, no doubt, the fact that Trieste was the only Adriatic, that is Mediterranean, channel for the whole of the Central European trade.
[3] Salandra, 246.
[4] Sonnino to Avarna, 8 April '15. *Italian Green Book*, No. 64, pp. 1299–1302. Articles VIII and IX are of secondary interest. Articles X and XI pledged Italy's 'perfect neutrality throughout all the present War with regard to Austria-Hungary and Germany' but significantly not Turkey—and a renunciation by Italy of 'all power subsequently to invoke Article VII of the ... Triple Alliance', provided Austria-Hungary did the same in respect of the occupation of the Dodecanese by Italy. The sweep of the Italian demands may be illustrated by the fact that, in the Trentino, for example, they included the big railway junction of Bozen (Bolzano) and aimed at severing the Merano line from the Brenner. The Note was handed by Avarna to Burián on 10 April '15.

for maintaining a neutrality to which we are already bound by Treaty. ... And for good measure we are demanding that they be carried out immediately, between to-day and tomorrow. One asks oneself whether the person responsible for these terms ... has a head on his shoulders at all'.[1] Indeed, he had. Only a few days previously Delcassé had presented his compromise,[2] and Italy was well launched on the way to agreement with the Entente. Sonnino's stipulations, therefore, as the American Ambassador has stated, were deliberately 'intended to be such—as to place it out of Austria's power to accept them'.[3]

Small wonder, then, that on April 16th Burián rejected outright the claims regarding Trieste, the Curzola archipelago, the Isonzo frontier (Gradisca, Gorizia) and Albania, ruled out 'immediate execution' and—though he consented to extend the cession in the Trentino—refused to accept the line indicated there by Sonnino, so that Italy would be left in her state of hateful inferiority.[4] On the 29th, since the Consulta had spurned these suggestions, he 'increased' his offer by adding Valona, which was already in Italy's hands, and proposed, instead of 'immediate execution', the appointment of a joint Commission ostensibly to settle the details of the territorial transfer, but really to bog down the issue.[5] Seeing that acceptance of the Consulta's demands would have disarmed the Dual Monarchy in the Alps, removed the defences of part of her littoral and several central provinces, deprived her of her greatest maritime outlet (Trieste), affected her 'most perceptible' interests in the Balkans, made Italy mistress of Dalmatia and the Adriatic, and reversed the whole equilibrium between the two Powers,[6] the paucity of Austria-Hungary's concessions is not surprising. What may seem astonishing, however, is the leisurely pace of Burián's proceedings and, even more, his 'strange delusion that the Royal [Italian] Government may end by being convinced of the great sacrifice made by the Imperial

---

[1] Bollati to Avarna, 14 April '15. *Carteggio*, LXII. III. 378–9. Avarna to Bollati, 23 April, expressed agreement with this view. *ibid.* LXII. III. 384. Even if allowance must be made for Avarna's and Bollati's bias in favour of the Triplice, their judgment at any rate casts a strong light on what was felt in the Central capitals. Cf. Burián, 53.
[2] See p. 347 above.
[3] T. N. Page, 204. A similar view was expressed at the time by the Rumanian Foreign Minister. See Poklevski to Sazonov, 10 April '15. *Internationale Beziehungen*, II. 7. II. No. 511, p. 511. Salandra, 248, has confessed that their only worry was lest Austria should accept and so jeopardize 'the magnificence of our hopes'.
[4] Avarna to Sonnino, 16 April '15. *Italian Green Book*, No. 71, pp. 1305–9. Salandra, 251. Burián, 53.
[5] Sonnino to Avarna, 21 April '15. Avarna to Sonnino, 29 April. *Italian Green Book*, NN 72, 75, pp. 1309, 1315–16. Burián, 53.
[6] Avarna to Sonnino, 16 and 29 April '15, reporting Burián's arguments. *Italian Green Book*, NN 71, 75, pp. 1305–8, 1314. Macchio, 103.

and Royal Government . . . and of the impossibility of its making further concessions. . . . He does not yet despair of arriving at an understanding. . . .'[1]

3

### THE CENTRAL POWERS WORK FOR A CHANGE OF CABINET IN ROME

Could this optimism have sprung merely from the happy-go-lucky Viennese temperament, or were there real reasons for it? Could it, for example, have had anything to do with Bollati's report that 'a distinguished representative of the highest Austrian feudal aristocracy, who is universally known for his hostile attitude to Italy, has approached . . . the [Russian] Emperor with the request to conclude peace with Austria. . . .'[2]? According to Paléologue's Diary, Nicholas II at the end of March 1915 had received a letter from Prince Hohenlohe, the Austro-Hungarian Ambassador in Berlin, who had previously served for 12 years as Military Attaché in Petrograd, containing the suggestion 'that a confidential envoy should be sent to Switzerland to confer with an emissary from . . . Francis Joseph'.[3] The heads of the Italian diplomatic missions in Nish, Sofia and Berlin soon echoed the rumours of a possible deal between the Dual Monarchy and Russia.[4]

It is unlikely that these were simply hares started in Vienna to blackmail the Consulta into moderation. By mid-April, Burián, outraged no doubt by Sonnino's pretensions, had mentioned to his intimates the word 'peace'.[5] On the 27th, Tisza wrote to the Foreign Minister: 'If we should find that we cannot straighten things out with the Italians, then, without waiting for their attack, we ought to approach the Entente with an offer of peace. Perhaps the latter, too, would find it pleasing, if the Italians and the Rumanians had to go empty-handed'.[6] As Russia was the only Power really concerned with

---

[1] Avarna to Sonnino, 25 April '15. Salandra, 251-2. The same telegram is given in the *Italian Green Book*, No. 74, p. 1311, though much abbreviated and with slight verbal alterations, presumably due to the censorship. Burián's optimism is also referred to by Avarna to Bollati, 23 April '15. *Carteggio*, LXII. III. 384; and 7 March '15. *ibid.* LXII. I. 76.

[2] Memorandum, Russian Foreign Ministry, 7 April '15. on a telegram from Bollati to Sonnino. *Internationale Beziehungen*, II. 7. II. No. 494, p. 495.

[3] 28 March '15. Paléologue, I. 314. This information, without mention of the agent's name, is confirmed in Carlotti's telegram to Sonnino, 29 March, 15. *Italian Green Book*, No. 51, p. 1293.

[4] 10, 13, 15 April '15. *Italian Green Book*, NN 66, 68, 70, pp. 1303-5. Bollati's telegram of the 15th refers also to Germany.

[5] Forgách to Macchio, 17 April '15. Macchio, 108.

[6] Tisza to Burián, 27 April '15. Tisza, I. 189. '1927' in this letter is an obvious misprint. Tisza also mooted the idea of peace in his Memorandum of 1 May '15. Tisza, I. 200.

baulking Rome and Bucharest[1], this was evidently a reference to her. But since it could be foreseen, and soon proved to be the case, that the Tsar, at this juncture, would not desert his Allies (especially if it was a question of saving Austria), it must have been an alternative idea which brightened the countenance of the Ballplatz. When Avarna commented on Burián's 'strange delusion' that war with Italy might be avoided even if Austria remained intransigent, the Ambassador added that this was 'due to information reaching him [Burián] . . . as to the frame of mind of the Royal Government and the Italian people'.[2] Already in March—as soon as Sonnino had mentioned 'immediate execution'—the men in the Vienna Foreign Office had begun to talk of a 'change of Cabinet' in Rome.[3] On April 17th, Tisza instructed Burián that 'we must do more to tone down the hostile feelings of the Italians'. If Sonnino 'shows himself intractable, then we must so direct matters that, by excluding his person, that political tendency, which combines the achievement of national aims with a peaceful settlement with us, can assert itself'.[4] It would seem, then, that by degrees Sonnino's harsh turns of the screw caused the Austro-Hungarians to drop some at least of their earlier reservations about Giolitti.[5]

The Wilhelmstrasse, meanwhile, appears to have finally decided in favour of the prophet of the *parecchio*. Nothing, in fact, could have demonstrated more plainly the impossibility of negotiating with Sonnino than his demands of April 8th. A letter from the Chancellor Bethmann to Bülow, and another from the Ballhaus to Macchio, indicate that the Germans considered the Italian postulates regarding Trieste, the Adriatic islands and immediate cession as unacceptable.[6] These went far beyond the encroachments on Austria to which the Reich was indifferent. They were a direct challenge to its own designs in the Adriatic. Bülow at once said to Salandra that Italy's clause on Trieste was a bid for annexation. Jagow, with studied irony, inquired of Bollati whether she 'wanted the Tyrol up to the Brenner'. The Italian Military Attaché was summoned by the Chief of Staff, Falkenhayn, who threatened that, if the Italians fought Austria, Germany would march against them and that she had ten army corps in reserve for this purpose.[7] But the desperate battle in the Carpathians was eating up large German reinforcements. Even when the Russian descent into Hungary was

---

[1] See pp. 131, 331 above.   [2] Avarna to Sonnino, 25 April '15. Salandra, 252.
[3] Merey to Macchio, 16 March '15. Machio, 106.
[4] Tisza to Burián, 17 April '15. Tisza, I. 186.   [5] See p. 302 above.
[6] Bethmann to Bülow, 16 March '15. Bülow, III. 225. Merey to Macchio, 17 April '15. Macchio, 107.
[7] Bollati to Avarna, 14 and 15 April '15. *Carteggio*, LXII. III. 379, 381. Salandra 247–8.

THE FINAL STRUGGLE  369

stopped in mid-April, fresh divisions had to be sent to contain the enemy and prepare the counter-offensive.[1] Hence, it was better not to have to commit German reserves to the Italian front. And when Sonnino and Salandra replied, in effect, that 'it was becoming increasingly difficult to persuade a large section of the public that we were justified in asking so little . . . and our proposals represented . . . the irreducible minimum',[2] Berlin could have found no difficulty in deciding that they must go.

The Ambassador Bülow, therefore, according to his predecessor Flotow, 'had closely allied himself with . . . Giolitti in order . . . to overthrow the existing Government'.[3] Their 'casual' December meeting in a Roman square[4] must have led, under the impact of events in the spring, to so intimate a liaison that, by March 1915, they were reliably reported to be negotiating the price of Italian neutrality.[5] Giolitti, at that time, was already universally regarded as the head of the Opposition which, ranging from the aristocracy and a section of the bourgeoisie to the vast mass of Catholics and Socialists, dominated the Senate and the Lower Chamber, and was supported by the bulk of the country.[6] Early in April, by the initiative of Joel, the Director of the Banca Commerciale Italiana, Bülow tried to induce a Senator—a leading financier—to influence an industrial group controlling the *Tribuna* (which, despite its Giolittian affiliation, had interventionist tendencies) to return to the fold. To advertise the value of the German connection, the Editor of an important Naples paper was informed that the Reich would offset the British blockade by supplying Italy cheaply with coal, and relieve Italian unemployed by engaging them in German coal mines.[7] A week after Sonnino had presented his final terms, Bülow persuaded the Senator Carafa d'Andria to transmit to Salandra an offer of Mediterranean benefits, including a concession in Adalia, and then to publicize their private conversation in order to embarrass the Government before the people. When *Avanti* printed an interview with an ex-Minister containing an accurate summary of Vienna's latest offers, this (so Barrère learned) was engineered by Bülow to win Socialist backing. And, in requesting the company of the leader of the Catholics taking part in Italian politics, he was attempting to consolidate the sympathies of the Curia.[8]

[1] Ludendorff, I. 138-9. Talenski, 45.     [2] Salandra, 251.
[3] Flotow 'Um Bülows römische Mission'. *Süddeutsche Monatshefte*, March 1931, p. 404.
[4] See p. 293 above.
[5] Poklevski to Sazonov, 5 March '15, quoting information received from the Rumanian Foreign Minister. *Internationale Beziehungen*, II. 7. I. No. 318, p. 292.
[6] Salandra, 190-1, 201, 313. Rodd, III. 244. Croce, 234.     [7] Salandra, 205.
[8] Salandra, 201-4, 206. The Russian Chargé d'Affaires in Rome to Sazonov, 24 April '15. *Internationale Beziehungen*, II. 7. II. No. 604, p. 599. Macchio, 116.

## 4
### VATICAN DIPLOMACY

The Vatican was put in a position of peculiar delicacy by the War. When Pius X died in August 1914, it was 'not of a broken heart ... as was romantically suggested'[1]—he succumbed to pneumonia. If he was, nevertheless, represented as one of the first victims of the world catastrophe which he had done nothing to avert, it was because among the millions of believers there must have been those who wondered why the Vicar of Christ had not raised a finger to stop the new crucifixion of Man. Nor did his successor, Benedict XV, do more than announce that

> 'We ourselves are resolved to leave nothing undone to hasten the end of this calamity. . . . The Rulers of peoples we earnestly implore and conjure to forget their differences for the sake of the salvation of human society. . . .'[2]

He lamented in his first Encyclical:

> 'Who would think that the nations thus armed against each other belong to the same human family . . . that they are brethren, children of the same Father in Heaven? . . . Therefore, we earnestly beseech Princes and Rulers that, moved by the sight of so many tears, so much blood, they delay not bring back . . . peace. . . .'[3]

But as the Princes and Rulers, of course, paid no heed, he devoted himself to other concerns. He proposed an exchange of incapacitated prisoners, and the repatriation of certain groups of interned civilians.[4] He also suggested, as a 'Christmas gift to the soldiers and their families',[5] a general truce on all fronts for December 24th-25th. This idea, welcomed by King George V and the Kaiser, was opposed by the Emperors of Austria and Russia. But, as Berchtold informed Conrad, 'the Curia has put it to us that we should accept the Pope's proposal. It would then make public the initiative taken by His Holiness and announce that Austria-Hungary, Germany, England and Belgium were prepared to give their consent, while Russia

---

[1] Salandra, 108. Also Sforza, 120.
[2] The Pope's 'Exhortation to all Catholics of the World', 8 Sept. '14. Johnson, *Vatican Diplomacy in the World War*, 13.
[3] All Saints' Day, 1 Nov. '14. Johnson, 14.
[4] 9 Dec. '14 and 4 Jan. '15. In May '15, the Pope put forward a scheme which resulted in transferring to Swiss hospitals some 30,000 wounded prisoners. He also announced his intention to contribute to the restoration of the Library of Louvain. Johnson, 14, 16. Poincaré, VI. 6.
[5] The Russian Minister at the Vatican to Sazonov, 28 Nov. '14. *Internationale Beziehungen*, II. 6. II. No. 567, p. 485.

declared that she could not agree'. The Austro-Hungarian Foreign Minister, therefore, was of 'the opinion that we could consent to this proposition *pro forma* in the sense suggested by the Cardinal Secretary of State; thus the odium of rejection would be placed on Russia, while our assent would have no consequences whatever'.[1] The 'vive sympathie' expressed by Francis Joseph[2] consummated this exercise in propaganda. Early in January 1915, a Pontifical Decree ordered that,

> 'in the entire Catholic world, humble prayers should be addressed to God to obtain from His compassion the peace which is so much desired.'

When the French bishops sent this brief to their dioceses, the Government prohibited its reproduction and dissemination. But the restraint was at once removed when, according to the Russian Minister at the Vatican, the Archbishop of Paris and the other French prelates

> 'did not hesitate to make clear in a pastoral letter that, by the peace the Pope is praying for, one need in no way understand an immediate peace ... but peace as the norm of human existence, a firm and lasting peace. Such a peace, however, can only be based on justice ... and the respect of mutual rights, and hence every believer, in praying for peace, is free to take it as the realization of the aspirations precisely of his fatherland. ...'[3]

This interpretation must have harmonized with the views of the Pope, for the Bishop of Nice (as he confessed to the Russian Minister and the latter reported) had convinced Benedict XV that

> 'the commentaries by the local pastors on the theme of the Papal prayer must go a little further than ... the general terms of the original text, and put into them just that meaning which is nearest to the heart of their flock. And the Cardinal Secretary of State ... said outright: " ... c'est à vous, Mrs. les évêques, à mettre les points sur les i" '.[4]

---

[1] Berchtold to Conrad and the High Command, 9 Dec. '14. Conrad, V. 724–5; also 693. Johnson, 14–15. Poincaré, V. 471–2, 478, 492, 499. The Christmas truce was also opposed by France.
[2] Conrad, V. 725.
[3] The Russian Minister at the Vatican to Sazonov, 4 Feb. '15. *Internationale Beziehungen*, II. 7. I. No. 131, pp. 117–9. Poincaré VI. 38–9. It is noteworthy that the formula of a 'paix solide et durable' based on 'le triomphe et le règne du droit', which Poincaré quotes from Cardinal Amette's letter, tallies exactly with official French Government pronouncements. The Papal decree was published in the *Acta Apostolicae Sedis*, Annus VII, Vol. VII. Rome, 15 Jan. '15, p. 8.
[4] The Russian Minister at the Vatican to Sazonov, 4 Feb. '15. *Internationale Beziehungen*, II. 7. I. No. 131, pp. 117–9. On the other hand, the strong revulsion against the War prevalent among important Catholic bodies was illustrated by the resolution in favour of peace passed by the Council of the International Society for Franciscan Studies at Assisi, shortly before Christmas '14. See *The Times*, 26 Dec. '14.

If the Holy Father prayed for peace, he did not protest against the War.

The reason for this probably was that, although deprived of the Papal State, he enjoyed 'the quality of a Sovereign, with all the honours and some of the privileges appertaining to it'.[1] He had his bank, his press trust—*Corriere d'Italia, Avvenire d'Italia*—and a wide network of social organizations. Like every Sovereign, he had ideological, business and diplomatic relations with his fellow rulers, and was deeply involved in international policy.[2] It is significant, for example, that Pius X had more than once regretted Vienna's failure to curb Serbia, and that the Cardinal Secretary of State Merry del Val approved 'unreservedly' of the Sarayevo ultimatum.[3] Since the followers of the Pope were divided between the two warring camps, the Vatican's reiterated proclamation of neutrality was a logical necessity. But the very words in which it was preached implied a departure from it. For the *Osservatore Romano*, the Curia's official organ, to 'regard it as a crime against the country to seek to enlarge the field of Italian enterprise in a way that might have dangerous consequences', or to denounce intervention as 'a political adventure, hazardous . . . and morally dishonest, into which a few unwise people wish to drag the country', or to declare that, 'as the Freemasons desire the War . . . as Freemasonry is the greatest enemy of the Italian people, the War, whatever its outcome, would . . . be a most serious misfortune for the nation . . .'[4], amounted to opposing the Salandra-Sonnio course and siding with the Central Powers against the Entente. It was because of this attitude that the Belgian Catholics were grieved by the lukewarm comfort offered them for their injuries[5]; and that, as Sir R. Rodd recollects, 'there were moments when the Vatican certainly appeared anything but friendly to ourselves'.[6]

Indeed, the Holy See distrusted 'Atheist' France, was indifferent

---

[1] The Italian interpretation to 'The Law of Guarantees', 1871. Salandra, 299.
[2] Conrad, IV. 683. T. N. Page, 185. Salandra, 312. Johnson, 20. The Banca di Roma was reputed to be controlled by clerics close to the Vatican. Megaro, 249. Hallgarten, II. 213, and *ibid.* footnote 1.
[3] The Austro-Hungarian Chargé d'Affaires at the Vatican to Berchtold, 29 July '14. Sforza, 121, footnote 1.
[4] Salandra, 109.
[5] Even when, mindful of Catholic opinion in Belgium, the Pope condemned 'every injustice by whatsoever side committed' (Consistorial Allocution, 22 Jan. '15), he was so anxious not to offend the Central Powers that so warm a sympathizer with the Holy See as H. Johnson has felt constrained to comment: '. . . we may perhaps feel tempted to regret that he did not see his way to speaking more explicitly'. (See *op. cit.* p. 16). According to Cardinal Mercier (Pastoral Letter, issued after his return from the Conclave, August-September '14), it was argued in Vatican circles that Belgium herself was responsible for her misfortunes. Johnson, 17.
[6] Rodd, III. 218. Also Johnson, 15.

to Protestant Britain, and was actively hostile to Orthodox Russia. The defeat of the latter, in particular, was expected to weaken the Greek Church and further the eastward spread of the Roman dogma. The new Pope ('an aristocrat by birth and a diplomat by profession'[1]) was alive, above all, to the importance of Southern Germany and Austria-Hungary as the principal bulwarks of Catholicism in Europe. Although he and most of the Curia were Italian, their real attachment, in this conflict at least, was with the Dual Monarchy—the last solidly Catholic Great Power. Abhorring as they did the prospect of its eclipse, and dreading a victory of the Italian lay State, which would affect the prerogatives of the Papacy, they were bound to oppose a clash which would bring about these contingencies.[2] Moreover, while the Habsburg recognized Benedict XV as his and his subjects' spiritual Father, he was in a very material sense his protector. Some of the largest revenues accrued to the Vatican from his Empire. Some of the world's biggest clerical societies crusaded under his aegis against Liberalism, Rationalism and Socialism.[3] Some at least of the bigger keys to the Sacred College were held by Francis Joseph who had the ancient right of vetoing any candidate for Pope. Since he had, in 1903, blocked the elevation of Cardinal Rampolla[4] (presumably because the latter was Francophil), it may be inferred that, as he did not wield this weapon in 1914, he must have considered Benedict *persona gratissima*. At any rate, it was not—despite the efforts of the French cardinals and the Quai d'Orsay—the favourite of France who was chosen.[5] And even though the new Pontiff appointed a Secretary of State not ill disposed towards the Entente,[6] still, he had to remember that, for his election, he was under an obligation to Vienna.

An interest at least as close tied him to Berlin. The Vatican had never reconciled itself to being a 'Sovereignty without a State'. More than once it had objected to, and tried to overcome, its exclusion from temporal affairs. But the Kingdom of Italy—jealous of its own undivided authority—had consistently denied the Pope any but strictly religious competence. He, therefore, availed himself of the war crisis to assert the hope that 'the abnormal position of the Head of the Church would be altered'.[7] By a coincidence, too good to be

---

[1] Poincaré, V. 304. Johnson, 11.
[2] Salandra, 232, 312. Tirpitz, 448. Croce, 224. Bülow, III. 222 Johnson, 9, 13, 17.
[3] Steed, 107-8. May, 148, 499. Johnson, 17: '... in no other European country, save Spain, did the Church retain so many of her medieval privileges'.
[4] Salandra, 300. In the light of this fact, Johnson's assertion, p. 8, that 'the veto was dead...' seems incomprehensible.
[5] Poincaré, V. 137, 140, 154, 304. Johnson, 8.
[6] Johnson, 13. Poincaré, V. 304. Rodd, III. 218.
[7] Encyclical, 1 Nov. '14. Salandra, 170; also 299-300.

true, this claim was preceded by a statement in a leading Spanish paper that, at the Peace Conference, the question of Temporal Power might be raised, and that paper, in Salandra's words, 'was notoriously in touch with the German Embassy in Madrid'.[1] It seems equally significant that Joel, the ever-present Director of the Banca Commerciale Italiana, conveyed to the Premier through an Italian business man a threat from Bülow that, if Italy took up arms against the Central Coalition, the latter would restore the Papal State.[2] And on November 11th 1914, the then German Ambassador, Flotow, told Salandra that the Pope was determined to attend the Peace Congress, that the formidable Catholic Centre Party in Germany demanded the solution of the Roman question as part of the coming readjustment of Europe, and that Berlin would have to consent to that. This was an attempt at blackmail, repeating—as Salandra was quick to see—'Bismarck's game . . . of shutting us once more within the gates of the Triple Alliance'. In fact, Flotow implied that only by friendship with Germany could Italy hope to restrain the Church.[3] What he did not say (although it must have been in the mind of the Wilhelmstrasse) was that, if the blackmail failed, and Salandra's 'friendship' was not to be had at the expense of the Curia, the Roman question would still be useful for the converse purpose of enrolling the Curia against Salandra.

It was obvious from 'unmistakable signs' received by the latter that Benedict was striving to bring about a change in his position. By December 1914, there were indications of an active Papal diplomacy to that end in Madrid. On the 25th, the U.S. Ambassador reported that the recent appointment of a British Envoy to the Holy See was 'in line with what some think is a strong effort on the part of the Vatican to strengthen itself with a view to the internationalization of its present status in Italy'. 'It is now thought by some that the Vatican is taking steps to be represented in the Peace Congress. . . .'[4] It must be presumed, therefore, that the movement of German Catholicism in this direction, and particularly Erzberger's

[1] Salandra, 169. The Russian Ambassador in Madrid mentioned to Sazonov, 19 Jan. '15, the pro-German sympathies of the Catholic clergy in Spain. *Internationale Beziehungen*, II. 7. I. No. 39, p. 37.
[2] Nov. '14. Salandra 168–9. This was, of course, before Bülow's appointment as Ambassador.
[3] Salandra, 168–9, 301. The quotation is from Salandra's book.
[4] T. N. Page to the Secretary of State, 25 Dec. '14. *The Lansing Papers*, I. 719. Although Delcassé, on 2 Dec. '14, declined Grey's suggestion of 30 Nov. that Paris, too, should send a mission to the Holy See (Poincaré V. 469–70, 475), special agents such as Jules Cambon were busy wooing its favours (Oct. '14. Tabouis, 282) so that T. N. Page, in the above report, could state: '. . . it is said that the relations between the Vatican and France are more amicable than they have been since the time of the separation'.

THE FINAL STRUGGLE 375

plans,[1] could not have matured without the knowledge, if not the encouragement, of the Nuncio in Berlin. If the Vatican in the 19th century could maintain Temporal Power by leaning on France, why should it not do so in the 20th by relying on the Reich? And why should the Reich not expect that, in return, the Pope would ally himself to the Kaiser? Why should the Pontiff not mould Italian opinion in favour of Giolitti, and influence Austria's politics towards effecting a compromise large enough to fit the *parecchio*?

Such must have been some, at least, of the thoughts underlying the activities of Bülow and, recalling in his Memoirs Benedict XV, he admitted that 'my efforts received his support. . . . At Easter, His Holiness sent my wife his apostolic blessing, with a message to me that he prayed for the success of my mission'.[2] The American Envoy mentions the current supposition that 'Giolitti and the anti-interventionists . . . were . . . encouraged by the neutralists of the Vatican'.[3] At the same time, the German Catholic Deputy Erzberger, during a visit to Rome in March, was reported to be busy persuading the Curia to bring pressure to bear on the Habsburgs to cede the Trentino.[4] In the same month, Admiral Tirpitz wrote in a letter: 'The Vatican and the Centre Party have banded together to induce the old Emperor Francis Joseph to be accommodating'.[5] Bülow's story that the Pontiff 'charged . . . Piffl, the Cardinal-Archbishop of Vienna, to speak in this sense to the old Emperor', and that the latter 'crimson with rage . . . literally thrust him from the room',[6] is denied by Macchio. But Macchio agrees with Salandra that an approach to the Emperor had certainly been made by the Nuncio in Vienna. Though unsuccessful at first, it contributed, in Salandra's words, 'to the belated [Austrian] offers in later days'. There was, as the Italian Premier has suggested, 'much that went on round and about the Vatican. . . .'[7]

5

ERZBERGER AS A GO-BETWEEN

But in much of it Bülow could not take a direct hand. Since he was accredited to the Quirinal, and the Quirinal had no relations with the Holy See, his position necessarily imposed restraints on him.

[1] Erzberger, 153-4. Erzberger's scheme for re-establishing the Pope's Temporal Power in the form of a diminutive Vatican State appears to have received a measure of support from the German Foreign Minister Jagow and the Austro-Hungarian Emperor. Johnson, 21, and *ibid.* footnote 2.
[2] Bülow, III. 222.     [3] T. N. Page, 189.
[4] Rodd, III. 240. Cf. Erzberger, 62.     [5] Tirpitz, 448.
[6] Bülow, III. 222.
[7] Salandra, 312, 232. Macchio, 63-4. According to the latter, a Bavarian Capucin had, on the initiative of Erzberger, also importuned Francis Joseph.

Yet there was an important body of Catholic deputies in Parliament. There were the Christian-Socialist circles. There was 'that minority —not very numerous but increasing, and of high social condition and connections—which had remained (since 1870) organized round the Vatican'. There was the hierarchy of the Curia. Some of them, bewildered by the Pope's neutral standing, were wavering; some were hostile to Salandra and Sonnino; others, though drawn to the *parecchio*, were still in close touch with the Cabinet; and yet others expected definite rewards for an action that would please Berlin.[1] The Ambassador, clearly, could not risk being caught intriguing with them against the Government for whom, formally, he professed friendship and goodwill. But Erzberger, the unofficial agent, could; and, armed with a special cipher code, he came several times to Rome, provoked restiveness in the Catholic press, paid— as Bülow has written—'many visits to the Vatican', kept 'me closely informed of his own political conversations', and altogether 'did me excellent service'.[2] And no sooner had he arrived again on May 2nd 1915 than—after quick soundings with Bülow and the Curia—he wired to Vienna:

'The affair is on a razor's edge. Assumption of Austrian Ministry that Government crisis here is near is erroneous. But even if correct, the present danger remains. For prospective successor would be Giolitti. He . . . has stated that he considers all offers made hitherto as in any event insufficient and military catastrophe inevitable unless the Italian demands are immediately fulfilled. Chief of Staff Cadorna wants the War . . . . Italy is quite ready. . . . Our common destiny, the future of the Habsburg Dynasty, the outcome of the whole War depends on the resolve to keep Italy calm by granting her demands'.

This telegram went to two Catholic priests and Prince Lichtenstein, the leader of the Austrian Christian-Social Party. The priests were enjoined 'to exert in this sense all the influence at your command' on two anonymous key personages given as 'Frau Schnell' and 'Frau Schwarz', and assured that 'you will meet thereby the explicit wish of the Pope'. The Prince was invited to press these considerations on Burián.[3] And on May 3rd, after a talk with Sonnino, Erzberger cabled to the Chancellor Bethmann: 'Within three days, we must

---

[1] Salandra, 206, 254, 311–12. *The Review of Politics (U.S.A.)*, April 1952, pp. 157–8.

[2] Bülow, III. 203–4. Also Macchio, 110. Erzberger, 41, 44–6, 54, 60, 62. Salandra, 207, 232; and 316: Erzberger 'continually trafficked with the Vatican . . . as he wished to make use of the Catholic element as a card in the great game'.

Although Prussia was represented by a Minister at the Holy See, he had, like Bülow, to observe diplomatic discretion.

[3] Tisza, I. 238–9. Erzberger, 48 (abbreviated for obvious reasons).

# THE FINAL STRUGGLE 377

force Austria categorically to yield. If this does not suffice, we shall have to be ruthless. . . . Otherwise our cause here is lost'.[1]

But the very fact of Erzberger's return, and all that it implied at this crisis, spurred Sonnino. He was all the more impatient with the irksome meddler because the Consulta had just failed in a last-minute attempt to brush away the web enmeshing its policy. As the Hungarian Premier Tisza informed Burián on April 27th, a Budapest doctor had shortly before been summoned to Italy by the Genoese Professor Bossi, a friend of the Italian Foreign Minister, for the purpose of transmitting an important communication. With Tisza's encouragement, the doctor proceeded to Rome with Bossi. The latter was received by Sonnino and given the following message for Tisza:

'. . . Hungary's interests were, are and always will be identical with Italy's. For it is in the interest of both countries alike that neither the German nor the Slav element should rise up to crushing preponderance in Europe. The Vatican co-operates with the German Centre Party—and therefore supports Germany. The Vatican has always been the enemy of both the Italian and Hungarian nations, and hence it is in the common interest of both to provide a counterweight to the activities of the Vatican. . . . Italy has every moral inclination and the interest to support the emergence of a Greater Hungary as free as possible of German influence, and it will be easy to accomplish a secret arrangement between Hungary, Italy and Rumania, which would satisfy the particular interests of these countries. . . . To achieve this aim . . . Tisza must, as soon as possible, strive by every means to bring about peace. . . .'[2]

Whether these were Sonnino's actual words or whether they had been embroidered by the messenger, this was a plan worthy of the craftsmen at the Consulta. Drawn up, apparently, on the very eve of the secret London Treaty, it was an attempt to avoid war in the eleventh hour, yet win the coveted prizes and, at the same time, prevent the dreaded Russian and French hegemony. Playing on the inordinate ambitions and phobias of the Magyar oligarchs, it was

---

[1] Erzberger, 49. Tisza, I. 240. The telegram was countersigned by Bülow.
[2] Tisza to Burián, 27 April '15 ('1927' here is an obvious misprint), and Sonnino's Alleged Statement to Prof. Bossi (according to a report made by the latter immediately after his visit). Tisza, I. 190–3, 265. Sonnino's message may have been prompted by a move of Tisza's. The latter, shocked by Italy's terms of 8 April '15, had written to Burián on 11 April that 'personal soundings with leading Italians would be absolutely essential'. On the same day he had sent a letter to Avarna assuring him 'privately' and with 'the frankness of a friend' of Austria's loyalty in making the concessions offered, holding out the prospect of 'the sincere friendship and lasting support of Austria-Hungary in all the important questions', and warning him, at the same time, that the spoils Italy could expect from joining the Entente would be offset by 'Russian hegemony in the East and French hegemony in the Mediterranean'. Avarna at once sent on the letter to Sonnino. See Tisza to Burián, 11 April '15. Tisza to Avarna, 11 April. Avarna to Tisza, 12 April. Tisza, I. 175–179. Salandra, 248–50.

designed to bring about, through the defection of Hungary, the dissolution of the Dual Monarchy, which would leave Italy in possession of the Trentino, Trieste and the Adriatic. Aimed at a new power combination, in which Budapest would dominate the Eastern Balkans (with a satellite Rumania enlarged at Russia's expense), and Rome the Western half of that Peninsula, it was a move to doublecross the Entente and checkmate Berlin, Vienna and the Vatican. But the Hungarian rulers appreciated the importance for their economy of Austria's food markets, industry and finance. They were well aware that only in conjunction with the Austrian magnates could they hope to repress their Slav subjects and neighbours. Only in conjunction with Austria could they extend their sway over the Danube and Eastern Europe. Only in conjunction with Austria could Hungary, as Tisza answered Sonnino, 'serve as a bulwark against the Slav wave. . . . The fate of Hungary is bound up with the existence of Austria-Hungary as a Great Power'. And hence the desired friendship between Italy and Hungary 'shall exclude for ever any hostile intention against Austria'.[1] This dictum made nonsense of Sonnino's policy. Besides, it said nothing about the Vatican. It chimed in with Burián's last ineffectual concessions of April 29th. It brought into relief the advantages of the London deal. It seemed to overlook that there was someone called Erzberger. Hence, on May 3rd 1915, the day when the latter sent his brutal telegram to Bethmann, Sonnino instructed the Ambassador Avarna to notify the Ballplatz that:

'. . . Italy exerted herself for several months to create a situation that should be favourable to the re-establishment between the two States of those friendly relations which constitute the essential foundation of all cooperation. . . . These negotiations did not lead, however, to any appreciable result. All the efforts of the Royal Italian Government met with the resistance of the Imperial and Royal Government. . . .

. . . In this state of things, the Italian Government must renounce the hope of coming to an agreement, and sees itself compelled to withdraw all

[1] Tisza's Reply to Sonnino's Message. Tisza, I. 193–4. The Editor of the Tisza volume notes: 'Since no allusion whatever to this matter has been found . . . either in letters or elsewhere, it can be assumed with certainty that it was terminated by Tisza's Reply which was communicated later' (p. 265, note 141). The Reply to Sonnino is undated. It is attached to Tisza's letter to Burián of 27 April '15, in which Tisza, after giving the gist of his answer, wrote: 'Now I am curious to know whether this business will have a sequel'. As it is unlikely that he could expect 'a sequel' from the few sentences of the resumé, it would seem that he must have sent the Reply before or on 27 April. But even if it had been given to Sonnino later, this must have been done before the denunciation of the Triplice by Italy, for it would have been pointless afterwards. Indeed, it would be surprising if Tisza, in a crisis as acute as this, had not answered at once. May he not have hoped that an immediate reply, with its reaffirmation of Austro-Hungarian solidarity, might still deter Sonnino?

its proposals for a settlement . . . Italy, confident of her just rights . . . proclaims that she resumes from this moment her complete liberty of action, and declares as cancelled and as henceforth without effect her Treaty of Alliance with Austria-Hungary'.[1]

One can almost see Erzberger and Bülow wringing their hands as they wired Berlin: 'If the Viennese goings-on continue as before, we shall have war in a few days' time. At such a time, inappropriate Viennese susceptibilities cannot be taken notice of'.[2] On May 9th, Erzberger—after 'many conferences . . . with parliamentarians, prelates, politicians and so forth'—cabled to the Chancellor Bethmann: 'Developments have convinced me of the necessity for the final exclusion of Macchio. May it please Your Excellency to see to it at once that he is directed this very day to fall ill. He must no longer leave the house, nor receive any visitors, or else he will be intriguing. . . . There can be no . . . consideration for Vienna. The miserable indecision of Macchio can be our doom. . . . The fate of millions, the fruits of the sanguinary sacrifices of the nation, the future of our fatherland cannot depend on the incapacity of a man who is undoing our work here. . . . If he falls ill . . . time will be too short for a substitute, and negotiations will of themselves pass into one hand. . . .'[3] But the Ambassador received no such uncharitable instructions. The Ballplatz knew perfectly well that, as Macchio wrote later, 'Austria-Hungary was to be cut out altogether, so that Germany could . . . without restraint dispose with Italy of the territory of the Dual Monarchy'.[4] And since his 'incapacity' and 'indecision' were, of course, not personal failings, but faithful compliance with Burián's deliberate policy,[5] it was of particular importance that he should be 'in good health' now that the diplomatic war of attrition between the two Allies was approaching its climax.

On the day in March when Burián accepted in secret the principle of territorial sacrifice, the *Deutsche Tageszeitung* had publicly urged the surrender of the Trentino.[6] Even though the Chancellor Bethmann recognized that 'Austria . . . has every reason for her fears that the more response she makes to Italian demands the more these demands are sure to increase. . . .',[7] he seconded Bülow's activities in Rome by tightening the vice on Vienna. Even though they quashed all suggestions, including those from Bollati, that William II should set an example to Francis Joseph by offering him a scrap from his

---

[1] *Italian Green Book*, No. 76, pp. 1316–18.
[2] 8 May '15. Tisza, I. 241. Erzberger, 51.
[3] Tisza, I. 241–2; also 240. Erzberger, 51.
[4] Macchio, 111.    [5] See Macchio, 108, 110.
[6] 9 March '15. *Internationale Beziehungen*, II. 7. I. No. 349, pp. 316, 419–20.
[7] Bethmann to Bülow, 16 March '15. Bülow ,III. 225.

own bounty[1]—the Under-Secretary Zimmermann visited Vienna in mid-April 'to extort [as the Ballplatz was aware] an additional cession at the Isonzo and the final renunciation of Albania'.[2] Even though the Germans refused, on the 24th, Burián's personal request in Berlin for joint military measures to meet the anticipated Italian attack, the Austrians were in for 'renewed and more insistent pressure'.[3] On May 4th—after the denunciation of the Triplice—Bethmann requested that Macchio and Bülow should at once be given 'carte blanche so that they can buy the necessary agreement as cheaply or as dearly as circumstances will permit, even if demands are raised that appear exorbitant (islands on the Dalmatian coast, immediate transfer . . . and so on)'.[4]

By May 7th—after a meeting between Bethmann, Falkenhayn, Conrad and Tisza—Habsburg resistance seems to have been worn down sufficiently for Tisza to write that 'we shall do the utmost possible . . . even if Italy's conditions should be quite unacceptable, to continue parleying on their basis in order to postpone the rupture'.[5] This was, however, not the only reason why Macchio was instructed, as he puts it, 'to prevent, at any price, the last thread from snapping'.[6] The Austro-Hungarian and the German High Commands, after the big break-through at Gorlice in North Galicia on May 2nd 1915, wanted to exploit their success without being diverted by an Italian attack. The victory, at the same time, enabled Vienna to make further concessions without fear of losing too much face. Nor did she, on Burián's subsequent admission, wish 'to take upon herself the odium of breaking off negotiations, or to help the Italian Government out of its embarrassments'.[7] But what must have been the decisive motive was contained in Tisza's argument that, whereas 'the present Italian Government is very hostile to us . . . serious

[1] The Polish coal-mining area of Sosnovice, and Berchtesgaden, were mentioned in this connection. Avarna to Bollati, 31 March and 23 April '15. Bollati to Avarna, 14 April. *Carteggio*, LXII. III. 375, 381, 385.
[2] Merey to Macchio, 17 April '15. Macchio, 107. Also Burián, 54.
[3] Avarna to Sonnino, 25 April '15. *Italian Green Book*, No. 74. p. 1311. Burián, 54. For Berlin's attempts to browbeat Vienna by withholding a much-needed loan see Tisza to Burián, 12 April '15. Tisza, I. 182; also 171, 204. German-Austrian relations were further bedevilled by continued arguments whether a decision should be sought primarily on the Eastern or the Western front, and by attempts to subordinate at least part of the Habsburg armies to the Hohenzollern command. See Conrad to Falkenhayn, 7 April '15. Falkenhayn to Conrad, 8 and 13 April. *Dokumente der Deutschen Politik und Geschichte von 1848 bis zur Gegenwart*, II. pp. 310–12.
[4] Bethmann to the German Consul-General in Budapest, 4 May, '15, mentioning a German démarche in Vienna. Tisza, I. 218; and 266, note 160. On the same day, Francis Joseph received a telegram from William II presumably to the same effect. Tisza, I. 207.
[5] Tisza to Czernin, 9 May '15. Tisza, I. 208.
[6] Macchio, 116; also 91. Burián, 56.
[7] Burián, 57. Also Macchio, 106, 116.

people, above all Giolitti, are condemning an adventurous policy. The question is whether this tendency can gain the upper hand by way of a Ministerial change. . . .'[1]

6

PLOT AND COUNTERPLOT

The 'coming man', as Macchio described Giolitti,[2] came to Rome—after a lengthy absence—on May 9th. In the preceding March he had still induced his followers to vote for Salandra, partly because, at that stage in the negotiations with Austria, he desired to leave the necessary rough spade work to him (as a friend of Germany he could clearly not expect to extort as much from Austria as Salandra and Sonnino), and partly because he did not like to identify himself with the Socialist motion of no-confidence. But, from his country house in Piedmont, he was, as the American Ambassador has noted, 'the inspiring spirit of the anti-interventionists'.[3] He was rumoured to have been in touch with Vienna, and he certainly maintained active relations with Bülow, for, on April 29th, he wrote to a friend of the Ambassador: 'The only method . . . to preserve peace is to persuade Austria to cede what she is in any way bound to lose. . . .'[4] And now, as soon as he arrived in the capital, a conference was 'convened with the greatest speed' by Macchio and Bülow at Villa Malta, and 'it was decided', according to Macchio, 'to write [out] at my dictation', as Bülow claims,[5] a 'list containing all our concessions' and endorsed by the signatures of the two Ambassadors. The list was at once sent to Giolitti, the Pope and to the King. It was, as Macchio has admitted since, 'certainly a . . . proceeding unprecedented in diplomatic usage for foreign Envoys . . . to approach in a solemn manner . . . influential politicians of a foreign country

---

[1] Tisza to Czernin, 9 May '15. Tisza, I. 208. Also Avarna to Bollati, 13 May '15. *Carteggio*, LXII. III. 387. Since Erzberger, at that time, was pinning his last hopes on a Cabinet crisis in Rome (Erzberger, 50), it would seem that the Austro-Hungarians, too, had embraced this alternative rather than relying on public 'pressure on the present Government' mentioned almost as an afterthought by Tisza. Burián, 56, has admitted that he wanted to 'give an opening to . . . a section of Italian opinion which was still observable'. Cf. also Rodd, III. 248: 'The enemy Missions, having now realized that it was too late to deflect Salandra and Sonnino . . . rested their hopes on displacing the Government. . . .'
[2] Macchio to Burián, 5 May '15. *The Austrian Red Book*, II. No. 173, p. 302. Also Salandra, 227.
[3] T. N. Page, 188, footnote 1. Also Giolitti, 393–4. Rodd, III. 240. Salandra, 318.
[4] Giolitti, 395–6. On 5 March '15, Poklevski reported to Sazonov that, according to the Rumanian Foreign Minister, Giolitti had submitted to Vienna a memorandum on Italy's terms. *Internationale Beziehungen*, II. 7. I. No. 318, p. 292. See also Trevelyan, *Scenes from Italy's War*, 15.
[5] 9 May '15. Macchio, 117. Bülow, III. 227.

as it were against the official authorities with whom they would ordinarily be negotiating'. But Giolitti, as Erzberger recollects, had 'let me know, through an intermediary, of his desire to have this Note in writing for his audience with the King' and for use among his fellow deputies and the press. The Pope, as Bülow assured the hesitant Macchio, had promised to attempt immediate mediation. And Victor Emmanuel had to be put in the right mood for his interview with Giolitti on the following morning.[1] It was not until 24 hours later (May 10th) that the document was transmitted to Salandra and Sonnino, and then only in order 'to avoid any appearance of intrigue against the Cabinet', and to 'drive a wedge into the Ministerial Council' which was to meet for crucial decisions on May 11th.[2]

The prophet of the *parecchio*, meanwhile, summoned his party friends and other pro-German deputies to Rome. His Turin mouthpiece, the *Stampa*, brought into the open the conflict, hitherto hidden, between him and Salandra and Sonnino. The *Corriere d'Italia* (May 8th et seq.) and other Catholic papers attacked the Government for suppressing Austria's proposals and called for Giolitti's intervention. On May 10th, his Rome organ, the *Tribuna*, sounded the first public note of his campaign. And on the 11th, at almost the exact hour when they were delivered to Salandra and Sonnino, the *Stampa* revealed Macchio's and Bülow's latest offers:

1. The whole of the Italian-inhabited part of the Tyrol.
2. The entire West bank of the Isonzo, wherever populated by Italians, with Gradisca.
3. Full municipal autonomy, an Italian University, and the status of a Free City for Trieste.
4. Valona.
5. The complete renunciation by Austria of her interests in Albania.
6. The protection of the national interests of Italians in the Dual Monarchy.
7. Goodwill in examining the wishes Italy may still express regarding the aggregate of questions, notably those affecting Gorizia and the Adriatic islands.

[1] Macchio, 117–18. Erzberger, 52; also 53. Salandra, 331. Tisza, I. 211. Erzberger, 51, writes of their 'hope that a great decision could incline the scales in favour of peace'. It follows also from a letter he wrote to one of his go-betweens in Vienna that 'the Holy Father has made most particular exertions in favour of this Austrian offer'. Tisza, I. 242.
[2] Macchio to Burián, 10 May '15. Tisza, I. 211; also 266, note 153. Macchio, 116–7. Salandra, 332. Erzberger, 53–4.

## THE FINAL STRUGGLE 383

8. Every guarantee by the German Reich of the faithful and loyal execution of the agreement to be concluded between Italy and Austria-Hungary.[1]

These tidings, as Erzberger has gleefully recorded, 'spread like wildfire. The effect was excellent'.[2] Coming as it did at a time when the failure at the Dardanelles, Russia's defeat at Gorlice, and Britain's threat to allow coal supplies only to her Allies, had lowered the prestige of the Entente, the sudden knowledge of Austria's substantial proposals boosted the anti-Government agitation in the country. The *Tribuna* drove home the fact that 'Giolitti's friends have received letters from magistrates, officials, professors, writers and scientists in every province of Italy expressing their sympathy and exalting his great patriotism'. Among the deputies the commotion was such that Salandra saw himself faced with a 'neutralist insurrection' in Parliament.[3] The Chambers, prorogued since March, were due to reopen on May 12th. As there was reason to believe that the Administration contemplated a postponement, the Opposition devised a demonstration which could not be punished by dissolution. No sooner had Giolitti appeared in Rome than nearly a hundred senators and well over three hundred deputies, by means of letters and telegrams sent in haste, or visiting cards left at his door, pledged their support for the *parecchio*. This unorthodox form of voting signified that, in a House with a membership of about five hundred, Giolitti had rallied more than an absolute majority.[4] The omens clearly were that, far from opting for war, Parliament would overthrow the Government. A dissolution was impossible, as fresh elections were certain to return more neutralists. The Cabinet was finally paralysed by internal rifts. Several Ministers, won over by Bülow and the Vatican, or antagonized by Salandra's and Sonnino's proceedings, dissented. Salandra relates that he 'passed a sleepless night. Finally, I arrived at a conclusion....' Late on May 12th, it was learned that the Government had resigned.[5]

---

[1] Salandra, 335. Macchio, 117. Bülow, III. 227. Erzberger, 53. On the same day, Salandra received another letter from Macchio and Bülow, signed 11 May, on 'the mode and form . . . for carrying into effect those concessions . . . (1) Signature of the agreement. (2) Guarantee of the concessions by the Empire of Germany. . . . (4) Institution of joint commissions which . . . represent the first steps in bringing into effect the agreement. (5) All military personnel native to the territories ceded to Italy will discontinue their service on the Austro-Hungarian front'. Salandra, 336. For Giolitti's activities and the newspaper campaign see Macchio to Burián, 10 May '15. Tisza, I. 211. Salandra, 334. Macchio, 116, 119.

[2] Erzberger, 53. [3] Salandra, 336–7. Also Erzberger, 52. Tisza, I. 212.

[4] Giolitti, 397. Rodd, III. 251. Salandra, 306, 318, 337–8. The Premier had 'letters from men of high rank . . . who reported public opinion in the cities and country districts . . . as being against the War.' *ibid*. 313.

[5] Salandra, 343; also 322–3, 342–5, 354. Macchio, 116, 125. Erzberger, 54, 56. Rodd, III. 251.

A 'breath of relief' went through Vienna and Berlin.[1] In Rome, Bülow was 'chanting victory',[2] and a press correspondent, unable to use cypher, wired to his paper: 'Schöner blauer Himmel' (lovely blue sky). But Salandra, on an intercepted copy, wrote tartly: '... it will rain tomorrow'.[3] Meanwhile, Rodd—and no doubt Barrère— had some of 'the grimmest moments I have ever experienced'.[2] Before the resignation, as Salandra recollects, the two Ambassadors, 'much disturbed by the activity of the Parliamentary neutralists, had gone to Sonnino. They suggested that before the 20th [the new date fixed for the opening of the Chambers] there should be some decisive act'. And they must have been emphatic enough for Sonnino to record the 'impression' that 'the Entente ... no longer believes in our good faith ... and will do something imprudent in order to compromise the situation irreparably. ...'[4] After the announcement of resignation, the *Temps* invited Victor Emmanuel to take a decision —'one of the most serious he will ever be called upon to take'. 'Barrère and Rodd went to call upon Sonnino for ... some indication of what to expect'. The Foreign Minister replied that 'the Ministry had conceived it to be its duty to place in the hands of the King the names of those persons who would have carried out the ... [London Treaty] obligations. ... If ... the Salandra Ministry were called upon to resume the helm, we should not change by so much as a single line the policy adopted by us. ...'[5] It was presumably after this interview that Poincaré noted on the strength of a telegram from the French Ambassador: 'Barrère considers that Salandra ought, as quickly as possible, to place the Chamber and the country before a *fait accompli*'.[6]

In the meantime, the interventionist movement had gained the momentum of a volcanic eruption, sweeping and scorching the land. Since April 11th, when violent unrest in Naples, Florence, Turin, Ancona, Rome and many other places was caused by those demonstrating for war and opposing pro-peace manifestations, a young worker was killed, and the near-octogenarian Luzzato called upon the King to 'cross the Isonzo',[7] the belligerent chorus had become a roar. With the approach of May and the maturing of the crisis, it was not enough simply to cease to discourage agitation. As the resistance of the neutralists 'became more open and tenacious', the authorities, in Salandra's frank admission, saw to it

---

[1] Macchio, 125; also 122. Tisza, anticipating the event, had spoken of 'the beautiful prospects inaugurated by the action of the peace party'. Tisza to Burián, 12 May '15. Tisza, I. 210.
[2] Rodd, III. 251.   [3] Salandra, 345.
[4] Salandra, 342; also 322. T. N. Page, 207, footnote 1. Macchio, 125.
[5] Salandra, 350–1.   [6] 14 May '15. Poincaré, VI. 206.
[7] Salandra, 214–5. Macchio, 86–7.

'that one tendency should definitely overpower the other. . . . We set to with a will to fulfil this complicated and difficult duty'.[1] Hence the scope allowed to D'Annunzio's furious tirades during the Garibaldi celebrations at Quarto on May 5th, which the American Ambassador likened to 'a firebrand stuck into a magazine charged . . . for the explosion'.[2] Hence the latitude given to the whipping up of emotions about the *Lusitania's* sinking, to the frenzied processions in Genoa, the wrecking of German shops and lighting of bonfires in Milan, the disorders in Turin and the incipient terror in Rome. Hence the attempts at physical intimidation of Giolitti in Turin, the 'Abbasso!' with which he was received in the capital, and the concerted press attacks on him and his party since May 9th.[3] And hence, promptly after the resignation of the Government, the deadly thrust in the *Messagero*:

'The Bülow-Giolitti Agreement.—We are in a position to announce that the definite Austro-German offer was notified, before its presentation to the responsible Ministers, to the Hon. Giolitti and his lieutenants. . . . So the Cav. Giovanni Giolitti treats, discusses, and pledges Italy behind the back of the King and Government. This grave news needs no comment'.[4]

On May 14th, the *Corriere della Sera* disclosed that the Triplice had been abrogated, and a Treaty signed with the Entente.[5]

'Giolitti and his friends are triumphant, the Prince von Bülow is more triumphant still. He has succeeded in bringing about the fall of the Ministry which was leading the country towards war. The party of which Giolitti is the head have proved admirable coadjutors . . . the Giolittian party does not want to fight Austria, but to surrender to her'.[6]

The indiscretions were designed to detract from the value of the Austrian concessions by showing that they had not been made until

---

[1] Salandra, 307; also 340–1. Macchio, 122–3.
[2] T. N. Page, 210; also 209. Rodd. III. 249. The King and the Cabinet were to have attended the ceremony. But, according to T. N. Page, they had received warning that, in their presence, D'Annunzio's oration would amount to a declaration of war, or provoke a political incident leading to it. 'For many reasons— not least the anxiety of the General Staff to avoid a sudden attack . . . which would seriously have disturbed . . . our mobilization—this would have been premature'. (Salandra, 321; also 320). On the other hand, it was undesirable to stop D'Annunzio, whose function was to produce a popular mood which Salandra could claim to have forced his hand. So Victor Emmanuel and his Ministers took the last-minute decision to stay away from the celebrations. Erzberger, 49, implies that this was due to the intervention of the Vatican.
[3] Giolitti, 396–7. Salandra, 334. Rodd. III. 248, 250. T. N. Page, 210.
[4] 13 May '15. The attack was coupled with one on Erzberger. Trevelyan, *Scenes from Italy's War*, 16.
[5] Rodd, III. 251.
[6] Quotation from the *Corriere della Sera*. Salandra, 346.

after the rupture. The slur cast on Giolitti was to discredit the Opposition and, with it, the very idea of peace. Already D'Annunzio, at a mass meeting in Rome, was inveighing against the 'traitors'.[1]

## 7
### D'ANNUNZIO, POET-MERCENARY

'The greatest living poet . . . that Italy could boast'—this was a tribute from Salandra—had so far lived in France where, thrown into a fever by the War, he had become one of its foremost bards. At the end of April 1915, unabashed by the extravagant luxury of his own living, he declared the hour to have 'struck for Italy to do and suffer. . . .'[2] In May, having returned amidst such glare and glamour as surrounds the 'heroes' in his plays, he told the Genoese that what they wanted was 'a greater Italy not through gain, but through conquest. . . . Viva la giusta guerra! Viva la piu grande Italia',[3] read a poem of 'faith and love' at Quarto,[4] detected in Rome, where he arrived on the night of Salandra's resignation, 'a certain odour of treason . . .'[5] and, at the height of the crisis, roused (to Poincaré's delight) storms of patriotic exaltation by proclaiming:

'No, we are not, and we will not be, a museum, an inn, a village summer resort, a sky painted with Prussian blue for international honeymoon couples, a delightful market for buying and selling, fraud and barter.'[6]

This new note of pride touched a chord in hearers smarting under an old sense of national humiliation. How were they to know that he had gone abroad in order to dodge his creditors at home; that he was financially dependent on, and deeply in debt to, the Editor of the interventionist *Corriere della Sera*, the mouthpiece of Milanese big business; that he received continuous subventions from, and since July 1914 had intimately collaborated in belligerent propaganda with, Luigi Albertini[7]; and that, when D'Annunzio came to Rome 'in a sort of triumphal procession, and for days spoke in a species of lyric frenzy from hotel balconies or in theatres to excited crowds',[8] his patron and mentor was in the background close by? How should it have occurred to the mob of Milan that there were those who paid for the tunes of Benito Mussolini—'that remarkable man', as the British Ambassador has styled him—whose agitations were 'not less zealous and effective in the critical hour'[9]? And who

---
[1] 14 May '15, at the Constanzi Theatre. Rodd, III. 251.
[2] *La Petite Gironde*, Bordeaux. Salandra, 309. A. Albertini, 136.
[3] 4 May '15. Poincaré, VI. 192.     [4] Salandra, 320.
[5] Salandra, 340.     [6] Trevelyan, *Scenes from Italy's War*, 20.
[7] A. Albertini, 134-9, 141.     [8] T. N. Page, 210.     [9] Rodd, III. 249.

could guess that, as Salandra admits, 'some organizer or other of street demonstrations may have been acquainted with the stairs of Palazzo Farnese', the seat of the French Embassy[1]?

'The Italian Government which . . . resigned . . . had made solemn engagements with another group of nations . . . a scheme of combined military action. . . . And now the . . . exertions of months upon months have been brought to nought by a sudden and ignoble onslaught, inspired, instigated and assisted by the foreigner. . . . It has been done . . . by Members of Parliament, in commerce with the stranger, in the service of the stranger, in order to dishonour, enthral and abase Italy for the benefit of the stranger'.[2]

This was enough to lash scores of thousands into fury, dash waves of the angry populace against Giolitti's house, drive them into invading and ransacking the Chamber and assaulting proponents of the *parrecchio*. They did not stop to think that behind D'Annunzio and Salandra and Sonnino, too, was a 'stranger'—only a different one. Neutralist deputies received letters threatening death. Erzberger was attacked in his car. Poison pens, evidently to someone's dictation, accused Giolitti of having taken a twenty million bribe from Austria and Germany. Though, to prevent the situation from getting out of hand, the capital was packed with troops—the *Fasci*, the Nationalists, the rioting gangs, the black-banner processions mourning the escape from war, had the freedom of the streets. The police, according to Giolitti, refrained from 'intervening however unruly these manifestations became'. For two days (May 14th, 15th) barricades, looting, and bloodshed held Rome and the country in terror. For two days, Salandra contrived that, 'while the neutralists held the field at Montecitorio [the Chamber], the interventionists occupied the piazzas'.[3] And as this went on, the crowds were incited not to 'countenance the presence behind the responsible Government of . . . the irresponsibles of Montecitorio who interfere with its work'.[4] This novel designation of the elected representatives of the people gave away the war-mongers' game. Baulked by the legal majority, they resorted to the old 'politics of the public square'. Against the will of Parliament they mobilized the piazza.[5]

---

[1] Salandra, 349.
[2] D'Annunzio at the Constanzi Theatre, Rome, 14 May '15. Salandra, 347.
[3] Salandra, 338; also 341, 347–8, 350. Giolitti, 400–1. Croce, 287. Rossi, 6. Rodd, III. 251–2. T. N. Page, 210–11. Tisza, I. 213. Erzberger, 55–7. Macchio, 123, 126.
[4] The Deputy Labriola in Rome. Salandra, 339.
[5] See Rodd, III. 220. Trevelyan, *Scenes from Italy's War*, 19. Croce, 287.

## 8
### PIAZZA POLITICS. KING AND CONSTITUTION

It was in this setting that the King dealt with the Cabinet crisis. 'As was only logical', Salandra had proposed that his successor should be Giolitti.[1] The advice was given, although the veteran statesman had made it plain that he did not immediately aspire to office. Owing to the part he had played in opposition, he could not take the reins without encouraging Vienna. Seeing a Government in Rome 'obviously set on neutrality', the Ballplatz, as Giolitti argued, 'would not make the concessions necessary to avoid war'.[2] This outcome, clearly, would destroy his prestige and position in the country. What he intended, therefore, was to force Salandra, by Parliamentary pressure on behalf of the latest Austrian offer, to jettison the worst warmongers like Sonnino and Martini and, as the head of a new Administration (including presumably himself), to tear up the compact with the Entente. He offered Salandra the support of three-fourths of the Chamber for the operation. Yet such a motion of confidence, based on the reversal of the policy pursued hitherto, would be equivalent to a vote of censure. Then, as soon as the inevitable bargain was struck with Vienna, Salandra would be finally displaced and Giolitti put in power as the man who had expanded Italy and yet saved her from war. This, as the Premier has reflected, 'was not the first time that Giolitti had preferred, at a difficult moment, to leave things to others'. But Giolitti was soon to discover that this was not the occasion for 'the usual Parliamentary manoeuvres'.[3]

For, by resigning, Salandra passed on the responsibility to his rival, yet prevented him from accepting it by moving the scene of struggle from Montecitorio into the market place. Even if Giolitti, constrained by the emergency, wished to take over the Government immediately, he could not do so. It was impossible to introduce what would at once be branded as an Austrophil Ministry, while 'Rome' roared for Austrian blood. It was unthinkable for a politician, hounded in the streets, accused of subverting 'legitimate authority' and execrated as a 'traitor', to challenge the mob without risking not only his own political (if not physical) death, but a general upheaval, the ruin of the régime, the end of the existing institutions. Late on May 15th, the Germans, as Erzberger noted, learned 'that

---

[1] Salandra, 345.
[2] Giolitti, 394. Also Croce, 276. *Carteggio*, LXII. III. 387.
[3] Salandra, 333; also 331–32, 344, 353. Macchio to Burián, 10 and 15 May '15. Tisza, I. 211, 214. Macchio, 125. A. Albertini, 156. Giolitti apparently also suggested two other candidates for the caretaker premiership. Giolitti, 400.

Giolitti can do no more. He has completely collapsed in mind and body'.[1] The King, therefore, after the customary consultations, acted upon Salandra's motives which the latter says he had 'faithfully explained' to him.[2] Victor Emmanuel, as Bollati confided to Avarna, shared Sonnino's and Salandra's predilections for war.[3] The Premier has himself shed light on the attitude of the dynasty by relating how the Queen Mother, listening 'from behind her curtains' to D'Annunzio's street oration, 'applauded the Poet's words'.[4] According to Macchio, the King received the Bard in private audience.[5] The House of Savoy, hypnotized by the prospect of revolution, believed that only by means of a great military diversion and sweeping conquests would it be able to retain the throne.[6] In Milan, Mussolini—already a leader of the *Fasci*—screamed 'War or the Republic!'[7] In Rome, Salandra whispered warnings of 'the disaster', as he puts it, which a last-minute halt 'would be to the Constitution'.[8] It may or may not be too much to speak, as some have done, of a palace intrigue against the Chamber.[9] But it is a fact that, as the British Ambassador was to write, the Cabinet 'had resigned because they had realized that they would not be supported by Parliament. The King . . . disregarding actuarial forecasts of the Parliamentary vote. . . .'[10] chose, one might say, the verdict of the piazza. On May 16th, it was announced that 'His Majesty . . . has refused to accept the resignation of the Salandra Ministry'. On the 17th, Giolitti left the capital, and Erzberger was expelled.[11] 'Beau joueur', a French journalist wrote of Salandra. Sir Rennell Rodd, recapitulating, breathes a sigh of

---

[1] Tisza, I. 242. Erzberger, 56. Also Salandra, 377. Macchio, 125.
[2] Salandra, 344; also 353.
[3] Bollati to Avarna, 12 Jan. '15. *Carteggio*, LXI. IV. 535.
[4] Salandra, 340.
[5] Macchio to Burián, 19 May '15. *Austro-Hungarian Red Book*, II. No. 196, p. 325.
[6] Burián to the Ambassador Hohenlohe, 1 May '15, quoting Victor Emmanuel's remark (reported by Bülow) that the War was a necessity for the dynasty. Tisza, I. 204. Tisza, in his letter to Burián, 4 May '15, speaks of the King's 'fear of revolution and his belief that the regeneration of the Italian nation demands a victorious war'. (Tisza, I. 206). In the first days of May '15, Erzberger wired to the Chancellor to the same effect. Erzberger, 48. Also Macchio, 124.
[7] Rodd, III. 252. 15 May '15, according to the *Encyclopaedia Britannica*, 1947. Vol. XVI. p. 29. Also Rossi, 6.
[8] Salandra, 330. Also Macchio to Burián, 16 May '15: 'His Majesty is said to have let himself be convinced that street demonstrations must be regarded as beginning of revolutionary movement, and salvation of throne could lie only in continuation of former policy'. (Tisza, I. 215). That such was the view of the Salandra Government was stated, as early as 15 Dec. '14, by Avarna in his letter to Bollati. *Carteggio*, LXI. III. 390.
[9] See Rossi, 7, 62.
[10] Rodd, III. 253.
[11] Salandra, 354–5. Giolitti, 400. Erzberger, 58.

relief: 'And so the great conspiracy failed'.[1] But the other side must have argued that a greater one had succeeded.

Still, for a few more days it refused to admit defeat. On May 16th, Tisza wrote to Burián: 'If the King should not accept the resignation, the peace-minded members of the present Government ought to ... make its life impossible by resigning again'. On the 17th, in the Hungarian Diet, he staged a manifestation of 'lasting friendship with Italy'. On the 18th, the Chancellor Bethmann, in the Reichstag, coupled an announcement of the Austrian concessions to Italy with a plea for an understanding. On the same day, speculating on the coming vote in the Italian Chamber, Tisza was still relying on 'Bülow's connections' and 'the tenacious activity of Giolitti, the Vatican circles and the Socialists'. Even while repressing the Labour movement in his own country, he had no qualms about banking on 'the anti-war demonstrations of the [Italian] workers'.[2] Erzberger, on the other hand, practically on the eve of his enforced departure, had been besetting one of his high-placed Catholic go-betweens in Vienna: 'Holy Father sends you most heart-felt thanks.... If war is to be avoided, immediate cession is absolutely imperative....'[3] Yet, when Bülow and Macchio, on the 18th, handed to Sonnino the draft of a new pact they had cheerfully drawn up for his would-be successor, it varied to Salandra's eyes 'from the former list of concessions only in slight rectifications of frontier and details'. A new clause provided that the mixed commissions to settle the mode of the transfer of territory 'shall begin work immediately after the signing of the agreement', and that the transfer 'will be completed within one month' of the ratification of their decisions by the two Governments. The Austrian claim to compensation for Italy's occupation of the Dodecanese was dropped.[4] But, as Salandra says, 'while it was textually progressive,' it left 'our principal requests unsatisfied'.[5] Indeed, it was not until May 21st that the Foreign Minister Burián acknowledged Italy's denunciation of the Triplice some three weeks before, and even then it was, in effect, only to emphasize 'the material impossibility of an immediate

---

[1] Rodd, III. 253. Also Salandra, 345. On 14 May '15, Paléologue noted in his Diary that the Salandra Cabinet had 'very cleverly' submitted its resignation so that Giolitti could be 'foiled'. Paléologue, I. 337–8.

[2] Tisza to Burián, 16 and 18 May '15. Tisza, I. 215–17. Andrassy, 133. Helfferich, II. 69. Salandra, 358.

[3] Erzberger to Pater Count Andlau, 15 May '15. Tisza, I. 242–3. Also Erzberger's telegram to Bethmann, 16 May '15. Erzberger, 57.

[4] Burián to Macchio, 17 and 18 May '15. *Austro-Hungarian Red Book*, II. NN 190, 192, pp. 322–3. Salandra, 357, footnote 1; also 352. Macchio, 126. Burián, 57. For the text of the draft see *Austro-Hungarian Red Book*, II. No. 188, pp. 318–21.

[5] Salandra, 357.

surrender of the ceded territory', and to declare that Sonnino's move was

'in absolute contradiction with the solemnly undertaken obligations which Italy assumed in the Treaty . . . and which fixed the duration of our Alliance to . . . 1920, with a right to cancel it only on a year's notice, and with no provision for abrogation . . . before that time. The Royal Italian Government having in an arbitrary manner freed itself from all its obligations, the Austro-Hungarian Government declines the responsibility for all consequences that may arise from this procedure'.[1]

### 9
### AUSTRIA-HUNGARY, LIKE ITALY, IS BENT ON WAR

Here, in the eleventh hour, was a threat which was only partly due to the fact that the die had been cast in Rome. It would be nearer the truth to suggest that Vienna, from the autumn of 1914 at any rate, and certainly since Burián's advent, was perfectly aware that the groups led by Salandra and Sonnino were spoiling for a fight. Although, of course, she had no knowledge of, say, the contents of the Avarna-Bollati correspondence, their letters only mirrored the impressions which the proceedings of the Consulta evoked in the minds of the informed. As far back as August 1914, Bollati, after a visit to Rome, expressed himself as 'convinced that, on our side, we are sliding fatally, indeed we intend to go, to war with Austria'. In September, referring to the gathering interventionist clamour in Italy, he said that 'neither in the Government nor in high places is there a desire to resist' it. By December, Avarna noted that the Government 'will not be able to meet the grave internal situation created—except by going to war with Austria'. In January 1915, Bollati found that the Consulta was 'conducting the negotiations not only without any desire that they should succeed, but with the intention of preventing their success'. In February, Bollati recorded that 'every line, every phrase of Sonnino's telegrams reveals his intention to bring matters to a head . . .', and Avarna wrote that the Austro-Hungarians 'have always had very little trust in us, but now they have lost it altogether. . . .' At the end of March, he commented: 'The present negotiations have no solid foundation for continuing . . . Burián himself ought not to be under the illusion that any sort of agreement can be arrived at'. From Sonnino's conduct, 'one can deduce that he is not negotiating in any serious sense, but that he just wants to draw the matter out and wait for a convenient moment

---

[1] Burián to Macchio, 21 May '15, containing Burián's Note to Avarna of the same day. *Italian Green Book*, pp. 1319–22. Also Burián, 55–6. Salandra, 361.

at which to break off the parleys'. Late in April, Avarna diagnozed the discussions, 'from the nature of our proposals . . . as a pure formality. . . .'[1] And in the Italian diplomatic documents, as the American Ambassador has pointed out, 'nothing is disclosed . . . to give reason to believe that Italy would have accepted any "compensation" which Austria . . . would have offered'.[2] It was, therefore, no mere wisdom after the event, if Burián pleaded in his Memoirs that neutrality 'was the curtain behind which Italy quietly completed her preparations for deserting her Allies and joining the Entente'. Sonnino's whole performance was 'obviously a tactical manoeuvre . . . devoid of any serious intention of effecting an understanding'.[3]

Nevertheless, it has been argued that a timely Austrian concession on the surrender of Habsburg property might have led to an agreement. Hoyos thinks that 'until the outbreak of the World War all Italian statesmen . . . had their minds first and foremost on acquiring the Trentino, and for such a prize they would, in 1914, still have been ready to consent to Austro-Hungarian territorial expansion in the Balkans'. In the spring of 1915, a genuine compromise might have made it possible for Bülow 'to put Giolitti in Salandra's place and so defer the date of the declaration of war'; this would have allowed Germany, by her victories in Galicia, Poland and Courland, to tilt the diplomatic balance.[4] Macchio, for his part, is convinced that, if the Ballplatz had been more forthcoming, 'the Italian Government, despite the pressure of the Entente, would have still attempted to prolong the talks with us and—considering the general temper of the country and the enormous hazards of a modern war—given very careful thought to whether there would not have been greater advantage in letting Austria-Hungary pay amply for its neutrality'.[5]

[1] Bollati to Avarna, 31 Aug. and 24 Sept. '14; 27 Jan. and 11 Feb. '15. *Carteggio*, LXI. II. 252, 259. IV. 558. LXII. I. 67. Avarna to Bollati, 15 Dec. '14; 5 Feb., 7 and 31 March '15. *ibid*. LXI. III. 389–90. IV. 562. LXII. I. 77. III. 376, 378. Avarna to Sonnino, 25 April '15. Salandra, 253–4. Cf. *Italian Green Book*, No. 74. Although Avarna and Bollati, as adherents of the Triplice, were critical of their Government's policy, the correctness of their judgments seems to be borne out by the developments as they emerge from this narrative. As early as 9 Aug. '14, moreover, San Giuliano, writing to Salandra (*Documenti Diplomatici*, 5. I. No. 151, p. 83) foresaw 'if not the probability at least the possibility that Italy must . . . attack Austria'. On 9 Sept. '14, the Russian Military Attaché in Rome reported that 'the preparation for war is being actively continued'. *Internationale Beziehungen*, II. 6. I. p. 166, footnote 2.
[2] T. N. Page, 204.
[3] Burián, 18–19. Cf. Hoyos, 66: 'After . . . the Marne battle there was no other policy for Italy that promised gain than to change front'. Macchio, 103, writes that the demand for immediate cession 'removed all doubts' about Sonnino's intentions.
[4] Hoyos, 51, 69. Bülow, III. 205, adds as another *sine qua non* of an agreement 'the autonomy of Trieste'.
[5] Macchio, 131–2.

Even if such reasoning had been too optimistic, such tactics would have enabled Burián to protract the negotiations, to postpone the start and slow down, perhaps obstruct, the progress of Sonnino's discussions with the Entente. It would have strengthened greatly the Giolittian, Catholic and Socialist Opposition in Italy. If nothing else, it would at least temporarily have upset Sonnino's plans.[1] Since it is inconceivable that Burián was not aware of this, there must have been a basic motive (apart from the specific ones governing concrete issues such as the Trentino or 'immediate execution') why his advent coincided with stiffening resistance, why he waited until he was forced in March to make his first hesitant advance, and why —even in the critical month of May—he continued his negative policy.

The hidden springs of Burián's actions would seem to have been deep in the imperialist relationships of Austria-Hungary with Italy and Germany. The whole intercourse between Vienna and Berlin was poisoned by the continuous German sponsorship of the Consulta's claims.[2] It was all very well for the Vice-Chancellor Helfferich to assert in retrospect: 'It was a matter of sacrificing pawns... lest the game for our survival should be lost'.[3] What the Hohenzollerns considered as 'pawns' were knights and bishops to the Habsburgs and, worse still, the Wilhelmstrasse was conscious of the futility of the sacrifice. As early as January 1915, Bollati recognized that the Germans were certain of the inevitability of the Italian attack. On April 14th, he reported that, 'with regard to the intentions of our Government, Jagow believes ... that it has continued the negotiations only with a view to completing military preparations and to concluding an agreement with the Entente'.[4] The rulers of the Dual Monarchy could not have been unaware of this appraisal of the situation[5] (it was, after all, identical with theirs), and since Jagow, nevertheless, through Erzberger and Bülow, High Finance and the Vatican, 'moved heaven and hell'[6] to extort the concessions, this only hardened the conviction on the Danube that what the Ally

[1] Avarna to Bollati, 7 March '15. *Carteggio*, LXII. I. 77. Macchio, 71–2, 130. Hoyos, 69–70. Rossi, 3–4.
[2] See Helfferich, II. 68, 70. Tirpitz, 437. Huldermann, 243. Hoyos, 68. Macchio, 132. Burián, 59. Bülow, III. 205. Also pp. 300–1, 310–11 above.
[3] Helfferich, II. 67.
[4] Bollati to Avarna, 12 Jan. and 14 April '15. *Carteggio*, LXI. IV. 552. LXII. III. 379. Helfferich cannot have been the only leading German to think that 'once the Italian Government had taken the road of betrayal and blackmail, it was driven perforce by the traitor's and blackmailer's distrust into the War'. See *op. cit.* II. 70.
[5] See, for example, Macchio, 24.
[6] Macchio, 116. Hoyos, 68. For an authoritative German opinion which supports Vienna's suspicions of Bülow see Wedel, 'Fürst Bülow und Österreich'. *Süddeutsche Monatshefte*, March 1931, pp. 407–8.

really intended was to offset, by the enforced surrender to Italy, the gains Austria-Hungary hoped to make in Russia, Poland and the Balkans.[1] From the Emperor's partners in his daily game of tarock to big business men, from Conrad and Tisza to the Ballplatz officials, everyone 'in the know' in Vienna was livid with wrath. The secret diplomatic papers bristle with bitter references and retorts.[2] The whole pent-up fury against Germany exploded in Tisza's denunciation of

> 'the undermining work of the Bülow-Erzberger clique . . . and the means they did not shrink from employing against us. . . . If it is established that the decision of the Italian Government to go to war had been brought about by impaired faith in the honesty of the [Dual] Monarchy's proceedings, and this impairment of faith has, in its turn, been caused by lack of accord between . . . our action and Bülow's promises, then this is the most devastating criticism of Bülow's truly ill-fated activity in Rome. No words can convey how damaging was Bülow's procedure . . . in always making promises at our expense, which he was not entitled to make and which, moreover, he knew to be contrary to our views. . . . We have repeatedly drawn the attention of the German Foreign Office to the dangerous consequences of these machinations. . . .'[3]

Indeed, even if Austria-Hungary had intended to compromise with Italy, then—as Macchio has written—'the never-ending pressures . . . from the . . . Wilhelmstrasse were the worst prelude for such a policy'.[4]

This fact, that Austria-Hungary was besieged by both her Italian foe and her German friend, and that resistance to the one was automatically resistance to the other, could only make her more intransigent. And what increased her staying power was the shrewd perception that the range of the Reich's batteries was circumscribed. There could be little doubt that (as Bollati forecast from his observation post in Berlin) 'Germany, if forced to choose between

[1] See pp. 279–80 above.
[2] See Berchtold to Macchio, 21 Nov. '14. Macchio, 53–4. Tisza to Czernin, 26 Nov. '14. Burián to Tisza, presumably 5 Jan. '15. Tisza to Burián, 5 Jan. '15. Tisza to Berchtold, 6 Jan. '15. Tisza to Conrad, 16 Jan. '15. Tisza, I. 114–15, 143, 140, 145–6, 156. Conrad to Tisza, 19 Jan. '15: '. . . the pressure of the Germans, who want to improve their position at our expense, must be resolutely met'. (Tisza, I. 160). Merey to Macchio, 1 Feb. and 17 April '15. Macchio, 96, 84, 107. Burián to Hohenlohe, 1 May '15: 'At this moment, recriminations between Vienna and Berlin appear to me . . . pointless'. Further concessions 'would touch the vital nerve of the [Dual] Monarchy'. (Tisza, I. 203). Francis Joseph to William II, 5 May '15: '. . . I have reached the utmost limit of imaginable concessions. . . . I am prevented from considering further Italian demands out of regard for the position of the [Dual] Monarchy as a Great Power, its permanent interests and future. . . .' Tisza, I. 207–8. Also Huldermann, 243.
[3] Tisza to the Archbishop of Kalocsa, 28 June '15. Tisza, I. 237.
[4] Macchio, 132.

them, would inevitably place herself on the side of Austria and not of Italy'.¹ At the height of the crisis he gave warning that, in a showdown, the Reich would stand by the Danubian Empire.² It was not only that, in Jagow's words, 'Austria is the last stronghold of the aristocratic tradition and conservative principles, whereas Italy is a democractic and revolutionary structure'.³ The stark truth was that, in this 'decisive War', as Conrad has stressed with pride, 'Austria-Hungary was Germany's only reliable Ally'.⁴ Hence, the Chancellor Bethmann was constrained to write to Bülow: '... we are saying in Vienna as much as is at all permissible with an Ally: had we proceeded further, and used threats, we should only have brought the Austrians to the point of laying down their arms, and might so have been left to face our enemies alone'.⁵ This is why Bethmann and Jagow lacked what Bülow calls the 'energy for any real pressure on Vienna'.⁶ And the latter, certain—as the Prince bitterly reflected—of the 'Pomeranian grenadier',⁷ could well afford not to capitulate to Italy.

On the contrary, Austria's rulers would appear to have desired that Italy should capitulate to them. Ever since Bismarck had imposed the Roman Alliance on them, it was universally regarded in Vienna as an act of 'self-abnegation' or 'a marriage of convenience'⁸ in which the advantages were monopolized by the other partner. It brought Austria the danger of conflict with France with whom she had no quarrel, without ensuring Italy's assistance in a clash with Russia. It compelled her to admit Italy to a parity of 'rights' in the Balkans without—as Szilassy, an old Ballplatz stalwart, grumbles—receiving 'the slightest *quid pro quo*'. It gave Italy 'a bill of exchange on Tripoli', without securing for the Austrians Albania. Although 'we even recognized our identity of interests in Albania', 'the Italians always ... complained, scolded, and demanded so much that ... in most cases we granted something on Germany's initiative. ... The Italian desires were numberless. I have counted some thirty during the thirty years' duration of the Alliance'.⁹ As Hoyos wrote

---

¹ Bollati to San Giuliano, 8 July '14. Salandra, 40.
² Bollati to Avarna, 4 May '15. *Carteggio*, LXII. III. 386.
³ Bülow, III. 233.
⁴ Conrad, IV. 214. The Habsburg Ambassador in Berlin, Hohenlohe, presumably dismissing Turkey altogether, went so far as to describe his country as Germany's 'only Ally'. See Berchtold to Conrad, 23 Dec. '14, transmitting a report from Hohenlohe. Conrad, V. 899. Cf. also Bollati's report, quoted in San Giuliano's telegram to Carlotti, 14 Sept. '14. Deciphered in the Russian Foreign Ministry. *Internationale Beziehungen*, II. 6. II. p. 499, footnote 3.
⁵ Bethmann to Bülow, 16 March '15. Bülow, III. 225. Ludendorff, I. 78, also speaks of German fears 'that Austria would make a separate peace with the Entente'.
⁶ Bülow, III. 205.  ⁷ Bülow, III. 185.
⁸ Macchio, 12, 15.  ⁹ Szilassy, 116–18, 120.

later, 'for years our Italian Ally was consistently . . . working to throttle us . . . in the Balkans'.[1] Rome, Conrad emphasized, was ever ready to thwart Vienna's designs against the Serbians.[2] Owing to her 'imperialist tendencies', as Macchio puts it, 'we were . . . facing in Italy a competitor resolved . . . to give the ominous Article VII extensive and arbitrary interpretations'.[3] That Article enabled the Consulta to make use of Austria's whole Eastern policy for its own ends. Time and again she had tried to obtain a rewording of the fatal clause, and failed. Since each of her steps brought on automatic claims for compensation, 'we were deprived of all freedom of movement' and, as Habsburg imperialism strained to be 'free', the whole Treaty became an intolerable stranglehold and, in Hoyos's words, 'an impossibility'.[4]

Despite their silence about the one-sided gains (Bosnia-Herzegovina) and the anti-Italian manoeuvres made by the Habsburgs, these pronouncements reveal the state of feeling on the Danube. 'At Court . . . in the Foreign Office . . . in aristocratic society; in the Army and Navy and especially in the Church, there have always been . . . influences and intrigues working for "the chastisement of Italy", and propagating the belief that only by fresh victories on the Lombard or Venetian plains or by another battle of Lissa, can the [Dual] Monarchy . . . gain a free hand in the Western Balkans'.[5] Compounded of distrust, hatred and contempt, this aversion was such that, as early as 1906, the German Ambassador informed Berlin: 'Only a war with Italy would be really popular' in Vienna.[6] It was then that Conrad started his persistent battle-cries against the Ally. During the Libyan War, he was supported by sabre-rattling among the Austrian clerical and military groups, big business and the Liberal press. In December 1912, writing to Berchtold, he lamented that 'we did not come to a reckoning with this unreliable neighbour years ago'. The defeat of the Ballplatz in the Balkan Wars, the frustrations in Albania, and the Consulta's share in both, converted this agitation into something like an inevitable and fixed resolve. Early in 1914, Conrad's dispatches were replete with references to fresh fortifications at Pola and the Isonzo, to rearmament, to 'negotiations' from strength with, and war against, the Italians.[7]

[1] Hoyos, 47.     [2] Conrad to the Emperor, 16 Jan. '14. Conrad, III. 755.
[3] Macchio, 22-3.
[4] Hoyos, 60-1. Also Pribram, *The Secret Treaties of Austria-Hungary*, II. 176.
[5] Steed, *The Hapsburg Monarchy*, 278-9.
[6] 12 Feb. 1906. *Die Grosse Politik*, XXI. 1, No. 6999, p. 159, May, 392. Macchio, 17. L. Albertini, II. 218. Salandra, 43.
[7] Conrad to the Emperor, 16 Jan. '14. Conrad to Berchtold, 18 March '14. Conrad to the Emperor, 25 March '14. Conrad to Berchtold, 22 June '14. Conrad, III. 560, 562, 694, 755, 771, 779; also 598, 676, 681. Macchio, 23. Pribram, *Secret Treaties*, II. 175-77. Steed, 276-7. Michels, 97; also 191, and *ibid.* footnote 3.

And after Sarayevo, Vienna's entire diplomacy in Rome would have been no different if her avowed aim had been to produce an ultimate break.

Some circles, such as Andrassy's may have been honest in wanting an understanding[1]; Berchtold, if he had remained Foreign Minister, might have submitted to German pressure; and even his successor Burián, in the event of a Carpathian disaster, might, as a temporary expedient, have adopted the required compromise.[2] But, as it was, by not consulting Italy before sending the ultimatum to Belgrade*, Berchtold did something that was tantamount to deliberately wrecking the Alliance. When Burián delayed and side-tracked the issue and, even in yielding, stopped short of 'immediate execution'— the one concession which, it might have been supposed, would satisfy Sonnino—he must have known that this would provoke an attack. Indeed, as early as August 1914, Tisza was 'convinced that even a slight resistance by German and Austro-Hungarian troops will hold up ... [the Italians] until the decision has fallen elsewhere'.[3] In February 1915, this theme of successful resistance, mingling with speculations on Italian difficulties at home and in her colonies, recurs in a Ballplatz letter.[4] In April, after the Constantinople Agreements had been reached by the Entente, the risks attendant upon war with Italy appeared mitigated by the hope that 'England ... will not permit Russia's undivided sway in Europe'.[5] And in May, as soon as Salandra had resigned and the full scope of the Gorlice break-through had become apparent, Burián tried to revoke the major offers tabled with his consent by Macchio and Bülow on May 9th.[6]

His 'boundless optimism' and 'delusions' about the feasibility of an understanding,[7] therefore, were camouflage. All his con-

[1] On 27 Jan. '15, Andrassy wrote in the *Neue Freie Presse*: 'If Italy wishes to settle the question that exists between us ... by means of a friendly agreement, and if Italy remains neutral, she can count with certainty upon Austria-Hungary as her constant Ally. ... It would be a mistake to assume that because Italy did not join us we entertained any bitter feelings against her. ...' He also aired this view in Italian newspapers. His chief argument was that Italian neutrality would enable Austria to grow so strong that her friendship would become an abiding Italian interest. Andrassy, 128, 130, 133–4.

[2] Even Tisza and Conrad, shaken by the military crisis in April and early May, appear to have been, for a short time, prepared to make 'heavy sacrifices'. See Tisza to Conrad, 16 April '15. Conrad to Tisza, 23 April. Tisza to Czernin, 28 April. Tisza to Burián, 4 May '15. Tisza, I. 184–5, 194, 207. Macchio, 131.

[3] Tisza to Berchtold, 10 Aug. '14. Tisza, I. 49.

[4] Merey to Macchio, 16 Feb. '15. Macchio, 97.

[5] Diary, 6 April '15. Redlich, II. 28. On 25 April, the *Neue Freie Presse* (No. 18, 201, p. 3) published an article by Count Lützow, 'Österreich-Ungarn und England', discussing Austria's attitude to Britain and pleading for an abatement of the hatred engendered by the War. See Redlich, II. 31.

[6] Erzberger to Pater Andlau in Vienna, 15 May '15. Tisza, I. 242. Cf. also Helfferich, II. 71. See p. 381 above.

[7] Macchio, 81, 131. Avarna to Bollati, 31 March '15. *Carteggio*, LXII. III. 376.

* See pages 165–6.

cessions were tactical manoeuvres to deceive public opinion, to throw the blame on Italy, to weaken the German pressure and, above all, 'to gain as much time as possible . . . and . . . make . . . preparations. . . .'[1] He had, as he has since confessed, 'confidential reports' on the conclusion of the secret London Treaty[2] and, quite obviously, his plans were laid. To set about liquidating Serbia, conquering Poland and marching on Salonika clearly does not square with the idea of sacrificing the Trentino, abandoning Trieste and forfeiting Albania. There was no point in fighting to drive Russia from the Balkans merely to make way for the Italians. It would have been senseless for Austria-Hungary to struggle for the re-division of South-Eastern Europe, and leave inviolate the Power which was not only disputing her hegemony but also burning to wrest territory from her. Tisza's subsequent admission that the Ballplatz had never been in earnest in its proposals to the Consulta[3] fits into the pattern of this policy. Far from intending to reward Rome for the 'betrayal', Vienna was bent on summary punishment. All the evidence available goes to show that Austro-Hungarian imperialism, like that of Italy, wanted war.[4]

And that, it would seem, was why the one really crucial point of 'immediate execution' was not conceded until May 22nd, when Sonnino replied that it was 'too late'.[5] In giving that answer, he 'referred to the demonstrations of the past few days and to the decisive vote in Parliament'.[6] The King, having just allowed the mob to overrule the Chamber, remembered his duty as Constitutional Monarch and, replying to a last-minute appeal from the Kaiser, told Bülow that he must abide by the verdict of the majority.[7]

---

[1] Burián, 38. Also Conrad, V. 331. Macchio, 96. On 26 Feb. '15, Redlich noted, on the strength of information received about Burián's intentions: 'We are ready for war and are gearing ourselves for it'. (Redlich, II. 19). According to Macchio, 115–16, Vienna's last proposals in May were made 'only' because the Austrian, like the German, General Staff pressed for delay. Also ibid. 126. Erzberger, 41, 47.

[2] Burián, 56. Other signs of the approaching *dénouement* were the retention of Italian vessels in their ports and the dispatch of a ship from Italy to Fiume for the repatriation of Italian residents in Austria. See 21 April '15. Redlich, II. 31. Avarna to Bollati, 13 May '15. *Carteggio*, LXII. III. 387.

[3] Speech in the Hungarian Parliament in 1916. See Musulin, 256. Erzberger, 130, states that, in July 1915, Tisza expressed relief at the failure of the negotiations with Italy.

[4] 'Granted the character of the Austrian State, which had its own logic and its own needs, it was to be expected that the final issue would be war'. Croce, 272.

[5] Even then Burián's proposal to meet 'Italy still further on the question of the putting of the cessions into effect' was coupled with the proviso: without 'immediate military occupation'. See Burián to Macchio, 22 May '15. *Austro-Hungarian Red Book*, II. No. 202, p. 333. Burián, 58. Also Erzberger, 58.

[6] Macchio to Burián, 23 May '15. *Austro-Hungarian Red Book*, II. No. 203, p. 334. Cf. also Salandra, 358.

[7] Bülow, III. 228.

## 10
### THE LAST OBSTACLE. THE BALANCE SHEET

But before Salandra could face the crucial Parliamentary ballot, one more obstacle had to be overcome. The Socialist Party, since Mussolini's expulsion in October 1914, had closed it ranks. The Executive, assuming the collective editorship of *Avanti*, proclaimed as 'our battle-cry, our avowal of faith. . . . Long live the Socialist International'.[1] Throughout the autumn and winter it campaigned against intervention, the equivocal policy of the Government and the expenditure of thousands of millions on arms: 'Salandra must go!' In March 1915, with the quickening of events, *Avanti* called upon the masses to prevent the war-mongers 'from disposing of you and your lives in the cause of your masters'. In the House, the Deputy Turati attacked the Cabinet with a censure motion, and in the big cities such as Milan the workers came out into the streets. The order to fire given to the soldiers, the bloodshed in Reggio Emilia and the prohibition of all public demonstrations were met by 'measures designed to protect Italian freedom'. On April 11th, despite the official veto, Rome, Naples, Turin, Florence, Ancona and other cities were swept by huge popular manifestations, and in Milan the funeral of a man killed in the street-fighting was turned into an impressive plea for peace. In the decisive May days, a wave of strikes, mass processions, denunciations of 'the interventionist squadrons swarming in Milan under the protection of Salandra's police', and active resistance against the Nationalists, the Fascists and other groups of *guerrafondai* showed that the working class was solidly opposed to war.

The leadership, however, was in the throes of dissensions and confusion. Although the Left was in control, the influence of reformism (Turati, Treves) was strong, notably in the Parliamentary fraction and the Confederation of Labour. The Party Executive, headed by Serrati and Lazzari, occupied a centre position between Henderson, Scheidemann or Renaudel who supported their own belligerent Governments, and Lenin whose programme was to 'transform the Imperialist War into civil war'. The Italian Socialist Party, therefore, even while inveighing against the resort to arms, refrained from either organizing or calling for a struggle. The current motto was 'neither support nor obstruction', and in practice, as Salandra says scornfully, 'their action was confined to words, manifestos, meetings, debates, fiery newspaper articles; little else'.[2] This made them easier to deal with. *Avanti* constantly bore the scars of censorship. There

[1] 20 Oct. '14. Balabanoff, 93–4.   [2] Salandra, 310–11.

were times when it was prohibited in twenty provinces. In May, more than 250 Socialists—if Macchio's figures are correct—were in prison. Outbreaks of unrest were quelled by troops. When the Confederation of Labour reacted to the reappointment of Salandra and Sonnino (on May 16th) by ordering a general strike, when industrial labour in many towns followed the lead of the metal-workers of Turin, the movement, as Salandra has recorded, 'was immediately repressed by transferring powers to the military authorities'.[1]

And so the stage was set in every respect for the Parliamentary session of May 20th. 'Access to the Chamber and to the Tribune was rigidly guarded . . . incidents were quickly suppressed'.[2] 'The galleries were packed. . . .'[3] Although Sonnino, two days previously, had promised Macchio to lay Austria's latest proposals before the deputies, they were told nothing. Salandra, as he has since revealed, had no intention 'of leaving the decision with the Chamber . . . we had made our decision. . . . Parliament could do no other than accept the consequences'.[4] Amid a tumult of acclamation—'only five rows of Socialists . . . remained seated and grimly silent'[5]—he tabled a Bill (in a single clause so as 'to shorten the discussion'[6]) granting him exceptional powers. On the eve of his resignation, in a provisional analysis of the strength in the House, it was estimated that 'not more than sixty were . . . in favour of the War: on taking the vote the number might rise to 150'.[7] But since then, the piazza had roared its verdict. Giolitti's huge majority, intimidated or mesmerized, deserted the fallen idol. Few had the courage of their convictions to stay away. Turati's was the only voice for the Opposition. The Bill was passed by 407 to 74, with two abstentions. The ballot in the Senate was almost unanimous. Only a few of its 300 members were absent or abstained.[8] And when the Chamber adjourned *sine die*, it had accomplished an extraordinary feat: elected by a swing to the Left, it produced what was, in effect, a dictatorship of the Right. Permeated by neutralism, it brought about intervention. Representing a people whose moral right and duty was to liberate its unredeemed kinsmen and complete the unification of the State, it sanctioned the predatory policy of 'the impudent minorities . . . that had dragged a nation into war against its will'.[9]

[1] Salandra, 354; also 172, 190, 196, 198–9, 214, 311, 319, 339, 350. *Avanti*, 20–23 May '15. Nenni, 50. Macchio, 127. Destrée, 80, 91. Megaro, 313. Tisza, I. 213. *Voprosy Istorii*, 1953. VI. 70–1.
[2] Salandra, 359.
[3] Rodd, III. 254.
[4] Salandra, 341–2. Cf. Rodd, III. 253.
[5] Rodd, III. 254.
[6] Salandra, 360. The quotation is from Salandra's book.
[7] Salandra, 343. The quotation is from Salandra's book.
[8] Salandra, 361: 'It is useless to inquire into the motives of such converts'. Also *ibid*. 355, 359–60. Rodd, III. 253–4. T. N. Page, 213–14. Macchio, 127.
[9] Giolitti, Election speech in 1919. Rossi, 63; also 3–7.

## THE FINAL STRUGGLE

On Whit Monday, May 23rd 1915, when the declaration of war went to the Austro-Hungarian Ambassador, Rome—save for some organized demonstrations outside the Entente Missions—was quiet[1] with fatigue and foreboding. But the Chancelleries of Europe were astir. The ten months of diplomatic strife had injured the partnership between Vienna and Berlin so gravely that it never recovered. The relations between Russia and the West, already impaired by the Turkish tangle, were further strained. Italy had become an Ally of the Entente on terms which made her no friend of France and Russia.[2] And, as one more item on the debit side, there was the fatal impact of the London Treaty on the remaining neutral States.

---

[1] Rodd, III. 255-6. T. N. Page, 215. Helfferich, II. 69.
[2] See Poincaré, VI. 230-2, 238. Also Schilling to Carlotti, 7 April '15. *Internationale Beziehungen*, II. 7. II. No. 494, p. 496.

# BIBLIOGRAPHY

## Documents

ADAMOV, E. A. (Edit.) *Konstantinopol i Prolivy po sekretnym dokumentam byvshevo ministerstva inostrannykh del.* (*Constantinople and the Straits*, according to the Documents of the Former Ministry of Foreign Affairs). Vols. I, II. Litizdat N.K.I.D. Moscow, 1925, 1926.

*The Austro-Hungarian Red Book.* No. 2. Diplomatic Documents Relating to the Outbreak of the European War. Part I. Edit. by J. Brown Scott. Oxford University Press, Inc. New York, 1916.

*British Documents on the Origins of the War, 1898-1914.* Vols. VI; X, part 2, and XI. Edit. by G. P. Gooch and H. Temperley. H.M.S.O. London, 1930, 1938, 1926.

*Il carteggio Avarna-Bollati Luglio 1914-Maggio 1915.* Edit. by C. Avarna di Gualtieri. *Rivista Storica Italiana.* Anno LXI, fascicolo II, III, IV. Anno LXII, fasc. I, III. Naples, 1949, 1950.

*Dardanelles Commission, First Report.* H.M.S.O., London, 1917. (Cd. 8490). *Supplement to the First Report.* H.M.S.O. London, 1917. (Cd. 8502). *The Final Report.* H.M.S.O. London, 1917. (Cd. 371).

*Die Deutschen Dokumente zum Kriegsausbruch.* I., IV. Band. Compiled by Karl Kautsky. Deutsche Verlagsgesellschaft für Politik und Geschichte m.b.H. Charlottenburg, 1919.

*Diplomatische Aktenstücke zur Vorgeschichte des Krieges 1914.* I. Teil. Ergänzungen zum österreich-ungarischen Rotbuch. Staatsdruckerei. Vienna, 1919.

*I Documenti Diplomatici Italiani.* 5. Serie: 1914-1918. Vol. I. Ministero degli Affari Esteri. Libreria dello Stato. Rome, 1954.

*Dokumente der Deutschen Politik und Geschichte von 1848 bis zur Gegenwart.* Herausgeber Dr. J. Hohlfeld. II. Band. 'Das Zeitalter Wilhelm II, 1890-1918'. Wendler und Co., Berlin.

*Die Geheimakten des Deutschen Aussenamtes (1914-1918).* Photostats and microfilms of the original documents. Public Record Office, London.

*Die Grosse Politik der Europäischen Kabinette 1871-1914.* Sammlung der diplomatischen Akten des Auswärtigen Amtes. Herausg. v. J. Lepsius, A. Mendelssohn-Bartholdy, Fr. Thimme. Vols. XI; XXI, part 1. Deutsche Verlagsgesellschaft für Politik and Geschichte m.b.H. Berlin, 1924, 1925.

*Die Internationalen Beziehungen im Zeitalter des Imperialismus.* Dokumente aus den Archiven der Zarischen und der Provisorischen Regierung, herausg. von der Kommission beim Zentralexekutivkomitee der Sovjetregierung u.d. Vorsitz von M. N. Pokrovski. Deutsche Ausgabe herausg. von O. Hoetzsch. Reihe II. 6. Band, I. Halbband, II. Halbb. 7. Band, I. Halbb., II. Halbb.

8. Band, I. Halbb., II. Halbb. Verlag der Reimar Hobbing G.m.b.H. Berlin, 1934, 1935, 1936.

*Iswolski im Weltkriege.* Der diplomatische Schriftwechsel Iswolskis 1914-1917. Neue Dokumente aus den Geheimakten der russischen Staatsarchive. Kommentar von Fr. Stieve. Deutsche Verlagsgesellschaft für Politik und Geschichte. Berlin, 1925.

*The Italian Green Book.* Diplomatic Documents Relating to the Outbreak of the European War. Part II. Edit. by J. Brown Scott. Oxford University Press, Inc. New York, 1916.

KLYUCHNIKOV, YU. V. i [and] SABANIN, A. *Mezhdunarodnaya politika noveishevo vremeni. (International Politics of Recent Times).* Part II. Litizdat N.K.I.D. Moscow, 1926.

*The Lansing Papers 1914-1920.* Vol. I. Papers Relating to the Foreign Relations of the United States. U.S. Government Printing Office. Washington, 1939.

*Österreich-Ungarns Aussenpolitik von der bosnischen Krise bis zum Kriegsausbruch 1914.* Diplomatische Aktenstücke des österreich-ungarischen Ministeriums des Äusseren. VIII. Band. Österreichischer Bundesverlag. Vienna, Leipzig, 1930.

*The Parliamentary Debates* (Official Report). 5th Series. Vol. LXX. Third Volume of Session 1914-1915. H.M.S.O. London.

PRIBRAM, A. F. *The Secret Treaties of Austria-Hungary 1879-1914.* Vols. I, II. Harvard U. P., Oxford U. P., 1920, 1921.

TISZA, GRAF STEFAN. *Briefe 1914-1918.* I. Band. Verlag Reimar Hobbing. Berlin, 1928.

*Das Zaristische Russland im Weltkriege.* Neue Dokumente aus den russischen Staatsarchiven über den Eintritt der Türkei, Bulgariens, Rumäniens und Italiens in den Weltkrieg. [Russisches] Vorwort von M. Pokrovski. Deutsche Verlagsgesellschaft für Politik und Geschichte m.b.H. Berlin, 1927.

## Books

ABBOTT, G. F. *Greece and the Allies 1914-1922.* Methuen and Co., Ltd. London, 1922.

ABDULLAH, KING OF TRANSJORDAN. *Memoirs.* J. Cape Ltd. London, 1950.

AGA KHAN. *The Memoirs.* Cassell and Co., Ltd. London, 1954.

ALASTOS, D. *Venizelos.* P. Lund Humphries and Co., Ltd. London, 1942.

*Albania.* Handbooks Prepared under the Direction of the Historical Section of the Foreign Office. No. 17. H.M.S.O. London, 1920.

ALBERTINI, A. *Vita di Luigi Albertini.* A. Mondadori. Rome, 1945.

ALBERTINI, L. *The Origins of the War of 1914.* Vols. I and II. Oxford University Press, 1952, 1953.

# BIBLIOGRAPHY

ALBRECHT-CARRIÉ, R. *Italy at the Peace Conference.* Columbia U. P. New York, 1938.

ALDROVANDI MARESCOTTI, L. *Guerre diplomatique 1914-1919.* Gallimard. Paris, 1935.

*Anatolia.* Handbooks Prepared under the Direction of the Historical Section of the Foreign Office. No. 59. H.M.S.O. London, 1920.

ANDRASSY, COUNT J. *Diplomacy and the War.* John Bale, Sons and Danielsson, Ltd. London, 1921.

*Arabia.* Handbooks Prepared under the Direction of the Historical Section of the Foreign Office. No. 61. H.M.S.O. London, 1920.

ARTHUR, SIR G. *Life of Lord Kitchener.* Vol. III. Macmillan and Co., Ltd. London, 1920.

ASQUITH, H. H. (The Earl of Oxford and Asquith). *The Genesis of the War.* Cassell and Co., Ltd. London, 1923. *Memories and Reflections 1852-1927.* Vol. II. Cassell and Co., Ltd. London, 1928.

AVERBUKH, R. A. *Italiya v pervoi i vtoroi mirovykh voinakh.* (*Italy in the First and Second World War*). Izd. Akademii Nauk S.S.S.R. Moscow, Leningrad, 1946.

BADEN, PRINCE MAX OF. *The Memoirs.* Constable and Co., Ltd. London, 1928.

BALABANOFF, A. *Erinnerungen und Erlebnisse.* E. Laubsche Verlagsbuchhandlung G.m.b.H. Berlin, 1927.

*The Balkans.* A History of Bulgaria, Serbia, Greece, Rumania, Turkey by N. Forbes, A. J. Toynbee, D. Mitrany, D. C. Hogarth. The Clarendon Press. Oxford, 1915.

BASTER, A. S. J. *The International Banks.* P. S. King and Son, Ltd. London, 1935.

BEAVERBROOK, LORD. *Politicians and the War, 1914-1916.* I. Thornton Butterworth Ltd. London, 1928.

BENTWICH, N. *England in Palestine.* Kegan Paul, French, Trubner and Co., Ltd. London, 1932.

BERTIE, LORD. *The Diary 1914-1918.* Vol. I. Hodder and Stoughton Ltd. London, 1924.

BETHMANN-HOLLWEG, TH. V. *Betrachtungen zum Weltkriege.* 2. Teil. Verlag Reimar Hobbing. Berlin, 1921.

BLAKE, R. *The Unknown Prime Minister.* The Life and Times of A. Bonar Law 1858-1923. Eyre and Spottiswoode Ltd. London, 1955.

BOWMAN, I. *The New World.* Problems in Political Geography. G. Harrap and Co., Ltd. London, 1922.

BRADY, R. A. *Business as a System of Power.* Columbia University Press. New York, 1943.

BRANDENBURG, E. *Von Bismarck zum Weltkriege.* Deutsche Verlagsgesellschaft für Politik und Geschichte m.b.H. Berlin, 1924.

BRÉAL, A. *Philippe Berthelot.* Gallimard. Paris, 1937.

BUCHAN, J. (Edit.). *Italy.* The Nations of Today. Hodder and Stoughton Ltd. London, 1923.

BUCHANAN, SIR G. *My Mission to Russia.* Vol. II. Cassell and Co., Ltd. London, 1923.

BÜLOW, PRINCE von. *Memoirs 1909-1919.* [Vol. III.] Putnam. London, 1932.

BURIÁN, COUNT STEPHAN. *Austria in Dissolution.* Ernest Benn Ltd. London, 1925.

BUXTON, N. and CH. R. *The War and the Balkans.* George Allen and Unwin Ltd. London, 1915.

CAMBON, P. *Correspondance 1870-1924.* Tome III. Éditions Bernard Grasset. Paris, 1946.

CARR, E. H. *The Bolshevik Revolution 1917-1923.* Vol. III. Macmillan and Co., Ltd. London, 1953.

CHÉRADAME, A. *L'Europe et la question d'Autriche au seuil du XX-e siècle.* Plon. Paris, 1901.

CHURCHILL, W. S. *The World Crisis 1911-1914.* Thornton Butterworth Ltd. London, 1923. *The World Crisis 1915.* Thornton Butterworth Ltd. London, 1923.

CHRISTOPHER, PRINCE OF GREECE. *Memoirs.* Hurst and Blackett Ltd. London, 1938.

COLOMBI, A. *Pagine di storia del movimento operaio.* Ed. di cultura sociale. Rome, 1951.

CONNELL, B. *Manifest Destiny.* A Study in Five Profiles of the Rise and Influence of the Mountbatten Family. Cassell and Co., Ltd. London, 1953.

CONRAD, FELDMARSCHALL V. *Aus meiner Dienstzeit 1906-1918.* Band III, IV, V. Rikola Verlag. Vienna, Leipzig, Münich, 1922, 1923, 1925.

CORBETT, SIR J. S. *History of the Great War.* Naval Operations. Vols. I, II. Longmans, Green and Co. London, 1920, 1921.

CORRADINI, E. *Il volere d'Italia.* F. Perella. Naples, 1911. *Stato liberale e stato nazionale.* Manifesti del Nazionalismo italiano. Ist. Ed. Italiano. Milan, 1916.

CRISPI, F. *Questioni internazionali.* Milan, 1913.

CROCE, B. *A History of Italy 1871-1915.* The Clarendon Press. Oxford, 1929.

CRUTWELL, C. R. M. *History of the Great War 1914-1918.* Oxford U. P., 1934.

CUMMING, H. H. *Franco-British Rivalry in the Post-War Near East.* Oxford U. P., 1938.

DESTRÉE, J. *En Italie avant la guerre 1914-1915.* G. van Oest et Cie. Bruxelles, Paris, 1915.

*Diplomaticheski slovar (Diplomatic Dictionary).* Vols. I, II. Edit. by A. Y. Vyshinski and S. A. Lozovski. Gosudarstvennoye Izdatelstvo Politicheskoi Literatury. Moscow, 1948, 1950.

DJEMAL PASHA. *Memories of a Turkish Statesman 1913-1919.* Hutchinson and Co. London.

DUMAINE, AMB. A. *La dernière ambassade de France en Autriche.* Plon-Nourrit et Cie. Paris, 1921.

EINSTEIN, L. *Inside Constantinople. A Diplomatist's Diary during the Dardanelles Expedition.* John Murray. London, 1917.

EMIN, AHMED. *Turkey in the World War.* Yale U. P., Oxford U. P., 1930.

*Encyclopaedia Britannica* 1929, Vol. XVI; 1947, Vol. XVI.

ERZBERGER, M. *Souvenirs de Guerre.* Payot et Cie. Paris, 1921.

FEDELE, P. *Why Italy is at War.* G. Bertero e. C. Rome, 1915.

FEIS, H. *Europe the World's Banker 1870-1914. An Account of European Foreign Investment and the Connection of World Finance and Diplomacy before the War.* Yale University Press. New Haven, 1930.

FISHER, LORD. *Memories.* Hodder and Stoughton. London, 1919.

FRANCKENSTEIN, G. *Facts and Features of My Life.* Cassell and Co., Ltd. London, 1939.

GEORGE, DAVID LLOYD. *War Memoirs.* Vol. I. Ivor Nicholson and Watson. London, 1933. *The Truth about the Peace Treaties.* Vol. I. V. Gollancz Ltd. London, 1938.

GIOLITTI, G. *Memoirs of My Life.* Chapman and Dodd Ltd. London, 1923.

GOOCH, G. P. *Recent Revelations of European Diplomacy.* Longmans, Green and Co. London, 1927.

GRAMSCI, A. *Il Risorgimento.* Einaudi. Turin, 1949. *Lettere dal carcere.* Einaudi. Turin, 1947.

GREY, SIR E. (Viscount Grey of Fallodon). *Twenty-Five Years 1892-1916.* Vol. II. Hodder and Stoughton Ltd. London, 1925.

GRIECO, R. *Problemi della riforma fondiaria.* Milano-Sera. Milan, 1951.

HALLGARTEN, G. W. F. *Imperialismus vor 1914.* Band I. II. Beck'sche Verlagsbuchhandlung. Munich, 1951.

HEADLAM-MORLEY, J. *Studies in Diplomatic History.* Methuen and Co., Ltd. London, 1930.

HELFFERICH, K. *Der Weltkrieg.* II. Band. Ullstein und Co. Berlin, 1919.

HENRI, E. *Hitler over Russia?* J. M. Dent and Sons Ltd. London, 1936.

HINDENBURG, MARSHAL VON. *Out of My Life.* Cassell and Co., Ltd. London, 1920.

HOYOS, GRAF A. *Der deutsch-englische Gegensatz und sein Einfluss auf die Balkanpolitik Österreich-Ungarns.* Vereinigung wissenschaftlicher Verleger. Walter de Gruyter und Co. Berlin, Leipzig, 1922.

HOURANI, A. H. *Great Britain and the Arab World.* John Murray. London, 1945. *Syria and Lebanon.* Oxford U. P., 1946.

JOHNSON, H. *Vatican Diplomacy in the World War*. Basil Blackwell. Oxford, 1933.
JONESCU, T. *Some Personal Impressions*. Nisbet and Co., Ltd. London, 1919.
KAROLYI, M. *Memoirs*. J. Cape. London, 1956.
LABRIOLA, ANTONIO. *Scritti vari di filosofia e politica*. Laterza e figli. Bari, 1906.
LABRIOLA, ARTURO. *La guerra di Tripoli e l'opinione socialista*. Scintilla (S. Morano). Naples, 1912.
LENIN, V. I. *Imperialism and Socialism in Italy*. Collected Works. Vol. XVIII. Martin Lawrence Ltd. London, 1930. *Imperialism the Highest Stage of Capitalism*. Collected Works. Vol. XIX. Martin Lawrence Ltd. London, 1942. *The State and Revolution*. Collected Works. Vol. XXI, book II. Martin Lawrence Ltd. London, 1932. *Sochineniya (Works)*. 3rd edit. Vol. XXV. Partizdat Ts. K.V.K.P. (b). Moscow.
LEWIN, E. *The German Road to the East*. William Heinemann. London, 1916.
LUDENDORFF, GEN. V. *My War Memories 1914-1918*. Vol. I. Hutchinson and Co. London.
MACCHIO, FREIHERR V. *Wahrheit! Fürst Bülow und ich in Rom 1914-1915*. Jung Österreich Verlag. Vienna, 1931.
MARCOVITCH, L. (Edit.) *Serbia and Europe 1914-1920*, George Allen and Unwin Ltd. London, 1920.
MAY, A. J. *The Hapsburg Monarchy 1867-1914*. Harvard U. P., 1951.
MEGARO, G. *Mussolini in the Making*. George Allen and Unwin Ltd. London, 1938.
MELAS, G. M. *Ex-King Constantine and the War*. Hutchinson and Co. London, 1920.
MENNE, B. *Deutschlands Kanonenkönige*. Europa Verlag. Zürich, 1937.
*Mesopotamia*. Handbooks Prepared under the Direction of the Historical Section of the Foreign Office. N. 63. H.M.S.O. London, 1920.
MICHELS, R. *Italien von Heute*. Orell Füssli Verlag. Zürich, Leipzig, 1930.
MILLER, A. F. *Ocherki noveishei istorii Turtsii*. (*Outline of the Recent History of Turkey*). Izdatelstvo Akademii Nauk S.S.S.R. Moscow, Leningrad, 1948.
MONELLI, P. *Mussolini, an Intimate Life*. Thames and Hudson. London, 1953.
*Montenegro*. Handbooks Prepared under the Direction of the Historical Section of the Foreign Office. No. 19. H.M.S.O. London, 1920.
MORGENTHAU, AMB. H. *Secrets of the Bosphorus*. Constantinople 1913-1916. Hutchinson and Co. London, 1918.

# BIBLIOGRAPHY

MOUKHTAR PACHA, GÉN. M. *La Turquie, l'Allemagne et l'Europe.* Berger-Levrault. Paris, 1924.

MUSULIN, FREIHERR V. *Das Haus am Ballplatz.* Erinnerungen eines österreich-ungarischen Diplomaten. Verlag für Kulturpolitik. Munich, 1924.

NAPIER, H. D. *The Experiences of a Military Attaché in the Balkans.* Drane's. London, 1924.

NENNI, P. *The Years of Tyranny in Italy.* George Allen and Unwin Ltd. London, 1932.

NETON, A. *Delcassé (1852-1923).* Académie Diplomatique Internationale. Paris, 1952.

NITTI, F. *Il capitale straniero in Italia.* Gius. Laterza e figli. Bari, 1915. *Peaceless Europe.* Cassell and Co., Ltd. London, 1922.

NOËL, L. *Camille Barrère, Ambassadeur de France.* Tardy. Paris, 1948.

PAGE, AMB. T. N. *Italy and the World War.* Chapman and Hall Ltd. London, 1921.

PALÉOLOGUE, M. *An Ambassador's Memoirs.* Vol. I. Hutchinson and Co. London, 1923.

PASCOLI, G. *La grande proletaria si è mossa.* Zanichelli. Bologna, 1911.

PEARS, SIR E. *Forty Years in Constantinople 1873-1915.* Herbert Jenkins Ltd. London, 1916.

PERRIS, G. H. *The War Traders.* National Peace Council. London, 1914.

PETRIE, SIR CH. *Mussolini.* The Holme Press. London, 1931.

PICCOLI, R. *Italy and the War.* T. Fisher Unwin Ltd. London, 1915.

POINCARÉ, R. *Au service de la France.* Vol. V. *'L'Invasion 1914'.* Librairie Plon. Paris, 1928. *Au service de la France.* Vol. VI. *'Les Tranchées 1915'.* Librairie Plon. Paris, 1930.

PORTER, CH. W. *The Career of Théophile Delcassé.* University of Pennsylvania Press. Philadelphia, 1936.

POTEMKIN, V. P. (Edit.) *Istoriya diplomatii.* (*History of Diplomacy*). Vol. II. OGIZ. Gosudarstvennoye Izdatelstvo Politicheskoi Literatury. Moscow, 1945.

PRATO, G. *Il Piemonte e gli effeti della guerra sulla sua vita economica e sociale.* Laterza. Bari, 1926.

PRIBRAM, A. F. *The Secret Treaties of Austria-Hungary 1879-1914.* Vol. II. Harvard U. P., Oxford U. P., 1921. *Austria-Hungary and Great Britain 1908-1914.* Oxford U. P., 1951.

REDLICH, J. *Das politische Tagebuch. Schicksalsjahre Österreichs 1908-1919.* Band I. II. Verlag H. Böhlaus Nachf. G.m.b.H. Graz, Cologne, 1953, 1954.

RENOUVIN, P. *La Crise européenne et la Grande guerre 1914-1918.* Librairie Félix Alcan. Paris, 1934.

RIESSER, J. *The German Great Banks and their Concentration in Connection with the Economic Development of Germany*. Government Printing Office. Washington, 1911.

RODD, SIR J. RENNELL. *Social and Diplomatic Memories*. (III. Series) 1902-1919. E. Arnold and Co. London, 1925.

ROSEN, BARON R. *Forty Years of Diplomacy*. Vol. II. George Allen and Unwin Ltd. London, 1922.

ROSMER, A. *Le Mouvement ouvrier pendant la guerre*. Vol. I. Librairie du Travail. Paris, 1936.

ROSSI, A. *The Rise of Italian Fascism*. Methuen and Co., Ltd. London, 1938.

RYAN, SIR A. *The Last of the Dragomans*. Geoffrey Bles. London, 1951.

SABINI, C. *Le Fond d'une querelle*. Documents inédits sur es relations franco-italiennes 1914-1921. Bernard Grasset. Paris, 1921.

SALANDRA, A. *Italy and the Great War*. From Neutrality to Intervention. E. Arnold and Co. London, 1932. *La neutralità italiana, 1914*. Mondadori. Milan-Verona, 1928.

SALVATORELLI, L. *A Concise History of Italy*. George Allen and Unwin Ltd. London, 1940.

SALVEMINI, G. *The Fascist Dictatorship in Italy*. Jonathan Cape. London, 1928. *Mussolini diplomate*. Bernard Grasset. Paris, 1932.

SANDERS, GEN. L. V. *Five Years in Turkey*. The Williams and Wilkins Co. for the U.S. Naval Institute. Annapolis, 1928.

SAVINSKI, A. *Recollections of a Russian Diplomat*. Hutchinson and Co., Ltd. London.

SAZONOV, S. *Fateful Years 1909-1916*. Reminiscences. Jonathan Cape. London, 1928.

SCHREINER, A. *Zur Geschichte der deutschen Aussenpolitik 1871-1945*. I. Band: 1871-1918. Dietz Verlag. Berlin, 1955.

*Schulthess' Europäischer Geschichtskalender 1896*. Beck. Munich.

SELDES, G. *Sawdust Caesar*. The Untold History of Mussolini and Fascism. Arthur Barker Ltd. London, 1936.

SERENI, E. *La questione agraria nella rinascita nazionale italiana*. Einaudi. Rome, 1946. *Agrarny vopros v Italii (The Agrarian Question in Italy)*. Moscow, 1949. *Razvitiye kapitalizma v italyanskoi derevnye 1860-1900. (The Development of Capitalism in the Italian Village 1860-1900)*. Moscow, 1951.

SFORZA, COUNT C. *Makers of Modern Europe*. Portraits and Personal Impressions and Recollections. Elkin Mathews and Marrot. London, 1930.

STEED, H. WICKHAM. *The Hapsburg Monarchy*. Constable and Co., Ltd. London, 1913. *Through Thirty Years 1892-1922*. Vol. II. William Heinemann Ltd. London, 1924.

STORRS, R. *Orientations*. Nicholson and Watson. London, 1937.

SUAREZ, G. *Briand. Sa vie, son oeuvre avec son Journal*. Vol. III. 1914-1916. Librairie Plon. Paris, 1939.

*Syria and Palestine.* Handbooks Prepared under the Direction of the Historical Section of the Foreign Office. No. 60. H.M.S.O. London, 1920.

SZILASSY, BARON J. V. *Der Untergang der Donaumonarchie.* Verlag Neues Vaterland. E. Berger und Co. Berlin, 1921.

TABOUIS, G. *The Life of Jules Cambon.* Jonathan Cape. London, 1938.

TALENSKI, MAJ. GEN. N. A. *Pervaya mirovaya voina.* (*The First World War*). OGIZ. Gosudarstvennoye Izdatelstvo Politicheskoi Literatury. Moscow. 1944.

THOMAS, B. *The Arabs.* Thornton Butterworth Ltd. London, 1937.

TIRPITZ, ADM. A. V. *Erinnerungen.* K. F. Koehler Verlag. Leipzig, 1919.

TOYNBEE, A. J. *Turkey: a Past and a Future.* George H. Doran Co. New York, 1917.

TOYNBEE, A. J. and KIRKWOOD, K. P. *Turkey.* E. Benn Ltd. London, 1926.

TREVELYAN, G. M. *Grey of Fallodon.* Longmans, Green and Co. London, 1937. *Scenes from Italy's War.* T. C. and E. C. Jack Ltd. London, 1919.

*Turkey in Europe.* Handbooks Prepared under the Direction of the Historical Section of the Foreign Office. No. 16. H.M.S.O. London, 1920.

VECCHIO, G. *The Moral Basis of Italy's War.* T. Fisher Unwin Ltd. London, 1917.

WINGATE, SIR R. *Wingate of the Sudan.* John Murray. London, 1955.

YERUSALIMSKI, A. S. *Vneshnyaya politika i diplomatiya germanskovo imperializma v kontse XIX veka.* (*The Foreign Policy and Diplomacy of German Imperialism at the end of the 19th Century*). 2nd Edit. Izd. Akademii Nauk S.S.S.R. Moscow, 1951.

PERIODICALS

*The Cambridge Historical Journal.* Vol. XI. No. 2. 1954. Pryce, R., 'Italy and the Outbreak of the First World War'.

*History.* Vol. XXV. No. 100. March 1941, London. Howard, Ch., 'The Treaty of London, 1915'.

*L'Idea Nazionale.* IV. No. 33. 13 Aug. 1914. Corradini, E., 'Il nostro dovere'.

*International Affairs.* Vol. XXVIII. No. 1. 1 Jan. 1952, London. Lewis, B., 'Islamic Revival in Turkey'.

*Istoricheski Zhurnal.* No. 12. 1942, Moscow. Miller, A., 'Turtsiya pod gnetom germanskovo imperializma v gody pervoi mirovoi voiny, 1914-1918'. ('Turkey under the Yoke of German Imperialism during the Years of the First World War, 1914-1918').

*Il Mondo.* 7 Jan. 1950, Rome. Salvemini, G., 'Mussolini e l'oro francese'.
*Politique Étrangère.* No. 4. October 1952, Paris. Rondot, J., 'Les Intérêts pétroliers français dans le Proche-Orient'.
*La Revue des Deux Mondes.* XCVII-e année, 7-e période. Vol. XLI. 1 Oct. 1927, Paris. ***, 'L'Italie et les responsabilités austroallemandes de la guerre'.
*La Revue des Deux Mondes.* CV-e année, 8-e période. Vol. XXIX. 15 Oct. 1935, Paris. Verax, 'Jules Cambon en 1914'.
*La Revue de Paris.* 15 July 1921. Bompard, Amb., 'L'Entrée en guerre de Turquie'.
*The Revue of Politics.* Vol. 14. No. 2. April 1952. Notre Dâme, Indiana (U.S.A.). Caponigri, A. R., 'Don Luigi Sturzo'.
*Rinascita.* No. 10. 1946, Rome.
*La Scintilla.* 11 Oct. 1911, Naples.
*The Slavonic Review.* Vol. XXXI. No. 76. December 1952, London. E. Walters, 'Austro-Russian Relations under Goluchovski, 1895-1906'. Unpublished Documents.
*Süddeutsche Monatshefte.* XXVIII. Jahrg. March 1931, Munich. Flotow, H. v., 'Um Bülows römische Mission'. Wedel, B. v., 'Die Daily Telegraph Affaire—Bülows römische Mission'. 'Fürst Bülow und Österreich'.
*The Times.* London, 23 Sept. 1912, p. 3.
26 Dec. 1914.
26 Feb. 1915, p. 10. Parliamentary Report.
15 Sept. 1952, Adm. Sir H. Kelly's Obituary.
4 Nov. 1952, p. 8.
21 July 1955, p. 12 Gulbenkian's Obituary.
17 Jan. 1955, L. de Rothschild's Obituary.
*Voprosy Ekonomiki (Problems of Economics).* No. 9. 1952, Moscow. Oborina, T., 'Ob agrarnykh otnosheniyakh v Italii'. ('On the Agrarian Relations in Italy').
*Voprosy Filosofii (Problems of Philosophy).* No. 1. 1953, Moscow. Yegerman, E. Y., ' "Literatura i natsionalnaya zhizn" A. Gramsci'. (' "Literature and National Life" by A. Gramsci').
*Voprosy Istorii (Problems of History).* No. 6. 1953. Moscow, Kirova, K. E., 'Massovoye dvizheniye v Italii protiv imperialisticheskoi voiny letom 1917 g.' ('The Mass Movement in Italy against the Imperialist War in the summer of 1917').
*The World.* New York, 6 Sept. 1915. p. 3. K. v. Wiegand's report.

### REFERENCE BOOKS

*Chi È.* 5th edit. Rome, 1948.
*Post Office London Directory,* 1914.
*Who Was Who,* Vol. III. Adam and Charles Black. London, 1941.

# INDEX

Abbazia Conference of 1914, 140, 159, 166
Abdul Hamid II, Sultan of Turkey, 21, 24, 30
Abdullah, son of Sharif Husain, 50-1, 67
Abruzzi, earthquake in, 294, 304, 359
Abyssinia, 136-7, 146-7, 179, 204, 213
Adalia, 146-7, 156, 204, 314, 317, 369
Adler, von, 210, 297
Adowa, battle of, 136-7, 146
Adriatic Sea, 155, 157-60, 173, 175, 189-90, 198-9, 201, 213, 219, 237, 241, 253-4, 258, 314-15, 320, 326-33, 331, 337, 342, 345, 354 364, 366, 378, 382
Aegean Islands, 28, 34, 36-9, 56, 64
Aehrenthal, Count, 250
Aga Khan, 56
Alaya, 156
Albania (also Saseno and Valona), 146, 157-9, 192-3, 195, 198-200, 204, 217, 235-8, 243-4, 251, 253-4, 304, 308, 314-16, 322, 326-7, 329, 331, 334-6, 350-1, 353, 364-6, 380, 382, 395-6, 398 See also London Conference of Ambassadors, 1913
Albertini, L., 168, 189, 385
Aldrovandi Marescotti, Italian Chargé d'Affaires in Vienna, 166-7, 190, 297, 354
Alexander, Crown Prince and Regent of Serbia, 349
Alexandretta, 67, 79-83, 101, 107, 113, 124
Algeciras Conference, 1906, 137
Alighieri Society, 155
Allgemeine Österreichische Bodenkreditanstalt, 209
Alliance and Trade Pact, 1880-83, between Austria-Hungary and Serbia, 257
Alp, Tekin, 28-9
Alp, Zia Goek, 28
Alphonso, King of Spain, 296
Ambris, see De Ambris
Amette, Cardinal, 126
Anatolia, 146, 256, 260, 310, 313
Anatolian Railway, 22, 53
Andrassy, Count J. jun., 397
Andrassy, Count J. sen., 257
Andria, see D'Andria
Angeli, E. de, 189
Anglo-Palestine Company, 20
Annunzio, see D'Annunzio

Ansaldo concern, 142
Antivari, 146, 190, 204, 330
Antivari-Virbazar Line, 155, 330
Arabia, 146, 317
Arabs and Britain, 49-51, 67, 97, 103
Ardahan, battle of, 89
Armenians, 31, 109-10
Armstrong concern, 19, 25, 42, 224
Askold, Russian cruiser, 115
Asquith, H., British Prime Minister, 45-6, 52-4, 79, 84-5, 96, 108, 120, 227, 243, 339-40, 343-5, 347, 350, 364
Assab, Gulf of, 146
Association of Italian Joint-Stock Companies, 142
Augagneur, French Minister of Marine, 81
Austria-Hungary, Adriatic and, 158, 160, 258, 364, 382
  Aegean and, 258
  agriculture in, 248
  Albania (Saseno, Valona) and, 157-9, 192-3, 195, 235, 244, 254, 304, 308, 364, 366, 380, 382, 395-6, 398
  Albania, investments in, of, 257
  Anschluss faction in, 262
  aristocracy in, 248-50
  Austrian rulers, 250, 252, 255-6
  Balkans and, 137, 156-61, 166, 170, 191, 193, 239, 242, 251-4, 256-9, 262-3, 275-7, 281, 306-7, 364, 366, 392, 394-6, 398
  Belgium and, 263
  bourgeoisie in, 249
  Bulgaria and, 264, 281
  Bülow and, 239-40, 282-3, 302, 304
  China, ambitions in, of, 256
  Christian-Social Party in, 246, 262, 311, 376
  Dardanelles Expedition and, 131, 309
  financial control in, 249-50
  France and, 203-4, 208-11, 263, 297-9, 354, 395
  France, investments of, in, 209-10, 262
  Galicia and, 60, 68, 248, 265-7, 273-5, 279, 298-9, 303, 380
  Germany, conflicts with, of, 135, 163-4, 171-2, 240-2, 260, 263-80, 282-3, 301-3, 310-11, 376-7, 379-80, 393-4, 401
  Germany, dependence (war-time) of, on, 394-5

413

Austria-Hungary—*cont'd*
  Germany, designs of, on, 153, 260-1, 278-80, 286, 306, 368
  Germany, economic, financial and political dependence on, of, 261-3, 310
  Germany, military dependence on, of, 268, 276-7, 310
  Germany, peace plans with Russia, of and, 274-5
  Germany, pressure on Italy's behalf, of, in, 163-4, 172, 191, 238, 240-2, 278, 282, 291, 293, 296, 300-2, 305, 310-11, 364, 379-80, 393-5, 398
  Germany, pressure for war, 1914, by, in, 165, 263, 281
  Giolitti and, 302, 368, 381
  Great Britain and, 201-4, 208, 210-11, 263, 353, 397
  imperialism of, 250, 256-9, 262-3, 378, 396
  industry in, 249, 256, 258
  Irredentism in, 251, 253
  Italy and, 135-7, 140, 152, 173, 353
  Italy, conflicts with, 135, 155-73, 175, 190-7, 210, 234-46, 251, 257-8, 265, 271, 276, 278, 281-3, 290-2, 294, 299, 302-11, 319, 321, 324, 327, 333, 361-8, 378-82, 385, 388, 390-8, 401
  Italy, 1915 offers to, by, 193, 195, 238, 305
  Japan and, 263
  Magyar rulers, 244, 247, 250, 252, 255-6, 282-3, 377-8
  military operations, 195, 235, 239, 242, 244, 264-76, 281, 299, 303, 305, 308-10, 363, 368-9, 380, 383, 397
  Montenegro and, 156-8, 254
  Montenegro, investments in, of, 257
  Poland, designs on, of, 257, 272-3, 276, 299, 394, 398
  régime (internal) of, 247-8, 250-2
  Rumania and, 60, 165, 244, 250, 257, 264, 271, 281-2, 299, 309, 362
  Russia, conflicts with, 158, 251, 258, 263, 275, 298-9, 327, 378, 394-5
  Russia, separate peace soundings with, by, 297-300, 367-8
  Salonika, designs on, of, 258, 398
  separate peace soundings by, 276, 296-7, 347
  Serbia, Alliance and Agreements (1880-83) with, of, 257
  Serbia, conflicts with, 157-9, 162, 164-9, 171, 251-5, 257-8, 292, 396

Austria-Hungary—*cont'd*
  Serbia, ultimatum to, by, 162, 16-5 6, 170-1, 201, 240, 281, 397
  Serbia, 1914 War against, of, 160, 166, 253-6, 259, 263, 275, 279, 281, 310, 398
  Slav restiveness in, 244, 251-3
  subject races, oppression of, by, 250-2, 378
  Trentino and, 157, 163, 193-4, 196, 239, 242, 244-6, 276, 281-2, 302, 308, 311, 362, 364, 366, 382, 393, 398
  'Trialism' in, 252, 261
  Trieste and, 258, 366, 382, 398
  Triple Alliance and, 135-6, 162-3, 167-8, 171-2, 391, 395-6
  Triple Alliance, Article VII of, and, 156, 162-6, 171-2, 191, 242, 305-7, 362, 396
  Triple Entente, Secret Agreement on Turkey of, and, 397
  Triple Entente, Secret Treaty with Italy of, and, 398
  Turkey and, 35-6, 60, 251, 256, 258-9
  Turkey, imperialist encroachments on, by, 156, 256, 260
  Ukraine, ambitions regarding, of, 257, 276
  Vatican and, 136, 151, 248-9, 373, 375, 382, 390
  war aims of, 255-6, 263, 276, 292, 299, 394
  working class in, 248, 390
  War of 1914, apologia for, by, 250, 255, 259
  Yugoslavs, conflict with, 250-1, 254, 258-9, 275, 378
  See also Central Powers, Triple Alliance
Austrian Lloyd, 257-8, 286
Austro-Prussian War of 1866, 135
*Avanti*, 181, 183-5, 369, 399
Avarna, Italian Ambassador in Vienna, 152, 154, 160, 166-7, 169-70, 173, 177, 191, 194-6, 221, 233, 241-3, 277, 282, 300, 304-5, 311, 318, 360, 362-4, 368, 378, 391-2
*Avvenire d'Italia*, 372
Azerbaidjan (Persian), 69, 73

Balfour, A. J., 84, 108, 119-20
Balkans, 60, 65, 85, 89, 92, 95, 103, 107, 121, 127-8, 130, 137, 153, 156-62, 166, 170, 175, 191, 193, 196, 236-7, 239, 241-3, 251-4, 256-9, 263, 275-7, 281, 285, 299, 306-7, 314, 316, 318-19, 323-4, 326-7, 330-1, 348, 350, 353-4, 364, 366, 378, 392, 394-6, 398

INDEX 415

Balkan Wars of 1912-13, 25, 27-8, 30, 34, 48, 56, 61, 63, 57, 158, 251, 253-5, 260, 396
Ballin, Albert von, 284, 300-1, 310
Balmoral, Sazonov's visit to, 67
Baltic, British naval project regarding, 78
Banat, 341
Banca Commerciale Italiana, 139, 142, 146, 226, 284, 288, 290, 330, 369, 374
Banca Commerciale Tunisiana, 146
Banque Bardac, 80
Banque de Paris et des Pays Bas, 209
Banque Périer, 20
Banque Populaire de Menton, 225
Barrère, French Ambassador in Rome, 206, 209-10, 214, 217-18, 229-30, 283, 334, 369, 384
Barthou, L., 209
Bata concern, 249
*Bataille Syndicaliste*, 229
Bazili, N.A., 63-5, 94, 96
Belgium, 37, 54, 177, 224, 227, 229, 263, 275, 363, 372
Belgium, investments in Italy, of, 224-5
Benckendorff, Russian Ambassador in London, 40-1, 45, 69-70, 96, 102, 115, 199, 202, 206, 297, 323, 338, 341, 351-2, 355-7
Bendzhin coal-bearing area (Poland), 273
Benedict XV, Pope, 229, 370-1, 373-6
Berchtold, Austro-Hungarian Foreign Minister till Jan. 1915, 140, 159, 162-6, 168, 171-3, 191-3, 195-6, 201, 210, 235, 238-44, 246, 253-6, 258, 260, 262-3, 268, 273-5, 281-2, 297, 370-1, 397
Bergamini, Editor of *Giornale d'Italia*, 212, 216
Berlin-Baghdad Railway, 20, 22-3, 41, 48, 56, 58, 80, 85, 87, 104, 124, 261
Bernezzo, General, 155
Bertie, Sir F., British Ambassador in Paris, 66-7, 86-7, 93, 100-1, 103, 108, 130, 205, 318, 322-4, 353
Bessarabia, 131
Bethmann-Hollweg, Th. von, German Chancellor, 140, 163, 165, 263, 284, 302, 310, 347, 368, 376, 378-80, 390, 395
Bilinski, Austro-Hungarian Finance Minister, 257
Birdwood, General Sir W., 101, 108
Bismarck, Prince Otto von, 135-7, 260, 374, 395
Bissolati, L., Italian Socialist, 180-2
Black Sea, 62-3, 66, 94, 103

Black Sea, Russian ports bombarded, in, 60
Blanqui, 185
Blohm und Voss concern, 32
Bodenkreditanstalt, 250, 255-6, 310
Bohemia, 248, 298
Bollati, Italian Ambassador in Berlin, 151-2, 159, 167-8, 174, 177, 189, 192, 195, 221, 228, 241, 277-8, 293, 296, 300, 307, 347, 360, 363, 365, 367-8, 379, 389, 391, 393-4
Bompard, French Ambassador in Constantinople, 37, 52, 98
Bonomi, I., Italian Socialist, 180
Bosphorus, 60, 68, 72, 75, 87, 104, 113, 115, 131
   See also Straits
Bossi, Prof., 377
Bosnia-Herzegovina, 38, 61, 157, 202-3, 242, 251, 253, 257, 298, 329, 336, 396
Bourgeois, L., 209, 215
*Bouvet*, French dreadnought, 102, 346
Boxer Rising, 256
Boyana river, 146, 257, 330
Bravi, Massini, Plata & Co., 330
*Breslau*, German cruiser, 43-8, 53-4, 57-8, 60, 88, 202
Briand, A., French Minister of Justice, 77-9, 82, 126, 209, 214, 216, 220-1
Britain, see Great Britain
British India Steam Navigation Co., 20
Buccari, 329
Buchanan, Sir G., British Ambassador in Petrograd, 40, 47, 70, 88, 97, 209, 235, 320, 322, 333, 335-6, 342-5
Bukovina, 72, 202, 257, 299
Bulgaria, 31, 36-40, 56, 60, 77, 79, 84-5, 96, 107-8, 113-15, 121, 127-9, 264, 281, 309, 313, 317, 323, 331
Bülow, Prince, German Ambassador in Rome from Dec. 1914, 138, 151, 220, 229, 239-42, 282-8, 292-4, 296, 300-4, 307, 310, 312, 322, 326, 361-3, 368-9, 374-6, 379-85, 390, 392-5, 397-8
*Bund, Der*, 263
Burgas, port of, 113-15
Burián, Austro-Hungarian Foreign Minister from Jan. 1915, 61, 242, 244-5, 283, 300-11, 361-2, 364, 365-8, 376-80, 390-3, 397
Busi, island of, 344, 365
Buxton, N., 66

Cadorna, Italian Chief of Staff, 173, 178, 232, 363, 376
Caillard, Sir Vincent, 21

Caisse de Crédit de Nice, 225
Cambon, Jules, French ex-Ambassador in Berlin, 229
Cambon, Paul, French Ambassador in London, 67, 74, 101, 323, 354, 356
Capitulations, see Turkey
Carcano, successor to Rubini as Minister of the Italian Treasury, 232
Carden, Vice-Admiral, 82, 102
Carlotti, Italian Ambassador in Petrograd, 88, 175, 198, 207, 217, 228, 234, 296-7, 313-15, 318, 327, 330, 332, 339, 345, 347
Carol, King of Rumania, 196
Cassel, Sir Ernest, 19, 102
Castelnuovo, 329, 350
Cattaro, Bay and port of, 157, 203, 326, 329, 331, 334, 337, 340, 342, 344, 350
Cavasola, Italian Minister of Agriculture, 215
Cazza, island of, 344, 365
Central Bank for Railway Securities, 262
Central Powers, 135
Central Powers, Bulgaria and, 127-9
  Dardanelles Expedition and, 109, 309-11
  Italy and, 135-8, 152-4, 159-60, 174-7, 190, 192-3, 195-8, 209, 217, 219, 221, 226, 231-2, 234-8, 241, 243, 277-8, 290, 292, 309, 361, 382, 384, 390
  Italy, 1914 military agreements with, 140
  Rumania and, 309
  strategy (military), 264
  Turkey and, 35-9, 62, 310
  Turkey, 1914 Treaty of Alliance with, 36, 46-7, 58-9, 62
  Vatican and, 136, 151, 154, 248-9, 301, 310, 369, 372-7, 382, 390, 393
  War of 1914, desire for, of, 165, 263
  See also Austria-Hungary, Germany, Triple Alliance, Turkey
Chamberlain, Sir Austen, 120
Chantiers de la Méditerranée, 20
Charles, Archduke, Crown Prince of Austria-Hungary after death of Francis Ferdinand, 256-7
Chiapelli, Alessandro, 148
China, 146-7, 256
Churchill, Winston, First Lord of the Admiralty, 42, 52-4, 68-9, 77-9, 81-6, 88, 92, 96, 102-4, 106-8, 113, 119-20, 127-9, 205, 313-14, 321, 327, 340
Clemenceau, Georges, 188, 213-16, 218, 221

Colonna, Prince P., 188
Compagnia di Antivari, 316, 330
Compagnie Générale des Eaux, 100
*Concordia*, 194, 300
Condouriotis, Greek Admiral, 44-5
*Confederazione Generale del Lavoro*, 180-1, 399-400
Conrad, General, Austro-Hungarian Chief of Staff, 157-8, 172-5, 192-3, 195, 239-40, 244-6, 253-9, 262-77, 281-2, 299, 301-3, 309, 311, 361-2, 370, 380, 394-6
Constantine, King of Greece, 44, 46, 95, 115
Constantinople, Bulgaria and, 40, 114-15
  commercial importance of, 66, 123-4
  Dardanelles Expedition, impact of, on, 109
  France and, 72, 96, 98, 100-3, 115, 122, 124-5, 130, 324-5, 343
  Great Britain and, 78-9, 83, 87, 97, 103, 107, 115, 117-8, 122-3, 125-6
  Greece and, 40, 95
  internationalization suggested, 91, 93, 95, 99-100, 130
  Russia and, 39-40, 47, 64-5, 69-72, 90-2, 95-6, 116-18, 123-5, 313, 319, 331, 333, 356
  Russia, Franco-British assurances to, regarding, 70-1, 73, 86, 97, 99, 101, 103, 105, 322, 333, 343, 347, 355, 357-8
  Vatican and, 126, 130
Corbett, Sir J., 104
Corradini, E., 148-9
Corridoni, F., 182, 186, 227
*Corriere della Sera*, 185, 189, 216, 220, 227, 360, 385-6
*Corriere d'Italia*, 130, 372, 382
Corsica, 135, 217-8, 316, 323. See also Italy.
Crawford, Sir R., 21
Crédit Lyonnais, 20
Credito Italiano, 139
Crespi, Italian cotton magnate, 142, 189
Creusot, Schneider concern, 20-1, 35, 253
Crewe, Lord, 67
Crispi, F., 330
Croatia, 207, 251-2, 298, 329, 332, 334, 352-4
Croato-Slovene Congress, 349
Croce, Benedetto, 147-8, 174, 186
Curzolari islands, 339-40, 344-5, 347, 349-50, 365-6
Custozza, battle of, 155
Cyprus and Britain, 74, 103

# INDEX 417

Czeczen, Austro-Hungarian Ambassador in Paris, 211
Czernin, O. von, Austro-Hungarian Minister in Bucharest, 166, 244, 255, 299
Czestokhowa coal-bearing area (Poland), 273

*Daily Chronicle*, 202
D'Andria, Carafa, 367, 369
D'Annunzio, G., 148, 186-8, 385-7, 389
Dalmatia, 105, 155, 207-8, 222, 314, 320, 322-3, 326-32, 334, 336-8, 340-2, 344, 350, 353, 366, 380
Danilov, Russian Quartermaster-General, 90, 117, 131
Dardanelles, Anglo-French Expedition to, 77-9, 81-7, 92, 95, 101-3, 106-8, 112, 114-16, 119, 121, 123, 127, 129, 131, 305, 309, 311, 313, 318, 321, 341, 346, 354, 356, 383
Dardanelles, Anglo-French Expedition to, Central Powers and, 109, 309-11
France and, 81-2, 96, 103, 112-13, 127, 129, 325
Italy and, 154, 305, 310, 313-14, 346, 354
Russia and, 75-6, 88-90, 95-6, 115-18, 131
political advantages expected from, 85-7
closure of, 57, 63
German cruisers in, 44, 46, 58
See also Gallipoli, Straits
Dardanelles Commission, 79, 82, 84-6, 108
Darmstädter Bank, 262
D'Atri, Salandra's *Chef du Cabinet*, 216-17, 222-3
De Ambris, A., Italian Syndicalist, 183, 186
Dedeagach, port of, 108, 114-15
Delcassé, Th., French Foreign Minister from 26 Aug. 1914, 52, 67, 74, 94, 96, 98-9, 100-1, 103-5, 110-11, 113, 117, 122-3, 125-6, 131, 155, 216-17, 220-2, 297, 299, 322, 324-5, 332, 335, 343, 346-9, 351-2, 355-7, 366
Degasperi, (A. de Gasperri), 195
Deloncle, French State Councillor, 100, 104
Deraa-Haifa Railway, 124
Deschanel, P., 209, 215
Destrée, J., Belgian Deputy, 227
Deutsche Bank, 23, 139, 260, 262, 310

Deutsche Nationalbank, 22, 139
Deutsche Orientbank, 22-3, 32
Deutsche Palästinabank, 21
*Deutsche Tageszeitung*, 379
*Die Bagdadbahn*, 23, 31
Discontogesellschaft, 22-3, 139, 256, 262
Disraeli, 88
Djavid Bey, Turkish Finance Minister, 37, 52, 55, 110-12
Djemal Pasha, Turkish Minister of Marine, 25, 29, 31, 34-6, 51, 54, 56-7, 59-62
Djibouti, port of, 323
Dnyestr river, oil wells on, 299
Dodecanese Islands, 147, 155, 157, 175, 213, 244, 304-5, 307, 313-14, 390
D'Oissel, Baron, 210
Douglas, General, Chief of Imperial General Staff, 78
Doumergue, G., French Foreign Minister in Aug. 1914, 42, 199, 205-6, 208-11, 214-17, 220, 263
Dresdner Bank, 22-3, 139, 262
Drin river, 337
*Dublin*, H.M.S., 44
Dumaine, A., French Ambassador in Vienna, 211, 247, 263, 278, 286
Dumas, Secretary to Guesde, 230
Durazzo, 315, 323, 326, 330, 336

Eastern front, 58, 60, 68-9, 75, 86, 116-17, 195, 235, 239, 264-76, 299, 301, 303, 305, 308-9, 312, 348, 351, 355-6, 363, 368-9, 380, 383, 392, 397
Ebergard, Russian Black Sea Commander, 114
*Echo de Paris*, *L'*, 218
Edward VII, 137
Egypt, 35, 56, 60, 81, 101, 121, 285, 315
Egypt, British protectorate established, 73-4
Einaudi, L., 142
Enos-Midia Line, the, 39, 56, 72, 92
Enver Pasha, Turkish Minister of War, 25, 27, 30, 32, 38-9, 60, 83, 88-9, 109
Epirus, the, 41, 175, 236-7
Eritrea, 146-7 154, 317, 323
Erzberger, M., 300-1, 310-11, 374-9, 382-3, 387-90, 393
Essad Pasha, Albanian leader, 159, 235, 243
Esterhazy, House of, 248
Ethiopia, see Abyssinia
Euphrates and Tigris Steam Navigation Co., 19

Falkenhayn, General, German Chief of Staff from Sept. 1914, 265, 269, 271, 273, 275-6, 302, 368 380
*Fasci d'Azione Rivoluzionaria*, 183, 186-7
Fasciotti, Italian Minister in Bucharest, 166, 196, 218, 279, 312, 320, 332
*Federazione dei Lavorotari della Terra*, 180
Ferdinand, King of Bulgaria, 114-5
Fiat concern, 142, 188
*Figaro*, 91
Fisher, Admiral, 1st Sea Lord, 79, 82-4, 86, 119-20
Fiume, 222, 258, 352-3
Flandin, P. E., 81
Floridsdorf Engineering Plant, 249
Flotow, H. von, German Ambassador in Rome till Dec. 1914, 164-6, 168-9, 171, 193, 279, 285, 369, 374
Forgách, Count, 190, 297
France, Albania and, 198-9, 335
 Austria-Hungary and, 203-4, 208-11, 263, 297-9, 354
 Austria-Hungary, investments in, of, 209-10, 262
 Austria-Hungary, soundings for a separate peace, of, with, 296-9
 Balkans and, 35, 66, 78-9, 103, 127-8, 130, 323-6, 354, 395
 Bulgaria and, 52, 96, 107, 309, 323
 Catholic hierarchy in, 371
 Constantinople and, 67, 72, 96, 98, 101-3, 115, 122, 124-5, 130, 324-5, 343
 Dardanelles Expedition and, 81-2, 96, 103, 112-13, 127, 129, 325
 German attempts to detach Russia, and, 105, 117-18
 Germany and, 298
 Great Britain, common interests with, 103-5, 325-6, 329
 Great Britain, conflicts with, 74, 80-1, 96, 101-4, 112-13, 123, 126, 137, 208, 317-19, 346
 Greece and, 96, 107, 309, 323-4
 Italy, agreements with, 137-8, 140, 147, 213-14, 220, 226
 Italy, conflicts with, 135-6, 138, 140, 147, 152, 175, 194, 198, 208, 211-12, 217-23, 232, 234-5, 315-16, 323-4, 346, 354, 357-8, 377, 401
 Italy, investments in, of, 225-6
 Italy, towards Alliance with, 198-200, 203-6, 208-9, 211-17, 229-30, 322, 324-5, 335, 347, 351-2, 354-6

France—*cont'd*
 Mediterranean and, 66, 100, 323-4, 329, 347
 military front of, 58, 60, 68-9,75, 77, 81, 102, 177, 194, 209, 215-19, 235-41, 265-7, 277, 312, 324, 334, 346-7
 Montenegro and, 323, 352, 354
 Morocco, protectorate established in, by, 74, 80, 137
 Mussolini, financed by, 184, 230
 Near East, overall policy in, of, 31, 48, 51, 82, 323, 347
 Rumania and, 98, 130-1, 324
 Russia, Alliance with, 226, 262, 316
 Russia, conflicts with, 39-40, 47-8, 66, 72, 78, 86, 91, 98-100, 103-4, 114, 122-7, 129-31, 205, 324-5, 333-5, 341, 343, 351-2, 354-7
 Serbia and, 315, 323-4, 343, 354
 Socialists in, 229-30
 Straits and, 72, 101, 130, 172
 Syria and, 67, 73, 80-2, 101, 104, 111, 318
 Turkey and, 31, 34-5, 41-2, 48, 51-2, 72, 124, 322-4
 Turkey, investments in, of, 20-1, 41, 80-2, 98
 Vatican and, 135, 229, 371-3, 374 (footnote 4), 375
 war aims of, 72-3, 80-1, 97, 99, 101, 111, 198
 See also Triple Entente, Tunis
Francis I, Emperor of Austria, 244
Francis Ferdinand, Crown Prince of Austria-Hungary, 168, 254, 258, 261
Francis Joseph, Emperor of Austria-Hungary, 65, 166, 169, 172, 188, 191, 193, 196, 202, 210, 240, 245-7, 249, 253, 262, 270-1, 282-3, 297, 299-301, 310-11, 327, 347, 367, 370-1, 373, 375, 379, 394
Franco-Russian Alliance of 1893, 226, 262
*Frankfurter Zeitung*, 300, 310
Franckenstein, G., Austro-Hungarian Commercial Counsellor in London, 202
Frederick, Archduke, Austro-Hungarian C. in Ch., 266, 270
French, Field-Marshal Sir J., 79

Galicia, 58, 60, 68, 248, 265-7, 273-5, 298-9, 303, 380
Gallieni, French General, 77, 103
Gallipoli, 78-9, 95, 107-8, 112-14, 119-21, 127, 129, 354, 356, 358
 See also Dardanelles.

# INDEX

Garibaldi, Bruno, 294
Garibaldi, General, 320
Garibaldi, Giuseppe, 188, 385
Garroni, Italian Ambassador in Constantinople, 168, 217
Gasparri, Cardinal Secretary of State, 126, 371
Gemlik-Brusa-Simav Railway, 256
General Confederation of Agriculture (Italy), 141
George V, 70, 99, 103, 202, 355, 370
George, David Lloyd, 67, 77-9, 83, 119, 291, 293, 319, 358
Germany, Adriatic and, 153, 220, 261, 279, 286, 368, 380, 382
  Austria-Hungary, conflicts with, 135, 163-4, 171-2, 240-2, 260, 263-80, 282-3, 301-3, 310-11, 376-7, 379-80, 393-4, 401
  Austria-Hungary, dependence (military) of, on, 268, 276, 310
  Austria-Hungary, dependence (war-time) on, of, 394-5
  Austria-Hungary, designs on, of, 153, 260-1, 278-80, 286, 306, 368
  Austria-Hungary, economic, financial and political control in, by, 261-3, 310
  Austria-Hungary, pressure on Italy's behalf in, by, 163-4, 172, 191, 238, 240-2, 271, 278, 282, 291, 293, 296, 300-2, 305, 310-11, 364, 379-80, 393-5, 398
  Austria-Hungary, pressure for War of 1914 in, by, 165, 263, 281
  Bulgaria and, 84, 264
  Catholic Centre Party in, 301, 310-11, 374-5, 377
  cruisers *Goeben* and *Breslau*, 43-8, 53-4, 57-8, 60, 88, 202
  Dardanelles and, 104, 117, 309, 311
  Eastern front and, 240, 264-76, 301, 368-9, 380, 383, 392
  Great Britain and, 137, 201, 203, 297-8, 301
  Italy and, 135-40, 150-1, 153-5, 163-4, 167-9, 171-2, 174-5, 240-1, 265, 277-80, 285-8, 291-2, 296, 305-7, 310, 362-3, 365, 368-9, 374, 378-80, 393
  Italy, investments in, by, 138-9, 225-6
  Italy, 1914-15 offers to, by, 277-8, 285-6, 322, 326, 337, 369
  Mediterranean and, 153, 261, 286
  Near East, designs in, 261
  Poland, designs on, 272-3, 275
  Rumania and, 36, 165, 264, 271
  Russia, separate peace approach to, by, 104-5, 117-18, 131, 339-40

Germany—*cont'd*
  Russia, separate peace plans with, of, 274-5
  Trieste and, 261, 279, 286-7, 365, 368, 382
  Trentino and, 240-2, 277-80, 286-7, 296, 300, 310, 333, 375, 379
  Turkey and, 30-3, 43-5, 54, 57-60, 84, 110, 112, 128, 154, 285, 369
  Turkey, investments in, of, 21-4
  Turkey, Treaty of Alliance with, 35-6
  ultimatum to France and Russia by, 171, 213
  Vatican and, 301, 310, 369, 373-7, 390, 393
  war aims of, 272-3, 277-9
  Western front and, 264-5, 269, 271-2, 275-6, 278, 301
  See also Central Powers, Marne, Triple Alliance
Giers, Russian Ambassador in Constantinople, and later in Rome, 38-9, 55, 207, 217-18
Giesl, Austro-Hungarian Minister in Belgrade, 253-4
Giolitti, G., 139, 142, 178, 231, 288-95, 301-2, 317, 361, 368-9, 375-6, 381-3, 385-90, 392, 400
*Giornale d'Italia*, 81, 188, 205, 212, 216, 232, 295, 318
*Giorno, Il*, 152, 194
*Gloucester*, H.M.S., 44
*Goeben*, German cruiser, 43-8, 53-4, 57-8, 60, 88, 202
Goltz, General von der, 129
Goremykin, Russian Premier, 347
Gorizia, 328, 336, 365-6, 382
Gorlice, battle of, 380, 383, 397
Gradisca, 336, 365-6, 382
Grandi, Italian Minister of War, 232
Great Britain, Arabs and, 31, 49-51, 67, 97, 103, 111, 317
  Austria-Hungary and, 201-4, 208, 210-11, 263, 297-8, 353, 397
  Austria-Hungary, separate peace soundings of, with, 296-8
  Balkans and, 31, 35, 66, 318-19, 350
  Black Sea and, 66, 103
  Bulgaria and, 85, 107-8, 114-15, 121, 309, 317
  Conservative Opposition in, 97, 119-20, 202
  Constantinople and, 66-7, 78-9, 83, 87, 97, 103, 107, 115, 117-18, 122-3, 125-6, 319, 322
  Dardanelles Expedition and, 77-9, 81-7, 92, 101-3, 106-8, 318
  Egypt, protectorate established in, by, 74. See also Egypt

Great Britain—*cont'd*
  France, common interests with, 103-5 325-6, 329
  France, conflicts with, 74, 80-1, 96, 101-4, 112-13, 123, 126, 137, 208, 317-19, 346
  German attempts to detach Russia, and, 104-5, 117-18
  German cruisers and, 43-8, 53-4
  Germany and, 137, 201, 203, 297-8, 301
  Government crisis, May 1915, in, 119-20
  Greece and, 35, 41-2, 85, 95-6, 107-9, 115, 121, 237, 309, 317, 350
  Italy and, 85, 136-7, 199-201, 203-9, 212, 228, 233, 236-7, 290, 317-19, 321-2, 325, 336-45, 350-2, 355-8, 364
  Italy, investments in, of, 142, 224
  Mediterranean and, 66, 202-3, 205, 318-19, 329
  Mesopotamia and, 19-20, 24, 31, 48, 50-1, 66, 79, 82, 87, 103-4, 128
  Montenegro and, 337, 352-3
  Near East, overall policy in, 31, 51-3, 87, 103, 128, 319
  Nejd and, 50
  *parecchio* and, 317
  Rumania and, 317
  Russia, conflicts with, 39-40, 47-8, 66, 69-70, 72, 78, 86-8, 91, 105, 107, 114, 117-18, 121, 126-7, 129-31, 201, 203, 205, 207-8, 236, 298, 318-19, 325-6, 333-8, 341-5, 351-2, 355-7, 397
  Serbia and, 201-2, 298, 318, 335-8, 340-1, 344, 350, 352-3
  Straits and, 66, 68, 78-9, 82-8, 97, 102-3, 126, 128, 319, 322
  Syria and, 79, 81, 318
  Turkey and, 21, 41-2, 48, 51-2, 68
  Turkey, investments in, of, 19-20
  Turkey, Naval Mission in, of, 21, 54, 58
  Vatican and, 373-4
  war aims of, 52-3, 66-7, 96-7, 101, 103, 111, 317
  See also Triple Entente.
Greece, 28, 34, 36-8, 40-2, 44, 79, 82-3, 85, 95-6, 98, 108, 115, 175, 237, 258, 309, 313, 317, 324, 331
Greeks, Turkish persecution of, 109
Greppi, Count, 151
Grey, Sir E., British Foreign Secretary, 41, 45-7, 52-3, 55-7, 62, 67-70, 73-4, 78-9, 84-5, 88, 91-2, 94-7, 100, 102-4, 106-7, 113-15, 117, 122-3, 126, 155, 199, 200-2, 204-6, 208, 210, 214, 221, 228, 236-7, 263, 297-8, 314, 317-21, 323, 325-6, 333, 335-8, 340-6, 350-3, 355-7, 365
Grimm, Prof. E. D., 87, 124
*Grossdeutschland*, 261
Guesde, J., French Socialist, 230
Gulbenkian, Calouste, 19, 23

Habsburg, Dynasty of, 135-6, 150, 195, 249-50, 253
Haldane, Lord, 202
Halil, President of Turkish Chamber, 29
Hamburg-America Line, 23
Hamilton, General Sir I., 102, 107-8, 113, 126
Hankey, Secretary of British War Council, 78
Hanotaux, G., 130
Haus, Admiral, C. in Ch., Austro-Hungarian Navy, 204
Helfferich, K., German Vice-Chancellor, 32, 393
Henderson, Arthur, 399
Heraclea mines, 20, 146-7, 315
Herzen, Alexander, 247
Hindenburg, General von, 266-70, 273, 278, 309
Hohenlohe, Prince, Austro-Hungarian Ambassador in Berlin after Szögyény, 267, 274, 367
Holy War of Islam, 35, 49, 109
Hoyos, A., 163, 165, 253-4, 259, 262-3, 282, 302, 392, 395-6
Hungary, 247-8, 250, 262, 283, 353, 377-8. See also Austria-Hungary
Husain, Sharif of Mecca, 49-51, 60, 67, 103

Ibn Saud, Emir of the Nejd, 49-51
*Idea Nazionale, L'*, 187, 360
*Ikdam*, 59
Imbros, island of, 34, 64, 70
Imperial Defence, Committee of, 1908 decision by, 66
Imperial Ottoman Bank, see Ottoman Bank
Imperiali, Italian Ambassador in London, 175, 203, 206, 208-9, 221, 227, 236-7, 319, 321, 323, 337-9, 345, 356
Inchcape, Lord, 20
Iron Gate blast furnaces, 262
Irredentism, see Austria-Hungary, Italy, Serbia, Turkey
Islam, 49, 59, 97, 103, 317 See also Mecca, Medina

# INDEX

Isonzo river, 155, 241, 300, 366, 382, 384
Istria, 155, 207, 304, 326, 328-9, 331-2, 334, 336, 352
*Italia Nostra*, 290
Italian Commercial, Industrial and Financial Corporation, 313
Italo-American Petroleum Co., 330
Italo-Rumanian Treaties of 1914-15, 309
Italy, Abyssinia and, 136-7, 146-7, 179, 204, 213
    Adriatic and, 155, 157-9, 173, 175, 189-90, 198-9, 201, 203, 213, 219, 237, 241, 314-15, 320, 326-33, 337, 342, 345, 354, 364, 366, 378
    Africa, expansion in, of, 146-7, 152-4, 156, 186, 204, 285, 317, 323, 325, 336,
    agriculture in, 141, 147
    Albania (Saseno, Valona) and, 157-9, 192-3, 198-200, 204, 217, 235-8, 243, 254, 304, 314-15, 323, 326, 329, 331, 335, 350, 353, 365
    Albania, investments in, of, 146, 330
    Arabia, enterprises in, of, 146
    armed forces of, 163, 178-9
    Austria-Hungary and, 137, 140, 152, 173, 353
    Austria-Hungary, conflicts with, 135, 155-73, 175-7, 188, 190-7, 200-1, 205, 234-46, 251, 257-8, 265, 271, 276, 278, 281-3, 290-2, 294, 302-11, 319, 321, 324, 327, 333, 361-8, 378-82, 385, 388, 390-8, 401
    Austria-Hungary, investments of, in, 138
    Austria-Hungary, 1515 offers by, to, 193, 195, 217
    Austria-Hungary, separate peace possibilities of, and, 296, 300, 347-8
    Austrophiles in, 151, 153, 179, 195, 289
    Balkans and, 137, 145, 153, 156-62, 175, 191, 237, 241-3, 285, 306-7, 314, 316, 319, 323, 326, 330-1, 353-4, 378, 395-6
    Belgium, investments of, in, 224-5
    Bulgaria and, 313, 351
    Catholics in, 145, 151, 154, 179, 186, 195, 289, 294-5, 369, 376, 382, 393
    Central Powers and, 135-6, 152-4, 159-60, 174-7, 190, 192-3, 195-8, 206, 209, 217, 219, 221, 226, 231-2, 234-8, 241, 243, 277-8, 290, 292, 309, 361, 382, 384, 390
    Chinese venture of, 146-7

Italy—*cont'd*
    Corsica, Nice, Savoy, claims to, of, 135, 152, 186, 217-19, 316
    Croatia and, 207, 222, 352-4
    Dalmatia and, 105, 155, 207-8, 222, 323, 326-32, 341, 350, 353, 366
    Dardanelles and, 154, 305, 310, 313-14, 321, 346, 354
    dictatorship, governmental, in, 359-60, 400
    economy of, 141-4, 147
    economy depressed by European War, 359
    emigration from, 143-4, 147
    Ententophiles in, 154, 294
    exports of, 143
    Fascists in, 187, 231-2, 294, 360, 387, 389, 399
    France, agreements with, 137-8, 140, 147, 213-14, 220, 226
    France, conflicts with, 135-6, 138, 140, 147, 152, 175, 194, 198, 208, 211-12, 217-23, 232, 234-5, 315-16, 323-4, 346, 354, 357-8, 377, 401
    France, investments of, in, 225-6
    France, towards Alliance with, 198-200, 203-6, 208-9, 211-17, 229-30, 332, 324-5, 335, 347, 351-2, 355-6
    Futurists in, 186
    Germanophiles in, 150-3, 179, 282, 284, 287-91, 294, 301, 382, 393
    Germany and, 135-40, 150-1, 153-5, 167-9, 171-2, 174-5, 240-1, 265, 277-80, 285-8, 291-2, 296, 305-7, 310, 362-3, 365, 368-9, 374, 378-80, 393
    Germany, investments of, in, 138-9, 225-6
    Germany, 1914-15 offers by, to, 277-8, 285-6, 322, 326, 337, 369
    governmental changes in, 231-2, 289
    Great Britain and, 85, 136-7, 153-5, 199-201, 203-9, 212, 228, 233, 236-7, 290, 317-19, 321-2, 325, 336-45, 350-2, 355-8, 364
    Great Britain, investments of, in, 142, 224
    Greece and, 237, 313, 331
    Hungary and, 353, 377-8
    imperialism of, 147-9, 155, 160, 180, 231, 290-1, 326, 331, 400
    imports of, 143, 153
    industry in, 142-3, 147
    intervention in World War I, reasons for, 154, 176-7, 234, 314
    interventionist elements in, 186-9, 234, 239, 295, 360, 384-7, 389, 399-400

Italy—*cont'd*
  investments abroad of, 144, 146-7.
    See also Albania, Arabia, Montenegro, Turkey
  Irredentism, 135-6, 152, 155, 187
    244-5, 307, 326
  Liberal Party in, 187, 231, 288-90, 295
  Libya and, 137, 147-8, 168, 313, 395
  Libyan (Tripolitanian) War of, 25, 28, 30, 51, 63, 67, 144, 147-8, 152, 157, 178-81, 185, 242, 288, 290, 313, 396
  Malta and, 152, 186-7
  mediation and, 174-6
  Mediterranean and, 135, 146, 152-3, 155, 160, 175, 194, 205, 213, 217, 219-20, 285-6, 313-16, 319, 322, 324-5, 329, 345, 353, 309
  Montenegro and, 156-7, 203, 306, 323, 331
  Montenegro, investments in, of, 146, 156, 190, 316, 330
  Nationalist Party in, 186-7, 231-2, 294, 387, 399
  neutrality of, 173-9, 194, 209, 232, 277, 291-2, 294, 312-13
  *parecchio* policy in, 294-6, 302, 361, 365, 375, 383
  partisans of peace in, 179, 181-2, 188, 197, 289-90, 295, 359-60, 369, 375, 381, 383-4, 387, 393, 399-400
  peasantry in, 141, 179
  preparations for war in, 178, 188, 196-7, 238-40, 246, 294, 303, 319, 360, 363
  press, influence of, in, 188-9, 194-5, 287, 360
  'Red Week' in, 154, 168, 180-1, 289
  Rumania and, 161, 198, 309, 331, 377-8
  Russia, Agreement (Racconigi) with, 137, 140, 327
  Russia, conflicts with, 105, 151-2, 175, 207-8, 228-9, 243, 314-16, 320-2, 325, 327, 331-4, 339-41, 345, 350-2, 356-8, 364, 368, 377-8, 401
  Russia, towards Alliance with, 198-200, 205-6, 208-9, 212, 320, 322, 334-6, 337, 342, 344, 348, 357
  Savoy dynasty, the, 135, 389
  Serbia and, 160-2, 169-72, 194, 203, 306, 327, 347, 396
  Serbia, conflicts with, 152, 157, 207, 323, 327-9, 331, 340, 345, 349, 353
  Socialist Party in, 154, 179-82, 185-7, 230, 289, 294-5, 360, 369, 381, 393, 399-400

Italy—*cont'd*
  social structure in, 141-2, 144-5
  Straits and, 234, 313-14, 320
  suffrage in, 144-5, 288
  Syndicalists in, 181, 183-4, 186-7
  Trentino and, 135, 153, 155, 163, 188, 193-4, 196, 198-201, 213, 217-20, 238, 240-1, 277, 287, 291, 304, 365-6, 378, 392
  Trieste and, 153, 188, 199-201, 213, 217-20, 222, 286-7, 291, 304, 326, 334, 353, 365-6, 378
  Triple Alliance (Triplice) and, 37, 135-8, 140, 150, 153-5, 162-3, 168, 170-1, 174, 194-5, 214, 217, 242, 277-8, 285, 294, 303, 378-9
  Triple Alliance, Article VII of, and, 156, 162, 165, 169-72, 191, 209, 216, 238-9, 242, 305-6, 362, 396
  Triple Entente and, 105, 107, 153-5, 175-7, 193, 197-201, 205-6, 209, 215-16, 219, 224, 226-7, 231, 233-8, 291-2, 311-58, 360, 363, 366, 378, 383-4, 389-90, 392-3, 401
  Triple Entente, Secret London Treaty with, 325, 354, 358, 377-8, 384-5, 389-90, 398, 401
  Tunis and, 135-6, 146, 152, 187, 217-19, 232, 313, 315-16, 320, 323
  Turkey, designs on, of, 135, 137 155-6, 175, 200, 204, 213, 234-5, 310, 313-14, 316-17, 320, 325. See also Arabia
  Turkey, investments in, of, 146-7, 200
  unpreparedness of, 178-9, 194, 196, 203, 205, 303
  unrest in, 141, 151, 154, 163, 179, 231, 238, 359-60, 384-5, 399-400
  Vatican (Pope) and, 135-6, 145, 151, 154, 288, 373, 375, 377-8, 382-3
  war aims of, 150, 155, 198, 200, 204, 217, 242-3, 245, 316-17, 323, 325-30, 345
  working class in, 179-80
  World War I and, 150, 291, 312-13, 351
  Yugoslavs, conflict with, 327-30, 349, 353

Izvolski, Russian Ambassador in Paris, 42, 72, 98, 105. 122, 127, 130, 198-9, 203, 206, 211, 297, 324, 332, 335, 343, 355, 357
Izzedin, Crown Prince of Turkey, 60

INDEX 423

Jackson, Sir, H., 82
Jagow, G. von, German Foreign Minister, 61, 117-118, 164-5, 167-8, 235, 240-2, 270, 272, 277, 284, 302, 307, 368, 393, 395
Japan, 118, 205, 263
*Jeune Turc*, 59
Jewish National Trust, the, 20
Jews, Turkish persecution of, 109
Joel, Director of Banca Commerciale Italiana, 139, 226, 284, 288, 369, 374
Joffre, Marshal, French C. in Ch., 79, 123, 318, 351, 354
*John Bull*, 202
Joly, Inspector-General of Finance in Turkey, 21
Jonescu, T., 61
*Journal des Débats*, 130
Jung, French ex-Resident in Tonkin, 51

Kaiser, see William II
Karolyi, House of, 248
Karolyi, Michael, 210, 353
Kerr, Vice-Admiral, 46
Khimara, 326, 334
Kitchener, Lord, Secretary of State for War, 49-50, 53, 56, 67, 75, 78-9, 82-4, 107, 113, 117, 119-20, 128-9, 355
*Kölnische Zeitung*, 307, 310
Kreditanstalt (Rothschild's), 249
Krka river, 334
Krupenski, Russian Ambassador in Rome, 189, 205-9, 228, 312-13, 320, 332, 334-5, 360
Krupp concern, 22, 32
Kudashev, N. A., 116-17
Kuwait, Sheikh of, 50

Labriola, Antonio, Italian Socialist, 147, 180
Labriola, Arturo, Italian Syndicalist, 148, 180
Lagosta, island of, 328, 344, 365
Lansdowne, Lord, 120
Lapeyrère, French Admiral, 44, 46
Law, Bonar, 119-20, 128
Lazzari, C., Italian Socialist, 181-2, 399
Lemnos, island of, 41, 64, 107, 115
Lenin, V. I., 181-2, 399
Lesina, island of, 347, 365
Levante-Kontor, 22
Libya, see Italy
Libyan (Tripolitanian) War of 1911-12, see Italy.
Lichtenstein, House of, 248
Lichtenstein, Prince, 376

Liebig, Austrian magnate, 249
Limpus, Admiral, 21, 54
Lissa, battle of, 396
Lissa, island of, 344, 365
London Conference of Ambassadors on Albania of 1913, 158, 235
London Secret Treaty of 1915, see Italy, Triple Entente.
Lombardy, 136
Loti, Pierre, 111-12
*Lotta di Classe, La*, 185
Lorand, G., Belgian Deputy, 227
Loubet, Émile, 137
Lovchen, Mount, 157, 159, 190, 235
Lublin, 266
Luchaire, Director French Institute, Milan, 227
Ludendorff, General von, 266-8, 270-2, 310
Lugano, Socialist Conference at, 1914, 182
*Lusitania*, 385
Luzzati, Luigi, 227, 384
Lynch, H. B., 22

Macchio, Austrian Ambassador in Rome from Aug. 1914, 158, 174, 191-5, 229, 232, 239, 241-2, 244, 246, 252, 277-8, 284, 296, 300, 302-5, 308, 368, 375, 379-82, 389-90, 392, 394, 396-7, 400-1
Macedonia, 39, 156
Mallet, Sir L., British Ambassador in Constantinople, 37-8, 50-1, 56-7 67
*Manchester Guardian*, 202
Mannesmann Tube Works, 262
Marcora, President of Italian Lower Chamber, 155
*Mare Nostro*, 157
Margherita, Italian Queen Mother, 151, 389
Marne battle, 58, 60, 68, 177, 194, 216-19, 235, 241, 265-7, 277, see also Western front
Marinetti, 186
Martini, F., Italian Colonial Minister, 212, 232, 388
Mary, Queen, 202
Massawa, 146, 156
*Matin, Le*, 80
*Matino, Il*, 152, 159, 194
Matsui, Japanese Deputy Foreign Minister, 118
Mauser concern, 22, 32
Mecca, 49, 81, 97, 103, 317
Medina, 49, 81, 97, 103, 317
Mediterranean, see France, Germany, Great Britain, Italy, Russia.

Mediterranean Alliance of 1887, 137
Mehmed V, Sultan of Turkey, Abdul Hamid's successor, 24, 35, 65, 109
Melas, G., 44
Meleda, island of, 347, 365
Melot, A., Belgian Deputy, 227
Mensdorff, Austro-Hungarian Ambassador in London, 201-2
Merey, Austro-Hungarian Ambassador in Rome till Aug. 1914, 159, 162-5, 169, 171, 174, 190-1
Mersina-Tarsus and Hedjaz-Adana Railways, 22, 124
Mesopotamia, 19-20, 24, 31, 48, 50-1, 66, 79, 82, 87, 103-4, 128
*Messagero, Il*, 188, 385
Metkovich, port of, 329, 340
Metternich, Princess Pauline, 250
Millerand, French Minister of War, 79
Milne, Admiral, 43-6
Milyukov, P., Leader Russian Liberal Party, 64, 66, 91, 94, 313
Minghetti, M., 144
*Mitteleuropa*, 260
Moltke, German Chief of Staff till Sept. 1914, 36, 174, 240, 264
*Momento, Il*, 185
Monelli, P., 184
Monro, General, 128
Montecatini Trust, 142, 188
Montenegro, 146, 156-8, 190, 203, 254, 257, 306, 316, 323, 330-1, 334, 337, 339, 342, 350, 352, 354, 356
Montenuovo, Prince, 249
Monts, Count, 242
Monzie, de, 221
Moravia, 248
Morgenthau, H., U.S. Ambassador in Constantinople, 27, 43, 46-8, 54-5, 109, 129
Morocco, 74, 80, 137
Moukhtar Pasha, Turkish Ambassador in Berlin, 30, 46, 48, 111
Murray, General, Chief of Imperial General Staff, 83
Mussolini, B., 183-7, 227, 230, 294, 360, 386, 389, 399

Naldi, F., 183-4, 230
Napoleon I, 185, 294
Napoleon III, 135
Narenta river, 326, 329, 336-7, 340-2, 344, 350
National Bank of Turkey, the, 19, 102
Nava, Italian Deputy, 216
Naval Agreements, Franco-British, 1912 and 1914, 81
Naval Agreement, Franco-Russian, 1912, 67

Naval Convention between Central Powers and Italy, 1913, 140
Naval Convention, British-Italian, 1915, 327
Nejd, the, 50
Neklyudov, Russian Minister in Stockholm, 91
Nemitz, Russian Chief of Black Sea Operations, 70
Nenni, Pietro, 184
Neuve Chapelle, battle of, 107, 334
Nice, 135, 217-19, 316, 323. See also Italy
*Nichi Nichi*, 118
Nicholas II, Emperor of Russia, 40, 62, 72-4, 78, 86, 95, 98-9, 101, 104, 106, 114-16, 118, 137, 140, 202, 228, 274, 299, 333, 339, 342, 348-9, 354-6, 367-8, 370, 333
Nicolson, Sir A., 357
Nikolai Nikolayevich, Grand Duke, Russian Generalissimo, 66, 76, 86, 116, 331, 348
Nitti, Francesco, 144, 147, 225, 231, 330
*Nouvelles de Basle*, 263
Novibazar, 258, 279

Obotti Co., 257
Ogadiri, Japanese Military Attaché in Petrograd, 88, 91
Olmütz, Archbishop of, 248
Oriental Railway, 22, 58, 256, 261, 310
Orlando, Italian Privy Seal, 142, 360
Orosdi Back concern, 20, 80
*Osservatore Romano*, 372
*Osmanischer Lloyd*, 59
Österreichische Bodenkreditbank, 209
Otranto, Straits of, 158, 204
Ottoman Bank, 20-1, 23, 80, 98, 102 Ottoman Empire, 19, 31, 33, 48-9, 67, 124. See also Turkey.
Ottoman Public Debt, 20-2, 25, 98, 124, 146
Ottoman Railway Co., 313
Ottomanism, 27

Page, T. N., U.S. Ambassador in Rome, 129, 179, 235, 292-3, 295, 331, 366, 374-5, 381, 385, 392
Paléologue, M., French Ambassador in Petrograd, 72, 88, 92, 99, 101, 103, 106, 209-10, 234, 297-9, 322, 332, 343, 367
Palestine, 67, 73, 80-1, 101
Pallavicini, Austro-Hungarian Ambassador in Constantinople, 35-6, 59
Palmerston, Lord, 88
Pan-German League, 260-1

## INDEX

Pan-Islamism, 29-30
Pan-Turanianism, 27-30, 61
Pashich, Serbian Prime Minister, 251, 253, 332, 349
Peano, Italian Deputy, 294
Pelagosa, island of, 344, 365
Persia, 35, 66, 69-70, 73-4, 97, 103
Persian Gulf, 48-50, 66, 97, 103
Petrie, Sir Ch., 185
Piffl, Cardinal-Archbishop of Vienna, 375
Pirelli, G. B., 142, 189
Pius X., Pope, 370, 372
Planka, Cape, 337-40, 342, 344, 350
Poincaré, R., French President, 34, 41, 47, 55, 62, 66-7, 74, 81, 98-9, 101, 103, 111, 121, 126, 175, 198, 210, 213-16, 218-19, 312, 318, 323-4, 335, 346, 351, 354, 358, 384, 386
Poklevski, St., Russian Minister in Bucharest, 218, 293
Pola, 100, 216, 218, 222, 328, 353, 396
Poland, 257, 266, 271-3, 275-6, 299, 394, 398
Pollio, General, 163, 173
Pope, the, see Vatican.
*Popolo d'Italia, Il*, 184-5, 230, 360
Porto Re, 329
Posqualini, Minister of the Italian Royal Household, 212
Przemysl, fortress of, 300, 309, 336-7, 339, 348, 363
Puglia Line, the, 330

Quarnero, Gulf and islands of, 326, 334, 336

Racconigi Agreement of 1909, 137, 140, 327
Radoslavov, Bulgarian Premier, 114-15
Ragusa, 329, 350, 352
Rampolla, Cardinal, 373
Railway Conventions, see Austria-Hungary and Serbia
Regia Co-interessata dei Tabacchi del Montenegro, 330
Renaudel, French Socialist, 399
*Reshadieh*, Turkish battleship, 42-3, 54
Resita combine, 249
*Resto del Carlino, Il*, 183, 230
Rhodes, island of, 217, 313, 330
Ribot, A., 221
Rifaat, Turkish Ambassador in Paris, 52, 60
Risorgimento, the, 135, 137, 144, 188, 231, 326
Robeck, Vice-Admiral, 102
Rodd, Sir R., British Ambassador in Rome, 44, 200, 205-6, 208-9, 227-9, 232-3, 285, 287, 293, 295, 318-19, 321, 327, 345, 350, 372, 384, 386, 389
Rodosto, port of, 114
Rohrbach, Dr. P., 23, 31
Rothschild, Alfred de, 227
Rothschild Bank, S.M. von, 249
Rothschild, Edmund de, 67
Rothschild (Austrian) House of, 250
Rothschild Syndicate, 262
Rubattino Company, 146
Rubini, Italian Minister of the Treasury, 231
Rudolph, Crown Prince of Austria-Hungary before Francis Ferdinand, 256
Rumania, 31, 36-8, 60, 77, 85, 98, 130-1, 161, 165, 244, 250, 257, 264, 271, 281-2, 299, 309, 317, 324, 331, 362, 367-8, 377-8
Ruspoli, Prince, 214
Russia, Albania and, 198-9, 236-7, 243, 314-16, 334-5, 351
Appeal to the Slavs, Aug. 1914, by, 66
Austria-Hungary and, 202-3, 251, 264, 276, 298-9, 327, 378, 394-5
Austria-Hungary, possibilities of a separate peace with, 297-300, 367-8
Balkans and, 38, 65, 75, 89, 151, 318, 348
Black Sea and, 62-3, 66, 75, 86, 94, 115
bourgeoisie, pro-Western, in, 68, 131, 313
Bulgaria and, 31, 39, 72-3, 113-15
Caucasian front, 75, 83, 89, 109
Constantinople and, 39-40, 47, 64-5, 69-72, 90-2, 95-6, 116-18, 123-5, 313, 319, 331, 333-4, 341, 356
Constantinople, Franco-British assurances regarding, to, 70-1, 73, 97, 99, 101, 103, 105, 322, 333, 343, 347, 355, 357-8
Croatia and, 298, 332, 334, 352
Dalmatia and, 207, 320, 322, 331-2, 334-5, 337, 340, 342, 344, 350, 352, 356
Dardanelles Expedition and, 75-6, 88-9, 95-6, 112-18, 131
Duma in, 58, 90-2, 107, 116, 313
Entente, dependence on, of, 39, 73, 125, 356
France, Alliance with, 226, 262, 316
France, conflicts with, 39-40, 47-8, 66, 72, 78, 86, 91, 98-100, 103-4, 114, 122-7, 129-31, 205, 298, 324-5, 333-5, 341, 343, 351-2, 354-7

Russia—*cont'd*
  France, military agreements with, 75
  General Staff, influence of, in, 40, 75-6, 89-90, 95, 113, 116, 348
  Germanophiles in, 68, 104, 131
  Germany, separate peace soundings by, with, 104-5, 117-18, 131, 274-5, 339-40
  Great Britain, conflicts with, 39-40, 47-8, 66, 72-3, 78, 86-8, 91, 105, 107, 114, 117-18, 121, 126-7, 129-31, 201, 203, 205, 207-8, 236, 298, 318-19, 325-6, 333-8, 341-5, 351-2, 355-7, 397
  Great Britain requested to act against Turkey by, 76-7, 89-90
  Greece and, 95-6, 114, 237, 314, 335
  Italy, conflicts with, 105, 151-2, 175, 207-8, 228-9, 243, 314-16, 320-2, 325, 327, 331-4, 339-41, 345, 350-2, 356-8, 364, 368, 377-8, 401
  Italy, Racconigi Agreement with, 137, 327
  Italy, towards Alliance with, 198-200, 205-6, 208-9, 212, 320, 322, 334-6, 337, 342, 344, 348, 357
  Japan and, 118
  Mediterranean and, 64-6, 100, 318, 329, 331
  military operations on East-European front, 60, 68-9, 75, 86, 116-17, 195, 235, 240, 264-76, 299, 301, 303, 305, 308-9, 312, 348, 351, 355-6, 363, 368-9, 380, 383, 392, 397
  Montenegro and, 334, 337, 350, 352, 356
  Near East, overall policy in, of, 64-5, 94, 331-4, 341, 343-4, 355-8
  Rumania and, 31, 131, 309, 367-8
  Serbia and, 39, 207, 237, 259, 314, 318-19, 327, 331-2, 334-5, 337-8, 340-2, 344, 348-52
  'steamroller' (Russian), Franco-British need of, 40, 47, 67-9, 75, 85, 98, 104, 127, 299, 347, 357
  Straits and, 39-40, 47, 63-5, 68, 70-3, 75-6, 90-2, 94-6, 99, 118, 131, 313, 319-20, 333-4
  Straits, Franco-British assurances regarding, to, 70-1, 73, 75, 78, 86, 97, 99, 101, 105, 322, 333, 343, 347, 355-8
  Turkey and, 31, 38-42, 60, 62, 89
  Vatican and, 154, 332, 370-1, 373
  Vladivostock contingent of, 116-18
  war aims of, 64, 68, 70-3, 90-1, 99, 101, 298, 331-4, 356

Russia—*cont'd*
  Yugoslavs and, 332-4, 342, 348-9
  See also Triple Entente.
*Russkoye Slovo*, 118
Ryan, Sir A., 48, 51

Sabbioncello, Peninsula of, 326, 336, 339-42, 344-5, 347-50, 352, 356
Sabini, C., Commercial Attaché, Italian Embassy in Paris, 175, 212-23, 233, 314
Sadowa, battle of, 135
Said Halim, Turkish Grand Vizier, 24, 37, 54-5, 60, 109-10
Salandra, A., Italian Prime Minister, 139, 150-1, 153-5, 157, 160, 166, 168-71, 174, 176-9, 182, 184, 187-9, 193, 196, 199, 206, 212, 215-17, 219, 222-3, 228-9, 231-4, 236-7, 241-2, 284-5, 287, 289-90, 292-6, 302, 312, 314, 325-6, 328, 339, 344-5, 347, 351, 358-61, 363-5, 368-9, 374-6, 381-4, 386-91, 397, 399-400
Salonika, 77-9, 82-3, 103, 127-8, 258, 398
Samothrace, island of, 64
Samuel, Sir H., 67
San Giuliano, Italian Foreign Minister till Oct., 1914, 140, 151, 153-5, 159-60, 162, 164-72, 174-6, 184, 190-6, 200-1 204-5, 207-11, 214, 216-17, 221, 229, 231, 240-2, 254, 289, 292, 296, 327
San river, oil wells on, 299
Sanders, General Liman von (Liman Pasha), 24, 33, 35, 58, 60, 112, 129
Sarakamysh, battle of, 89, 109
Sarayevo, 34, 154, 160, 162, 166-8, 202, 254-6, 261-2, 283, 397
Saseno, island of, 192, 235, 237-8, 326, 336, 365. See also Albania, Austria-Hungary, Italy.
Savoy, 135, 217, 219. See also Italy.
Sazonov, S., Russian Foreign Minister, 38-41, 43, 45, 62-5, 68-73, 75-6, 88-92, 94-7, 99-105, 107, 110-11, 113-18, 122-3, 125-7, 155, 175-6, 179, 198-9, 201, 205-8, 217-18, 228, 236-7, 243, 297-9, 313-16, 318, 320-22, 326, 328-9, 331-45, 347-52, 354-7, 364
Schaaffhausenscher Bankverein, 22
Scheidemann, Ph., German Social-Democrat, 182, 399
Schichau ship-yards, 23
Schneider-Creusot concern, 20-1, 35, 253

### INDEX

Schönborn, House of, 248
Schratt, Frau, 310
Schwarzenberg, House of, 248-9
Scutari, Lake and town of, 146, 330
Sebenico, 334-6
*Secolo, Il*, 182, 185, 188, 329, 360
Second International, 181-2, 399
Secret Agreements of Triple Entente regarding partition of Turkey, 1915, 97, 99, 101, 106, 357-8, 397
Secret London Treaty between Triple Entente and Italy, 1915, 358, 377-8, 384-5, 389-90, 398, 401
Sedan, battle of, 57, 135, 265
Sella, Italian textile magnate, 142
Serbia, 38, 84, 127-8, 256, 279, 318, 323, 337, 341, 398
   Adriatic and, 253-4, 328-9, 331
   Albania and, 251, 253-4, 327
   Austria-Hungary, Alliance and Agreements with, 257
   Austria-Hungary, 1914 War of, against, 160, 166, 253-6, 259, 263, 275, 279, 281, 310, 398
   Austria-Hungary, conflicts with, 157-9, 162, 164-9, 171, 251-5, 257-8, 292, 396
   Austria-Hungary, ultimatum of, to, 162, 201, 240, 281, 397
   Dalmatia and, 314, 328, 332, 349
   France and, 315, 323-4, 343, 354
   Great Britain and, 201-2, 298, 318, 335-8, 340-1, 344, 350, 352-3
   Irredentism (Serbian), 253
   Italy and, 160-2, 169-72, 194, 203, 306, 327, 347, 396
   Italy, conflicts with, 152, 157, 207, 323, 327-9, 331, 340, 345, 349, 353
   Montenegro and, 159, 251, 327
   rise of, 251-4
   Russia and, 39, 207, 237, 259, 314, 318-19, 327, 331-2, 334-5, 337-8, 340-2, 344, 348-9, 351-2
   Sarayevo and, 254-5, 261
   Yugoslav unification and, 251-3, 327, 332, 349
Serrati, Italian Socialist, 181-2, 399
Servizi Marittimi Co., 330
Shevket Pasha, General Mahmud, 32
Sieghart, Governor of Bodenkreditanstalt, 310
*Simplicissimus*, 272
Skoda concern, 209-10, 249, 253, 273
Smyrna-Aidin Railway, 19, 313
Società Commerciale d'Oriente, 146, 313, 316, 330
Société Générale, 209
Sokol organization, 251

Somaliland, 146-7, 154, 317, 323
Sonnino, Italian Foreign Minister from Nov. 1914, 189, 212, 322-6, 238-9 241-3, 245, 283-4, 286-7, 289-93, 295-6, 302, 304-8, 310-12, 314-19, 321-3, 325-6, 331, 333-6, 339-40, 344-5, 347-8, 350-4, 357-8, 360-4, 366-9, 376-8, 381-4, 387-93, 397-8, 400
Sosnowice coal-basin, 311
Souchon, Admiral von, 54, 58, 60
Spalato, 329, 336, 338-9, 356
Sporades islands, 155, 313
*Stampa, La*, 138, 188, 293, 382
Starhemberg, House of, 248
Steed, Wickham, 286
*Stefani* news agency, 228
Steyr armaments concern, 209, 249
Storrs, Ronald, 50-1
Stinnes, Hugo, 22
Straits (Narrows), the, Conventions of 1356 and 1871 regarding, 46
   France and, 72, 101, 130, 172
   Great Britain and, 66, 68, 78-9, 82-8, 97, 102-3, 126, 128, 319, 322
   Great Britain and France, assurances to Russia, of, regarding, 70-1, 75, 75, 78, 86, 97, 99, 101, 105, 322, 333, 343, 347, 355-8
   internationalization or neutralization, question of, 91, 93-4, 99-100, 130
   Italy and, 234, 313-14, 320
   Russia and, 39-40, 47, 63-5, 68, 70-3, 75-6, 90-2, 94-6, 99, 118, 131, 313, 319-20, 333
   Russia's demand for, 70, 72, 92, 94, 99, 313
Strempel, German Military Attaché in Turkey, 33
Stürgkh, Austrian Premier, 247, 255, 263
Stylos, 326, 334
Südekum, Dr., German Social-Democrat, 182
Suez Canal, 53, 58, 93-4, 103, 146, 261
*Sultan Osman*, Turkish battleship, 42-3, 54
Suphi, Mustapha, Turkish Socialist, 27
Supilo, Franco, Dalmatian leader, 332, 349
Switzerland, investments in Italy, of, 138-9
Syria, 50-1, 79-82, 101, 104, 111, 318
Szilassy, Austro-Hungarian Minister in Athens, 156, 395
Szögyény, Austro-Hungarian Ambassador in Berlin, 165, 263

Talaat, Turkish Home Minister, 25, 32, 37, 56, 60, 109, 111
Tannenberg, R., 261
Tannenberg, battle of, 266
Tardieu, André, 80
*Temps, Le*, 80, 91, 216, 384
Tenedos, island of, 34, 64, 70
Thomson, French Minister for Industry and Commerce, 220
Thrace, 38-9, 56, 72, 78, 99
Tiber floods, 359
*Times, The*, 202
Tirpitz, Admiral A., German Minister of Marine, 274-5, 279, 375
Tisza, Stefan, Hungarian Premier, 60, 193, 195, 240, 244-7, 250, 255, 268, 279, 282-3, 301-3, 305, 308-9, 311, 361-2, 367-8, 377-8, 380, 390, 394, 397-8
Tittoni, Italian Ambassador in Paris, 176, 203, 212, 214-17, 221-3, 237, 312, 346
Torre, A., Italian Deputy, 212
Trans-Balkan Railway project, 146, 330
Trans-Caucasia, 66
Transylvania, 72, 202, 244, 282, 299
Trentino, 135, 153, 155, 157, 163, 188, 193-4, 196, 198-201, 203, 213, 215, 217-20, 238-42, 244-6, 276-82, 286-7, 291, 300-2, 304, 308, 310-11, 322, 362, 364-6, 378, 382, 392-3, 398
Treves, Italian Socialist, 181, 399
*Tribuna*, 294, 369, 382-3
Trieste, 153, 188, 199-201, 213, 215, 217-20, 222, 258, 261, 279, 286-7, 291, 304, 322, 326, 328, 334, 336, 353, 365-6, 368, 378, 382, 398
Triple Alliance (Triplice), 135-6, 140, 150
  Article VII of, 156, 162-6, 169-72, 191, 209, 216, 238-9, 242, 305-7, 362, 396
  Austria-Hungary and, 135-6, 162-3, 167-8, 171-2, 395-6
  Germany and, 136, 285
  Italy and, 37, 135-8, 140, 150, 153-5, 162-3, 168, 170-1, 174, 194-5, 214, 217, 242, 277-8, 285, 294, 303
  members, conflicts among, see Austria - Hungary, Germany, Italy
Triple Entente, Albania (Valona, Saseno) and, 198-9, 235-7. See also France, Russia.
  Balkan States and, 77-8, 85, 107, 130, 309, 317. See also France, Great Britain, Russia.

Triple Entente—*cont'd*
  Bulgaria and, 56, 127, 309. See also France, Great Britain, Russia.
  Greece and, 95, 175, 199, 309. See also France, Great Britain, Russia.
  Italy and, 85, 105, 107, 153-5, 175-7, 193, 197-201, 205-6, 209, 215-16, 219, 224, 226-7, 231, 233-8, 291-2, 311-58, 360, 363, 366, 378, 383-4, 389-90, 392-3, 401
  members, conflicts among, see France, Great Britain, Russia.
  peace approach by Austria-Hungary to, 296-7
  peace approach by Turkey to, 110-12
  Rumania and, 77, 85, 198, 309, 317. See also, France, Great Britain, Russia.
  Secret Agreements on Turkey of, 97, 99, 101, 106, 357-8, 397
  Secret Agreements on Turkey of, and Italy, 313, 316, 318, 320, 357-8
  Secret Treaty of London with Italy, of, 358, 377-8, 384-5, 389-90, 398, 401
  Serbia and, 199. See also France, Great Britain, Russia.
  Turkey, designs on, of, 31-2, 48-51, 56-7, 64, 67, 70-3, 90-7, 101
  Turkish orientation and, 34-5, 37-42, 51-7, 62, 68, 78. See also France, Great Britain, Russia.
Tripolitania, 61, 136, 147, 180, 395. See also Libya.
Tripolitanian War, see Libyan War under Italy.
Troubridge, Rear-Admiral, 44-5
Trubetskoi, Russian Minister to Serbia and High Commissioner designate for Constantinople, 90, 125, 279, 296, 349
Trubetskoi, Prof. E. N., 64, 91
Tsar, see Nicholas II.
Tschirsky, German Ambassador in Vienna, 163-5, 240, 242, 263, 277, 281-2, 301
Tugan-Baranovski, Russian economist, 64
Tunis, 135-6, 146, 187, 217-19, 232, 315-16, 320, 323
Tunisia, 74, 80, 152, 323
Turati, Italian Socialist, 181, 399-400
Turk Jourdou (Turkish Hearth) Association, 28
Turkey (Ottoman Empire), agriculture in, 26
  Arabs and, 49-51

# INDEX 429

Turkey (Ottoman Empire)—cont'd
 armed forces of, 58, 112
 Austria-Hungary and, 35-6, 60, 251, 256, 258-9
 Austria-Hungary, imperialist encroachments by, on, 156, 256, 260
 Black Sea ports (Russian) bombarded by, 60
 Bulgaria and, 38, 40, 115, 313
 Capitulations in, 25, 31, 36-7, 39, 41, 56, 59
 Caucasian front, 75, 33, 89, 109
 Central Powers and, 35-9, 62, 310
 Central Powers, 1914 Treaty of Alliance with, 36, 46-7, 58-9, 62
 diplomatic soundings, autumn 1914, 36-8
 economic structure of, 25-6
 Egypt, invasion of, by, 60
 foreigners holding Turkish official posts in, 21, 24
 France and, 31, 34-5, 41-2, 48, 51-2, 72, 124, 322-4
 France, investments of, in, 20-1, 41, 80-2, 98
 Germany and, 30-3, 43-5, 54, 57-60, 84, 110, 112, 128, 154, 285, 369
 Germany, investments of, in, 21-4
 Germany, Treaty of Alliance with, 35-6
 Great Britain and, 21, 31, 41-2, 48, 51-2
 Great Britain, investments of, in, 19-20
 Greece and, 28, 34, 37-8, 40, 95, 313
 Irredentism (Turkish) abroad, 28-9
 Italy, designs of, on, 135, 155-6, 175, 200, 204, 213, 234-5, 310, 313-14, 316-17, 320, 325, 336
 Italy, investments of, in, 146-7, 200. See also Arabia.
 orientation of, Triple Entente's attitude to, 34-5, 37-42, 51-7, 62, 78
 Pan-Islamism in, 29-30
 Pan-Turanianism in, 27-30, 61
 partitioning of, 31-2, 48-9, 51, 56-7, 67, 71-3, 96-7, 100-1, 155
 peace approach to Triple Entente by, 110-12
 persecutions in, 109-10
 Ottomanism in, 27
 railways in, 19-20, 22-3, 25, 58, 80, 256, 258, 310, 313
 Russia and, 31, 38-42, 60, 62, 89
 Socialism in, 27
 Triple Entente's Secret Agreements on, 97, 99, 101, 106, 357-8, 397

Turkey (Ottoman Empire)—cont'd
 U.S. interest in, 93 (footnote 2)
 See also Arabia, Constantinople, Dardanelles Expedition, Mesopotamia, Palestine, Straits, Syria
Turkish Petroleum Company, 19, 23
Tyrrel, Sir William, 318

Ukraine, 63, 56, 250, 257, 276
Ulk, 227
Ungarische Bank-und Handelsgesellschaft, 256
Ungarische Escompte-und Wechslerbank, 262
Uniate Church, 257
U.S.A. and Turkey, 93 (footnote 2)

Val, Merry del, Cardinal Secretary of State before Gasparri, 372
Valona, 158, 164, 175, 193, 198-201, 204, 217, 220, 235-8, 243, 304-5, 307, 315, 322, 326, 328-30, 335-6, 353, 365-6, 382. See also Albania, Austria-Hungary, Italy, Triple Entente.
Van, fall of, 109
Vandervelde, Belgian Socialist, 182
Vasilchikova, Mme. M.A., 104, 117-18, 339-40
Vatican, Austria-Hungary and, 136, 151, 248-9, 373, 375, 382, 390
 Belgium and, 372
 Central Powers and, 136, 151, 154, 248-9, 301, 310, 369, 372, 374, 382, 390-3
 Constantinople and, 126, 130
 France and, 135, 229, 371-3, 374 (footnote 4), 375
 Germany and, 301, 310, 369, 373-7, 381-2, 390, 393
 Giolitti and, 375
 Great Britain and, 373-4
 Italy and, 135-6, 145, 151, 154, 288, 373, 375, 377-8, 382-3
 neutrality of, 372
 Russia and, 154, 332, 370-1, 373
 Serbia and, 372
 Spain, activities in, 374
 Temporal Power, the Pope's striving for, 135-6, 154, 372-5
 Triple Entente and, 130, 151, 154, 372
 1914 War and, 370-2
Venetia, 135-6
Venizelos, E., Greek Prime Minister, 95-6, 107
Vickers concern, 19, 21, 23, 35
Vickers-Terni, 142, 144, 224, 360

Victor Emmanuel III, King of Italy, 137, 140, 155-6, 172, 176, 188, 229, 285, 289, 348, 381-2, 384-5, 388-90, 398
*Victoria*, 194, 300
Villa Malta, Rome, 284-5, 293, 301, 381
Viviani, R., French Premier (also Foreign Minister in June-July, 1914), 34-5, 98, 103, 215, 219-20
Volosca, 326, 334, 336, 352
Volpi, G., Italian financier, 315-16
Voyusa river, 326, 337-9, 352

Wangenheim, German Ambassador in Constantinople, 33-5, 43, 52, 58-60, 109-10, 129, 168
Wars, see Austro-Prussian, Balkan, Libyan.
Warsaw-Ivangorod, battle of, 268-70
Wechselstuben A/G 'Merkur', 262
Wedel, Prince, 301
Western front, 58, 60, 68-9, 75, 77, 81, 102, 107, 121, 177, 194, 209, 215-19, 235, 263-7, 269, 271-2, 275-8, 301, 312, 324, 334, 346-7, 355
*Westminster Gazette*, 202
Wied, Wilhelm v., Prince of Albania, 158-9, 235, 254
Wiedenfeld, Prof., 31
Wiener Bankverein, 210

William II, Emperor of Germany, 21, 30, 32, 35-6, 44, 46, 59, 104, 109, 117-18, 138, 140, 171-2, 174, 177, 188, 196, 218, 239-40, 263-4, 266, 268-70, 276, 284, 286, 302, 360, 370, 375, 379, 398
Williams, General, British Military Attaché in Russia, 89
Wilson, Sir Arthur, 84
Witkowitz Coal and Iron Works, 249
Woods, H., 21
*World, The*, 86, 130

Yanushkevich, General, Russian Chief of Staff, 75
Yemen, 317
Young Turk Committee of Union and Progress, 24, 27-8
Young Turks, 26-7, 29-31, 37, 48, 56, 110-12
Ypres, first battle of, 269, 271
Ypres, second battle of, 355
Yugoslavs, 250-4, 258-9, 275, 298, 327-30, 332-4, 342, 348-9, 353, 378

Zara, 328, 334-6, 338, 341-2, 344
Zimmermann, E., German Under-Secretary for Foreign Affairs, 192, 275, 277-9, 301, 307, 380
Zupelli, General, Italian Minister of War, 232, 363